# THE IDEA
# OF
# DECLINE
# IN
# WESTERN
# HISTORY

◆

## ARTHUR HERMAN

**THE FREE PRESS**

*New York   London   Toronto   Sydney   Singapore*

THE FREE PRESS
A Division of Simon & Schuster Inc.
1230 Avenue of the Americas
New York, NY 10020

THE FREE PRESS and colophon are trademarks
of Simon & Schuster Inc.

Designed by Carla Bolte

Manufactured in the United States of America

10   9   8   7   6   5   4   3   2   1

Library of Congress Cataloging-in-Publication Data

Herman, Arthur
    The idea of decline in Western history /
Arthur Herman.
        p.   cm.
    Includes bibliographical references and index.

    1. Civilization, Western—Philosophy.   2. Regression
(Civilization)   I. Title.
CB245.H429   1997
909'.09912—dc20                                    96–36285
    ISBN-10: 1-4165-7633-9                            CIP
    ISBN-13: 978-1-4165-7633-4

FOR BETH

# CONTENTS

PART THREE

## THE TRIUMPH OF CULTURAL PESSIMISM

# INTRODUCTION

Every time I mentioned to friends or acquaintances that I was writing a book on the decline of Western civilization, the response was almost invariably, "Well, is it or isn't it?" I then had to point out that this was a book about the *idea* of Western decline as part of modern thinking, not a pronouncement on whether modern civilization was actually doomed or not.

I would point out that while intellectuals have been predicting the imminent collapse of Western civilization for more than one hundred and fifty years, its influence has grown faster during that period than at any time in history. Western cultural ideals and institutions enjoy more prestige now than they did during the heyday of European colonization and empire. The West's essential contributions to our contemporary world include the role that science and technology play in enhancing material life, our belief in democracy, the rights of the individual, and the rule of law, as well as the liberating effects of free market capitalism and private ownership of property. As we now approach the twenty-first century, these beliefs seem to be more and more the unshakable pillars of the modern global outlook.

Yet when I point this out as evidence that, to paraphrase Mark Twain, reports of the demise of the West might be greatly exaggerated, I usually meet with strong skepticism. It became apparent to me that if I took a poll among my lecture audiences at the Smithsonian Institution—which tend to be older than my college audiences—the vote would be

1

overwhelmingly in favor of the verdict that civilization, that is, the modern West, stands on the brink of dissolution.

We live in an era in which pessimism has become the norm, rather than the exception. Two decades ago John Kenneth Galbraith remarked that every publisher wants his author's book to be entitled "The Crisis of American Democracy"—because he knows that that title will sell. That observation seems even more true today. A long string of "crisis" books have appeared, preparing us for the twenty-first century as an erea of deep dislocation and uncertainty, with the West, which largely means the United States, increasingly unable to exert any influence on the outcome. America and Europe have lost their long-held position of global dominance, they argue; we had all better prepare for the worst rather than the best. Here is a standard opening:

> Hardly more than a quarter-century after Henry Luce proclaimed "the American century," American confidence has fallen to a low ebb. Those who recently dreamed of world power now despair of governing the city of New York. Defeat in Vietnam, economic stagnation, and the impending exhaustion of natural resources have produced a mood of pessimism in higher circles, which spreads through the rest of society as people lose faith in their leaders. The same crisis of confidence grips other capitalist countries as well.

These words come from the preface to Christopher Lasch's *Culture of Narcissism*. Published in 1979, it warned that "bourgeois society has lost both the capacity and the will to confront the difficulties that threaten to overwhelm it" and that "the political crisis of capitalism reflects a general crisis of western culture." Lasch quoted distinguished historian David H. Donald: "The age of abundance has ended," ushering in "the bleakness of the new era."[1]

Less than a decade later, American and European politics witnessed a massive return to the virtues of free enterprise, bourgeois values, and a new "age of abundance," as oil prices fell and non-Western countries began to turn to American-style capitalism, not socialism, to invigorate their industrial economies. Yet already Paul Kennedy was arguing in *The Rise and Fall of the Great Powers* (1987) that Americans were about to face the same fate as the British at the end of the nineteenth century: their decline as a world power. The United States was suffering from what Kennedy called "imperial overstretch," and was being squeezed by the same inexorable forces that had wrecked the *Pax Brittanica* and led to World Wars I and II. Trapped by its Cold War military commitments and by new economic challengers along the Pacific Rim, America's dominant position in the world was over. "The task facing American statesmen over the next decades," Kennedy wrote, will be "to 'manage' affairs so that the relative erosion of the United States' position takes place slowly and smoothly."[2]

Kennedy's prediction of Cold War overstretch proved correct—but for the Soviet Union rather than the United States. Less than three years after Kennedy's book appeared, the Soviet empire (which he had scarcely mentioned) disappeared, while America moved into position as "the world's sole superpower."

Of course, facts alone cannot make or unmake a theory of history. Pessimism and optimism are attitudes the scholar brings to his analysis of events, not conclusions that arise from that analysis. Kennedy's claims about "imperial overstretch" fit in too well with the prevailing gloom about the fate of American society as it approached the end of the twentieth century. Political analyst Kevin Phillips used Kennedy to compare Washington, D.C. to imperial Rome and nineteenth-century London, the bloated, "arrogant capital" of an declining empire ruled by "abusive and entrenched elites." "Too much of what happened then is happening again," he wrote. "Economic polarization" and "a declining middle class" move hand in hand with "an expansion of luxury and moral permissiveness," "loss of old patriotism," and "complaints of moral decay"—the diagnosis of decline (as in Phillips's own writings) standing as evidence of decline itself.[3]

The black critic Cornel West used Kennedy's image of "the eclipse of U.S. hegemony in the world" as the backdrop for his own summary of America's woes in *Race Matters* (1993). West warned that American society was being ravaged by a "silent depression" of declining industrial jobs and sinking incomes, and a collapse of community. "Cultural decay in a declining empire" had created "rootless, dangling people" and a "powerless citizenry that includes not just the poor but all of us."[4] West's book, and Phillips's *Arrogant Capital* and *Boiling Point*, joined other books on America's future with depressing titles such as *The Twilight of Democracy, The Democracy Trap, Democracy on Trial, Giving Up on*

*Democracy, The Frozen Republic, The Selling of America, The Bankrupting of America, The Endangered American Dream,* and *Who Will Tell the People*.[5]

For all their supposed topicality, however, many of these claims about decline and doom have an air of déjà vu about them—or at least a ring of familiarity. If Kevin Phillips's dire warnings about the Reagan era's "decade of greed" sound like the verbal assault on America's Gilded Age of Boston Brahmins like Henry Adams, then Paul Kennedy's warnings that the twenty-first century will usher in a struggle of "the West against the rest," with "fast growing, adolescent, resource-poor, undercapitalized, and undereducated populations" on one side "and demographically moribund and increasingly nervous rich societies" on the other, sounds very much like Arnold Toynbee, Oswald Spengler, Benjamin Kidd, or any number of other gloomy prognosticators in the first decades of this century. Those same writers, in fact, had originally coined the term "Western" to describe a faltering European civilization that, they believed, was steadily fading away, like a brilliant sunset against the western sky.

Then Charles Murray and Richard Herrnstein's widely publicized *The Bell Curve* (1994) presented a picture of America's future highly reminiscent of the writings of eugenicists and "race scientists" at the end of the nineteenth century—the *fin de siècle* in which the image of Western decline first took decisive shape. Charles Murray warned that America's overly mobile society was about to split in two, based on IQ and cognitive ability. The United States was fast becoming "two nations," a detached and culturally isolated elite holding the bulk of economic and social resources and an increasingly cretinized underclass, both black and white, incapable of taking care of itself. The political measures to deal with this bifurcation of society "will become more and more totalitarian," Murray predicted, with increased police powers, the spread of racial antagonisms and resentment, curtailed personal freedoms, and the creation of "a lavish and high-tech version of the Indian reservation for a substantial minority of the nation's population." He concluded that "unchecked, these trends will lead the U.S. toward something resembling a caste society," adding that, "like other apocalyptic visions [of America's future], this one is pessimistic, perhaps too much so. On the other hand, there is much to be pessimistic about."[6]

As if these worries were not enough, there are the current fears about environmental degradation and its consequences for the survival of modern Western society, and even of the planet itself. These reached a kind of crescendo with the publication of Vice President Albert Gore's *Earth in the Balance* in 1992.

Unless we "embrace the preservation of the earth as our new organizing principle," Gore wrote, "the very survival of our civilization will be in doubt."[7] Global warming, the depletion of the ozone layer, the destruction of the rain forest, extinction of endangered species, poisoning of air and water pose mortal threats to our very existence. In response, "we retreat into the seductive tools and technologies of industrial civilization, but that only creates new problems as we become increasingly isolated from one another and disconnected from our roots." Instead, people around the world need to "take a hard look at the habits of mind and action that reflect—and have led to—this grave crisis." Among those habits is modern acquisitive capitalism, which has been blind to its destruction of the environment.[8] Then there is the nature of technological civilization itself:

> The edifice of civilization has become astonishingly complex, but as it grows ever more elaborate, we feel increasingly distant from our roots in the earth. In one sense, civilization itself has been on a journey from its foundations in the world of nature to an ever more contrived, controlled, and manufactured world of our own initiative and sometimes arrogant design.

That civilization now faces a "collective identity crisis," Gore suggests, and evidence is accumulating that "there is indeed a spiritual crisis in modern civilization that seems to be based on an emptiness at its center and the absence of a larger spiritual purpose."[9]

"It is easy," Gore says, "to feel overwhelmed, utterly helpless to effect any change whatsoever" when faced by an impending catastrophe of this size. A few people, however, proved willing to take up that challenge.

On April 21, 1995, a letter bomb exploded in the Sacramento office of timber industry executive Gilbert Murray, killing him instantly. The police investigation concluded that the murder was the work of the so-called Unabomber, a legendary renegade who had killed three people and injured and maimed twenty-three others in a one-man guerrilla campaign against "the corporate state." In fact, this time the Unabomber followed up his attack with a 35,000-word manifesto, entitled "Industrial Society and Its Future," which summed up virtually every pessimistic view regarding the future of modern society, and the future of America and the planet, that had appeared in the past several decades.

"The Industrial Revolution and its consequences have been a disaster for the human race," the Unabomber began. It had "destabilized society, made life unfulfilling, subjected human beings to indignities, and psychological damage (in the Third World to physical suffering as well) and severe damage on the natural world." "There is no stable framework" left for humanity, he concluded, only relentless and ceaseless change. The chief villains were technology, capitalism with its "drive for endless material acquisition," and science, which "marches on blindly, without regard to the real welfare of the human race," in obedience to the commands of government officials and corporate executives. Together they had created a society in which "only minimal effort is necessary to satisfy one's physical needs." Industrial society deprived people of their personal autonomy and their links to what the Unabomber called "the power process," the personal experience of place and purpose in the world. As a result, true freedom had disappeared.

The Unabomber accused modern Americans of leading the lives of "decadent leisured aristocrats": they were "bored, hedonistic, and demoralized." People had been brainwashed into a state of conformity and docility comparable to "domesticated animals," with every aspect of their lives dictated and controlled by the technological corporate elite. The Unabomber was calling for nothing less than a global revolution, "to overthrow not governments but the economic and technological basis of the present society." Then a new ideology "that opposes technology and the industrial society" would have to arise, "so that when and if the system collapses, the remnants will be smashed beyond repair, so that the system cannot be reconstituted." He believed radical environmentalism was such an ideology. (In fact, the FBI would later find a dog-eared, heavily marked copy of Gore's *Earth in the Balance* in his cabin when he was arrested in April 1996.) But he had no illusions that creating the new, ideal society would be easy: speaking for himself, "our goal is only to destroy the existing form of society"—the modern West.[10]

Some people talk about the decline of civilization. Others live it. This is a book about the origins and diffusion of an intellectual tradition, the idea of "the decline of the West." We will see how it formed the dark underside of modern European thought in the nineteenth century and how it became arguably the single most dominant and influential theme in culture and politics in the twentieth century. Not only has it affected peoples' lives in unexpected and startling ways which we will examine in some detail, but it may also be inseparable from the idea of civilization itself.

But we will also see that the idea of decline consists of two distinct traditions. For every Western intellectual who dreads the collapse of his own society (like Henry Adams or Arnold Toynbee or Paul Kennedy or Charles Murray), there is another who has looked forward to that event with glee. For the better part of three decades, America's preeminent thinkers and critics—from Norman Mailer, Gore Vidal, Thomas Pynchon, Christopher Lasch, Jonathan Kozol, and Garry Wills to Joseph Campbell, Joan Didion, Susan Sontag, Jonathan Schell, Robert Heilbroner, Richard Sennett, Noam Chomsky, Paul Goodman, Michael Harrington, E.L. Doctorow, and Kirkpatrick Sale, not to mention Cornel West, Albert Gore, and the Unabomber—have advanced a picture of American society far more frightening than anything pessimists like Charles Murray or Kevin Phillips could come up with. As a critique of Western industrial society, it dates back to the nineteenth century. In this point of view, modern society appears as greedily materialistic, spiritually bankrupt, and devoid of humane values. Modern people are always displaced, rootless, psychologically scarred, and isolated from one another. They are, as the Unabomber puts it, "demoralized." The key question now becomes not *if* American society or Western civilization can be saved, but whether it deserves to be saved at all.

We will term this darker, more radical vision of decline "cultural pessimism." Cultural pessimism embodies a particular view of modern history, exemplified by the title of Oswald Spengler's gloomy masterpiece, *The Decline of the West*. The modern world and modern man, the cultural pessimist claims, are trapped in a process of deterioration, exhaustion, and inevitable collapse. Cultural pessimism draws heavily on the philosophy of Friedrich Nietzsche and on his sweeping condemnation of the European society of his day as "sick" and "decadent." "There is an element of decay in everything that characterizes modern man," Nietzsche wrote in 1885. In fact, a straight line of descent runs from Nietzsche and his disciples Martin Heidegger and Herbert Marcuse, to the Unabomber and beyond: a line of descent that produced a single view of the modern West, summed up in Herbert Marcuse's *One Dimensional Man*: "A comfortable, smooth, reasonable, democratic *unfreedom* prevails in advanced industrial civilization, a token of technical progress." For the cultural pessimist, the momentous issue for the future is not whether Western civilization will survive, but what will take its place.

In its original European context, cultural pessimism cut across the political and ideological spectrum. Marcuse was a Marxist; Heidegger turned to Hitler with enthusiasm, Oswald Spengler with misgivings. Nietzsche despised all conventional political labels. Cultural pessimism is an attack on modern Western culture that predates and transcends adherence to any Marxist or socialist creed. If the leading voices of the antimodern chorus in America today come from the Left, figures like T.S. Eliot, William Faulkner, Evelyn Waugh, Walker Percy, Malcolm Muggeridge, Alexander Solzhenitsyn, and Thomas Molnar have managed to sustain the refrain from the Right as well.

Regardless of the country, regardless of the era, and regardless of political persuasion, all these authors have shared the same prophetic vision: the capitalist bourgeois civilization of their day, whether in 1846 or 1886, 1946 or 1996, is doomed to self-destruction. Capitalism is not just painful or difficult for those excluded from its benefits, or capable of enormous physical destruction, or prone to outbursts of crassness and vulgarity, or forgetful of "the higher things" and its own spiritual traditions. Cultural pessimism insists that the ordinary, normal course of civil society on the Western model, as a capitalist or "commercial" society, resting on rational and scientific principles, democratic political institutions, and self-consciously "modern" cultural and social attitudes, awaits its own secular apocalypse. An inevitable doom hovers over its products and achievements: as Oswald Spengler put it, by living in modern society we must be "resigned to the fact of a late life."[11] Modern man lives in a world that is sliding ever deeper into the slough of despond, until some entirely new redemptive order arises.

This cultural pessimist tradition has shaped our view of ourselves and our own society in ways that we can scarcely realize. The ideas of the Unabomber, Third World Marxist revolutionaries, Afrocentric scholars, Vice President Gore, Greenpeace, Robert Bly, and Madonna all reflect, in different ways, its principal beliefs and assumptions. From our current obsession with questions of "identity" and "diversity" to modern psychoanalysis and what is called "the therapeutic society," cultural pessimism has given us a rich and pungent, but ultimately a crabbed and self-limiting, view of modernity and change.

Yet as the reader will discover, at the heart of this tradition is a fascinating paradox. On the one hand, it contains a sobering message of gloom and doom: modern society is systematically destroying itself. That declinist component has had its own despairing practitioners, such as Jacob Burckhardt, Henry Adams, and Arnold Toynbee. But cultural pessimism goes further and includes, paradoxically, a message of hope. Like his Marxist colleagues, the cultural pessimist assures us that when our corrupt modern society has finally ruined itself and vanishes, something better will replace it. This new order, however, will not be primarily economic or political; it will involve instead the demolition of Western culture as a *totality*.

This new order might take the shape of the Unabomber's radical environmental utopia. It might also be Nietzsche's Overman, or Hitler's Aryan National Socialism, or Marcuse's utopian union of technology and Eros, or Frantz Fanon's revolutionary *fellahin*. Its carriers might be the ecologist's "friends of the earth" or the multiculturalist's "persons of color," or the radical feminist's New Amazons or Robert Bly's New Men. The particular shape of this future order will vary according to taste; however, its most important virtue will be its totally non-, or even anti-Western, character. In the end, what matters to the cultural pessimist is less what is going to be created than what is going to be destroyed—namely, our "sick" modern society.

For the cultural pessimist, then, bad news is actually *good* news. He greets economic depression, unemployment, world wars and conflicts, and environmental disasters with barely concealed glee, since these events all foreshadow the final destruction of modern civilization. Like the biblical prophets of old, the modern prophets of pessimism know that the worse things get, the better they will be.[12]

Most people today are barely aware of this other, almost sadistically redemptive, component of the pessimist tradition. Instead, the sowing of despair and self-doubt has become so pervasive that we accept it as a normal intellectual stance—even when it is directly contradicted by our own reality.

PART ONE

# THE LANGUAGES OF DECLINE

## CHAPTER 1

# PROGRESS, DECLINE, AND DECADENCE

Everything degenerates in the hands of men.
—Jean-Jacques Rousseau

The idea of decline is actually a theory about the nature and meaning of time. So is the idea of progress. The notion of history as progress stands largely discredited today among intellectuals, and especially among historians. They debate instead the origins and history of "the idea of Progress" and how it has served as a powerful cultural "myth" in Western thought.[1] The origin and significance of the myth of decline have attracted less notice. Yet the two ideas are actually opposite sides of the same coin. Every theory of progress has also contained a theory of decline, since "inevitable" historical laws can just as easily shift in reverse as move forward. Likewise, whenever we meet a theory about the decline of Western civilization, we can probably find lurking underneath a theory of progress.

Virtually every culture past or present has believed that men and women are not up to the standards of their parents and forebears. In the earliest Greek literature, Homer's *Iliad*, we find a description of Ajax picking up with one hand a chunk of stone, "which the sturdiest youngster of our generation would have found difficult to lift with both hands."[2] Two hundred years later, in the seventh century B.C., the poet Hesiod saw the entire cosmos governed by a process of generational decay, beginning with a golden age when gods ruled and men lived in peace and harmony, followed by a silver age, a bronze age, and finally an iron age when men are forced to live by the sweat of their brow and suffer their fate (at the hands of landlords, kings—and wives). The resemblance of Hesiod's iron age to the expulsion from the Garden of Eden is striking; but "iron age" is also the translation of the *Kali Yuga* of Hindu and Vedic religion, the last and worst of all human epochs, when "the strong, the cunning, the daring, and the reckless" rule the world. Similar myths appear in Confucian China; among the Aztecs, Zoroastrians, Laplanders, and numerous Native American tribes; and in Icelandic and Irish sagas, not to mention the Book of Genesis.[3]

> *To whom can I speak today?*
> *The iniquity that strikes the land*
> *Has no end.*

> *To whom can I speak today?*
> *There are no righteous men,*
> *The earth is surrendered to criminals.*[4]

The sentiments seem recognizably modern, even though the author actually lived in Egypt's Middle Kingdom, circa 2000 B.C.

Why is this sense of decline common to all cultures? It may simply reflect the human experience of bodily changes from childhood to maturity and the inevitable decay of physical and mental capacity in old age. The collective memory of the past tends to be of a world endowed with powers that now seem lost. In fact, those endowments and losses seem to form the key stages of human existence itself, which Shakespeare would sum up as the Seven Ages of Man.

The genius of the Greeks was to expand this basic physical self-awareness into a philosophy of the nature of time and change. For the Greeks, time *is* change: what we were and what we have now—good, bad, or indifferent, but perhaps especially good—comes to an end. The philosopher Heraclitus saw the entire cosmos as governed by a single law of change: "Everything is in flux, and nothing is at rest." Sophocles' Oedipus understood this all too well:

> *Time destroys all things,*
> *No one is safe from death except the gods.*
> *The earth decays, the flesh decays,*
> *Trust among men withers, and distrust takes its place.*

*Friends turn on friends,*
*And cities upon cities,*
*With time all things change: delight*
*Into bitterness, even hatred into love.*[5]

The Greek word for time, *chronos*, was also the name of the god who devoured his own children.

A sense of the transitory nature of human existence permeated both Greek and Roman literary culture.* It underlay the myth of Arcadia, the imaginary pastoral paradise where shepherds and shepherdesses enjoyed the pleasures of life with none of the sorrows, as well as the motto *carpe diem*. Life was too short, and happiness too fleeting, to permit any postponement of gratification.

*Tomorrow, do thy worst, for I have lived today;*
*Be fair or foul or rain or shine,*
*The joys I have possessed in spite of Fate are mine . . .*[6]

But the Greco-Roman view of time also contained the conviction that events do not occur at random but according to a repetitive cycle, from birth, life, decline, and death to rebirth. The Greek term for this cycle was "revolution," *anakuklosis*. Plato saw the Greek city-states evolving according to a recurrent cycle. The Greek historian Polybius theorized that political systems followed a series of revolutions as monarchy decayed into tyranny, leading to aristocracy, which decayed into oligarchy, which led in turn to democracy followed by anarchy, requiring the restoration of one-man rule or monarchy.[7] The medieval version of this cycle was Fortune's wheel. Man was held in the hands of fate like the thread on a spinning wheel. By rotating the wheel, Fortune raises some men up as kings and heroes and popes, and then with another turn of the crank sends them back down again. Their fame is purely "fortuitous," with no rhyme or reason.†[8]

Man's one resource in the face of Fortune and blind circumstance

---

* For example, Marcus Aurelius observes in his *Meditations*: "Reflect how speedily in this life the things of today are buried under those of tomorrow, even as one layer of drifting sand is quickly covered by the next."

† It says something about the fundamental optimism of American culture that it transformed "the wheel of Fortune" from a symbol of bleak fatalism into the chance for instant cash.

was his virtue. Originally, *virtus* meant courage in battle, but it came to include manly integrity in all spheres of life. Virtue was the inner strength necessary to overcome the "slings and arrows of outrageous Fortune," as Shakespeare put it, and to forge one's own destiny. Virtue's emblem was Hercules, the hero and slayer of monsters whose physical strength enabled him to defy impossible odds. Hercules was by far the most popular god both in the ancient world and during the Renaissance, the hopeful symbol of the individual's ability to determine the direction of his own life against blind fate.[9] In the Middle Ages, virtue took on Christian overtones and Fortune became identified with sin, the realm of corrupt flesh and the Devil. In the Renaissance, Machiavelli revived the opposition between Virtue and Fortune in pagan guise. As the author of *The Prince* explained, "Fortune is a woman," who requires a strong man to tame her and control her. For that reason, "she is always well disposed toward younger men, since they are less cautious and more aggressive."

Virtue versus Fortune, virtue versus corruption, and still later the clash between *Kultur* and *Zivilisation*: in each case, history is determined by an inevitable conflict between human character and impersonal fate. The ancient Greeks believed that this conflict made possible the growth of knowledge and the arts, as man struggled against primal nature and the surrounding darkness, as in the myth of Prometheus. Similarly, Plato's philosopher struggles against the forces of ignorance and opinion as he ascends from the shadowy Cave of Illusions to the pure Realm of Ideas. The historian Thucydides saw the same struggle transforming Greece from rude barbarism to the city-state or *polis*.[10] In the end, however, there was no escape from fate. Even the gods were ruled by its decrees; all must eventually return into the primal darkness, or *chaos* in Greek, and start anew.

That is, until one day someone arrives who has so much virtue (plus the unanimous support of the gods) that he manages to halt the relentless cycle of doom and set it in reverse, restoring the lost Golden Age. In the classical world, that man turned out to be Augustus Caesar; the restored Golden Age was imperial Rome:

*Ours is the crowning era foretold in prophecy;*
*Born of time, a great new cycle of centuries*

*Begins. Justice returns to earth, the Golden Age*
*Returns, and its first born comes down from heaven . . .*
*With him shall hearts of iron cease, and hearts of gold*
*Inherit the whole earth . . . Thus have the Fates spoken,*
*In unison with the unshakeable intent of Destiny.*

Virgil's "Fourth Eclogue" was composed in 40 B.C. to celebrate Augustus's victory at Actium over Marc Antony and Cleopatra. Virgil proclaimed that fate, instead of being pitted against humanity, was now on its side. With destructive Fortune stopped in its course, there was no limit to the possibilities for empire, both in time and space.

*Caesar Augustus, son of a god, destined to rule . . .*
*his empire shall expand*
*Past Garamants and Indians to a land beyond the zodiac*
*And the sun's yearly path.*

The cyclic motion of Fortune and history now becomes the "translation of empire" from east to west following the course of the sun, from the empires of the Orient, Egypt, and the Middle East (whose rulers likewise conjoined a heavenly and earthly order) to the Greeks and then to Augustus and his successors.

The myth of universal empire sustained Roman imperial propaganda until the age of Justinian. It proposed a new role for human rulers: creating a dominion based not on conquest or even heroic virtue, but on universal harmony—"to practice men in the art of peace" by dissolving contingent difference into a single immortal whole. The human arts and sciences would flourish and any hint of conflict—or decline—would vanish. For premodern Europeans, then, empire and imperialism had positive, not negative, connotations. Imperial Rome's various successors and imitators took up the mission of establishing a universal empire that would be global, permanent, and harmonious. It influenced that central Christian image of Christ on Judgment Day, the "king of kings" into whose universal empire all previous and present ones would be dissolved. To late-antique Christians, Rome's universal empire had seemed to presage Christ's Catholic (in Greek, the *katholikos* or "universal") Church:

What is the secret of Rome's historical destiny? It is that God wills the unity of mankind. . . . Hitherto the whole earth from east to west had been rent asunder by continuous strife. To end this madness God has taught the nations to be obedient to the same laws and to all become Romans. Now we see mankind living in a single city. . . . This is the meaning of all the victories and triumphs of the Roman Empire: the Roman peace has prepared the way for the coming of Christ.[11]

Charlemagne and the German Holy Roman emperors all strove to build this single "Christian empire" during the Middle Ages, while in the age of absolutism a series of secular rulers, from England's Elizabeth I to the "sun king" Louis XIV, appealed to the same expansive, irenic ideal.[12]

For the pagan world, the best that could be hoped for in a world governed by fate was a fixed stability in time. Universal empire was a kind of stalemate with history: it promised that the future would bring nothing bad, but also nothing new. But Christianity, through its Hebrew antecedents, introduced a different perspective. Time was governed not by fate but by the will of Yahweh. History's movement was no longer cyclical but linear, running from Genesis to Judgment Day, according to God's purpose. "I am the Alpha and the Omega," He tells His faithful. "I am the first and the last." In the new linear view, the future becomes more important than the past in determining man's meaningful relations with other men, as humanity pushes irresistibly forward to Christ's Second Coming. A future event and final purpose—the millennium or return of Christ to govern his universal empire—directs all of history and our actions in it.[13]

The central text for the millennialist perspective on history was the New Testament's Book of the Revelation of St. John, or (in its Greek version) the Book of the Apocalypse. From the apocalyptic perspective, the things in the world are never as they seem. The beast with seven heads and ten horns, symbolizing the Roman Empire under Nero, seems powerful and immortal. All the world "worshiped the beast, saying, who is like unto the beast? Who is able to make war with him?" (13:4). But the beast is actually weak and insignificant, because he has no place in God's final purpose. As the angel explains, "The beast that thou sawest was, and is not; and shall ascend out of the bottomless pit, and go into perdition; and they that dwell on the earth shall wonder . . ." (17:8).

The Empire of the Beast and the Scarlet Woman will, improbably enough, be destroyed by the Lamb and his followers, the then tiny Christian sect, since they are the Lord's Anointed. In history, it is the rebel, not the ruler, who finally emerges victorious. "These shall make war with the Lamb, and the Lamb shall overcome them; for he is Lord of lords, and King of kings; and they that are with him are called, and chosen, and faithful" (17:14). The apocalyptic prophet brings comfort to the oppressed and afflicted by pronouncing God's doom on the status quo, and announcing what will take its place.

This apocalyptic view found its first practical application in A.D. 410 when Saint Augustine, bishop of Hippo in North Africa, learned that Rome had fallen to the Visigoth barbarians. Augustine told his dismayed parishioners that this was not the end of the world, but a glorious new beginning. He announced that the fall of Rome opened the way to the building of a Christian world order to replace the corrupt earthly Babylon of paganism. He called this future eternal city the New Jerusalem, in which all the faithful will be finally united with God once and forever.

Augustine's *City of God* became the foundation of Christian theology in the medieval West. The Catholic Church, which already had established its base in Rome, quickly identified itself with this New Jerusalem, and the notion that papal Rome was indeed the Eternal City became an imperishable part of the Church's self-image. But all through the Middle Ages a tension remained between a Church establishment that identified itself as the new universal empire and the apocalyptic identification of earthly empire with the Antichrist. A succession of prophets and rebels—Joachim of Fiore, John Wycliffe, Jan Hus, and Savonarola—insisted that the Roman Apostolic Church in fact bore the mark of the beast. More often than not these rebels ended up at the stake, and the Church's claim to power remained unshaken. But then one managed to elude his persecutors and create his own "true Reformed church." For Martin Luther, the Catholic Church was nothing more or less than Babylon—"it would be no wonder," he wrote in 1520, "if God would rain fire and brimstone from heaven and sink Rome into the abyss, as He did Sodom and Gomorrah of old"—and the pope the Antichrist. "If he is not," Luther exclaimed, "then somebody tell me who is!"[14]

Protestants and Catholics alike explained the religious wars of sixteenth-century Europe in terms of the Apocalypse and the struggle against a menacing Antichrist. Salvation seemed to require the violent and catastrophic destruction of everything that had come before, as massacres and atrocities mounted on both sides. Only with the ebbing of sectarian passions in the seventeenth century did a new, less catastrophic vision of history as redemption emerge: the idea of Progress.

## PROGRESS AND CIVILIZATION

On the eve of the modern era, then, there were numerous ways that Europeans could talk about change, time, and history. There was the myth of the Golden Age, with its appeal to what the poet Petrarch called *dolce tempo della prima etade* ("that sweet time of man's first stage") and its awareness of the relentless decay of time. There was the cyclical *anakuklosis* of the Greeks, refurbished as Fortune versus virtue and then as virtue versus corruption. There were invocations of universal empire, particularly among Europe's absolutist rulers, and of millennium and apocalypse among their opponents. Yet despite their great differences, all these theories of time remained ultimately pessimistic about the fate of the world of the flesh. Any true hope for man, they taught, lay in the world of the spirit, with God and His law of eternity.

However, by the Renaissance, thinkers were recognizing that the world of the flesh was subject to its own God-given natural laws. The idea of natural law meant that the will of God governs our daily affairs in the form of divine Providence, that benevolent and curiously detached vigilance God keeps over all His creatures. The great natural law philosophers—Hugo Grotius, John Locke, Samuel Pufendorf, and Giambattista Vico—were all working on variations of this single simple insight, that the natural laws governing human behavior were also the laws of God.[15] And since God's will always works to good ends, the same must be true of the laws governing our individual lives and, even more significantly, our collective history. The Neopolitan churchman Giambattisto Vico saw all of human history moving through three successive *corsi* ("cycles") under the guidance of God's will as Providence.[16] Vico also started the custom of dividing history into distinct civilizations, each of which illustrated Vico's Christianized *anakuklosis*. Every historical people, he claimed, began with an archaic age of kings and priests and primitive myths, followed by an age of heroes and epic struggles, leading to an age of empire and universal dominion, which then broke apart and declined into barbarism, causing the cycle to begin again.

Vico's empirical historical bent remained unusual, but his penchant for using cross-cultural comparisons to construct a single "universal history" typified the Englightenment. The Enlightenment mind also embraced Vico's other assumption, that human society was part of a larger rational and benevolent natural order.

Living in the shadow of the religious wars, Thomas Hobbes had concluded that men's natural instincts led to a "war of all against all." A half century later, the natural law philosopher Francis Hutcheson argued that human society grew out of man's innate sociability or desire to be with others—the "natural bonds of beneficence and humanity in all." Hutcheson served as mentor to a generation of Enlightenment thinkers, including David Hume and Adam Smith. Although these men would become more skeptical about humanity's prospects than their great teacher, the so-called Scottish school did remain true to Hutcheson's basic supposition. A single, universal set of natural bonds underpins all human communities throughout history, and these develop in increasing complexity—from family, tribe, and clan to community and empire—according to the same regular pattern. This was Europe's first secular theory of Progress, or "civilization."

Being "civilized" had originally meant living under Roman, or "civil," law; but at the dawn of the Renaissance it had come to denote a way of life and law distinct from that of barbarism. It included prohibitions against murder, incest, and cannibalism; belief in a transcendant creative divinity; respect for property and legal contracts; and essential social institutions such as marriage, friendship, and the family. How did people learn these standards? Through collective reason, since these "laws" were not written down or dictated, but discovered directly in people's daily dealings with each other. These laws were referred to as "natural," suggesting that being civilized meant, above all, learning to live in accordance with natural law rather than mere instinct or habit.

The term *civilisation* originally appeared in France. At first *civilisé* was synonymous with providing good government or being "well policed" (*policé*). Soon, however, *civilisation* denoted more than just a specific form of government; it referred to a process that moved people from customs (*moeurs*), institutions, and a material existence that was identified as primitive, to one that was more sophisticated or "civilized." Civilization was an historical process. It had a beginning and an end; it made people different, but also better, than they had been in their primitive or savage state.*

Civilization made its forward march from primitive solitude and barbarism to modern or "civil society" in four stages. In his presocial solitary *state of nature*, man roams helpless and alone; then he forms primitive *pastoral and nomadic* communities, such as the Hottentot bushmen and Plains Indians of America; the third stage is the *agrarian* stage, in which men make their living from fixed possession of the land; which leads finally to the *civil* or *commercial* stage, in which men shift their social and economic lives from the village and farm to the city and its urban attributes.

This progress is first of all an economic advance, as men and women earn their living in increasingly productive ways, from foraging to herding to agriculture to trade and industry. But it also involves a steady cultural advance. Man finds himself connected to more and more people in more complex and mutually beneficial ways; other human beings are no longer just competitors for a bone to gnaw on or the meager fare from the day's hunt. They are family and friends, customers and colleagues, fellow citizens in a common enterprise in whom we recognize the best part of ourselves. The rational part of man's personality increasingly discovers new and exciting outlets.[17] This results in the development of the arts and sciences, literature and poetry: "The more these refined arts advance," wrote philosopher David Hume, "the more sociable men become."

Civil society, or modern civilization, encompassed a human transformation that Enlightenment thinkers summarized in the four catchphrases of civil society theory. The first was the refinement of manners. Manners formed a society's collective character or virtue. "Manners," Edmund Burke exclaimed, "are of more importance than laws" in the

---

* There was also some resistance to the term. James Boswell visited Samuel Johnson in 1772 as the latter was revising his famous dictionary, and the new word came up. "He [Johnson] would not admit *civilisation*," Boswell wrote afterwards, "but only *civility*. With great deference to him, I thought *civilisation*, from *to civilize*, better in the sense opposed to *barbarity*, than *civility*." From the point of view of later English usage, it was Boswell who won the argument.

secure foundation of human society. "They aid morals, they supply them, or they totally destroy them."[18] Voltaire made them the principal subject of history itself. As men become more rational, and as their society's horizons become less narrow, their manners lose their earlier parochialism. Society's tastes in literature and the arts become, in a word, civilized (in fact, the French simply translated the English word "refinement" as *civilisation*). Refinement of manners brings a tolerance for those of different political and religious views: no more Inquisitions or religious wars. Men look for a rational rather than mythic understanding of the workings of nature, which we call science. Refinement also encourages a more sympathetic appreciation of the intrinsic worth of other human beings, including (or especially) women, who were, the Englightenment agreed, an important influence on raising the standard of society's manners and morals.[19]

Refined manners were closely connected with the second important virtue of civilization, the rise of politeness, a word with the same root as "polished" and "finished." The third Earl of Shaftesbury, English moralist and philosopher, used the term to describe people as well as objects, and saw it as the happy result of modern urban life: "We polish one another, and rub off our corners and rough sides by a sort of amicable collision." These multiple contacts teach us that we must treat others with respect, or civility, and that we owe a due regard for their interests as well as our own.[20] Politeness was more than just a question of good manners (as we would say today). It opens up our true nature as rational, social, and moral beings.

Yet the cultural and social transformations of refinement and politeness were only symptoms of a third phenomenon that served as the central mechanism of human improvement: the growth of commerce. Modern civil society was above all a commercial society. The systematic exchange of goods and services with others opened up a dimension of the rational mind that remained closed under more primitive economic conditions. "Commerce tends to wear off those prejudices which maintain distinction and animosity between nations," historian William Robertson wrote in 1769. "It softens and polishes the manners of men. It unites them, by one of the strongest of all ties, the desire of supplying their mutual wants."[21]

It became a commonplace to say, as we do today, that a market economy depends on people pursuing their own self-interest. But self-interest to a student of civil society such as Adam Smith did not mean avarice or greed. Those were the typical antisocial attitudes of a more primitive state of economy and society, in which the fear of material scarcity is genuine and real. Instead, self-interest in a civilized or "polite" society involves the rational desire to provide goods and services at a profit to an equally self-interested consumer. For the eighteenth century, commerce not only produced the "wealth of nations," it was also the primary mechanism of achieving human progress and turning men from beasts into civilized beings.

In 1803, the liberal political economist Francis Jeffrey identified the middle class or "middling ranks" as the social stratum in which this progress took place. The reasonable, sober, polite, and industrious manners of the middle classes (in French, *la bourgeoisie*), Jeffrey argued, form the cutting edge of civilization's moral, economic, and social improvement, which trickles down to the other ranks of society.[22]

Civilized commercial society brings one final crucial advance. This is the capacity for self-government or liberty. Each previous stage of the civilizing process had likewise created its appropriate form of governance, from no government at all in the state of nature, to the patriarchal chieftain and clan leader, to the feudal lord and king of Europe's Middle Ages. As commercial society encourages men to be autonomous and responsible in the economic and cultural sphere, so it encourages the same capacity in the political sphere, as men learn to throw off "servile dependency upon their superiors."[23] Dependency, especially on political and religious authority, is the distinguishing mark of a barbarous and primitive society, while autonomy—liberty—is the mark of a modern and civilized one. Adam Smith and his contemporaries saw the British constitution and its American offshoot as products of "modern liberty" and the ongoing political advance of civil society. For the French liberal historian François Guizot, the same advance reached the European continent via the French Revolution, when the bourgeoisie was finally able to assume a political role to match its importance in Europe's economic progress. Among those who agreed with that judgment (although little else) would be Karl Marx.[24]

From the point of view of civil society theory, then, history consisted of a general movement toward modern commercial "opulence," as

Adam Smith termed it, conjoined with mankind's ascent from the ignorant savage to the modern Londoner or Parisian. As Guizot put it, the idea of progress was inseparable from the idea of civilization. Progress gave the modern European urban-dweller his taste for fine art and music, his scientific rational understanding of the world, and his instinctive distaste for violence, cruelty, superstition, and political despotism. It was this "onward march," as another British philosopher, Arthur Balfour, explained more than a century later, "which for more than one thousand years had been characteristic of Western civilization."[25]

The first thinker to suggest that this civilizing process had reached its height in modern Europe was the French philosopher A.R.J. Turgot. More than any other society or civilization in history, Turgot argued, Europe had managed to overcome the barbaric and savage part of its collective personality. Its ongoing rational and scientific character was the emblem of its success. At the same time, that in no way implied that progress was exclusively a European possession. Turgot and his disciple Condorcet looked forward to a day when, thanks to "the successive changes in human society," the sun will shine "on an earth of none but free men, with no master save reason; for tyrants and slaves, priests and their stupid or hypocritical tools, will have disappeared." After all, Turgot's friend the baron d'Holbach argued, "the savage man and the civilised; the white man, the red man, and the black man; Indian and European, Chinaman and Frenchman, Negro and Laplander have the same nature. The differences between them are only modifications of that common nature produced by climate, government, education, opinions, and the various causes which operate on them."[26] The German philosopher Johann Gottlieb Fichte pointed out that "the most civilized nations of modern times are the descendants of savages," and so present-day primitive peoples will in future become civilized in their turn. "It is the vocation of our race to unite itself into one single body," he wrote in 1800, "all possessed of a similar culture," which will be the highest and most perfect (that is, the most civilized) in history.[27]

European civilization had a dual and paradoxical nature for the Enlightenment. On the one hand, it sprang from very particular and distinct historical processes, involving differences of "climate, government, education, opinions, and the various causes which operate on them." But on the other, it provided a universal standard for the benefit of all humanity everywhere. The result was a kind of natural convergence of human progress and Europe's dominant role in the world. As "the human mind [is] enlightened," A.R.J. Turgot explained, "manners are softened and isolated nations are brought closer to one together. Finally commercial and political ties unite all parts of the globe; and the whole human race . . . advances, ever slowly, towards greater perfection. . . . At last all the shadows are dispelled; and what a light shines out on all sides! What a host of great men in every sphere! What perfection of human reason!"*[28]

Civilization's progress created a momentum of its own; like Augustine's Heavenly City, it existed apart from human wishes.[29] As the cliché says, You can't stop progress. The English writer William Godwin declared in 1798, "As improvements have long continued to be incessant, so there is no chance but that they will go on." Yet there was also a keen awareness that this improvement could be a transformative as well as a cumulative process, in which each stage of civilization's advance required the destruction of what came before. Edward Gibbon made this the central theme of the most famous work of Enlightenment history, *The Decline and Fall of the Roman Empire* (1776).

Gibbon took up the central episode of the apocalyptic and Augustinian view of history, the fall of the Roman Empire, and turned it inside out. In one sense he proved Augustine correct: the rise of modern Europe did require the destruction of its corrupt ancient predecessor. But Gibbon's historical view was triumphantly secular. The decadence of Rome turned out to be an economic and political crisis rather than a moral one. Rome's global dominion had produced a bankrupt ruling class, an impoverished peasantry, an insolent and overconfident army, and an emperorship that had become the plaything of madmen and degenerates. Gibbon suggested that "instead of inquiring why the Roman empire was destroyed, we should rather be surprised that it had subsisted so long."

Huge, shambling, and ill-conceived, the Roman Empire had insolu-

---

* Voltaire summarized the same position more succinctly and prosaically in his *Age of Louis XIV* (1751): "We may believe that reason and industry will progress more and more; that the useful arts will be improved; that of the evils which have afflicted men, prejudices, which are not their least scourge, will gradually disappear among all those that govern nations."

ble problems that left it exposed to its enemies: not only barbarous Goths, Vandals, and Huns, but also Christianity. "The decline of Rome was the natural and inevitable result of immoderate greatness," Gibbon declared.*

Gibbon's conception of the Roman Empire as doomed to self-destruction by its own success had a profound impact on the modern historical imagination. All great empires and societies reach an end point, it suggested, a point of no return, after which they must inevitably be replaced by something else. "The course of empire" necessarily embodied a cycle of growth, decay, and destruction. This was described by historian John Anthony Froude in these terms: "Virtue and truth produced strength, strength dominion, dominion riches, riches luxury, and luxury weakness and collapse—fatal sequence repeated so often." The possibility that modern civilization might one day disappear despite its material and political endowments would haunt the later eighteenth century, and marked a sharp detour from the earlier, more optimistic view of the European future.[31]

Of course, no civilization completely disappears. Even the most remote and archaic leaves behind physical evidence in the form of ruins. The later Enlightenment was fascinated by ancient ruins. Recent archeological discoveries in Athens, Pompeii, and Egypt fed speculation about the fate of empires and civilizations. Gibbon himself was sitting in the ruins of the Roman Forum when he was inspired to write his *Decline and Fall*. These ancient monuments stood as mute warnings to the eighteenth-century imagination, symbols of past worlds not unlike our own, which likewise was heedlessly heading to its doom.[32]

Count Constantine de Volney's *Les Ruines*, published in 1787, proved enormously popular and influential. It even inspired Napoleon to take Volney with him on his expedition to Egypt in 1798. Subtitled "Medita-

---

* Did Rome's fate await the modern British Empire, as many of his contemporaries predicted? Gibbon himself said no. Material progress, politeness, and refinement—"the system of arts and laws and manners which so advantageously distinguish, above the rest of mankind, the Europeans and their colonies"—made such a repeat performance impossible. A modern, civilized, and commercial society like Britain was not, *could* not be, ancient Rome. "The experience of four thousand years should enlarge our hopes and diminish our apprehensions," Gibbon wrote. "No people, unless the face of nature is changed, will relapse into their original barbarism."[30]

tion on the Revolution of Empires," *Les Ruines* was a reverie on the fragile nature of civilization itself, and an important document of early Romanticism. Standing in front of a pile of broken marble columns at the edge of a great desert, Volney mused:

> Here once flourished an opulent city; here was the seat of a powerful empire. Yes! these places, now wild and desert, were once animated by a living multitude; a busy crowd circulated in these streets now solitary. Within these walls, where now reigns the silence of death, resounded incessantly the noise of the arts, and the shouts of joy and festivity; these piles of marble were regular palaces; these fallen columns adorned the majesty of temples. . . . here industry, parent of enjoyments, collected the riches of all climates . . . and now behold what remains of this powerful city; a miserable skeleton! . . . The wealth of a commercial city is changed into hideous poverty, the palaces of kings become the den of wild beasts . . . Ah, how has so much glory been eclipsed! how have been annihilated so many labours! Thus do perish the works of men! thus vanish empires and nations![33]

Volney had turned the ancient motif of the destructiveness of time against civil society itself. When the Swiss historian Carl Vollgraff later described all of human history as a "colossal collection of ruins,"[34] he was expressing the same sense of melancholy fatalism that Volney first injected into the Romantic imagination.

So there was an inevitable price to be paid for progress. In 1794, the Reverend Robert Malthus worried that commercial society's growth in affluence, and consequent rise in population, must eventually outstrip its ability to feed itself. The result would be starvation, destitution, and ruin. "The great question is now at issue, whether man shall henceforth start forwards with accelerated velocity toward illimitable and hitherto unconceived improvement; or be condemned to a perpetual oscillation between happiness and misery."[35] Malthus also introduced the disturbing image of modern commercial society's "accelerated velocity," spinning it mindlessly on toward more and more progress, both exhilarating and disorienting to those caught up in it. Civil society's linear progression was beginning to resemble the rapid revolutions of Fortune's wheel. One hundred years later, the sight of a giant rotating electric dynamo—

"revolving within arm's length at some vertiginous speed"—would become for Henry Adams the symbol of progress itself.*

Jean-Jacques Rousseau drew up the definitive balance sheet of civilization and barbarism for the late Enlightenment. Originally a native of republican Geneva and a self-styled lover of political liberty (in 1762 he published *The Social Contract*), Rousseau attacked virtually every "progressive" aspect of his own century. Everything his predecessors had praised about the civilizing process Rousseau subjected to a harsh and critical analysis. Refinement in the arts and sciences, politeness in social relations, commerce and modern government were not improving men's morals, Rousseau proclaimed, but making them infinitely worse. Luxury, greed, vanity, self-love, self-interest were all civilization's egregious by-products. "Man is born free," he wrote in the first sentence of *The Social Contract*, "and is everywhere in chains"—the chains imposed by civil society.

Rousseau reversed the poles of civilization and barbarism. His paeans of praise for primitive man, the "noble savage" (not his term) who lives in effortless harmony with nature and his fellow human beings, were meant as a reproach against his refined Parisian contemporaries. But they were also a reproach against the idea of history as progress. "All subsequent progress has been so many steps *in appearance* towards the improvement of the individual," he wrote, "but so many steps in reality towards the decrepitude of the species." Ownership of property gave birth to competition and exploitation; complex social interaction gave birth to pride and envy. The arts made men soft and effeminate. Human beings became physically weak, unhappy, and highly strung. Worst of all, the progress of civil society brought not political freedom, but its opposite. It "irretrievably destroyed natural liberty, established for all time the law of property and inequality . . . and for the benefit of a few ambitious men subjected the human race henceforth to labor, servitude, and misery." He concluded one early essay with this ironic prayer: "Almighty God, deliver us from the Enlightenment, and restore us to ignorance, innocence, and poverty."[36]

Rousseau was the first great critic of capitalism and the prophet of the

---

* See Chapter 5.

failure of civil society.* His example proved irresistible. On the eve of the French Revolution, Rousseau's disciples proclaimed that true happiness did not involve integration into normal society, but liberation from it. When Rousseau's dictum that "man is everywhere born free, but everywhere in chains" joined forces with the notion of the *Volkstum*, or "nation," as an historically rooted community older and stronger than commercial society, the result was Romantic liberalism. As a political faith it inspired figures such as Robespierre and Napoleon, and later swept along figures like Byron, Shelley, and Giuseppe Mazzini. Personal freedom was the goal of human progress, Romantic liberalism asserted, and democratic revolution was the means to attain it.

By 1800, the Enlightenment theory of civil society was not discredited, but it had split apart. Man's social progress and his moral advance now stood at odds. His virtue and his innate desire for liberty now had to fight against the surrounding forces of corruption, which included the sociopolitical order and civilization itself.

## PROGRESS TRIUMPHANT

The golden age is not behind us, but in front of us.
    —Henri de Saint-Simon

The nineteenth century faced an ambiguous legacy. On one side was civil society theory, teaching that human society makes men better. On the other stood Rousseau, proclaiming that it makes them worse. Although to their detractors the great nineteenth-century prophets of progress such as Hegel, Auguste Comte, and Herbert Spencer appear smug and self-assured, in fact they were trying desperately to balance both sides of this Enlightenment heritage. Their great goal was to banish any contradiction between advancing human institutions as defined

---

* It is worth remembering that Adam Smith had no illusions about what the triumph of the commercial spirit and the division of labor's emphasis on specialization might mean for those who were part of it. "Another bad effect of commerce," he wrote in *The Wealth of Nations*, "is that the minds of men are contracted, and rendered incapable of elevation. Education is despised, or at least neglected, and heroic spirit is almost utterly extinguished. To remedy these defects," Smith concluded, "would be an object worthy of serious attention."

by civil society theory and man's natural human aspirations as defined by Rousseau.

The great nineteenth-century prophets of progress proclaimed that what we must be—time-bound social beings—and what we want to be—happy and free—will one day be the same. They rejected both the political anarchy of romantic revolution and the "spiritual anarchy" of a self-interested market society. They proclaimed a different future, which was also historically predetermined. This was Progress with a capital P, embossed with a metaphysical reality all its own.

At the same time, the nineteenth-century version of progress made explicit an issue that had been only implicit in the Enlightenment. This was that the lone individual did not have much choice in these matters. The social and economic processes that make up civil society are large, complex, and inexorable. Those processes are themselves governed by hidden but inevitable laws, including that of Progress itself. The civilized individual is their product, rather than the other way around. One cannot choose to remain outside the grip of those processes by deciding to turn oneself into a noble savage or Pericles, or by trying to recover the lost virtues of a previous human epoch. Human beings have become cogs in the wheels of history as they inevitably grind forward.

The advice of the nineteenth-century prophets of Progress was to enjoy the ride. But there was another, more frightening possibility. If those wheels grind on beyond a certain optimum point and history begins to move *downward* rather forward, as it had in the case of other great civilizations in the past, then the human being becomes as helpless in the face of decline as he was in the face of progress. He is trapped, like medieval man riding Fortune's wheel, with no future and no escape.

Of course, the great founders of the nineteenth-century theories of Progress had no such worries. Georg Friedrich Hegel, a distinguished professor of philosophy at the University of Berlin until his death in 1831, used his famous theory of the dialectic to keep both aspects of the Enlightenment's view of man's fate in society in focus. In the dialectical perspective, things that seem to be opposites are in fact only prior stages of a final reconciliation or synthesis. History is the story of the progress of civil society *and* the story of human freedom, Hegel asserted. Humanity moves progressively toward its own idea of freedom, which is the "self-contained existence" of each individual.* The development of civil society does not put chains on the individual, as Rousseau claimed; step by step, stage by stage, it strikes them off by giving him an understanding of his own independent, creative powers. Art, literature, religion, science, and philosophy are all transformed by the same historical process, which is to say Progress. Progress, Hegel proclaimed, "is the boundless impulse of the world-spirit—the goal of its irresistible urging." Understanding how the spirit of Progress reaches every society and continent on the globe required seeing world history as "founded on an essential and actual aim, which actually is, and will be, realized in it—the Plan of Providence."

"The first phase" of Hegel's universal history of civilization "is the East." The civilizations of China, India, and the Middle East—the "Orient"—form the "childhood of history." It was they that first laid bare the rational nature of the universe, created the first systematic religions, and invented the notion of the state. The Greeks, who "may then be compared with the period of adolescence," invented the notion of the free individual. "The consciousness of freedom first arose among the Greeks," Hegel explained, "and therefore they were free, but they, and the Romans likewise, knew only that *some* are free—not man as such. The Greeks," Hegel added, "therefore had slaves."[38]

The Romans ushered in the "maturity" of humankind, when those same free individuals (and their slaves) created a great material and political empire. Then came the "German" or European world. "This," Hegel noted, "would answer in comparison with the periods of human life to Old Age. However, the Old Age of Nature is weakness; but that of *Spirit* is its perfect maturity and *strength*." By teaching that all men are by their nature free, modern civilization represents the culmination of Progress. "Europe is absolutely the end of history," Hegel proclaimed, since "the History of the World is nothing but the development of the Idea of Freedom."[39]

For Hegel, modern Europe gives us the spectacle of man's progress

---

* "If I am dependent, my being is referred to something else which I am not; I cannot exist independently of something external. I am free, on the contrary, when my existence depends on myself."[37]

both as *a subject*—as an autonomous rational and ethical being—and in terms of his *objective* relations with others in civil society. Both of these branches of his progress culminate, neatly enough, in the emerging nation-state.

As one prominent critic has said, Hegel is the father of the historical theory of the nation, as well as of historical progress.[40] Hegel believed that any remaining discrepancies in commercial society—all the issues that worried Rousseau, Malthus, and others about inequalities of wealth, runaway self-interest, and the loss of human purpose—would be finally and definitively resolved by this national state. "The state power," he explained, "is the achievement of all."[41] Greed and poverty disappear. People become participants in a solid, stable "ethical social realm" (*Sittlichkeit*) created by the expansion of the state's powers and its professional and enlightened civil servants. They learn that freedom and reason are not at odds, as Rousseau had warned, but one and the same: "In the ethical social realm, a human being has rights insofar as he has duties, and duties insofar as he has rights." In Hegel's exalted view, this is what history teaches, reason confirms, and the state makes possible.[42]

Hegel's version of progress not only focused the nineteenth century's political imagination on the role of the state, which Hegel called "the march of God on Earth." It also gave new impetus to the idea that mankind could rationally construct its own salvation. Man's final happiness is not some distant dream, Hegel announced, but is taking place here and now, arising from the irresistible confluence of the progress of human institutions and human aspirations. One of those he inspired in this direction was Karl Marx.

Karl Marx certainly qualifies as one of the nineteenth century's most influential prophets of Progress. His theory of history was constructed on the same foundations as Hegel's: the irresistible march of man's freedom. However, Marx identified economics, rather than politics, as the key that unlocks man's progress through the law of class struggle. Unlike Hegel, Marx denied that commercial society was the final stage of man's economic relations. A further stage lay beyond capitalism: socialism. For Marx and his collaborator Engels, "the authority of the political state dies out," because in a classless society no one will require coercion to get what he wants. "Man," Engels wrote, "[will be] at last the master of his own form of social development. [He] becomes at the same time the lord over nature, and his own master—free."[43]

As with Hegel's nation-state, Marx's Communism is the final reconciliation of man's desires and his relations in society. However, the transformation is more apocalyptic. Capitalism faced a "day of reckoning," Marx warned—misery and exploitation would increase, to the point that the explosion of revolution would become irrepressible. Marx saw bourgeois society as doomed to destruction "by its immoderate greatness" (as Gibbon would have put it), but a new redemptive paradise, "the dictatorship of the proletariat," would take its place. The closing words of the 1848 *Communist Manifesto*—"The proletarians have nothing to lose but their chains. Workers of the world, unite!"—echo Rousseau as well as the aspirations of Romantic liberalism.

For both Hegel and Marx, history as Progress reaches an end point, beyond which it can go no further. For Hegel's contemporary Henri de Saint-Simon, it was not history but technology and science that provided the key to human existence and happiness. Originally a supporter of the French Revolution, Saint-Simon had become disillusioned by its more radical excesses and turned away from politics. Instead, he became convinced that the modern scientific mind would be able to create a new spiritual community in which all conflict and unhappiness would disappear.

As in Hegel, an enlightened bureaucratic elite would organize this perfect society. But whereas Hegel's bureaucrats are homegrown boys as it were, who have a keen understanding of their society's institutions and traditions, Saint-Simon's dwell entirely in the realm of abstract reason and material science. Their guiding principle is the inevitable and infallible "law of Progress," which determines human affairs just as the law of gravity determines nature. "All we can do," Saint-Simon suggested, "is to obey this law with understanding, taking into account the course it prescribes for us instead of being blindly pushed by it." He termed it "our veritable Providence."[44]

"Bureaucracy" and "technology" would later become disparaging and sinister terms. But for Saint-Simon and his intellectual heir Auguste Comte, they seemed to promise a new age of human progress and rational understanding of the world, akin to a new religion. Comte's "positive" philosophy delivered a redemptive message very similar to Hegel's. Our moral nature and social progress are not at odds, Comte explained, but the same. "All human progress, political, moral, or intellectual, is inseparable from material progression," he wrote, meaning the growth of industry and science. Comte termed the principles of man's progressive social development "social physics." He saw it as only one part of a steady growth of a rational order in the universe, which will eventually guarantee "a perfect harmony" in nature as well as society. "Ideas of order and progress are, in social physics, as rigorously inseparable as the ideas of organization and life in biology."[45]

Auguste Comte considered man's perfection through modern society to be more than just a utopian ideal. Because all existence enjoyed a relentlessly forward momentum, perfection was inevitable, if not imminent. His English counterpart, Herbert Spencer, agreed: "The ultimate development of the ideal man is logically certain." For English thinkers of the mid-nineteenth century like Spencer, progress was no longer an arguable issue. It had become an unquestioned metaphysical assumption. The historians Thomas B. Macaulay and W.H. Lecky, philosophers Jeremy Bentham and John Stuart Mill, and political economists David Ricardo and Nassau Senior—the founding fathers of classical nineteenth-century liberalism—all drew inspiration and sustenance from it.

Herbert Spencer personified this faith in progress and the optimistic outlook associated with it. An engineer by training, Spencer had no difficulty seeing modern industrial Britain as at the cutting edge of progress. His version of civilized progress was self-consciously evolutionary, with individual liberty and social solidarity gradually melding together into the perfect liberal society. "Man has freedom to do all he wills," Spencer wrote, "provided he infringes not on the equal freedom of any other man."

The overall purpose and direction of Spencer's version of Progress is the organic evolution of matter from "homogeneity" into differentiation and "heterogeneity." That development, he believed, encompassed biology, psychology, chemistry, and geology as well as the two fields of study that were beginning to command the attention of students of

Progress: political economy and sociology. Like Comte, Spencer saw Progress governing not only human history but everything in the universe.

When Charles Darwin's theory of biological evolution first appeared in *The Origin of Species* in 1857, Spencer was quick to seize on it as proof of his own theory. But in fact Spencer's ideas on the organic evolution of society predated Darwin. It was Spencer, not Darwin, who first coined the term "the survival of the fittest," and it was Spencer who concluded that evolution meant that a gradual perfectibility was possible for human beings as well as other organisms. As in Darwin, man was part of nature, not above it. But Spencer's version of nature was not "red in tooth and claw" (as it would be for later, more pessimistic Darwinians). It was instead a realm of boundless energy and possibilities, where the human individual inevitably finds his powers growing "in dealing with all that comes within the range of experience," until finally he becomes happy and free.

Hegelians and Marxists despised Spencer for his laissez-faire view of the nineteenth century and its awesome expansion of man's material wealth and bourgeois liberty. Yet what strikes us in retrospect is how similar Spencer and Marx were in their expectation of, and dogmatic insistence on, the inevitability of man's progress. Eventually, Spencer believed, all remaining unfitness and deficiencies in society must disappear. For Spencer as for Marx, the existence of evil, man's cruelty and brutality, was merely the remnant of earlier social imperfections. Humanity was like a wrinkled shirt: a few passes of the iron of modern civilization and the imperfections would disappear forever.

Under Spencer's and Comte's influence, a series of "scientific" historians now stepped forward, offering to show how these laws of Progress were played out in the history of civilization itself. Henry Thomas Buckle was an English disciple of Comte. He related the entire course of European and British history to the unfolding of Progress according to regular, fixed, and indubitable laws. In the same year that Spencer declared the "evolution of the simple into complex" to be the universal law of "Society, Government, Manufauctures, Commerce, Language, Literature, Science, and Art," Buckle published his *History of Civilization in England* (1857). Buckle argued that "the progress Europe has made from barbarism to civilization" was due entirely to the growth of man's knowledge and mastery of the world around him, by which he meant science and technology. Other earlier yardsticks of progress, such as the refinement of manners or the growth of politeness, were now set aside or forgotten. Buckle's Progress is first and foremost the imposition of man's rational control over his material environment.

In the early or primitive stages of man's development, for example in nomadic or primitive farming societies, Buckle's human being soon learns that climate, geography, and other external surroundings have the upper hand, and he is forced to adapt accordingly. But as his knowledge and intellectual powers expand in later stages, man takes the driver's seat. The projection of his faculties through science and technology increasingly takes precedence over all other forms of rational activity, and comes to characterize civilization in its European form.[46]

Far from being threatened by a comparative perspective on the relative strengths and weaknesses of European civilization, Buckle and his contemporaries strongly welcomed it. They were able to draw on a wide range of new sources for comparison, including recent archeological discoveries such as Heinrich Schliemann's ancient Troy, Sir Austen Henry Layard's Nineveh, Sir Arthur Evans's Minoan Crete, and, still later, Lord Carnarvon's Egypt. The steady growth of "Oriental studies" provided valuable new data about the past and present civilizations of the Middle and Far East, while pioneering studies of primitive peoples and institutions, such as E.B. Tylor's *Primitive Culture* (1871) and James G. Frazier's *The Golden Bough* (1890), helped to clarify the distinction between "civilized" and "savage" societies. Yet all this material, no matter how startling or interesting, never seemed to contradict the same basic picture: the intrinsic superiority of European civilization over its predecessors and contemporaries.

Whether one examined its scientific achievements, its enormous economic and industrial productivity, its forms of government, or simply its remarkable historical progression from its own savage past, Europe enjoyed an unsurpassed, almost preordained, superiority to its global counterparts. It even became customary to treat the terms "civilization" and "modern Europe" as equivalent, as if all the others were simply second-rate predecessors or flawed imitations of the original. In 1854, John Henry Newman was forced to conclude that European civilization was "so distinctive and luminous in its character, so imperial in its extent, so imposing in its duration, and so utterly without rival upon the face of the earth" that it could justifiably "assume to itself the title of 'human society,' and its civilization the abstract term 'civilization.' "[47]

The real problem for historians was not explaining why Europe had succeeded to primacy, but why the others had all failed or wandered into decrepitude and decay. European and American scholars presented a bewildering number of explanations for this systematic failure of the rest of the world to be like them. Some appealed to differences of climate and geography, others, more notoriously, to racial inferiority and physiological degeneration. Still others pointed to differences in collective psychology and to the role of religious and cultural beliefs.[48] Compared with China, Persia, Ottoman Turkey, and once great but now decadent centers of European culture such as Greece and Italy, or with the primitive jungle-dwelling tribes still scattered in remote parts of the world, only Western Europeans seemed to have achieved the level of material and moral progress that constituted true civilization.

Who could have predicted that by the end of the century scholars would regularly be applying those same terms—decadence, decrepitude, and degeneracy—to Europe itself? Yet this was not so surprising as it must have seemed. After all, if all civilizations rise and fall according to scientifically certain historical laws, then it was only logical and inevitable that the same laws must apply to the European version as well. It is easy to imagine Herbert Spencer's distress in 1858 when he was told that the second law of thermodynamics, the so-called law of entropy, implied that endless progress was not possible, since all energy in the universe must eventually dissipate and life itself cease. "I remember being out of sorts for some days afterwards," he wrote to his informant. "Your assertion that when [final] equilibrium was reached life would cease, staggered me . . . I still feel unsettled. . . ."[49] If our expectations about the future depend on the flawless execution of a preordained and unalterable historical destiny, then we are bound to feel "out of sorts" when forced to conclude that destiny is working against, rather than for, our happiness.

Faith in the law of Progress now opened up the possibility of reversal. Thomas Buckle's American counterpart and fellow Comtean John W. Draper added to the history of progress the new final stage of Decrepitude, when the forces propelling society and man forward suddenly lose energy and begin to run in reverse. He warned readers in *The Intellectual Development of Europe* (1864) that smug comparisons with non-Western societies might not bear too close a scrutiny. "Europe is hastening to become what China is," he suggested. "In her we may see what we shall be like when we are old."[50]

Draper's warning and Spencer's fear of entropy pointed the way to the pessimistic determinism of Henry and Brooks Adams. But a powerful counterweight to the faith in progress had already appeared, in the artistic and literary movement called Romanticism.

## THE ROMANTIC BREAK

Hope, hope, fallacious hope; where is thy market now?

    —J.M.W. Turner

Romanticism's pessimism was largely the result of the French Revolution. The poet William Wordsworth was ecstatic when revolution broke out in 1789. "Bliss was it in that dawn to be alive, but to be young was very Heaven," he wrote, but then: "What disappointment of elevated hopes!" Hopes of a return to Rousseau's world of innocence and freedom dissolved in the Reign of Terror and Napoleon's military dictatorship—a new and preposterous form of despotism disguised as universal empire. Wordsworth, William Blake, the landscape painter J.M.W. Turner,[51] and Adam Smith's disciple James Mackintosh initially were enthusiastic but soon realized their mistake. Another intellectual heir to civil society theory, Edmund Burke, wrote his *Reflections on the Revolution in France*, which became the Bible of nineteenth-century English liberals as well as of Romantic conservatives.

German Romantics were hit especially hard. Friedrich Schiller's expansive "Ode to Joy" in 1785 was followed by this in 1799: "This century in tempests had its end/the new one now begins with murder's cry." Friedrich von Schlegel feared that the French Revolution and Reign of Terror had ushered in a terrible new era of "unselfish crimes," when men commit horrible atrocities out of a love not of evil but of virtue. To the nineteenth-century imagination, the French Revolution became what the Holocaust is to the twentieth: an image of man's deliberate betrayal of his highest nature and ideals. Just as the critic Theodor Adorno claimed that there could be no art after Auschwitz, so did Schlegel suspect one hundred and fifty years earlier that the atrocities of the Reign of Terror meant that the "drama of human history" was actually nearing its end. One Swiss scholar in 1818 even seriously suggested making Iceland a museum of European cultural artifacts before civilization vanished completely.[52]

Like radical intellectuals in the thirties and forties who became disillusioned with Communism under Stalin, the new Romantics came to appreciate virtues in their own society that their previous political faith had taught them to condemn. The result was the rise of a new generation of conservative Romantics, including Schlegel, Joseph de Maistre, and the poets Chateaubriand, Novalis, and Samuel Taylor Coleridge. They looked at the institutions the French Revolution and its Enlightenment predecessors had attacked—the Catholic Church, the monarchy, the traditional aristocracy—with a new respect. These now appeared as important landmarks of an older and nobler cultural heritage, which both the French and Industrial Revolutions had put at peril. One could call these figures conservative Romantics, but "reactionary"—as a reaction against the whole notion of progress—is probably more accurate.

At the same time, Romanticism's loss of confidence in the future was matched by a growing nostalgia for the premodern past. Romantic poets and painters had a strong taste for history. But history for them was not the story of progress but the narrative of the past and its vanished glories. It is no coincidence that the most popular novelist of the first half of the century was Sir Walter Scott. Schooled in the tradition of German Romanticism, his first runaway bestseller was the historical novel *Waverley* (1814). The idea of setting a story in the Middle Ages or the Scottish highlands and populating it with "barbaric" characters such as crusading knights, monks, Anglo-Saxon maidens, and clan chieftains would have seemed ridiculous to Scott's Enlightenment predecessors. But Scott turned the genre of the historical novel into a mass-market industry. A string of imitators appeared, including Alexandre Dumas, Victor Hugo, and the young Jules Verne.

Scott turned his home into a veritable museum of Scottish and English history, with a collection of armor, banners, and religious relics that served as a visual tribute to the values of heroism and virtue that his own industrial age seemed to have lost. A fashion for neo-Gothic architecture that swept over England at the same time attempted to recreate visually the sense of community and sanctity of a Middle Ages destroyed by its modern commercial successor.[53]

The Romantics were also shocked by commercial society's latest permutation, industrialization. Factories, steam engines, and smokestacks became veritable images from hell. Blake spoke of the "dark satanic mills," Thomas Gray of the "daemons at work" at the iron foundry, and Robert Southey of "infernal noises and infernal occupations" of the factory, which "the devil has fixed upon . . . for his own nursery-garden and hot-house."[54] Blake's description of early industrial London contrasted sharply with the image the Enlightenment gave of the city as the summit of urbane "politeness" and civilization:

> I wander through each chartered street,
> Near where the chartered Thames does flow
> and mark in every face I meet
> Marks of weariness, marks of woe.
>
> In every cry of every man,
> in every infant's cry of fear,
> In every voice, in every ban,
> The mind-forged manacles I hear.

Wordsworth gloomily surveyed England in 1806 with these thoughts:

> The world is too much with us; late and soon,
> Getting and spending, we lay waste our powers.
> Little we see in nature that is ours;
> we have given our hearts away, a sordid boon!
>
> For this, for everything, we are out of tune;
> it moves us not. Great God! I'd rather be
> a pagan suckled in a creed outworn;
> So, might I, standing on this pleasant lea,
> Have glimpses that would make me less forlorn.

Robert Southey contrasted the new era of materialism and greed with an earlier England, when "the benevolent squire called his tenants around the crackling fire" and everyone shared in the benefits according to his station. It was a world where human beings were united by ties of tradition, religion, and a sense of community. But then "a trading spirit gradually superseded the rude but kindlier principle of the feudal system; profit and loss became the rule of conduct; in came calculation, and out went feeling."[55]

This would prove to be Romanticism's most enduring legacy: its alienation from its own time and era. "No poetry can bloom in the modern soil, the drama has died. . . . The ecstatic dream which some twelfth-century monk cut into the stones of the sanctuary is reproduced to bedizen a warehouse; the plan of an abbey is adapted to a railway station." This was not Wordsworth or Southey speaking, but the American lawyer Brooks Adams in 1893. Romanticism taught everyone that the middle-class makers of modern civilization (including, of course, professional men like Brooks Adams himself) might be decent, hard-working, and respectable, but they had also become philistines.

Meanwhile, others were seeing in what used to be civilization's most prized achievement, "refinement" and the "softening and polishing of men's manners," something equally sinister—the rise of decadence. The principal target of those fears was, ironically, Romanticism itself.

Decadence literally means "a falling away," which ancient Romans used to describe the loss of an earlier fixed norm or standard of literary excellence. Like "decline," the word became inseparable from the image of the fall of the Roman Empire. It was and is a term of abuse, not analysis.[56] But decadence also implied that a decline in intellectual and moral standards was related to larger social and economic changes.* Decadence starts at the top, when an elite loses its desire to maintain the old order. Instead of resisting the impending collapse, "decadent" politicians, artists, and aristocrats accept and embrace it. Arthur Balfour put it this way in 1903: "When in an ancient and still powerful state, there spreads a mood of deep discouragement, when the reaction against recurring ills grows feebler, enterprise slackens and vigour ebbs away, then as I think, there is present some process of social degeneration," which can be called decadence.[57]

In the nineteenth century, decadence became the watchword for a conservative reaction against the excesses of Romanticism. The Ro-

---

* As in Montesquieu's *Considérations sur le Grandeur et Décadence des Romains* (1734).

mantic appeal to strong emotions and the bizarre and irrational shocked people who were used to more staid standards. At the end of his life, Goethe had pronounced that classicism was health and romanticism disease. Then, in 1834, Desiré Nisard published *Studies on the Manners and Critiques of the Roman Poets of the Decadence*, which purported to show that the bizarre decadence of modern Romantic literature was only a reflection of the larger decadence of moral and social values of modern society. Soon everyone was using the term. In 1845, a Parisian magistrate wrote in a report to his superiors, "I believe that our society is suffering from a profound malaise." Romantic literature had, he concluded, "given license to the worst instincts. . . ." Everywhere he saw the same thing: "immediate gratification of the appetites, the search for pleasure, a monstrous egotism . . . If we continue like this . . . the days of the Roman decadence will return."[58]

Two years later, Thomas Couture unveiled his painting "The Romans of the Decadence," setting off a storm of comment and controversy in Paris. It showed a Roman orgy in a sumptuous palace, surrounded by the luxuries and delicacies of superfluous wealth. But the faces of the participants betray their boredom; as they go through the motions of sensual delight, they are spiritually dead. Material comfort and opulence had drained away all creativity and life. Couture attached this subtitle from Juvenal's "Sixth Satire":

*Luxury, more vicious than any foreign foe,*
*lays its heavy hand upon us, and avenges*
*the world we conquered.*[59]

Civilized society's success brings an overabundance of commodities and comforts to a population that no longer has to struggle and strive to survive; it becomes soft and "effeminate," as Rousseau had charged almost a century earlier: "True courage is enervated . . . [and] the dissolution of morals in turn leads to the corruption of taste."[60]

Lurking behind this moral critique was a critique of the orthodox principles of political economy. As the inexorable forces of the division of labor bring specialization to its most acute point, civilization reaches its most developed or "late" stage. The decadent artist and the philistine businessman both reflect a human personality shrunk to its narrowest and basest level, pursuing objects now readily at hand to the exclusion of all else: money in the case of the latter and self-gratification in the case of the former. In both cases, creative energy recedes and the grossly material triumphs over the spiritual. "The whole no longer lives at all" was Friedrich Nietzsche's diagnosis of decadence, "everywhere paralysis, arduousness, torpidity or hostility and chaos." Decadent society, like decadent art, Nietzsche concluded, "is composite, calculated, artificial, and artifact."[61]

What were supposed to be positive developments—the growth of wealth and industry, the spread of self-government, the rise of technology and the decline of religion—now became harbingers of "the last hours of civilization." Europe here had entered an "impressive old age," according to the twenty-five-year-old Victor Hugo in 1827. Its civilization was now "ancient," other French Romantics insisted; it was "played out," "decaying," "senile," and even "dying."[62] Progress took on a bitterly ironic meaning, as in Théophile Gautier's discussion of progress in the arts in his *Preface to Mademoiselle de Maupin*: "Some centuries ago we had Raphael and Michelangelo," Gautier wrote scathingly, "now we have M. Paul Delaroche, and all because we are progressing."

Yet in ridiculing the idea of Progress, Hugo and Gautier betrayed the same basic assumption as Comte or Spencer. This was that societies and civilizations had a fixed life span and function as a biological organism just as its members do. "The human race as a whole has grown, has developed, has matured, like one of ourselves," Hugo remarked. "It was once a child, once a man, and now we are looking on at its impressive old age." Hugo echoed an organicist tradition that dated back to Giambattista Vico (whose writings were enjoying a new vogue in Paris literary circles) and ultimately to Plato and the Greeks. Just as old age eventually overtakes each of us, the organicist view argued, so must it overtake European civilization. Almost two decades before John Draper warned that in Chinese civilization "we may see what we shall be like when we are old," both the Romantics and their opponents were arguing that Western Europe was already there. It was a commonplace on both sides of the Atlantic that Europe was the Old World, in contrast to the New World of America. Even Europe's unchallenged power and influence around the globe became suspect, since it only confirmed that the era of dynamic growth was already past; the only future left was maturity sliding into overripeness and decay.

In a profound sense, the nineteenth century's fear of decadence re-flected its fear of its own success. European civilization's awe-inspiring power took on a quality of "overmuchness," a surfeit of easy wealth, so-cial mobility, material comfort, and complacency—as well as a surfeit of change and destruction of what had come before. "Progress has atro-phied in us all that is spiritual," Charles Baudelaire wrote.[63] The same "excesses" that repulsed radical Romantics like Gautier also earned the wrath of their conservative opponents. Six years after Couture's canvas was unveiled, one of those conservatives, Count Arthur de Gobineau, gave the attack on progress a profoundly new and startling twist.

## CHAPTER 2

# AFLOAT ON THE WRECKAGE

*Arthur de Gobineau and Racial Pessimism*

> The fall of civilizations is the most striking, and at the same time, the most obscure, of all the phenomena of history. . . . Every assemblage of men, however ingenious the network of social relations that protects it, acquires on the very day of its birth, hidden in the elements of its life, the seed of an inevitable death.
>
> —Arthur de Gobineau, *Essay on the Inequality of the Human Races*

Joseph Arthur de Gobineau began life despising two things: revolution and the bourgeoisie. He was born on July 14, 1816, the anniversary of Bastille Day, proof, he later wrote with grim amusement, that "opposites attract." The great loves of his life were books, especially poetry and literature, and himself—or rather, his own aristocratic lineage. As Count Gobineau, he enjoyed casting himself as the last survivor of an ancient Norman noble family. He even constructed a family tree purporting to show that the Gobineaus were direct descendants of Normandy's Viking conquerors, the same stock that had produced William the Conqueror.\* His mother likewise claimed descent from an illegitimate son of Louis XV, which may also have contributed to Gobineau's lifelong obsession

---

\* This was his *Histoire d'Otto Jarl*, privately printed in 1879. The truth was very different. The Gobineaus were a family of prosperous Bordeaux merchants who became ennobled in the eighteenth century by holding royal office. The comtes de Gobineau were, in short, proof of the virtues of social mobility, the very quality of modern "commercial society" that Gobineau most affected to despise.

with blood, heredity, and race as well as his distaste for the era into which he had been born.

Arthur's father, Louis de Gobineau, had fought loyally on the royalist side during the French Revolution and had been imprisoned under Napoleon. However, his failure to receive any pension or recognition from the restored Bourbon monarchs deeply embittered him. Forced to live hand-to-mouth as a half-pay army officer, he passed his own bitterness and self-pity on to Arthur. "My own situation [is] as one defeated," Louis wrote in his relentlessly self-justifying memoirs for his teenaged son. "My humiliation is that men should see my sword snatched away because of my obedience to my prince."[1]

At nineteen, the young Arthur de Gobineau was determined to succeed where his father had failed. He decided he would reverse the family's fortunes, not by following his father into the army but as a poet, playwright, and eminent man of letters—a French Goethe. Picking up his father's metaphor, he wrote thus to his sister in 1834: "The sword that this age has shattered will be replaced by my pen. . . . Knowing how to preserve my independence at all cost, I shall give lie to all the world—and I shall succeed." In a franker moment he confessed, "I must succeed or die."[2]

When Gobineau left his native Normandy and arrived in Paris in 1835 to launch his literary career, he was, like his father, a conservative Catholic royalist. But in poetic and artistic matters he was modern down to his fingertips. His tutor (who had also been his mother's lover) had surrounded him with the works of contemporary German poets such as Hölderlin and Novalis, and he had a keen interest in what would soon come to be called the "avant-garde."[3] At the time, there was nothing unusual about this combination of conservative politics and avant-garde tastes. For every artistic and political radical, or "bohemian," living and working in Paris, such as Georges Sand or Théophile Gautier, one could just as easily find a Chateaubriand serving as a minister of state under the Bourbons, or an Alfred de Vigny gracing the ultraroyalist literary salon of the duchess de Cayla, along with the young Victor Hugo.[4]

Despite their political differences, bohemians and conservative Romantics alike shared the same contempt for modern French society. In the wake of the Industrial and French Revolutions, a new ruling class of merchants, bankers, and industrialists came into prominence, which, unlike its predecessor under the Old Regime, seemed to have neither the time nor the interest to appreciate the arts. The German poet Hölderlin had introduced the term "philistine" to describe this supposedly narrow and anti-intellectual middle class. Among French Romantics another term did just as well: *bourgeoisie.*

The French bourgeoisie were, as Hölderlin said of the German middle class, "barbarians." But they were modern, not primitive, barbarians, the collective products of "industriousness and science." As a class they were "deeply incapable of every divine emotion."[5] Charles Baudelaire viewed his own society as "the most stupid of societies," a world of "asinine Romantic hypocrisy [and] the home of imbecility." "Commerce," he stated, "is, by its very essence, satanic." Many besides Gobineau, both radicals or reactionaries, would have agreed with him.[6] One of Gobineau's literary models, the novelist Stendahl, wrote that the sight of a businessman or lawyer or successful doctor, made him want to "weep and vomit at the same time."[7] The bourgeois credo was, Gustav Flaubert sneered, that "man is born to work." The artist's credo, by contrast, came from Théophile Gautier's novel *Mademoiselle de Maupin,* published in 1834, the year before Gobineau arrived in Paris: *l'art pour l'art,* or "art for art's sake."[8] To be an artist or writer was to be by definition antibourgeois: in another of Gautier's famous phrases, the writer's cultural role was *épater la bourgeoisie,* or "to shock the bourgeoisie." The artist, like the aristocrat, stood apart and above the petty aspirations of the "tobacconists, grocers, and dealers in potato chips" who formed the nucleus of modern commercial society. Instead, the Romantic artist looked elsewhere for inspiration and spiritual kinship.

As discussed in Chapter 1, romantic alienation prompted a nostalgic fascination with the Middle Ages, the same epoch that the Enlightenment despised as the Dark Ages and attacked as an era of superstition and clerical tyranny.

The other escape route from modernity was geographic, to the non-Western cultures of the Middle East, India, and Asia. Ever since scholars had accompanied Napoleon on his conquest of Egypt in 1798 and the linguist Jean-François Champollion had deciphered the Rosetta Stone in 1822, Paris had been one of the leading centers of Orientalist studies, feeding the artistic and intellectual ferment that had overtaken the city. At one level, Orientalism prompted an interest in the ancient civilizations of the Middle East and India and in comparative linguistics. The Paris Asiatic Society (1822), London's Royal Asiatic Society (1823), and the American Oriental Society (1842) were major centers for research and translation of non-European literature and texts. But the exotic flavors of Orientalism also appealed to the Romantic aesthetic imagination. The leading lights of French Romanticism—Chateaubriand, Gautier, Gérard de Nerval—were all profoundly affected by European scholars' translations of the Hindu Upanishads, the Indian drama *Shakuntala*, and the Persian epic *Shah-Nameh*, as well as many Chinese and Arabic classics. The philosopher Friedrich Schlegel, who came to Paris to study Sanskrit in 1803, proclaimed that "it is in the Orient that we must seek the highest Romanticism."*

Romantic Orientalism gave a new twist to the age-old belief in civilization's inevitable westward course. Out of disillusionment with the results of modern European civilization, the Romantics acquired a new fascination and respect for its eastern predecessors. Leading exponents of Orientalism such as the painter Eugène Delacroix and later Gobineau himself were struck by the fact that, while Western Europe was ostensibly more "progressive" than the "decadent" civilizations of the East, those older cultures had preserved spiritual values that seemed lost in their own society. Delacroix had left Paris for Morocco just the year before Gobineau arrived, in search of new aesthetic outlets and sensations, just as Gobineau would later travel to Persia and Gauguin to Tahiti later still.

Above all, these non-European peoples, like their pre-modern European counterparts, seemed to radiate a vitality that modern civilization had either dissipated or destroyed. As Gobineau's contemporary Charles Baudelaire explained: "There are but three groups worthy of respect: the priest, the warrior, and the poet. To know, to kill, and to create."[10] All three were vanishing from modern life. Its most characteristic product, the Romantics claimed, was *ennui*, the lethargy or "drowsy nausea" that resulted from an overcivilized life-style. Thomas Couture's

---

* Edgar Quinet, scholar of Chinese literature and professor at the University of Paris, noted in one of his lectures the impact of Oriental studies on Romantic aesthetics: "Germany: Herder, Hebraic poetry, Persian influence (Jean-Paul); Goethe. . . . England: Lake School, Coleridge, Shelley completely Indian; Byron &c."[9]

"Romans of the Decadence" suffered from *ennui*; so did the cold, bored young men of Balzac's novels. *Ennui* was the opposite of what the German Romantics called the "life-feeling," and the enemy of artistic creativity. Baudelaire summed up the dichotomy between the modern and the primitive this way: "Nomad peoples and even cannibals may all, by virtue of their energy and personal dignity, be the superiors of our races of the West."[11] Or as Théophile Gautier put it, "Better barbarism than boredom!" It was a sentiment that Gobineau would turn into a new theory of history.

Gobineau turned to history largely to explain to himself why his literary career ended up a failure. When he arrived in Paris, he discovered thousands of other young men with similar literary ambitions who were trying to succeed.* Since Gobineau had no connections to help him, his plays and poems failed to find an audience. He was forced to take a clerical job in a Parisian gas company. Angry and humiliated, he began to echo a familiar theme in his letters home: "Our poor country lies in Roman decadence," he wrote in 1840, "we are without fibre or moral energy. I no longer believe in anything." He also knew who was to blame: "MONEY HAS KILLED EVERYTHING," he wrote in large capital letters.

Like Balzac, a writer he admired, Gobineau learned to see the City of Lights as ruled by only two forces, "gold and pleasure." He gave vent to his frustration in a letter to his sister: "Money has become the principle of power and honor. Money dominates business; money regulates population; money governs . . . money is the criterion for judging the esteem due to men." France had become a "kingdom of bankers. . . . How I despair of a society which . . . has no heart left."[12]

Two other events confirmed him in his pessimism. In 1843, Gobineau managed through some German friends to meet one of the leading lights of the liberal intellectual establishment, Alexis de Tocqueville. Tocqueville hired him as a research assistant for a massive research project on the origins of manners and morals in modern Europe. Tocqueville hoped to show that nineteenth-century liberalism, for all its self-consciously secular character, still kept the moral teachings of

---

* One observer estimated that there were at least forty thousand young writers looking for government clerical jobs in Paris in 1831.

Christianity at its foundations. The equality of all human beings before God, "the duty of those who have more to help those who have less," and the intrinsic worth of the individual—these were still, Tocqueville believed, the guiding principles of liberal society.[13]

However, as Gobineau spent his days poring over the works of the leading progressive philosophers of the day—Jeremy Bentham, Joseph Priestley, William Godwin, the French socialist Charles Fourier, Kant, Hegel, and Fichte—he was driven to a conclusion directly opposed to that of his employer. Traditional Christianity, he complained, "the chain which unites men through their beliefs," had obviously fallen apart. Greed, self-interest, falsehood, and material gain were the dominant forces of the day. At the same time, Gobineau blamed Christianity for this moral bankruptcy. Instead of valuing strength, valor, and self-sacrifice, as the ancients had, Christian morality "has expressly declared that it prefers the weak and lowly to the strong."[14] This had allowed a certain feebleness of spirit to enter the cultural mainstream of Europe at the expense of more active and vital principles, leaving a trail of mediocrity in its wake.

The other event was a wave of popular revolutions that broke out all across Europe in 1848. In February crowds of students and workers overthrew the monarchy of Louis Philippe in violent street demonstrations in Paris. By March the revolutionary fervor had spread to Germany and Austria. In November the Pope was expelled and his government replaced by a new Roman Republic. However, the revolutionaries' hopes of a "new world order" of national self-determination and liberty soon collapsed. The new nations and republics formed from the ruins of fallen empires—Germans, Czechs, Poles, Hungarians, Serbs, and Croats—quarreled among themselves over borders and territories. Middle-class liberals discovered that the forces of social discontent that revolution had allowed to spill out into the streets could not be suppressed except by force. One by one the new republics collapsed and the old powers returned to their thrones to protect law and order. In France itself the Second Republic willingly gave way to a dictatorship under Louis Napoleon (later Napoleon III), a nephew of the great Napoleon, amid a series of bloodily suppressed worker and peasant uprisings across the country.[15]

Like the revolutions of 1968, 1848 came to define the politics of an entire generation. As one supporter put it, "Never have nobler passions moved the civilized world, and yet all this was to end in failure." Moderate liberals like Tocqueville, the self-conscious heirs to Enlightenment ideals about civilization and progress, were deeply shaken by the upheavals and violence. By contrast, radicals such as Karl Marx and Friedrich Engels concluded that the violence had not gone far enough. True freedom and progress now required the complete and inevitable destruction of capitalism, as well as of the political status quo. "Let the ruling classes tremble at a Communist revolution," they wrote in their *Manifesto of the Communist Party*, "the proletarians . . . have a world to win."

The revolutions of 1848 also destroyed Romanticism's liberal aspirations. Poets such as Lamartine, who helped found the French Second Republic, and Charles Baudelaire; historians such as Jules Michelet, who had just published a soaring paean of praise to the French spirit of unity and brotherhood entitled *The People*; musicians such as the young director of the Dresden Opera, Richard Wagner; and a host of other writers and intellectuals had rallied to the call for liberty and equality. They were appalled by the results. Michelet said, "I should never write *The People* now." Wagner, who had supported the outbreak of socialist revolution in Dresden, was forced to flee abroad when it sputtered out and died. He remained in exile for twelve years and refused to have anything to do with politics again.[16]

The revolutions drove the final wedge between Gobineau and society; his attitude toward both the revolutionaries and their opponents was "a plague on both your houses." Gobineau, like many other observers, dismissed the revolutionary crowds as "barbarians." But whereas Tocqueville and other liberals viewed the "barbaric" riots and "savage" violence of 1848 as a reversion to an earlier, precivilized state, for Gobineau there was something peculiarly *modern* about what had just occurred.

*Manfredine* was a verse play he had begun in 1842 but now completely revised in the wake of the 1848 uprisings. Set in 1647, its Sicilian heroine, Countess Manfredine, leads a popular revolt against Spanish rule not in order to free the masses, for whom she feels nothing but contempt, but to avenge her brother Roger, whom the Spanish had unjustly murdered. In the end, however, the demagogue Masaniello takes over the revolt, and it degenerates into a socialistic *jacquerie*. Gobineau portrays Masaniello and the rebellious mob in vivid antidemocratic terms as we might expect. But thoughtless brutality and untrustworthiness extends to all the other characters, as well. Whether rich or poor, Spanish noble or Sicilian peasant, all are the corrupt products of a society beyond redemption.*

Only the countess herself is spared this irretrievable decay. Like Gobineau, she is the blood descendant of Sicily's Norman conquerors in the Middle Ages, and before that of "barbarian" Viking freebooters who, over the course of generations, have passed their valor and vitality on to her. She is, in short, the last of a virtuous race; her innate superiority shields her against the inevitable degeneration of her age—just as Gobineau fancied of himself. By the time he finished *Manfredine*, Gobineau had concluded that there was a direct causal link between his aristocratic lineage and his alienation from bourgeois society. The blood of France's ancient *noblesse de race*, he (erroneously) believed, still flowed through his veins, providing a buffer against the typical money-grubbing decadence of his own era. As he explained years later, "I discovered that it was not I who was growing old and degenerate, but the society around me."[17]

His mission now was to translate this insight into a more general, historical form. He would show that the Germanic invaders of the Roman Empire were the true founders of Europe's greatness. The Vandals, Visigoths, Franks, and Vikings had destroyed Roman decadence and brought a nobility and inner vitality to an exhausted ancient world. He would demonstrate in telling detail how the ancient aristocracy of Europe, those who were "born to the sword and shield, who will hate and despise repose to the marrow of their bones," progressively disappeared from the modern world, taking with them its vitality and strength. The research he had done for Tocqueville, along with his Orientalist studies in comparative religion and civilization, gave him a solid scholarly framework for the kind of sweeping thesis he had in mind. In a letter to his sister from February 1851, he mentioned "a large book that I am do-

---

* As Countess Manfredine's chaplain observes:
    *When a people have fallen, nothing can regenerate them,*
    *Neither prosperity, nor excess of hardship,*
    *Nor even the efforts of a great and noble master.*

ing on the Human Races."[18] Two years later the "large book" appeared before the reading public as *The Essay on the Inequality of the Human Races.*

## RACE AND THE ARYAN MYTH

In 1853 the idea of "race" was still relatively new.* At the very beginning of the nineteenth century, Johann Friedrich Blumenbach and Georges Cuvier had both proposed a threefold division of humanity into the Oriental or Mongol, Negroid or "Ethiopian," and White or Caucasian races. The scholarly discipline Blumenbach and Cuvier created, anthropology, tried to understand the origins of these essentially physiological differences and to decide whether the races were in fact distinct species or merely variations on the same human type.[19]

Soon, however, Europeans began to use racial or physiological differentiation to explain *cultural* differences. Descent from one race or another, it was assumed, meant acquiring the mental and moral traits of that people, which were played out in their cultural activities. Civilization, the forward march from barbarism to modern civil society, now seemed to acquire a new and empirical base: that of race. To its adherents in the early nineteenth century, racial theory merely seemed a scientific extension of the Enlightenment's "universal history" of mankind, in which the entire panoply of human progress turns out to be related to a single underlying cause. Long before Darwin, race theory was arguing that the unifying laws of progress were not political or economic (as they would be, for example, in Marx's *Das Kapital*), but biological.

All racial theories before Gobineau's *Essay* had classified human races according to a hierarchy, with whites on top and blacks on the bottom. Carl Gustav Carus, who strongly shaped Gobineau's ideas, argued that since Europeans more closely resembled the classical ideal of physical beauty than non-Europeans, this was a sign of their preordained superiority over other, uglier peoples. White Europeans were the "day people," Carus stated, the lightness of their skin reflecting the life-

---

* Until the eighteenth century the term was a synonym for "lineage," or persons descended from a single individual, as in "the race of Abraham" or the French concept of *noblesse de race*, the idea being that true nobility (as opposed to noble status acquired by office or purchase) was based on the transmission of certain key aristocratic virtues, such as a sense of honor, through the generations.

giving light of the sun. Negroid people, on the other hand, were the "night people," whose ebony skin revealed their dark, inchoate nature.[20] Carus and other theorists all agreed that whites enjoyed innate mental and physical advantages over their brown and yellow counterparts.

This assumption of white superiority is, of course, the most notorious aspect of race theory to the twentieth-century mind. But at the time it was by no means the most important, or even the most interesting, aspect of racial thinking. What intrigued the nineteenth-century imagination was race theory's proposition that the *natural* history of man as a biological species had also produced the *cultural* history of mankind as social and creative beings. Racial classification seemed to unlock the mysteries of the civilizing process by explaining why some societies made that forward march more easily and quickly than others.

Gustav Klemm published his ten-volume *General Cultural History of Mankind* between 1846 and 1852, the year before Gobineau's *Essay* appeared. Klemm insisted that all the cultural developments in history consisted of the diffusion and development of distinct racial types. He argued that the crucial difference between the races was not skin color but "active" and "passive" traits. An active racial type displays in its early stages (during what Klemm called man's savagery) an inner strength and will, which it uses to overcome the material obstacles in its path and to conquer other, more passive (and hence inferior) races. Conquest then inevitably brings miscegenation, as the conquerors settle down and lose their fierce independence and will. The original dominant group disappears and a new racial type is formed followed by a new stage of civilization.[21]

For Klemm and Carus, history is inevitably the story of racial mixing. But this mixing was a good, not a bad, thing. Following the Enlightenment view of universal cultural progress, Klemm believed that European man's steady advance from savagery to freedom could be traced to successively higher levels of racial breeding and intermingling. Others disagreed. But the consensus among racial theorists was that the history of race was one of progress, of the steady advance of white dominance and the spread of political freedom for all whites (or at least white males) in its European, racially patterned form.

For this reason, the chief appeal of racism in the nineteenth century was its politically progressive, even liberal, message. If all whites (or white males) were equal by race, there was no excuse for social or economic discrimination among them. Race theory shattered the claims of an aristocratic class to privilege and authority. Instead, all Frenchmen or Englishmen or Germans were endowed from birth with the same cultural gifts, regardless of social origin. And even as European society itself was moving in this happy, egalitarian direction, so must white cultural power naturally extend itself over the nonwhite world.[22] In short, the whole direction of racial thinking in Europe was one of liberal egalitarian optimism, even self-satisfaction.

The word "race" had only appeared once before in Gobineau's writings, in 1849.[23] In framing his discussion he relied heavily on his German predecessors, particularly Klemm, Carus, and Christian Lassen.* Gobineau accepted the hierarchical white-yellow-black racial classification and the notion of racial history as cultural history. Yet when he put his own ideas about race on paper, his Romantic despair and alienation, not to mention his sense of aristocratic exclusiveness, took over. Instead of being the apex of man's biological progress, modern Europe turned out to be a cesspool of racial degeneration. With one stroke Gobineau radically reoriented the whole direction of European thinking about race.

In the *Essay*, contemporary white Europeans are, of course, still superior to their Negroid or Oriental counterparts. As Gobineau explains, the white man enjoys a greater harmony of physical energy, intelligence, and moral scruples. Of all the existing races, he remains the most vital—and it is this vitality, a life force or essence passed from the living organism to its descendants, that lies at the origin of all human creativity and civilization.[24]

The bearers of this organic vitalism were the aboriginal forebears of the European white race, whom Gobineau called "Aryans." The term came from the world of Orientalist studies, and had an interesting history of its own. In 1788 Sir William Jones, a civil servant with the British East India Company, established the deep grammatical similarities between Latin, Greek, Persian, and Sanskrit, as well as the Germanic and

---

* Christian Lassen was the student of Friedrich Schlegel's brother, August Wilhelm, who was a leading Romantic Aryanist. Lassen had studied in Paris with many of the same Orientalist scholars whom Gobineau met and admired. Lassen's work on the Aryan heritage in India (1858–1862) gave an enormous boost to the links between race theory and the Aryanist thesis.

Celtic languages. Jones suggested that all these peoples may have originally shared the same language, and perhaps other cultural traits as well.[25] Friedrich Schlegel took the argument a step further when he came to Paris in 1803 to pursue his studies in Indian philosophy. He proposed that Sanskrit was the original language shared by *all* civilizations both East and West, and that its historical speakers, the Aryan nomadic conquerors of India, were the true ancestors of the Greeks, Romans, and other founders of Western culture.

As it happens, Schlegel was wrong. However, his conclusion that all civilizations had originally been one seized the imagination of Orientalists and philosophers across Europe. The idea of a vanished race of perfect beings endowing the world with all their knowledge dated back to the Greeks and the myth of Atlantis. It was another variant of the Golden Age myth. The year of Schlegel's arrival in Paris marked the heyday of the fascination with ancient Egypt as well as with "primitivism," the belief that an ancient and superior race of philosophers, inventors, and artists had once inhabited the planet and created a vanished supercivilization. Primitivism had prompted serious scholarly debate in the age of Rousseau, inspiring intense interest in Neolithic monuments such as Stonehenge.[26]

Schlegel was an important figure not only in Orientalism and Aryanism but in the Romantic movement as well. His Aryan thesis swiftly took root in that fertile imaginative soil. The Aryans became the original founders of civilization, predating the Greeks, Romans, and Egyptians. By 1813, scholars had invented the term "Indo-Europeans" to describe these Aryan forerunners, a restless and adventurous people who left their original homeland to set off on a historic mission. As they wandered, they spread their cultural gifts from east to west, since "the march of culture," August Friedrich Pott explained, "has always followed the sun's course."[27]

For Christian Lassen at the University of Berlin, these wandering Aryans displayed all the virtues of a bygone, prebourgeois Europe. They had great physical beauty and courage, a strong sense of personal honor (*arya* meaning "man of honor" in Sanskrit), and they expressed their nobility of spirit and vitality in epic poetry from Homer and *Beowulf* to the *Mahabharata*. They were men of great intellectual gifts, able to balance imagination with reason, unlike the inferior peoples they conquered (such as the Dravidians of ancient India and the Semitic peoples of the Middle East). Above all, they were men of the soil, with deep emotional roots in the land rather than in large urban centers and commerce. The Aryans were, in short, the opposite of "polite" in the Enlightenment sense. Instead, they were virtuous in Rousseau's sense, unspoiled by corruption and false values. That virtue was both their birthright and their legacy to their descendants.

At this point, of course, Aryan or "Indo-German" theory merged into racial theory. The wandering Aryans were the prime example of Klemm's active races. And following the assumptions of racial vitalism, Lassen and other Aryanists also agreed that those Aryan peoples closest to the original bloodline preserved more of its vitality and heroic qualities. The Persians, Hittites, Homeric Greeks, and Vedic Hindus in ancient times and the Germanic tribes and Vikings somewhat later had carried an heroic civilization far from its original home. In the Romantic Aryan myth, an heroic, virtuous past replaces the civilized present as the means of determining the worth of a race—or a civilization.

The intermingling of Aryan theory and racial theory gave Gobineau grounds for claiming that all European culture was drawn from a single biological type, the white Aryan or Indo-German. And not only in Europe. History, he said, "shows us that all civilizations derive from the white race, that none can exist without its help. . . ." The last three volumes of the *Essay* surveyed the civilizations created by Aryan blood. The range is breathtaking in its scope.

Gobineau delineated ten great historical civilizations descending from the Aryan war bands. "Of the multitude of people who live or have lived on the earth . . . the remainder have gravitated around these [civilizations] more or less independently, like planets around their suns." The first was India, home of Aryan civilization properly speaking; then came Egypt and Assyria, including Persia, all of which were supposedly founded by a single invading race of white Aryans who subjugated and colonized the indigenous Semitic peoples. Next came Greece, Rome, and the Germanic invaders who founded Western Christendom.

Among these founding "white" civilizations Gobineau included China, arguing that it was actually founded by a colony of Aryan warriors from India. Even more amazingly, the civilizations of pre-Columbian America also turned out to be the product of the same

Aryan colonizing spirit. As in the case of the Chinese, the cultural attainments of the Aztecs and Mayans were never their own; their laws, customs, and mathematical and technological skills all had to be the legacy of "a finer race that has long disappeared." For Gobineau, the logic of racial vitalism was obvious. Wherever we find culture, we have to assume the white man's presence, for "history springs only from contact with the white man."

Having bestowed the gifts of civilization, then, the Aryan peoples promptly vanished as a distinct group. They left behind only their language (Gobineau's one concession to the Indo-European linguists) and a certain higher biological strain in the peoples they conquered. This racial remnant became each civilization's aristocracy, from the Brahmins of India, the Zoroastrian nobility of Persia, and the heroic Achaeans of Homeric Greece to the Frankish warriors of Charlemagne's Europe. For Gobineau, it was not economics but race that created a ruling class. "A society is great and brilliant only so far as it preserves the blood of the noble group that created it."[28]

In the end, the Aryan racist myth was for Gobineau the fantasy of his own aristocratic breeding writ large. The *Essay on the Inequality of the Races* created an idealized French aristocracy, unsullied by revolution or trade, on a truly global scale. This is also why it later became so important for Gobineau to trace his lineage to Otto-Jarl, the half-mythical Viking conqueror of Normandy. As with the fictional Countess Manfredine, Aryan descent insulated him from the "philistines" and their degenerate, mongrel society. For Gobineau, "the white race has disappeared from the face of the earth," having "lost their complete purity by the time of Christ." Aryan-based racial vitality had become "degenerate and exhausted." The Germanic tribes and Vikings were its last gasp. Civilization has been running on borrowed time—and borrowed vitality—ever since.[29]

As the Aryan race vigorously expanded its domain through war and conquest (which are, after all, signs of racial vitality), it also became diluted in numbers and power. Through their distant and diverse conquests, the once great Aryan nations became "rich, commercial, and civilized." Conquerors found themselves cheek to jowl with the conquered. The "natural" repugnance of different races for each other asserted itself but ultimately faded, until the subjugated inferiors no longer looked ugly (as in Nietzsche, moral and aesthetic distinctions and conquest are part of the same value-forming process). Cross-breeding occurred and "the blood of the civilizing race is gradually drained away," parceled out among its many racial inferiors.[30]

The civilizing process was for Gobineau a process of corruption, symbolized by racial miscegenation. The conquerors fall victim to their very genius for creating a stable political and social order. This is the "seed of an inevitable death" that Gobineau most feared—it is the curse of civilization. For Gobineau, the inevitable mingling of peoples in a complex society is a source of creativity but also of instability. Civilizations try to prolong their lives by becoming empires, fusing different peoples and cultures into a single whole. But this multicultural fusion cannot survive because, in the end, blood tells. Gobineau's favorite example is the Greeks and Persians of the Hellenistic age who, despite Alexander the Great's best efforts, went their separate ways after his death. Racial destiny also explains why, according to Gobineau, savages will remain savages even after prolonged contact with superior, civilized beings. The historical process alone cannot transform barbarians into civilized men; nor, for that matter, can it reduce the civilized to savagery. Only race can do that.[31]

For Gobineau, race "imposes on populations their modes of existence. . . . It dictates their laws, their desires, their loves and their hates." It leads peoples and civilizations "like blind slaves" to their greatest victories—and their greatest catastrophes.[32] As the dominant race dilutes its blood with inferior stock, its offspring lose the ability to control events. Civilizations collapse, Gobineau concludes, literally because they are no longer in the same hands. "The blow cannot be turned aside, it is inevitable. The wise man can see it coming, but can do nothing more. The most consummate statesmanship cannot for a moment counteract the immutable laws of the world," which are the laws of racial vitality.

This degenerative fate had now overtaken nineteenth-century Europe. To Gobineau's mind, European civilization had no upward linear progression from barbarism to civility or from slavery to freedom. It moved instead in a circle, as peoples closer to the original Aryan source, and hence more vital, conquered those more removed from that source, only to intermingle with their inferiors and lose their own racial purity.

History turns out to be an endless cycle of wars, miscegenation, and conquest—Gobineau's racist version of *anakuklosis*. There are no winners in history, only—in the long run—losers:

> Our civilization may be compared to the temporary islands thrown up in the sea by underwater volcanoes. Exposed as they are to the destructive action of the currents, and robbed of the forces which had once sustained them, they will one day break up, and then fragments will be hurled into the all-conquering waves.

"It is a sad end," Gobineau admits, "and one which many noble races before ourselves had to meet." But it is the inevitable fate of the modern, mongrelized European population, the ignorant and ignoble heirs to a once great racial heritage.[33]

Following the Aryan Germanic invasions, premodern Europe had been blessed with a racially homogeneous ruling class that persisted from the fall of the Roman Empire until the later Middle Ages. "Blond" and "broad shouldered," as Gobineau describes them, and "reared upon the essence of a pure and severe religion, of wise politics, and a glorious history," these Germanic warriors preserved for a time the vitality of the aboriginal Aryans.[34] Then, foolishly, the Catholic Church taught this still racially intact feudal nobility "pliancy" and "reasons for sociability."[35] That sociability ("politeness" in the Enlightenment sense) turned out to be their doom. Instead of fighting and ruling over their serf populations, the conquerors learned to marry them. Eventually Germans, Latins, and Gauls intermingled, and Europe's ruling elite sank into Gobineau's inevitable cycle of racial corruption and decay.

A new class of Europeans sprang up at the end of the Middle Ages. This was an urban middle class that earned its living by trade rather than by war and land; but it was also a "middle" class in the sense of being a racial hybrid of conqueror and conquered. The remainder of European history then became a struggle between the remnants of the original German-Aryan aristocracy and this rising bourgeois order, a struggle that, thanks to its cunning and superior numbers, the bourgeoisie increasingly wins. From Gobineau's perspective, the French Revolution marked the final defeat of racial exclusivity. Now the middle class's demands for liberty, equality, and "the liberal dogma of human brotherhood" proved irresistible. Europe's once sacred social order, of aristocracy, crown, and altar, was defeated and ruined—as in the case of Gobineau's own family.

It may seem strange to consider the French Revolution as an essentially racial conflict, yet Augustin Thierry had done so twenty years earlier in his *History of the French Revolution*. In Thierry's history, the French Revolution culminates a centuries-old struggle between two distinct races or peoples, the Gauls and the Franks. The Gallic majority eventually win, freeing themselves from their oppressive Frankish masters in the dramatic events of 1789. For Thierry, racial history is again the triumph of freedom and equality.[36] Gobineau, on the other hand, takes away the happy liberal ending, while the racial aspect of the struggle is entirely hidden from the antagonists. The revolution is a stage where, in Matthew Arnold's phrase, "ignorant armies clash by night," as Jacobins, royalists, Bonapartists, and other degenerates struggle among the ruins left by their more vital ancestors.

The image of ruins runs all through the *Essay*. Ruins were, to Gobineau's mind, the visible traces of a people superior to (because prior to) ourselves, who were nonetheless as blind to their own inevitable fate as we are to ours. "All the civilizations before our own . . . believed in their own immortality. The Incas and their families . . . were certainly convinced that their conquests would last forever. Time, with one blow of his wing, has hurled their empire, like so many others, into the uttermost abyss."[37]

Gobineau's racial pessimism is not so much a theory of history as a work of Romantic art. Today, Gobineau wrote, "there are no longer classes, there are no longer peoples, but only certain individuals who float like wreckage upon the flood"—like Gobineau himself. Yet even as the bourgeoisie triumphs, fresh hordes of mongrelized masses emerge from the rural darkness to descend on the cities and towns. The inevitable result was 1848, and worse is to follow. As for America, which optimists such as Tocqueville had seen as eventually bearing the torch of civilization after it passed from European hands, that country actually represents the bottom of the racial drain. There the human refuse from other nations and peoples—Africa and Asia as well as Europe—gathers and collects. America represents "the last possible form of culture."[38]

As the original Aryan blood is further diluted, even these mongrelized masses will eventually be totally absorbed. "The white species will disappear henceforth from the face of the earth." Other races—yellow, brown, and red—will rise up and take their places, obliterating their memory forever. But the creative period for humanity will be over. Human beings "will not quite have disappeared but will have completely degenerated . . . deprived of strength, beauty, and intelligence." As Gobineau gloomily concludes, "Perhaps that fear, reserved for our descendants, would leave us cold if we did not feel, with secret horror, that the hands of destiny are already upon us."[39]

## RACIAL PESSIMISM AS A DOCTRINE

When the *Essay* appeared, the response was—indifference. Or so it seemed to Gobineau. Much to his consternation, the book failed to set off a major storm of controversy. France's anthropologists and racial theorists were distinctly lukewarm, even hostile, to Gobineau's approach. Even more embarrassingly, authors who were his leading sources—including Carus and August Pott—condemned his work as incompetent and wrong-headed.[40] On one level, Gobineau could dismiss these criticisms as predictable. As he told an intimate, "I never supposed that I can tell people today, 'you are in a state of complete decadence, your civilization is a swamp, your intelligence a smoldering lamp, you are already halfway to the grave,' without expecting some opposition."[41] But since the book never commanded a French readership or made his reputation as a great philosopher or historian, he was also disappointed.

In Gobineau's own mind, the *Essay* was a work of exact science, in its way as revolutionary as Copernicus's discovery that the sun and not the earth is at the center of the solar system. He had established once and for all the racial principles underlying all history, which now would force men to reconsider everything they knew or thought they knew about the rise and fall of civilizations. "We need to include history in the natural of natural sciences," he had written, "and give it all the scientific precision of this form of knowledge." The parallel between Gobineau and Karl Marx, who at the time was still toiling away in the British Museum on the first draft of *Das Kapital*, is striking: if history is to be of any value, it must be as a science, with the power to predict as well as analyze events.[42] However, these claims to predictive power and omniscience did not impress Gobineau's former patron, Alexis de Tocqueville.

Tocqueville was the product of an aristocratic heritage and outlook very different from Gobineau's. His family really were ancient Norman nobility. The Tocquevilles traced their lineage back to the twelfth century and had served the French monarchy by sword of arms for more than seven hundred years. The milieu in which Alexis de Tocqueville had been raised was not one of penurious pretentions and bitter memories, but of practical responsibilities and civic duties.[43] In political matters Tocqueville was a liberal, but his liberalism, like that of his father, was tempered by a respect for custom and tradition in the vein of Edmund Burke. His *Democracy in America*, published in 1835, had argued that although the forces of social and economic change could be destructive, it was still possible through energetic attention and reform to preserve the best of the past. Indeed, Tocqueville concluded, a truly free society required both.

In contrast to Gobineau's self-absorbed and self-dramatizing Romanticism, Tocqueville's outlook was resolutely that of the Enlightenment: rational, skeptical, and at times sardonic, yet hopeful for the future. As he wrote to Gobineau years later, "Yes, I sometimes despair of mankind. Who doesn't. . . . I have always said that it is more difficult to stabilize and maintain liberty in our new democratic societies than in certain aristocratic societies in the past. But I shall never dare to think it impossible."[44]

Gobineau had sent him a copy of the *Essay*, although he must have known that any response he might receive could hardly be encouraging. As Tocqueville said, "There is an entire world between our beliefs." This was even truer than he could know. The *Essay* and Tocqueville's response mark a dividing line in the European spirit between the Enlightenment tradition of rational liberalism, which was now finding itself on the defensive, and a new outlook in which Gobineau's racial pessimism would play an increasingly important part.

Tocqueville was repelled first of all by Gobineau's racist perspective, which he saw (correctly) as a repudiation of the essential equality of all men before God. Tocqueville also understood that the belief in racial superiority was a result, not a cause, of specific historical circumstances. "I am sure that Julius Caesar, had he had the time, would have willingly written a book to prove that the savages he met in Britain did not belong to the same race as the Romans, and that the latter were destined by nature to rule the world, while the former were destined to vegetate in one of its corners. . . ."[45] Two thousand years later, of course, the reverse had come to pass, with industrial England dominating the European continent as well as much of the world.

Then there was the issue of Gobineau's doom-laden pessimism. Tocqueville worried that a sense of despair about the future of civilization, especially after the debacle of 1848, could become a self-fulfilling prophecy. Perhaps the previous century had had too much faith in progress, Tocqueville admitted. Now, however, the failures of the French Revolution and of 1848 have "led us to the opposite extreme. . . . After having excessive pride, we have now fallen into excessive self-pity; we thought we could do everything, and now we think we can do nothing." Pessimism "is the great sickness of our age," he warned. Tocqueville believed that in proclaiming Europe's decline to be racially predestined, Gobineau was encouraging a fatalism that sapped energy, confidence, and the will to achieve. "If one morning my doctor came and said, 'My dear sir, I am honored to announce that you are mortally ill and . . . that there is absolutely no chance of any kind of recovery,' " Tocqueville said, "I would see nothing else for it than to put my head beneath the covers and . . . prepare myself for eternal life. But for societies there is no eternal life."[46]

However, the aspect of the *Essay* that most repelled Tocqueville was Gobineau's stony fatalism, the racial determinism that abolished human freedom. Individuals cut a puny figure in the *Essay*, compared to "the immutable laws" of race history and brute nature that lead them "like blind slaves" and dictate their choices. In Gobineau's formulation, the organic life of a society or civilization stands totally apart from the human beings who make it up. Individuals play no conscious part in either a society's creation or its preservation.[47]

Since man is rendered helpless in Gobineau's historical scheme, he is also not accountable for the disaster that inevitably occurs. "There is nothing" in the fate of his own civilization "for which he can be held accountable," Gobineau concluded, because there is nothing to be done. Tocqueville was appalled by both propositions. "To me," he explained, "human societies, like persons, only become something worthwhile through their use of liberty. . . ." The great gift of civilized society was freedom, freedom in the sense of the individual's moral responsibility for what happens to himself as well as to others. Gobineau had abolished that freedom with one stroke of biological determinism. Indeed, Tocqueville sensed that Gobineau had abolished individual freedom because he was in a profound sense frightened by it.

Gobineau sharply reacted. He wrote:

> I am not telling people "you are acquitted" or "you are condemned"; I tell them: "*You are dying.*" What I say is that you have spent your youth and you have now reached the age of decline. . . . Establish kingdoms, dynasties, republics, whatever you want; these things may be possible and even inevitable. . . . But in the final account, the causes of your enervation are gathering . . . And no one in the world will replace you when your degeneration is completed.

"If I am wrong," he added, "nothing will remain of my four volumes. If I am right, the facts will not be suppressed by the desire of those who do not wish to face them."[48]

Gobineau had no interest in changing the world. His *Essay* and subsequent works remained at their heart acts of Romantic rebellion, gestures of defiance aimed at what he saw as a bourgeois-dominated social order that had rejected him. Yet Gobineau had drawn a sharp, and in Tocqueville's opinion fateful, distinction between men's "social aptitudes," the collective psychological forces that led them to create great civilizations, and the "qualities that make moral truths operative"—honesty, integrity, compassion, and a sense of right and wrong. Social aptitudes for Gobineau drew on the vital power transmitted by blood and race. Moral qualities, on the other hand, were arbitrary and conventional—and ultimately dispensable. In Gobineau's scheme of things, man's ethical stance was irrelevant to the larger process of history. A society or civilization "carries no morality," he had written, "it is neither virtuous nor vicious . . . it simply exists."

Gobineau was not simply denying any necessary link between purposeful public action and the dictates of ordinary morality—Machiavelli, after all, had made that point three hundred years earlier. He was asserting that public action and the exercise of power *had no moral con-*

*tent whatsoever.* They were instead dictated by blood, race, and biology. The vitality and value of a civilization depended entirely on its ability to generate the necessary patterns of power and domination, which sensitive or squeamish moral considerations tended to impede. Failure to follow the dictates of power, whether by preserving one's racial identity or killing a captured enemy, was a sign that society's vital foundations were rotting away.

Moral principles are the opposite of vitality and creativity—what Friedrich Nietzsche would call "the will to power." In Gobineau's later writings, particularly his *Renaissance* (1877), genuine creative power always sweeps aside issues of morality. According to him, the Renaissance marked the last triumph of Europe's Aryan aristocracy over the bourgeois forces rising up against them. The result was a final spasmodic eruption of vitality not only in the artistic sphere—Michelangelo, da Vinci, Raphael—but in the politics exemplified by Cesare Borgia and Machiavelli as well.

Gobineau's cultural hero is entirely amoral. Conventional standards, whether aesthetic or moral, are for the weak and timid:

> Know then that for that kind of person whom fate summons to dominate others, the ordinary rules of life are reversed. . . . Good and evil are lifted to another, to a higher region, to a different plane. . . . Leave to small minds, the rabble of underlings, all slackness and scruple.

"Power is everything, the master key," Gobineau later wrote to Richard Wagner. "It destroys everything in its path, and leaves nothing behind."[49] It is, as Nietzsche would later say, "beyond good and evil."

Gobineau died in Turin on February 14, 1882.* Toward the end of his life, the prospect of civilization's apocalyptic collapse into the abyss seemed to fill Gobineau with a kind of ghoulish Romantic *Schadenfreude.* "An avalanche of Chinese and Slavs," he wrote just before his death in the preface to the second edition of the *Essay on Inequality,* "mottled with Tartars and Baltic Germans, will put an end to the stupidities and indeed to the entire civilization of Europe. . . . I foresaw and predicted these strange phenomena a number of years ago. . . . But I

---

* Ironically, he suffered a heart attack while boarding a train, the symbol of the new industrial age he despised.

must admit that I did not then expect these things to come about so quickly."

## GOBINEAU AND NEO-GOBINIANS IN GERMANY

France's overwhelming defeat in 1870 by the new German Empire, and the civil war and Commune of the following year, set off a wave of fears about French national degeneration that, if not borrowed directly from Gobineau, certainly made him appear more right than wrong. Yet Gobineau never caught on in France as a racial theorist, and the language of degeneration was never linked to any specific Gobinian perspective. Its roots lay elsewhere, in the kind of "scientific" and positivist liberal racial theory that Gobineau had repudiated. However, when Gobineau first lamented the failure of his *Essay on the Inequality of Races* in France, Tocqueville had predicted that he would find a better response in Germany, which turned out to be correct.

Gobineau's success there was due to a single individual. Richard Wagner became interested in Gobineau's works in 1876 while preparing for his first performance at Bayreuth. They met soon afterwards and became close friends; Wagner once described Gobineau to his wife Cosima as "my only true contemporary."[50] Although Gobineau's racial ideas appeared too late to have any effect on Wagner's operas, the composer did relentlessly push the French count's theories on the coterie of young artists, musicians, and intellectuals in his Bayreuth circle. Two in particular, Ludwig Schemann and Houston Stewart Chamberlain, would take up Gobineau and turn his ideas into a political gospel for a modern Germany, to accompany the artistic gospel of Wagnerism.

Ludwig Schemann was thirty-seven when he first read *The Renaissance*. That led him to the *Essay on Inequality*, which, he would tell everyone later, transformed his life. He was particularly struck by the uncanny resemblance of Gobineau's ideas to those of the key figure in the ultranationalist volkish or Germanic movement, Paul Anton Bötticher, whom Schemann and others knew under his French-sounding pseudonym Paul de Lagarde.

Lagarde's ideas were an unstable mixture of Herder, Fichte, the brothers Grimm, and the German Romantic *Lebensphilosophie* that had also influenced Gobineau. "The core of man is not his reason, but his will," he wrote, "whose driving force is love." The German nation, he believed, had a will of its own, the expression of its *Seele*, or "collective soul." In Germany's case, that soul was being destroyed by materialism, middle-class greed, and the industrialization that was moving across the landscape of the Rhine and Ruhr valleys. As Germany became a unified nation and moved into the modern mainstream, Lagarde warned, the real Germany, rooted in the rural customs and traditions of the common *Volk*, was being overwhelmed. The result was a cultural crisis that would deprive the German people of their unique heritage and identity. Lagarde's view of the future was gloomy in a Romantic, even Gobinian, sense. "We are face to face with [spiritual] bankruptcy," he wrote in 1881. "We shall all sink into nothingness."

Lagarde reflected the bitterness of the culturally conservative successors to the German Romantics, who saw progress as the Trojan Horse of a soulless bourgeois future. Mechanization, philistinism, socialism, and liberalism were all of a piece; true spiritual health meant escaping from their malign influences. Lagarde saw true German culture as being under direct assault from liberals, with their insistence on individualism at the expense of volkish solidarity, and from Jews, the Catholic Church, industrialists, and a range of other "un-German" elements. In "this new Germany that is so powerful, so liberal, and so utterly un-German," Lagarde wrote, "we worship foreign gods—that is our undoing."[51]

Schemann realized at once that what Lagarde and others were trying to define in cultural and national terms Gobineau had understood in racial terms. Lagarde's German national soul was actually its Aryan identity, a heritage reaching back to the forests and bogs of northern Europe and Scandinavia and extending forward to the rural communities and traditions of the German *Volk*. Schemann became a man possessed; as he put it, an "instrument of higher powers." Although he never met Gobineau, Schemann wrote an admiring two-volume biography (he later did the same for Paul de Lagarde), edited the French aristocrat's unpublished essays, and created the Gobineau Archives at Strassburg, with over six thousand volumes on race and race theory. In 1894, Schemann and a group of enthusiasts met in his rooms at the University of Strassburg to found the Gobineau Society and to raise a subscription for a new translation of the *Essay on Inequality*. He introduced Gobineau's doctrines of racial Aryanism to the Pan-German League, a major right-wing nationalist lobbying group, which proceeded to distribute copies of the *Essay* to all chapter libraries.[52]

Although the Gobineau Society never enjoyed a large membership (in 1914 there were still only three hundred and sixty official members), it attracted attention from German politicians and intellectuals. It came to exercise a disproportionate influence on cultural matters and gave a new racial cast to Pan-German nationalist feeling. Schemann and the neo-Gobinians would make it plain that Germany, and Germany alone, stood agaist modern Europe's cultural, social, and racial disintegration. German folk culture was the last surviving remnant of the original Indo-German Aryan peoples, and the German people their last descendants and heirs. As members and admirers of the Bayreuth circle, the neo-Gobinians identified Wagner's operas, particularly the Ring cycle, as authentic recreations of the original Aryan myths. Bayreuth became an annual festival where Aryan-Germans could participate in "their primeval mysteries," rediscover the origins of their *Kultur*, and be restored to spiritual health.[53]

The issue of rejuvenation became crucial for the neo-Gobinians. In the hands of Schemann and his influential successor Houston Stewart Chamberlain, Gobineau's Aryan myth acquired a happy ending. The blond, broad-shouldered, vital and free Aryans do not disappear. They become "Teutons," the modern-day descendants of the ancient Germanic tribes. Modern culture remained in crisis, of course; Lagarde's (and Gobineau's) fear that "everything of value was in decline" was too rhetorically effective to be abandoned. However, the degenerative and soul-destroying processes of modern civilization now had an antidote: the pursuit of racial purity.

Turning Gobineau into a central figure in the Pan-Germanic pantheon required glossing over certain inconvenient points. Gobineau's despair for his own French homeland had been matched only by his contempt for Germany and Prussia. He regularly portrayed modern Germans as humorless bourgeois philistines, using the same scathing, excoriating tones that Nietzsche would later employ. The idea that Wilhelmine Germany in any way reflected the virtues and vitality of the ancient Aryans would have struck him as ridiculous, yet this was precisely what Schemann and the Pan-Germanists were to argue.[54] Gobineau's German admirers also narrowed his historical perspective, dropping the comparative elements that derived from his Orientalist studies. The Aryan heritage now belonged only to Europe, specifically to Western Europe and Scandinavia. Even the term "Aryan," with its too-obvious association with Vedic India, began to be replaced with Nordic or Indo-German.[55] Both Schemann and Chamberlain would dismiss Gobineau's speculations regarding the Aryan origins of Chinese and pre-Columbian civilizations as mere fantasy. The progenitors of civilization were emphatically and exclusively white Europeans, and specifically German.

While Schemann's writings remained limited to a small (although very distinguished) audience, Houston Stewart Chamberlain reached out to a much larger one. An English Germanophile who had married Wagner's daughter, Chamberlain became the most influential of the Bayreuth circle and the neo-Gobinians. In 1899 he published *The Foundations of the Nineteenth Century*, a sweeping, rambling survey of European history that intended, as Chamberlain put it, to "make the past part of the present." The debt to Gobineau's *Essay* was profound and obvious. Yet the differences overshadow the similarities.

In the *Foundations*, all of European civilization is a product of the Aryan race, who are now identified as Teutons or modern ethnic Germans. The aboriginal Aryan has also shed the aristocratic hauteur and exclusiveness conferred by Gobineau; instead, he exhibits two outstanding virtues, "freedom and loyalty," meaning loyalty to himself as well as to others through an instinct for maintaining his racial identity and autonomy. Exuding "physical health and strength, great intelligence, luxuriant imagination, untiring impulse to create," the Germanic peoples appear at the end of the Roman Empire like Siegfried setting off on his Rhine journey in Wagner's *Götterdämmerung*, "glowing with youth, free . . . endowed with all the qualities which fit them for the very highest place."[56]

"The Teuton entered history," Chamberlain wrote, "not as a barbarian but as a child." But their supreme confidence and naive innocence proved to be their downfall. "Every power was set in motion to betray them," like a "child that falls into the hands of old experienced libertines." Old Europeans—Latins, Gauls, Mediterranean Greeks, and Jews—conspired against the Germanic newcomers. Over the course of time the conquerors were deluded into embracing their deadliest enemies. They "contaminated their pure blood by mixture with the impure races of the slave-born." By the beginning of the Enlightenment, the original Teutonic blood of the German people faced dilution and oblivion, and European civilization hung in the balance.

All this seems familiar from Gobineau; however, Chamberlain now introduced a new corrupting element, the principal villains behind the destruction of Teutonic vitality—the Jews. Chamberlain's anti-Semitism stemmed from Wagner and volkish ideologues like Lagarde, not Gobineau.* Wagner, like Karl Marx, despised Europe's Jews as symbols of soulless commercial society. The hooknosed dwarf Alberich in Wagner's *Ring*, who renounced love and beauty out of greed for gold, became the enduring symbol of the antinatural, antispiritual Jew. Wagner's views struck a deeply responsive chord with all of his Bayreuth circle (which, curiously, included several Jews) and became a cornerstone of neo-Gobinian racial theory.†

For Chamberlain, the Jews were a hybrid Asiatic race. Following the Swiss anthropologist Vacher Lapouge (who was another Gobinian racial pessimist), Chamberlain defined the "Jewish race" as the mongrelized result of cross-breeding between Bedouins, Hittites, Syrians, and Aryan Amorites in the Fertile Crescent of the Old Testament. "Their existence is a crime against the holy laws of life," he proclaimed. As a result, they were the opposite of *Lebensgefühl* and vitality. Jews were "born rationalists. . . . The creative element, the real inner life is almost totally wanting in them." Compared to "the infinitely rich religious life of the Aryans," their religion is "rigid," "scanty," "sterile." Jews were, in short, without soul.[58]

The Jews became for the Germanic neo-Gobinians what modern-day Europeans had been for Gobineau: a tainted race. Aware of the curse they bore, the Jews consciously worked to pollute the civilization their Teutonic superiors had built. Capitalism, liberal humanitarianism, and sterile science—"Jewish science," as Chamberlain called it (referring to

---

* Anti-Semitism had played no part in Gobineau's own ideas; he considered the Jews to be part of the white race and in fact saw their survival as a people through the Diaspora as an example of the virtues of racial purity.

† One of the Jewish members of the circle was the conductor Hermann Levy.[57]

Albert Einstein and other proponents of the new theory of relativity)—
were all forms of race pollution, the modern instruments of the Jews' revenge. The history of Europe is no longer Gobineau's cycle of conquest,
corruption, and reconquest, but becomes an apocalyptic power struggle
between Aryan Teutons and their Jewish antagonists. As one contemporary English reviewer put it, Chamberlain's book is "the *Iliad* of
Aryans versus Jews," a sweeping epic of racial conflict with magnificent
Aryan heroes, such as Martin Luther, Dante, and Jesus Christ (whom
Chamberlain "proves" was an Aryan and not a Jew), and a miscella-
neous cast of anti-Aryan villains such as Ignatius Loyola (a degenerate
Basque as well as the founder of the Jesuits).

Wherever we find energy, vitality, creativity, and innovation, as in
medieval Christianity or during the Renaissance, there we can also find
Teutonism as a racial-historical force. Where we do not, we see the bale-
ful effects of racial and cultural anarchy, or *Völkerchaos*. Chamberlain's
term brings us back to Gobineau's image of racial degeneration in the
*Essay*, which "ends in utter impotence, and leads societies down to the
abyss of nothingness." Yet in Chamberlain's account, there remains a redemptive escape route. Civilization ends in a final stage of regeneration,
an inner process of rebirth in which man's basic nature is transformed
from death to life. Racial purity is a matter of personal rejuvenation as
well as collective salvation.

Chamberlain could make this sweeping claim because he no longer
defined race purely in terms of heredity. It was a spiritual rather than
physiological force, an intricate unity of physical, mental, and vitalist attributes. Belonging to a race meant having "a special way of thinking
and feeling." One did not have to be born Jewish to be a Jew: "It is necessary only to have frequent intercourse with Jews, to read Jewish newspapers, to accustom oneself to Jewish philosophy, literature, and art."
Given this possibility of cultural pollution, Chamberlain concluded, "we
have the right and the duty to take—without unfriendliness—strenuous measures against such a dangerous alien."

Where the struggle [between the races] is not waged with cannon balls,
it goes silently on in the heart of society by marriages . . . by the varying
powers of resistance in the different types of mankind, by the shifting of

wealth, by the birth of new influences and the disappearance of others. . . . But this struggle, silent though it is, is above all a struggle for life and death.[59]

In 1927 Chamberlain met the man who would undertake that life-or-death struggle. Adolf Hitler had been raised on the Austrian version of Pan-Germanism, which was deeply anti-Jewish as well as anticlerical. However, at the same time that Hitler was growing up in Austria, neo-Gobinianism was sweeping through the German-speaking world. Chamberlain's *Foundations of the Nineteenth Century* was part of the standard history curriculum in Prussian schools, while the Gobineau Society worked to distribute copies of Gobineau's *Renaissance* to German soldiers—like the young private Hitler—as they marched off to World War I.[60]

Hitler does not seem to have actually read any Gobineau then or later. However, when he returned from the war he met Alfred Rosenberg and Dietrich Eckhart, who introduced him to Chamberlain's views as well as to other Aryanist racial doctrines. During Hitler's stay at Landsberg Prison after the 1923 *putsch* attempt, neo-Gobinianism became a fixed part of his world view. In *Mein Kampf* Hitler would state categorically that "all culture, art, and civilization were the achievements of the culture-bearing Aryan race," while his pronouncement that "all great cultures of the past perished only because the original creative race died out from blood pollution" captured the original spirit of Gobineau's racial pessimism.[61]

Yet Hitler also shared Chamberlain's Wagnerian hope of redemption. Germany could achieve a new racial destiny through purity of blood and a rejuvenation of its collective soul. This became Hitler's goal and the neo-Gobinian promise of the Nazi movement. In 1927 Hitler at last came face-to-face with his new intellectual mentor, Houston Chamberlain. Joseph Goebbels, an eyewitness, described it as a "shattering scene." The old man, paralyzed in a wheelchair since a stroke thirteen years earlier, clutched Hitler's hand; Hitler addressed him as his "spiritual father."[62] A few days later, Chamberlain wrote to Hitler: "With one blow you have transformed the state of my soul. That Germany, in her hour of need, brings forth a Hitler—that is proof of her vitality. Now I will be able to sleep peacefully and I shall have no need to wake up again. God protect you!"

Chamberlain did not live to see Hitler come to power. But Ludwig Schemann did, and on his eighty-fifth birthday would receive Germany's highest literary award, the Goethe Medal, from the Third Reich.

## CHAPTER 3

# HISTORICAL AND CULTURAL PESSIMISM

*Jacob Burckhardt and Friedrich Nietzsche*

> Wait and you will see the sort of spirits that are going to rise out
> of the ground in the next twenty years. . . . We may all perish;
> but at least I want to discover the cause for which I am to per-
> ish, namely, the old culture of Europe.
>
> —Jacob Burckhardt, 1846

> If you see something slipping, push it.
>
> —Friedrich Nietzsche, 1886

By tradition, the city of Basel used to set its clocks exactly one hour behind the rest of Europe. In the eighteenth century, several re-formers tried to get the citizens of Basel to wake up on time but they all failed. Then, in 1797, Basel suddenly became part of the French Revo-lution. French troops swept into Switzerland and, with the help of lead-ing liberals in cities such as Berne and Basel, established the Helvetian Republic. The revolutionaries finally set Basel's clocks right, and when Basel's traditional ruling class returned to power after the fall of Napoleon in 1814, they decided to leave the clocks as they were. Nonetheless, when Jacob Burckhardt was born there four years later, the bells and chimes in Basel's clock towers welcomed him to a deeply conservative and independent city that was only reluctantly becoming part of modern Europe.[1]

Basel, like the rest of nineteenth-century Switzerland, was prosper-ous and economically active, although it had escaped the rigors of large-scale industrialization and democratic political change. Basel was still governed by old patrician families like the Burckhardts, who had served as pastors in its churches and professors in its university (the oldest in Switzerland) since the sixteenth century. Jacob Burckhardt was brought up in a world of orderly and pious values, where a tradition of intellectual and spiritual labor was passed on from generation to generation. The young Burckhardt would have acknowledged the truth of Edmund Burke's observation that "there is an order that keeps things fast in their place. It is made to us and we are made to it."

Everyone assumed that Jacob would follow his father and grandfather into the ministry. However, Protestant theology was everywhere in an uproar. The old, solid Lutheran and Calvinist faiths were under siege from the Enlightenment's emphasis on the secularizing power of reason and from the so-called higher criticism in biblical studies. Close scholarly examination of the Old and New Testaments had exposed enormous gaps and inconsistencies in the texts, undermining the claim that the Bible was the literal word of God. Higher criticism taught that, for better or worse, the Bible was an historical document like any other text from antiquity, and subject to the same interpretive freedom. David Strauss, a critic at the University of Tübingen, published his controversial *Life of Jesus* in 1835, arguing that most of the New Testament Gospels was a fabric of myth and legend, like the founding myths of other religions.*

Exposed to these hammer blows, Jacob Burckhardt's belief in Christianity never recovered. Burckhardt did not become an atheist or agnostic; he never abandoned his belief in a God, and he kept his loss of faith a secret from his parents until their deaths. Instead, he became one of a growing company of university-educated intellectuals in the nineteenth century who found they could no longer believe in Christianity (or Judaism) as a system of revealed truth. They included Matthew Arnold, Emile Durkheim (whose father was an Orthodox rabbi), Søren Kierkegaard, Friedrich Nietzsche, Wilhelm Dilthey, and somewhat later, Martin Heidegger. The collapse of the religious and moral certainties of their boyhood was a deeply shattering experience, leaving them casting

---

* Ironically, Strauss would later come under fire from Nietzsche, in one of his early *Untimely Meditations*, for criticisms directed at Nietzsche's mentor Richard Wagner.

about for new faiths to cling to. Some would find that faith in the philosophies of Hegel and Kant, just as many would later turn to Karl Marx. Others found it in the reigning academic disciplines of the modern university—in other words, a rational or even scientific truth to substitute for the one revealed by God. For Emile Durkheim, this was sociology; for Friedrich Nietzsche, philology, the intensive study of Greek and Latin according to rigorous scientific principles. For the young Jacob Burckhardt, the alternative path to truth became the study of history.

In 1838 he set off for the University of Berlin, where two professors, Theodor Droysen and Leopold von Ranke, were transforming historical scholarship. Burckhardt was enthralled. "Every day in the course of my work I am discovering new sources of greatness and beauty," he wrote. "I am really determined to devote my life to it." His teachers presented a sharp contrast in style and outlook. Droysen was the typical "progressive" historian of the time. According to Droysen, European history was the story of the emergence of the nation-state and political liberty. Like Hegel, Droysen believed history was a process by which human aspiration and destiny are finally and definitively reconciled in the state. "God's hand guides events, both great and small, and the science of history has no higher task than to justify this faith . . . and belief in the fatherland." Droysen was the sort of historian Burckhardt later came to dislike, one who smugly assumed that "our own time is the culmination of all time . . . [and] that the whole past may be regarded as fulfilled in us" as the epitome of human progress.[2]

Ranke was a very different case. To Ranke's mind, partisanship or present-mindedness was the cardinal sin of historical writing. He rejected the notion of linear progress or historical laws of any sort, whether in Hegel's terms or those of Comte and the so-called Positivists. He was skeptical of grand philosophic schemes that tried to impose a large purpose and direction on the human past, and he understood the difference between claiming to see a *pattern* in past events and claiming to have discovered an underlying *law*. Instead of looking for laws, Ranke said, the historian's task was to reveal the past *wie es eigentlich gewesen ist* ("as it truly happened")—the phrase became the trademark of the Rankean or German historical school.[3]

"Nor," Ranke added, was the only significant issue in the study of history "the often dubious advancement of civilization. . . . There are forces and indeed spiritual, creative forces, nay life itself, and there are moral energies, whose development we see. . . . In their interaction and succession, in their life, in their decline and rejuvenation . . . lies the secret of world history."[4] The place where historians would find the most vivid interplay of these creative forces, Ranke believed, was in the arena of politics. On the one hand, Ranke had great scorn for scholars who allowed contemporary political issues and passions to distort their historical accounts. Ranke was a conservative who, as an historian, could feel sympathy for the aspirations of the men who made the French Revolution; a German Protestant who could understand the ambitions and fears of the medieval papacy.* He believed that the historian's job was not to judge but to observe and analyze the past. This conviction made a deep impression on the young Burckhardt, who would later state that historians needed to find an "Archimidean point outside events," and that history had to be written in a "spirit of contemplation" rather than confrontation.[5]

However, Ranke and Burckhardt also agreed that human beings display the same character, regardless of place or culture. The historian finds in every epoch the same unwillingness to allow reason to guide the passions, the same disordered jumble of hopes and fears. Ranke's studies had convinced him that religion and politics provided necessary systems of belief and order, allowing human beings to find coherence and a stable balance in their collective lives through institutions specific to their time and place. The historian had to realize that man's historical destiny has many faces, not just one. "These many separate, earthly-spiritual communities called forth by moral energy, growing irresistibly . . . each in its own way! Behold them, these celestial bodies, in their cycles, their mutual gravitation, their systems!"[6]

In Ranke's "organicist" view of history and society, the nation forms "a living thing," not an abstract principle; it was "an individual, a unique self." But Ranke had also turned his back on German Romanticism's vitalism. Unlike Gobineau (whose works he despised), Ranke did not see

---

* Ranke was pleased when his *History of the Papacy* (1834–1836) generated criticism from leading Protestants for being too sympathetic to the Catholic Church and from leading Catholics for being too severe.

society's organic changes coming from the brutal biological imperatives of a mysterious life force. Instead, societies are rational wholes, the parts of which fit and grow together in a balanced, orderly way and in "a creative, unifying sense."[7]

But Ranke's organicist view also faced one large difficulty. Like any living organic system, society's ordered process of development could sometimes fail. Under certain conditions, it could lose the delicate balance between the parts and the whole. Unless the society's members are then able to summon up the spiritual strength to restore the overall balance, disorder will follow and energy stream out not "in a creative, unifying sense" but as "dissolution." This is what had happened, Ranke argued, at certain critical junctures in the European past, such as at the end of the Roman Empire and again, before the Reformation.[8]

But what if such evidence of breakdown and dissolution appears not at the end of the Roman Empire, but in our own time? Suddenly dynamic contemporary trends assume a terrible new significance. What other people unthinkingly accept as "normal" the trained observer recognizes as warning signs of impending collapse. In this case, Ranke's organicist view of society and history produces a particular kind of pessimism about the future, which can be called "historical pessimism." The historical pessimist sees the present as *systematically* undoing the achievements of a creative and ordered past. Institutions that used to be in harmonious balance are now out of sync, and social development becomes chaotic and destructive. At the same time, individuals are helpless to do anything to avert the disaster about to happen. Unless the system somehow repairs itself, the historical pessimist concludes, its breakdown is virtually preordained. Pessimism turns to fatalism, and the only option is resignation and withdrawal.

Burckhardt had been a passionate supporter of German liberal nationalism during his stay in Berlin. However, a wave of political violence and democratic upheaval that struck his beloved Basel and the other Swiss cantons in the 1840s, and the European debacle of 1848, reversed his earlier enthusiasm. One of his closest friends, Gottfried Kinkel, was tried and executed in the German revolution's aftermath. Burckhardt's grief turned to disgust with the Romantic idealism that had brought him and Europe to the brink of disaster. "I have given up all political activity forever. . . . The whole business is alien to me," he wrote to one of his

German friends. "I am tired of the modern world. I want to escape them all, the radicals, the communists, the industrialists, the overeducated, the fastidious, the imitative and the abstract, the absolutists, the philosophers, the sophists, the state fanatics, the idealists, the -ists and -ers of every kind."[9]

For Gobineau, the violent dawn of modernity was something that had happened to his father's generation, during the French Revolution. It assumed the status of myth, like Adam's fall from grace. Burckhardt experienced that fall directly and personally. The stable, secure world he knew had changed horribly before his eyes, leaving him frightened and disillusioned. "I have no hope at all for the future," he wrote to a friend. "It is possible a few half-endurable decades may still be granted to us, a sort of Roman imperial time."[10] Burckhardt withdrew into a monkish solitude, finding refuge in his love for history and art. He made an eye-opening trip to Italy, where he became enraptured with the masterpieces of Michelangelo, Raphael, and Titian. He returned to write a book on the artistic culture of Italy—the *Cicerone*—and to accept a post at the University of Basel as professor of history. From 1885 until his death thirty-four years later, he never again left his hometown, except for vacations in his beloved Italy. Living modestly and dressed in a modest black suit, his hair prematurely white, Burckhardt could easily have been mistaken for a minister, which indeed he might have been had he not lost his religious faith. Even when his fame as an historian grew, he refused to venture outside. In 1871 the University of Berlin offered him the chair of history once occupied by his beloved teacher, Leopold von Ranke. Burckhardt turned it down.[11]

For the ivory tower of his study, surrounded by his books and manuscripts, Burckhardt struggled to place the events of 1848 within the wider historical context of European civilization. Like Gobineau, Tocqueville, and many others, Burckhardt thought the revolutions and the violent middle-class reaction marked the rise of a modern barbarism. But Burckhardt also disagreed with vitalists such as Gobineau and the Swiss Romantic historian Ernst von Lasaulx, who tried to distinguish between an "ancient" barbarism, the expression of energetic and dominant races such as the Germanic tribes and Vikings, and a "modern" or decadent version, in which the life force has exhausted itself. Burckhardt believed that the vitality of a people or a race did not determine the health of a society, but the other way around. A primitive people can be as enervated and sterile as their modern counterparts. What matters is the state of the larger social order: whether it is still growing and developing, or whether it has achieved overripeness, with the "inward degeneration and decrease of life" that marks the end of the old and the beginning of the new.

All societies and civilizations, Burckhardt argued, are a dynamic balance among three social elements or powers. Two he borrowed from Ranke, religion and the state. The third was culture (or what the Enlightenment would have called "manners"), "that process by which the spontaneous and unthinking activity of a race or nation is transformed into considered action." Each element follows a course of "growth, bloom, and decay," as new social groups and forces come and go with the passage of time. "During epochs of high civilization, all three powers exist simultaneously at all levels of mutual interaction." However, when they collide or conflict with each other, "a crisis in the whole state of things is produced," which affects entire peoples and populations. Burckhardt's history does not present us with a smooth and progressive working out of human forces and movements, but instead with a recurring tension among the three elements, expressed in periodic "crises." In a crisis, "the historical process is suddenly accelerated in a terrifying fashion. Developments which would otherwise take centuries seem to flit by like phantoms in months and weeks, and are fulfilled."[12]

The fall of the Roman Empire was one such crisis. Burckhardt's first extended historical work, *The Age of Constantine the Great* (1852), showed how the power of the Roman imperial state had expanded at the expense of other social institutions to the point that civilization itself broke apart. The barbarian invasions did not cause the fall of the Roman Empire, Burckhardt argued; they simply exacerbated a crisis that was already under way in Roman society itself. The "youthful, very prolific" Germans smashed through a vulnerable imperial frontier, prompting a series of ruthless military emperors to seize power. It was these emperors and their legions, not the German tribes, who destroyed the ancient world's civic life as they tried to prop up their great, sagging dominion.

As a result, another power, religion, rose up to replace the state. When the Catholic Church abused its authority, once again overbalancing the system, the result was the Reformation. A new historical force, the nation, rose up to topple the Church's might.

Now, Burckhardt believed, European civilization was undergoing another similar crisis. This time it was a cultural crisis, as the national movements and ideals unleashed by the nineteenth century destroyed their own future.

## BURCKHARDT: DEMOCRACY, INDIVIDUALISM, AND THE EUROPEAN CRISIS

One of those self-destructive forces, Burckhardt believed, was modern democracy. The French Revolution had established the principle that the rule of the people is the only legitimate form of political power. From Burckhardt's perspective, that principle galvanized the great unwashed masses from town and countryside in the form of public opinion, and made them part of the political fabric of the nation (as was happening to the working class in his beloved Basel). But it had also increased social resentment and demands for social and economic leveling. Men hoped "to find salvation in demolishing and rebuilding the whole [social] structure" in the name of progress and reform. This is what set off the radical and socialist revolts in 1848; in the aftermath, political institutions and politicians learned to submit. "Statesmen no longer seek to combat 'democracy,'" Burckhardt wrote in 1873, "but in some way or other to reckon with it" and manipulate its awesome power for their own purposes.

However, demands for the destruction of the old continue unabated. "In the end people believe that if the state power were completely in their hands they could fashion a new existence." The masses join forces with the dynamic power of commercial society, "big business," industry, and the thirst for "property and money-making." Business turns to the power of the state to protect and extend its interests, while the masses want the state to provide the benefits they cannot acquire on their own.[13] From these twin pressures the all-powerful modern state emerges, along with its new power wielders. Burckhardt saw in France's Napoleon III an example of the archetypal rulers of the future: "the terrible simplifiers" as he called them, military dictators and their henchmen who reduce the fragile complexity of human experience to the single reality of power.[14] The masses learn to acquiesce. "They want their peace and pay," Burckhardt wrote sardonically, and will accept them from whatever political form will deliver, even if it means a "long, voluntary servitude" to a brutal dictatorship.

Of course, Burckhardt's conclusion that democracy inevitably gives way to dictatorship was as old as Plato and Aristotle. But Burckhardt added to this traditional antidemocratic critique a new fear, which would be the foundation stone of all subsequent critiques of "mass society": that popular rule threatens the cultural life of society as a whole. "The decisive new thing that has come into the world through the French Revolution," he explained, "is the permission and will to change things" simply because the masses wish it. The uneducated mass man uses his political ascendancy to set his own mediocre stamp on all human activities, because he now defines the priorities of society. This was the true "despotism" unleashed by the French Revolution, Burckhardt believed, "the unfettering of . . . all passions and selfishness." Burckhardt saw the events of 1848 and the subsequent rise of nationalism as proof of this larger trend; the new democratic despotism would "serve as the model for every despotism for all eternity."

"Democrats and proletarians *must* submit to an increasingly harsh despotism," Burckhardt asserted, as their intellectual and moral corruption draw down "all the hellishness of human nature." As political, intellectual, and moral standards collapse and a rising class of bureaucrats snatch away all freedom and autonomy, society will not be able to withstand the ruthless, ambitious wielders of modern military power. Society must become one great "military factory," Burckhardt predicted, with the masses conscripted into great and destructive armies and its rulers dealing out mass death in the same way as its industries deal out mass production and its press mass propaganda.[15]

Jacob Burckhardt was not only the first prophet of the totalitarian state and the military-industrial complex. He was also describing the triumph of a debased mass culture that comes to dominate all of society. That culture destabilizes the social order, with its traditional and organic balance of institutions and ideals. Modern democracy was destroying a European civilization that he believed was "decadent" and had lost its *raison d'être*. But democracy was incapable of producing anything constructive to replace it. This was indeed a "purely negative and destructive barbarism."

In a democracy, people learn to reject their assigned role as parts of the systematic whole; individual striving helps to unravel the fabric of society and culture. Modern man wants to break the rules, while true freedom for Burckhardt was the desire to live within them—just as Burckhardt himself and his family had done for generations in Basel.

Yet ironically, as Burckhardt was forced to admit, this desire to break the rules had also produced one of the high points of European civilization, the Renaissance. His most famous work, *The Civilization of the Renaissance in Italy* (1859), revealed how in the Renaissance for the first time "man became a spiritual individual and recognized himself as such." The result was a momentous release of human activity from the constraints of medieval ideals and traditions, providing the impetus for the modern age. That release had obvious positive results: great works of art, the rediscovery of the values of ancient Greece and Rome, and a passion for political freedom. The Renaissance established the modern principle that it is not birth but achievement that counts. In the Renaissance, as in the modern world, "talent and audacity win the great prizes."

But the Renaissance also revealed the negative side of individualism. Burckhardt was not an unqualified admirer of the Renaissance. Personally he preferred the Middle Ages, with its sense of organic unity and spiritual community.* The Renaissance, to his mind, gave rise to the shameless worship of power. Burckhardt wrote, "For the first time we detect the modern political spirit of Europe . . . often displaying the worst features of an unbridled egoism, outraging every right, and killing every germ of a healthier culture." Rulers like the Borgias shed their sense of moral responsibility. "Where individuality of every sort attained its highest development we find instances of that ideal and absolute wickedness which delights in crimes for their own sake."[16]

The Renaissance of Michelangelo was also that of Machiavelli. This

---

* As he remarked in *On History and Historians*: "The Middle Ages are not responsible for our present decline! It was a time of natural *authority*. It is not its fault that we no longer have this or can regain it, but are instead flooded by waves of *majority* from below" (p. 32).

is the dark specter that haunts *The Civilization of the Renaissance in Italy* and, Burckhardt believed, modern Europe. The book was, as he told a friend, "a child of sorrow." Yet Burckhardt could not find the answer to a larger question: what if the two sides of individualism, its creative virtue and its destructive evil, were one and the same thing? In Gobineau's *Renaissance*, the question does not arise. Blood tells all: where we find the actions of a racial elite, however cruel and savage they may seem, there we also find vitality and health. "Go straight ahead. Simply do as you please, insofar as it serves your interest. Leave weakness and scruples to the petty minds and the rabble of underlings."[17]

Burckhardt could not accept such a monstrous conclusion. For all his historical pessimism, he remained as much an heir to the Enlightenment as Tocqueville. Burckhardt was convinced that the distinction between good and evil had to be something more than just personal whim; it somehow had to be revealed in man's inner nature. But if civilization and progress did not necessarily destroy man's moral nature, as Rousseau and the Romantics claimed, Burckhardt conceded that they did nothing to contribute to it either.[18] Once again, societies and nations existed to fulfill their purpose as collective organisms; they stood above and apart from the moral questions that vexed their individual members.

So where did the difference between good and evil reside, if it existed at all? Burckhardt could no longer answer or even face that question in his own work. His young colleague Friedrich Nietzsche, however, would press it to its limit.

## NIETZSCHE, SCHOPENHAUER, AND WAGNER

One of Burckhardt's favorite images of encroaching modern life was the railway locomotive. The first rail line into Basel opened in 1844, connecting the city to Berlin and the rest of Germany. On April 19, 1869, the train from Berlin brought a new professor of philology to the University of Basel, the twenty-four-year-old prodigy Friedrich Nietzsche. As he disembarked from the train, Nietzsche presented an unprepossessing figure in a drab suit, with thick spectacles and diffident manners. He hardly looked like a man about to set off a revolution that would shake Europe even more profoundly than the events of 1848. However, this was to be a revolution not in the streets but in the mind.

Like Burckhardt's father, Nietzsche's had been a Lutheran pastor. He died when Nietzsche was only five. Nietzsche's formative years as an intellectual would involve a series of intense but ambivalent relationships with a series of older and distinguished father figures.[19] His family had expected the bookish and withdrawn Friedrich to follow in his father's footsteps and enter the ministry. He received extensive training in Greek and Latin at one of Prussia's most distinguished preparatory schools.* But Nietzsche's faith in Christianity did not survive his matriculation at the University of Bonn and, like the young Burckhardt, he had to find another outlet for his intellectual energies. This turned out to be classical philology, the intensive study of Latin and Greek grammar according to rigorous scientific principles and the central pier of humanistic education in the nineteenth century. A brilliant and precocious doctoral scholar at the University of Leipzig, Nietzsche's appointment to the University of Basel made him one of the youngest professors in the German-speaking world. His inaugural lecture at Basel on May 28 was a ringing defense of the value of philology as a means of unlocking the secrets both of Greek and Latin literature and of Europe's ancient past.[20]

But the speech already belied Nietzsche's own doubts. Privately he had decided that, despite his obvious competence as a philologist, he had become a classical scholar not by choice but by default. Accepting the position at Basel with its rigorous teaching duties would require him to set aside his blossoming interest in philosophy, comparative literature, and music. Although he proved to be a popular teacher, Nietzsche was unhappy and restless. As he explained years later, he felt that he was wasting his time in Basel. University life seemed nothing more than an idle holding pattern as he waited for some greater inner awakening to stir him out of his lethargy.[21]

One small ray of light broke in on his boredom and restlessness in Basel: his growing friendship with Jacob Burckhardt. Although Nietzsche and Burckhardt were thirty years apart in age, they established an

---

* This was Schulpforta, where Ranke had also been educated.

immediate rapport. They took to attending each other's lectures, and even planned to write a book together on the culture of ancient Greece. Nietzsche regularly sat in on Burckhardt's lectures on modern history, where he witnessed the older man's vigorous attacks on "our old friend, the idea of Progess."

The guiding principle of this new modern age, Burckhardt told his audience, was equality. "Equality before the law, equality of taxes and . . . equal eligibility for offices" shared the same democratic podium with equal opportunity for property and material affluence. Yet with all the advantages of the modern world—equality, wealth, rapid communication, and "the great influence of public opinion on all events" through the modern press—"it is doubtful whether the world has on the average become happier."[22] Capitalism, with its worship of "absolute, ruthless acquisition," had created new miseries in the squalor and exploitation of industrial labor. High culture and creativity had become debased in a world where "money becomes and remains the great measure of things, [and] poverty the greatest vice." Certainly, "at our present moment of history . . . we have no business sitting in judgment on any past age." This included the Middle Ages, which for all its faults had been "without . . . threatening national wars, without forced mass industry with deadly competition, without credit and capitalism." Burckhardt concluded, "Our life is a business, theirs was living."

Today, "hurry and worry are spoiling life. Through universal competition everything is forced to the greatest speed and struggle for minimal differences." Underneath this "strong change in the pulse beat" of the nineteenth century, Burckhardt recognized the "prevalent optimism" of the Enlightenment, a "blind will to change" that results from a faith in progress. However, he argued, as people come to realize that their fondest hopes for wealth and happiness will never be realized, that optimism will turn sour. "It is conceivable that a shifting of that optimism to pessimism may take place" in the near future, he concluded, "such as happened at the end of antiquity" and the fall of Rome.[23]

"Yesterday evening," Nietzsche wrote to a friend, "I had the pleasure of hearing Jacob Burckhardt. . . . I am attending his weekly lectures on the study of history, and believe I am the only one of his sixty hearers who understands his profound train of thought. . . . For the first time in my life I have enjoyed a lecture: and what is more, it is the sort of lecture I shall be able to give when I am older."[24] Although he and Burck-hardt belonged to different generations, Nietzsche already shared the older man's disillusionment with post-1848 Europe. Nietzsche had also read the philosopher Eduard von Hartmann, who predicted that the world of the future would be one of material wealth but spiritual poverty.[25] Nietzsche, too, saw industrial capitalism and its socialist alternative as a "distinction without a difference," since both relied on a gross materialist view of the world and both placed the same demands on the omnipotent power of the state.*

Burckhardt's gloomy predictions became Nietzsche's guide to the future of modern European civilization, particularly its political future. Burckhardt argued that the triumph of democratic nationalism marked the final collapse of freedom. For Nietzsche, nationalism marks the end of politics as such. Far from bringing a new sense of unity and solidarity, the nation-state completes the divorce between individual and community that characterizes the entire modern age. Democracy makes a stable civic life impossible. As Nietzsche's Zarathustra says, "I turned my back on those who rule when I saw what they call ruling: higgling and haggling for power with the rabble."

The socialist delusion is the *reductio ad absurdum* of democracy. The collapse of the traditional social order and "the absence of superior presence," the "notorious vulgarity of manufacturers with red, fat hands," convinces the common man that he too should have a chance at running the state.[26] Democracy, nationalism, socialism—for Nietzsche they formed a single continuum, extensions of a meaningless and debased modernity. His mature works were liberally sprinkled with attacks on modern Germany and its leading figures, particularly Bismarck and the kaiser, which later admirers had to excise for publication.[27]

At the same time, Nietzsche remained optimistic while Burckhardt had given up hope. Nietzsche believed European civilization might still be saved, although not on the terms familiar to Burckhardt and other

---

* He also shared wholeheartedly Burckhardt's fear of modern militarism. As a student he had served briefly in the Prussian reserve horse artillery, and had taken a fall from a caisson that ended his service and gave him a loathing for the military that lasted all his life. Nietzsche even went so far as to renounce his Prussian citizenship when he moved to Basel. However, when the Franco-Prussian War broke out, he quixotically decided to volunteer as a medical orderly. His experiences at a field hospital during the siege of Metz did not lead him to revise his low opinion of war and soldiering.

old-fashioned Enlightenment liberals. In his opinion, European culture required a revolution that would reverse the nineteenth century's course, with the submission of the bourgeoisie and the masses to a new elite—and Nietzsche had just met the man who could lead it.

Nietzsche was an adolescent when he first encountered the emotional power of Richard Wagner's music. However, it was not until 1868, at a performance of the overtures to *Die Meistersinger* and *Tristan und Isolde*, that he fell under the Wagernian spell. "My every fiber, every nerve vibrates to this music. And I have hardly had such a lasting feeling of release as upon listening to this overture [to *Die Meistersinger*]." Later that year, Nietzsche attended a dinner party with the composer, and was so nervous that he tore his new dinner jacket up the back as he was putting it on.[28] But the composer was taken with the young philology student and invited him to his home at Triebschen near Lucerne; Nietzsche would make several visits during his tenure at Basel.

Wagner was then engrossed in his great life work, the *Ring des Nibelungen*. His household was what contemporaries would have called bohemian: he was living with Cosima von Bülow, a woman who was not his wife who was also bearing his child. In fact she was the wife of his friend Hans von Bülow, and Wagner's power of personality was such that von Bülow remained Wagner's dedicated (one might even say abject) disciple, continuing to conduct his works for an increasingly admiring public.[29] Wagner's operas had already made him the cultural hero of an entire generation of late Romantic artists and writers in both Germany and France, and he was at the brink of becoming a symbol of artistic creativity and philosophic profundity on a par with Goethe and Shakespeare. He was also the same age as Nietzsche's father would have been had he been alive.

Nietzsche was enthralled by Wagner's expansive personality and boisterous self-confidence, which contrasted sharply with Nietzsche's own diffidence, as well as with the self-effacing irony and melancholy of Nietzsche's other mentor, Jacob Burckhardt. Richard and Cosima Wagner opened up a new world for Nietzsche, one in which, despite his peculiarities and introversion, he seemed welcome and accepted.* Wag-

---

* Even after he had turned against Wagner years later, Nietzsche would admit, "I should not want to give away at any price my days at Triebschen."[30]

ner, in turn, appreciated the worshipful attention of a brilliant university professor. Here, Wagner thought, was a willing disciple who could defend his works and present his theory of aesthetics in respectable academic language. At the heart of that theory were the ideas of the chief German philosophic critic of nineteenth-century progress, Arthur Schopenhauer.

Schopenhauer is a good example of how the spell of Orientalism in the early nineteenth century could transform a thinker's life. As a young philosophy student, Schopenhauer had stumbled on a French translation of the Indian *Upanishads,* and he became enthralled with Hindu and Buddhist doctrines regarding renunciation. Schopenhauer's one major philosophic work, *The World as Will and Idea* (1818), pitted this Eastern mystical version of wisdom against the Enlightenment's faith in reason, science, and civilization.

The world we perceive around us, Schopenhauer explained, "the world as idea," is a creation of our self-centered ego. It is an illusion, the projection of our hopes and fears. Schopenhauer agreed with German Romantic philosophers that the only reality is the human will. However, Schopenhauer's Eastern influences pushed him to a more radical position. The subjective human will is the source of all striving, for money, love, and power. It is also the source of all our anguish. We must learn to abandon it, renounce it, in order to escape what Schopenhauer called "the sickness" of our lives in the world. The wise man's final goal is what Buddhists called *nirvana,* or "emptiness," a final release from will and desire that leads finally to extinction and death. "Life," he was often quoted as saying, "ought *not to be*"—meaning life according to the secular European or Western tradition.

Schopenhauer directed his philosophy of radical renunciation at two principal targets. The first was the Enlightenment, with its false optimism and its empty faith in reason and progress, epitomized by the philosophy of Hegel.* Schopenhauer's second target was Christianity, or more precisely the Judeo-Christian tradition. Most Romantics understood the Enlightenment and organized religion to be mutual enemies.

---

* Shortly after the publication of *The World as Will and Idea,* Schopenhauer offered a series of lectures at the University of Berlin, scheduled at the same time as Hegel's, to expound his doctrines. No one came.

Schopenhauer, however, saw them as allies. Both urged men to strive for their salvation in *this* world, whether through scientific rationalism, or the nation-state, or through adherence to religious law. Schopenhauer was particularly antagonistic toward the Jews in this regard. Judaism, Schopenhauer believed, had permanently infected Christianity with the illusion of "will as idea": the striving to change or alter the world to fit a set of religious and moral preconceptions, which the Jews and then the Christians called the laws of God.*

Now only one path of liberation remains. This is art, and particularly music. Art becomes a new way of knowing the world, immune from the remorseless desires of the ego and the "world as will." Through aesthetic experience, such as looking at a painting or listening to a symphony, we both experience the world in a new way and obtain a momentary release from the prison house of desire. Art and music provide moments of pure contemplation, uncorrupted by contact with the gross materiality that surrounds us. They must remain so, Schopenhauer stated, if they are to be "true philosophy."

Schopenhauer's book remained virtually unread for forty years, until Romantic disillusionment after 1848 brought him a new and willing audience. One disciple was Burckhardt. Another was Eduard von Hartmann, who in the *Philosophy of the Unconscious* (1869) turned Schopenhauer's remorseless human will into the "unconscious," a concept that Sigmund Freud later adopted and revised. Meanwhile, the young Nietzsche discovered a copy of *The World as Will and Idea* in a used bookshop in Leipzig in 1865. A shared admiration for Schopenhauer's philosophy was the starting point of Nietzsche's friendship with Burckhardt, for whom Schopenhauer would always be simply The Philosopher.[32]

Richard Wagner was yet another convert. His operas *The Flying Dutchman*, *Tannhäuser*, and *Tristan und Isolde* revolved around Schopenhauer's central idea, that the world of human activity is one of suffering

---

* The only parts of Christianity of any lasting value—its self-denying asceticism and its pessimism regarding the world of the flesh—were, Schopenhauer claimed, derived from Hindu India. Jesus, he concluded triumphantly, had been raised by Brahmin teachers during his flight into Egypt and absorbed their message of renunciation and spiritual release. Like the doctrines of another great spiritual teacher, Gautama Buddha, "Christian doctrine [was] born of Hindu wisdom," Schopenhauer wrote, and eventually "completely covered the old trunk of a grosser Judaism uncongenial to it."[31]

from which the soul yearns to be freed.* When Nietzsche paid his first visit to Triebschen in May 1869, he could hear torturous piano chords through an open window. Wagner was working that morning on the final scene of the Ring cycle, the suicide of Brünnhilde, whose acceptance of her fate finally releases her and the world from the endless cycle of rebirth, desire, and death. The scene was pure Schopenhauer:

> *I shall proceed to the most hallowed chosen land*
> *beyond both desire and illusion*
> *the end of the earthly journey.*
> *Do you know how I attained*
> *the blessed goal*
> *of all that is eternal?*
> *The pain of grieving love opened my eyes*
> *I saw the world end.*

Schopenhauer had stressed that music allowed human beings to transcend, albeit only temporarily, the will's relentless grip. Wagner explained to Nietzsche that he believed his operas could provide a more permanent respite. The *Ring des Nibelungen* would transform opera into a new revolutionary art form, he declared, one that combined music, drama, poetry, and the plastic arts in a single *Gesamtkunstwerk*, or "complete work of art." Wagner's operas would literally redeem a corrupted modernity through a combination of emotional catharsis, transcendent musical experience, and mythic ritual.

The breathtaking arrogance of this vision went with an equally audacious plan to construct a huge theater in which the *Ring* could be presented as an annual event, part artistic festival and part religious service. This theater would be built on German soil, at Bayreuth in Upper Franconia. As the months passed and the friendship between Nietzsche and Wagner grew, the composer found in his young professor friend a willing ally in his plan to launch a new beginning for art and humanity. For the next two years, 1870 and 1871, while continuing his round of lectures and duties at Basel, Nietzsche eagerly threw himself into this new, much larger undertaking: the literal salvation of Europe

---

* Schopenhauer even inspired Wagner to plan an opera on the life of Buddha.[33]

through Wagner's music. In the following year he published his first book, *The Birth of Tragedy*. It was ostensibly about Greek drama and religion; but in truth it was a celebration of Wagner's conception of the relation between art and society. The book also represented Nietzsche's first provisional answer to the question that would preoccupy him for the rest of his life: how to prevent the decay of modern civilization.

All of Nietzsche's writings from the 1870s, including *The Birth of Tragedy* and his four *Untimely Meditations*, took shape from Schopenhauer's view of the futility of human will and from Burckhardt's bleak picture of the modern industrial age. "The waters of religion are ebbing away and leaving behind swamps or stagnant pools," Nietzsche wrote in "Schopenhauer as Educator." As a general war threatens to destroy Europe, "the educated classes and states are being swept along by a hugely comtemptible money economy." He declared that "the world has never been more worldly, never poorer in love and goodness."[34] Men of intellect have made matters worse by encouraging a belief in the illusion of progress instead of being "beacons or refuges in the midst of this turmoil of secularization." They have persuaded the masses to believe that the final improvement of mankind lies somewhere in the future, and "that happiness lies behind the hill they are advancing towards." Nietzsche concluded in Burckhardtian fashion: "Everything contemporary, art and science included, serves the coming barbarism. A winter's day lies upon us, and we dwell in high mountains, in danger and in poverty."[35]

But Nietzsche also rejected Rousseau's primitivist solution to modern civilization. Any "return to nature" is for Nietzsche only a return to poverty and hopelessness. History would always have a forward momentum, even if it was only toward limited horizons. However, social life and the civilizing process are expressions not of our higher nature but of our base animality, an unvarying continuum of humdrum human experience. It cannot be improved upon but only, as Schopenhauer suggested, transcended.[36] So while Nietzsche accepted Burckhardt's diagnosis of modern civilization as doomed, as riddled with "degeneracy" and "weakness," he modified the historian's larger assumption that society as a whole followed a regular course of organic development. Every nation or civilization is for Nietzsche, as it was for Burckhardt, a dynamic unit of forces and counterforces that balance or displace each other over time.[37] This means that the present is an irrevocable unfolding of the past. "The best we can do," he proclaimed, "is to confront our inherited and hereditary nature . . . and implant in ourselves a new habit, a new instinct, a second nature, so that our first nature withers away." His adherence to Schopenhauer then compelled him to add, "Every past is worthy to be condemned—for that is the nature of human things."[38]

This was where Nietzsche parted company with Burckhardt. He gave the older man credit for recognizing the forces that have led to the decay and breakdown of the old order, but Burckhardt had failed to see that the fault lay not in the individual components but in the weakness of the old order itself—European civilization according to its traditional, Judeo-Christian pattern. Burckhardt still worshipped at the shrine of the old society. He still hoped to save the "polite" conventions of manners and morality of his fellow Basel burghers, as well as their trust in a good and just God. Burckhardt's blindness was the blindness of the nineteenth century. "It knows only how to preserve life, not how to engender it. . . . Its motto is: 'let the dead bury the living.' This is precisely why our modern culture is not a living thing." Modern Europe has not lost its vital spark of greatness, Nietzsche proclaimed; in a crucial sense, it never had it. In order to break free of this dying world, men must now push on to a new culture, with new habits and "new instincts."

Nietzsche's antidote to Burckhardt's historical pessimism was Romantic heroism. He issued an appeal to those he called "men of redemption"—philosophers, artists, and writers—"selected individuals . . . who are equipped for great and lasting works." A new cultural elite will step forward, Nietzsche argued, and deliberately turn their backs on the prevailing materialistic direction of modern civilization. They will toil to produce a true "Schopenhauerian culture," in which "one giant calls to another across the desert intervals of time and, undisturbed by the chattering dwarfs who creep about beneath them, the exalted spirit-dialogue goes on."[39] Nietzsche suggested to his readers that one such "man of redemption" was already living in their midst: Richard Wagner. Wagner's operas would renew civilization and release man's great vital instincts by overcoming the fateful division that lay at the foundation of European culture itself.

In his study of ancient Greek culture, *The Birth of Tragedy*, Nietzsche drew what would become a famous distinction, between the Dionysian spirit, the untamed spirit of art and creativity, and the Apollonian, that of reason and self-control.[40] The story of Greek civilization, and all civilizations, Nietzsche implied, was the gradual victory of Apollonian man, with his desire for control over nature and himself, over Dionysian man, who survives only in myth, poetry, music, and drama. Socrates and Plato had attacked the illusions of art as *unreal,* and had overturned the delicate cultural balance by valuing only man's critical, rational, and controlling consciousness while denigrating his vital life instincts as irrational and base. The result of this division is "Alexandrian man," the civilized and accomplished Greek citizen of the later ancient world, who is "equipped with the greatest forces of knowledge" but in whom the wellsprings of creativity have dried up.

Modern European man is the direct descendant of Alexandrian man.[41] He is the epitome of civilization according to a Thomas Buckle or an Auguste Comte. His belief that he can discover reality by reason alone leads directly to "the spirit of easy optimism which is the germ of the destruction of our society," as well as of its misplaced faith that science and institutions can make men happy and free.[42] Nietzsche saw Wagner's operas as a momentous return to European man's original wholeness, the world of "tragic culture" that accepts both human helplessness and human triumph, the monstrous and the sublime. With one hundred such men, "the whole noisy sham-culture of our age could be silenced forever" and the human mind and spirit become one again.[43]

On May 22, 1872, crowds trudged up the hill at Bayreuth amid a day-long downpour to witness the dedication of Wagner's new theater. Nietzsche and Richard Wagner, "a man who lives out idealistic speculations in an age when the world is ruled by speculation on the stock exchange,"[44] rode side by side in the carriage. Nietzsche glanced at Wagner: "He was silent and he seemed to be gazing into himself with a look not to be described in words. . . . Everything that had gone before was a preparation for this moment." To both men it seemed literally the dawn of a new age.

## NIETZSCHE AND CULTURAL PESSIMISM

"Only he who has attached his heart to some great man is by that act *consecrated* to culture"—unfortunately, as work began on the Bayreuth theater that summer, so did Nietzsche's first doubts. At first he limited his misgivings to his private notebooks. "Wagner's art speaks a *theatrical* language . . . a popular language, and as such it is bound to coarsen even the noblest sentiments." He decided that Wagner was a "misplaced actor." Later on he concluded that "none of our great composers was such a poor musician at the age of 28 as Wagner," and in a final outburst that "his music is not worth much, nor is the poetry, nor is the plot, the dramaturgy is often mere rhetoric."[45]

Nietzsche's worst fears were confirmed at the first Bayreuth festival in 1876. Its audience were the fashionable bourgeoisie and aristocracy whom Nietzsche despised and whom he had thought Wagner also despised. Wagner's biggest publicity coup, however, was the appearance of Kaiser Wilhelm I himself. As Nietzsche watched the kaiser applaud at the end of a scene and then turn to his military aids to remark, "Deplorable! Deplorable!" Nietzsche's patience snapped. Wagner had sold out, Nietzsche told himself. Bayreuth had become a showcase for all the shallow, bourgeois, patriotic sentiments that Nietzsche most detested (although these were the very qualities that would draw Ludwig Schemann, Houston Chamberlain, Nietzsche's future brother-in-law Bernhard Förster, and other admirers into Wagner's orbit). Nietzsche's new assessment of his erstwhile idol was reflected in the title of his next book: *Human, All Too Human.*

Meanwhile, Jacob Burckhardt was beginning to be concerned about his young friend. On April 5, 1879, he wrote to Nietzsche, thanking him for having sent a copy of *Human, All Too Human* and praising him for the book's profundity and "freedom of mind." To others, however, he worried about Nietzsche's deteriorating physical and mental state, his "very weak sight, constant headaches, violent attacks [of nausea] every few days." Nietzsche deteriorated to the point that he was forced to take a leave of absence from the University of Basel that summer. He never returned.[46]

The end of Nietzsche's father-son relationship with Wagner led to a searching self-examination (how could he have made such a mistake about Wagner?) and launched him on the philosophical journey that would consume the rest of his life. Nietzsche had decided that Wagner's art suffered from the same disease that afflicted Alexandrian man in *The Birth of Tragedy* and the rest of modern society: decadence.

What is . . . decadence? That life no longer dwells in the whole . . . the vibration and exuberance of life is pushed back into the smallest forms. . . . The whole no longer lives at all; it is composite, calculated, artificial, and artifact.

Here Nietzsche echoed the criticisms by Nisard, Couture, and other conservative critics forty years earlier. Above all, the decadent work of art or decadent person lacks "authenticity," a term that Nietzsche would make famous. "No one dares to appear as he is, he masks himself as a cultivated man, as a scholar, as a poet, as a politician"—or a musician. As proof of his diagnosis, Nietzsche could point to Wagner's own popularity, which reached new heights after the composer's death in 1883. "In declining cultures, wherever the decision comes to rest with the masses, authenticity becomes superfluous, disadvantageous . . . Only the actor [Wagner] still arouses great enthusiasm."[47]

All of Nietzsche's later influential works—his *Joyful Science, Genealogy of Morals, Beyond Good and Evil,* and the brooding epic parable *Thus Spake Zarathustra*—were in a profound sense a search for the origins of decadence in European culture. As Burckhardt himself astutely observed, what Nietzsche wrote was not so much philosophy in the normal sense as history.[48] Nietzsche's point of departure was the same as Burckhardt's: the rise of a mass democratic and capitalist age, precipitating the breakdown of European society and its "values" (another term Nietzsche would make famous).

But Nietzsche arrived at a conclusion much closer to Gobineau's: modern Europe has lost the vital life force necessary for the creation of values and "the overflowing riches" of a truly strong culture. That life force Nietzsche called "the will to power." The historical root of modernity's "declining life," Nietzsche concluded, was not racial miscegenation (although he did not rule it out as a contributing factor) but instead "the birth of morality." This is why he would later describe his entire philosophy as a "campaign against morality"—and a celebration of the will to power.[49]

Nietzsche understood man's will to power to be something far broader and more pervasive than a conscious desire to exercise control over others, as in politics or master-slave relations. The latter were merely manifestations of what is in a sense a part of life itself; as philosopher Richard Schacht explains, the will to power is "the basic tendency of all forces and configurations of forces"—in man, society, or nature—"to extend their influence and dominate others." These forces "collectively constitute the reality of the world as it actually exists." The will to power is the origin of all that exists and all that man has made, from the most sublime works of art to the most violent and horrific crimes.[50] The healthy, vital individual, like the healthy society, is aware of his will to power. It gives him, Nietzsche wrote, "a feeling of plenitude, of dammed-up strength" and well-being that "permits [him] to meet with courage and good-humor much that makes the weakling shudder."[51] Sickness and decadence, by contrast, are horrified by and shun the instinct for life and power; "life, equal vitality, is pushed back into the smallest forms." The larger whole loses energy and decays, entering a state in which "one loses the power of resistance" and a "weary nihilism" sets in. "Wherever the will to power declines in any form there is also a physiological regression, a decadence."[52]

For Nietzsche, all of history becomes a metaphysical struggle between two groups, those who express the will to power and the life instinct, and those who do not. "Those poor in life, the weak," impoverish culture; "those rich in life, the strong, enrich it."[53] Nietzsche explained that all civilization is the work of "men of prey who were still in possession of unbroken strength of will and lust for power, [who] hurled themselves on weaker, more civilized, more peaceful races . . . or upon mellow old cultures whose last vitality was even then flaring up in splendid fireworks of spirit and corruption."[54] These men of prey Nietzsche called the Aryans—Gobineau's term—who become the ruling class of the new society. "The noble caste was always the barbarian caste," Nietzsche wrote, because they are literally more alive and complete human beings than the jaded sophisticates they conquer.

Nietzsche's Aryans breathe a vitalism that Gobineau would easily have recognized. In fact, the evidence of Gobineau's influence on Nietzsche may be indirect but it is convincing.[55] Like Gobineau, Nietzsche admired the aristocrat as the paragon of society's vital life force. "Every enhancement of the type 'man,'" he wrote, "has so far been the work of an aristocratic society—and it will be so again and again." Nietzsche's earlier "Schopenhauerian culture" of genius and contemplation yields to the vital, spontaneous world of the Japanese samurai and Homeric hero, and to early Germany and Viking Scandinavia, where strength, honor, and a contempt for inferior forms of life predominate.

However, Nietzsche's vital Aryan "blond beast" is not a racial type but a cultural one. His chief characteristic is his ability to spontaneously "create values" for himself and his society. The strong aristocratic class creates its own definition of honor, duty, and beauty (which is whatever looks the way the aristocrats do). It creates its own version of right and wrong and decides what counts as true and false. These values the conquerors then impose on the conquered, just as they confiscate their land and property as spoils of war. Nietzsche does not deplore the brutality of conquest in history. On the contrary, he admires it, because "life itself is *essentially* appropriation, injury, overpowering of what is alien and weaker."*

Vitality and creativity, including the creation of values, is the "privilege of the strong," that is, of conquerors, aristocrats, and, Nietzsche adds, artists. Morality, on the other hand, is the creation of the underclass, their revenge on their vital superiors. Nietzsche's paradigm of the vital individual in European history is the same as Gobineau's: Cesare Borgia. Nietzsche exalts him and all the Borgias precisely because their victims and later generations condemned them as criminals and sadistic monsters. Nietzsche is not impressed by these labels; the more vital the individual, the more he will shock and horrify the inert majority. In the aristocratic society, such as samurai Japan or Homeric Greece, the warrior's deeds and murders are celebrated and enshrined in art and poetry (as in the *Iliad* or *Nibelungenlied*); in the decadent or democratic society, he is vilified as a monster. The Aryan warrior "emerges from a disgusting procession of murder, arson, rape, and torture, exhilarated and undisturbed of soul," even as his resentful victims and inferiors secretly plot his downfall. Since they cannot defeat him on the battlefield, they do it through culture. They produce what the Enlightenment called politeness and sociability and what Nietzsche calls the "slave morality."

On one side, then, stands the master morality of the aristocratic warriors. It values the "proud, exalted states of the soul," which are experi-

---

* "Exploitation does not belong to a corrupt or imperfect and primitive society; it belongs to the essence of what lives, as a basic organic function; it is a consequence of the will to power, which is after all the will to life."[56]

enced firsthand through "war, adventure, hunting, dancing, war games, and in general all that involves vigorous, free, joyful activity." The master morality shapes a world view that is necessarily self-centered; "such a morality is a self-glorification."[57] On the other side is the slave morality, born from the resentment (Nietzsche uses the French term *ressentiment*, with its connotation of a reactive response) of those exploited and controlled by their natural, vital superiors. "That sheep dislike birds of prey does not seem strange," and so the sheep pretend that the aristocrats' happiness is not genuine. Real happiness and virtue, they proclaim, depend on helping the oppressed. "Pity, the complaisant and obliging hand, the warm heart, patience, industry, humility, friendliness, are all honored" by the victims of the Aryan "blond beast," in order to shame and defeat him.[58]

In stark contrast to the master morality, "slave morality is essentially a morality of utility." The word "utility" is crucial. *All* material civilization and economic progress, Nietzsche is saying, including that of middle-class Europe, is based on the slave morality. It nourishes the virtues of the herd animal, who "gives himself the appearance of being the only permissible kind of man, and glorifies his attributes, which make him tame, easy to get along, useful to the herd." The new social imperatives become kindness, self-effacement, and conformity—and mediocrity. "Everything that elevates an individual above the herd and intimidates the neighbor is henceforth called evil."

The entire civilizing process is the victory of the weak majority over the vital minority, the sacrifice of aristocratic perfection for the sake of the common man. Nietzsche did not require Gobineau's appeal to biological racial mixing to explain this process of corruption; instead, the herd deliberately waters down and pollutes society's cultural values. But society also pays a fatal price. By civilizing its aristocratic elites, it introduces "a will to the denial of life" into the whole, "a principle of disintegration and decay."[59]

The blame for this "slave revolt" falls squarely on Christianity. Like Gobineau, Nietzsche concludes that Christianity is "the anti-Aryan religion par excellence," but again, not for racial reasons. Instead, like his mentor Schopenhauer, Nietzsche saw the spirit of Christianity and the Enlightenment faith in material progress ("the principle of utility") as one and the same. Both restrict and constrict the human will, instead of releasing creative energies and generating new values. They turn will to power in on itself, producing guilt and shame. "The Christian resolve to find the world ugly and bad has made the world ugly and bad. . . . Only the most mediocre flourish while the higher kind miscarries. Faced by this so-called 'civilization,' [it] loses courage and submits."[60]

"Morality negates life." Nietzsche's conclusion is not just an ethical or philosophical judgment, but an historical one. The breakdown of civilization is not a move backward to an inchoate savage state—barbarism in Burckhardt's sense—but a movement forward to decadence and meaninglessness. "We can see nothing today that wants to grow greater, we suspect that things will continue to go down, down, to become thinner, more good-natured, more prudent, more comfortable, more mediocre, more indifferent, more Chinese, more Christian—there is no doubt man is become 'better' all the time." The progress of this poison through "the entire body of mankind seems irresistible," precisely because the masses identify this repression of the life instinct as progress.[61] By embracing Christianity, science, and liberal humanitarianism, Western culture has embraced its own destruction. "For some time now, our whole European culture has been moving as toward a catastrophe." The modern West is *sick*, a term Nietzsche uses in a literal and diagnostic sense. "Are we not straying as through an infinite nothing? Do we not feel the breath of empty space? Has it not become colder? Is it not night continually closing in on us?"

By the time he finished *On the Genealogy of Morals* in 1887, Nietzsche's own illness was closing in on him, destroying both his body and (as he was realizing) his mind. He would sit at his desk, face and spectacles pressed to the paper, writing furiously about the "proud, exalted states of being" of a vanished Aryan aristocracy and the joys of war and hunting, and then spend three days at a time in bed, with blinding headaches and vomiting. Yet he was convinced that there was still a way out for culture and humanity. This was to ride the decadence of modern civilization out to the bottom, to "descend to the depths" of meaninglessness and nihilism. Humanity's last hope now rests with the enemies of conventional values, "those who blaspheme God, the immoralists, the nomads of every type, the artists, Jews, musicians—at bottom, all disreputable classes of men. . . . We immoralists are today the *stronger power*." The nihilist and the immoralist break through the false facade of good and evil. Total disbelief is "an ideal of the highest degree of power-lessness . . . to this extent, nihilism, as the denial of a truthful world, of being, might be *a divine way of thinking.*"[62]

Then a new dawn will break, as Nietzsche spelled out in his most popular book and his only work of fiction, *Thus Spake Zarathustra*. While Nietzsche's other books were the product of struggle and agoniz-ing self-reflection, *Zarathustra* was literally an inspired work. He wrote it with incredible speed, finishing each of the first three parts in only ten days in 1881 (the fourth and concluding part was completed a year later). It is a parable of humanity at the end of modern civilization. Just as Wagner's *Ring* revealed the death of a world ruled by gods and the be-ginning of a world ruled by men, so *Zarathustra* described the death of "the last man"—Western man.*

Nietzsche chose the ancient Persian religious prophet Zarathustra (Zoroaster) as his main character. Zoroaster had proclaimed the uni-verse to be divided into light and darkness, life and death; to Nietzsche's mind he is a symbol of the vitalism of ancient Aryan religion. In the story, he is also Nietzsche himself. After ten years of mountain solitude, Zarathustra (like Nietzsche ten years after his visits to Wagner at Trieb-schen) returns to the world of men to announce that *God is dead.* Ra-tionality and science have killed Him off; modern culture rests on a core of unbelief, an absence of faith. Modern man's lack of faith has de-stroyed his capacity to value and his power to create new values to re-place the dead myth of Christianity.

On his journey, Zarathustra encounters the last man, the final egre-gious product of decadent bourgeois society. He is an insect in compar-ison with his predecessors—"his race is as ineradicable as the flea-beetle"—yet thanks to his command over the material world and doctrine of progress, "the last man lives the longest." Zarathustra comes to the marketplace, the symbol of modern man's pettiness and empty values, where "everyone wants the same; everyone is the same; whoever wants different goes voluntarily to the madhouse." Although the last man claims that modern man "invented happiness," what he has actu-

---

* The parallels between Wagner's *Ring* and Nietzsche's *Zarathustra* are striking, and there is reason to believe that Nietzsche hoped his book would become the subject of annual ritual performances, complete with sets and music, at a sacred site in the manner of Wagner's Bayreuth.

ally done is to destroy it by banishing the will to power: exertion, creativity, and striving. It is a society with "no shepherd and one herd."[63]

Zarathustra also encounters his earlier father figures, Schopenhauer and Wagner, as cultural archetypes. The Magician (Wagner) at first appeals to Zarathustra for help, then admits he is only pretending to be in distress. "Stop it, you actor! You counterfeiter! You liar from the bottom!" Zarathustra shouts at him, recalling Nietzsche's description of Wagner as a "misplaced actor."[64] The Magician then confesses that he, too, is waiting for Zarathustra to tell him how to live in a world without God, that is, in a world without moral certainties.

The Soothsayer (Schopenhauer) preaches a doctrine of "the great weariness." "All is the same," he intones, "nothing is worthwhile, the world is without meaning, knowledge strangles." In fact, his nihilism is justified. In modern society, "the world has become small . . . the last man makes it small." However, all this is about to end. Zarathustra brings news of the end of the last man and the birth of the Overman. The motto of the last man is "There are no higher men . . . before God, we are all equal." But Zarathustra can now tell them the terrible truth. "Before God! But that god has died." Modernity has destroyed all conviction in its own principles: what might once have been a source of despair has now become a source of release. "You higher men, this god was your greatest danger. It is only since he lies in his tomb that you have been resurrected. Only now the great noon comes; only now that the higher man becomes—lord."[65]

The *Übermensch* is the Overman in the sense that he has *overcome* within himself those characteristics that make him timebound, a helpless part of the endless ebb and flow of history and "animality" described with such loathing in Nietzsche's early essays. The Overman triumphs over decadent civilization not in a physical sense, in the way the Aryans conquered antiquity, but in a psychological and cultural sense. He has conquered the chaos of his passions; as Nietzsche said of Goethe, "he disciplined himself to wholeness, he *created* himself." He creates his own values, his own master morality, since the morality of the bourgeois world turns out to be a fraud. He is the *total* man, "a spirit who has become free."[66] Above all, the Overman has freed himself from the restraints and obligations of civil society, since he recognizes that they are the products of history and therefore meaningless and empty.

The Overman realizes that history has no larger meaning because it is governed by the law of eternal recurrence.* The only significant change in human society is the movement from vitality, an abundance of will to power and energy, to decadence, the ebbing away of that energy. Since the totality of energy in the universe always remains the same, Nietzsche insisted, that movement must be cyclical. The law of eternal recurrence is Nietzsche's vitalist version of the Greek "circle of doom." It "means that all events are repeated endlessly, that there is no plan or goal to give meaning to history or life. . . . The eternal recurrence is the epitome of 'a tale told by an idiot, full of sound and fury, signifying nothing.' " The true Overman has entirely reconciled himself to this bleak truth. Zarathustra says, "I come again, with this sun, this earth, this eagle, this snake—not to new life or a better life or a similar life: I come again to *this same life*. . . ." Since there is no final goal, only the choice of the individual matters: "Live [so] that you must desire to live again."[67]

"My hour is come," Zarathustra says, "this is my morning, my day is breaking; rise now, rise, thou great noon!"

*I slept I slept*
*I have woken from a deep dream*
*The world is deep, and deeper than day imagined.*

"This is my great harvest time," Nietzsche wrote to a correspondent in the autumn of 1888. "On questions of decadence I am the highest court of appeal." He had moved that summer to Turin, in Italy, "a superb and beneficent city." It was the city where Arthur de Gobineau had died six years earlier, as Nietzsche knew (he asked the locals about the house where Gobineau stayed before he died).[68] With the final onslaught of his disease, Nietzsche's grasp on reality was dissolving. In his last published work, *The Antichrist*, his attacks on Christianity went to new extremes. He called it "the one immortal blemish of mankind . . . it has made of every value a disvalue, of every truth a lie." Nietzsche even announced that he was himself the Antichrist. "Since the old God is abolished, I am prepared to rule the world."[69]

---

* Some scholars call this the myth of the eternal return. In fact, however, it is not a myth or a "noble lie," as Nietzsche sometimes calls other socially useful beliefs. Instead, Nietzsche takes it seriously as an objective scientific truth.

On October 15, 1888, Nietzsche celebrated his forty-fifth birthday. "No moment in history has been more important. . . . Everybody glances at me as if I were a prince—there is a special distinction in the way doors are held open for me, meals set out." In reality, his stay in Turin was a lonely existence: he would sit for hours by himself in the parlor of his boardinghouse, playing the piano. According to his landlord's daughter, what he played most often was—Wagner.[70]

In his own long and tortuous intellectual journey, Nietzsche had turned decisively away from two of his intellectual mentors: Wagner and Schopenhauer. But Nietzsche never severed relations with his other great father-mentor, Jacob Burckhardt. Nietzsche continued to send him copies of his books almost until the end, even when Burckhardt could no longer acknowledge or recognize his young friend in the nihilist philosophy he espoused. With the last one, *The Case of Wagner*, Nietzsche wrote in a pathetic note, "A single word from you would make me happy." Yet Burckhardt found himself unable to reply. In Nietzsche's last letter to Burckhardt, written after his final mental breakdown in January 1889, he confessed, "You are our great greatest teacher."[71]

The figure of Nietzsche towers above the history of twentieth-century thought. He is the great prophet of "cultural pessimism." In an important sense, however, Nietzsche's pessimism stemmed from Burckhardt's earlier view of the fate of modern civilization. Burckhardt's historical pessimism sprang from a view of society that he inherited from Ranke, the view that it is a complete and organic whole that must eventually face decline and death just as any living organism does. Confronted by the new, unfamiliar forces of the nineteenth century—democracy, industrial capitalism, the reach and power of the nation-state—Burckhardt concluded that these represented the breakdown of an earlier social harmony. The nineteenth century did not signal some different future order, even if its nature was still vague and hard to predict. It was merely the harbinger of future disorder.

The historical pessimist sees a decaying or decadent present systematically undoing the achievements of the past. The Nietzschean cultural pessimist sees the present as simply an extension of the same corrupt and meaningless values of the past; true cultural health, he concludes, requires the rejection of both. The imminent collapse of a decadent civilization is not a tragedy but a cause for celebration. It clears the way for something new and unprecedented, a rejuvenated cultural order built on an entirely new principle.

That new principle could be racial. After all, Nietzsche's philosophy proceeded from the same vitalist assumptions as Gobineau's. Every civilization, they both stated, relied on a reservoir of organic life force for its existence, or will to power. But Nietzsche's most decisive influence would not be on racial thinkers but on cultural critics and artists. Nietzsche would inspire them to think of themselves as a counterforce to a decadent social order. The modern artist did not pretend to be the savior of modern society (Percy Shelley had called poets the "future legislators of mankind"), since there was nothing worth saving. Instead, Nietzsche encouraged the notion that attacking the Western cultural and moral tradition was in itself an expression of health and renewal. Critical thinking in Nietzsche's sense was the first stage in a "revaluation of all values."[72] The antiestablishment critic, the artist, and the "immoralist"—from Picasso and Bertolt Brecht to the Sex Pistols and Madonna—form a new vitalist aristocracy in the modern cultural void.

None of them, however, can hope to find a foothold unless the historical pessimist has already pronounced the earlier tradition dead, or at least moribund and dying. As Nietzsche's mentor, Burckhardt had predicted the rise of the last man almost two decades before Nietzsche. Like Nietzsche and later cultural pessimists, Burckhardt saw modern democracy as "manufactured consent," the masses being mere tools of more powerful interests, such as industrial corporations and military dictators. The possibility that popular participation and growing material affluence might serve as a barrier to the growth of the totalitarian state never occurred to Burckhardt. Instead, he concluded, "I know too much history to expect anything from the despotism of the masses except tyranny, which will be the end of history."

Nietzsche's philosophy deplored the same nineteeth-century trends—nationalism, industrial capitalism, and the growth of mass culture—that Burckhardt did. Yet, paradoxically, Nietzsche's philosophy of the will to power and a master morality seemed to Burckhardt to point precisely in the same direction, toward brutality and despotism. Nietzsche's twisting of Burckhardt's own adage that "power is by its nature evil" into a positive faith appalled him.* The fate of civilization, Nietzsche argued, depended on vitalist forces that lay "beyond good and evil." Burckhardt, like Tocqueville, still believed in the necessity of social rules and conventions, in the need for human beings to have a conscience and a sense of moral restraint, and in free will.

Yet in confronting what he saw as the distasteful direction of modernity, Burckhardt himself could only recommend withdrawal. At his university, Burckhardt enjoyed a life undisturbed by any outward events or excitement, a life of sweet repose surrounded by scholarship, art, music, and beauty. However, he always remained uneasy about the developments taking place beyond his door, about which he felt he could do nothing. As he confessed to a friend, "I, at least, say to myself daily, this could all end in an hour." His one hope was that at some remote future date, human beings might once again discover the humanist culture of old Europe, the place where "the richest formations originate, a home of every contrast . . . where everything that can be thought has been given voice and expression."[74]

---

* Burckhardt never confronted Nietzsche directly on this point, although in one letter he did meekly ask whether Nietzsche's observation that willingly inflicting great suffering "belongs to greatness" didn't seem to advocate the "eventual tyranny" of the totalitarian state.[73]

## CHAPTER 4

# DEGENERATION

## *Liberalism's Doom*

We are accustomed to regard ourselves as necessarily progressing . . . and as destined to progress still further. . . . it is well to
remember that we are subject to the general laws of evolution,
and are as likely to degenerate as progress.

—Edwin Lankester, *Degeneration: A Chapter in Darwinism*, 1880

My good friend John, let me caution you. You deal with the
madmen. All men are mad in one way or another.

—Bram Stoker, *Dracula*, 1897

In November 1870, a young Italian doctor named Cesare Lombroso
was preparing to conduct a postmortem at the Pavia hospital. This
was no ordinary autopsy: the body was that of the notorious bandit Villela, the Italian Jack the Ripper, who had defied authorities and horrified the public for decades before finally being caught and executed. For
Lombroso the postmortem was also a matter of more than casual interest. He was deeply interested in the link between deviant behavior and
physiognomy. He had noted that many violent criminals liked to wear
elaborate tattoos, often with "indecent designs," and he had noticed
how a sadistic murderer he had once examined exhibited the cannibalism usually associated with the South Sea Islands rather than modern
Italy.

Now, as he worked in the gloom of the late autumn evening, he noticed something else. The occipital section of Villela's skull revealed a

pronounced indentation where it joined the spine, the same kind of indentation as that found in "inferior animals including rodents." Lombroso raised his eyes from the body. "I seemed to see all of a sudden, lit up as a vast plain under a flaming sky, the problem of the nature of the criminal—an atavistic being who reproduces in his person the ferocious instincts of primitive humanity and the inferior animals. . . ." The murderer's body revealed the distinctive characteristics shared by "criminals, savages, and apes." These included enormous jaws, high cheek bones, insensibility to pain, extremely acute eyesight, tattooing, "excessive idleness, love of orgies, and the irresponsible craving of evil for its own sake. . . ."[1]

Lombroso was convinced that he had found the key to an issue that had begun to worry other members of the medical profession. This was the fear of "degeneration," the possibility that the population of Europe was no longer physically capable of sustaining the demands of civilized life. Gobineau had used the term to refer to the results of racial mixing, or miscegenation; his modern man was a "degenerate" because of cross-breeding between Aryans and less vital human types. This new fear of degeneration, however, took hold in the same liberal circles that rejected Gobineau's fanciful racial theories. To the trained observer, the economic and social advances of the nineteenth century suddenly seemed to be working against human progress, rather than for it. Degeneration theory presented a pessimistic picture of the outlook for modern civilization that would ultimately be more influential than anything propagated by Gobineau, Nietzsche, or their disciples. By the turn of the century, degeneration theory had cut deep into European liberalism's confidence in the future, leaving it exposed to its enemies.

Degeneration was defined as the morbid deviation from an original type. "When under any kind of noxious influences an organism becomes debilitated, its successors will not resemble the healthy, normal type . . . but will form a new sub-species," which passes its peculiarities on with increasing frequency to its offspring.[2] Could this debilitation, under the proper conditions, happen to modern man? Doctors, biologists, zoologists, and anthropologists—the leading members of the new scientific professions—were the first to raise the alarm. By 1890 there was a growing consensus that a tide of degeneration was sweeping across the landscape of industrial Europe, creating a host of disorders in its wake that included a rise in poverty, crime, alcoholism, moral perversion, and political violence.

The scientists most concerned about degeneration were, with few exceptions, strongly progressive, even socialist, in their political views. They were far from being the conservative defenders of the status quo that historians sometimes present them as being.[3] Lombroso, for example, was for a time a member of the Italian Socialist Party and built his career combatting poverty and malnutrition among Italy's poorest sharecroppers, which earned him the lasting hostility of the aristocracy and large landowners.* The opponents of his theory that heredity determined social behavior came not from the Italian Left but from what we would today call the religious Right, the Catholic Church and its traditionalist allies.

Max Nordau, the author of the influential *Degeneration*, was a committed egalitarian democrat and admirer of the French Revolution. He detested aristocracy, social snobbery, religion, and inherited wealth as much as he loved science and reason. Much the same could be said for many of the leading eugenicists, who took their impetus from degeneration theory. Ernst Haeckel was a founding member of the National Peace League as well as the Society for Racial Hygiene, while Karl Pearson, director of the Galton Laboratory, was a socialist. Indeed, the threat of degeneration became one of the issues on which late-nineteenth-century socialists, radicals, and liberals strongly agreed.†

The degeneration scare raised the possibility that modern industrial society might be creating a new "barbarian within." Liberals were forced to draw a similar conclusion to that of their socialist colleagues: the normal social and economic transformations of modern civilization no longer constituted progress, but its opposite. Modern society would not survive without the forceful intervention of modern science—and the bureaucratic state.

---

* It was Lombroso who first established that pellagra was the result of poor diet, rather than heredity, among Italy's most destitute classes.[4]

† Among those interested, even fascinated, by degeneration was Friedrich Engels.[5]

## DARWIN: PROGRESS VERSUS DECLINE IN HUMAN HISTORY

That conclusion might seem to contradict the most important and characteristic biological theory of the nineteenth century, Charles Darwin's theory of evolution. Darwin's theory stressed that all species, including man, evolve through natural selection, the fittest specimens surviving according to their ability to adapt to their environment. Those adaptive features are passed on to their offspring, leading eventually to the progressive development of higher biological species (such as *Homo sapiens*) from lower, simpler ones. The analogy between evolution and civilization in the classic liberal sense, as a continuous process of improvement, was marked and obvious.[6] But there was also another, darker aspect to Darwin's theories that modern critics sometimes overlook, but that his contemporaries immediately grasped. Evolution meant that the natural history of species, including human beings, was no longer fixed and immutable. The study of evolution could trace not only the *rise* of species over time but, like that of ancient empires and civilizations, their decline and fall. A species might, at some point in its history, find itself losing ground to one better adapted to the current environment, or external circumstances could suddenly and drastically change, rendering its original adaptive features obsolete.

Proof of this came with the growing study of dinosaur fossils, as well as the discovery of the remains of Neanderthal man in 1856. Both were evidently powerful creatures, in their own ways the lords of creation, yet both had become extinct.* In fact, the modern fascination with dinosaurs starts with the Darwinians. The dinosaurs became a cautionary tale for modern society, the zoologists' equivalent of the fall of the Roman Empire, in which "immoderate greatness" leads to decline and extinction. Thomas Huxley, Darwin's disciple, conducted pioneering research into dinosaur fossils that led him to conclude: "It is an error to imagine that evolution signifies a constant tendency to increased perfection. . . . Retrogressive is as practicable as progressive metamorphosis."[7]

---

* The first remains of Neanderthal were discovered in the Neander Valley near Düsseldorf in Germany, only three years before the publication of *Origin of the Species*. In 1841 Sir Richard Owen gave the name "dinosaur" to the giant lizards whose bones had been discovered across Europe and North America since the 1770s.

The mechanism behind this "metamorphosis," was, of course, natural selection, the relentless struggle of individuals for survival. In the process they created a species adapted to its environment. Natural selection could, of course, be viewed as a process that inevitably improved a species.* This was the optimistic view of natural selection usually associated with Social Darwinism, according to which, in the words of the nineteenth-century biologist W.R. Greg, "the best specimens of the [human] race . . . continue the species and propagate an ever-improving and perfecting type of humanity."[8]

But in Darwinian evolution the environment itself does not directly improve the race or the species' adaptability.† Instead, everything depends on the innate characteristics of the individuals themselves, who, if they survive, pass those traits on to their offspring. On the other hand, the environment can do serious damage, by interfering with the normal competition for resources or desirable mates or by otherwise preventing the best specimens from coming to the fore. This was particularly true of society's man-made environment, which brought new artificial elements to the evolutionary equation. In his later *Descent of Man* (1871), Darwin himself voiced doubts about whether the growth of civilization might actually serve to undermine natural selection.[9]

At the same time, heredity was not fixed. It, too, was constantly evolving. Even before Gregor Mendel, every student of genetics knew that reproduction was a complex process of *similarity*, by which white swans produce white swans, but also of *diversity*, by which white swans from time to time produce black swans. For the Darwinian, the interplay of diversity and similarity was overshadowed by one undoubted fact: all human beings, regardless of their race or cultural status, were descended

---

* Darwin himself wrote, "Thus, from the war of nature, from famine and death, the most exalted object which we are capable of conceiving, namely the production of the higher animals, directly follows."

† Before Darwin, theories of evolution were influenced by the theory of the eighteenth-century biologist Lamarck that animals could pass on acquired characteristics through heredity. Lamarck's favorite example was the giraffe, which by stretching its neck to reach for food acquired a longer neck and passed this trait on to its offspring. Darwin himself was not immune to the Lamarckian view of evolution, nor was the French degeneration theorist B.A. Morel. However, the net effect of Darwin's theories, combined with the genetic research of German zoologist August Weismann, was the final defeat of Lamarckianism as a serious theory (although it would resurface in the twentieth century in the theories of the notorious Soviet geneticist Profim Lysenko).

from apes. This opened up the possibility that physical and mental traits that had allowed man to adapt to a savage environment, whether in the remote past (of the Neanderthal hunter) or in the present (of the Watusi warrior), could inadvertently be passed on to his modern civilized descendants. The Darwinian zoologist Henry Maudsley explained this with the chilling observation that there is "truly a brute brain within the man's," making it possible to "trace savagery in civilization, as we can trace animalism in savagery."[10]

Nineteenth-century biologists called this brutish survival "atavism," after the Latin word *atavus*, or remote ancestor. Atavism taught that every organism had certain "lost" characteristics that were ready to reappear under certain conditions and would then be passed on to offspring. Atavistic theory had existed before Darwin, but his theory of evolution only seemed to confirm it, as did Mendelian genetics later on. Atavism would be the foundation stone of degeneration theory.

Atavism did not just present the terrifying image of the healthy middle-class family suddenly producing a brutish throwback, as in the traditional myth of the changeling (Heathcliffe in *Wuthering Heights* and *Rosemary's Baby* are both modern variants on that theme). Most theorists agreed that atavism of this sort was an exceedingly rare event: one of Lombroso's contemporaries, the Italian anthropologist Morselli, calculated its chances as no more than one in eight million.[11] But what if specific conditions brought these lost characteristics to the surface all at once for the *entire species*, which then haplessly passed them on to their offspring? The process of heredity might suddenly and inexplicably work *against* the best interests of the species. Natural selection would then become a trap, with the worst indiscriminately breeding more of the worst in an atavistic meltdown of the human race, approaching Houston Chamberlain's *Völkerchaos*.

In fact, Gobineau's racial pessimism played no part in degeneration theory—or at least not at first. But Darwinism and degeneration did finish off any lingering notion that civilization could serve as a refining and improving process for the species. In the end, the formal institutions of civilized life play no significant role in shaping man's fate; instead fate is determined by hidden biological processes. As Lombroso put it, "We are governed by silent laws which never cease to operate and which rule so-

ciety with more authority than the laws inscribed in our statute books."
Western man was faced with the possibility that under his sunny, civilized surface lay an explosive mixture of barbarism and cruelty. A powerful image came to haunt the liberal imagination: that inside every man
lay a sleeping beast that might, if conditions went awry, suddenly spring
out of its lair into the light of day.

## LOMBROSO AND THE LOMBROSIAN REVOLUTION

Cesare Lombroso claimed that this savage throwback was in fact the
modern criminal. Following his postmortem on Villela, his research
rapidly expanded to include hundreds of prisoners, convicted criminals
(including women), and Italian army recruits. He used all the techniques and instruments that were the latest rage in anthropology and
racial theory. The craniometer and calipers to measure the width of the
skull and to calculate the all-important cranial index, the aesthetome-
ter and algometer to test tactile sensitivity, as well as the dynamometer,
campimeter, and a host of other scientific-sounding devices (including
a forerunner of the polygraph) all became standard equipment in
Lombrosian-style criminology.[12] Lombroso combined his anatomical
studies with an almost magical faith in quantitative data. By counting
the number of appearances of a certain characteristic, he and his disciples assumed, the scientist will discover something significant about *why*
it appears. This quantitative barrage became the most impressive part of
Lombroso's theories, and to superficial observers the most convincing.
He recited numerical data, displayed complicated charts and graphs,
and endlessly created new indices and computational formulae. Lombrosian criminology reflected the new fascination with numbers of "social science" during the latter part of the nineteenth century, which
would also surface in economics, in sociology (in Emile Durkheim's statistical study of 1897, *Suicide*), and then in eugenics and "race science."

Lombroso's underlying assumption was the same as that of racial anthropologists: physical characteristics such as the length and shape of
the skull and facial features were clues to cultural or psychological difference. Like other scientists of his era, Lombroso assumed that whites
were superior to nonwhites by heredity. However, he used a step-by-step

evolutionary model borrowed from Darwin (although Darwin was not his only source) to explain racial difference, instead of a diffusionist or Gobinian one. Lombroso considered Africans to be the original humans, but then the species followed an inevitable upward development, from black and brown through yellow to white. Racial developments paralleled the course of civilization from primitive to modern.

White Europeans were the evolutionary apex of the human species and the embodiment of man's intellectual and moral gifts. "Only we white people have reached the ultimate symmetry of bodily form," Lombroso wrote in *The White Man and the Colored Man* (1871), echoing Gustav Klemm almost three decades earlier. "Only we have [bestowed] the human right to life, respect for old age, women, and the weak."[13] Those civilized attainments were under attack, however, from biological reversion. From time to time within the general population, atavistic individuals appeared whose savage and irrational behavior set them apart from the standard evolutionary norm. Their deviance from that norm made them criminals in civilized society, whereas in savage society they would have attracted little or no notice.*

For Lombroso, criminality in modern civilization was an anachronism, a survival of behavior from a more primitive age. The criminal exhibited specific pathological symptoms that Lombroso and later degenerationists termed "antisocial" behavior, because it undermined the structure and needs of modern civilized society. The born criminal was as remote from evolved modern man as a Borneo headhunter: both were throwbacks to an earlier stage of human evolution. Lombroso could say of his subject, "He was born a criminal because he was born a savage" and mean it literally.[14]

How can we distinguish these savages in our midst? Lombroso pointed to certain physical signs or "stigmata" that revealed to the trained observer the atavism of the born criminal, the "morally insane." These included a low, sloping forehead; hard, shifty eyes; large, handle-shaped ears; a flattened or upturned nose and a forward projection of the jaw ("as in Negroes and animals"); large middle incisors; prehensile

---

* One of Lombroso's more controversial claims was that "crime, with the savage, is not an exception, but the general rule." See the response from Emile Durkheim in *The Division of Labor in Society*, pp. 164–65.

toes and feet and long simian arms; and a scanty beard and baldness.*
The born criminal, like the savage, also displayed an insensitivity to pain
(Lombroso liked to tell the story of African tribesmen who, confronted
with shoes for the first time, casually cut off their toes to make them fit)
and a tendency to vindictiveness, idleness, and treachery. The criminal
maintained a cynical attitude toward life and had a generally low intelligence. Lombroso even listed specific physical characteristics that were
linked to specific crimes: thieves generally had twisted or flattened "Negroid" noses, for example, while those of murderers were straight and
aquiline, "like the beak of a bird of prey." Murderers and rapists tended
to have bushy eyebrows, while small eyes, a large nose, and a "singular,
stereotyped expression of amiability" denoted the forger and counterfeiter. Lombroso even claimed that by looking at an Italian army draftee
he could predict whether he would end up in the stockade.[15]

If it is hard to take Lombroso's ideas seriously as science, it is worth
remembering that neither did many of his contemporaries.[16] Yet when
his *Criminal Man* first appeared in 1876, Lombroso found a receptive
audience in progressive intellectual and political circles both inside and
outside Italy. His theories contrasted the criminal degenerate with an
idealized "normal" European male, the proud product of liberal progress. All around these normal types, whom Lombroso identified as "our
fellow countrymen," were people who still bore the marks of a backward
and brutal past. Having lived and worked in impoverished southern
Italy, Lombroso was acutely aware of the gulf that still separated his
country's rural peasant from the typical Turin businessman or Milanese
lawyer of the industrialized North. Some of his contemporaries even
classified the typical Sicilian or Neapolitan slum dweller as the racial
equivalent of the African Negro.[17]

Lombroso and his peers did not think that the distinction they made
between deviant and normal was invidious or arbitrary. To their minds,
it arose from the forces of historical development. Modern civilized man
stood at the point of intersection between two inexorable evolutionary
processes: his biological ascent from the apes, and his progress as a social being from barbarism to civility. The great nineteenth-century de-

---

* All of these would become part of the stock description of criminals in a new genre of late-
nineteenth-century literature, the detective story.

bate about nature versus nurture lay at the heart of degeneration theory, but no one seriously claimed that the influence of one excluded the other. Anthropologists and biologists were too aware of the importance of history, and of man as the product of history through evolution, to insist on a single simple answer.

As a strong positivist and believer in progress, Lombroso saw the intersection between man and his modern environment as essentially benign. His theory of an inborn criminal tendency did not exclude the influence of the man-made environment. Lombroso discussed how broken families, as well as illegitimacy and even poverty, could foster crime, although he argued that the importance of poverty was "exaggerated." He was particularly concerned about alcoholism as a trigger for atavism and criminality.* However, he insisted that better results could be obtained by concentrating on the nature rather than the nurture side of the equation.

Degeneration was something fixed and limited in scope, Lombroso argued, and like crime itself it would eventually disappear under modern scientific methods. The true born criminal, the avatistic, "morally insane" individual, only constituted one-third of the entire criminal population. The rest were "criminaloids," people who are not physically distinct from the normal population but in whom a variety of environmental factors could trigger an atavistic response. In Lombroso's view, there was nothing to be done about the true born criminal, except capital punishment:

> The fact that there exist such beings as born criminals, organically fitted for evil, atavistic reproductions not simply of savage men but even of the fiercest animals . . . steels us against all pity. . . . We feel justified in their extermination.[19]

In the case of the habitual occasional criminal, however, there was an opportunity for a more humane scientific response. Lombroso's penal reform movement of the 1880s and 1890s called for nonimprisonment for minor offenses or crimes of passion, a probation and penal system that stressed rehabilitative work and treatment rather than punish-

---

* Lombroso solemnly cited a German study purporting to show that even bees, those most innately social of all creatures, can become dishonest when their honey is mixed with brandy.[18]

ment, special regard for female criminals (the subject of a separate work of 1898, *The Female Offender*), a separate juvenile justice system, and even court-appointed legal aid for poor offenders—all the goals, in fact, of progressive penal reform over the next hundred years.

Lombroso's theories became an obsession among progressive-minded politicians and intellectuals in Italy, England, and particularly the United States.[20] He inspired a fascination with the link between heredity and criminal behavior that would consume social scientists for at least a half-century.* Under the Lombrosian umbrella, the range of hereditable antisocial or atavistic behavior rapidly expanded to include impotence, masturbation, homosexuality, and even nervous disorders (or neurasthenia) and hysteria. However, according to the Lombrosian approach, all these forms of social deviance were diseases, like epilepsy. The criminal or social deviant required treatment, not punishment. The impulse to *punish* the offender for his actions was itself a primitive instinct, Lombroso argued, which had no place in an enlightened civilized community. Lombroso died in 1909 and did not live to see his ideas incorporated directly into legal practice. But his assistant Enrico Ferri would play a major role in reshaping the legal code of Italy—under Benito Mussolini. The 1930 Fascist legal code, with its Lombrosian stress on the "treatment" and rehabilitation of offenders, was among the most admired and progressive of all of Mussolini's reforms.[21] In the final analysis, the criminal's or the pervert's behavior was not his fault. As one of Lombroso's followers revealingly argued in 1884, thanks to the new criminal anthropology, "moral responsibility [is] disappearing . . . from penal science."[22] Instead, a heavy dose of determinism took its place, along with a new therapeutic approach to social ills that spilled over into other spheres of modern life.

## DEGENERATION AND INDUSTRIAL SOCIETY

At first, the Lombrosian vocabulary of evolutionary degenerationism was applied only to the criminal underworld; inevitably, anthropolo-

---

* For example, the dismal history of the notorious "degenerate" Jukes family of upstate New York was summarized succinctly in later editions of *Criminal Man:* "Ancestor Max Jukes: 77 criminals, 142 vagabonds, 120 prostitutes; 18 keepers of houses of ill-fame; 91 illegitimates; 141 idiots or afflicted with impotency or syphilis; 46 sterile females."

gists, criminologists, and sociologists began to use it to describe other classes and groups. By the end of the century, some would find Lombroso's atavistic and antisocial degenerate not just in the deviant and criminal but in modern man himself.

These early "social scientists" all assumed that biological heredity and social development acted upon each other in a predictable way. If man lived at a primitive stage of development, like the African Hottentots or the Indians of Tierra del Fuego,* then he was a savage, regardless of whether he was a strong or weak biological specimen. If he lived in an advanced and civilized society and was of healthy stock, then he became "normal" (a term originally coined by the English radical progressive thinker Jeremy Bentham). If, on the other hand, he lived in an advanced society and brought with him a morbid or "retrogressive" biological inheritance, then he would become a degenerate or throwback—and pass that same affliction on to his offspring with ever greater frequency. This last point, at least, was the conclusion of the founder of the so-called French school of degeneration theory, Benedict Morel. Morel and his followers did not see the intersection between man and his modern environment in the benign light that Lombroso did. They saw it as potentially dangerous, producing problems that could threaten civilized life itself.

Lombroso himself had used Morel's studies of cretinism (mental retardation) from the 1850s in developing his own theories. Morel, however, gave the theory of hereditary reversion a much darker cast.† For Morel, degeneracy was not isolated or fixed in certain families, as it was for Lombroso; instead, it was part of a larger process, a rising stain of morbidity on the face of modern industrial society. Morel and his followers argued that environmental factors could be even more important than heredity in triggering the process of degeneration, which was most apparent among the lower classes. Workers, the poor, the unem-

---

* The southern tip of South America, a favorite place for early comparative anthropologists to observe "savage man" in his natural environment.

† In many respects, his views resemble those of Arthur de Gobineau, whose *Essay on the Inequality of Races* appeared just a year before Morel's *Treatise on Degeneration*. Both men were also well-read in German, which put them in touch with German racial theorists such as Blumenbach and Carus; both were deeply affected and appalled by 1848, and both held an outlook on the world that can be described as Ultra-Catholic antimodernism.

ployed—what Marx called the proletariat and French liberals referred to as "the dangerous classes"—these were the carriers of the stigmata of progress. They were "the invalids of civilization" who now threatened to engulf society with their growing numbers.[23]

The Franco-Prussian War of 1870–1871, which brought France sudden and complete defeat at the hands of the Germans, civil war, and the destruction of Paris by the radical working-class revolutionaries of the Commune shocked and terrified France's intellectual elite. French critics described the events in the same apocalyptic terms that Gobineau's generation had used to describe 1848.* However, they turned to the language of science, rather than to vitalist power and racial myth, to explain what had happened. Fear of *la France dégénerée* (the title of an anonymous pamphlet from 1872) permeated debates on every aspect of social policy, including alcoholism, illegitimacy, crime, and low birth rates, as well as political corruption. The result was an orgy of national self-examination and reproach, in which both Morel and Lombroso were applied indiscriminately to explain why France was supposedly on the brink of moral and cultural collapse.[24]

The historian Hippolyte Taine, for example, was a great admirer of Lombroso. His massive study, *The Origins of Contemporary France*, which he began in 1873 and completed in 1894, argued that the entire nineteenth century, from the Revolution to the Commune, revealed the forces of physiological degeneracy undermining France's cultural and political health. Taine claimed that destructive "germs" (the nineteenth-century term for genes) had entered the French bloodstream through the revolutionary crowds of 1789, "causing fever, delirium, and revolutionary convulsions." As a result France had found itself in a chronic state of political instability and social crisis ever since.[25]

In *Degeneracy and Criminality* (1888) Charles Féré insisted in Morellian fashion that environmental factors explained the rise of social deviancy. Modern urban life, with its unhealthy conditions, hectic pace, and complex demands, overstimulated the nerves of the weak-minded and the lower classes, leaving them exhausted and prone to commit ir-

---

* "What barbarism! What a disaster!" wrote that former enemy of the bourgeois status quo, Gustav Flaubert, to a friend during the Commune. "I was hardly a progressive . . . but I had my illusions! And I did not believe that I would live to see the end of the world. But this is it."

rational acts, including crime. Féré concluded that industrial society was creating a garbage heap of "pathological capital," just as a working coal mine accumulates slag. "The impotent, the mad, criminals or decadents of every form, must be considered as the waste-matter of adaptation, the invalids of civilization" who had to be somehow controlled or cleansed away before they overwhelmed their productive hosts.[26]

Taine and Féré were both political conservatives. At the other end of the political spectrum, the radical Emile Zola conceived of his twenty-volume series of novels on the Rougon-Macquart family as an actual experiment in the study of degeneration and of the interaction between heredity and environment. Through his fictional family, Zola showed how Lombroso's degenerative stigmata could be traced through successive generations, culminating in the political and social "debacle" of 1870–1871, the title of the last novel in the series. In Zola's view, the "barbarism" of the French peasantry and industrial working class was more than matched by the rapacious "cannibalism" of their capitalist bourgeois oppressors and by the physiological decline and loss of nerve of France's ruling class. For Zola, degeneration was a collective catastrophe, trapping all of society in its death embrace. In 1870 decadent France had found itself led by a clinical degenerate, Napoleon III, whom Zola described in *The Debacle* as "a wraith with a cadaverous face, lacklustre eyes, drawn features, and colorless mustache." The emperor presided over a defeat that was as much medical-physiological as military-strategic: "What a breakdown of this sick man's whole being, this sentimental dreamer, silent while dully awaiting his doom!"[27]

Similar images of degeneration and atavism across the Channel in England, permeated two new literary genres, the detective novel and the horror story. Robert Louis Stevenson's *Dr. Jekyll and Mr. Hyde* (1886) vividly presents the evolutionary duality of modern man, with the civilized and socially useful self (Doctor Jekyll) suddenly confronted by his atavistic self, Mr. Hyde. Hyde's Lombrosian-style simian features, hairy hands, and barbaric appetites mark him as a figure of horror ("God bless me," one character remarks, "the man hardly seems human! Something troglodytic, shall we say?"). Jekyll himself realizes that it is the "curse of mankind" that "in the agonized womb of consciousness, these polar twins should be continuously struggling." Civilization, Stevenson is forced to conclude, rests on repression of the animal within—"My devil had long been caged," Jekyll says, "he came out roaring"—a conclusion similar to the one that Sigmund Freud would reach a few years later.

Sherlock Holmes was also well-acquainted with Lombroso. Like his creator Arthur Conan Doyle, Holmes is trained in medical pathology, in which the search for telltale physical signs of disease closely parallel Lombroso's search for evidence of criminality. The same search for stigmata or visible clues, lies at the core of Holmes's technique as a detective. The detective story also presents us with a Jekyll-and-Hyde duality in its basic plot: the transformation of "normal" circumstances (such as Wilkie Collins's and Agatha Christie's English country house or Conan Doyle's London) by a sudden pathological outbreak in the form of a murderer (or of a monster in the classic horror story).

"The Case of the Creeping Man" moves Holmes to note the darker implications of man's evolutionary nature. When a scientist attempts to ward off old age by injecting himself with monkey glands, he transforms himself instead into a hideous apelike throwback. Holmes, surveying the ghastly scene, remarks: "The highest type of man may revert to the animal if he leaves the straight road of destiny." But the power of modern science to alter that destiny, by preventing "natural" death or extending "unnatural" life, leads to this sober speculation:

> There is a danger there—a very real danger to humanity. Consider, Watson, that the material, the sensual, the worldly would all prolong their worthless lives. . . . It would be the survival of the least fit. What sort of cesspool may not our poor world become?

The Jekyll-and-Hyde transformation of civilized man into beast appears most dramatically, however, in the *fin de siècle* images of the wolfman and the vampire. Bram Stoker wrote *Dracula* in 1897, shortly after Max Nordau's *Degeneration* had popularized Lombroso's theory of degeneracy before a wide audience. Count Dracula is the last of a long aristocratic line; he could in fact be Gobineau's alter ego, except that his lineage is stamped with the mark not of the heroic but of the degenerate. Stoker gives us a close description of the count's "very marked physiognomy," which carefully follows Lombroso's textbook descriptions of the regressive type, noting as it does Dracula's high-domed forehead, his "peculiar arched nostrils" and pointed ears, and eyebrows that almost meet at the bridge of the nose. Dracula's prominent canine teeth also serve as a stigma in the Lombrosian sense, marking his primeval origins and his cannibal-like appetite for blood.[28]

Dracula is not possessed by any demonic or supernatural force, as he would have been in an earlier Romantic Gothic story. Like Lombroso's thief and counterfeiter, he is the deviant product of amoral nature. "The Count is a criminal and of criminal type," one character even says. "Nordau and Lombroso would so classify him."[29] He is also a parasite, like Charles Féré's "invalids of civilization," attached to the productive host of middle-class society. Doctor Van Helsing, Dracula's enemy and normal countertype, points out that vampires appeared in all the ancient great civilizations, from Greece and Rome to China. Dracula poses, however, a particular danger in what Van Helsing calls "our scientific, skeptical, matter-of-fact nineteenth century," because he has left his remote hideout in rural Transylvania for London, the great, teeming industrial city. There, he can spread his parasitic disease throughout the urban population, draining it of its vitality and creating a kingdom of the Undead at the very heart of modern society.

The human characters in *Dracula* find themselves engaged in a war for civilization, in which they are forced to turn to extreme and brutal methods. It is a war that they both win and lose: before killing Dracula, they lose the book's heroine, Lucy Westenra (her name can be read as "light of the West"), to the count's monstrous powers. She is permanently transformed from a model of normal and civilized womanhood into a ravenous beast. The shocking appearance of Lucy as vampire, her lips dripping blood, her "sweetness turned to adamantine, heartless cruelty, her purity to voluptuous wantonness," becomes Stoker's parable of how the process of degeneration destroys the supposedly safe and secure bowers of civilized life.[30]

The fear of degeneration changed popular perceptions of great industrial cities such as London and Paris, which no longer seemed a productive matrix of social mobility and opportunity. Instead, they became dangerous places, a lair of criminals, paupers, and debased humanity, a world of Draculas and Jack the Rippers. Civilized and "polite" urban life found itself restricted to only a few outposts, such as London's Mayfair and the West End, where wealth and exclusiveness could still hold back the floodtide of degeneration.[31] An 1880 issue of *The Lancet*, England's premier medical journal, noted: "He who would find the centres of decay in a nation, still on the whole robust and active, must seek them at the points of social tension. The proofs of pressure, starvation, and atrophy, of vice and brutal reversion, and of their results are all to be found there."[32] The self-image of the nineteenth century began to undergo a radical change, and that "feeling of dread" that Gobineau had evoked in the face of history now gripped the middle class itself.

## DEGENERATION AND CULTURE: FROM MAX NORDAU TO EMILE DURKHEIM

By 1890 degeneracy was no longer being treated as an anomaly. Thinkers were concluding that it was an inevitable part of modern life, just as Charles Féré's underclass was the natural product of industrial civilization. Its challenges took a variety of new and startling forms. In 1892 the Hungarian doctor and journalist Max Nordau published his *Entartung* (Degeneration), which he dedicated to Cesare Lombroso. Despite its size (almost six hundred pages), the book became an international bestseller and soon appeared in a dozen languages. Nordau had expanded the Lombrosian analysis to show that "degenerates are not always criminals, prostitutes . . . lunatics; they are often authors and artists." Charles Baudelaire and the French "decadent" poets, Oscar Wilde (Bram Stoker's original model for Count Dracula), Manet and the Impressionists, Henrik Ibsen, Leo Tolstoy, Emile Zola, as well as Wagner and Friedrich Nietzsche—all the leading lights of *fin de siècle* culture, in fact—came under Doctor Nordau's critical microscope. He concluded that they were all victims of diseased "subjective states of mind." The modern degenerate artist, like his criminal counterpart, lacks a moral sense: "For them there exists no law, no decency, no modesty." Emotionalism and hysteria, as well as that old disease of Romanticism, *ennui*, pervade their works and outlook, Nordau proclaimed, because of their enfeebled nervous state. "The degenerate and insane," he wrote, "are the predestined disciples of Schopenhauer."[33]

Echoing Tocqueville forty years earlier, Nordau wrote that "pessimism is the keynote of the age."[34] He sensed a deep resentment on the part of men like Gobineau and Nietzsche at the changes that the nineteenth century had brought. Like the conservative Catholic anti-Semites of Nordau's own Austria-Hungary (Nordau was Jewish), these intellectuals sneered at the century's achievements in scientific knowledge, economic growth, and popular democracy. But Nordau launched his counterattack from his medical laboratory, claiming that pessimism was the result of a larger physiological corruption infecting modern society. Europe's artistic and intellectual elite were forced by evolution to produce "degenerate art," a term that Nordau would, unhappily, make famous. He even claimed that the Impressionist painters like Monet and Seurat painted with vivid purples and blues as a result of a nervous disease called nystagmus, or "trembling of the eyeball," which blurred and distorted their vision.[35]

Nordau was forced to conclude that the only hope for European civilization lay with its working people. Europe's aristocracy and wealthy classes were virtually beyond hope since "degenerates are found principally among the upper classes."[36] Instead, farmers, laborers, and *petit bourgeois* householders, men who worked with their muscles and women who stayed home to raise their children, would preserve the vitality of the species, as well as a sense of traditional morality. His ultimate conclusion (a strange one for a professed admirer of modern industrial society), was that Europe's affluence had ruined vitality and self-confidence, leaving a trail of nervous wrecks and moral degenerates. On the other hand, the active life and physical labor would lead to a "civilization of truth, love of one's neighbor, and cheerfulness."[37]

Nordau's praise of physical exertion became part of a widespread campaign in the later nineteenth century for exercise and physical fitness. Strenuous outdoor exercise, doctors, teachers, philanthropists, and even politicians decided, could counteract the dangerous forces of degeneration. Its physical benefits would boost moral well-being, in addition to reviving the racial stock. The result was a rage for sports and fitness. Athletic clubs sprang up all across Germany, while the German Youth Movement became identified with hiking and backpacking in the woods and mountains. The craze for bicycles and bicycle racing in France (which lives on today in the Tour de France), for rugby and football in England, and for national parks and baseball in America were all part of the same desire to create a society of healthy men and women who, in Nordau's words, "rise early and are not weary before sunset, with clear heads and hard muscles."[38] Nordau himself helped found the

*Journal of Jewish Gymnastics* and stressed the importance of creating a culture of "muscular Judaism" to counter charges that the Jews were a race of physical degenerates.[39]

Nordau's theories gave a new twist to the question of how man's biological evolution and society's historical evolution intersected. A fourth and disturbing possibility now presented itself: even healthy human specimens living in advanced civilized society would, *unless corrective steps were taken*, degenerate into a lesser physical and moral type. Nordau, like Lombroso, remained optimistic about the future, but the grounds for optimism were steadily shrinking. Degeneration theory forced many to conclude that modern industrial society was moving toward a level of "progress" with which the human species could no longer keep up. A series of thinkers stepped forward in the 1890s to suggest that modern civilization was in the grip of hidden forces that the normal social and political order could no longer control. Lombroso's claim that "we are governed by silent laws which ... rule society with more authority than the laws inscribed on our statute books" would gain a new significance in the work of Gustav Le Bon, Emile Durkheim, and Max Weber.

Gustav Le Bon published *The Crowd* in 1895. It proved immensely influential. Le Bon was a leading doctor and admirer of the French medical expert on degeneration, Jean Martin Charcot, who was also Sigmund Freud's mentor. Le Bon had done some early physiological research on skull and brain size, and "established" that, in modern society, men's brains tend to grow larger—a sign of increasing intellectual capacity—while those of women shrink.[40] He then set down his callipers and craniometer and turned his attention to collective behavior in industrial society, particularly that of crowds.

Le Bon claimed that when individuals assemble in the street or at a political meeting, they spark in each other a mass reversion to a primitive state: "By the mere fact that he forms part of an organized crowd," Le Bon wrote, "a man descends several rungs in the ladder of civilization." By himself, "he may be a cultivated individual; in a crowd, he is a barbarian"—and becomes capable of the sort of irrational and brutal actions that characterize a street riot or lynch mob. "He possesses the spontaneity, the violence, the ferocity," but also the "enthusiasm and heroism of primitive beings."[41] Since modern urban life and democratic politics create a wealth of opportunities for this kind of mass reversionary behavior (what another theorist, William Trotter, would call "the herd instinct"), enormous dangers loomed ahead for European industrial society. As Le Bon explained, echoing Jacob Burckhardt, "the advent of power of the masses marks one of the last stages of Western civilization . . . Its civilization is now without stability. The populace is sovereign, and the tide of barbarism mounts."[42] Therefore, the "true" character of mass democracy required a new approach to politics. Traditional parliamentary or legal institutions can no longer control the masses, Le Bon warned. What the crowd looks for, in its atavistic way, is instead a leader, a single powerful figure who can direct its irrational energies to constructive ends.*

The crowd's natural leader, Le Bon concluded, radiated the same personal power that distinguished the chieftain or witch doctor of a primitive tribe from his inferiors. Le Bon termed it "prestige," while Max Weber would call it "charisma." Weber never expressed a great interest in degeneration theory, and his ideas took form in a very different context from the debates of the 1870s and '80s between Italian criminologists and French medical professionals. However, his theory of charisma and his famous contrast between charisma's primitive creative force and institutions based on rational (and debilitating) routine had an enormous affinity with degeneration thinking. For Max Weber, rationalized routine defined modern civilization. For the individual, however, it could become an "iron cage," as limiting as any primitive society.[43]

Emile Durkheim, on the other hand, was deeply interested in the main features of degeneration theory and the effects of what he called "hypercivilization" on modern man. His great fear was that modern civilization would destroy its own human materials by disrupting the basic equilibrium of "vital forces" that keep the social organism alive. If the social organism is strong, Durkheim argued, "individuals have more vigor, more force of resistance" to the traumas of social change. If the social whole loses its balance, then individuals feel the effects in their own mental and physical health. In short, people become sick because their

---

* Not surprisingly, two close readers of *The Crowd* would be Adolf Hitler and Benito Mussolini.

society is ailing. "Organic causes are often social causes transformed and fixed in the organism," he claimed, producing unhealthy trends across society such as a declining birth rate and a rising rate of suicide.[44]

Durkheim's landmark work, *Suicide* (1897), sprang directly out of the matrix of degeneration theory. Like Lombroso, Durkheim did not see the pathological and the normal as mutually exclusive opposites. Suicide, like crime, stood at the extreme end of a sliding scale of responses to modern industrial society. First comes neurasthenia ("The individual can maintain himself in a society only by possessing an equal mental and moral constitution. This the neurasthenic lacks."), then depression, and finally *anomie*, the sense of alienation and despair leading to suicide, which, Durkheim suggests, is "the ransom-money of civilization."

> The hypercivilization which breeds the anomic tendency and the egoistic tendency also refines nervous systems, making them excessively delicate; through this very fact they are less capable of firm attachment to a definite object, more impatient of any discipline, more accessible both to violent irritation and to exaggerated depression.[45]

For Durkheim, civilization in the classic sense—of economic progress, scientific and technological knowledge, and progress in the arts—is devoid of moral content. The old Enlightenment categories, the rise of politeness and sociability and the refinement of manners, are thrown out. Commercial and industrial society is structured to supply man's physical and material needs, but "far from serving moral progress, it is in the great industrial centers that crimes and suicides are most numerous." Work and the division of labor impose a harsh discipline and a uniformity on people's lives that are unknown in more primitive communities. Material progress propels them along with little choice: "They move because they must move."[46]

For Durkheim, the solution to the debilitating effects of industrial society lay not in the individual but in the group. While modern society has destroyed or spoiled the old bases of moral action—moral strictures, self-restraint, religion—a new one in the form of group solidarity has taken its place. The bourgeois family, the corporation, the trade union, the state—these form an ascending order of social organisms created by modern society, in which individuals can discover an organic connection to others and gratify their needs as sociable beings, rather than feeling alone and abandoned.

Words like unity, solidarity, and community came to symbolize the hopes of figures like Durkheim, Nordau, Weber, and Lombroso. They and many others believed that these collective social virtues could make whole what modern industrial society was supposedly destroying: man himself. Lombroso passionately argued that true national unity would stamp out economic disparities, as well as degeneration and criminality, across Italy. Nordau believed that man's true moral progress was his ever-expanding sense of group solidarity; ultimately all of humanity would form "a collective organism of which you form one cell. . . . Its vital energies produce you and maintain you until you die, its elevation carries you upward with it."[47] Durkheim, however, pointed out that the sense of unity that modern society needs will not spring up spontaneously. The state must provide the unifying function for the entire social organism, which the division of labor tends to fragment and break apart. Quoting Auguste Comte, Durkheim concluded that government alone enjoys the capacity for "fittingly intervening in the habitual accomplishment of all the diverse functions of social economy, so as to recall to them unceasingly the feeling of unity and the sentiment of common solidarity."[48]

The fear of degeneration had now altered the horizons of nineteenth-century liberalism. Progress in the classic sense of civilized man's economic and scientific advance no longer seemed enough to provide for a safe, stable society. By 1880 classical liberalism was, as many commentators noted at the time, in crisis, its old individualistic tenets having fallen out of fashion across Western Europe. Instead, a series of new movements arose to try to save liberal society, borrowing elements from both socialist and conservative political creeds. These included the so-called New Liberalism of late Victorian England, the "armchair socialists" in Wilhelmine Germany, and the Progressive movement in the United States.[49]

A key factor in this "postliberal persuasion" was precisely the fear of degeneration. The assumption that modern civilization is psychologically debilitating became a standard axiom of the social sciences and social psychology, as did the claim that underneath modernity's self-generating decline lurked the primitive and backward part of the human soul. "We see by what a very thin and precarious partition," opined *Blackwood's Magazine* in 1892, "are we divided from the elements of violence which underlie all civilized societies."[50] Modern liberal civilization seemed to be dooming itself to extinction. Although *fin de siècle* liberals may have continued to resist "vulgar" Gobinian racial theories or Nietzschean nihilism, they were becoming convinced that the only way to avert a crisis was by turning to solutions that would supplement, if not actually replace, laissez-faire liberalism.

EUGENICS AND THE STATE

One of those solutions would be eugenics. Postliberal sociologists, economists, and philosophers like Durkheim in France, Gustav von Schmoller in Germany, and Thomas Hill Green in England reexamined that fateful intersection of modern society and modern man from the social development side of the equation. They and their peers tried to show how altering man's *social conditions* could produce a fundamental change in all of society's members and in effect save civilization from itself. Eugenics examined the problem from the other side, investigating how man's *biological potential* might be altered so that he could live and prosper in modern society.

Eugenics owes much of its notoriety to its association with Nazism. Thanks to Hitler's Final Solution, the term "racial hygiene" today has a chilling sound. But the eugenics movement began benignly enough, as a humane and progressive corrective to what was believed to be the physiological deterioration threatening Europe and America. It was part of an effort to construct what progressive-minded liberals in the 1860s called a "social economy," a harmonious society that would overcome the inequalities arising from modern industrial capitalism. The entire social reform movement in Europe and the United States, from public hygiene and slum clearance to temperance and women's emancipation, was always closely associated with eugenics and rested on the same postliberal assumptions.[51]

The birthplace of the eugenics movement was Darwin's England, in Darwin's own family. His cousin Francis Galton coined the term in 1883 to refer to a science of breeding the "well-born." Galton always insisted that eugenics was merely the practical side of theoretical Darwinism. Along with other Darwinians such as Thomas Huxley, Galton worried about the "retrogressive" dark side of the evolutionary process, but his concerns were more specific and socially grounded. Galton was concerned that the intellectual talents and abilities that made for civilization's progress were very unevenly distributed in modern society and were under direct threat as a growing population overwhelmed England's cities. The rise of "mass man," which Burckhardt saw as the triumph of cultural mediocrity, seemed to Galton to guarantee a biological mediocrity as well.

To represent the distribution of intelligence in the general population, Galton produced a chart using a large bell-shaped curve; hereditary genius, like hereditary idiocy, was found only at the very extreme end of the curve. Only one person in four thousand had the talents necessary for the advance of civilization, he concluded. The vast majority showed a mediocre intelligence at best. If the members of that most-talented group (which included judges, statesmen and prime ministers, clergy, military officers, scientists, university scholars, writers, musicians, and, interestingly, professional wrestlers and championship rowers) failed to reproduce themselves in sufficient numbers, the result would be social catastrophe.[52]

This imminent talent gap was linked to Galton's fears of the disruptive effects of modern society. Anticipating Durkheim's concerns about hypercivilization, Galton was worried that industrial Britain was expanding too quickly and becoming too complex for human beings to keep up. "The average citizen is too base for the every day work of modern civilization."[53] The modern social environment was taxing the powers of human evolutionary material beyond its limits; everything suggested that the best were not in fact renewing themselves, but that the mediocre and the worst were.

For Galton and other eugenicists, normal population growth had actually become a form of negative natural selection.[54] Another Darwinian zoologist affected by the same concerns, Edwin Lankester, explained that society was threatened by "excessive reproduction of the reckless and hopeless, the poorest, least capable and least desirable members of the community." The lower classes would become a parasitic mass, a sort of permanent underclass of proletarian Draculas eating away at the social fabric of industrial society.[55] The solution was eugenics. The plan itself was simple enough: "If talented men were mated with talented women . . . generation after generation, we might produce a highly-bred race" and eliminate the risk of reversion or atavism. Eugenics had the inestimable advantage of correcting the degeneracy of the West by a method both scientific and humane. "Eugenics cooperates with the workings of nature by securing that humanity shall be represented by the fittest races," Galton proclaimed. "What nature does blindly, slowly, and ruthlessly, man may do providentially, quickly, and kindly."[56]

But not haphazardly. Galton developed a complicated system for identifying the most talented people in the British population and the least talented—"true imbeciles and idiots"—based on observable characteristics that were to be studied, quantified, compared, and filed away. He enthusiastically threw himself into cerebral physiology à la Lombroso, arming himself with a device for creating composite photographs of ideal human types, or "stereotypes," epitomizing criminality, talent, and stupidity—as well as Jewishness. He attempted to construct a "beauty map" of Britain by counting the recurrence of lovely features in the population (London scored the highest, Aberdeen the lowest). He even tried to develop a quantitative index for measuring boredom. Galton's research, as one modern scholar puts it, "pushed the physical explanation of culture to its limit."[57]

At first, in the late 1860s, Galton's research met with no response. Later, degeneration anxieties helped to trigger strong support for Galton's eugenics among radicals and socialists, including George Bernard Shaw, H.G. Wells, Sidney and Beatrice Webb of the Fabian Society, sexologist Havelock Ellis, and the American feminist Margaret Sanger. The fiercest opposition, and Galton's chief critics, came from religious conservatives and Catholics. The traditional Christian message to "be fruitful and multiply" seemed hopelessly out-of-date to Galton and other eugenicists, and even dangerous in a world threatened by degeneration. Like birth control later on, eugenics was supposed to provide an antidote to antiquated and misguided notions about human reproduction.[58]

Part of Galton's radical appeal was that he did not identify the most talented with the well-born; on the contrary, he specifically excluded them from its ranks. "Rank and wealth," one of Galton's colleagues proclaimed, "inherited without effort and in absolute security, tend to produce enervated and unintelligent offspring."[59] Galtonian eugenics, like Nordau's muscular populism, turned all aristocrats into latent degenerates. They might not be Count Draculas, exactly, but they could certainly fit the Oscar Wilde stereotype: human beings bred to indolence, with various nervous disorders and the aesthete's decadent tastes. Somewhat later, they would turn into a phalanx of Bertie Woosters, with dim brains, narrow shoulders, and receding chins. Eugenicists generally agreed that Europe's hereditary ruling class was as much a product of genetic bankruptcy as the mentally retarded, or "mongoloid idiots"—or the Irish.[60]

Eugenics made other unusual converts during its brief heyday.* It also scored some "successes" in such areas as the forced sterilization of the retarded and mentally ill in both England and the United States, before enthusiasm and scientific support began to recede. However, the death blow to eugenics came only with the discrediting of all theories of race as a reliable basis for social science.[61] By World War II, eugenics in the English-speaking world had lost its scientific and politically progressive trappings and was absorbed into Gobinian racial pessimism.

The same transformation took place earlier on the Continent, where eugenics mingled with a variety of influences very different from the liberal positivist ones that had influenced Galton. If the British and American eugenicists were attracted to the "soft" side of eugenics— government encouragement of selective breeding—their Continental counterparts were more forthright about its "hard" side, including abortion, sterilization, and euthanasia.[62]

Chrétien Vacher de Lapouge, a Swiss anthropologist strongly influenced by Gobineau's racial views, was a leading member of the French Société d'Eugénique and the author of *Social Selection* (1896), which advocated a particularly stark vision of natural selection, including euthanasia and infanticide.[63] Ludwig Woltmann was originally a doctrinal Marxist, but his enthusiasm for Darwin eventually converted him to a racialized eugenics, in which state-organized natural selection would

---

* One was W.R. Inge, dean of St. Paul's Cathedral and author of *Christian Mysticism;* another was H.G. Wells. In 1912 Galton's disciple and successor Karl Pearson (who himself a socialist) organized the first International Eugenics Conference, chaired by Charles Darwin's son Leonard and attended by a host of important personages, including a young Liberal Member of Parliament named Winston Churchill.

both lead to social justice and reassert Aryan racial superiority. Both Woltmann and Lapouge were deeply concerned about Western cultural decline as well as degeneration. Both were enthusiastic advocates of state socialism, the form of government best able to undertake the coercive steps necessary for a serious eugenics program. Both also listed Europe's Jews as an important target for such an anti-degeneration program.

After 1880, and particularly after the trial of Dreyfus in 1893, the Jews were increasingly identified as Europe's leading degenerates. Under the microscope of theories of degenerative morbidity, Jews revealed inborn tendencies toward all the diseases of modern life, such as hysteria, nervous disorders, and syphilis. Some theorists argued that the Jews were actually European Negroes.[64] The charges became so prevalent that Cesare Lombroso, who was Jewish, was forced to refute them, arguing that anti-Semitism was itself a form of degeneration.[65] Unfortunately, this ingenious argument convinced no one, and anti-Semitic political parties began to take root in France, Germany, and Austria.*

In order to combat such claims and fears, the great German biologist and founding member of the German Anthropological Society, Rudolf Virchow, conducted a massive craniological study of German schoolchildren, carefully noting which were of Jewish origin and which were not. The results, published fifteen years later in 1886, showed conclusively that there were no physiological differences between Jews and non-Jews and that the supposedly Teutonic racial type—blond hair and blue eyes—constituted less than a third of the German Empire's population, and actually included many Jews. Virchow, a steadfast liberal of the classic variety, believed that he had finished off the myth of an Aryan or Teutonic race once and for all. Instead, his study was subjected to a whirlwind of dismissive attacks, including charges that Virchow himself was a Jew (which he was not). In any case, Virchow's antiracial views steadily lost ground in German anthropological and biological circles as the turn of the century approached.

---

* That storm grew fiercer in 1903 when Otto Weininger published his *Sex and Character.* Weininger stridently proclaimed that Jews were an effeminate and degenerate race that was currently spreading its sickly lack of spiritual and national feeling through modern society. Like women, Jews were "emotion, sexuality, and irrationality incarnate." What made Weininger's fierce anti-Semitic claims particularly chilling—and convincing to some—was that he was himself Jewish.

Instead Virchow's leading opponent, Ernst Haeckel, became the leading figure in both German eugenics and racial biology. Born in 1834, Haeckel was a zoologist at the University of Jena when he first brought Darwin's theories to Germany. His work on race exuded the intellectual atmosphere of Lombroso and the laboratory, rather than that of the neo-Gobinians and *Götterdämmerung*. His most influential book, *The Riddle of the Universe* (1899), proclaimed that modern civilization, with its enormous scientific and technological advances, had acquired an entirely new evolutionary character. At the same time, however, civilization had made virtually no progress in social or moral principles. The same antiquated institutions and assumptions remained in place, especially religion—for which Haeckel reserved a special loathing—individualistic morality, and traditional taboos about sex.

The result was that "superstition and stupidity reign instead of right and reason." Haeckel observed that "an uneasy sense of dismemberment and falseness" had settled over Europe in the last year of the century, giving rise to fears of "great catastrophes in the political and social world."[66] The root of this unease, he claimed, was the same as the root of all the errors that permeate traditional European culture: the anthropocentric view that man is somehow special and separate from the rest of nature. "The boundless presumption of conceited man has misled him into making himself 'the image of God,' claiming an eternal life . . . and imagining that he possesses unlimited freedom of will."

Modern man must abandon "this untenable illusion" if he is to realize his true destiny. Haeckel's new man is entirely one with nature and the "ecology" (a term that Haeckel invented). For Haeckel, the entire history of Western civilization is simply one part of the "stem-history of vertebrates," which he laid out in twenty-six evolutionary stages from the formation of carbon molecules to *Homo erectus*.[67] Charles Darwin had made biological evolution a function of natural selection, which was the real mechanism for change in nature. In Haeckel's philosophy, just the opposite happens. Natural selection, the life-and-death struggle for dominance and power, becomes a function of evolution, a single system of organic growth permeating all of nature, which Haeckel called "monism." Although Haeckel scoffed at older Romantic versions of vitalism, his monistic view of nature and society was permeated with it.

Monism was a deeply deterministic vitalism in which all forces move toward a single totality, including the human community.[68]

*The Riddle of the Universe* sold a hundred thousand copies in its first year of printing. By the end of the First World War it had gone through ten editions and had been translated into twenty-five languages. Haeckel founded the Monist League, which spread the gospel of evolution and natural selection in German lower-middle and working-class circles. Haeckel also became a leading spokesman for eugenics as the key to a new unified and biologically fit humanity. Selective scientific breeding, euthanasia, and defenses against degenerate elements such as Jews and Negroes became social imperatives, which the modern state would have to turn to in order to save civilization.[69]

Liberal opponents such as Virchow accused Haeckel's deterministic vitalist eugenics of pointing the way to socialist dictatorship. Haeckel strenuously denied this; his views were not in any sense proto-totalitarian or even proto-Nazi. He dismissed with contempt writers such as Houston Chamberlain, whose *Foundations of the Nineteenth Century* appeared the same year as *The Riddle of the Universe.** Nonetheless, when the great German armaments magnate Alfred Krupp sponsored an essay contest in 1900 on the question, "What can we learn from the principles of Darwinism for application to domestic political development?" almost every contestant stressed the importance of expanding the role of government in order to transform the physiological destiny of the German race. "Otherwise," pointed out one essayist, "we will all become like the Jews."

Four years later the Society for Racial Hygiene was founded, with Ernst Haeckel as honorary chair. By 1907 there were over a hundred branches across Germany. After the First World War, many eugenicists and racial biologists joined the growing consensus that Germany's political future required some sort of state socialism. One of that future state's priorities, they argued, would have to be a policy regarding eugenics and "controlled selection" to preserve the German race.

Not all German eugenicists were anti-Semites—Alfred Ploetz, for example, who founded the Society for Racial Hygiene in 1904, even ar-

---

* The neo-Gobinians, in turn, ignored Darwin and monism in their own writings.

gued that Jews were racial Aryans. An admirer of Francis Galton, he had coined the term "controlled selection" to refer to a more humane alternative to Darwin's natural selection, so that human beings in a civilized society could propagate the species without fear of genetic catastrophe, including degeneration.[70] But the main thrust of political opinion was in a more radical direction, with the popular success of Chamberlain's *Foundations* and the political clout of groups such as the Pan-German League. Although scientists concerned about physiological Jewish degeneracy tried to distance themselves from what they called "vulgar race propaganda," one leading member of the Society for Racial Hygiene, Eugen Fischer, warmly praised Ludwig Schemann's book on Gobineau's racial theories when it appeared in 1910. Schemann himself became a member of the Society for Racial Hygiene and an enthusiastic eugenicist.

A number of other German race scientists and anthropologists formed the Ring der Norda, which combined the mystical overtones of Bayreuth with the promotion of health and sports to cultivate Teutonic physical specimens. Scientific speculations on the racial future of Germany became infused with a Gobinian pessimism: "Today in Italy, Spain, and Portugal, the Germanic blood, the Nordic race, has already disappeared," wrote Ploetz in his 1913 textbook *Anthropology*. "[National] decline, in part, insignificance, is the result. . . . Then it will be our turn . . . if things go on as they have and are going today."[71]

Inevitably, volkish nationalism, neo-Gobinian vitalism, and racial eugenics overlapped in complicated and striking ways. Racial hygiene remained a sober matter of public health, on the one hand, and the rich expression of cultural vitality and power on the other. The Ariosophists were neo-Gobinian mystics who appeared on the scene shortly before the First World War and enthusiastically took up the cause of eugenics. Max Sebaldt von Werth's multivolume *Genesis*, which appeared between 1898 and 1903, combined appeals to Aryan racial purity with an almost pornographic interest in eugenic sexual breeding. Jörg Lanz von Liebenfels was a former Cistercian monk (and Orientalist scholar) and a fanatical convert to Ludwig Woltmann's radical racial Social Darwinism. His *Theozoology* (1905) concluded that the real chosen people of the Bible were the Aryan-Teutons. The fall of Adam became for Liebenfels a parable of Aryan contamination by miscegenation; the entire Old

Testament, he asserted, was a cautionary tale about racial-mixing, as the Semitic peoples of Canaan and Palestine engaged in deviant sexual orgies with subhuman Mesopotamian love-pygmies (in German, *Buhlzwerge*). Liebenfels proclaimed that modern European man was the mongrelized descendant of these bestial unions. However, through rigorous eugenics, it would be possible to restore modern man (Anthropozoa) to his original status as god-man (Theozoa), with superior powers of sight and hearing, telepathy, and even command of the electrical energy of the cosmos. However bizarre these theories might have seemed to respectable scientists at the time, the Ariosophist outlook influenced the Nazis' court philosopher Alfred Rosenberg, and its visionary eugenics programs directly inspired Heinrich Himmler's *Lebensborn*, the Aryan breeding farms for his SS elite.[72]

The major figures in scientific eugenics and the Society for Racial Hygiene were at first neutral toward the Nazi Party but then became supporters. Alfred Ploetz, who had once argued that Jews were Aryans and that anti-Semitism was doomed to disappear under the glare of scientific research, cooperated with the Nazis' anti-Jewish campaigns and forced sterilization law of 1933. Eugen Fischer, who at one point in his career praised racial mixing (a good example of how difficult it is to find a consensus on any scientific issue in the nineteenth century), came under fire from the Nazis as the director of the Kaiser Wilhelm Institute. Seeing which way the wind was blowing, he then helped to sponsor research at the institute to find scientific evidence that Jews were an inferior race like Negroes and Orientals.[73]

The fate of German eugenics and race sciences illustrates how the fear of degeneration, and appeals for collective state solutions, could drive progressive practitioners into the arms of those willing to marshal the forces of the state to "save" civilization—regardless of the cost.* Eugenics, after all, made heavy demands on the powers of government: identifying "higher" and "lower" human types, selecting and matching suitable specimens for breeding, sterilizing or destroying the weak and infirm, and restraining those who for religious or moral reasons refused

---

* Nor was this true only in Germany. Galton's successor, Karl Pearson, became an admirer of the Nazis, while in the United States the Eugenics Record Office, founded in 1912, kept close touch with the German Society for Racial Hygiene and provided the practical inspiration for the 1933 sterilization law.

to cooperate. These were powers that the postliberal state of the future was equipped to exercise and responsibilities that, at least in the case of Nazi Germany, it was prepared to accept.

## SIGMUND FREUD: CIVILIZATION AND DEGENERATION

By 1900 influential sections of the mainstream intellectual community had lost faith in Western civilization's powers of self-renewal. The modern social fabric no longer seemed to provide any protection for the human species. On the contrary, it was widely assumed that civilization's complex workings would suddenly trigger a reversionary turn for the worse, a descent into chaos more terrible than anything experienced during precivilized "savagery." Even for the most self-confident Darwinian, man's evolutionary past constituted a hereditary burden. It burdened mankind with a host of savage and irrational traits, which science through eugenics or some other means had to carefully weed out and cut back in order for the human race to survive. As Gustav Le Bon put it, "The future is indeed within us and it is woven by ourselves. *Not being fixed, like the Past,* it can be transformed by our own efforts."[74] An alternative perspective—that man's past is not a burden, but a necessary support to civilized life—never occurred to them.

This failure is particularly true for Sigmund Freud. He was, like Nordau, a Jew in a polyglot empire (Austria-Hungary) for whom liberalism had served as a safeguard against traditional forms of persecution and discrimination, as well as providing freedom from the most insular kinds of orthodox Judaism. The liberal positivist bias in favor of rational science, and against religion and other forms of "superstition," remained part of Freud's outlook until his death. Included in the category of superstition was anti-Semitism: from his early days as a medical student, Freud struggled against the increasing focus of degeneration theory on "the Jewish problem" in Austria and elsewhere. The link between anti-Semitism and the fear of degeneration probably encouraged Freud to turn his back on the entire approach and to strike out in his own, startlingly original, direction.

Freud received his medical training in a field that was crucial to degeneration theory, neurology. In 1885 he went to Paris to study the "secondary atrophies and degenerations" of children's brains. He engaged in the same debates, and studied under the same professors, that Max Nordau had a decade earlier.* Eventually, however, Freud gave up trying to understand degenerative disorders on the basis of their physiological-organic causes. He concluded, as most of the medical profession would later, that degenerationist accounts of "diseases" such as neurosis and hysteria were "a judgment of value, a condemnation instead of an explanation," and hence lacking in scientific rigor and objectivity.[75]

Inevitably, though, degeneration theory and its implicit opposition between the forces of civilization and a healthy humanity found its way into Freud's theories. His first path-breaking work, *The Interpretation of Dreams*, was published in 1899, the same year as Haeckel's *Riddle of the Universe* and only two years after Durkheim's *Suicide* and Stoker's *Dracula*. Freud's picture of the human personality presented a tension between the ego and superego of civilized man and their primitive counterpart, the id. The id, like Stevenson's Mr. Hyde, remains hidden or repressed in the normal healthy human being. "The ego represents what one may call reason and deliberation," Freud wrote in one of his later works, "in contrast to the id, which contains the passions."[76]

The id establishes its hidden domain in the unconscious, a Lombrosian underworld of fantasies and dreams, of myth and primal urges (what Freud's disciple Carl Jung would call the realm of the archetypes). The neurotic, according to Freud, has allowed this hidden realm to intrude into his normal psychic environment—he has *regressed*, just as criminality to Lombroso was a form of regression. However, Freud's theory of *psychological* regression replaces *physiological* degeneration in explaining the movement from reason and order to irrationality and disorder. Regression occurs in the individual, but also in society as a whole.† Every child relives in his own development the psychic development of the human race as a whole, from irrational and simple to ra-

---

* Freud would later praise his teacher Jean Martin Charcot, France's greatest specialist in nervous disorders and degeneration theory, as "one of the greatest physicians, a genius."

† Freud was a convert to Ernst Haeckel's law of recapitulation, which stated that the growing embryo repeats the entire history of the species' past evolution in its own development. This is sometimes expressed in the maxim that ontogeny recapitulates phylogeny. It was a view held by many evolutionary biologists but that Haeckel raised to the level of a universal law.

tional and complex.[77] Conversely, human societies display the same psychological principles that apply to ordinary individuals—or to neurotics—as Freud argued in *Totem and Taboo* (1912) and *Moses and Monotheism* (1937–1939). Just as the individual bears the psychic scars of early childhood, relations with parents, and other traumas experienced throughout his life, so does society's inner psychological life bear similar scars and burdens, dating from the very moment of its foundation.

Like Nietzsche, Freud found the fatal flaw in civilization at its origin. For Freud, that origin is patricide. This primal act of savagery, and the collective guilt felt for the death of the father, lingers on in guilt-generating institutions such as religion and in social conventions such as taboos. Hence, primitive society's successor, modern society, is not immune to the savage and irrational. Its original urges and crimes survive in its collective memory and in the institutions that give social life its structure and meaning. As Freud put it, "The primitive mind is, in the fullest sense of the word, imperishable."[78]

The primitive and savage remain part of the individual psyche in the form of the id. They remain with man as a social creature in the instinct of the primal horde, which as Le Bon and Trotter had shown comes fully to the surface in modern democratic institutions. For Freud, in short, man's cultural formation gives the lie to the claim that civilization is a distinctly different state from barbarism, since the inner psychological structures of both are actually the same. Sir James Frazier's massive comparative study of primitive religion, *The Golden Bough* (which profoundly influenced Freud), had already suggested that the role of "irrational" myth and ritual had not disappeared from civilized societies. As race theory receded from the liberal purview in the twentieth century, anthropologists began to turn to Freud's theories for a reappraisal of the distinction between civilized and primitive cultures. A new generation of anthropologists—Franz Boas, Margaret Mead, and Ruth Benedict—dedicated themselves to elevating the cultural status of primitive societies vis à vis their "advanced" counterparts (now carefully hedged within quotation marks). Their field work revealed the deep similarities and affinities between the two, and it suggested that primitive peoples, in Romantic Orientalist fashion, often preserved the vitality and psychological health the civilized West had lost (the best example is Margaret Mead's *Coming of Age in Samoa*).[79]

*Civilization and Its Discontents* was Freud's last testament to the enlightened liberal society in which he was born and raised. Published in 1930, it closed an era in European thinking about human history as a civilizing process and the consequences of progress for modern man. It is perhaps not surprising, then, that the first arresting image in the book is that of the ruins of ancient Rome.

The Roman Forum represents for Freud the ongoing nature of historical development, as each distinct epoch (early republic, Augustan era, late empire, and Renaissance) succeeds and obliterates its predecessors. An archeological expert on early Rome can "at most point out the places where the temples and public buildings of that period once stood." The ruins that occupy those sites are not even ruins of the same buildings, but of later imperial ones and of "restorations after fires and destruction," which are themselves hedged in and obscured by "the jumble of a great metropolis which has grown up in the last few centuries since the Renaissance."

"Suppose," however, Freud suggested, "that Rome is not a human habitation but a psychological entity with a similarly long and copious past." Then we would discover that "nothing that has come into existence will have passed away." Not only would "the palaces of the Caesars be rising to their old height on the Palatine" and each building still be decorated by "the beautiful statues which graced it until it was besieged by the Goths," but ancient Roman temples would be standing in the middle of Christian basilicas and Renaissance palazzi. "The observer would perhaps only have to change the direction of his glance or his position" to see the ancient city simultaneously with its modern counterpart.[80]

Civilization as a material process transforms and alters what came before; as a psychological process, a "civilizing process," it does not and cannot. For Freud, the civilized man retains the basic instincts of his earlier savage existence. On the positive side, his social evolution brings, in Freudian terms, maturity and independence. He overcomes the infantile sense of helplessness of primitive man and the need for protective paternalistic figures such as gods, popes, and kings.[81] Civilization invests individuals with a sense of their own autonomy and their place in a larger community of order and moral duty. But this process also involves conflict with their primitive life-giving instincts:

> It is impossible to overlook the extent to which civilization is built upon a renunciation of instinct, how much it presupposes precisely the non-satisfaction . . . of powerful instincts. This "cultural frustration" is, as we know . . . the cause of the hostility against which all civilizations have to struggle.

In fact, this self-repression can advance to the point where vitality itself vanishes from the cultural landscape. Man and his social progress reach a new and fateful point of intersection, where civilization's conquest of its own vitality becomes so unbearable that it finally pushes the barbarian within to the surface, a "return of the repressed." This can happen in the individual—in the neurotic and other "discontents"—or, more frighteningly, in the society as a whole as it lurches back to its brutal, aggressive precivilized state, in which only the strong rules, with no restraints beyond "the sense of his own interest and instinctual impulses."[82]

By the time Freud published *Civilization and Its Discontents*, in 1930, humane and liberal values seemed to be flickering out all across Europe. Degeneration's greatest nightmare—an uprising of the debased, criminalized masses, the triumph of primitive delusion and passion over reason—seemed about to come to pass.

> The fateful question for the human species seems to me to be whether and to what extent their cultural development will succeed in mastering the disturbance of their communal life by the human instinct of aggression and self-destruction.

Freud added in a postscript a year later, "But who can foresee with what success and with what result?" Two years after that, in 1933, Adolf Hitler became chancellor of Germany.

PART TWO

# PREDICTING THE DECLINE OF THE WEST

CHAPTER 5

# GILDED AGE APOCALYPSE

*Henry and Brooks Adams*

America is therefore the land of the future, where, in the ages
that lie before us, the burden of the World's History shall reveal
itself.

—G.F. Hegel, 1830

I am myself more than ever at odds with my time. I detest it, and
everything that belongs to it, and live only in the wish to see the
end of it, with all its infernal Jewry. I want to put every money
lender to death, and to sink Lombard Street and Wall Street
into the ocean.

—Henry Adams, 1894

The American belief in progress drew upon a rich heritage of millennialist thought from the nation's Calvinist past. Like the Jews
and Christians in ancient times and the English in the sixteenth century, the Puritans and Pilgrims had seen themselves as the people or
"race" that God had selected as His instruments in the world. The New
England settlements of the early seventeenth century all claimed that
status of chosenness by virtue of their sworn covenant with God. Being
a chosen people was both a destiny and a responsibility. God's divine
purpose had to be reflected in every aspect of the conduct and actions
of the community, including proclaiming His gospel to the other peoples
of the earth.

147

America was the "redeemer nation," with a special mission to the rest of the world.[1] That redemptive mission justified America's westward expansion throughout the nineteenth century as part of its "manifest destiny." The arrival of Europeans on the shores of North America and their push beyond the Alleghenies seemed to represent a momentous shift—even *the* definitive shift—in world history. It made America part of a much older process, the westward movement of civilization and universal empire:

> *Westward the course of empire takes its way;*
> *The four first acts already past*
> *A fifth shall close the drama with the day,*
> *Time's noblest offspring is the last.*[2]

Today the term "empire" conjures up images of imperialism and exploitation. However, by strict definition an empire is simply a series of disparate and distinct geographical units governed by a single political sovereignty. That sovereignty might be a single person, an emperor—but it might also be the people themselves. For this reason the *Federalist Papers* could refer to the new American republic as an empire with no sense of contradiction. The new American republic acquired an expansive imperial mission to match its redemptive one.

Thomas Jefferson called America an "empire of liberty," which would spread the message of popular sovereignty and foster virtue as it moved farther and farther west. In 1809 Jefferson doubled the size of the country with his Louisiana Purchase, creating the physical space necessary for such an empire.[3] Secretary of State John Quincy Adams said that America's "proper dominion [is] to be the continent of North America" and gave that dominion universal characteristics. It would, he wrote, "proclaim to mankind the inexhaustible rights of human nature, and the lawful foundations of government. Its motto is *Freedom, Independence, Peace.*"[4]

More than any other people, Americans enjoyed a sense that their nation, "the land of the free and home of the brave," held center stage in a world-historical process. "Here Empire's last, and brightest Throne shall rise," wrote Timothy Dwight, the president of Yale College, after America won its independence, "and Peace and Right, and Freedom, greet the skies."[5] The Declaration of Independence, J.Q. Adams declared in 1821, was "destined to cover the globe." In 1858 *Harper's Monthly* observed, "Everything connected with our position, history, and progress point out the United States of America as the land of the future.[6] From the Puritan fathers and the Founding Fathers to what the *Time* magazine publisher Henry B. Luce would call "the American century"—the twentieth—the history of the United States formed a single, inspiring, and forward-looking story. America represented the highest, culminating stage of civilization and progress.

Strictly speaking, the idea of progress implied a secular as opposed to a Christian view of history. In Europe these two views of historical change clashed constantly from the Enlightenment to Marx (who called religion the opiate of the masses) and Auguste Comte, who believed his Positive Philosophy would replace Christianity altogether. However, the key figures of the American Enlightenment, such as Jefferson and Benjamin Franklin, simply grafted their goals onto those of the Calvinist redeemer nation. America became "dedicated" to a basic Enlightenment principle, that "all men are created equal." The chosen people also now enjoyed rights and capacities as individuals. These rights, "life, liberty, and the pursuit of happiness," were divinely endowed even though they also were part of man's rational place in nature.[7]

A rational understanding of nature meant, of course, science. Science and technology, therefore, occupied an important place in the American panorama of redemptive progress and liberty. "Do not fear science," Yale geologist James Dwight Dana wrote in 1865, because science has shown that "progress through organic growth was God's law and plan . . . progress is upward as well as onward, to clearer and clearer visions of infinite beneficence." So it came as no surprise that Charles Darwin found enthusiastic support in the United States from Henry Ward Beecher and other churchmen, a group that had greeted Darwin's theory with revulsion and suspicion in his own country. Lombroso, Francis Galton, Ernst Haeckel, and other "scientific" social theorists scored similar successes when their works reached American shores.[8]

In 1907 Gina Lombroso-Ferera issued a new edition of her father's *Criminal Man*, citing examples of prisons and reformatories where Lombroso's theories had been put into successful practice. Each one came from the United States. Thirty years later, on the eve of the Second World War, Harvard criminologist and anthropologist Earnest Hooton was still using Lombroso's methods to classify criminal offenders. With his optimistic claims to quantitative accuracy and scientific certainty, Lombroso appealed to the nineteenth-century American confidence in science and progress as forces of the future.[9]

There was, however, another American tradition that grew out of the same Calvinist roots and the same belief in an "empire of liberty." This tradition saw an underlying tension between liberty as an American birthright and the possibility of corruption arising from the exercise of that liberty, especially in the political and moral spheres. Its great spokesman, and a staunch opponent of American Enlightenment optimists like Jefferson and Madison, was the second president of the United States, John Adams.

Adams had become concerned about America's inevitable corruption and fall even before the American Revolution broke out. His earliest political work* described how the colonists had come to the shores of North America out of "a love of universal liberty and a hatred, a dread, a horror" of the "infernal confederacy" of the corrupt English monarchy and the Anglican Church. The forces of "temporal and spiritual tyranny" had managed to destroy men's liberties in England; now the British Empire was "sunk in corruption" and "teetering on the brink of destruction." Then that same "wicked confederacy" set out to subjugate the colonies, Adams wrote in 1775; Americans had to secure their virtue and natural rights by breaking free from "the mighty ruin of a once noble fabrick," which was Hanoverian England.[10]

Adams's hopes that the American people would preserve their independence and virtue disappeared almost as soon as the revolution ended. By 1785, even before the ratification of the Articles of Confederation, Adams declared that Americans "never merited the Character of a very exalted Virtue," and he had been foolish to expect "that they would grow much better." The sudden rush of the low-born and obscure into the political system convinced him that America was doomed.

---

* *A Dissertation on the Canon and Feudal Law* (1765).

There was "no special Providence for Americans," he told his friends, "and their nature is the same with that of others"—in other words, greedy, vicious, stupid, and ambitious.[11]

Adams was evoking a transatlantic version of historical pessimism, in which Americans of the past are always free, independent-minded, and charged with moral purpose, while those of the present are carelessly about to destroy their birthright. He drew heavily upon the American Calvinist tradition of the "jeremiad," in which Plymouth and Boston ministers harangued their congregations for their egregious collective sins. In Adams's terms, an unworthy American electorate had made itself vulnerable to "wicked confederacies" of "lying priests and knavish politicians," who continually try to use their powers to gain ascendancy over the minds of the people.[12] John Adams was in effect the United States's first great conspiracy theorist, the author of what is termed "the paranoid style" in American politics.

The paranoid style sees vast, organized, and malign conspiracies operating "as *the* motive force in historical events," recalling apocalyptic fears of a world in which the Antichrist directs events for his own evil purposes. At stake are "the birth and death of whole worlds, whole political orders, whole systems of human values."[13] Waves of conspiracy theories struck across the bow of American politics in the early nineteenth century, with an anti-French Jacobin campaign in the 1790s, the formation of an anti-Masonic political party in the 1820s and '30s, and nativist attacks on Irish immigrants in the 1840s that were driven by a fear of Roman Catholicism—"that system of holy lies and pious frauds that has raged and triumphed for fifteen hundred years," as John Adams described it.

The paranoid style sees time as forever running out. "Party spirit," Adams wrote in 1814, "sects, factions, threaten our existence in America at this moment."[14] The conspiracy theorist demands action *now*. But unlike his apocalyptic predecessor, the conspiracy theorist understands that history is a secular, not a sacred, process. For John Adams, the success or failure of these conspiracies depended on the American people themselves; if they refused to exert the energy to save themselves, no one else would save them either. In that case the conspiracy would achieve its terrible object and, as an Adams ally put it in 1798, "the earth can be nothing better than a sink of impurities, a theater of violence and murder, and a hell of miseries."

John Adams's descendants became the principal carriers of this fear of America's collective moral failure. It could be a powerful stimulus to action. John Adams's son, John Quincy Adams, moved New England's Whigs to see slavery as the single great betrayal of the Founding Father's legacy. His grandson, Charles Francis Adams, brought the mission of ending slavery to the Republican Party and Abraham Lincoln's presidential victory in 1860. But when the moral burden of chosenness became too much, the imperative of duty could dissolve into self-doubt. The result was that "chilly and isolated sense of moral responsibility" that Henry James saw as typical of Americans, particularly New Englanders, and that weighed momentous public issues with "an uncertain hand and a somewhat agitated conscience."

For Charles F. Adams's sons, Henry and Brooks, America's world-historical mission had been dissolved by collective unworthiness. They watched the social changes of their own time—the growth of industrialization, immigration, and mass democratic politics—with deep disquiet and became convinced that America's belief in progress would destroy its very soul.

We saw that by the late nineteenth century many Europeans had reached the same conclusion about modernity. But they had an escape hatch: the premodern past. The cultural achievements of earlier epochs, such as the ancient world and the Middle Ages, were available either to bolster and secure modern European civilization, as Tocqueville and others argued, or to provide a source of resistance and escape, as they had been for the Romantics and Gobineau. But for the American liberal mind, no such options existed.* *All* positive American values were, by definition, progressive and modern. So when the fruits of progress, including the growth of learning and science, individual autonomy, and a moral sense shaped by the necessities of social interaction (manners and politeness) rather than biblical injunction, seemed under attack from the social and economic forces that were supposed to gen-

---

* It is striking and significant that neither Adams had the slightest interest in the one place where an American *ancien régime* might be said to exist, namely the antebellum South.

erate progress in the first place, the future seemed closed. "I see ruin in the pole star," Henry Adams wrote, and he meant it.

## HENRY ADAMS: TRADITION AND PROGRESS

One day when he was seven years old, Henry Adams tells us in his autobiography, he decided that he would no longer go to school. No amount of persuasion or threats could move him. The angry shouting and arguing took place at the bottom of the stairs leading to the study of his grandfather, ex-President John Quincy Adams. Suddenly "the door opened and the old man slowly came down. Putting on his hat, he took the boy's hand without a word, and walked with him, paralyzed by awe, up the road to the town." As they marched along, Henry still thought he might escape, figuring that "an old gentleman close on eighty would never trouble himself to walk near a mile on a hot summer morning over a shadeless road to take a boy to school. . . . But the old man did not stop" until he had escorted young Henry into the school building. "Not til then did the President release his hand and depart." During their long walk "he had said nothing . . . he had shown no concern in the matter; hardly even a consciousness of the boy's existence."[15]

For the rest of Henry Adams's life, his grandfather remained the emblem of the Adams family tradition of civic duty and responsibility. That tradition was an unyielding and inexorable force, impersonal in its demands and expectations. To the mature Henry Adams, it became an impossible burden to bear. When his brother Brooks published John Quincy Adams's diary in 1907, the seventy-one-year-old Henry confessed, "I go all to pieces whenever I attempt to handle it," since the image of the old man was "a psychologic nightmare to his degenerate and decadent grandson."[16]

Henry and Brooks grew up in a Boston dominated by certain families of Puritan descent known as the Brahmins—Lodges, Lowells, Lymans, Saltonstalls, Crowninshields, Cabots, and Brookses, the family of the Adams brothers' mother. The Brahmins married amongst themselves and maintained a virtual monopoly on public and intellectual life. In 1815 their orthodox and Unitarian wings had split apart. The outlook of Unitarian families like the Adamses was more worldly and nonsectarian than that of their orthodox opponents, but they lived up to their civic obligations with the same Puritan earnestness. The men belonging to the circle of the Adams brothers' father, Charles Francis, such as James Russell Lowell and Senator Charles Sumner, not only came from the best families but held the same progressive bourgeois views as European liberals such as Tocqueville and John Stuart Mill. They were the forerunners of what would come to be known as the "genteel tradition," with Harvard College as their intellectual base. Henry Adams described their outlook this way: "Human nature worked for God, and three instruments were all she asked—Suffrage, Common Schools, and [the] Press—[for] leading a virtuous, useful, unselfish life."[17]

If 1848 was a watershed for European liberalism, it was no less so for the New England variety. In January John Quincy Adams died: "The glory of the family has departed," the grief-stricken Charles announced to his children. That spring, Charles Francis Adams led a revolt against the national political parties on the issue of slavery. The antislavery "Whigs of conscience," as they were called, organized the Free Soil Party and Charles was nominated as its vice-presidential candidate. Although the ticket was soundly defeated in the 1848 election, it marked the beginning of abolitionism's rise from a fringe movement to a national moral crusade.*

Four years later another Boston Unitarian, Harriet Beecher Stowe, published *Uncle Tom's Cabin*, and the American redeemer nation had found a new outlet.

Antislavery, like politics itself, was a central part of the Adams family heritage. It had been John Quincy Adams's consuming passion and his greatest burden. The persistence of slavery in the United States, his grandson Brooks later said, "injected into his mind the first doubt as to whether there were a God, and whether this life had a purpose."[18] Now the banner and the burden had passed to his son. Nicknamed the Archbishop of Antislavery, Charles Francis led his Free Soil stalwarts into the new Republican Party, which swept to victory under Abraham Lincoln in the election of 1860. The outbreak of war against the "slave powers of King Cotton" (Charles's favorite description of the South) one year

---

* That same year, Walt Whitman was dismissed as editor of New York *Eagle* for his abolitionist views.

later seemed to mark the beginning of a national moral cleansing. Lincoln selected Adams as his ambassador to London in March 1861, to argue the case for the war and to persuade Britain not to recognize the Confederacy. As his private secretary, Charles Adams took along his son Henry, fresh from Harvard College.

The Adamses's supporters among English liberals included Richard Cobden and John Bright, who combined a commitment to democracy and laissez-faire principles with a passion for justice for the working man; Charles Dickens and Matthew Arnold; Nassau Senior, editor of the English edition of the works of the late Alexis de Tocqueville; and John Stuart Mill, whose *On Liberty* was the definitive statement of the principle that liberty—economic, social, political, and intellectual— should be the sole criterion governing relations between the individual and society. Henry Adams would later have harsh things to say about Mill's brand of classical liberalism.[19] At the time, however, he carefully read another of Mill's works, *The Positive Philosophy of Auguste Comte.* Comte's basic conclusion, that man's progress obeyed exact dynamic laws and moved in conformity with the natural forces governing the universe, filled Adams's imagination and shaped all his subsequent historical thinking. "Any science of history must be absolute like other sciences," he explained in a paper he wrote thirty years later entitled *The Tendency of History* (1894), "and must fix with mathematical certainty the path which human society has got to follow."[20]

Under Comte's influence, Henry Adams came to hold a strong organicist view of social and political progress. American society, like all societies and nations, was more than just the sum of its parts; it formed a single systematic whole. However, he also took an impersonal mechanical, even deterministic, view of its workings.

In contrast to American Darwinians like John Fiske of Harvard, Adams agreed with Ernst Haeckel that the truth of evolution drained moral purpose not only from nature but from human society as well. At some future date, he would write years later, "psychology, physiology, and history will join in proving man to have as fixed and necessary development as that of a tree; and almost as unconscious."[21] Studying progress in society required Comtean-style quantitative, even mechanical, calculations rather than "inexact" moral judgments. Energy, force, dynamism, and their opposites, Adams believed, were nature's, and therefore society's, only realities. As an historian and writer, Henry Adams abandoned what had been a major tenet of American liberalism: that the moral life of the individual lay in conformity with, not opposition to, human nature as it appeared in the world.

At the same time, the individual still had to bear the burden of a moral life. Determinism did not turn Henry Adams into an out-and-out hedonist: the old Puritan tradition of the Adams family continued to assert itself. The individual still had to uphold a higher vision for man and society. During his stay in England, Henry Adams had met Thomas Carlyle. An orphan of Romanticism, Carlyle denounced the liberal capitalist society so admired by Henry's father's friends as "profoundly, irremediably immoral."[22] Carlyle's views deeply impressed the young Adams.

The other critic of the bourgeois version of progress whom Adams encountered was Karl Marx. In 1863 he attended a London trade-union meeting organized by Marx, and he became intimately acquainted with the German socialist's writings. Marx, incidentally, was attracting the interest of other American liberals. In 1851 Horace Greeley had hired Marx as his European correspondent for the *New York Herald*, and Greeley's editor Charles A. Dana paraphrased passages from the *Communist Manifesto* in his own editorials.[23] Like Adams, they had taken up Marx's writings not for their value as an economic or historical dogma—*Das Kapital* did not appear until 1867—but as powerful expressions of their own indignation at the inequities of industrial society. Henry Adams later complained that Marx had not been part of his education at Harvard; he also admitted that after Comte, Marx was the writer who most influenced his own thinking.[24] Above all, Marx provided him with the indelible image of an industrial capitalist world sinking inevitably into decline. "At the end of the vista," Adams mused ruefully, "in any and all contingencies, stands ruin for Western Europe."

And for the United States, if it became infected with the same desire for economic competition and material wealth. In that case, all the forces that governed society's development would contradict its moral traditions. The upright individual would have to carry on totally alone, in the face of the indifference, and perhaps the hostility, of society at large. In Henry Adams's mechanistic universe, the burden of generating moral meaning fell entirely on the individual, even while the individual was reduced by that same theory to a puny, solitary status relative to the whole. "The atom might move," Adams would write later, "but the general equilibrium does not change."

## ARISTOCRATS AND ANGLO-SAXONS

"The atom might move"—those words might have seemed appropriate to Henry Adams as he returned home in 1865. Enormous changes had swept across the American landscape during his absence and would gather strength in the coming decades. Rapid industrialization brought a raw new material affluence, while the Civil War had greatly expanded the size and character of the federal government. In addition, the last impediments to mass political participation had been removed. Where there had been one voter in the presidential election in 1824, there were twelve in 1872. Propertyless working-class males, black freedmen, immigrants, and Irish Catholic tenement dwellers in cities such as New York and Boston served as the moving parts of a new kind of democratic politics, which would come to be called "machine" politics. A new political elite stepped forward, made up of urban political patrons and party bosses, while the older political elite of New York Knickerbockers, Philadelphia Quakers, and Boston Brahmins found itself on the defensive.[25]

Signs of resentment and disillusionment began to surface in Eastern intellectual circles soon after the Civil War. The earlier vision of a progressive redeemer nation was of an agrarian paradise of endless waves of amber grain, where, as historian George Bancroft wrote, "the yeoman, living like a good neighbor near the fields he cultivates, glories in the fruitfulness of the valleys." In 1878, two decades later, Henry Parkman could write: "Now . . . the village has grown into a populous city, with its factories and workshops, its acres of tenement-houses, and thousands and thousands of restless workmen, foreigners . . . to whom the liberty means license and politics means plunder . . . ."[26] Economist Henry George wrote similarly in *Progress and Poverty* (1871): "The great city, here are to be found the greatest wealth and the greatest poverty. And it is here that popular government has most clearly broken down."[27] A new fear of democracy, and of its underlying revolutionary social implications, broke the surface among the old patrician elite of the United States, just as it had in Europe.

What to do? New England and New York liberal circles, including Henry Adams and his brothers, organized groups like the Reform League to attack the "spoils system" and the nefarious political "rings."* The reformers' motto was "good government" (hence the nickname "goo-goo liberals"). Their lobbying efforts concentrated on specific issues such as civil service reform and changes in the nation's monetary and tariff policy. Underneath their reform agenda, however, lay a deep conviction that the new forms of democratic politics were imperiling the nation's moral integrity. To the reformers' minds, government was falling into the hands of vulgar millionaires (the Vanderbilts, Fiskes, and Goulds), ignorant immigrants who traded votes for bribes and drinks, and corrupt elected officials whose loyalty was to their party bosses rather than to the larger public good.[28] Henry George warned that a new ruling class had arisen, "men of power, whose favor the ambitious must court" and who commanded voting wards and nominating conventions. "Who are these men? The wise, the good, the learned?" George asked. The answer was an emphatic no. "They are gamblers, saloon keepers, pugilists, or worse. . . . They stand to the government of these cities as the Praetorian Guards did to that of declining Rome." That fear prompted the president of Harvard, Charles W. Eliot, to claim that the very foundations of law and order in America were under threat, and that something must be done to lessen the influence of the new democratic politics.[29]

Henry Adams had returned to America in the hopes of launching a political career. He assumed that a new Republican administration under Ulysses S. Grant would welcome the services of the son of one of the party's most illustrious founders. However, postwar turmoil and arguments over Reconstruction froze out the Adams dynasty. Disappointed, Henry Adams instead turned his hand to political journalism. He wrote a series of articles for E.L. Godkin's *The Nation* that, not surprisingly, lambasted the Grant administration for its lack of political judgment. To Adams's mind, he and other well-born liberals constituted what John Adams half a century earlier had called a "natural aristocracy," which

---

* These included the notorious Tweed Ring that dominated New York City politics until 1874 and the so-called Whiskey Ring, which involved several members of President Ulysses S. Grant's cabinet.

could save American democracy from itself. "By aristocracy," John Adams had explained in 1814, "I mean a citizen who can command or govern two votes or more in society, whether by his virtues, his talents, his learning, loquacity" or other outstanding characteristics. This aristocracy, he wrote, can never be "more than one fifth—no, not one tenth—of the men regularly educated to science and letters." Without them, however, the people can be as "unjust, tyrannical, brutal, barbarous, and cruel" as any tyrant.[30]

Beginning in 1870, an influential group of New England intellectuals and reformers took up this idea that a natural aristocracy could guide the forces of American democracy in a constructive direction. Important organs of liberal opinion such as Godkin's *Nation* and the *North American Review* lamented the failure of persons of the "best class" to enter politics.[31] Their liberal vision of a natural aristocracy was never meant to be elitist in any invidious sense. It was not the fault of its members that persons of "honor, education, and property" tended to come from the same families and to be educated at the same schools (in 1896, Harvard's President Eliot estimated that there were five hundred and sixty such "family stocks" at Harvard and four hundred and twenty at Yale). Nor did this Eastern-bred elite necessarily exclude others who might exhibit the same characteristics; in fact, Eliot insisted, the task of democracy was to multiply their numbers.[32]

In classic Aristotelian terms, the wellborn Few would balance the irrational passions of the Many. They would provide a guide as well as an anchor for the ship of state as it entered uncertain and treacherous waters. Most of these well-born and educated leaders would not even have to run for office. Instead, America's elected politicians would learn to depend on them as "preachers, teachers, jurists . . . scholars, men of science, historians, inventors, economists, and political philosophers." During his forty-year tenure as president of Harvard, Eliot's mission was to turn the college from a Unitarian seminary into a training camp for this new generation of American leaders, who would later come to be called "the best and the brightest." Other Protestant denominational colleges, such as Yale, Princeton, and Dartmouth, followed suit, while in 1884 the Reverend Endicott Peabody founded the Groton School for the same purpose.

Eliot had been struck by the articles Henry Adams was publishing on the dire situation in Republican Washington, in which he warned that without reform "our Government and Union will go to pieces."[33] Adams wrote scathingly about the corruption in Congress, while President Grant himself became a favorite target for abuse. "His ideas of political economy were those of a feudal monarch a thousand years ago," he wrote; what hope was there for a political system that chose such a benighted simpleton for president? "The progress of [human] evolution from President Washington to President Grant," Adams sneered years later, "was alone evidence to upset Darwin." And the corruption was embedded in modern democracy itself. "The more I study its workings," he wrote to an English friend, "the more dread I feel at the future."[34]

A corrupt democracy seemed to Adams to be the natural extension of an economic system that was (and here he was clearly borrowing from Marx) "divided into two classes, one which steals, the other which is stolen from." He went on: "Never in the world's history" had so much economic power "been trusted in the hands of mere private citizens," who will "ultimately succeed in directing government itself." Adams's most hard-hitting article, "The Gold Conspiracy of New York," was the forerunner of the muckraking journalism of the 1890s. It nearly brought a libel suit against Adams but it moved Charles W. Eliot to offer him a teaching post at Harvard and the editorship of the main organ of enlightened opinion, the *North American Review*. Finding himself stranded in Washington, "a place he did not love, and before a future which repelled," Adams accepted and left politics behind forever.[35]

Eliot had brought Henry Adams to Harvard to help revamp the curriculum so that America's natural aristocracy might be prepared for its leadership mission. Adams found the assignment congenial. He had written to his brother Charles that "we want a national set of young men like ourselves or better to start new influences not only in politics, but in literature, in law, in society, and throughout the whole social organism of the country." To Adams's mind, this included exposing his students to the latest historical theories coming out of the German and English universities. Adams turned his seminar in medieval history (his students included the future senator from Massachusetts Henry Cabot Lodge and the future monetary historian J. Lawrence Laughlin) into a laboratory for investigating the so-called Anglo-Saxon thesis, the latest twist to the Aryanist revision of history.

In 1850 the German philologist Friedrich Max Müller gave new life to the old claim that the English tradition of liberty and constitutional government was the gift of Britain's Anglo-Saxon inhabitants when he brought to Oxford his version of the Aryan origins of civilization. Max Müller was a fierce opponent of the racial theories of Aryanism that were percolating among his German colleagues.* But he did argue that a single linguistic-cultural tradition linked all Aryan-descended societies past and present and had produced parallel religious, political, and economic institutions in each one. The English historians whom Max Müller influenced—Henry Maine, Frederick Pollock, James Bryce, and E.A. Freeman—labored to show that the Germanic Anglo-Saxons had brought to Britain from the forests and bogs of Scandinavia a primitive form of democracy, which lay at the origin of Parliament and modern political freedom.

These liberty-loving Teutonic forebears were no longer envisioned as Gobinian warrior-aristocrats, however. They had been domesticated to match the middle-class expectations of their Oxford and Cambridge admirers. They were sober farmers and husbandmen, with an instinct toward self-reliance and independence; their notion of liberty implied a democratic setting.† Adams simply transferred that Anglo-Saxon legacy to the shores of America, where English-speaking colonies made it the foundation of their societies beginning with the Mayflower Compact. Adams and his students published a series of papers in 1876 on how the American traditions of law, rights, and democracy were part of a heritage belonging to free Germanic peoples in Europe as well as in the New World. The Aryan farmer and Anglo-Saxon freeholder were revealed as the direct ancestors of Jefferson's self-reliant yeoman.[37]

The term "Anglo-Saxon democracy" quickly became part of the stock vocabulary of American scholars and politicians. Its influence was spread through John Fiske's highly successful lectures on "American Political Ideas" in 1880, James K. Hosmer's *History of Anglo-Saxon Freedom* (1890), and the speeches of politicians like Henry Cabot Lodge, Albert

---

* "To me an ethnologist who speaks of Aryan race, Aryan blood . . . is as great a sinner as a linguist who speaks of a dolichocephalic dictionary. . . . It is more than a Babylonian confusion of tongues. It is downright theft," he wrote in *Biographies of Words* (1888).[36]

† Represented by the Anglo-Saxon *witangemot*, or council of elders.

Beveridge, and Theodore Roosevelt.* The English-speaking peoples, including Americans, formed the leading westward edge of the migrations of Aryan peoples across Europe and Asia. Scholars had already seen that migration as a crucial turning point in the history of civilization. Now it became a central event in the history of American liberty as well. The white Anglo-Saxon Protestant, or "Wasp," turned out to be the true founder of America's world-historical role as redeemer nation.

The Anglo-Saxon thesis appealed to Henry Adams. He was pleased to see that the American Constitution was not the product of circumstance or individual whim, but of a cultural instinct and the heritage of Germanic freedom. As a political doctrine, the Anglo-Saxon thesis also appealed to a conservative Burkean view of liberty and constitutions that Henry Adams and many nineteenth-century liberals shared. The members of the Anglo-Saxon or English "race" had been the builders of an ancient house of liberty. It was now incumbent on their successors to learn and practice the habits, customs, and traditions that would maintain that structure so that the legacy of freedom could continue to flow unhindered.

However, the influence that *tradition* won in the history of modern liberty was an influence that *progress* lost. America's legacy of political freedom and constitutional government existed apart from the confluence of its social and economic forces. Society's own development did not add to or expand the original German heritage; on the contrary, that development could only undermine its primitive foundations. Adams reserved his own judgment on these issues for an anonymous novel he published in 1880 entitled *Democracy*. Its main character, the Washington political hostess Mrs. Lee, articulates the book's underlying theme with these words: "I must know whether America is right or wrong." By the end of the book, Henry Adams has tried to convince his reader that what was once valid about American democracy has been overwhelmed by what is fundamentally, irretrievably wrong.

The novel demonstrates that the republic Washington and Jefferson founded no longer exists. It has transformed itself into a social and po-

---

* James Hosmer's cousin Frank was principal of the high school in Great Barrington, Massachusetts, and would pass the Anglo-Saxonist version of American history on to his favorite student, the young W.E.B. Du Bois.

litical chaos, as well as into "moral paralysis." An air of Oriental decadence hovers over the novel: scenes and characters are surrounded by the Gilded Age gaudiness of a brothel, with "embroidered carpets and woven gold from Japan and Teheran" and "a strange medley of sketches, paintings, fans, embroideries, and porcelain." The most admirable characters in the book are all from distinguished lineages, families in which, as Harvard's President Eliot would put it, "gentle manners, cultivated tastes, and honorable sentiments are hereditary." Several cling to their status as part of this natural aristocracy and, like Adams's own "goo-goo" liberal friends, enthusiastically advocate reform. However, they are helpless, ineffectual amateurs in a society where, as one character puts it, "scum floats on the surface of politics."

Patronage and corruption have become the lifeblood of the nation. Presidential elections have decayed into mindless popularity contests: when the president and his wife appear at a party, they seem like "mechanical figures . . . their faces stripped of any intelligence [but] representatives of the society that streamed past them." Money and greed have replaced virtue and public-spiritedness as the motive forces in Washington. The most corrupt figure in the book, Senator Ratcliffe, is also the most powerful. He is a master politician precisely because he understands that "the issue now involved was not principle but power"; his followers understand that "their principle must be the want of principle." "In politics," Ratcliffe admits to his visitor Mrs. Lee, "we cannot keep our hands clean."

In listening to Ratcliffe, Mrs. Lee "felt as though she had gotten to the heart of politics, so that she could, like a physician with his stethoscope, measure the organic disease." That disease, she decides, is "moral paralysis . . . an atrophy of the moral senses by disuse." Was this paralysis the product of "moral lunatics" like Ratcliffe, or something larger? "Are we for ever to be at the mercy of ruffians and thieves?" she muses. "Is a respectable government impossible in a democracy?" The other sympathetic characters provide her with little help. When she asks Carrington (the spokesman for Henry Adams himself) if he would bring back the "old society" of the Virginia squirearchy of Jefferson and Washington to save the republic, he replies "What for? It could not hold itself up. General Washington himself could not save it. Before he died he had lost his hold in Virginia, and his power was gone." No amount of personal leadership, not even the best and the brightest, can withstand a corruption that has penetrated into the very workings of American society. No amount of reform can cleanse democracy, Carrington avers, "as long as the American citizen is what he is." The Bulgarian ambassador, Baron Jacobi, sums up the situation this way:

> In all my experience I have found no society which has the elements of corruption like the United States. The children in the street are corrupt, and know how to cheat me. The cities are all corrupt, as are the towns and counties and the State legislatures and judges. Everywhere men betray trusts both public and private, steal money, run away with public funds.

In one hundred years, Baron Jacobi predicts, Washington will become like Rome under the Medici popes, or Caligula. In despair and disgust, Mrs. Lee moves to Europe, leaving the New World for the old one, which at least has the courage to face up to its own corruption. She sighs, "Democracy has shaken my nerves all to pieces."

*Democracy* was a bestseller, both in the United States and in England, but Henry Adams never wrote a sequel. Instead, he threw himself into discovering how and when this disastrous transformation of America took place. His *History of the United States of America During the Administrations of Jefferson and Madison* appeared in nine volumes between 1889 and 1891. It was the product of twin personal tragedies that deepened his own pessimism: the suicide of his wife in 1887 and the death of his father. At the work's core was Adams's revelation of the moment when corruption replaced virtue in American history—when its original Anglo-Saxon legacy of freedom disappeared forever. That moment was the War of 1812, when the Founding Fathers' original ideal of America's world-historical role dissolved into a squalid scramble for land, money, and empire.

Adams detailed how Americans started the war against Britain and Canada out of desire to expand their borders, to create an empire not of liberty and "the march of mind," in John Quincy Adams's phrase, but of greed and conquest. In the process, America's natural aristocracy degenerated into either self-seeking demagogues, like Jefferson's former vice president Aaron Burr, or lackeys of the new wielders of industrial wealth. After 1815 America's physical and economic growth would continue unabated, but "the American people went to their daily tasks without much competition or mental effort . . . the result was a matter for a census rather than for history." Americans after 1815 presented "no evidence that the human being, any more than the ant and bee, was conscious of a higher destiny," Adams wrote bitterly. Progress would now be measured in purely mechanical rather than spiritual terms, symbolized by Robert Fulton's steamship. The new imperial, materialistic face of the American national character was fixed forever.[38] He quoted Jefferson's warning when the war against Britain was declared: "Our enemy has indeed the consolation of Satan on removing our first parents from Paradise; from a peaceable and agricultural nation, he makes us a military and manufacturing one."[39]

Adams's narrative of corruption in *The History of the United States* is driven by the impersonal historical forces that Comte and Darwin helped to define but were now colored by Adams's pessimism. In American history the "evolution of the race" becomes a "bloody arena" in which the struggle for life becomes the battle of nations and peoples for ultimate supremacy. Even powerful individuals, such as a Jefferson or a Madison, could leave no trace against the "contrary direction to modern civilization" or evade "the laws of Nature and instincts of life." Yet a single deterministic, Comtean-style law that would explain the decline of American civilization as a totality still eluded Adams. Then, four years later, when his brother Brooks presented him with a large, hastily written manuscript, he realized he had found it.

## BROOKS ADAMS: THE LAW OF CIVILIZATION AND DECAY

If America's political changes triggered Henry Adams's pessimism, its economic changes stirred Brooks Adams to take up the issue of "decline." Those changes had indeed been cataclysmic. In 1870 America's farms still produced more wealth than its factories; by 1900 industrial production was three times the value of agriculture. Within ten years of the Civil War, all the major personalities and institutions of the modern industrial age were suddenly in place. The transcontinental railroad was completed in 1869, and one year later John D. Rockefeller created Standard Oil Company in the oil fields of western Pennsylvania. The following year J. Pierpont Morgan founded Drexel, Morgan and Company and became the most powerful banker in the world. In 1876 Andrew Carnegie created the prototype of all industrial corporations, United States Steel, Thomas A. Edison opened his lab at Menlo Park and Alexander Graham Bell presented his first working telephone at the Philadelphia Centennial Exposition. The exposition itself stood as a striking symbol of the dominance of the engine and machine over the new American landscape.[40] During the same period the nation's population doubled. Most of the increase was due to the first great wave of mass immigration, bringing to American shores more than ten million people between 1860 and 1890. In the next wave, from 1890 to 1914, another fifteen million would join them, drawn from Russia and southern Europe and including large numbers of Jews.

These transformations were a double blow to a social and intellectual elite that had already been caught off guard by mass democratic politics. The power of corporations, trusts, and monopolies seemed as decisive and menacing a threat to traditional American values as Whisky Rings and machine politics. In the year following the Centennial Exposition a series of punishing railway strikes erupted, and large-scale financial panics broke out in 1873, 1893, and 1906. Industrial concentration, financial uncertainty, and labor unrest became the hallmarks of the Gilded Age (a name invented by Mark Twain)—the image suggesting glittering material splendor covering up a deep moral and social decay.

To young Albert Jay Nock growing up in New York, the country seemed to be in the grip of what Nock called "economism," which "interpreted the whole of human life in terms of the production, acquisition, and distribution of wealth." Its new motto was "Go and get it!" which was "the morale of the looter, the plunderer." Looking at the great figures of the new industrial age, the Carnegies, Rockefellers, and Fricks, Nock asked himself "whether any amount of wealth would be worth having if—as one most evidently must—if one had to become just like these men in order to get it. To me, at least, decidedly it would not."[41] Nock saw himself as being in general agreement with the other "highly developed minds" of his day, among whom he included William Dean Howells, Mark Twain, Walt Whitman, John Hay, Henry Cabot Lodge—and Henry and Brooks Adams.

A combination of moral outrage and intellectual snobbery prompted these men to turn against America's propertied class and millionaires—"a gaudy stream of bespangled, belaced, and beruffled barbarians," according to E.L. Godkin—and toward the labor movement, even in its more radical forms. The editor of *Harper's Monthly*, William Dean Howells, presented a strongly sympathetic view of radical labor in his widely read novels, as Henry James did in *The Princess Casamassima*. The latter appeared in 1886, the same year that seven policemen were killed by a bomb at an anarchist labor rally in Haymarket Square, Chicago. When the anarchists who spoke at the meeting were sentenced to death for murder, Howells, Henry Adams, and Oliver Wendell Holmes publicly pleaded for mercy for the condemned men. In response to the Haymarket sentence Howells said, "After fifty years of optimistic content with 'civilization' . . . I now abhor it." Howells believed that America could only save itself now if "it base[d] itself anew on a real equality."[42]

Literary figures and social reformers voiced concerns that would come to sound familiar over the next century. They condemned the highly visible poverty of urban slums and workers' tenements. They railed against the supposedly widening gap between rich and poor and lamented the disappearance of America's middle class. Henry George's *Progress and Poverty*, which became the bible of the Progressive movement, crystallized these worries. "The association of poverty with progress is the great enigma of our times," George explained to his readers. "It is the riddle which the Sphinx of Fate puts to our civilization, and which not to answer is to be destroyed."[43]

This was the riddle that perplexed Brooks Adams and that he set out to solve. Originally trained as a lawyer, he became attached to the same Comtean-Darwinian social determinism as his brother Henry (he and Henry would be co-founders of the American Social Science Association). In his own mind at least, Brooks Adams viewed the workings of American society without any false moral sentiment. In a stable civil order, Brooks Adams stated in an article for the *North American Review*, "laws are made by the strongest, and they must and shall be obeyed."[44] During his brief tenure as a teacher at Harvard Law School from 1882 to '83, Brooks helped found the school of legal thinking called legal realism, which would be most closely associated with his friend Oliver Wendell Holmes. For lawyers of the Holmes-Adams persuasion, the rule of law was "the natural enemy of anarchy and despotism," but also of the "incorporated power and greed" of men like the Morgans and Rockefellers.[45]

Brooks's interest in restraining the growth and power of private industrial capital drew him, as it did his older brother Henry, toward socialist and even Marxist ideas. Political or legal reform would never be enough by itself, he had concluded. Like the old-fashioned, naive faith in democracy, laissez-faire economic principles were no longer applicable in the modern age. Classical liberalism, with its "absurd" hopes for a free and equal society, Brooks explained, failed to account for the growth of power available in modern industrialized society, both in the private and the public sector. Free competition only enabled the large to devour the small, creating monopolies of private power that threatened the public good.[46] In a world that had evolved beyond laissez-faire, Brooks believed, the law and the national power of the state became the iron hoops that would hold a hypertrophied industrial society together, even as other forces—such as monopolies and trusts on the one side and anarchism and communism on the other—threatened to pull it apart.* Indeed, Brooks balefully explained to his brother, anarchy would be the inevitable result if the disequilibrium created by American industrial capitalism continued unabated.[47]

Brooks's warning led his brother to break with the Republican Party their father had helped to found. Brooks insisted that Republican presidential candidates were merely puppets of the monopolists and plutocrats, and as early as 1884 he tried to swing liberal and independent Republican colleagues like Henry Cabot Lodge, E.L. Godkin, and President Eliot to the Democratic Party. In 1892 Brooks and Henry actively campaigned for Democratic presidential candidate Grover Cleveland as the people's champion against Wall Street and its international banking allies. Brooks delivered a speech to the Tariff Reform League entitled "The Plutocratic Revolution," a stinging attack on what his friend and fellow patrician Theodore Roosevelt would later term "the malefactors

---

* As for American democracy—when President Eliot attended one of his lectures at the law school and remarked that Brooks did not seem to have much respect for democratic rule, Brooks burst out, "Do you think I'm a damned fool!"[48]

of great wealth." Brooks warned that the growth in the size and power of capitalist enterprises was feeding the forces of resentment among the poor and downtrodden. The new Populist Party, which drew support from midwestern and southern farmers as well as working people, would lead inevitably to revolution unless something were done to restrain the forces of economic competition and concentration.[49]

Then, in May 1893, the failure of the National Cordage Company sent the stock market into a tailspin. As if confirming Adams's warnings about the dangers of international capitalism, the British banking house of Baring, a major creditor for American businesses, collapsed at the same time. This prompted a massive hemorrhaging of capital and gold out of the country, and the financial panic turned into a full-scale depression. Over fifteen thousand businesses failed, while five hundred and seventy-two banks closed their doors and a full quarter of America's railroad capital went into receivership. It was the precursor of the crash of 1929, and for young progressive-minded intellectuals like Lincoln Steffens, who covered the events for New York's *Evening Post*, it was a lesson in the consequences of "unfettered" capitalism they would never forget.[50]

It was also a stern lesson for the Adams family. Like other affluent critics of capitalism past and present, they were heavily invested in it. The collapse of Boston's State Street Bank threatened to wipe out the Adams holdings. Henry Adams was in Europe when he received a letter from his brothers warning that they were all about to be made bankrupt. Henry rushed home to the family seat at Quincy on August 7. As it happened, the scare turned out to be nothing more: the family money was safe. But the trauma left its mark, especially on Brooks. Not long afterwards, he stopped his brother as they passed in the hall and gave him a large bundle of papers. "Please read this manuscript for me and tell me whether it is worth printing or whether it is quite mad," he said.[51]

Henry took it out into the garden and read it through as Brooks paced around his chair. No, Henry assured him when he had finished, the manuscript was not the "dream of a maniac." What Brooks had done was to put the events of the 1893 panic in a world-historical perspective worthy of a professional historian. Even more remarkably, he had accomplished what Henry had tried to do seven years earlier.

Brooks Adams had established a definitive "scientific" principle of social growth and decline in the modern age, which he called (and as his book was entitled) "the law of civilization and decay."

Brooks Adams later claimed that *The Law of Civilization and Decay* was not inspired by the 1893 panic and the near loss of the family fortune. Instead he insisted that the idea came to him on a visit in 1889 to the monumental Roman ruins at Baalbek in Syria. As he gazed at the massive capitals and fallen columns, "the conviction dawned on me . . . that the fall of Rome came about by a competition between slave and free labor and an inferiority in Roman industry."[52] The scene, of course, places Brooks in the grand historical tradition of Gibbon among the ruins on the Capitoline Hill and the pessimistic Romanticism of Volney or Gobineau. But it also echoed the opening of his brother's *History of the United States*, in which Henry Adams imagines a traveller to the Washington of 1800 gazing at the unfinished columns of the United States Capitol and reflecting on how a new Rome will rise up to the destiny of the old.

Both Adams brothers were convinced that the forces of economic expansion were dissolving America's unique status. Americans in the Gilded Age had become "like all other people," as their great-grandfather John Adams had mournfully lamented one hundred years earlier, "and shall do like other nations."[53] The redeemer nation was now an industrial and commercial empire like its older European counterparts. Therefore, both of them concluded, it must suffer the same inexorable eclipse. Brooks Adams told his brother he seriously considered calling *The Law of Civilization and Decay* "The Path to Hell."[54]

Brooks Adams had forged his brother's Comtean and Darwinian principles into an ironclad deterministic vitalism and then plunged it into the heart of civil society theory. The history of civil or commercial society is the history of money as a *physical* force, nothing more and nothing less. "As money accumulates, society concentrates into nations. As the amount of money dwindles, civilization decays." Brooks Adams abolished the crucial distinction Adam Smith and others had made between economic activity in its premodern and modern forms. There was no difference, because all forms of money-making were based on the same animal instincts, namely fear and greed. "At the moment of action, the human being almost invariably obeys an instinct, like an animal."

These hereditary instincts were governed by infallible physical laws, for "history, like matter, must be governed by law."[55] Fear and greed determine the individual's "rise and fall in the social scale," just as they dictate the rise and fall of the market. Those instincts also determine the rise and fall of nations in Brooks Adams's own version of Fortune's wheel, a repetitive cycle of expansion, concentration, and collapse.[56]

Adams's view of the economic history of the Roman Empire became a parable of the struggle between capital and labor in Gilded Age America. The concentration of wealth and growth of empire destroyed the Roman freeholder, who was, like the Jeffersonian agrarian yeoman and the Anglo-Saxon farmer, arms bearing and liberty loving. The disappearance of small farmers, Adams concluded, increased the power of the senatorial landowners and agricultural "capitalists." As the Roman people sank into serfdom and destitution, the senatorial class had to hire mercenary soldiers to defend their wealth and shore up an increasingly unstable frontier against Rome's enemies. The Roman martial spirit declined, the mercenary hirelings became dictators, the frontier collapsed, and the barbaric hordes poured into the empire. In Brooks Adams's theory, as Charles Beard later observed, Rome's "whole imperial, bureaucratic, centralized system dissolves into ruins" thanks to untrammeled capitalism.[57]

Then Brooks described how the Dark Ages descended on Europe for seven centuries. Under the barbarians, Europe's money economy abruptly ended. Then, slowly and painfully, the process of monetary concentration began again, first in medieval towns during the Crusades, then among the Medicis and other merchant princes of the Renaissance. In accordance with Adams's theory of money as energy, the extraction of bullion from the New World launched European civilization into the modern age, when the concentration of wealth and the concentration of state power went hand in hand, as in imperial Rome.

But now a crisis has again been reached. Britain's victory at Waterloo had marked the beginning of an age of even more concentrated energy and wealth, with British and Jewish international bankers dominating the European scene. In the nineteenth century, "capital is autocratic, and energy vents itself through those organisms best fitted to give [its power] expression," namely the modern business corporation. The vital instincts also decline in other spheres. "The scientific intellect is propagated, while the imagination fades, and the emotional, martial, and the artistic types of manhood decay." Meanwhile industrialization, fed by demand from the prosperous urban classes, depresses agricultural prices and the independent farmer disappears in Europe and America, just as he did in the age of Trajan.[58]

Then came what Brooks Adams considered to be the final blow to modern civilization: the adoption of the gold standard, first by Great Britain in 1876 and then in short order by the other leading industrialized countries.* The gold standard concentrated all the remaining vital energy of society in the hands of what his brother Henry maliciously termed "Wall Street, State Street, and Jerusalem." For Brooks Adams, the gold standard was simply the final victory of capitalist civilization over itself. The remaining characteristics and institutions of modern civil society—material affluence, free markets in goods and labor, the nation-state—would lose their remaining energy, bringing stagnation and collapse of which 1893 was only a foretaste. In the end, "the survivors of such a community" will lack the energy necessary to resuscitate the social process: the monopolistic power of gold and industrial wealth will have literally drained it out of them. "Because the energy of the race has been exhausted" it must "remain inert," Brooks Adams concluded in a chilling closing passage reminiscent of Gobineau, "until supplied with fresh energetic material by the infusion of barbarian blood."[59]

Brooks Adams's zero-sum law of vitality, and the deterministic direction of force, energy, and instinct, rendered the entire notion of civilization meaningless. All societies and all civilizations obey the same mechanical laws, regardless of origin, manners, or moral character.† Not only had America's claim to be the redeemer nation vanished; the very notion was an illusion. In societies past and present, "there is but one

---

* The intricacies of the political battle over bi-metallism in the 1890s cannot concern us here. However, Henry Adams made it very clear that his own prosilver stance sprang less from a concern for midwestern and southern farmers than from a hatred of large-scale capitalism (*Education*, p. 355), while Brooks's *Law of Civilization and Decay* first appeared in the United States as a prosilver pamphlet entitled *The Gold Standard*, in 1895.

† "The velocity of the social movement of *any* community is proportionate to its energy and mass, and its centralization is proportionate to its velocity" (emphasis added).

moral, the moral of success." Or as he grimly put it in a letter to his brother in 1898, "The form of society which perishes is always in the wrong, and the form of society which survives is always in the right."[60]

*The Law of Civilization and Decay* had an enormous impact on Henry Adams at the same time that he discovered Max Nordau's *Degeneration* in a Washington bookstore.[61] Henry was now convinced that there really was no hope left for America, Britain, and Europe—what other scholars were starting to call "Western" civilization. His despair anticipated later prophets of disaster like Paul Ehrlich. "Two [more] generations should saturate the world with population," Adams wrote in 1898, "and should exhaust the mines. When that moment comes, economical decay, or the decay of economical civilization should set in."[62] The Adams brothers agreed that for industrial societies the survival of the fittest meant the survival of the cheapest, with those nations that had the cheapest sources of labor and natural resources destined to prevail. Therefore Mexico must eventually outstrip the United States, as China and Asia would overtake Britain and Europe.[63]

They also saw, in true Adams fashion, the outline of a powerful conspiracy leading the United States and Western civilization to destruction. "England is as much governed by the Jews of Berlin, Paris, and New York, as her own native growth," Brooks wrote. "It is in the nature of a vast syndicate, and by control of London, they control the world." Henry pointed out that the Cleveland administration was trapped "between the Jews and the Gentiles" on Wall Street, while Brooks responded that the last great battle for control of the world's economic resources would have to be fought in America, since it was only in the United States that the "Jews" could count on an "exhaustless mine of gold."[64]

Theodore Roosevelt described Brooks's malicious melancholy during a visit to his home in the mid-1890s: "He is having a delightful time here, and simply reveling in gloom over the appalling social and civic disasters which he sees impending."[65] Henry, meanwhile, began formulating his own series of explicitly declinist "laws of dissipation." Drawing heavily on his brother's *Law of Civilization and Decay*, Henry also turned to two other, seemingly contradictory sources for inspiration. The first was Ernst Haeckel's *Riddle of the Universe*, with its suggestion that everything is expanding and moving toward an ever greater totality. The other was the second law of thermodynamics, the so-called law of entropy, which stated that the energy in the universe is finite and running down. Henry Adams happily concluded that the human race was stuck on an ever-accelerating evolutionary course that must end in extinction and death. Not only modern society but the planet and entire solar system were exhausting themselves of heat and energy. By 2025 at the latest, the planet would be reduced, like its sun and moon, to a cold and lifeless lump of matter hurtling through the nothingness of space.[66]

"I will not deny that the shadow of this coming event has cast itself on me. . . ." His yearning for a sacred refuge in the midst of impending chaos drew him to the European Middle Ages, inspiring his most famous historical work, *Mont-Saint-Michel and Chartres* (1904). Like his European Romantic counterparts, Henry Adams could only find safety from "the present evils of the world—its huge armaments, its vast accumulations of capital, its advancing materialism and spiritual degradation" in a kind of nostalgic withdrawal.[67] His hero Thomas Carlyle had said industrial society was in the grip of "the rapidest motion and self motion: with convulsive energy as if possessed by a Devil." Modern civilization's mindless energy and power, symbolized by the mighty turbine he had seen at the Chicago Exposition, stood in opposition to the spiritual serenity of the past, symbolized by the medieval cult of the Virgin Mary. "All the steam in the world could not, like the Virgin, build Chartres." However, Henry Adams refused to allow *Mont-Saint-Michel and Chartres* to be printed, except privately, until after his death. He made the same decision about his autobiography, *The Education of Henry Adams*. Like Burckhardt, he could see no cure for the ills he had diagnosed except resignation and withdrawal. In the face of the clamoring forces of modernity, he decided, "beyond a doubt, silence is best."

## FRONTIER, IMPERIALISM, AND THE POSTLIBERAL STATE

In 1893, the same year as the financial panic and the genesis of Brooks's law of civilization and decay, a young American historian named Frederick Jackson Turner presented a paper to his fellow historians entitled "The Significance of the Frontier in American History." Turner argued that the "winning of the West" was not just a part of American history but its central episode, just as it was central to America's progressive character and self-perception as the redeemer nation. The frontier had been, Turner declared, "the meeting point between savagery and civilization." But that boundary was dynamic rather than static. For three hundred years it had represented "a new field of opportunity, a gate of escape from the bondage of the past; and freshness, and confidence, and scorn of older society." In short, it had been the escape route from corruption. Through its promise of free and open land, the Western frontier had continually renewed Americans' sense of being a free and virtuous people.[68]

Now, however, for the first time in American history, the frontier was gone. With the disappearance of the last unclaimed public lands (the Cherokee Strip) in 1889 and events such as the capture of Geronimo and the battle of Wounded Knee, America's continuous expansion had ended. The frontier as a source of renewal was closed forever. The consequences, Turner warned, could be dire. Consciously or unconsciously echoing George Berkeley, Turner declared that "the west looks to the future, the east toward the past." America was in danger of becoming part of the past, rather than a beacon for the future.

Turner had restated the old problem that the Adams family had struggled with for generations—the redeemer nation confronting the inevitability of its own corruption—in terms of the end of America's "empire of liberty." The end of westward expansion meant the loss of the country's perpetual expansion, which Jefferson and others had envisaged as the guarantor of America's freedom and progress. With it the sense of American progress must also end, along with its claims of universal empire.

Or must it? Even as Turner was publishing his views, a coterie of influential Americans was beginning a search for a new empire of liberty beyond the shores of California to the Pacific. In 1893, Congress had debated annexing the Hawaiian Islands, where naval facilities were stationed at Pearl Harbor. The measure was defeated but as one of its proponents, Captain Alfred Thayer Mahan, warned, "Whether they will or no, Americans must now begin to look outward. . . . The United States by her geographic position must be one of the frontiers from which, as from a base of operations, the Sea Power of the civilized world will be energized."

Other believers in the "new imperialism" were key members of the Adams brothers' Boston circle, including Theodore Roosevelt, Henry Cabot Lodge, and Albert J. Beveridge. By 1898 the ranks included Brooks Adams himself. "The civilization which does not advance declines," Brooks wrote in 1900. Echoing Turner's frontier thesis, he explained that "the continent which . . . gave a boundless field for the expansion of Americans, has been filled" and must be supplanted by "the organization of a western empire which will stretch over into Asia."[69] With a Pacific empire, Brooks Adams had decided, America could save itself from the inevitable decline that he had confidently predicted only two years before. Some American enthusiasts for empire even began to speak of Hawaii and the Pacific Rim as the "New America."[70]

This idea of imperialism as renewal certainly animated Theodore Roosevelt. Roosevelt had written a review of *The Law of Civilization* for *Forum* magazine, praising it for its "very ugly element of truth. . . . The resemblance between the world as it is today, and the Roman world under the empire." Like Adams, Roosevelt was worried about the direction in which America was heading, with the growth of an urban underclass and its "deification of the stock-market, the trading-counter, and the factory."[71] But as a student of degeneration theory, he believed this decline could be reversed through healthy and vigorous action, both at the personal level—in hunting, shooting, riding, and outdoor exercise—and at the political level by America's taking on a more assertive role in world affairs. Empire, in Roosevelt's confident opinion, would provide a check on the "grave signs of deterioration in the English-speaking peoples."[72]

The pursuit of a Pacific empire could be self-renewing in another sense. It would force a harmony of domestic interests in American politics, including big capital, by redirecting society's energies outward. In a letter to Brooks Adams of July 18, 1903, Roosevelt noted that keeping Asian markets open to American industry necessarily meant maintaining control over the nation's links to those markets: "It is merely to state an axiom to say that the public must exercise some control over the great highways and avenues of commerce." If the capitalists—"the Morgan-Hill people and their sympathizers"—resist, the only alternative will be direct state ownership.[73] Far from being deliberate tools of capitalist interests, as critics charged, American colonies and dominions in far-off tropical places would be a salutary counterweight to those interests at home.

Here Henry and Brooks Adams parted company. Henry treated the Spanish-American War and "jingoism" as part of the same corrupting forces that had set in motion the War of 1812, and saw America's new rise to globalism as further evidence of its decline. Brooks saw it, on the contrary, as a sign of civilizational health. This empire, as he explained in *The New Empire* and *America's Economic Supremacy*, pointed to the United States's future as a military industrial state.

Brooks seized on the coming of war with Spain in 1898 as proof that his original theory of monetary concentration had in fact been premature; the final distribution of global energy and force had still not been achieved. By acquiring colonies from one "dying civilization" (Spain) and supplanting the economic power of another (Great Britain), the United States would be able to put off the onset of decline indefinitely. In the coming Darwinian struggle for world resources, success in empire-building would become the ultimate test of strength for modern civilizations.* However, if expansion were to cease, he argued, the only remaining outlet for virile and vital energies would be economic competition, which would only benefit the capitalists.†

In retrospect, many of Brooks Adams's predictions in *America's Economic Supremacy* seem remarkable. He predicted that the European balance of power, which had endured since the Congress of Vienna, would collapse into war fourteen years before it actually did. He prophesied the decline of Great Britain as a world power—"for nearly a hundred years

---

* "We are a conquering race," his friend Senator Albert Beveridge had proclaimed in a famous speech in Boston in April 1898. "In the Almighty's infinite plan . . . debased civilizations and debased races" must disappear "before the higher civilization of the nobler and more virile types of man." Quoted in B. Tuchman, *The Proud Tower* (New York, 1970), p. 177.

† A similar point of view inspired the liberal imperialists in England and the Pan-German League's lobbying on behalf of a German Empire in Africa and Asia. See H.C. Matthew, *The Liberal Imperialists* (Oxford, 1973).

England has acted as the containing power, or balance wheel, of the world . . . that time appears to have passed"—and the rise of Germany, as well as a future Anglo-Saxon alliance to counteract Germany's geopolitical ambitions. He even suggested that the great economic battle of the future would be between the West and the Pacific Rim. But when examined closely, the predictions turn out to be the flawed products of Brooks's own deterministic laws. For example, he insisted on casting Germany's future geopolitical role in the pseudoscientific jargon of his *Law of Civilization and Decay*: "The Germans cannot increase their velocity because they cannot extend their base, and augment their mass— we can and do." He envisaged the future Anglo-Saxon alliance centering not on the Atlantic but in India and Asia, while his discussion of the confrontation between East and West was couched in typical Orientalist terms.

To the very end, Brooks Adams remained tied to the assumption that a civilization, like a society, "is a complete living organism, with circulation, heart, and members." He even compared financial exchanges to the heart and commercial trade to the body's arteries.[74] Vitality, he earnestly argued, was busily flowing out of one such living organism, the British Empire, and into another, the United States. "The United States must shortly bear the burden England has borne," he wrote. "Few Americans can feel confident that the antiquated administrative machinery we have inherited from the last century is adapted to meet such a strain. In that case social reorganization may lie before us."[75]

If overseas expansion was to serve as an antidote to American decline, then it also required a new state to complement the new empire. A vastly expanded governmental machinery would have to marshal the resources, discipline, and power necessary for a competitive imperialism. Its organizing principle, Brooks added, would have to be state socialism. Brooks, like his brother Henry, did not see the advent of socialism in class terms; to put it crudely, both had too much to lose. Instead, socialism simply applied the same principles of efficiency to the state that they imagined had already been achieved in the private sector when monopoly capitalism replaced laissez-faire.[76] Like other postliberal thinkers in Europe and America, Brooks Adams was convinced that the twentieth century was about to unleash massive growth in the scale of power and the capacity for collective action. Size would become the key to everything. "From the retail store to the empire, success in modern life lies in concentration." In fact, government in the future would simply be "a gigantic corporation whose business is to materially benefit its members" through the power of administrative cadres and bureaucracies.[77]

Like many later Progressives, Adams lamented how far America had fallen behind other European countries in terms of growth in the size and power of government.[78] He was a particular admirer of Wilhelmine Germany, where the state managed to be both efficient and self-sustaining, while also imposing a military-style discipline over its members. He later welcomed America's entry into World War I in 1917 precisely because he believed it would force America to make the hard choices involved in building the omnipotent administrative state, as Germany already had.[79] In his novel *Democracy*, Henry Adams had evoked George Washington as the symbol of a graceful, aristocratic social and moral order that had vanished forever. By contrast, Brooks Adams evoked General Washington as an example of what the fusion of military and political power could accomplish in the future.

And who would run the new leviathan, America's military-industrial complex? It is not difficult to discern in Brooks Adams's "powerful administrative minds" a postliberal version of America's natural aristocracy, organizing and adjusting a relentlessly interventionist government in accordance with the dynamic social forces of the future. These best and brightest would not be cultivated gentlemen of letters, however. Instead, they would be a trained technocratic elite, "the highest vehicle of energy" in society; their watchwords would be "success," "adaptability," and "the maintenance of an open mind" in a world where "nothing is permitted to stand as fixed." Brooks Adams's technocracy anticipated on the one hand the views of Progressives such as Walter Lippmann and Herbert Croly, who looked forward to a classless American social democracy organized and run by the "best minds." On the other hand, it foreshadowed Oswald Spengler's engineers, technicians, and soldier-workers, men "with Prussian instincts" and "discipline, organizing power, and energy"—in effect, the new Fascist man of the twentieth century.[80]

## EPILOGUE: THE RISE OF AMERICAN RACIAL PESSIMISM

"Civilization's going to pieces. . . . I've gotten to be a terrible pessimist
about things. Have you read 'The Rise of the Coloured Empires' by this
man Goddard?"

"Why, no," I answered, rather surprised by his tone.

"Well, it's a fine book, and everybody ought to read it. The idea is if
we don't look out the white race will be—will be utterly submerged—
It's all scientific stuff; it's been proved."

"Tom's getting very profound," said Daisy.

—F. Scott Fitzgerald, *The Great Gatsby*

State socialism was one solution to the dark, seemingly inexorable
forces by which many in America felt hemmed in at the end of the century. Another grew out of the Anglo-Saxon thesis that Henry Adams
had brought to influential academic and political circles two decades
earlier. This solution pointed to race as the key to national decline. Its
proponents made Gobineau's Aryanist myth part of the American political scene for the first time, as well as other racialized versions of degeneration theory.

In its original version, the idea of "Anglo-Saxon democracy" did not
carry any sense of racial exclusiveness.[81] After all, once the Anglo-
Saxon house of liberty was established, it hardly mattered who occupied
it, just as long as they preserved the original owners' legacy of free and
responsible self-government. But what if the character of the succeeding owners was drastically and catastrophically different from that of the
original builders? What if the customs and habits needed to maintain as
well as build that house of liberty depended on certain inborn instincts,
which only those of Anglo-Saxon descent could bring to bear? These
were nagging questions that lent themselves to volkish conclusions as
well as volkish solutions.

In April 1894, Henry Adams read a book entitled *National Life and
Character*, which foresaw the eclipse of the white Aryan and Anglo-
Saxon races by other races from Asia, Africa, and the Middle East.
Henry Adams had to agree. "The dark races are gaining on us," he
mused with some relish, and the white races must either "reconquer the
tropics by war and nomadic invasion or be shut up, north of the fortieth
parallel." [82] Brooks Adams, too, had worried about infusions of "barbarian blood" polluting an "old native American blood," which was not re-
producing itself in sufficient numbers.[83] But true racial pessimism in

America gained real impetus when *economic* mobility—rampant capitalism and its "gaudy stream of bespangled, belaced, and beruffled barbarians"—seemed less of a threat to American civilization than the *ethnic* mobility of the millions of new immigrants who had arrived in the wake of industrialization.

The two were related, of course. After 1870 foreign-born immigrants formed the majority of the industrial labor force. The idea that immigrants joined a "melting pot" of American cultural identity was nonexistent in the nineteenth century. The great waves of immigration at the end of the century were, as one modern scholar has pointed out, "a major differentiating force" in American society, separating "those who bear the mark of foreign origin or inheritance from those who do not."[84] So even as Frederick Jackson Turner's virtue-renewing frontier was closing forever, strange-sounding, strange-looking, and even strange-smelling "aliens" were arriving in ever greater numbers, concentrating in ever denser masses in the cities and workers' tenements.

The reaction took the form of fears and degeneration and racial catastrophe. The original anti-immigrant movements, such as the Know-Nothings of the 1840s and '50s, had focused on the threat foreign-born Catholics posed to a Protestant chosen people. They ignored Jews and had no interest in other forms of ethnic distinction or identity.[85] Immediately after the Civil War, however, the "gathering hordes" from eastern and southern Europe "in the squalid quarters of great cities," with their "tiger passions" and alien customs, made members of America's natural aristocracy like Harvard professor Charles Eliot Norton feel like exiles in their own country.[86]

Writers began to point to a link between a freedom that was Anglo-Saxon in its historical foundations and an American Anglo-Saxon racial presence or "stock," which supplied the necessary "spirit" or "blood" to sustain that freedom in the face of disruptive change. A permanent line seemed to separate Anglo-Saxon "native Americans" (as they called themselves) on one side from foreigners and nonwhites on the other. The socialist Jack London, who evoked the threat of the "yellow peril," stood at one political end of this nativist consensus. Brooks Adams's patrician friend Henry Cabot Lodge stood at the other.

A keen student of degenerationist theorist Gustav Le Bon, Lodge took the Anglo-Saxon thesis he had learned as a student in Henry

Adams's seminar directly into politics. In 1894, the same year Nordau's *Degeneration* appeared, he helped to found the Immigration Restriction League. He evoked the threat to America's native Anglo-Saxon stock to mobilize support for strong anti-immigration legislation—although President Grover Cleveland promptly vetoed it. Lodge's principal targets were Slavs, Italians, and East European Jews ("the rotten, unsexed, swindling, lying Jews," in Henry Adams's own colorful phrase). Lodge, the Immigration Restriction League, and various Progressive spokesmen such as Josiah Strong and E.A. Ross saw these immigrant groups as literal carriers of degeneracy into the American population. Ross described the foreign immigrant in Lombrosian terms as "hirsute, short in stature . . . in every face there is something wrong." Allowing these inferior physical specimens into the country would have a catastrophic effect on "our pioneer stock," producing atavism, criminality, and disease in the major industrial cities. Lax immigration laws, Ross warned, amounted to "race suicide," a term he made into one of the most popular slogans of the next two decades.[87]

Henry Adams died in 1918, Brooks in 1923, and Lodge a year later. The generation that succeeded them turned to more potent support for their warnings about the threat posed by immigration to America's Anglo-Saxon heritage. Lothrop Stoddard, a Boston native and son of the distinguished lecturer and writer John L. Stoddard, had worked for Henry and Brooks's cousin Charles D. Adams in his law firm in Boston. He became attracted to the works of Madison Grant, a New York socialite and founder of the New York Zoological Society. Grant had published *The Passing of the Great Race* in 1916, borrowing heavily from Houston Chamberlain's *Foundations of the Nineteenth Century.* Grant's works and Stoddard's own *Clashing Tides of Color* (1922) and *Revolt Against Civilization* (1922) used the neo-Gobinian idea that the Teutonic race was the source of all civilization to give a new vitalist dimension to the idea of Americans as the chosen people.

Grant's *Passing of the Great Race* had purported to show that American history was the creation of the Teutonic, or "Nordic," race via its Anglo-Saxon branch. In *Conquest of a Continent* (1922), Turner's frontier becomes a Nordic saga, with Teutonic-American pioneers pressing on in their great westward migration with the same vitalistic energy as their original Aryan forebears and attaining their destined *Lebensraum.*

Now, Grant argued, the rising tide of non-Aryan immigration threatened their racial and cultural vitality. A drastic crisis required drastic solutions: "This generation must completely repudiate the proud boast of our fathers that they acknowledged no distinction in 'race, creed, or color,' or else the native American must turn the page of history and write: FINIS AMERICAE."[88]

Just as Grant borrowed heavily from Houston Chamberlain, so did Stoddard borrow heavily from Grant in *The Revolt Against Civilization*, adding generous doses of Lombrosian-style statistical surveys to prove that the new immigrants were systematically undermining the racial future of America.* Stoddard's Nordic type exhibited a remarkable fusion of neo-Gobinian and specifically American virtues. Nordic man was "at once democratic and aristocratic. . . . Profoundly individualistic and touchy about his personal rights, neither he nor his fellows will tolerate tyranny." He was naturally averse to degeneration: "He requires healthful living conditions, and pines when deprived of good food, fresh air, and exercise." His racial purity becomes the key to progress as well, since "our modern scientific age is mainly a product of Nordic genius." All the nations with high infusions of Nordic blood were, according to Stoddard, "the most progressive as well as the most energetic and politically able.[89]

But Stoddard also dared to confront the paradox that underlay the Gobinian confrontation between cultural vitality and civilization. Even as a healthy racial stock generates society's material wealth and cultural attainments, Gobineau had claimed, its openness to change and diversity sows the seeds of its own destruction. Ultimately the people discover that "their social environment has outrun inherited capacity." The Anglo-Saxon heritage cannot sustain itself in the future without its racial stock. (Grant was also a keen eugenicist.) "The more complex the society and the more differentiated the stock," Stoddard insisted, "the graver the liability of irreparable disaster."

Grant and Stoddard presented a frightening picture of the future, a neo-Gobinian oil sketch based on Brooks Adams's geopolitical vision.

---

* One graph, for example, indicated that the average Italian immigrant child, although supposedly white in skin color, had an IQ score only one point higher than that of most Negroes. See *The Revolt Against Civilization*, p. 63.

Western civilization's Nordic stock would be overwhelmed by inferior Mediterranean and "Alpine" (meaning south-central European) types, while vast "colored empires" would arise from Asia, India, and the Middle East to Africa. As always with racial pessimist fears, a drastic crisis required drastic solutions. Grant embraced eugenics as the corrective to racial decline. Stoddard turned to an organization he helped to bring to his native Massachusetts and for which he served as court philosopher: the Ku Klux Klan.[90] The Klan's explosive growth in the early '20s from a moribund ex-Confederate terrorist group into a national movement was driven precisely by this fear that immigration was threatening the end of Wasp America. The new Klan, with its large base north of the Mason-Dixon line, had as its principal target not blacks (who were still a tiny minority in northern cities) but Jews, Slavic Bolsheviks, and other degenerate foreign-born elements. Stoddard's racial pessimism gave the Klan's motto, "one hundred percent Americanism," the trappings of a struggle for the soul of Western civilization. The Klansman of the '20s did not see himself as a racist redneck. He was the guardian and shield of a civilization whose most precious jewel was the American ideal of freedom. He was, in effect, America's new natural aristocrat.

He is recognizable in Scott Fitzgerald's Tom Buchanan from *The Great Gatsby*, which was written as the Klan craze was just passing its peak. We do not know if Buchanan is a member of the Klan, of course, but in real life he could well have been (in 1922 even President Warren G. Harding, a man respected for his "liberal" views on the American Negro, had become an honorary member).[91] With his gloomy view of the future of the West and his pretensions to a modern scientific understanding of the relations between race and culture through "that man Goddard" (Lothrop Stoddard, obviously), Buchanan captures the new American racial pessimism and its hunger for a redemptive solution to the threat of decline. In the end, the solution came in the form of bureaucratic regulation. An alarmed Congress passed new restrictive immigration laws in 1921 and 1924, which not only excluded aliens from Asia and southern Europe but also attempted to fine-tune America's racial stock by encouraging immigration from northern European nations.[92]

However, the neo-Gobinian craze and the Klan faded almost as quickly as they had begun. After World War II and the Holocaust, both anti-Semitism and racial theories fell into deep disrepute, and nativist sentiments lost ground to the idea of America as "a nation of immigrants" (the title of a book by the young senator John F. Kennedy). The last American neo-Gobinians took up the battle on a different front: that of white versus black. Self-educated and brilliantly mad, Francis Yockey committed suicide in prison in 1960. His 600-page *Imperium* (1948) became the bible of the neo-Nazi movement of George Lincoln Rockwell and is dedicated to the spirit of Adolf Hitler, "the hero of the twentieth century."[93] Yockey's picture of modern society—"the life of the material . . . of power, giant economies, armies and fleets"—and his conviction that a hierarchical national socialism imposing a discipline of work and duty was the prescription for its salvation—are strongly reminiscent of Brooks Adams (just as Adams's law of civilization and decay would resurface in the economic theorizing of Lyndon Larouche).

Yockey was also as deeply ambivalent about America's role in history as any of the Adamses had been. It promoted on the one hand the energies and ideals of Anglo-Saxon individualism and on the other a false materialism that "dissolves the whole collective life into a miserable, soulless, endless battle for money." In the end, however, Yockey's redeemer nation turns out to be the Aryan nation, that "blond and strong-willed primitive stratum" that he insisted was the foundation of all Western culture.

Ernest Siever Cox enjoyed a longer career as the founding father of the white supremacist movement, from the publication of *White America* in 1925 until his death in 1963. Cox rediscovered in an American context all the elements of Gobineau's original analysis of Western decline. He even managed to recover some of the Romantic vitalism of early racial theories. "The white man is the sun that lights the world," he exclaims at one point, "the luster of other races is but reflected glory." Cox's racial history of America involved many of Gobineau's themes, such as a dominant civilizing Aryan aristocracy (the early American colonists) and the racial threat posed by Christianity in its encouragement of racial mixing.

However, Cox no longer recognized that racial threat in inferior Mediterranean or so-called Alpine types. His obsession was with the "negroidization" of America, which he believed required more drastic solutions than simply segregation or institutionalized white supremacy.

The only permanent solution, to Cox's mind, was to return all American Negroes to Africa and allow new waves of white Teutonic pioneers to spread into the empty spaces—in effect recreating Turner's American frontier, now preserved forever through racial purity.[94]

As it happened, Cox would find support for this plan from a strange and surprising quarter.

## CHAPTER 6

# BLACK OVER WHITE

## W.E.B. Du Bois

The future will, in all reasonable probability, be what colored men make it.

—W.E.B. Du Bois, *The Negro*, 1915

It will be a terrible day when black men draw the sword to fight for their liberty, and that day is coming. . . . the day of the war of the races.

—Marcus Garvey, 1919

In 1889, just as the second volume of Henry Adams's *History of The United States* was appearing in Boston bookstores, a young undergraduate arrived at Harvard College. Small and elegant, with aristocratic manners and a command of Latin, Greek, and German, he held the kind of clearheaded and "realistic" political views that a Brooks Adams would have approved and admired. His role model was Otto von Bismarck, chancellor of Germany, whose career demonstrated "what a man can do if he will." He also suffered no doubts about himself: he told one of his professors that he had chosen to go to Harvard because "I foresaw that such discipline would best fit me for life. . . . I believe foolishly, perhaps, but sincerely, that I have something to say to the world. . . ."[1] The only thing that distinguished him from the other well-bred young men milling about Harvard Yard was that William Edward Burghardt Du Bois had black skin.

W.E.B. Du Bois stands at the source of contemporary thinking about race and culture. Despite Martin Luther King's reputation, Du Bois remains the paramount African-American thinker: the very currency of the term "African-American" reflects his influence. Working tirelessly as a sociologist, historian, and journalist, Du Bois transformed America's "Negro problem" from a residual issue of Civil War and sectionalism into the central paradigm for interpreting not only American history but the history of Western civilization itself. In doing so he created a new secular cultural identity for the non-Western world that stood in direct opposition to the modern West. In 1903, Du Bois predicted that "the problem of the twentieth century will be the problem of the color line." What Lothrop Stoddard most feared in his book *The Clashing Tides of Color* was precisely what Du Bois anticipated and desired. What gave Du Bois this sense of confidence about the future? It was the growing pessimism about the fate of the West among Western intellectuals themselves. Western civilizations, he learned from his teachers at Harvard and the University of Berlin, was a society at war with its own soul.

European and American thinkers alike were regrouping in the face of fears of degeneration and social decay. Brooks and Henry Adams in America, Emile Durkheim and Gustav Le Bon in France, Francis Galton and Benjamin Kidd in England, Adolf Wagner and Gustav von Schmoller in Germany (both of whom would have a decisive influence on Du Bois's own outlook), and many other scholars and academics, were busy confronting what they perceived to be the limits and the human costs of their own modern industrial society, what Durkheim termed "hypercivilization." Everyone was searching for an explanation for what was happening and for a solution.

Race theory, in either its neo-Gobinian or its "scientific" guise, provided both. Du Bois wrote his most influential works at a time when eugenics and racist doctrines were taking Europe and the United States by storm. Skin color was becoming a badge of civilization or the lack thereof. More and more respectable thinkers were accepting that white skin signified inner vitality and the capacity to move civilization forward against the inevitable undertow of degeneration. Conversely, dark or "colored" skin (which particularly sensitive observers believed to include the complexions of Europe's Jews) signified an absence of, or even a threat to, those qualities.

What Du Bois did, by various stages and strategies, was to turn those claims upside down and in effect revise the color line. Whether framed in terms of his theory of a Negro "talented tenth," or his Pan-African nationalism after 1911, or his hopes for a Marxist overthrow of imperialism in the 1930s, Du Bois's underlying assumption was the same. Africans, Asians, native American Indians, and other "persons of color" possessed an artistic and cultural creativity distinct from, or even superior to, that of their white antagonists and oppressors. They exhibited a deeper inner vitality and humanity that Du Bois's German mentors called the "life-soul," or *Seeleleben*, and Du Bois would translate as "soul." As a character explains in Du Bois's novel *Dark Princess*, "the darker peoples are the best—the natural aristocracy, the makers of art, religion, philosophy, life, everything"—he adds significantly—"except the machine."

Du Bois's view of race was more complicated than this blast of typical romantic Orientalism suggests, although, as we will discover, he owed more to that Orientalist heritage than some current admirers are willing to admit. His theories, however, were based on his reaction against the doctrines of white supremacy circulating at the time and against what he saw as their most significant consequence: the growth of European colonial empires. To Du Bois, imperialism was the West's most characteristic product, the natural outgrowth of European civilization's own peculiar qualities. And its evils were now the evils of the West—including the United States, a nation created and sustained by imperialism's institutional predecessor, slavery.

In 1914, Du Bois and other non-European nationalists, such as Mohandas Gandhi of India and the young Marcus Garvey of Jamaica, still lived in a world in which 80 percent of the earth's land mass was dominated by Europeans or their descendants. The outlook for freedom was bleak, to say the least. But what if that dominance, and imperialism itself, bore the marks not of an ascending, but a *declining*, Western civilization? That was the question Du Bois asked himself, and in the process of answering it he gave racial pessimism a new and wholly different meaning.

## W.E.B. DU BOIS: RACE AND CIVILIZATION IN AMERICA

Like Henry and Brooks Adams, W.E.B. Du Bois was a New Englander, born in 1868 in Great Barrington, Massachusetts, where his mother's family had lived as "free blacks" since the American Revolution. Free blacks constituted 12 percent of the African-American population in antebellum America in the North and the South combined. Although they were subject to various forms of petty discrimination and in some states were not allowed to vote, many free blacks were prosperous and became a fixed part of civic life in cities such as Boston and New York, as well as in small towns like Great Barrington. One of Du Bois's grand-fathers had been a well-to-do landowner; the other was a retired merchant in New Bedford, Massachusetts.[2] Alexander Du Bois's aristo-cratic bearing and opulent home in New Bedford, with its gleaming silver plate, cut-glass decanters, and lace tablecloths, always remained for his grandson a glittering vision of what successful blacks in America might achieve.

The whole issue of race in nineteenth-century America and the South hinged on the complicated issue of white supremacy as a social doctrine, which Jim Crow symbolized and perpetuated. In fact, there were four types of racial thinking circulating in America when Du Bois was growing up, each with a distinct origin and its own social implica-tions.

The first was the color line that applied to all slave-owning societies, not only the American South but also the Caribbean, Brazil, and Latin America, in which a hierarchy of skin color defined social status. A gamut of traditions and taboos secured these color caste societies, with whites on top and those with the darkest skin on the bottom. The prod-uct of long-established practice rather than disembodied theory, these traditions would survive in America in ritual lynchings for racial trans-gressions and in an obsession among many affluent blacks with having light skin and straight hair. It was an obsession from which Du Bois (who was very light-skinned) himself was not immune.[3]

This was understandable, since the color line was an unambiguous barrier but also a permeable one. Thanks to racial mixing, light skin could serve almost as well as white. The result was a residual category of persons of Negro ancestry whose skin was light enough for them to "pass" as white. A large and largely free mulatto class was part of all slave societies, including the Deep South. It was a class that, thanks to the color line, enjoyed rights and privileges denied to unfree blacks.[4] Du Bois himself came from just such a light-skinned mixed-blood family, which had emigrated to America from Haiti. His idea in the 1910s of the "talented tenth" of the Negro population one day leading their race to liberation dimly reflected the long-standing aspirations of this mulatto elite.

Superimposed on the color line was the second way of thinking about race, the "race science" of the 1840s and '50s promoted by Robert Knox and James Hunt in Britain and by Josiah Nott and George Glidden in the United States.[5] These race scientists claimed to prove that white and Negro, and hence master and slave, were in fact distinct species, as distinctly superior and inferior as monkey and man. This pre-Darwinian "proof" of white supremacy remained largely theoretical, and although glancing through Josiah Nott's *Types of Mankind* may have provided additional comfort to some thoughtful Carolina planter, the ideas it contained bore no real connection to the realities of slave society.* Nott's translation of Gobineau's *Essay on the Inequality of the Races*, published in 1859 on the eve of the Civil War, excited neither interest nor a popular audience. However, the arguments remained available for later use, and when the popular clamor for segregation began to grow at the end of the century, Nott and Glidden seemed to support the conclusions of more topical books such as Charles Carroll's *The Negro a Beast* (1900).

The third type of racial thinking was exemplified in the racial theories of conquest and expansion borrowed from Europe and transplanted onto American soil, including the Anglo-Saxon thesis. These theories tended to divide nations or "races" (both white and nonwhite) into the categories of stronger and weaker, and inevitably of superior and inferior. Much has been made of this Romantic nationalism as the foundation for racism in modern America.[6] But its guiding force, even in its most chauvinistic forms, always remained historical rather than biological. The destiny of a "founding race," such as the Anglo-Saxons or Teutons, and the ethnic struggles that underlay its development—Franks

---

* In fact, Nott and Glidden argued that since whites should not live in the natural tropical habitats of nonwhites, plantation slavery in the South was doomed.

versus Gauls, Normans versus Anglo-Saxons, Anglo-Saxons versus Celts, Germans versus Slavs—were played out in the arena of political institutions and geopolitical conflicts. Compared to events on this scale, the issue of status as defined by physical difference was too puny and too unstable to carry any weight. To the Romantic nationalist, skin color obeyed the laws of history rather than vice versa.

But this kind of Romantic racial thinking did affect concrete racial issues in one important way. It pressed members of the nation together as equals, lifting its lowest members over the traditional social barriers of class or social status and creating a new democratic solidarity. As this solidarity overthrew social barriers between co-nationals, it erected new ones against outsiders. Rousseau had anticipated, even welcomed, this development as part of his free (and anti-Enlightenment) ideal republic. "Every patriot hates foreigners," Rousseau wrote in *Emile, or On Education.* "Among strangers the Spartan was selfish, grasping, and deceitful, while peace, harmony, and brotherhood ruled within his walls."

It also opened the door for the fourth and most forbidding racial perspective, a racial pessimism derived from Gobineau and his German followers, and now sharpened by Darwinian and degeneration theory. By the end of the nineteenth century, this European-style racial thinking had found its way into American public life thanks to anti-immigration and anti-Semitic sentiment. It had gloomily pointed out the dangers inherent in an unsupervised multiethnic society. Although a relative newcomer to the United States, racial pessimism would invigorate and galvanize traditional American thinking about race in both the North and the South in the 1890s. It cast blacks not merely as inferior, but as a direct challenge to civilization's survial.[7]

Racial nationalism, like Aryanism, appealed to a remote, hypothetical past; but racial pessimism pointed to what was happening before one's very eyes. Issues such as racial mixing or whether free blacks should be allowed to vote suddenly became charged with vast significance. Mulattoes were no longer light-skinned Negroes, but degenerate whites, corrupted by black blood. Once this view was superimposed on earlier ways of seeing race, it generated a cultural outlook more racialized than at any time in history, in Europe but particularly in the United States. Thomas Dixon's best-selling novels romanticizing the Ku Klux Klan, such as *The Leopard's Spots: A Tale of the White Man's Burden*

(1902) and *The Clansman* (1905), and the national fascination with D.W. Griffith's *Birth of a Nation* in 1915 reflected flourishing fears about "race suicide."

It was W.E.B. Du Bois's fate to grow up and receive his schooling just as this racialized outlook reached its climax. At his high school in Great Barrington, he learned the Aryanist Anglo-Saxon version of American history from his principal, Frank Hosmer. At the same time at Fiske University, a leading black college, he encountered the sons and daughters of affluent African-American mulatto families, who received a humanist education in Greek and Latin, science and mathematics, and who thought of themselves as much the members of a social elite as any Boston Brahmin or New York Knickerbocker. As the Fiske *Herald* proclaimed in 1889, "We are not the Negro from whom the chains of slavery fell a quarter of a century ago. We have learned what the privileges and responsibilities of citizenship are."[8] Yet that same year the first Jim Crow laws were implemented in Florida. They soon spread to the other states of the former Confederacy. These laws would ruin that natural black aristocracy that Fiske had cultivated and to which Du Bois belonged, transforming its members into second-class citizens and leaving them at the mercy of poor-white voters and mobs. It was a blow that Du Bois would never forgive and to which he would return again and again. A recurring image in his later writings is the humiliation of the segregated railway car, in which well-to-do blacks (such as himself) are forced to ride in filth and squalor while the lowest white farmhand travels in comfort. The black person in America, as he summed it up later, "is the person who travels third class."

Du Bois managed to retain this elitist self-image when he entered Harvard on a scholarship. Prim and proper, he presented himself as a cultivated gentleman of what his teacher George Santayana called the genteel tradition. He was conservative in his politics—he had applauded the harsh reprisals following the Haymarket bombing three years earlier, which men like Oliver Wendell Holmes and William Dean Howells had publicly protested—but sensitive and passionate on issues of race. The automatic association between antiracism and leftist politics did not yet exist. For Du Bois and others with enlightened views on the "Negro question," violent antiblack feelings were associated with the populism of demogogic politicians like Tom Watson and "Pitchfork

Ben" Tillman. It was easy for members of a natural black aristocracy to conclude that "vulgar democracy" was revealing its own true face both in Jim Crow laws and in the brutal and irrational actions of the lynch mob.[9]

Harvard did nothing to change Du Bois's views on these and other matters. Instead, Du Bois's intellectual transformation, and his radical recasting of the relation between race and civilization, began elsewhere, in *fin de siècle* Germany.[10]

## DU BOIS IN GERMANY, 1892–1894

Du Bois arrived in Germany as a scholarship student at a critical time in the newly unified nation's history. Wilhelm II had dismissed Du Bois's old idol, Bismarck, and installed the liberal Count Caprivi as chancellor. Caprivi cut agricultural tariffs and nudged the German industrial economy in the direction of free trade. He experimented with what today would be called "industrial policy," and with social welfare programs such as workers' compensation and unemployment insurance. In its approach to domestic as well as foreign affairs, imperial Germany expressed the new postliberal confidence in the ability of the national state to reshape and even reorganize industrial society.

Du Bois became a great admirer of Germany's postliberal direction. He even grew a Kaiser Bill mustache to salute his new hero and role model, and he "thrilled at the sight" of the kaiser on parade down Unter den Linden. Du Bois also found that in Germany he was free from the kind of racial discrimination and petty humiliations he had had to endure at home. Everywhere he was unquestioningly accepted for what he wanted to be: a serious and brilliant young scholar with exquisite manners and striking masculine looks. Released from the "hard iron hand" of American race prejudice, as Du Bois put it, he discovered in himself the stirring of a sense of autonomy and personal destiny. In February 1893 he wrote in his diary:

> Is it egoism—is it assurance—or is it the silent call of the world spirit that makes me feel that I am royal and that beneath my scepter a world of kings shall bow. The hot dark blood of that forefather—born king of men—is beating at my heart—I am either a genius or a fool.[11]

That new sense of inner freedom may have made him even more receptive to the exciting ideas circulating among his teachers at the University of Berlin, particularly the two men who had helped to shape
Germany's new postliberal outlook, Gustav von Schmoller and Adolf
Wagner.

Founders of the German Social Policy Association in 1872,
Schmoller and Wagner led a group called the "armchair socialists," who
rejected laissez-faire liberalism and called for a new "ethical economics."
They viewed entrepreneurial capitalism as the amoral "pursuit of Mam-
mon," devoid of any sense of social responsibility or moral uplift.[12] Like
New Liberals in England and Progressives in America, they worried
about a growing disparity between rich and poor in industrial society.
Schmoller, Wagner, and their adherents regularly compared modern industrial workers to slaves (which undoubtedly struck a responsive chord
with Du Bois). "Hunger makes almost a perfect substitute for the whip,"
wrote K.J. von Rodbertus-Jagetzow in *Shedding Light on Social Questions*
(1875), "and what was formerly called fodder is now called wages." If
one left the banker or steel manufacturer to his own devices, the armchair socialists argued, his greed for profits would force the other social
classes to turn to revolution and extremism. Echoing Brooks Adams's
concerns, they asserted that a corrective force was needed, and this had
to be the modern state.

Adolf Wagner pushed hard for the complete nationalization of Germany's major industries and accepted the designation of armchair socialist with pride. To Wagner's mind, there was no such thing as private
enterprise: all forms of economic production involved the exercise of
public power and therefore required public supervision and control.
Schmoller, who became Du Bois's true mentor in Berlin, was less convinced that statism was the answer. But he was sure that the "free market" was an institution whose time was past.

Far from being a reflection of universal human needs and desires,
Schmoller wrote, market economies occupied a very small and limited
space in the overall scheme of human history. "The idea that economic
life has always been a process mainly dependent on individual action . . .
satisfying individual needs, is mistaken." Now an alternative model for
economic life was desperately needed. "We preach neither the upsetting
of science nor the overthrow of the existing social order," Schmoller

wrote in 1872, "but we do not wish to allow the most crying abuses to become daily worse." A tremendous crisis would strike the industrial West unless it dissolved the inequities and private concentrations of power that modern capitalism seemed to entail.[13]

Schmoller's image of a laissez-faire capitalism doomed to self-destruction deeply impressed Du Bois, as did the armchair socialists' shining ideals of a planned economy and "scientific control" of industry. They also impressed a slightly later generation of German students, including the young Oswald Spengler.* Spengler and Du Bois also understood that the objections to capitalism were not entirely, or even principally, economic. Everyone agreed that a free market economy produced more material wealth, more goods and services, than any of its predecessors. The most important objections were social and cultural. Schmoller and Wagner worried that the rapid expansion of industrialization would displace the cultural center of German society, its farmers, artisans, and peasants. So by a strange twist, Du Bois's teachers (particularly Adolf Wagner) found themselves, despite their progressive views, the political allies of reactionary volkish ideologues such as Ludwig Schemann.[14] That unlikely alliance reflected a deeper consensus among German intellectuals regarding the conflict between culture and civilization, or *Kultur* and *Zivilisation*. No discussion of Du Bois's own ideas can be complete without an understanding of that basic conceptual conflict, which was so important and so dear to the German academic tradition.

In many ways it was an updated version of the old split between virtue and Fortune or virtue and corruption.† *Zivilisation* was the world of politeness and sophistication, but also of commerce and urban society. It was constantly changing, materialistic, and even superficial (the French were great exemplars of *Zivilisation*, just as they were the first to coin the term "civilization"). *Kultur*, by contrast, was permanent and spiritual. One of Schmoller's students, sociologist Georg Simmel, ex-

---

* Defenders of the free market in the German-speaking world made up one last embattled bastion at the University of Vienna. There classical economists like Conrad Menger and Eugen von Böhm-Bauwerk passed on their belief in the virtue of free enterprise and the dangers inherent in a command economy to a generation of students that included Ludwig von Mises and Freidrich Hayek. (See Chapter 1.)

† See Chapter 1.

plained it this way: "We speak of culture whenever life produces certain forms which it expresses and realizes itself: works of art, religion, technologies, laws and innumerable others." When Burckhardt had spoken of culture, he meant it in precisely this sense, which included the achievements of civilization in the normal use of the term.

But *Kultur* could also be used in the anthropological sense, to signify the artistic, literary, and material heritage of an historical people, a *Volk*. As one commentator put it, "the concept of *Kultur* delimits," stressing national differences and group identities and histories.[15] Early German Romantics such as J. G. Herder had proposed that the *Volk* had produced a living "folk culture" that, despite its humble beginnings among peasants and artisians, defined all "true" German art; poetry, epic, music, and myth.[16] Folk culture, then, contained the seeds of the *Volksgeist* (or "folk-spirit") of the German people.

Extreme nationalists like Paul de Lagarde seized on this idea, linking *Zivilisation* to the Jews and other undesirable foreign elements. However, even serious social scientists like Schmoller, Adolf Wagner, Friedrich Ratzel, and, somewhat later, Ernst Troeltsch and Georg Simmel, all agreed that the modern age was the triumph of superficial civilization over an organic, transcendent culture; Georg Simmel defined the entire nineteenth century as "the disintegration and perversion of *Kultur.*"[17] Ferdinand Tönnies produced a landmark study contrasting forms of social organization based on communal purpose and organic solidarity, or *Gemeinschaft*, and those based on self-interested utility and the application of means to ends, or *Gesellschaft*. The history of the modern West, in Tönnies's view, could be summed up as the advance of *Gesellschaft*, symbolized by the industrial corporation, at the expense of *Gemeinschaft*, the world of the village and small town—which also happened to be the seedbed of *Kultur.*[18]

Another group of German university professors who profoundly influenced Du Bois, the so-called Leipzig school of historical geographers, such as Friedrich Ratzel, Wilhelm Wundt, and Leo Frobenius, epitomized this declinist version of cultural history. Modernity, they claimed, took away the *Volk*'s organic solidarity, its folk-soul, or *Volksseele*. Ratzel suggested that the rural peasant and artisan engaged in a diverse range of activities that produced a well-rounded personality conducive to *Kultur*, while the worker in a Stuttgart factory or Silesian coalfield was chained to the "monotonous, repetitive turn of the cogwheel" of the machine.[19] This industrial version of Fortune's wheel made him an affectless automaton. Dragged from his original homeland, cut off from the social forces that made for cultural health, the individual in industrial society found himself alone and afraid.

In his own way, Du Bois gathered up these ideas from the German academic tradition and fed them back into the race issue at home. Schmoller had encouraged him to embark on a new "scientific" study of race relations, which resulted in his first important book, *The Philadelphia Negro*. The conflict between culture and civilization also underlies *The Souls of Black Folk*, even as Du Bois adapted Ratzel's theories to explain the experience of blacks in white society. On his return to the United States in 1894, Du Bois launched black American intellectual life in a new, volkish direction. In an 1897 speech entitled "The Conservation of the Races," he explained that history was the story of eight great races—Slavs, Teutons, Anglo-Saxon English, Latins, Semits, Hindus, Mongolians, and Negroes—"each striving in its way to develop for civilization its particular message, its particular ideal." American blacks served as "the advance guard" of that Negro race, "a vast historic race that from the very dawn of creation has slept, but half awakening in the dark forests of the African fatherland."[20]

But whereas in Germany racial and neo-Gobinian doctrines were essentially attacks on modern *Zivilisation*, Du Bois lumped racism and modernity together as allies. He became convinced that for the Negro and other nonwhite peoples, notions of *Volksgeist* and racial solidarity could be useful counterweights against "the whiteness of the Teutonic today" and point the way toward a new black nationalism.

## MANIFEST BLACK DESTINY: DU BOIS AND BLACK NATIONALISM

The dominant figure on the American black nationalist scene was the Reverend Alexander Crummell. "Tall, frail, and black he stood," Du Bois wrote later, "with simple dignity and an unmistakable air of good breeding."[21] Born in New York as a free black, educated at Yale and Cambridge, Crummell had for nearly four decades led a chorus of black intellectuals advocating the return of black Americans to Africa in order to discover a glorious new destiny, both for themselves and for the

so-called Dark Continent. While Crummell and his fellow Negro nationalists—Bishop Henry M. Turner, Martin Delany, and Edward W.
Blyden—failed to set off the great migration that they desired, they did
inspire many young black intellectuals with the vision of a black man's
Africa as powerful as, if not superior to, modern European civilization.

They exuded the same optimistic liberal nationalism that had flourished in European and American intellectual circles before 1848. Crummell preached what amounted to a black version of Manifest Destiny.
"The principle of growth and mastery in a race, a nation or people, are
the same all over the globe," he argued. Just as Anglo-Saxons and Germanic Teutons had forged a modern society out of the soil of their native land, so would "the destined superiority of the Negro" proceed
along similar lines in Africa. From the free state of Liberia, he predicted,
a race of "adventurous, enterprising colored men" would spread "religion and the great purposes of civilization" across the African continent.[22] Native African culture did not fare very well on Crummell's
scale of civilized values or indeed on that of other "civilizationist" nationalists.* Their goal was to raise the masses of the African continent
to full civic consciousness. This required a powerful outside agency,
whether black or white. Much as he detested European imperialism,
Crummell considered it far preferable to the primitive conditions that
had prevailed in Africa before Europeans arrived. Bishop Henry Turner
even saw slavery as a blessing in disguise, because it had taken blacks
out of savagery and thrust them into the modern world.[23]

Nineteenth-century black nationalists steadfastly rejected any notion of white supremacy and stressed black racial pride. In Bishop Henry
Turner's words, "Every colored man who is not proud of himself, his
color, his hair . . . is a monstrosity . . . and does not deserve the breath
he breathes, much less the bread he eats." At the same time, Crummell
and his counterparts were unashamed of the cultural debt they believed
black people owed to whites. Crummell saw Christianity, science, philosophy, and the rules of civilized moral conduct as gifts that would ultimately transform the lives of blacks as well as whites. The last speech he

---

* The important exception was Edward Blyden, who defended indigenous African culture and held
to the apocalyptic vision of the end of white civilization. H.R. Lynch, *Edmund Wilmot Blyden: Pan-
Negro Patriot.*

ever gave, one that Du Bois heard at the Negro Academy in Washington in 1897, was characteristically titled "Civilization, the Primal Need of the Race." Crummell told his audience that for black men to raise themselves to the same level as their former white masters they had to harness the forces of progress:

> Uplifting the crudeness of laws, giving scientific precision to morals and religion; stimulating enterprise, extending commerce, creating manufactures . . . producing revolutions and reforms; humanizing labor; meeting the minutest human needs . . . All these are the fruits of civilization.

Without them, he warned, blacks would lose their place "in the world of culture and enlightment."[24]

Du Bois took to heart Crummell's warning that American blacks "are a nation set apart in this country."[25] Yet Du Bois's Germanic perspective led him to reject Crummell's optimistic civilizationist thesis out of hand. To his mind, Crummell seemed to worship *Zivilisation* in its most superficial form. In modern civilization, Du Bois would later assert, "we are buried beneath our material wealth . . . Real culture depends on quality not quantity."[26] Just as the hope of establishing a racial homeland in an Africa dominated by white colonial powers was a retreat from reality, so did Du Bois conclude that black men and women in America, or at least the talented tenth, must look instead to the permanent values of *Kultur.* They must stand for "the *best* thought, the most unselfish striving and the highest ideals" against the laissez-faire individualism symbolized by the Declaration of Independence, Adam Smith, and a "mad money-getting plutocracy."[27]

This perspective influenced his famous rivalry with Booker T. Washington over the future of the Negro movement, which raged until Washington's death in 1915. In the final analysis, Washington saw "the Negro problem" with optimistic American eyes, Du Bois with *fin de siècle* European ones. The president of Tuskegee Institute envisioned a nation of black Horatio Algers, quietly pushing their way up from a hardscrabble existence similar to the one he had known, through "the glory and dignity of common labor" and adherence to a capitalist ethos. The politics of segregation would take care of themselves, he believed, once the underlying realities were changed—and they would change, as economic progress remorselessly pushed blacks onto an equal footing with the rest of American society.

To Du Bois's mind, Washington's concentration on material advancement would only make blacks part of soul-destroying capitalism. He accused Washington of being duped by "the speech and thought of triumphant commercialism" and of selling out to "the ideals of material prosperity."[28] Washington, he thought, ignored the importance of race as a source of group identity. Race was *the* central fact in world history, Du Bois announced in 1897, and "he who ignores or overrides the race idea in human history ignores or overrides the central thought of all history." Du Bois's African *Volksgeist* would enjoy a final triumph over white civilization, rather than succumbing to the same social and economic demands.[29]

The need to distance black culture from white civilization animates Du Bois's most influential work, *The Souls of Black Folk.* Published in 1903 at the height of his conflict with Booker T. Washington, the book presents American blacks as a *Volk* in the German sense. By the "souls" of the title, Du Bois meant *Volksseele*, the collective soul that the German social psychologist Wilhelm Wundt had argued determines a nation's mentality at a certain stage in history. The collective soul included a collective memory, made up of fragments of past myths and experiences that a people retain and pass on to their descendants.[30]

For Du Bois, the taproot of the collective soul of black Americans was the Negro spiritual. It was to the African-American what the *Nibelungenlied* is to the Teuton or *The Odyssey* to the Greek, the expression in an archaic poetic idiom of the *Volk's* spiritual strivings, revealing an inner strength that has endured enslavement and persecution. Just as German "folk psychologists" explained that a people's past, recycled as myth, could become a permanent part of their collective "soul experience," Du Bois now suggested that this was what had happened with slavery. Far from being relegated to the past, it determined all subsequent meaningful cultural activity for black people. Having black blood in America meant having the soul experience of being a slave, even if (as in the case of Du Bois) none of one's family members or ancestors had actually been in bondage.

This cultural legacy of slavery, "the accumulated sloth and shirking and awkwardness of decades and centuries," now shackled the modern Negro's hands and feet. "The very soul of the toiling, sweating black man," Du Bois wrote, "is darkened by the shadow of a vast despair." Yet "in the somber forests of his striving his own soul rose before him, and he saw in himself some faint revelation of his power, his mission." Indeed, black Americans, Du Bois contended, have *two* souls. One is the American or civilized soul, which is modern and pliable in the face of change. The other, the Negro soul, is vital and permanent. Having black blood, Du Bois stated, also means belonging to a black culture that is both distinct from its white counterparts and beautiful. "This race has the greatest gifts of God, laughter. It dances and sings: it is humble; it longs to learn; it loves men; it loves women. It is frankly, baldly, deliciously human in an artificial and hypocritical world."[31] Du Bois connoted these vital, creative qualities by the word "soul." In short, soul became for Du Bois what *Kultur* was for the German critics, a permanent source of vital religious, social, and political structures that point the way to the future—and away from an "artificial" and "hypocritical" European civilization.

Du Bois summed up his new approach to black culture in *The Negro*, published in 1915. Following in the footsteps of early Romantic nationalists, Du Bois treated Africa as a cultural and historical whole. Its great geographic diversity, ethnic diffusion and rivalries, and nearly two thousand languages and dialects crisscrossing the continent became side issues. Africa is "at once the most romantic and the most tragic of continents." Romantic because of the vital and creative peoples who inhabit it, tragic because of the fate that befell them at the hands of European slave traders.[32]

*The Negro* presented African blacks as "one of the most ancient, persistent, and widespread stocks of mankind." Their typical appearance is not the "black, ugly, and wooly haired Negro" portrayed in white propaganda, but the noble figures who appear as statues in the Egyptian Room of the British Museum: "The larger gentle eye, the full but not overprotruding lips ... and the good-natured, easy sensuous expression. This is the genuine African model." In fact, the typical African became the light-skinned mulatto, like Du Bois himself. "Africa is primarily the land of the mulatto," thanks to the constant admixture of races and peoples across the continent. For Du Bois, Africans are a vital aristocratic race *because* of racial mixing rather than in spite of it.[33]

Du Bois followed anthropologists like Franz Boas and Melville Herskovitz, who by 1915 had demolished the claim that racial classifications had any biological significance. However, Du Bois found another, more culturally centered use for race. Anticipating the position Oswald Spengler would take in *The Decline of the West* just three years later, he stated that "race is a dynamic and not a static conception." Over the course of history, a race is physically "changing and developing"; nonetheless, it "forms a mass, a social group distinct in history, appearance, and *to some extent in spiritual gift* [emphasis added]."[34] According to Du Bois, the Negro provided the basic racial stock for all the great cultures of the ancient Fertile Crescent, as well as those of Europe. The Negro's skin "was early bleached by the climate [of Europe], while in Africa it was darkened." *The Negro* is, in fact, Gobineau turned inside out.[35]

The pure, primeval origins of culture lie with the Negro, not the Indo-European or Teuton. The Negro enjoys the same "well-rounded" personality that Friedrich Ratzel described as typical of a rooted *Volk*. This well-roundedness is reflected in the Negro's artisanal and metallurgical skills and his instinct for trade and commerce, "the leading implement of civilization." However, Du Bois's Negro is also the embodiment of the higher spiritual values of *Kultur* tinged with an Orientalist exoticism. His art and folkloric tradition are a reflection of "the Negro's deep and delicate sense of beauty in form, color, and sound." Quoting from Leo Frobenius, Du Bois notes that "ceremony and courtesy mark Negro life" and that Negroes exhibit a "delicacy of feeling" and "a deliberateness, a majesty, a dignity, a devoted earnestness . . . with every gesture, with every fold of clothing." Meanwhile, the African Negro religion, fetishism, corresponds with the race's inner vitalism: "It is not mere senseless degradation. It is a philosophy of life." And since this vital Negro blood has been diffused everywhere, Du Bois concludes, "we may truthfully say that Negroes have been among the leaders of civilization in every age of the world's history from ancient Babylon to modern America."[36]

But then, as in Gobineau's Aryan myth, the historical forces of corruption disrupt the primeval vital center, Africa itself. First African cultural unity began to fall apart. Then Arabs and European slave traders intruded into a continent where overpopulation and political turmoil had already taken their toll. African slavery, which had been a merely local custom, became part of Europe's international economy and human beings became the most valuable commodity Africa could offer. Under such circumstances, Du Bois lamented, "there could be but one end: the virtual uprooting of ancient African culture, leaving only misty reminders of the ruin in the customs and work of the people."[37]

After four hundred years of slavery and colonial dominion, Africa found itself in the iron grip of white men determined "to use the organization, the land, and the people, not for their own benefit, but for the benefit of white Europe." Now, however, Du Bois could sense a change in the wind.

> There is slowly arising not only a curiously strong brotherhood of Negro blood throughout the world, but the common cause of the darker races against the intolerable assumptions and insults of Europeans . . . Most of the men in the world are colored. A belief in humanity means a belief in colored men. The future world will, in all reasonable probability, be what colored men make it.[38]

## THE DARK NATIONS AND THE END OF THE WEST

When Du Bois finished *The Negro* in 1915, he was already a famous figure in African-American circles. He had helped found the NAACP in 1906 and now was serving as editor of its monthly magazine, which he had created. Its title, *The Crisis: A Record of the Darker Races*, reflected a new direction in his thinking. Over the next decade and a half, Du Bois would abandon any exclusively American focus and take up a more global, world-historical pespective on the Negro problem. The possibility that "colored men"—not only black but brown and yellow and red—might join together to challenge the dominant European and American order seemed close to realization.

Three events combined to encourage his optimism. The first was the death in 1915 of Booker T. Washington, which left Du Bois as the unchallenged leader of the Negro civil rights movement in America. The second was the coming of the First World War, which shook to the core

Europe's position of preeminence in the world. From 1914 to 1918, four years of grisly conflict and slaughter left 8.5 million Europeans dead. Characteristically, Du Bois viewed matters from his own black nationalist perspective. On the eve of America's entry into the war, he wrote in *The Crisis* that the true origin of the Great War lay in the imperialist scramble for Africa, "the jealous and avaricious struggle for the largest share in exploiting darker races." With the coming of the armistice in 1918 and the Versailles settlement, in which Germany was forced to surrender its colonial possessions, Du Bois forsaw a new opportunity for nonwhite nationalisms of all types. He even organized the first Pan-Africanist Congress in Paris in 1919, to coincide with the peace conference's deliberations on the question of self-determination for all peoples, white and nonwhite. "Out of this chaos," he wrote, "may be the great awakening of our race."

The third formative event in Du Bois's thinking was the triumph of Communism in Russia. Du Bois followed the events in Lenin's Soviet Union closely, and they inspired him to take a closer look at the writings of Karl Marx and to make the Marxist view of history part of his own world view. In all these respects, the world in 1919 looked very different from the way it had four years earlier. Du Bois adjusted his hopes and plans accordingly. White Teutons and Anglo-Saxons have had their day of dominance and the yellow race and the Slavs are about to follow, Du Bois confidently stated. Japan and Russia were beginning their struggles for empire in Asia. Next it would be the Negro's turn.[39]

Slavery had not only turned the Negro himself into a commodity and his productive labor into something owned by someone other than himself. It had also made him an unwilling part of a growing, seething, materialistic white European *Zivilisation*, its tentacles reaching out and overturning the vital cultural order in every part of the globe. For Du Bois, slavery was merely one expression of the capitalist economic relations that characterized all of European civilization. "Modern African slavery was the beginning of the modern labor problem."[40] As plantation slaves, "the black workers of America bent at the bottom of a growing pyramid of commerce and industry," which eventually connected the slaves of the South to the exploited workers of the industrialized North as well as Britain and Europe.[41]

Like his German counterparts, Du Bois never saw the wealth of industrial society in economic terms, as the result of increased productivity. He saw it only in cultural terms, as the fruit of a process that violated human creativity and ruined happiness. Du Bois's Negro, like the volkish ideologue's German peasant, stood poles apart from the values of Western capitalism, even as he was forced to submit to them. The balance of cultural power in the world was clear. While Egypt gave the world its astronomy and science, China its art, and Mesopotamia its religion, the sole contribution of Nordic civilization was the factory. "As a system of culture," Du Bois announced, white civilization "runs chiefly to marvelous contrivances for enslaving the many, and enriching the few, and murdering both."[42]

The epitome of this corrupt white civilization was nineteenth-century colonialism. In Du Bois's writings, imperialism stands for more than just a political or economic system of exploitation. It represents a marauding instinct, a reflexive malignant response to the outside world that permeates every aspect of Western culture. Later multiculturalists would call this "the negation of the Other." Du Bois saw it principally in geopolitical terms. Indeed, like Brooks Adams, he believed that the West had to expand or die.[43]

It is ironic that while Du Bois was a penetrating critic of white racist stereotypes of *blacks*, he would always accept uncritically the picture presented by those same racial pessimists of whites.[44] Du Bois's white civilization is always Teutonist and almost Nietzschean in its unremitting thirst for conquest and domination, its "individualism coupled with the rule of might."[45] The white European world had "overrun the earth and brought not simply modern civilization and technique, but with it exploitation, slavery, and degradation to the majority of men. They have broken down native family life, desecrated homes of weaker peoples and spread their bastards over every corner of land and sea." European capitalism and imperialism have polarized humanity into two worlds. One is "that dark and vast sea of human labor in China and India, the South Seas and all Africa; in the West Indies and Central America and the United States," which contains "that great majority of mankind . . . driven, beaten, imprisoned, and enslaved in all but name." The other is the European world, the seat of "world power and universal dominion and armed arrogance."[46]

The marauding imperialist instinct was once the West's chief strength, enabling it to seize and build upon the achievements of prior civilizations. However, by 1919 Du Bois was convinced that imperialism, with its "lying and brute force," would ultimately prove to be the West's greatest weakness. World War I, he asserted, had begun with the imperial competition for control of Africa and had ended with the bloodbaths of Verdun and the Somme. "This is not aberration nor insanity," he wrote, "this *is* Europe; this seeming Terrible is the real soul of white culture."[47]

"The Dark World is going to submit to its present treatment just as long as they must and not one moment longer."[48] Unless European civilization makes amends, the colored people of the world will rise up, "and the War of the Color Line will outdo in savage inhumanity any war this world has seen." However, whether in peace or war, "a belief in humanity is a belief in colored men," Du Bois stated, echoing the theme he had set forth in *The Negro*. "If the uplift of mankind must be done by men, then the destinies of this world will rest ultimately in the hands of darker nations." The postcolonial world of the twentieth century will inevitably be a post-Western world; the collapse of empire must also bring about the collapse of Western civilization itself.

Du Bois believed what Oswald Spengler concluded at virtually the same time: imperialism had sounded the death knell of modern civilization. Like Joseph Conrad, Du Bois believed that colonialism had exposed European man's own heart of darkness. And like Spengler's *The Decline of the West*, Du Bois's vision for this postcolonial, post-Western world meant a return to vital *Kultur*. Like its Pan-Germanic counterpart, Du Bois's Pan-Africanism was born of a desire to escape the death embrace of a dying world. Beginning in the 1920s, W.E.B. Du Bois urged his readers to return to what would come to be called their "roots." This return to Africa would not be a physical exodus, as Alexander Crummell and other Negro nationalists had believed; it would be a psychological exodus, purifying the soul and washing away the corruption left by a moribund white civilization.

Du Bois made his first visit to Africa in 1923, and it inspired him to Romantic lyricism: "Africa is the spriritual frontier of human kind." The city where he disembarked, Monrovia, Liberia, was more beautiful than any European capital, he claimed; the people displayed a gaiety and a delight in life that was evident in their song, dance, and "perfect, unhidden bodies." What superficial Europeans would see as signs of poverty and unemployment really meant that "these folk have the leisure of true aristocracy, leisure for thought and courtesy, leisure for sleep and laughter." The isolation of village life brings "a deeper knowledge of human souls . . . Africans know fewer folk, but know them infinitely better." Du Bois's enthusiasm lifted him to poetic flights of racial vitalism: "The spell of Africa is on me. The ancient witchery of her medicine is burning in my drowsy, dreamy blood. . . ."[49]

Du Bois wrote his most personally revealing work, *Dark Princess*, in 1928, just before his Pan-African vitalism yielded to his allegiance to Communism and Stalin. *Dark Princess* was Du Bois's *Thus Spake Zarathustra*: an allegorical fantasy that is part poetic autobiography, part apocalyptic vision of the death of the corrupt society around him.[50] A gifted black American medical student, Matthew Towns, finds himself transformed by white racism "into a man whose heart was hate." He leaves America for Europe. In London he saves an elegant colored woman from the insults of a vicious white American tourist. She turns out to be a Hindu princess, whose natural breeding and sophistication clearly mark her superiority to the artificial civilization around her. She proceeds to introduce Matthew to a secret society of nonwhite expatriates, the Great Council of the Darker Peoples, who are planning the bright future of the planet once white imperialism and its institutions have collapsed.

The Great Council in fact symbolizes the talented tenth of the Third World, of which Towns becomes the representative for black Africa: "How humorous it was to Matthew to see the tables turned; the rabble now was the white workers of Europe; the inferior races were the ruling whites of Europe and America!" Towns returns to the United States to try to work for racial justice (including a plan to blow up a train carrying members of the Ku Klux Klan) but becomes entangled in the corruptions of American life. "Our machines make things and compel us to sell them," he laments. "We are rich in food and clothes and starved in culture. . . . All delicate feeling sinks beneath floods of mediocrity. The finer culture is lost; lost; maybe lost forever."[51]

Finally, two people save him. The first is his aged mother, an ex-slave and the gnarled yet vital and powerful representative of Towns's African soul: "She is Kali, the Black One," his Hindu princess intones, "Mother of the World!" The second is the princess herself, who returns to marry the hero in a proto-New Age ceremony containing Hindu, Buddhist, Judaic, and Moslem elements—every religion, in fact, except Christianity. A new colored elite arises to summon forth "a real and darker world. The world that was and is to be."

In Du Bois's fictional vision the world of *Zivilisation*, of the political and economic realities that surrounded him, is a world created entirely for and by whites. As such it shrinks to insignificance. Nor is this surprising. In all racial thinking, civilization retreats as a socializing and refining influence. Heredity comes to determine everything; the vitalism of an ancient race supplies all the necessary sources of true *Kultur* and creativity. The Pan-Africanist Du Bois found himself in agreement with white neo-Gobinians. Liberal society on the Western model destroys the integrity of race and virtue, whether it does so through racial mixing, atavistic degeneration, or slavery and imperialism.

This fear, then, became the guiding principle of Du Bois's views on black America. It led Du Bois to sever connections with the NAACP in 1934, because its members insisted on trying to eliminate segregation rather than pursuing his racial utopia. Even as Du Bois became more isolated from the civil rights movement, however, he remained adamant. The black *Volk* had to separate itself from whites because of the white man's soul-destroying world view. Its destructive power constantly manifested itself in exploitative economics, repressive social conventions, a manipulative political culture of false choices, and a mindless popular culture of advertising and radio.* Even if blacks were to achieve full civil rights and political equality in America, he told an audience in 1960, they still should not adopt the ideals of Americans. "This would mean we would cease to be Negroes as such and become whites in action"; this would encourage physical integration (i.e., miscegenation), destroy all "physical evidence of color and racial type," and thus "we would lose our memory of Negro history."[52]

---

* And of television, which Du Bois dismissed at the end of his life as "entertainment for morons."

The words may be by W.E.B. Du Bois, but the sentiments are those of a Houston Chamberlain or a Madison Grant. In fact, in Du Bois's view, black culture's chief virtue was its contradiction of bourgeois liberalism, both in Africa—where women travel bare-breasted and village life brings an "intimate human knowledge the West misses, [by] sinking the individual in the social"—and in black America itself. He wrote in 1926, "We are the supermen who sit idly by and laugh and look at civilization. We, who frankly want the bodies of our mates and conjure no blush to our bronze cheeks when we own it." The Negro's sense of humor and his sense of leisure, his refusal to work as if "daily toil is one of the Ten Commandments," which Du Bois had seen thirty years earlier as one of the most damaging legacies of slavery, had now become proud gestures of cultural defiance.[53]

## LET MY PEOPLE GO: MARCUS GARVEY AND THE DU BOIS LEGACY

Despite his reputation as America's greatest living black American, Du Bois's ideas drew more respect outside the United States than among his fellow citizens, whether black or white. Some of this influence and recognition pleased him; some of it did not. One disciple who definitely did not make him happy was the Jamaican immigrant Marcus Garvey. For the better part of a decade, Garvey's "back to Africa" movement convulsed black opinion in Jamiaca and the United States. It outraged Du Bois, who called Garvey "without doubt the most dangerous enemy of the Negro race in America and the world." Yet Garvey's movement simply gave Du Bois's vision of the final victory of the "darker nations" over white civilization a concrete, albeit crude, form. Despite their bitter personal rivalry, their similarities in outlook outweighted the differences.

A master printer by training and extremely well-read and traveled, Marcus Garvey was a leading black nationalist when, in 1914, he set up the United Negro Improvement Association in his native Jamaica. The UNIA, he believed, would spawn a series of anticolonial independence movements in the Caribbean and also provide a means for New World blacks to return to their original homes in Africa. Garvey visited the United States in 1916—the same year that Madison Grant's *Passing of* *the Great Race* was published—and thereafter decided to abandon his Jamaican base and set up the UNIA in New York City, in Harlem.*

The back to Africa movement took most of its support from Harlem's large black working class, which had emigrated from the South and the West Indies. The community's affluent middle class and the self-confident intellectuals of the Harlem Renaissance, such as Du Bois, Claude McKay, Countee Cullen, Langston Hughes, and Zora Neale Hurston, treated Garvey with contempt and scorn. He was mercilessly pilloried in the Marxist *Messenger* as "squat, fat and sleek, with small bright pig eyes and . . . bull-dog-like face," while one wealthy black physician was overhead to say that UNIA stood for "ugliest Negroes in America."[54] Instead, it was working-class blacks and West Indian immigrants who bought Garvey's newspaper, *The Negro World*, attended his rallies to sing Garvey's African national anthem, "Ethiopia, Thou Land of Our Fathers," and surrendered their wages for membership in the UNIA. Black nationalism, which had been a debating issue among the Talented Tenth, now found a new home among poor blacks.

At first glance, Garvey's Pan-African nationalism mirrors the assumptions of nineteenth-century predecessors like Alexander Crummell and Henry Turner, not to mention Du Bois. For example, the emphasis on racial pride: "Your hair is wooly, your nose is broad, your lips are thick," he told his listeners. "This difference must also be intended in your outlook and in your viewpoints of life."[55] Garvey proclaimed that Africa "was once the greatest race in the world" and had become the cradle of civilization while "the Teutonic race" was still clad in animal skins, and that returning to an African homeland would mean a rebirth of these ancient glories. He also insisted, in the Crummell tradition, that the new united Africa must be a modern industrial nation. "Africa will be completely colonized by Negroes, as Europe is by the white race," Garvey proclaimed, and a hardy stock of black American and West Indian pioneers would "assist in civilizing the backward tribes of Africa." Garvey founded the Black Star Steamship Line, a commercial joint venture that would prove that black entrepreneurs could be as

---

* Ironically, Garvey had traveled to the United States to meet Booker T. Washington, whose autobiography, *Up From Slavery*, made a deep impression on him. However, Garvey's own Pan-African ideology owed far more to figures like Du Bois and Crummell than to the Wizard of Tuskegee.

successful as whites—and would also provide the physical means to transport American blacks back to their homeland.[56]

But Garvey also reflected a late Darwinian cast of mind, which was entirely absent in the earlier nationalists and linked him as much to Brooks Adams as to Du Bois. Garvey believed that the fate of the black race was part and parcel of a larger "evolutionary struggle" among nations that would determine the future of the twentieth century. The black man had to become a strong, dominant power or be left behind. "The race that is able to produce the highest scientific development," he stressed, "is the race that will ultimately rule."[57] If, as Du Bois had claimed, history was the story of the stronger races, then blacks must learn to act like a strong race, as "master and owner and possessor of everything that God has created in this world." If empire was the enduring mark of an expansive civilization, then the Negro, too, must "become imperial" and construct a "racial empire" on which "the sun will never set."[58]

Garvey was also as obsessed with racial purity as any neo-Gobinian.[59] "I believe in a pure black race just as how all self-respecting whites believe in a pure white race," he remarked in *The Philosophy of Marcus Garvey*.[60] Like Du Bois, he unquestioningly assumed that modern European civilization was essentially Teutonic in origin and organized around the single principle of white supremacy. "The attitude of the white race," he wrote, "is to subjugate, to exploit, and if necessary exterminate the weaker peoples with whom they come in contact." Garvey accused whites of indoctrinating blacks so that they would believe they were useless for anything except manual labor in the shadow of white-owned capitalist enterprise, because economic exploitation was cheaper and more efficient than actual extermination (such as the Indians and African blacks had endured).*

Fortunately, that "soulless" white civilization had now become decadent and weak. Garvey explained to his audiences that Europe was teetering at the edge of economic bankruptcy. In America bread riots and mob violence were imminent as whites prepared to throw blacks into

---

* In Garvey's antiwhite rhetoric are the threads of what would later come to be known as "the Plan," a gigantic conspiracy to exterminate blacks (whether through the spread of drugs or AIDS or both) in a final effort to prevent the Caucasian race's own downfall.

"economic starvation." Four hundred million black Africans, he told his Harlem listeners, were now organizing to reclaim their heritage. "The fall will come," Garvey announced at a rally in 1919, "a fall that will cause the universal wreck of the civilization we see." A mighty apocalyptic struggle was about to break out "between black and white on the African battle plains."[61] Garvey lingered lovingly over the vision of a global race war, of black against white and white against yellow—although he held out the possibility that blacks might help whites out against the resurgent Asian empires of Japan and China in exchange for political freedom. However, the destruction of white civilization would provide blacks with the tools they needed—science, technology, and weapons of war—to create their own empires. A mighty African nation would emerge from his vast and bloody Armageddon, in which "the Negro must be united in one Grand Racial Hierarchy."[62]

Garvey told a reporter that he represented the future of black nationalism, while Du Bois represented the past.[63] That future, he believed, hinged on what he was convinced would be the future of twentieth-century politics: mass politics, mass propaganda, and the power of the disciplined and mobilized nation. That conviction drew him to the figure of Benito Mussolini. Garvey expressed great admiration for the Italian dictator until he invaded Ethiopia in 1936. He even claimed that far from his movement's being patterned after Mussolini's Blackshirts, the influence flowed the other way around: "When we had 100,000 men and were training children, Mussolini was still unknown." Garvey would insist that "the UNIA were the first Fascists."[64]

He reserved the same admiration for Adolf Hitler. For Garvey, Jews were the symbol of the "lying, wheedling" West, and Jewish international finance was a power that "can destroy men, organizations, and nations." No black was safe from that power, he warned his followers. The "Protocols of the Elders of Zion" taught "that a harm done by a Jew to a Gentile is no harm at all, and the Negro is a Gentile." Anti-Semitism and the appeal of modern mass movements also led him to seek a partner in an unusual quarter: the Ku Klux Klan. To the stunned outrage of Du Bois, the NAACP, and virtually every other Negro leader, on June 25, 1922, Garvey arranged a meeting with the KKK's Grand Dragon. Both men agreed that a black exodus from the United States would protect the purity of both races.[65] In short, racial pessimism formed a bridge between these two forms of radical nationalism, one black and the other white. In 1925 Garvey told the neo-Gobinian white supremacist Ernest Siever Cox that every good black nationalist should read Cox's *White America*. "The White American Society," he wrote, "the Anglo-Saxon Clubs, and the Ku Klux Klan have my full sympathy in fighting for a pure race, even as we are fighting for a pure black race." Both of them, he warned Cox, faced the same enemies: "the Jewish groups fighting me, and the NAACP."[66]

Indeed, Garvey's "black empire" collapsed almost as swiftly as it began. In 1923 he was convicted of mail fraud by a Federal court; he spent four years in prison until President Coolidge gave him a pardon and ordered his immediate deportation. Later, Garvey tried to revive his Negro fascist movement under the banner of "African fundamentalism." Two years before his death in 1940, he established the School of African Philosophy in London. Garvey's curriculum rejected all "white" anthropology and social science as racially biased and taught an African version of the Book of Genesis, in which Adam and Eve were black and their Negro offspring the first chosen people.[67]

After Garvey's deportation, radical black nationalism in America languished. Then, in 1933, a follower named Elijah Poole took over an obscure sectarian offshoot of the Moorish-American Science Temple called the Nation of Islam. From its pulpits he preached a millennialist version of Garvey's black Genesis. White Caucasians were a "degenerate race," he announced, to whom God had given six thousand years of domination in order to test the strength and endurance of His black children, the true chosen people. However, the end of this Babylonian Captivity was at hand. The Caucasian white devils and their satanic religion, Christianity, were about to disappear forever.

Poole changed his name to Elijah Mohammed and rapidly expanded the Nation of Islam's membership. He preached that God, Allah Himself, was a black man, "the Supreme Being among a mighty nation of divine black men," while the Negro was "the first and the last, maker and owner of the universe."[68] In 1948 one of his recruits explained to a young hoodlum named Malcolm Little that "the white man is the devil." As a black man, he said, "you belong to a race of people of ancient civilizations, . . . rich in gold and kings" from whom the white dev-

ils had stolen everything, including his real name. Malcolm was convinced. He changed his last name to X to symbolize his lack of identity
as a black man in white America and immediately became famous.

Malcolm X resolved Du Bois's dilemma of the African-American's
two souls. There was only one soul, a black African one, that whites
tried to obliterate and destroy, as they had destroyed any trace of blacks'
original African greatness. Although Malcolm X later broke with Elijah
Mohammed and the Nation of Islam, he always maintained its Du Bois-
Garveyite apocalyptic perspective. "The western world today faces a
great catastrophe," he declared in an early speech; "it stands on the
brink of disaster." Years later, in his autobiography, he declared, "Two-
thirds of the human population is telling the one-third minority white
man, 'Get out!' And the white man is leaving. . . . I believe that God is
now giving the world's so-called 'Christian white society' its last opportunity" to atone for its crimes.*[69]

In the sixties, Garvey's fascist emphasis on politics as power resur-
faced in the Black Power movement, and his uniformed paramilitary
guards, the African Legion, would become the Fruit of Islam, the body-
guards of Elijah Mohammed and then of his successor, Louis Farrakhan.
Farrakhan himself would recall that when he was eleven years old, he
saw a picture of a black man on the wall at his uncle's house and asked
who it was. He was told it was Marcus Garvey: " 'That is a man who has
come to unite all black people.' "[70] Every aspect of Farrakhan's Black
Muslim movement—his charismatic leadership style, his insistence that
blacks must become independent business owners, his anti-Semitism
and sympathy for Hitler's war against the Jews—all replay, at a slightly
more intense volume, the major themes of Garvey's Pan-Africanism.

"Garveyism" also reached far beyond the United States. *The Negro
World* and collections of Garvey's speeches and editorials resonated with
educated and nationalist-minded African youth in a way that the more
staid and old-fashioned Du Bois never did. Kenneth Kuanda of Zambia,
Harry Thuku of Kenya, and Nelson Mandela of South Africa were all di-

---

* Malcolm X then adds a rhetorical question that is pure Du Bois: "How *can* white society atone
for enslaving, for raping, for unmanning, for otherwise brutalizing *millions* of human beings, for centuries? What atonement would the God of Justice demand for the robbery of the black people's labor, their lives, their true identities, their culture, their history?"

rectly or indirectly influenced by Garvey's doctrines.* Another leader, Kwane Nkrumah of Ghana, would later write, "The book that did more than any other to fire my enthusiasm was the *Philosophy of Marcus Garvey*." This was ironic, since Nkrumah would serve as the final role model for Garvey's bitterest enemy, W.E.B. Du Bois himself.

## DU BOIS, COMMUNISM, AND THE END OF THE WEST

In 1946 the seventy-eight-year-old Du Bois wrote:

> We are face to face with the greatest tragedy that has ever overtaken the world. The collapse of Europe is to us the more astounding because of the boundless faith we have had in European civilization.

Of course, Du Bois was speaking ironically. For more than half a century Du Bois had impatiently awaited the eclipse of white civilization, which his teachers in Berlin in the early 1890s had taught would happen, *must* happen, as *Zivilisation* demeaned and undermined the vitality of *Kultur*. It had inspired his peculiar Pan-Africanist universal history in *The Negro* and other works, which would in turn inspire the Afrocentrist movement. His real attention had been fixed on what would come after modern European civilization collapsed.

For a brief period, from 1900 to 1910, Du Bois had evoked the image of a talented tenth of Negro intellectuals and politicians, who would assert a sense of racial pride by building a record of cultural achievements without "bow[ing] a knee to Baal."[71] Then he had turned to Pan-African nationalism and then to black separatism, according to which American blacks would build their own independent economy parallel to that of whites, again with no invidious profit motive.

Finally, in the thirties, he turned to Marx and Communism. He had learned a good deal about Marx during his stay in Germany in 1892 to '94 and visited the Soviet Union in 1924. His own analysis of imperialism had anticipated V.I. Lenin's *Imperialism, The Highest Stage of Capitalism*, which argued (wrongly) that the scramble for Africa was due to surplus capital, and that late capitalism could only derive its profits from

---

* Among the resolutions of the 1925 meeting of the African National Congress was one calling for Garvey's immediate release from prison. *Philosophy*, pp. xxxviii–xxxix.

an expanding colonial empire.* For a time after World War II, Du Bois even worried that the capitalist world, in its final death agonies, would crush out the cause of liberation of nonwhite people.[72] Then the British granted independence to India, the United States forced the Dutch to leave Indonesia, and the European powers began to shed their colonies—and prospered. Du Bois was forced to learn that Western capitalism would get along very well without imperial dominion.

In the end, what attracted Du Bois to Marxism is what attracted many other intellectuals in the twentieth century: its status as a form of cultural liberation. The victory of Marxism seemed to promise a moral cleansing of the modern world, as the corruptions of bourgeois civilization would be washed away in the revolutionary flood. By 1935 Du Bois had convinced himself that Soviet Communism would destroy the last vestiges of a sclerotic West and consolidate a new non-Western cultural order.

In *The World and Africa* (1946), Du Bois made it plain that Europe's decadence was the direct product of imperialism and colonial dominion. Anticipating multicultural theorists like Edward Said, Du Bois asserted that the entire tradition of polite culture had developed in order to disguise the horrors of imperialism, producing a "delicately poised literature which treated the intellectual problems of the rich and the well-born" and neglected "the weightier ones of law, mercy, justice, and truth."† This superficial *Zivilisation* made it "impossible for charming people in Europe to realize what their comforts and luxuries cost in sweat, blood, and despair" to the colored peoples of the world. Imperialism had also generated all the problems that degeneration theorists had been worrying about when Du Bois was a young student: a world of effete aristocrats who no longer need to do honest work for a living; "ugly and horrible" industrial cities riddled with crime, disease, and labor unrest, and a decline of intellectual standards. "This," Du Bois grimly concluded, "is a fair picture of the decadence of that Europe which led human civilization during the nineteenth century."[73]

---

* Both drew on the same source, the British journalist J.A. Hobson's harsh attack on the British Empire in Africa, entitled *Imperialism* (1902). On this point, see Chapter 7.

† How Du Bois decided that Oscar Wilde or Anthony Trollope were more representative of nineteenth-century literature than Leo Tolstoy, Fyodor Dostoyevsky, George Eliot, Emile Zola, Victor Hugo, or Charles Dickens is unclear.

Although he did not become an official member of the Communist Party until 1961, shortly before his death, Du Bois served as an apologist and fellow-traveller well before that. He celebrated Stalin as "a great and simple man," and even the revelations of Khrushchev's 1956 secret speech never caused him to falter in his conviction that Stalin's regime was "a glorious victory in the uplift of mankind" and that Stalin was "one of the great men of the twentieth century."[74] The Cold War, in Du Bois's view, was a capitalist-imperialist plot to hold "the darker peoples" and white workers in thrall and bring on another world war. "The organized effort of American industry to usurp government," he angrily wrote in 1954, "surpasses anything in modern history, even that of Adolf Hitler from whom it was learned."[75] In 1959 he journeyed to the Soviet Union, where he received the Lenin Prize, and to Communist China, where he did a series of broadcasts for Radio Beijing urging the new nations of Africa to turn their backs on Western capitalism and look instead to Russia and China as the shining models of the future. "I have seen the world," he declared, "but never so vast and glorious a miracle as China."*

One African leader who heeded his call was Kwame Nkrumah, who the next year invited Du Bois to come to Ghana (formerly the Gold Coast) and serve as his elder statesman and advisor. Du Bois and Nkrumah should have met several years earlier, at the Bandung Conference in Indonesia in 1955, a watershed event in the history of the postcolonial world. It was at Bandung that the term "Third World" was introduced to describe the newly independent nations of Africa and Asia, which were nothing more or less than Du Bois's darker nations of thirty years earlier—the collective symbol of humanity's bright future. Nkrumah was one of the postcolonial leaders who had attended, along with Gamal Abdel Nasser of Egypt, Jawaharlal Nehru of India, Prince Sukarno of Cambodia, Sihanouk of Indonesia—and Adam Clayton Powell, Jr., of Harlem. Du Bois was to present the conference's opening address, but the U.S. State Department withdrew his passport because of his Communist affiliations. The speech he sent to be read to the Ban-

---

* This was at the end of Mao's Great Leap Forward, during which somewhere between ten and twelve million Chinese peasants starved to death.

dung delegates returned to the themes that had permeated his work since his return to the United States from Berlin in 1894:

> We colored folk of America have long lived with you yellow, brown, and black of the world under the intolerable arrogance and assumptions of the white race. . . . We hereby warn the world that no longer can Africa be regarded as pawn, slave, and property of Europeans, Americans, or any other people.

Du Bois brought back a phrase he had coined in 1922, "Africa for Africans": "Hereafter it will no longer be ruled by might nor by power, by invading armies nor police, but by the spirit of all its gods and the wisdom of its prophets."[76]

Nkrumah was typical of the new leaders coming to power in postcolonial Africa. At the University of London he had been taught to believe that the capitalist West, like the British Empire it underpinned, was doomed to self-destruction. He also practiced a Garvey-style charismatic politics, ruthlessly crushing any opposition to his single-party state. When he became president of Ghana in 1956, Nkrumah gave himself the title of Osagyefo, or "the Redeemer," and made himself the leading spokesman for a united Africa. His goals for Ghana were as much symbolic as practical: "A Ghanaian nation will stand out," he wrote, "as a shining example before the rest of the world of the African's ability to manage his own affairs."[77]

When Du Bois accepted Nkrumah's invitation to move to Ghana he was ninety-two, having outlived one era and foreshadowed another. He had abandoned any hope for America, which seemed trapped in an endless and meaningless decline for blacks as well as whites. His volkish racist approach had been rendered obsolete by Martin Luther King's civil rights movement, just as his Stalinism made him few friends in the mainstream NAACP.[78] It was no surprise that Du Bois, who had found unblemished virtue in Stalin and called Harry Truman the greatest mass-murderer since Hitler,[79] should find a new hero in Nkrumah the Redeemer. He immediately launched a massive project for an *Encyclopedia Africa*, which was to be the great intellectual and historical archive for the new emerging Pan-African civilization, and served as Nkrumah's most distinguished apologist—or perhaps his most distinguished dupe.

Du Bois laid down the pattern that would become familiar over the next twenty years, of the Western intellectual who "discovers" in the Marxist dictatorship of a remote country a showcase for a new egalitarian society.[80]

To Du Bois's mind, certainly, African soul and Marxism had now happily joined hands in Ghana. One of Du Bois's very last writings is a paean of praise for Nkrumah, in the form of a Negro spiritual entitled "Ghana Calls":

*I lifted my last voice and cried*
*I cried to heaven as I died . . .*
*From reeking West whose day is done*
*Who stink and stagger in their dung*
*Toward Africa, China, India's strand*
*Where Kenya and Himalaya stand*
*And Nile and Yang-tze roll*
*Turn every yearning face of man.*

*Awake, awake O sleeping world,*
*Honor the sun;*
*Worship the stars, those vaster suns*
*Who rule the night*
*Where black is bright*
*And all unselfish work is right*
*And Greed is sin.*

*And Africa leads on*
*Pan Africa!*

Du Bois died on August 28, 1963. Three years later, the Ghanaian military, fed up with Nkrumah's incompetence, which had destroyed the country's economy and standard of living, toppled the Redeemer in a coup.

## CHAPTER 7

# THE CLOSING OF THE GERMAN MIND

*Oswald Spengler and* The Decline of the West

Anyone who cannot face up to "stark pessimism," to use
Nietzsche's phrase, is not fitted for life's great tasks.

—Oswald Spengler, 1931

As he left his boarding house in Turin on January 3, 1889, Friedrich
Nietzsche saw a cab driver beating a horse in the Piazza Carlo
Alberto. Nietzsche rushed to the horse's defense, and then suddenly
collapsed in the street. After onlookers had carried him back to his
lodgings, he began wildly shouting and pounding on the piano, the same
one on which he had mournfully been playing chords from Wagner's operas only days before. A friend was summoned and brought him back to
Basel, drugged into passivity. There a doctor examined him and diagnosed Nietzsche as suffering from "mental degeneration," an ironic condition for the man who had once said, "What do we consider bad and
worst of all? Is it not degeneration?"[1]

Two weeks later Nietzsche was released in the custody of his mother.
Despite the doctor's and friends' urging, she had decided to move her
son to her home in Jena. Nietzsche took the train from Basel for the last
time and underwent a three-day confinement for psychological observation. His behavior varied from megalomaniacal delusions (he insisted
he was the kaiser) to screaming rages. He became convinced that his
confinement had been ordered by Bismarck himself, and he smashed a
window in an escape attempt. Slowly, however, his rages lapsed into

lethargy and catatonia. From his release a year later until his death in 1900, Nietzsche lived as a virtual vegetable, under the care first of his mother and then of his sister, Elisabeth.

Unlike her mother, Elisabeth Förster-Nietzsche took an active interest in her brother's philosophy. She had married another intellectual from the Wagner circle, Bernard Förster, who was also a great admirer of Gobineau. Förster had even conceived a fantastic Gobinesque plan to set up a colony of Aryan-German settlers in South America called New Germania. Like a character from a Werner Herzog movie, Förster took Elisabeth and a small band of followers to the jungles of Paraguay in 1887 to recolonize the New World with sturdy, racially pure Nordic pioneers.[2] The result was a fiasco. Förster was charged with defrauding the colonists and committed suicide, leaving Elisabeth to pick up the pieces. In 1892 she returned to Germany to take care of her stricken brother, becoming his nurse and permanent guardian.

However, Elisabeth Förster-Nietzsche was also determined that her brother's philosophy not be forgotten. She was convinced that, despite his illness, a market existed in Germany for his writings.* Now she moved to obtain sole legal control over his published works and unpublished papers, forcing her mother to sign a document to this effect in December 1895. She wasted no time in creating a Nietzsche Archives on the ground floor of their house and wrote a worshipful two-volume biography of her brother, drawing from the material in his still unpublished *Ecce Homo*. The Nietzsche home became a shrine, with Nietzsche, now sunk into complete immobility, on permanent public display for distinguished visitors. After his death, his unpublished notebooks and manuscripts became available for study, all under Elisabeth's exclusive control.[3]

Förster-Nietzsche was determined that her brother be recognized as Germany's greatest genius since Goethe. She carefully edited and excised politically sensitive statements and slighting references to the monarchy and Bismarck from the materials she released. Any suggestion that Nietzsche had seen imperial Germany as the epitome of modern decadence or had admired the French, was rigorously suppressed or

---

* The volkish ideologue Julius Langbehn had shown up two years earlier, hoping to become Nietzsche's literary executor.

explained away. Despite Nietzsche's extreme anti-Christian views, his funeral in 1900 was a traditional Lutheran one, a crucifix solemnly laid on his coffin and various disciples and dignitaries in attendance. Förster-Nietzsche also brought about a reconciliation with the Bayreuth circle after twenty years of bitterness and silence. Nietzsche's philosophy became linked once again with the name of Richard Wagner, Germany's most recent cultural hero. By 1900, two great temples dominated the modern German cultural landscape, each with its all-powerful high priestess: Cosima Wagner at Bayreuth, the center of Germany's musical establishment, and Elisabeth Förster-Nietzsche at the Nietzsche Archives in Weimer.

After thirty years of political unification and industrialization, Germany had achieved the status of a modern European power. To the rest of Europe, Germany symbolized the triumph of science, technological know-how, and economic and political dynamism. Its Prussian military tradition, skilled and efficient civil service, and educational system were admired by people as diverse as Brooks Adams and Emile Zola. Yet Germany's success had also bred a sense of frustration and discontent. The revival of Nietzsche's philosophy struck an emotional chord with intellectuals and artists across Germany, as it would later spread across the rest of Europe.

W.E.B. Du Bois left Berlin in 1894 without encountering any of Nietzsche's ideas; had he stayed two years longer, he would not have been able to avoid them.* In 1896 the sociologist Georg Simmel pronounced Nietzsche's philosophy as important an intellectual revolution as Copernicus's theory of the solar system. Historian Kurt Breysig saw Nietzsche as the historic equivalent of Buddha, Jesus Christ, and (appropriately enough) Zarathustra: the founder of a new religion of will to power and action. While old-fashioned liberals like Max Nordau had pointed to Nietzsche's insanity as proof that his philosophy could not be taken seriously, Nietzsche's defenders now insisted that his madness was in fact a state of spiritual transcendence, the result of his having perceived a truth beyond rationality and bourgeois standards of common sense.[4]

---

* Du Bois makes one fleeting reference to Nietzsche's Superman in his *Dusk of Dawn*, p. 663. Otherwise, nothing.

Richard Strauss's tone poem *Also Sprach Zarathustra* premiered in Frankfurt in 1896, and within ten months it was being performed in Paris, London, New York, and Chicago. Its famous opening trumpet notes, heralding the dawn of the Superman, made Nietzsche the most recognizable philosopher in the musical world. That same year Gustav Mahler completed his Third Symphony, which he originally titled "The Gay Science" after Nietzsche's *Fröhliche Wissenschaft*. Meanwhile, in the realm of the written word, terms such as *Übermensch*, "will to power," "master-slave morality," "transvaluation of all values," and "blond beast" now became standard parts of the vocabulary of intellectuals and political writers.

All in all, it was an amazing turnaround. A member of the Förster-Nietzsche circle at the Nietzsche Archives, Count Harry Kessler, described the impact of Nietzsche this way: "The desert was in our hearts, and suddenly, like a meteor, Nietzsche appeared."[5] Nietzsche's writings now became the stock in trade for the entire range of ideological camps in Germany after 1900. Socialists enjoyed his attacks on the bourgeoisie and organized Christianity. Pan-Germanists were able to exploit his attacks on Judaism; since Elisabeth Förster-Nietzsche was herself deeply anti-Semitic, Nietzsche became (without his knowledge) a spokesman for anti-Semitic Aryanism. Likewise, an engraving of the convalescent Nietzsche, with his massive moustache and intense gaze (which disguised a total emptiness of mind), became a favorite pinup poster among nonpolitical avant-garde German writers such as Hermann Hesse and Stefan George.

Nor was his influence limited to Germany. George Bernard Shaw presented London theatergoers with *Man and Superman*, which Oswald Spengler later praised as a masterly as well as entertaining exposition of Nietzsche's doctrines.[6] In America Nietzsche strongly influenced H.L. Mencken, who wrote a book explaining his philosophy. In France he inspired the anarchist Georges Sorel, who passed him on to both revolutionary Marxists and Fascists like Benito Mussolini, while in Spain his works prompted a major philosophical upheaval through the writings of Miguel de Unamuno and José Ortega y Gasset, author of *The Revolt of the Masses*.[7] Nietzsche suddenly became *the* antiliberal philosopher for the twentieth century. He proved to be more important in this regard than Karl Marx, because while Marx's theories became hostage to the fortunes of the Communist Party after 1917, Nietzsche remained a shared cultural icon of the Left and the Right. This was especially true among adherents to the emerging modernist style and Expressionism, like the poets Stefan George and Gottfried Benn, who believed that an artistic-spiritual elite would lead a future overturning of the hypocritical bourgeois order. As one of them put it: "Nietzsche was a prophet not for the *Volk* but a prophet for the prophets."[8]

This was the Nietzsche—"the prophet for the prophets"—who would inspire Oswald Spengler and shape his view of the fate of Germany and Western Europe in his gloomy masterpiece, *The Decline of the West*. Yet in crucial respects, Spengler's Nietzsche was an expurgated Nietzsche. Without his knowledge or approval, Nietzsche had been turned into a spokesman for German radical nationalism and linked to another antiliberal tradition, that of volkish racial pessimism. Belief in the will to power served to justify authoritarianism at home and military aggression abroad, while Nietzsche's "master morality," which he had modeled on the vanished aristocracies of feudal Europe and Japan, merged with the image of Teutonic Germans as the new *Übermenschen* of postbourgeois Europe.

Spengler's vision of the *Decline of the West*, therefore, was not a matter of despair but, like the opening notes of Richard Strauss's tone poem, the heralding of a new dawn. Spengler's Western civilization is one that W.E.B. Du Bois would have recognized: soul-destroying *Zivilisation* at its worst. From its collapse, Spengler believed, would arise a new Europe centered not on the old decadent powers of the nineteenth century— France and Great Britain—but on Germany. The combination of *Kultur*, military discipline, and Nietzschean will to power would create "leader natures" to forge a new destiny. It would be difficult; "much blood must still flow," he wrote in the wake of the First World War. But even after Germany's defeat, Spengler was confident that "the master race . . . is faced by a task to which it is equal."[9]

## OSWALD SPENGLER AND THE
## CULTURAL IDENTITY OF GERMANY

Oswald Spengler was born in 1880 in Blankenburg. He spent an unhappy middle-class childhood with cold and emotionally distant parents. In self-defense he retreated (not unlike Arthur de Gobineau) into his own world of fantasy and intellectual rebellion. Like many educated middle-class adolescents in Wilhelmine Germany, his heroes were the founding fathers of modernism, the leaders of what one contemporary called "the great war of liberation against bourgeois dullness, prudery, and hypocrisy"—which for Spengler was the world of his parents. Spengler developed an admiration for the Norwegian dramatist Henrik Ibsen, whose plays (A *Doll's House*, *Ghosts*, and *Pillars of the Community*) both shocked and fascinated the bourgeois audiences they vilified. Richard Wagner was another hero along with Ernst Haeckel, whose vision of man's history as part of an organic totality deeply influenced Spengler's later thinking.[10]

The other role model was Friedrich Nietzsche. Spengler devoured Nietzsche's works as a high school student and found in them what the young novelist Thomas Mann had also found, a sense of "self-transcendence." The student Spengler also absorbed the philosopher's pessimism. In 1901, the year Spengler completed his degree at the University of Halle, a collection of Nietzsche's notebooks appeared as *The Will to Power*. Although carefully edited and expurgated by Elisabeth Förster-Nietzsche and her assistants, *The Will to Power* contained a trenchant critique of decadent bourgeois society. Nietzsche grimly urged that the will to power could serve as "a mighty . . . hammer" with which to "break and remove degenerate and decaying races to make way for a new order of life." He continued:

> A doctrine is needed powerful enough to work as a breeding agent; strengthening the strong, paralyzing and destructive to the weak. The annihilation of the decaying races. . . . dominion over the earth as a means of producing a higher type.

The Nietzschean nihilist could "implant into that which is degenerate and desires to die a longing for the end"—in other words, by planting the idea of decline in society one could actually hasten its demise.[11]

Certainly the members of Spengler's generation sought to break through what they saw as stifling bourgeois conventions and taboos to a new reality. It became fashionable to point to a generation gap: what was needed to save the world, one young Nietzschean wrote, was "an insurrection of the sons against the fathers." The image inspired Wilhelm

Hasenclever to write a play about a son who murders his father, which became a smash hit. At the University of Berlin, Georg Simmel explained to his students that revolutionary historical changes "have always been carried out by youth." Whereas adults, "because of their weakening vitality," concentrate their attention on material and social comforts, youth desires "to express its power, and its surplus of power" without regard for conventional forms of values. Simmel, who was also a keen admirer of Nietzsche, told German youth that it was their destiny to carry "this cultural movement toward life and its expression alone."[12] Nietzsche himself had called young men "the explosive ones." Youth became the symbol of creativity and cultural rebirth; in fact, Spengler and other intellectuals would continue to refer to themselves as representatives of German youth until they were well into their forties.[13]

For all their complaints of being oppressed and suffocated by their elders, Germany's university students were actually part of a privileged elite. In 1880, at a time when Germany's population was over forty-seven million, less than 1 percent received any education beyond primary school. Of this small group, less than one in ten had any chance of studying at a university. The professors themselves, the *Ordinarien*, were men of enormous public prestige. Full professors enjoyed the same status as councelors of state and were as much a part of the governing class as politicians or members of the Reichstag.[14]

However, the German mandarins in the universities were in as much turmoil as their students. German universities had always seen themselves as champions of certain higher spiritual values and of the cultivation of the individual intellect (*Bildung*). The *Bildung* ideal descended from the classical and humanist past. It was not incompatible with a rational Enlightenment outlook—its greatest heroes, after all, were Goethe and Kant—but it was primarily concerned with the spiritual and aesthetic rather than the scientific. It tended to deprecate the merely practical, technical, and utilitarian, as well as money-making. People who pursued these interests (which inevitably meant most people) were thought to lack "depth."*

Yet when professors in university towns such as Berlin or Heidelberg

---

* In this respect, Nietzsche's own attacks on philistines were part of, rather than a dissent from, this aspect of university snobbery and elitism.

or Bonn looked around them, their great spiritual citadel seemed under siege. Educational reformers and middle-class radicals argued for expanding the number of technical schools and introducing university students to practical modern subjects, such as physics and engineering, rather than Greek and Latin. These changes, along with the expansion of the nation's industrial base, seemed to portend a cultural crisis for German society as a whole.[15] Du Bois's teachers, the armchair socialists, were among the first to sound the alarm, in 1872. Indeed, each decade from 1870 until 1914 would be described as *the* critical decade in which the German nation would be forced to choose between its cultural integrity and health, or destruction at the hands of modernity.

The academic tradition of *Kulturkritik*, or cultural critique of modern society, rested, of course, on the old distinction between culture and civilization, which we have already encountered.[16] However, the Nietzschean revival gave this old problem a new twist. In Nietzsche's *Will to Power*, the confrontation between vital *Kultur* and superficial *Zivilisation* was illuminated by the issue of decadence. "Civilization has aims different from those of culture," he had said. "The period when the taming of the human animal ('civilization') was desired and enforced were times of intolerance against the boldest and most spiritual natures." Culture, on the other hand, finds its apogee in times that are, "morally speaking, times of corruption," such as the end of the nineteenth century.[17]

A civilization in decline was, therefore, both a tragedy and an opportunity, not only for Du Bois's darker nations but for the strong individual who could break free from its dying embrace. If the orthodox image of *Kultur* had always been personified in great figures from the German past such as Martin Luther or Hans Sachs,* the symbol of Nietzschean *Kultur* in the late 1890s became Zarathustra, the lone and willful prophet creating his own order out of the wilderness. The Nietzschean symbol of *Zivilisation*, on the other hand, was Venice in Thomas Mann's *Death in Venice*: glittering and sophisticated but corrupt and decaying, reeking with the stench of dissolution.

The second challenge to German culture came from technology. In 1911 the sociologist Werner Sombart published an essay entitled "Technology and Culture," which claimed that the mechanical and the hu-

---

* The virtuous medieval shoemaker-poet of Wagner's *Die Meistersinger*.

man dimensions of life were locked in irresolvable conflict. Much as Henry Adams was arguing at the same time in *Mont-Saint-Michel and Chartres*, Sombart stated that machines and mechanical power were the enemy of the organic and spiritual. The impulse toward technological change pushed the human being beyond "the limits of living nature." The machine was capitalism's handmaiden, Sombart argued, an expression of its cold and calculating rationalism. Technology's triumph would bring an "oozing flood of commercialism," he gloomily warned, and the mass production of "hard, cold, lifeless" objects that only served to profit the businessman.[18]

In the tradition of German cultural criticism, industrial machinery is not an emblem of progress but of alienation and degradation. Modern technology, like Du Bois's version of slavery, divorced the worker's livelihood from his higher creative self. The worker became wedded to the machine rather than to his organic community, the true source of creative power. Modern technological advance has brought matters to a point where, as Spengler would say later in *Man and Technics*, "civilization itself has become a machine." The powerful images in Fritz Lang's film *Metropolis*, of human beings being symbolically sacrificed to the industrial machine, reflected this fear that technology would come to control its users rather than vice versa.

The third and final challenge to cultural vitality came from liberalism, the belief in limited government and individual rights that emanated from Tocqueville, Mill, and Herbert Spencer. Cultural critics on both the Right and the Left agreed that laissez-faire liberalism was anathema to Germany's deepest cultural values, just as Adolf Wagner and Schmoller had argued that laissez-faire capitalism was an attack on the idea of organic community and rural life. "Liberals see themselves as isolated individuals," Arthur Moeller van den Bruck wrote later. "They seek only their own personal advantage in the present." Werner Sombart saw liberalism as the ideology of materalism and big business. It rationalized "all the lower instincts of men—covetousness, acquisitiveness, the quest for gold," creating a moral universe of what Sombart's students called *Lug und Trug*, "lying and cheating."[19] Sociologist Georg Simmel saw liberalism as depriving human beings of any ultimate meaning in their lives.[20] "[It] has undermined civilizations," wrote Moeller, "has destroyed religions, has ruined nations."[21]

The countries most closely identified with this destructive liberal world view were the United States and Great Britain. Britain was "the nation of shopkeepers," a phrase that was not meant to flatter. According to the young Thomas Mann, English liberalism marked the triumph of democratic mediocrity.[22] Ernst Troeltsch argued that Englishmen and Americans defined freedom in a purely negative sense, as freedom *from* constraints and responsibility. Their social goal was essentially a negative one, of "live and let live" rather than building a strong and vibrant community. On the eve of World War I, Werner Sombart penned an influential essay entitled "Heroes and Traders." He claimed that these were the two great opposite human types in history, the representatives of *Kultur* and *Zivilisation*, respectively, who now found their respective symbols in Germany and Britain. "The trader approaches life with the question, what can you give me . . . the hero approaches life with the question, what can I give you?"[23] The hero willingly sacrifices himself for the sake of others and sees the world around him in terms of duty and obligation to the community and *Volk*. The trader only sees opportunities for personal profit; commerce and business are the only institutions he respects. Indeed, in the community of true culture, the trader is a *stranger* (the title of a famous essay by Georg Simmel).[24]

The stranger's habitat is the anonymous and technologically sophisticated metropolis, what Spengler in *The Decline of the West* would call the cosmopolis: "the symbol of the formless . . . Here money and intellect celebrate their latest and greatest triumphs."[25] Sombart explained that "through city-life the original congenial bonds between man and nature are severed":

> The child of the city . . . no longer knows the song of the birds and has never examined a bird's nest; he knows not the significance of the clouds, drifting across the sky; he no longer hears the voice of the storm or the thunder . . . The new race lives an artificial life . . . an involved mixture of scholastic instruction, pocket-watches, newspapers, umbrellas, books, sewage disposal, politics.[26]

By contrast, German culture preserved those same qualities that were being destroyed in the rest of Western Europe and America. Antimodernism and gloomy fears for the future were already prevalent in other countries besides Germany by the turn of the century. Even Americans like Henry and Brooks Adams, and Britons like William Morris and Leslie Stephen, reflected the same pessimism, as had Jacob Burckhardt decades earlier. What was extraordinary, however, was the degree to which Germans before World War I saw themselves as *outside* European or Western civilization. As the young novelist Thomas Mann put it, "In Germany's soul, Europe's intellectual antitheses are carried to their limit. . . ." Nineteenth-century civilization represented an implicitly foreign set of values. "Whoever would aspire to transform Germany into a middle-class democracy in the Western sense," Mann wrote, "wishes to take away from her all that is best." Germany's separateness was her saving grace and "her national destiny."[27] As Werner Sombart concluded in 1911, Germany would soon show the rest of Europe "what to do with our masses . . . and how to save human nature from the machine."

## SPENGLER: DISAPPOINTMENT AND OPPORTUNITY

War regenerates degenerate peoples.
　　—Benito Mussolini

In the meantime, Oswald Spengler had suffered a crushing personal blow. Having completed his studies in natural science and philosophy at the universities of Halle and Munich, he had gone on to the University of Berlin to complete a doctoral thesis in 1903. When he presented his thesis, however, his professors failed him, saying that he had included too few scholarly references.[28] He managed to pass the next year, but it was a disastrous setback. The high road to a post at a leading university was now closed forever. In 1905 Spengler suffered a complete nervous breakdown and dropped out of life for a year.

Thereafter, he was condemned to a life teaching in local high schools, the *Realgymnasiums*, moving from job to job with mediocre colleagues and students more interested in making a living than in *Lebensphilosophie*. Against his will he was relegated to a world of hack writers, journalists, and disappointed scholars. Nonuniversity intellectuals in Germany were famously envious and resentful of their university counterparts, but they also drew their cues and attitudes from them. While the *Ordinarien* in the ivory tower were undermining their own self-confidence with fears of cultural decay, below them flourished a sub-culture of writers, intellectuals, and literary hacks who pressed their more radical wares on a growing reading public.

Germany's cultural crisis and the issues that obsessed the university giants—the links between *Kultur, Geist,* and *Volk*—took on even more radical and esoteric permutations. This was the period when the Monist League was introducing vitalist Darwinism into working-class circles, and Pan-Germanists were pushing the myth of Aryan superiority into German politics. In their hands, the notion of *Volksgeist* took on specific racial and Gobinian overtones. Chamberlain's *Foundations of the Nineteenth Century* was published in 1899 and, while largely ignored by university academics,* it was eagerly consumed by a large popular audience. Like Spengler's *Decline of the West* two decades later, it found numerous foreign translators when serious thinkers such as Ferdinand Tönnies and Ernst Troeltsch could not.

After six unrewarding years of teaching, Spengler decided to move to Munich to launch his own writing career, although he had no idea what he would write. At the time, Munich was the center of nonuniversity intellectual life in Germany, and it was seething with literary and cultural discontents. Houston Chamberlain's publisher, Bruckmann Verlag, was based in Munich. The poet Stefan George and his circle of young poets had brought the Nietzschean revival to Munich's cafes and restaurants, while another young resident Nietzschean, Thomas Mann, had just finished *Death in Venice*. A few doors away the painters Franz Marc and Paul Klee were leading lights of the German Expressionist movement, while two years later another artist—Adolf Hitler—would turn up in Munich to try to make a living.

Also living in Munich was the anti-Semitic journalist and member of the Pan-German Thule Society Dietrich Eckhart. Eckhart was a morphine addict and like Spengler was an early admirer of Nietzsche and Ibsen (he once staged a production of *Peer Gynt* using the inmates of a lunatic asylum where he had been confined). He became editor of a Pan-Germanist scandal sheet, *Auf Gut Deutsch* ("In Plain German"), and hired as a writer another anti-Semite, Alfred Rosenberg, who after the war would introduce Eckhart to Hitler when the latter returned

---

* One exception was the economist Johann Plenge. J. Muller, *The Other God That Failed*, p. 61, n. 14.

from the Western front.[29] Hitler's own *Mein Kampf* was a typical product of this low end of nonuniversity intellectual culture. Like his academic intellectual superiors, Hitler wrote of the nation's "creeping sickness" and "decay," and lamented the signs of "our declining culture and our general collapse." Hitler's generation was the first European generation raised on cultural pessimism. It cultivated the same hatreds (industrial capitalism, soulless liberalism, cultural degradation) as its academic mentors, and many of the same goals. There was, however, one important difference. Radicals like Eckhart, Rosenberg, and Hitler were willing to contemplate direct action to overturn what they saw as a sick civilization, not just talk about it.

They were also in agreement with their intellectual superiors on one essential point: the need for Germany to assert itself on the international stage. Nationalism was, as it were, their last bourgeois illusion—some even saw in Kaiser Wilhelm II the living image of the Nietzschean Superman. But their nationalist aspirations had a very different object than the conventional patriotism of the officials and professors who joined groups such as the Navy League or the Pan-German League.[30] For the cultural radicals it was struggle itself, rather than any geopolitical objectives, that was important. Struggle was a recurrent theme—*Mein Kampf* means "My Struggle"—a test of vital forces in the arena where, as Ernst Troeltsch put it, "the fullness of contending national spirits . . . unfold their highest spiritual powers." Thomas Mann saw Germany as perpetually engaged in "the terrible, perilous, irrational struggle against the world *entente* of civilization."[31] As in Ernst Haeckel's Darwinism, struggle implied the emergence of the vital and creative and the weeding out of the weak—that is, the bourgeois West. Years before, Nietzsche had welcomed the growing "military development" and "anarchy" of great-power Europe, a general war being a possible route of salvation. "Only fighting yields happiness on earth," Nietzsche had said, "the barbarian in each of us is affirmed; also the wild beast." "War is the father of all" was the maxim of Nietzsche's favorite Greek philosopher, Heraclitus—who also happened to be the subject of Spengler's doctoral dissertation.[32]

The crisis came in 1911, the same year that Spengler moved to Munich. In May, the German cruiser *Panther* put in at the port of Agadir to prevent a French takeover of Morocco. The crisis brought Europe to the brink of war, until the French government, with active British backing, forced the German government to back down. It was a national humiliation, and the result was an explosion of resentment against the chancellor and foreign minister. The president of the Pan-German League, Heinrich Class, published the pamphlet *If I Were the Kaiser*, calling on the kaiser to dissolve the government and establish an absolute dictatorship. Similar sentiments were voiced throughout Germany and in Spengler's Munich.[33]

The news of the Morocco crisis came to Spengler as a revelation. He decided that he and other Germans were witnessing a "world-historical shift" in the Heraclitean flux of national destinies.[34] The European civilization that rational science and the Enlightenment had made, and that France and Britain represented, was breaking apart. Germany may have lost the battle, but it was destined to win the war that was certainly coming, a struggle between cultural life and death, that is, between Germany and the liberal West.

Spengler began feverish work on a massive project to elucidate his insight, which to his mind amounted to a Nietzschean reevaluation of all history. In fact, the first title he chose for the project was "Conservative and Liberal." But stopping outside a Munich bookstore one day, he saw in the window a volume on ancient history entitled *Die Untergang des Antiktum*, or "The Decline of Antiquity." Spengler now had his title: *Die Untergang des Abendslands*, usually translated as *The Decline of the West*. A more accurate translation, however, would be the "twilight" or "sinking away" of the West, like the sun sinking below the horizon. History, Spengler had decided, was an inexorable natural process remote from human purposes and desires. Destiny was now leaving the Occident (the West or "evening lands") behind, and a cold black night was about to descend on its institutions and monuments.

The sense that Europe was indeed on the brink of catastrophic change, and the yearning for a new beginning, was widespread in Germany and Europe even as Spengler was working away. German Youth Movement leaders held a huge meeting in the Meissner Mountains in October 1913 calling for the "spiritual rejuvenation" of the nation, while French students calling themselves "the Generation of 1912" clamored for a national revival to transform a decadent French society. The twenty-three-year-old German Expressionist poet Georg Heym raged in his diary, "Everything is always the same, so boring, boring, boring. Nothing ever happens, absolutely nothing. . . . If someone would only begin a war, it need not be a just one." Another young Nietzschean wrote that "perpetual peace would be intolerable—it would be boredom, a yawning that would give us merely the philistine."[35] The experience of battle, they assumed, would dispel boredom and the cultural decadence that caused it. As war loomed closer in the summer of 1914, Spengler wrote to a colleague entering the army, "I envy the people who can volunteer and then *experience* the war." "Experience" became a key catchphrase, inspired by the Nietzschean enthusiasm for tapping one's will to power through strong emotions and contact with the elemental.* Others claimed that through danger and hardship, the "unrelieved bondage of loneliness" of German youth in bourgeois society would be replaced with feelings of purpose and unity.[36]

As for their elders, the years of worry about decline, decadence, and degeneration had finally reaped their harvest. War, they believed, would bring only a welcome death to a moribund civilization. Chancellor Bethmann-Hollweg had read Nordau's *Degeneration* and was resigned to the conclusion that "the existing world [is] very antiquated." The coming of war, he wrote in his diary on July 17, 1914, "will result in the uprooting of everything that exists."[37] The economist Johann Plenge celebrated 1914 as the definitive end of the "atomized, critical, disorganized" nineteenth century. "We are the twentieth century," he declared, about to launch forth on a great adventure.[38] Georg Simmel told his students as they marched off to war that the world crisis was part of "the struggle of life" against the old, decayed forms that tried to constrain it. The war formed "what we might call an absolute situation," he proclaimed. Life choices in bourgeois society "had something relative" and provisional about them, Simmel said: now men were faced with a stark Nietzschean choice between the old and the new, between life and death.[39]

All these hopes and expectations drove Spengler to finish *The Decline of the West*. As he explained in its preface, the book had become "a

---

* When war finally came Thomas Mann wrote to a friend: "Shouldn't we be grateful for the totally unexpected chance to experience such mighty feelings?" *Letters of Thomas Mann 1889-1955*, p. 67.

commentary on this great epochal moment," the coming of world war. "What I wrote in the storm and stress of those years," Spengler concluded, "was . . . a new outlook on history and the philosophy of destiny."[40]

## THE DECLINE OF THE WEST AND ORGANIC HISTORY

However, *The Decline of the West* was not as original as Spengler liked to pretend, or as readers sometimes thought.* The work was a great summing up of a half-century of historical pessimism and cultural discontent. Spengler relied heavily on the tradition of cultural criticism with its arcane vocabulary and metaphysical concepts, such as *Volksgeist* and "race memory." He also drew on the nineteenth-century organicist view of historical development, which he fused with the vitalist tradition he inherited from Nietzsche. In his view, every historical culture formed a whole because it had its own inner life force, which made it part "of the Living with all its immense fullness" and determined its future destiny. Spengler claimed that he had moved to a new level of historical thinking, not merely describing civilizations as a whole, but actually predicting their future development and fate. "In this book is attempted for the first time the venture of predetermining history," he explains, "by establishing the future destiny of the only Culture of our time and on our planet which is actually in the phase of fulfillment—the West-European American."[41]

Spengler distinguished eight world civilizations worthy of notice. These were the Babylonian, the Egyptian, the Chinese, the Indian, the pre-Columbian Mexican, the Classical or Graeco-Roman, the Western European, and the "Magian," which included the Arabic, Judaic, and Byzantine cultures.† In the end, Spengler did not have the time or inclination to devote a large part of *The Decline of the West* to non-Western civilizations such as China and India. But they nonetheless occupy a crucial part of his overall plan, because Spengler intended to write a

---

* One reviewer, Hans Freyer, pointed this out when the book first appeared. J. Muller, *The Other God That Failed*, p. 78.

† The Magian culture represented Spengler's tribute to the Orientalist tradition of Schopenhauer and Schlegel, according to which the East is the "true" creative source of Christianity and the West's religious and philosophical wisdom.

"universal history" that would for the first time relegate Western Europe to a small place in the overall story of mankind. His mission was to present a new world picture, which "admits no sort of privileged position to the Classical or the Western culture as against the Cultures of India, Babylon, Egypt" or other non-European civilizations. Spengler's history involved as much of a racial and cultural redistribution as anything W.E.B. Du Bois might have wished for. As "separate worlds of dynamic being," non-Western civilizations "count for just as much in the general picture of history," often surpassing classical culture or the West "in spiritual greatness and soaring power." To give the West any intrinsic importance outside "its narrow limits" would be Eurocentric—although Spengler did not use the term, it was implicit in his approach.[42]

Every civilization, including the West, is the fulfillment of a distinct culture. Each is a seething, breathing, and blossoming thing: "Each culture has its own new possibilities of self-expression, which arise, ripen, decay and never return." Each is "aimless" and each assigns its own weight and value to things, to time, and to space: the only thing with intrinsic meaning is the life force and its organic logic. Instead of continuity and progress in history, there are only discontinuities and sudden and rapid departures from "a boundless mass of human Being, flowing in a stream without banks" from which arises from time to time a self-conscious *Kultur*.* A culture's living existence over the centuries is "an inner passionate struggle to maintain the Idea against the powers of Chaos." Then, as more time passes, "it mortifies, its blood congeals, its force breaks down, and it becomes Civilization." In the terms of his German predecessors, Spengler sees *Zivilisation* as *Kultur*'s old age. This led Spengler to his famous analogy between the individual's life cycle and civilization: "Every culture has its childhood, youth, manhood, and old age."[43]

In its early vital stages ("spring"), culture draws individuals together into an organic unity, a *Geist*, or "spirit" "the inwardly lived experience of the 'we.' " However, like W.E.B. Du Bois's soul, spirit is a matter of feeling rather than reason—"the deeper this feeling is, the stronger the living force of the people." It depends on *roots*, symbolized by the village

---

* "A Culture is born in the moment when a great soul awakens out of the proto-spirituality of ever-childish humanity, a form out of the formless. The birth of culture brings the gift of selfhood."

with "its quiet hillocky roofs, its evening smoke, its wells, its hedges, and beasts." All great peoples begin as villagers, fitting their collective fate to the contours of the land, in recognition of their close affinity with Mother Nature. The second requirement is *race*. World history is no longer the Enlightenment's linear story of civilization. It is instead, in the fashion of Gobineau, the story of the rise and fall of nations and races. But Spengler, like Du Bois, rejects Gobineau's claim that all cultural advance involves the diffusion of a racial type. As Spengler puts it, "races do not migrate, men migrate." Instead, race for Spengler is a matter of feeling, through "the greater or lesser communicability of intuition, sensations, and thoughts from one to another" in words, symbols, and artifacts. That communication inevitably forms "a common world-feeling," which links the race's successive generations together into one whole.[44]

At its beginnings, a great culture (such as Homeric Greece or Zoroastrian Persia) remains austere, controlled, intense, because it is infused with soul as the life force. In the next stage ("summer") this vital cultural consciousness spreads from the dominant classes—Homeric heroes and the Aryan warriors of Vedic India, for example—to the rest of the population. Incipient urban centers, like the Greek city-states and Florence and Venice during the Renaissance, produce great works of art and literature, as well as the first stirrings of criticism of the older (now called "classical") forms. Yet already signs of future decay begin to appear. The medieval walled town already foreshadows the cosmopolitan world city:

> Looking down from one of the old towers upon the sea of houses, we perceive . . . the end of organic growth and the beginning of an inorganic and therefore unrestrained process of massing without limit. . . . *World history is city history.*[45]

At the stage we call civilization ("autumn"), culture still takes its form and strength from the continuity of race in Spengler's spiritual sense, but it has no independent life of its own. "Pure civilization, as a historical process, consists of a progressive exhaustion of forms that have become inorganic or dead." As in the Hellenistic kingdoms of the fourth century B.C. or the Arabian empire of the Umayyads, "the fire in the soul dies down." The culture continues, "like a worn-out giant of the primeval forest," to "thrust decaying branches towards the sky," often for centuries or even millennia, as in the case of ancient, "petrified" civilizations such as Egypt, India, and China.[46]

Mature civilization ("winter") has become a total parasite. It clings to the once living roots of culture, which are its own forebears. "[Civilization] is a conclusion . . . death following life, rigidity following expansion. . . . petrifying world-city following mother-earth. . . ."[47] The vital springs of culture rest on a series of reconciliations through "the mysterious power of the soil": between man and nature, human being and *Volk*, and individual and community. Civilization at its mature stage, by contrast, brings tension rather than harmony. It denies the existence of the sacred in society by severing its connections with nature. If the intellectual core of culture is religion, that of civilization is irreligion and its attendant displacement of values and identity. What Nietzsche believed was characteristic of a declining West, "the transvaluation of all values," is in fact a prime characteristic of *all* late civilizations, from Buddhist India to Hellenistic Greece to Taoist China: a deliberate unsettling and disturbing of what was once solid and harmonious. The achievements of such a civilization can be grandiose and sophisticated, but it is always on the verge of neurosis.[48]

Spengler announced that Europe had reached this sterile winter stage in the nineteenth century. All its achievements were merely the vitality-sapping thrashings of a dying world. "An incredible total of intellect and power has been squandered in false directions." Facile philosophies of optimism—Comte, Herbert Spencer, and Marx—sprang up to disguise the vital decline, only to be negated by the skeptical pessimism of Schopenhauer, Wagner, and Nietzsche. The nineteenth century had to confront "the cold, hard facts of a late life. . . . Of great paintings or great music there can no longer be, for Western people, any question."[49] Spengler does not use the term "degenerate," but that certainly describes his civilized man. The "parasitical city dweller" relates to others "unstably in fluid masses. . . . [He is] traditionless . . . religionless, clever, unfruitful." These "amorphous and dispirited masses of men, scrap-material from a great history," drift aimlessly through cities like London, Paris, and New York with no ties to community or soil. In short,

Spengler's vitalist critique of *Zivilisation* easily merged with the clichés of degeneration theory to create a vivid image of modern society on the brink of self-extinction.

Spengler's term for this modern Western culture is not Aryan or Teutonic, but "Faustian." Like Goethe's hero, it restlessly pursues knowledge and change. Its chief product, science, is merely the concretization of this indomitable Western will, which it then projects onto the rest of the world in mechanical, rather than organic, terms.[50] Spengler insisted that the Western mechanical view of time, nature, and history stands in opposition to organic reality. The result is an illusion of limitless expansion and improvement over time, symbolized by clocks and space and represented by Newtonian physics and Western man's "irrepressible urge to distance." Until 1800, Spengler explained, the expansive tendency of Faustian culture was directed toward pushing out the frontiers of inner knowledge through art, literature, and the development of the political state. After 1800, as the West entered "the early Winter of full civilization," it began its remorseless expansion outward, through capitalism with its ever-growing markets and technological processes, and finally through empire.[51]

"Imperialism is civilization unadulterated." Spengler's view paralleled that of W.E.B. Du Bois but also that of Thomas Mann, who spoke of the "imperialism of civilization" encircling and threatening the German spirit.[52] But whereas past empires were built through conquest and absorption of other peoples, Spengler believed, European empires were built on the conquest of space, conceived as markets. Spengler agreed with Du Bois, Lenin, and J.A. Hobson that imperialism was primarily the product of business. The Western businessman's frenetic Faustian appetites—Cecil Rhodes punching open the African jungle and savannah with iron railways and tearing open the earth with gold and diamond mines—is merely "the prelude of a future which is still in store for us." Spengler grimly announced, "The expansive tendency is a doom, which grips, forces into service, and uses up the late mankind of the world-city stage."[53]

The history of modernity was *closed*, limited by its own exhaustion of cultural vitality. "We have to reckon with the cold hard fact of a *late* life," Spengler said, which imposes iron limits on what may be done. "We have not the freedom to reach to this or that, but [only] the freedom to do what is necessary or do nothing." If his audience did nothing, Spengler warned, then Germany would be dragged down into extinction along with the rest of the West. Once the vital life force was dead, "all that remains is the struggle for mere power, for animal advantage per se." The post-Western world appears on Spengler's speculative horizon as a frozen, savage landscape, an atavistic struggle for life and death between uprooted nations and classes. "In late civilization even the most convincing . . . idea is only the mask of purely zoological striving."[54]

But there is a possibility of escape from doom. For Spengler history is a kind of millrace where "all things are in flux." Heraclitus's motto rules the river of life force as it constantly "overflows its banks." All objects are eventually swept downstream, but at certain moments it is possible to snatch at fortune and by flexing "the will to fight," to drag a new *Kultur* free from the enclosing chaos. Spengler believed history had reached decisive moments such as this many times in the past. One was the death of Napoleon, the other the death of the Roman Republic in the era of Julius and Augustus Caesar. One created the Roman Empire, the other the British. "These epochs left behind them a world changed to its depths."

Now, Spengler believed, it was Germany's turn. "[Germany] may not be able to produce new Goethes," he wrote, "but it can produce new Caesars."

## SPENGLER AND WEIMAR: WAR, POLITICS, AND DEMOCRACY

We latecomers to Western civilization have become skeptics. . . . We no longer want ideas and principles. We want ourselves.

—Oswald Spengler, 1919

Spengler completed *The Decline of the West* in 1914, but the coming of war interrupted any final revisions. Adolf Hitler later wrote of August of that year: "As for me, as for every German, there now began the greatest and most unforgettable time of my earthly existence. Compared to the events of this gigantic struggle, everything past receded to shallow nothingness."[55] Due to his poor eyesight and weak heart Spengler was unable to enlist in the army, but he quickly became caught up in the war effort. On October 25 he wrote to his friend Hans Klores: "I am a thorough-going optimist. We shall win. . . ." He worried that a victorious Germany might become infected with the same "soulless Americanism," the worship of "technical skill, money and an eye for facts," as the rest of Western civilization at its twilight stage. But otherwise he remained confident about the future, as he began revising the final text.[56]

The first volume of *The Decline of the West* finally appeared in April 1918, in the midst of the last great German offensive. Big Bertha was raining artillery shells on Paris, and German armies seemed poised for success. Even the death of his brother-in-law that same week did not dampen Spengler's conviction that Germany would carve a mighty empire out of the ruins of a decadent Europe and extend its power eastward to the Urals. Then came one crushing disappointment after another, not only for Spengler, but for everyone who had a stake in Germany's final redemptive victory.

That summer, the Lüdendorff offensive collapsed under Allied counterattacks and units began streaming toward the rear. By the end of October Germany's allies—Turkey, Austria, and Bulgaria—had given up and the British, French, and American armies were closing on Germany's borders from the west and south. On November 3, the imperial German navy mutinied at the naval base at Kiel, followed by units of the army. On the ninth the kaiser abdicated; on the eleventh an armistice stopped the inexorable Allied advance.

With the swift collapse of central authority, revolutionary sentiments spread from Bolshevik Russia to Germany. Sailors and soldiers formed armed committees, or "soviets," followed by workers in Munich and Berlin. Beginning in early December 1918, Germany's major cities were governed at gunpoint as Soviet republics. The government had ceased to exist, while at the Versailles conference civilian officials had no choice but to make concession after concession to the victorious Allies. Finally, the left-wing party that founded the Weimar Republic, the Social Democrats, were forced to bring in their old enemy, the army, to restore order. From January to May 1919, the army and volunteer units of veterans (the *Freikorps*) crushed the uprisings in Berlin, Munich, and other cities. Thousands were killed, many in cold blood. Spengler was in Munich during the entire squalid episode: "Nothing but hunger, looting, filth, danger and rascality [*Trottelei*] without parallel," he wrote to a friend.[57]

Spengler's first reaction was despair: "Everything which I have profoundly esteemed and held dear" had collapsed. "Why must this fate come to us?" The old political order of Wilhelmine Germany, with its traditional Prussian discipline and virtues, had died in the trenches. Yet with time, Spengler was able to see a silver lining through the clouds of doom and despair. "I see in the revolution the means to save us, if those who will build our future know how to make use of it." The revolution of 1919 was the bloodiest and most violent that Germany had ever experienced. The destruction and death toll were far worse than in 1848, and many compared it to the Paris Commune of 1871 or even, as Spengler would do, to the French Revolution of 1789. The builders of the future whom Spengler had in mind were the veterans and the army, which had saved Germany from Bolshevism and now constituted, he and others believed, the center of "discipline, organizing power, and energy" in society.[58]

Germany's returning soldiers seemed imbued with a purifying power. One of them, Ernst Jünger, described himself and his fellows as "a new generation, a race that has been hardened and inwardly transformed by all the darting flames and sledgehammer blows of the greatest war in history."[59] Through them the pre-1914 ideal of youthful rebellion managed to survive the war. On the other hand, every other institution in German society was discredited by defeat. The new Weimar constitution was immediately suspect: "a standard issue English suit," as one scholar, Carl Schmitt, quipped, implying that it represented a false foreign liberalism.[60] The universities, which were official pillars of the Weimar Republic, were deeply split. Radical cultural pessimism no longer stood outside their gates; it was now an active force within. Classes and curricula became the battleground of a new culture war between those who tried to salvage something from the wreckage and those for whom the inevitable triumph of *Kultur* over *Zivilisation* had only been suspended by Germany's collapse.

As an instrument of destruction and renewal, revolutionary Marxism, too, had proved a dead end. The Spartacist revolt of 1919 cost the Communist Left the support of the most valuable constituency of postwar Germany, the veterans, who had helped to suppress it. For the wartime generation of university-trained intellectuals—men like Carl Schmitt, Hans Freyer, Martin Heidegger, and Arthur Moeller van den

Bruck, as well as Oswald Spengler—Germany's renewal now had to come from a revolution of the Right, not the Left. It would come not from a return to the old conservatism of Bismarck and Wilhelmine Germany but from a new, radical Right galvanized by the disasters of 1918 and '19 and inspired by icons of cultural pessimism like Lagarde, Nietzsche, and now Oswald Spengler.

The period 1918 to 1919 proved a disaster for the political future of Germany but it made Spengler's reputation. He had predicted to friends that the effect of *The Decline of the West* would be "like an avalanche in a shallow lake" and he was right, although not quite in the way he expected. *The Decline of the West* sold at once at a rate that forced the publisher to bring out a second printing. The reaction from the old university mandarins was predictably negative.* But younger scholars like Hans Freyer were more respectful of its method and aims. Thomas Mann acquired a copy in the summer of 1919 and spent all of July reading it through. He compared its emotional effect on him to that of reading Schopenhauer for the first time, and he thought it "the most important book" of the era. It also encouraged his pessimism about the immediate future: "What's coming now is Anglo-Saxon dominance of the world, that is perfected *Zivilisation.*"[61]

The Viennese philosopher Ludwig Wittgenstein read *The Decline of the West* and was thunderstruck; Spengler's book may even have played a part in steering him away from logical positivism into an entirely new approach to philosophy.[62] Max Weber was less impressed. He decided Spengler was nothing more than a "very ingenious and learned dilettante," but invited him to talk to his sociology seminar at the university in Munich. Spengler accepted. He and Weber, one of the authors of the Weimar constitution, squared off in December 1919 for a day-and-a-half debate. Although Weber behaved with perfect courtesy, his left-leaning students were less cordial, tearing "stone after stone" out of Spengler's "intellectual construct." Spengler was not daunted—he knew his book was a *succès de célèbre* in the circles he wanted to impress.[63]

At the end of 1919 Elisabeth Förster-Nietzsche read *The Decline of*

---

* Adolf von Harnack, the grand old man of the "higher criticism" school of biblical studies, told Spengler in a letter that he found the book "dubious, arbitrary, and unproven." *Letters,* pp. 85–6.

*the West* and was so overwhelmed by it that she arranged for Spengler to receive the prestigious Nietzsche Prize. Spengler was now a public figure. Unused to celebrity, he was forced to impose a three-day waiting list on the endless stream of visitors. However, he also wanted to use his position to shape the new political scene. Accordingly, he now published an article entitled "Pessimism," which was a reply to critics of *The Decline of the West* like Arthur Moeller van den Bruck, who accused him of being a fashionable spreader of gloom and doom. On the contrary, Spengler argued, he saw himself as the prophet of a nationalist resurgence for Germany—and with it the extermination of the last of the corrupt West, including the Weimar Republic itself.

Shortly on the heels of *The Decline of the West*'s success, Spengler decided to turn his talents to political commentary. The result was *Prussianism and Socialism*, which appeared at the beginning of 1920. It turned Spengler into a formidable intellectual apologist for Germany's revolution of the Right. Just as Moeller van den Bruck was moving German nationalism out of the older Bismarckian tradition,* so was it Spengler's goal to take socialism away from the Marxists. Like Brooks and Henry Adams, Spengler had concluded that only a top-down socialist command economy could save modern society. He hoped that he could now reconcile the "respectable working classes," including ex-veterans, with the vision of a Nietzschean German nationalism. Together workers, soldiers, engineers, and right-wing intellectuals would team up to crush the international financiers and the mob. They would substitute a "dictatorship of organization" to replace "the dictatorship of money" in postwar Germany.[64]

What offended Spengler and other figures of the revolution of the Right about Marxist socialism was not that it empowered the working

---

* Although Moeller wrote a critical review of *The Decline of the West*, his own view of Germany and history was not much different. He rejected pre-1941 Bismarckian German nationalism as old-fashioned and inadequate. In 1922 Moeller composed his own idealized vision of Germany's future, of a great Middle European Germanic empire that would reconcile all social classes and all the contradictions of German history, which he dubbed the "third Reich." This third Reich (following the medieval German empire, or first Reich, and the second Reich of the Hohenzollerns) would be animated by the vital younger generation of the war: "They have Darwin and Nietzsche on their side." Until 1932 the term "third Reich" was associated not with Hitler and the Nazis, but with Moeller van den Bruck.

class and smashed big business and finance—they were planning to do that themselves.[65] They turned away from Marxism because they saw it as part of a dying civilization. To think of society in terms of categories like proletariat, bourgeoisie, and class struggle was antiquated: it was, as Hans Freyer put it, "the schema of the day before yesterday." A new society and a new culture required new political categories, and Spengler now provided a crucial one with *Prussianism and Socialism*.

Spengler shattered liberalism, the guiding ethos of modernity, along its central axis by splitting the desire for equality from the need for liberty. Liberty, he pointed out, was a dead end; it only led to cultural decadence and a loss of vitality as in England and America, nations inhabited by people "without roots and therefore without a future." Equality, on the other hand, sprang directly out of the old Prussian military tradition. "King Friedrich Wilhelm," he announced, "not Marx, was the first socialist." The Prussian tradition of discipline and self-sacrifice could build a modern, unified community of equals, men joined together by obedience, service, and instinct. This "true socialism" would destroy capitalism *and* Marxism, since both were false and degenerate ideologies of the past.

Prussian socialism, or "nationalist socialism" as he called it, would channel and direct the vital energies of the German people into a new seamless and organic whole, as German intellectuals had always dreamed. Such a community "is an expression of sublime strength and freedom, something which the outsider can never understand." Men would learn to exchange "practical freedom" of the English and American sort for an "inner freedom," which comes through discharging obligations to the organic whole. "The organization of production and communication by the State; everybody to be a servant of the State . . . Each citizen is assigned his place in the totality. He receives his orders and obeys them."[66] The nationalist socialist man's motto is not (like that of Werner Sombart's liberal) "every man for himself, but 'every man for every other man.'" Spengler called for a new elite to rise up in Germany, made up of young people who ignored "worthless political verbiage" and who "are capable of grasping what is potent and invincible in our nature, and who are prepared to go forward, come what may."[67]

Spengler's vision of a new nationalist socialism became almost as influential as his *Decline of the West*. Spengler himself noted that it found a strong following among younger politicians and industrialists.[68] Moeller van den Bruck borrowed from it heavily (just as Spengler had borrowed from Moeller's earlier *The Prussian Style*) and argued in a similar vein that a future "third German Reich" must be socialist, in the sense of enjoying a self-sacrificing organic unity as well as being an enemy of decadent capitalism. A militant and military socialism now loomed as the great signpost for the German future. Ernst Jünger wrote a political tract with a strikingly Marxist title, *The Worker*, which pointed to the affinities between workers and soldiers as cooperative builders of the future. Spengler very much praised Jünger's work, and soon the strong and virtuous worker was no longer a rallying symbol of the Marxist Left but of the radical Right.

Inevitably, this image of the free but rooted German worker merged with the Aryan-Teutonic free warrior of neo-Gobinian myth. Spengler's *Decline of the West* hit a responsive chord with his fellow Municher, the mystical anti-Semite Dietrich Eckhart. In January 1919 Eckhart and a group associated with the Pan-German Thule Society formed a new political party, the German Workers' Party. The Thule Society's emblem of Aryan vitalism, the swastika, now became an overt political symbol. When Alfred Rosenberg joined the German Workers' Party in May, he brought along his friend Adolf Hitler, who soon became its dominant spokesman. Rosenberg was also a Spengler convert, and both he and Eckhart impressed Hitler with Spengler's importance as a "true" German thinker, along with other figures such as Gobineau and Houston Chamberlain. In 1920 Hitler changed the Workers' Party name to the National Socialist German Workers' Party, reflecting the two themes of the revolution of the Right, volkish nationalism and Spengler's German socialism.

The second volume of Spengler's *Decline of the West* appeared in May 1922, amid military coups and political unrest. It was even more relevant and directly political than the first in its handling of the themes of the death of liberalism and the suicide of the West. Spengler attacked liberalism as the outdated and bankrupt ideology of a dying *Zivilisation* and its endangered species, the commercial-minded bourgeoisie. Bourgeois democracies operate by shameless flattery of the audience, fantastic lies about opponents . . . by games and presents, by threats and blows, but above all by money. Money organizes the process in the interest of those who possess it, and election affairs become a preconcerted game that is staged as popular self-determination.[69]

If Spengler's first volume presented history as the story of peoples and nations, the second presented the future as "the struggle of, not principles but men, not ideals but race-qualities, for executive power is the alpha and omega." Napoleon, Caesar, Alexander appear not just as kings or commanders of armies, but as creators of peoples. "Political talent," he wrote, "is nothing but confidence in its leaders." Caesarism, not constitutions, would become the keynote of politics in the new age. The power of the modern state would pass into the hands of egotistic "adventurers, self-styled Caesars, seceding generals and barbarian kings" for whom the *Volk* and nation are "only part of the landscape." Already, he thought (writing in 1922), such a one had appeared in Russia in Leon Trotsky. "In our Germanic world," Spengler added, "the spirits of Alaric and Theodoric will come again" to break "the dictatorship of money and its political weapon, democracy. The sword will triumph over money."[70]

Spengler's sequel prompted an ambiguous response. The distinguished ancient historian Eduard Meyer gave it strong marks, and although he expressed doubts about Spengler's method and evidence, he agreed with the book's general conclusions. In fact, he said, "I look perhaps even more pessimistically toward the future of our people than he does."[71] Other admirers such as Thomas Mann clearly saw Spengler's authoritarian political agenda for the first time, and were put off by it. Mann now referred to Spengler as Nietzsche's "clever imitator" (literally, "his apish imitator") and began to treat his works with indifference and even contempt. At the same time, Mann grasped Spengler's larger purpose in writing *The Decline of the West*: to make himself Nietzsche's successor in the practice of the philosophy of nihilism. Spengler intended to turn history itself into (as Nietzsche might say) "a mighty hammer" in order to "break and remove degenerate and decaying races to make way for a new order of life." In that sense, *The Decline of the West*, as Spengler told several correspondents, "has had the effect I had hoped."

Spengler believed a nationalist socialism was coming that would reach far beyond a political coalition of veterans and the working class. "Every German is a worker," he wrote in *Prussianism and Socialism*, "it is part of his way of life." This included army officers as well as machinists and artisans, industrialists and military contractors—even government officials and professional men. Such men would lose their status as stereotyped bourgeois, "small-minded, thought-stifling, and degrading," and become the indispensable managers of the machinery of industry and the state.[72] Spengler's vision of the future socialist nation bears a strong resemblance to that of Brooks Adams, with a disciplined technocratic elite of engineers and other practical-minded individuals leading Germany out its "feudal-agrarian narrowness." Like Adams, too, Spengler invested this socialist future with the awesome authority of historical inevitability; there was no sense in protesting against their version of the future, both writers assured their readers, because it was predetermined by destiny.

However, underneath Spengler's elite also beat the harsh, steady rhythms of Nietzsche's will to power. The complete overturning of society through socialist principles would be a true transvaluation of all values, Spengler believed, as everything would be transformed into a single *totality* of state, man, and machine. "We do not need ideologues anymore," he insisted, "we need hardness, we need fearless skepticism, we need a class of socialist master men." He added melodramatically, "Once again, socialism means power, power, and yet again power."[73]

Spengler sought to reconcile socialist equality with volkish nationalism. His effort profoundly affected left-leaning converts to Hitler's National Socialist Party like Josef Goebbels and Gregor Strasser. In June and July of 1925 Strasser wrote two letters to Spengler, one long and one short, expressing admiration for the latter's works and urging him to take note of the similarities between the ideals of the Nazi Party and his own. The Nazis, too, wished to bring about "a German revolution by a German socialism," Strasser said. Despite Hitler's failed 1923 coup in Munich and his imprisonment, Strasser announced, "the great political idea of National Socialism had not failed, but is only now beginning."[74] Spengler had his doubts. Like Moeller van den Bruck and other radical nationalists, Spengler's initial judgment of Hitler and the Nazi Party was resoundingly negative. "The pathfinder must be a hero," he sniffed when discussing Hitler, "not a heroic tenor." His own hopes centered on various German generals and on Fritz Seldte, the head of the veterans' group Stahlhelm. Hitler, on the other hand, seemed weak and indecisive; Spengler complained that the Nazis could not make up their minds whether they were rightists or leftists.[75]

He also held very different views on the issue of race from the Nazis. Spengler frequently used terms such as "master race" and "blood." But his idea of race was in the end subordinate to his ideal of *Kultur*. In this he resembles no one so much as another German-university-trained scholar, W.E.B. Du Bois. Both saw race as the organic involvement of human beings in the spiritual reality of their people, the *Volk*. Race was a matter of spirit, not mere biology. Others, of course, become impatient with this sort of academic distinction. Hitler, Rosenberg, and the other Nazi leaders were in the grip of a potent neo-Gobinian racial pessimism directed against the Jews. Their insistence on racial purity and Aryan descent stood in sharp contrast to the attitude expressed by Spengler's friend Fritz Seldte: "We say to hell with rank and status. . . . We look only at the man himself. Only character should count."[76]

As Spengler's most perceptive critic, H. Stuart Hughes, has pointed out, a certain snobbery also played its part in Herr Doktor Spengler's hostility toward Hitler, a low-bred radical bohemian. Hitler's response was quick and direct: "They accuse me of being a barbarian," he said to one of his associates. "Of course, we are barbarians. We are proud to be barbarians."[77] But perhaps Spengler's ultimate objection to Hitler was that the Nazis' vision of salvation through a mass movement offended his Nietzschean sense of historical relativism. A true student of *The Genealogy of Morals* and *Zarathustra* could only look skeptically on the possibility of mass political enthusiasm transforming what fate has decreed. In 1924 he gave a speech at the University of Wurzburg on "The Political Duties of German Youth," in which he warned that today "national politics are regarded as a kind of inebriation," in which marches and processions had replaced serious thought about Germany's future. "Undoubtedly, these things are satisfying to the emotions, but . . . trumpeters are hardly generals."[78]

However, when the Great Depression hit Germany, leaving one-third of its workers unemployed by 1932, the ensuing political choice between Communism and Hitler moved Spengler and other doubters into the

National Socialist camp. That year Ferdinand Fried, the editor of the conservative nationalist newspaper *Die Tat*, published his immensely popular *End of Capitalism*, which stated in Spenglerian tones that capitalist society had finally played itself out and would have to be reabsorbed by society through its agent the state. Werner Sombart asserted there was now a general consensus that Europe in the nineteenth century had "experienced a period of decline"—a consensus beginning, he noted, with Jacob Burckhardt and Nietzsche. "We who live at the end of this decline can now for the first time measure the extent and depth of the devastation" in the political, social, and spiritual life of Germany. "Only he who believes in the power of the devil," Sombart concluded balefully, "can understand what has taken place in western Europe and America in the last hundred and fifty years."[79] The one hope was Adolf Hitler, another sociologist said, who "will do away with the ossified remnants of the nineteenth century and free the way for the history of the twentieth." Hitler himself made it clear that he was prepared for this kind of demolition work in order to stop the "creeping sickness" of the age. "There must be no half-measures," he had written in *Mein Kampf*. "The gravest and most ruthless decisions will have to be made."[80]

In the 1932 election Spengler brought himself to vote for Hitler and even hung out the swastika flag from the window of his Munich home. Hitler was still "a fool," he believed, "but we must not abandon the movement." In 1933, following Hitler's accession to power, the enthusiastically pro-Nazi Hans Freyer, acting as head of the Institute for Historical Research at the University of Leipzig, wrote to Spengler offering him the Chair of Culture and Universal History. Spengler's great dream, a university professorship, was now his for the asking. But he was forced to refuse, partly, as he told Freyer, to preserve his solitude, but also, one suspects, to preserve his independence from an intellectual environment that was rapidly being politicized.

For the Nazis were determined to bring Germany's prestigious universities under their control. The story of the Nazi takeover of Germany's academic and intellectual life is the story of pressure from within as much as from without.[81] The party's first big success had been among university students, and through them the Nazis gained control of the National Student Union. Students in brown shirts and swastika armbands were a normal sight in classes well before 1932; afterwards they turned into violent mobs, burning books and demonstrating against Jewish professors.

Nor were many professors shocked or even disappointed—at least at first. At the University of Bonn, the sociologist Eduard Spranger claimed that the Nazi students represented a "genuine national movement," even if their tactics were at times "undisciplined."[82] Although the new National Socialist government refused to grant its student supporters the power they demanded to hire and fire professors, it did make job tenure a matter of political ideology. Over seventeen hundred faculty members were dismissed as pacifists and leftists, while academic disciplines that the Nazis considered "impractical" or "apolitical" were stripped of funds and personnel. In these matters they had considerable help from faculty members themselves. The distinguished philosopher and rector of the University of Freiburg, Martin Heidegger, helped ferret out Jews from academic positions. The legal theorist Carl Schmitt helped draft new laws discriminating against the Jews, "the deadly enemy of every genuine productivity of every other people." Werner Sombart and Hans Freyer represented a politically correct Nazi sociology at international conferences.[83] And as we have already seen, anthropologists and biologists like Eugen Fischer and Alfred Ploetz would cooperate fully with the Nazis.*

Of course, these were men with positions to protect. Spengler could afford to be more independent. He was coming under increasing fire from party hacks for his "pessimism," which really meant his unwillingness to back the Hitler regime. In the summer of 1933, under pressure from friends and political allies, Spengler finally agreed to meet Hitler, appropriately enough at the Bayreuth Festival.

It was a strange moment. These two men, the veteran turned anti-Semitic demagogue and the university scholar turned political magus, found themselves on the same hilltop Richard Wagner and Friedrich Nietzsche had climbed together in the rain in 1876, almost sixty years earlier. They stood at the confluence of two deep and swift channels running through the German cultural landscape: one flowing from Gobineau to Wagner and Houston Chamberlain, the other from Nietzsche and his radical nationalist followers. Both Spengler and Hitler were in

---

* See Chapter 4.

their own ways prophets of cultural pessimism. Both now looked forward to the Götterdämmerung of the old European order—the twilight of the idols of the liberal West—from which a new age would be born. Yet the meeting itself turned out to be an anticlimax. They discussed policy toward France—and the Catholic Church. Hitler tried to praise and flatter the older man, saying something about the need to draw non-Party members into the Nazi movement. But Spengler must have realized that the dictator had his own plans, which no longer included the likes of him.

The following spring Spengler published *The Hour of Decision*. It was a deeply gloomy book. Most of it had been written before Hitler's election as chancellor the previous year, but Spengler decided to change nothing.* Spengler reiterated his view that Germany was now the key nation in the world, situated as it was between Asia and the great revolutions taking place there (in Russia and China) and Western Europe and the economic decline taking place there. The world was about to be torn apart, he said, between class warfare in the West and the new colored nations and empires of the East. The German nation was still "young enough to experience world-historical problems" and solve them. But the simple "desire to fight" was no longer enough. He called the Nazis "everlasting youths," lacking the maturity and thoughtfulness needed to resolve the crisis of the West. Hitler had abandoned the tried-and-true traditions of Prussianism, of army and aristocracy, and was moving to a dangerous kind of socialism that was still untested. "Those in nationalist circles who have picked up the word as a slogan have to this day not understood that socialism is an ethos, not an economic policy."[84]

*The Hour of Decision* was hardly a call to overthrow Hitler; it was merely the Germanic equivalent of Brooks Adams's *America's Economic Supremacy*, the sort of now-or-never call to arms in the coming global struggle that would come to dominate declinist literature in the age of mass publishing and eventually replace it altogether. But in the intellectual climate of the Third Reich, anything less than full endorsement was the same as outright criticism. Although the publisher managed to finish his first run, the book was immediately banned and copies scooped

---

* He did send a copy to Hitler when it was published.

off of bookstore shelves. The attacks on Spengler in the press increased, as did his sense of isolation. As one of Spengler's few remaining friends wrote to another after *The Hour of Decision* was banned, "He is gradually making himself into a mythic figure; ill, not leaving his room for weeks on end, more and more incapable of tolerating men and humanity."[85]

With the universities and intellectuals tamed, the Nazis next imposed Aryan racial standards on the German army in February 1934, over the protest of many generals. Four months later came the purge of Ernst Roehm's Brownshirts and veterans' groups, the so-called Night of the Long Knives. Several leading conservatives and generals were also shot, along with the one Nazi Spengler had respected, Gregor Strasser. In October 1935 Spengler gave up his honorary position with the Nietzsche Archives. Elisabeth Förster-Nietzsche, now eighty-nine years old, had less than a month to live. She had been a firm supporter of Hitler almost from the moment his name hit the headlines.* His elevation to power in 1933, she told a friend, had left her "drunk with enthusiasm." She turned the Nietzsche Archives into a virtual Nazi shrine, with ceremonies and receptions attended by Hitler and other Nazi celebrities— but not Spengler. Now she wrote a letter to him, expressing puzzlement regarding his withdrawal from the archives and his reluctance to support Hitler. Hadn't the "great Fuhrer" achieved the same ideals and goals that Spengler had spoken of in *Prussianism and Socialism?* Spengler never sent a reply.

In November Elisabeth Förster-Nietzsche died; Hitler attended her funeral, as he had Houston Stewart Chamberlain's seven years earlier. The following March, Oswald Spengler suffered a massive heart attack and died in his apartment. At fifty-six, his passing went virtually unnoticed. One of the few who did notice was Thomas Mann. Mann was living in Zurich, in exile from the Nazi regime he despised. After reading Spengler's obituary, Mann noted in his diary that when he first read *The Decline of the West* almost twenty years earlier he had sensed "a certain kinship in spiritual values." Spengler "too had drawn his concept of decline principally from Nietzsche—what concerned him most was the

---

* Everyone who worked at the archives, according to one observer, from Förster-Nietzsche to the doorkeeper, was an enthusiastic Nazi.

decline of cultural values." But once Mann saw the depths of Spengler's underlying "contempt for human freedom" he had learned to hate him. Mann concluded:

> He died young in bitterness and sorrow I should think. But he did terrible things to pave the way for what was to come, and early sounded the notes which deafen us today.[86]

## CHAPTER 8

# WELCOMING DEFEAT

## Arnold Toynbee

> I am conscious of having a certain "down" on Western civilization
> and have often tried to think out why I have it. . . . Partly it is the
> feeling that the Ancient World is the real home of the human
> spirit, and that what came after is rather a pity—like dog Latin.
>
> —Arnold Toynbee to Gilbert Murray, 1930

One of the first people to buy a copy of *The Decline of the West* when it appeared in London bookstores was a young historian at the University of London named Arnold Toynbee. Toynbee found the book both exhilarating and dismaying. Each page teemed "with firefly flashes of historical insight" on the very problem that Toynbee himself had been planning to undertake: the rise and fall of civilizations. As he wrote long afterwards, "I wondered at first whether my whole inquiry had been disposed of by Spengler before even the questions, not to speak of the answers, had fully taken shape in my own mind."[1] But in the end Spengler's book served as a prompt to action. That summer Toynbee drew up the basic outline for what was to become *The Study of History*, a description of the entire history of mankind from Hammurabi to Hitler in twelve thick volumes. Eventually it would even eclipse *The Decline of the West* as the best-known assessment of Western civilization's place in world history.

Arnold Toynbee was the product of an intellectual tradition very different from Spengler's, and one that Spengler largely despised: that of late-nineteenth-century English liberalism. However, that did not prevent Toynbee from sharing many of the German scholar's assumptions and sympathies. Like Spengler, Toynbee took as his symbol of the modern West the British Empire. Like Spengler's *Decline of the West*, Toynbee's *Study of History* was shaped by the conviction that Great Britain's role in that history was coming to an end. On a tour of Crete in 1912 Toynbee had come upon an elaborate Baroque palace built by a Venetian merchant prince shortly before the island was overrun by the Turks. As he stood gazing at its ruined shell, Toynbee wrote later, the thought suddenly struck him: "If the Venetian Empire had perished, the British Empire could not be immortal." That melancholy insight would remain with him all his life: the fragility of human hopes and expectations, including his own, in the face of the larger forces of history and time.

Toynbee belonged to a generation of disenchanted intellectuals who dominated the English scene between the First and Second World Wars. They saw the British Empire as representing the discredited values of a "smug" and "hypocritical" Victorian age, and waited impatiently for its demise. But they shared more of that Victorian outlook than they cared to admit. The liberal optimism of the early Victorians had been evaporating long before Toynbee was born. This was due in large part to the degeneration scare, which had cast serious doubt on the future of civil society in the industrial age. If the fear of degeneration had driven English liberalism into retreat, then the trauma of World War I completed the rout. In the minds of interwar British intellectuals, their nation and the modern West were summed up in the title of T.S. Eliot's famous poem: *The Waste Land*.

Some turned to Marxism to create a new social order; a few others, like the artist Wyndham Lewis and the novelist D.H. Lawrence, turned to an irrational vitalism bordering on fascism. But Toynbee and many of his generation turned to another alternative, which flowed out of the New Liberalism of the later Victorians and its postliberal assumptions. Instead of demolishing the West, they would refurbish it as a community of shared moral values, what the Enlightenment would have termed "polite" values. Tolerance, compassion, humanitarian concern, and reasonable compromise would define this new Western civilization; its chief virtues would have a spiritual rather than a material basis. The British Empire, and by extension Europe and the West, would accept their political eclipse, as non-Western nations with their teeming millions rose up from the horizon. However, this kinder, gentler West would establish in effect a new universal empire of peace and harmony, with its humane, civilized values serving as the basis for a world government and unity among peoples everywhere.

This pacific new vision for the modern West proved to be immensely influential, and not only in England. It dominates the geopolitical outlook of modern liberals to this very day. Arnold Toynbee, in his *Study of History*, supplied it with a new version of universal history, called "world history," which it could use to justify its claims to a kind of spiritual grace and its implicit acceptance of Western decline.

A dangerous intellectual rift began to appear. At the center of the rift was the conviction, which everyone shared, that twentieth-century Western civilization was in crisis. Yet while cultural pessimists like Spengler looked to vitalism and militarism to regenerate the West, Toynbee and other liberals of the 1920s and 1930s looked to the exact opposite. Renouncing force and violence became a moral imperative for the heirs of liberal humanism, just as celebrating force and violence became the imperative of their opponents. What seemed to men and women like Toynbee, Lionel Curtis, Virginia Woolf, the pacifist Vera Brittain, Kingsley Martin of *The New Statesman*, and many, many others to be expressions of civilized restraint appeared to their enemies to be only further evidence of the West's decadence and cowardice. From appeasement and the League of Nations, to the Committee for Nuclear Disarmament and the Euromissile protests of the 1980s, twentieth-century liberalism proved more adept at encouraging its enemies than at protecting those it claimed to represent.

Constructed over the course of four decades, Toynbee's *Study of History* stands as a kind of monument to this modern liberalism. It reflects its virtues, its failures, and the deep historical pessimism that underlies it.

## PROGRESS, DECLINE, AND EMPIRE IN VICTORIAN BRITAIN

The dark leading edge of that pessimism first appeared in Britain in 1869, when Matthew Arnold published *Culture and Anarchy*. Arnold was the product of Victorian culture in its most vigorous and self-confident form. His father, Thomas Arnold, had been the headmaster of the Rugby School, where generations of young boys learned the upright values of the English "Christian gentleman," celebrated in the novel *Tom Brown's School Days* (1857). Thomas Arnold had seen those traditional values as easily embracing and absorbing the new middle class of industrial Britain. His son Matthew did not. He warned that "the course taken . . . by the middle classes of this nation will probably give a decisive turn to its history." In Matthew Arnolds view, the tobacconists, grocers, and aldermen of Liverpool, Manchester, and Birmingham lacked any cultural compass. They "believe that our greatness and welfare are proved by being very rich" and nothing more, Arnold charged. He gave them their immortal label: philistines.[2]

Arnold worried that an upwardly mobile middle class would pollute the wellsprings of culture. His definition of culture owed more to Enlightenment notions of politeness and learning than to German *Kultur*; it constituted a realm of "sweetness and light," an "endless growth in wisdom and beauty," and "the idea of perfection as an inward condition of the mind and spirit." However, the enemies of culture were the same: "mechanical and material civilization," with its blind faith in technology. Like Henry Adams, Arnold worried that an affluent industrial society would lose a sense of "subordination and deference" toward the superior individual of culture. "New and democratic forces" were swamping the boat, which the laissez-faire liberalism of Adam Smith and John Stewart Mill could no longer steer. He warned: "If [the middle class] will not seek . . . their own elevation, if they go on exaggerating their spirit of individualism . . . [it] will not prevent them getting the rule of their country for a season, but they will certainly *Americanize* it." They "will rule [Britain] by their energy, but they will deteriorate it by their low ideas and want of culture."[3]

Matthew Arnold's pessimism and air of aristocratic disdain reminds us of Henry Adams, a figure he in many ways resembles (they were also close friends). However, despite the earlier spread of a similar pessimism among English Romantics, which had touched isolated figures like Thomas Carlyle, this was something new to the English liberal mind. In fact, by 1870 the robust and active circles of liberal intellectuals in London, Oxford, and Cambridge that the young Henry Adams had found so congenial were breaking apart. Self-confidence had begun to turn to doubt and fear.

The leading spokesmen of classical English liberalism had also begun to die off, with no one stepping forward to take their place. Henry Adams's old mentor, John Stuart Mill, had died in 1873, while historian Thomas Macaulay had passed away in 1859. Parliamentary reformer Francis Brougham died in 1868, and the untiring advocate of liberal optimism and "muscular Christianity," Charles Kingsley, in 1875. Instead, the most articulate figures on the political landscape now tended to be critics of progress and liberalism, such as John Henry Newman and Benjamin Disraeli.[4] Liberalism itself was entering a new, more detached, "scientific" phase, represented by men like Walter Bagehot and Thomas Henry Buckle. Francis Galton, and Charles Darwin in his last influential work, *The Descent of Man* (1871), had already indicated scientific liberalism's future direction: concern about the debilitating effects of civilization on man's forward evolution and fears of degeneration.*

The rise of socialism also helped to fragment old-fashioned liberalism, drawing off many working-class reformers who had once rallied around the liberal banners of progress and free trade. A succession of groups such as the Chartists, the London Working Men's Association (founded in 1866), the Trades Union Congress (1869), the Independent Labour Party (1893), and finally the British Labour Party (1906) moved British labor step-by-step away from liberal and toward collectivist principles. Some liberals themselves turned to socialism, forming the so-called Fabian Society, the unofficial think tank of the Labour Party and a major voice in the intellectual circles in which the young Arnold Toynbee grew up and moved.

The decline in religious belief at Britain's leading universities had also sapped the old sources of confidence in the future. The term "agnostic" first appeared in the same year as *Culture and Anarchy*. In 1871 both Oxford and Cambridge abolished the religious test for entry into the university, permitting professed "freethinkers" and even atheists to

---

* Darwin's old rival, Alfred R. Wallace, wrote in 1890: "In one of my last conversations with Darwin he expressed himself very gloomily on the future of humanity, on the ground that in our modern civilization natural selection had no play, and the fittest did not survive." Quoted in Kevles, *In the Name of Eugenics*, p. 70.

hold academic positions. Yet at the same time that faith in a benevolent personal God was disappearing among Britain's intelligentsia, a sense of man's underlying sinfulness remained. Deprived of the traditional outlets, the Calvinist conscience searched out new arenas in which to vent its moral anxieties.[5]

One of these was the "discovery" of urban industrial poverty, which threw into severe disrepute British liberalism's central tenet, that human progress involved the unfettering of the forces of economic growth and production throughout society.[6] Poverty, of course, had existed before the nineteenth century, but it had remained largely out of sight in rural areas. Now industrial cities such as Liverpool, London, and Manchester spawned slums and filthy workers' tenements, shocking and disgusting middle-class observers (including the young Friedrich Engels).[7] In the view of outraged critics, this poverty *had* to be the result of the sudden and jolting transformation of Britain's economic life from agriculture to manufacturing. Indeed, the term "industrial revolution" was coined by one of these critics to dramatize its sudden and devastating effects. That critic was Arnold Toynbee's uncle, Arnold Toynbee, Sr.

As tutor at Balliol College, Oxford, the elder Toynbee had practically invented the field of British economic history. Like the German armchair socialists, he believed that the modern faith in free market capitalism ran counter to the rest of man's historical development. However, it had managed to do considerable damage in a very short time. The Industrial Revolution, Toynbee told his readers, was "a period as disastrous and terrible as any through which a nation ever passed."[8] His image of the Industrial Revolution as the *systematic* exploitation of men, women, and children at the hands of a mill-owning bourgeois class became classic, and remained a standard part of the new pessimistic liberalism.

Like their American counterparts, English liberals of the 1870s and '80s worried that industrial society would create two nations of rich and poor. Fears that industrial growth had impoverished its working class fed fears of degeneration. Industrial capitalism made people "unhealthy, poor and likely to perish," wrote John Ruskin, Slade Professor of Art and author of the influential anti–laissez-faire tract, *Unto This Last*.[9] Gloom about the future did not consume just socialists like Ruskin and William Morris, or conservatives like Benjamin Disraeli, who coined the term "two nations." It struck at major pillars of the Victorian establishment, including its poet laureate Alfred Lord Tennyson. In 1842, in his poem "Locksley Hall," he had written the lines, "Forward, forward let us range/ Let the great world spin for ever down the ringing grooves of change." Forty years later he returned to this theme in a very different mood:

> Good, this forward, you that preach it,
>     is it well to wish you joy?
> Is it well that while we range in Science,
>     glorying in the Time,
> City children soak and blacken
>     soul and sense in city slime?
>
> There among the glooming alleys
>     Progress halts on palsied feet,
> Crime and hunger cast our maidens
>     by the thousands on the street.
>
> Forward, forward, aye, and backward,
>     downward too into the abysm!

That same year, Arnold Toynbee, Sr., wrote in *The Industrial Revolution:* "The times are troubled, [and] old political faiths are shaken."[10] Beginning in the 1880s, Parliament passed a series of economic measures that began to roll back the old classical principle of laissez-faire.* Drawing inspiration from the German philosopher Hegel, the so-called British Idealists—Toynbee, Thomas Hill Green, R.B. Haldane, and Bernard Bosanquet—pressed for using the powers of the modern state to create an economy that would be "social" as well as "political." Like American Progressives and German armchair socialists, they believed that the day of the free market was over. Liberalism, they argued, must build a new future for Britain, one that reflected higher moral aspirations than "selfish" individualism and the sanctity of private property.

Steeped in the classical education of the English public schools and Oxford and Cambridge, the British Idealists looked back nostalgically to the age of Periclean Athens. The Athenians had combined self-

---

* Among these were the Irish Land Bill, the Agricultural Holdings Act, and the Employers' Liability Act.

government with great achievements in art, literature, and drama; they had managed to be commercially minded without being philistines. Most importantly, ancient Athens had cultivated the virtues of civilization, while retaining a strong sense of unity and tradition—something modern democracies, it was felt, had failed to do. Green and his disciples believed that Britain could achieve that same sense of enlightened community, drawing together rich and poor alike, through the ministrations of Hegel's bureaucratic state or what would later be called "the welfare state."[11]

The Idealists rejected the classic economic model of the autonomous individual, whose personal rights need to be protected from outside interference and whose rational self-interest serves as the motive engine for civilization's ascent. "Individual freedom," Green had written, "is valuable only as a means to an end." Instead he argued for a moral model in which the person chooses ends that "we enjoy in common with others" and that benefit others as well as himself (which, it was assumed, the businessman or industrialist never does).[12] The good citizen ("citizenship" was a crucial term for Green and the later New Liberals that conjured up images of Plato's *Republic* and Periclean Athens) was actively committed to extending the helping hand of the political community to "the less favoured members of society." As one disciple put it, "The power of the good state empowers the citizen, and the power of the good citizen empowers the state."[13]

In Athens, of course, citizens extended that helping hand themselves. In the modern age, the state had to take over citizenship's moral burden to provide for the welfare of others, discharging it for the society as a whole. As Sir Henry Jones explained: "The essence of society is moral. It is only on moral grounds that we can determine the nature and limits of its functions."[14] Wrote another leading Idealist, "Imagine that all human beings felt permanently and universally to each other as they now do occasionally to those whom they love best." The result would be a community "in which there would be no individuals at all, in which there will be a universal being in and for another . . . a common consciousness." In short, a modern universal empire—or what Graham Wallas of the London School of Economics called "the Great Society"— built not on conquest and competition, but on permanent love and fellowship.[15]

Green's most impassioned pupil was Arnold Toynbee, Sr.[16] Toynbee's historical research was fired by a crusading moral fervor—and a heavy dose of what might be called liberal guilt. In 1883 he tearfully confessed to a working-class audience in London that "we—the middle classes, I mean, not just the rich—have neglected you . . . but I think we are changing. If you will only believe it and trust us, I think that many of us would spend our lives in your service. . . . You have to forgive us, for we have wronged you; we have *sinned* against you grievously. . . ." On the way home Toynbee suffered a nervous collapse, and died less than two months later.[17]

Toynbee's spectacular demise made the British Idealists famous. Herbert Spencer made one last plea for the old individualistic ideal in *Man Versus the State* in 1884; otherwise, the statist assumptions of the New Liberalism swept all before it. New Liberalism was more than a political creed, it was "a new faith," as *Oxford Magazine* put it, "with Professor Green as its founder, [and] Arnold Toynbee as its martyr." Its leading spokesman was L.T. Hobhouse, the first professor of sociology at the University of London and a major force on the editorial staff of the *Manchester Guardian*, the virtual house organ of the New Liberalism, which was dedicated, in Malcolm Muggeridge's later phrase, "to all Good Causes and uplifting the spirits of the Downtrodden everywhere." Another wing of the New Liberalism, the Fabian Socialists, predicted that the ministrations of the bureaucratic welfare state would eventually replace the capitalist system altogether. Socialism, one of the Fabians' founding members, Sidney Webb, explained, was more than just an economic and political doctrine. "It expresses the real recognition of fraternity," and stood in sharp contrast to what the historian R.H. Tawney called "the acquisitive society," the hard, cold world of greedy businessmen, who sacrificed the public good for individual profits.[18]

Fabianism and the New Liberalism inspired a growing number of civil servants and social workers to venture forth into Britain's mines, factories, and city streets. Men like Henry Jones and women like Beatrice Potter (later Beatrice Webb) wrote tracts advocating nationalization of the gas works and electrical utilities, gave lectures to working men and women at Toynbee Hall in Manchester, named after the movement's martyr, and went about their duties with his last appeal to the working class echoing in their ears: "We work for you in the hope and trust that if you get material civilization, if you get a better life, you will really lead a better life." As Hobhouse put it in *What Is Liberalism?* (1910), "We are all socialists today." By the turn of the century the Liberal and Labour parties often accused each other of stealing the other's programs. Later they would also compete in their lavish praise of the Soviet Union.[19] But one issue split them across the bow: the British Empire.

The year that *Culture and Anarchy* appeared, 1869, also witnessed the opening of the Suez Canal and the expansion of British imperial dominion into a new and unprecedented phase. By 1890 it covered nearly one-quarter of the habitable globe. The old liberal attitude toward imperialism had been ambivalent at best: the British Empire, with its exotic trappings of imperial splendor, durbars and jubilees, and "maps painted red," was largely the creation of Benjamin's Disraeli's Conservatives. Among those of a New Liberal persuasion feelings ran deeper and sharper.[20] Webbs and the so-called liberal imperialists stressed that Britain's empire meant jobs at home and room for her unemployed masses abroad. They were untroubled by the implications of Britons being an "imperial race."* To empire's liberal supporters, it was possible to set against Tennyson's troubled vision of the future a far more optimistic one:

> *Land of hope and glory, mother of the free,*
> *How shall we extol thee, who are born of thee?*
> *Wider still and wider shall thy bounds be set;*
> *God who made thee mighty, make thee mightier yet . . .*

Liberal enthusiasm for empire was an extension of the older Anglo-Saxon thesis. The English-speaking peoples were Europe's "civilizing race," and dominion over places as diverse as India, Egypt, South Africa, Hong Kong, and Australia gave Britons the duty to raise up "backward" races and peoples, as well as opportunity for profit. Sir

---

* This was Sidney Webb's phrase. The notion of the British Empire as a kind of "virtue-renewing frontier," solving the problems of industrial society, attracted some unexpected supporters: Gothic revival guru John Ruskin used his inaugural lecture as Slade Professor of Art at Oxford in 1878 to summon his students on the great British mission to spread their race around the globe. The lecture impressed at least one listener: the young Cecil Rhodes.

James Bryce, a former student of Max Müller and ambassador to the United States, saw Britain's imperial system as operating on a Roman model, in which diverse religions and races, rich and poor, civilized and savage, would eventually merge under a single sovereignty. "All mankind is fast becoming one people," he explained, and the British Empire would provide the lead in that next crucial step for civilization. At the same time, Bryce recognized that such an empire would be inherently unstable, as Western ideas of nationalism spread to the brown, yellow, and black people living under its sway.[21]

The coming of the Boer War in 1899 forced liberals to choose between Britain's imperial mission and its civilizing one. While some joined conservative figures like Rudyard Kipling in supporting the effort to subdue South Africa's white farmers, others, including Bryce, sided with the Afrikaners. (Ironically, those same Afrikaner whites would appear as the chief villains in a later progressive crusade against apartheid.) One of the war's most strident opponents was a journalist for the *Manchester Guardian* named J.A. Hobson. In 1902 he published a polemical piece loaded with specious statistics and charts entitled *Imperialism*, in which he argued that the "economic taproot" of the British Empire was pure and simple greed. British and other capitalists needed to find an outlet for their surplus capital, Hobson wrote, left over from chronic poverty and underconsumption at home. As a result, a conspiracy of financiers and industrialists had whipped up nationalist feelings in order to create an overseas empire where their wealth would be safe and secure. He termed it "a debacle of Western civilization." Hobson's *Imperialism* decisively changed the image of empire among progressive-minded intellectuals around the world. It inspired Lenin to write *Imperialism, the Highest Stage of Capitalism*, and it influenced the views of W.E.B. Du Bois and anti-imperialist American Progressives such as Woodrow Wilson.[22] Imperialism and colonialism became, and remained, nasty epithets in the progressive lexicon.

Yet Hobson's theory, which proved so persuasive and long-lasting, also drew heavily from degeneration theory. Jingoism and the popular support of imperial adventures were a form of "atavistic lust," he believed, reflecting the "mob mind" that Le Bon had analyzed in *The Crowd*. "The stamp of parasitism is upon every white settlement" among "the lower races" of Africa and Asia, he warned.* The important carriers of this parasitism were the Jews, whom Hobson believed directed international finance as well as the British Empire. Johannesburg, the center of South African capitalism, was "essentially a Jewish town"; there "every form of private vice flourished unchecked," he wrote, with gambling halls, saloons, and brothels. The Jews and their imperialist allies were "an alien body of sojourners . . . destined to extract wealth from the country and retiring to consume it at home." Yet their desperate scramble for cheap profit was ultimately doomed, he concluded, since nature's laws "doom the parasite to atrophy, decay, and final extinction."[23]

There were, therefore, two contrasting liberal images of the British Empire as the twentieth century began. One, bitterly negative, was Hobson's: imperialism was an evil and degenerative system built on capitalist exploitation of natives abroad and the expansion of poverty and the armaments industries at home. Like the "acquisitive society" that fostered it, it was doomed to self-destruction. The other was summed up by novelist John Buchan in his memoirs:

> I dreamed of a world-wide brotherhood with the background of a common race and creed, consecrated to the service of peace; Britain enriching the rest out of her culture and traditions, and the spirit of the Dominions like a strong wind freshening the stuffiness of the old lands. . . . Our creed was not based on antagonism to any other people. It was humanitarian and international; we believed we were laying the basis of a federation of the world.[24]

## THE HOLLOW MEN: ARNOLD TOYNBEE'S LOST GENERATION

By birth and education, Arnold Toynbee, Jr., was a sterling product of the New Liberalism. His college at Oxford, Balliol—which he entered in 1907—was its epicenter. Balliol's famous master, Benjamin Jowett, had brought Thomas Hill Green there in 1874 to help breed an elite

---

* Racial egalitarianism played no part in Hobson's rejection of imperialism—rather the opposite, in fact. "Biology demands as a condition of world-progress that the struggle of nations or races continue," Hobson insisted; he became an enthusiastic supporter of eugenics.

"aristocracy of talent" that would carry out the postliberal agenda (in fact, Jowett's Balliol was the direct model for the Harvard of Charles W. Eliot and Henry Adams). Toynbee's uncle, Arnold Senior, had been tutor and bursar at Balliol. Its distinguished alumni included not only leading liberal intellectuals like Bernard Bosanquet and L.T. Hobhouse, but the chancellor of the exchequer as well as the foreign secretary, a former viceroy of India, and Lord Milner, the principal architect of British policy in South Africa. Graduating in 1911 with first-class honors, the brilliant young Toynbee immediately won a position at Balliol as tutor in Greek history and married the daughter of the most respected classical scholar of the age, Gilbert Murray. His future, like that of Britain itself, seemed assured.

"It was assumed as a matter of course," he wrote half a century later, "that the framework of the coming world-order would be the Western civilization. . . . Other civilizations had risen and fallen, had come and gone, but Westerners did not doubt that their own civilization was invulnerable."[25]

This brittle confidence of Toynbee and his generation was shattered by the coming of war in 1914. In terms of sheer numbers—702,410 dead—Great Britain suffered no more in World War I than Italy. But Britain's casualties were disproportionately drawn from society's elite: one third of the Oxford class of 1913 died in the war, and the death of many promising young Balliol men cast a pall over the British establishment. Out of the shock and sense of loss would emerge the myth of the "lost generation," which haunted British intellectual culture and policymaking for the next two decades.[26]

World War I was for Great Britain what Vietnam would be for America, the breaking of the morale of its political elite. As a character in an Aldous Huxley novel remarked, "The bottom has been knocked out of everything."

Among those broken was Arnold Toynbee. "My illusion that I was the privileged citizen of a stable world," he wrote afterwards, "had been shattered," and he would view neither his own society nor the West in the same light again.[27] Yet Toynbee managed to escape the ordeal unscathed. Although he initially supported "the war for civilization," his mother's encouragement and the help of influential family friends enabled Toynbee to evade service with a trumped up medical deferment. While fellow collegians were fighting and dying in Flanders and Salonika, Toynbee remained safe at Balliol, discussing Hellenistic history with his students over tea and sherry and writing a pamphlet calling for a negotiated peace.*[28] Guilt over his compromised position plagued Toynbee for the rest of his life. Almost as if in reaction, he became a committed pacifist who detested everything smacking of military valor, heroism, patriotism, or other "antiquated" notions of the prewar Victorian past. "In 1914," he wrote long afterwards, "I became convinced that war was neither a respectable institution nor a venial sin, but was a crime." His antipathy probably was not mitigated by the fact that his wife remained devoted to the memory of one of the war's heroes, her former lover Rupert Brooke, which drove a permanent wedge in their marriage.

In January 1918 Virginia and Leonard Woolf had dinner with Toynbee, and Virginia noted afterwards that he "knew the aristocratic heroes who are now all killed and celebrated, and loathed them."[29] Nor was he alone. The Woolfs and their friends, the so-called Bloomsbury group, set a new tone for Britain's intellectual class: socially bohemian, sexually promiscuous, politically radical, and resolutely pacifist (many in Bloomsbury had protested against the war and one, Bertrand Russell, even spent time in jail). They were angrily contemptuous of the old respectable values of the past. Bloomsbury's outlook was summed up in Lytton Strachey's sneering exposé of bourgeois Britain in *Eminent Victorians*, and in novelist E.M. Forster's famous maxim, "If I had to choose between betraying my country or betraying my friend, I hope I would have the courage to betray my country."

While never a full-fledged member of Bloomsbury, Toynbee shared many of its enthusiasms, including, for a time, socialism.[30] However, he was also passionately caught up in the new internationalism that swept through Europe's liberal intelligentsia after the war. Toynbee attended

---

* As his mother wrote to him regarding military service, "Everything is against you: your poor physique, your consequent lack of high spirits and animal courage: everything which arises out of the physical vigour of life which we've always unduly despised." The pamphlet in question was *Nationality and the War*, which proposed giving Germany most of the former Hapsburg Empire in central Europe.

the Versailles Peace Conference in 1919 and became a firm supporter of the League of Nations (its two British organizers, Walter Phillimore and Robert Cecil, were also pacifists).[31] The other institution Toynbee turned to for ideological sustenance was the Royal Institute of International Affairs. Its founder, Lionel Curtis, was a dedicated disciple of both T.H. Green and the senior Toynbee. As the idea of an Anglo-Saxon racial mission disappeared after 1918, and belief in imperial dominion faded, only liberal imperialism's vision of a single international community remained. Even before the war, Curtis had been steadily pushing the idea of transforming the British Empire into a voluntary "commonwealth" of independent nations. Britain would extend "free and ordered institutions" to its former dominions, and offer peace and harmony instead of exploitation and strife. In short, Britain would preserve the good features of liberal empire while avoiding the disasters and horrors described by men like J.A. Hobson or Joseph Conrad in *Heart of Darkness*. As hopes for a strong and effectual League of Nations foundered, liberal-minded internationalists turned to Curtis's commonwealth ideal by default.[32]

Curtis and his Round Table group (which included such influential men as the editor of the London *Times*) had consciously abandoned Bryce's Roman model of imperial sovereignty for one proposed by one of their members, drawn once again from classical Greece. Alfred Zimmern was professor of ancient history at Oxford and author of *The Greek Commonwealth*, which described how Periclean Athens had used its hegemony in the Greek world to spread the values of freedom and civility. Zimmern's vision of a civilizing commonwealth inspired Curtis to appropriate the term for himself; Zimmern was also a close friend of the young Toynbee. In 1915, Zimmern had written an essay entitled "German Culture and the British Commonwealth." Like many other Oxford figures, he believed that the Great War was not just a struggle over empire, as Du Bois, Spengler, Lenin, and other critics were claiming. It was also a war to defend liberal civilization against brutish Teutonic barbarism and tyranny. Zimmern contrasted Germany's belief in a Prussianized *Kultur* with Britain's belief in the rule of law and free institutions. Such ideals "are not the monopoly of Great Britain," Zimmern wrote. "They belong to civilized humanity as a whole." A British commonwealth would make spreading that message its most important goal.[33]

Curtis agreed, but he also saw that mission in more elitist terms. "Destiny," he wrote, "has placed on the shoulders of this Commonwealth an overwhelming share of the duty imposed on Europe—that of controlling its relations with races more backward than its own." The English-speaking peoples would retain their special civilizing mission in the world, but as diplomats and bureaucrats rather than as explorers, soldiers, and industrialists. Curtis even set up a joint Anglo-American enterprise in New York, called the Council on Foreign Relations, to provide enlightened advice on world affairs. Its London branch, the Royal Institute of International Affairs, resided at Chatham House. In 1921, Curtis brought Arnold Toynbee, Zimmern's young Oxford colleague and the nephew of his own great hero, to Chatham House as director. For the next twenty years Toynbee would devote himself to editing and publishing a thick annual survey of world affairs in addition to his own historical writings.

Toynbee, Curtis, and the rest of the "Chatham House set" were bitterly opposed to the sort of nationalistic and racial views that animated men like Spengler, Hitler, and the German "revolution on the Right." In 1921, Toynbee visited Crete on a mission for the League of Nations and saw firsthand the grisly results of Greek and Turkish fighting for the island. It reinforced his pacifism and gave him a horror of nationalism that never left him.[34]

Yet Toynbee and his colleagues agreed with their fascist counterparts on one point: World War I marked the end of the old European order and the dawn of a new. Only the Chatham House vision of that new order was placid, one might even say passive, by comparison. Its general shape was set forth in Benjamin Kidd's *Principles of Western Civilization* (1902), in which Kidd asserted that Western civilization had brought science, economic affluence, and political and cultural freedom to their summit. In its formative stages, Western civilization had exhibited the strong, self-assertive qualities of any great civilization, reflecting the virtues of "its virile vanguard race," Europe's Nordic stock. Now, however, Kidd warned that those self-assertive and competitive qualities had to disappear if modern civilization was to sustain itself. Individualism would have to give way to an ethic of social responsibility and duty.*[35]

Now, after the experience of the Great War, the New Liberal consensus asserted that the nation-state, too, would have to disappear, along with its war-making powers. At one time, Toynbee wrote later, Europe's nation-states could afford to expand both as "welfare states" and as "war-making states." In the twentieth century, they could no longer afford to do both and would have to make a choice. However, by shedding absurd claims of national sovereignty and joining with other nations to promote peace, they could concentrate on their primary duty: feeding, clothing, and elevating the lives of their own citizens.[36] Toynbee believed that only a diminished Britain, rid of its colonies and its military establishment, could play a constructive role in a peaceful world order. This would be a world order built around its former empire, the Commonwealth, and the League of Nations. Inevitably, Britain and Europe would no longer occupy center stage. Europe herself, Toynbee told an audience at the Fabian Society in 1926, "is in the process of being dwarfed by the overseas world which she herself has called into existence" through empire. The unchallenged predominance of Western civilization was a "recent and unprecedented" development, he pointed out, and one that the Great War had decisively brought to an end.[37]

Toynbee's own field of study, ancient history, also convinced him that Western domination had to come to an end. He remembered Edward Gibbon's famous prediction in *The Decline and Fall of the Roman Empire*: whereas ancient empires like Greece, Rome, and Assyria had collapsed into darkness, "modern" ones like Britain enjoyed a level of material progress and a "system of arts and laws and manners" that made collapse into barbarism impossible. "August 1914," Toynbee said, led "me to question Gibbon's judgment." He put it more indelicately in a private letter: "We shall be 'dagos' too when civilization centres in China."[38] His interest in the comparative method of studying ancient civilizations, inspired by Eduard Meyer's *History of Antiquity* (1884–1902), prompted him to ask a simple question: what if that comparative method were turned on the history of the West? How would it now compare with civ-

---

* "Duty" was a favorite word among the New Liberals, reflecting the impact of British Idealist F.H. Bradley's influential essay, "My Station and Its Duties," published in 1876.

ilizations, such as China and the Middle East, that the Orientalist tradition had once described as "decadent" and "decayed"?

Then, in the spring of 1920, had come Spengler. Although Toynbee proved unsympathetic to its harsh determinism, *The Decline of the West* galvanized him into action, determined to outdo Spengler at his own game in discovering the "laws of history" and the secret of Europe's decline. While Toynbee was researching and writing his comprehensive annual surveys for Chatham House by day, at night he was launched on an intensive reading program, devouring books on ancient and modern Chinese history, Japan, pre-Columbian America, Russia, and Eastern Europe, as well as the latest works in ethnology and anthropology. He was determined to master those areas of non-Western history that Spengler had only brushed upon, and tried to draw careful scholarly distinctions where Spengler had tended to dogmatic generalization.

After a decade of research, Toynbee distinguished twenty-one (later twenty-six) distinct societies or "civilizations" that constituted the history of mankind,* of which five had managed to survive to the present day: the Hindu or Indic; the Islamic in both its Iranian and Arabic forms; the Sinic, which combined China, Japan, and their cultural dependencies; the Orthodox Christian of Russia and Eastern Europe; and, of course, the Western. Toynbee left Africa out of his discussion entirely, which became a subject of some controversy and which Toynbee later regretted.[39] However, no racial or ethnocentric bias was at work in Toynbee's mind; indeed, he wanted to give non-Western societies their full due, which led him to write a work almost six times longer than Spengler's *Decline of the West*. Like Spengler, however, Toynbee was determined to create a comparative science of civilization that would cast the West in a diminished, if not an actually eclipsed, role. "We have to look at history with new eyes," Toynbee would write, and this meant casting off a Eurocentric perspective that placed Western civilization at the center of human progress.[40]

At the same time, of course, Toynbee also rejected Spengler's racial-vitalist views. The notion that Western civilization was Teutonic in ori-

---

* These were the Western, Orthodox Byzantine and Orthodox Russian, Iranic, Arabic, Hindu, two separate Far Eastern centering in Japan and Southeast Asia, Hellenic, Syraic, Indic, Sinic, Minoan, Sumeric, Hittite, Babylonian, Andean, Mexican, Yucatec, Mayan, and Egyptian.

gin, the creation of "pure races" of conquerors whose blood still invigorated and ennobled their supposed descendants, had been clearly overturned by the facts of archeology and linguistics, he said. Toynbee specifically dismissed Gobineau's theories as "nonsense."[41] Toynbee also rejected Spengler's Nordic (and anti-Christian) bias against the ethnic melting pot of the ancient Mediterranean. As befitted an Oxford classical scholar and son-in-law of Gilbert Murray, Toynbee reasserted the clear cultural linkage between modern Europe and the ancient Greeks and Romans that Spengler had denied.

But societies like black Africa did fall on the wrong side of the line that Toynbee drew between human "cultures" (in the anthropological sense), of which there existed hundreds at any given time, and "civilizations," which were distinguished from other kinds of societies by a single characteristic. This was their capacity for growth, not in an economic or material sense but in a spiritual sense. A civilization's growth moved it toward that "perfection as an *inward* condition of the mind and spirit" that Matthew Arnold had seen as the most important quality of Western culture, and which Toynbee now made the principal object of all human history.

## THE STUDY OF HISTORY: MATTER, SPIRIT, AND CIVILIZATION

Toynbee stated that all great civilizations in history had unconsciously moved toward a single higher goal, which he called "self-determination." His notion of self-determination came from his British Idealist precedessors; it was an ideal that was cultural and social, rather than political.[42] It meant that a civilization acquires a unique and self-conscious identity that it articulates through its members, who then acquire their own full sense of identity and purpose as conscious contributors to the whole.

However, this self-determination was the product of a spiritual "élan" that moved each civilization "from challenge through response to further challenge" and shaped the direction of civilization as a whole. Toynbee borrowed the notion of the *élan vital* from the French philosopher Henri Bergson.* Bergson's vitalism was not an outward projection

---

* See Chapter 9.

of the will to power, but an inward, self-contemplative introspection that raises the mind to a higher spiritual plane. It releases "the surging spiritual forces" of the individual and causes the world as it is understood by science and empirical reality, the world of *mécanisme*, to fade away.

Toynbee transferred this upward ascent of self-introspection from the individual to the collective experience of societies. In doing so he scrapped Spengler's Germanic view of the civilizing process as a threat to the vitality of *Kultur*. Instead, Toynbee presented *Zilivisation*'s sophistication and manners as advanced expressions of this inward-turning *élan vital*.

The result was startling. The civilized man in Gobineau's vitalist history is reduced to a racial mongrel; in Spengler's he is a clinical degenerate. In Toynbee's *Study of History*, by contrast, he is the purest expression of vitality and spiritual health. In fact, the human ideal turns out to be someone rather like Toynbee himself: diffident, sensitive, religious in a contemplative and otherworldly sense, a man who shuns the world of violence and barbarism to pursue the "etherealization" of himself and society.

The history of civilization, then, has a dual aspect. At one level, Toynbee describes the cyclical succession of outward political forms. Politics emerges from the darkness of prehistory in the form of "warring states," which engage in the constant quarrels of primitive warlords and petty princes until one—a Caesar Augustus, for example—emerges to forge a single "universal state." This is inevitably followed by invasion and internal division, which return civilization to the anarchy of warring states. In this sense, Toynbee's *Study of History* is yet another version of the course of empire: that repetitive cycle of conquest, dominion, and decline of which Great Britain seemed the latest example.

History at this level—the story of political institutions, rulers, statesmen, and wars—sparked little interest in Toynbee, except for an occasional outburst of indignation. He pointed to the rise of militarism and great armies and navies as infallible signs of civilization's *decline* rather than success. The military spirit is "suicidal" and an "aberration" in developed societies. It "has been by far the commonest cause of the breakdowns of civilizations," he concluded, the memory of the Great War still fresh in his mind. "In this suicidal process the entire social fabric becomes fuel to feed the devouring flame in the brazen bosom of Moloch." Democracy, too, especially in its modern form, came in for some pointed criticisms.[43]

However, the real history of civilization exists at a higher level, and is the chronicle of man as a spiritual being. Its first episode involves the robust confrontation between man and his immediate environment. Civilization's founders, like the ancient Egyptians, Sumerians, or Mayans, manage to carve out a human community from nature's wilderness by sheer force of will. The decision to do so is not an easy one; Toynbee even compares the agony and suffering it may cause to the expulsion from the Garden of Eden.[44] However, the ability to overcome these physical barriers is what separates an incipient civilization from a primitive society, which, like that of the Eskimos or pygmies, remains trapped by its environment and cannot grow beyond the brute facts of nature.*

Massive irrigation projects and the building of great temples dominate the lives of the founders of a great civilization. These challenges, Toynbee suggests, cause an initial outflow of the *élan vital*, which transforms the culture; indeed, for the most vibrant civilizations, "the greater the difficulty, the greater the response." In the *early* stages of civilization, Toynbee concedes, war and conquest contribute to that same vital growth, as a people consolidate their gains against a hostile environment. Over time, however, the process of self-assertion shifts its focus from "other-directed" challenges—nature and other peoples and nations—to "inner-directed" ones, which is to say the rational ordering of the community itself. "When a series of responses to challenges accumulates into a growth . . . the field of action is shifting all the time from the external environment into the interior of the society's own body social." Eventually, in fact, the field of action becomes the very soul of the individual.[45]

Toynbee was in effect reversing the all-important distinction between culture and civilization. For Toynbee, the vital forces of *Kultur*, of will to power and self-confident striving, are temporary and superficial; true permanence and stability come when more enlightened, reflective val-

---

* Toynbee later dropped this distinction as too redolent of Social Darwinism. No society or people should be excluded from the potential for civilization, he decided, and therefore none was in his later, more inclusive, version of the civilizing process. Cf. *Reconsiderations*, pp. 553–54.

ues take their place. Therefore, it is at the *civilized* stage that a society achieves true self-determination. Human energies are freed by the simplification of processes that in the past had tied up considerable time and effort, such as gathering and growing food, organizing religious cults, and creating systems of governance. Simplification triggers "a consequent transfer of energy . . . from some lower sphere of action to a higher."[46] Toynbee called this transfer self-determination; Adam Smith had called it division of labor. In fact, Toynbee's prime example of self-determination through simplification is the classic transformation of civil society from rural to urban production and from handmade artisanal to manufactured goods. But Toynbee also wanted to see this simplification process at work in other spheres, in the member of the king's household becoming the civil servant, the itinerant merchant the modern businessman, and the priest the university scholar.

Of course, none of these changes happens by accident. Like his predecessors, Toynbee believed that the progress of every society depended on its elites and aristocracies. But Toynbee's ideal aristocracy was not a military caste or even a political class in John Adams's terms. The flourishing civilizations of Athens, Renaissance Florence, and Elizabethen England were built by a spiritual elite, Toynbee claimed, which he called society's "creative minority":

> Growth is the work of creative personalities and creative minorities; they cannot go on moving forward themselves unless they can contrive to carry . . . the uncreative rank and file of mankind, which is always the overwhelming majority, with them in their advance.

They do this literally by setting a good example, which their spiritual inferiors accept and follow. Like good Balliol men, members of the creative minority live a set of principles—of honor, bravery, compassion, and truth—that inspire the rest of society. "The leader's task," Toynbee opines, "is to make his fellows his followers" by example and persuasion, rather than by coercive authority. A creative minority pushes an ascending society forward through its political, intellectual, and religious leadership. "In a growing and healthy society, the majority is drilled into following the minority's lead *mechanically*."[47]

However, the mechanical imitative process also poses a danger. Toynbee's fear of the mechanical extended far beyond anything connected with industrial technology: it included all forms of constant repetition in which routine replaces creative power. For Toynbee, as for his Blooms-bury contemporaries, all established custom and tradition (particularly in their recognizably British forms) represented spiritual sterility. Toyn-bee's civilizing process "is really a leap forward" into the unknown, while tradition implies caution and hence stagnation. Similarly, mechanical repetition—from the repetitive strokes of an engine piston to Max We-ber's routinization of political power to the rote performance of social roles, conventions, and rituals—eventually constrains a society's growth.* The dependence of the masses on the superior minority now backfires. "When the leaders cease to lead," Toynbee wrote, "their tenure of power becomes an abuse." They change from being a "creative minority" to a "dominant" one. Their privileges, like those of the ruling classes of imperial Rome and China, become an intolerable burden rather than a gift of trust; Balliol's aristocracy of talent becomes as life-less as Matthew Arnold's philistines, obsessed with bureaucratic tech-nique and careerism.

The process of civilization's growth is an upward spiral for Toynbee, as challenge leads to response and success, which in turn produces an-other challenge. Decline forms a similar downward spiral, as institutions lose the ability to respond to crises and break down, leading to new crises. Toynbee saw decline as arriving in three stages. The first is the initial breakdown, when self-determining power is replaced by the spirit of the mechanical. Unfortunately, Toynbee was forced to conclude, this was the point at which the modern West found itself in the nineteenth century, its spiritual progress replaced by the twin aspects of modern *mé-canisme*: industrialization and mass democracy.

As a result, the character of Western culture was irrevocably de-formed. Industrial society enabled man to "decisively overcome Nature by his technology; but . . . man has merely exchanged one master for an-other." Industrialization distorted the right to property into hideous in-equities, creating what Toynbee called "two nations," one of great

---

* One has a sneaking suspicion that Toynbee's original model of mindless *mécanisme* was the dreary daily routine of an English public school, like his own Winchester, with its early morning calis-thenics and endless drills in math and Latin verbs.

wealth and the other of great poverty. It also made available new technologies of mass death, which the modern nation is able to employ for its own short-sighted purposes. "War has now become 'total war,' " Toynbee lamented, "and it has become so because parochial states have become nationalist democracies." Toynbee's image of modern democracy, like Henry Adams's, might be summed up by the term "machine politics." Modern democracy has foolishly promised "to perform the miracle of the loaves and fishes" for the desperate masses by redistributing the benefits taken from them by capitalism. However, its failures soon degenerate into a virulent and mindless "parochial" nationalism, with each little linguistic and cultural group "striving desperately for economic autarky [self-sufficiency]."[48] It also creates a demeaning mass culture, reflected in radio, newspapers, and the cinema.

Civilization has now reached its second stage of decline: disintegration. The two nations become polarized into a self-regarding and self-satisfied mandarinate and an "internal proletariat" permanently excluded from civilization's material and spiritual benefits.[49] The elitist minority abandon the spiritual values that once animated society, while the internal proletariat, society's underclass, soon learn that they are not alone. There is also another, "external proletariat," growing along the fringes of the civilization's borders. This is the product of the other symptom of civilization's disintegration, the growth of empire.

Even more than Spengler or Du Bois, Toynbee passionately attacked the West's expansionist impulse. *The Study of History* condemned all empire-building as an attempt to distract popular attention away from society's internal decay.[50] Toynbee drew a picture of civilization acting as "a radiation of destructive intensity" into the barbarian hinterlands. Some "barbarians" are completely overwhelmed and willy-nilly become part of the civilization turned empire, like the Celts of Roman Britain and Gaul. Others, like the Germanic tribes beyond the Rhine frontier, resist—and if they resist long and successfully enough, they become society's external proletariat, excluded from civilization's benefits like the underclass but poised to strike when the civilization collapses.

For primitive societies in Toynbee's schema, the depredations of an empire such as imperial Rome or Victorian Britain presented a stark choice: between "being carcass or vulture."[51] But Toynbee suggested that civilization itself, already in the stage of disintegration, also faces a fateful decision. It must either abandon its imperial ambitions and risk complete internal collapse and revolt by its hungry underclass, or transform itself into an all-encompassing universal state. The universal states like imperial Rome form the most spectacular stage of Toynbee's process of decline, "when a disintegrating civilization purchases a reprieve by submitting to forcible political unification." But even with its vast colonial empire and its sweeping claims to universal dominion, the declining civilization remains split along an inner and an outer axis. It can no longer resolve its internal challenges and achieve a new equilibrium, which leads to unrest, riots, and revolutions. The dominant minority becomes barbarized by their contact with the outer fringes of primitive life; they become Jamaican planters or North American plainsmen, persons from a "Protestant Western Christian social heritage" who are willing to commit horrible atrocities in their struggle against the external proletariat.* Easy wealth corrupts the rest.

Toynbee provided this familiar downward course of empire with identifiably modern trappings. The ruling elite eventually becomes a class of Oscar Wildes, combining decadence of manners with sexual promiscuity and perversion; degenerate art à la Max Nordau raises its deliberately ugly head; language degenerates into slang and vulgar colloquialisms, and religion into syncretic mystery cults and occult magic. Can there be any doubt, Toynbee asked in 1939, on the eve of World War II, that all these are now leading characteristics of the modern West? "Nationalistic internecine warfare," Toynbee related "[and] the combined drive of energies generated by the recently released forces of Democracy and Industrialism" have let loose the forces of chaos. "These considerations and comparisons suggest that we are already far advanced in our time of troubles."

Eventually Western civilization will reach the last stage of decline, dissolution. "There is no known law of historical determinism," Toynbee wrote, that has consigned the West, like past civilizations, to "the slow and steady fire of a universal state where we shall in due course be re-

---

* Toynbee's source for these examples was, ironically enough, Frederick Jackson Turner.

duced to dust and ashes." However, "such precedents from the histories of other civilizations and from the life-course of nature are bound to appear formidable in the sinister light of our present situation."[52] At the same time, the "precedents from the histories of other civilizations" did point to a saving grace. Although imperialism gives civilization only a temporary reprieve, it does leave behind a universal church, a spiritual movement that takes on empire's highest ideals—universal peace and harmony, a cosmopolitan lack of discrimination between peoples under its sway, and aspirations toward permanence and eternity—and passes them on in theological form.

In the case of China, the theological form was Confucianism; in India, it was Buddhism; and in Rome, Christianity. That universal church draws together the internal proletariat, who unconsciously absorb the spiritual values abandoned by the mandarins, and the external proletariat into a single spiritual mass. Eventually, the self-awareness it inspires becomes a call for liberation. "At length," civilization's marginalized peoples "break free from what was once [their] spiritual home, but has now become a prison-house," and rise up to destroy the institutions of empire.

But the universal church survives. Indeed, this is the ultimate gift from previous higher civilizations to their primitive successors: so did Christianity illuminate the Dark Ages and Islam civilize the nomadic tribes of the Arabian desert. Likewise the modern West's legacy to non-Western peoples would not be its material technology—which Toynbee saw as the certain path to self-destruction, symbolized by Communism's failure in Soviet Russia[53]—but its spiritualized humanitarianism. The morality of the Sermon on the Mount, of humility, compassion, and turning the other cheek, would serve as the spiritual bridge between East and West, North and South.

For Toynbee, this was *The Study of History*'s great message of hope. On the one hand, Toynbee had redeemed the Enlightenment's progress of politeness as part of civilization. But now, he was saying, that progress must disappear, at least in a secular form. A universal spiritual creed of love, humanity, and commonality would survive instead, transcending all political and cultural boundaries. Even as "our post-Christian Western secular civilization" was moving inevitably toward its material decline and demise, he speculated, it might also be moving toward spiritual triumph.

## THE WHEELS OF THE CHARIOT: TOYNBEE AND THE END OF WESTERN CIVILIZATION

Chapter 62: A *Bad Thing*: America was thus clearly Top Nation, and
History came to a [stop].
    —W.C. Sellar and R.J. Yeatman, *1066 and All That* (1930)

World War I had not only shattered conventional liberalism in England; it had also thrown the profession of history into confusion. H.A.L. Fisher wrote in the preface to his history of Europe in 1934, "Men wiser than I have discerned in history a plot, a rhythm, a predetermined pattern. These harmonies are concealed from me. I can see only one emergency following upon another as wave follows upon wave."

That same year the first volume of *The Study of History* appeared, and it immediately provided what Fisher and others had lost: the sense of plan and purpose in history. Almost at once the sweep and clarity of Toynbee's historical judgments, as well their implications, prompted comparisons with Gibbon's *Decline and Fall of the Roman Empire*.[54] In fact, however, Gibbon's work had symbolized the triumph of the Enlightenment's secular vision of human history over its predecessor, a Christian God-directed history. Now Toynbee reversed the process once again. After describing the dire situation facing the modern world in his sixth volume, published in 1939, Toynbee concluded with the startling words: "We may and must pray that a reprieve which God has granted to our society once will not be refused if we ask for it again in a humble spirit and with a contrite heart."[55]

Toynbee had reached this conclusion in the wake of the failure of the League of Nations to restrain Mussolini and Hitler, at the advent of the policy of appeasement. Toynbee himself had been an enthusiastic supporter of appeasement, like many of his colleagues at Chatham House.[56] He was invited to meet Hitler for a personal interview in 1936, and he came away deeply impressed. He told listeners on his return to England that he was convinced of Hitler's "sincerity in desiring peace in Europe and close friendship with England." Like many other English liberals, it was not until after the Munich Agreement that Toynbee realized that

Hitler's aggression was not the result of too much Western pressure against him, but not enough.[57]

On the eve of the invasion of Poland Toynbee convinced himself that the West's failure to deal effectively with Hitler had nothing to do with pacifism or appeasement but with the character of the modern West itself. In this sixth volume of *The Study of History*, the last to appear before the war, he stated that Europe had pursued a new, unprecedented path among civilizations. It had abandoned belief in an immortal God and His laws and pursued material satisfactions at the expense of spiritual ones. "The spirit of man abhors a spiritual vacuum." The inevitable result was "tribalistic" and "parochial" nation worship, and the rise of men like Hitler and Mussolini to direct it.[58] "The only constructive thing to work for," he explained, "would be to get beyond national sovereignty—and I should follow that thread a long way." With another catastrophic world war looming on the horizon, the only hope left seemed to be a major spiritual redirection of all of Western culture, away from self-aggrandizement, material affluence, and the "spiritual inadequacies of the Enlightenment"—and toward God.

As in the case of Henry Adams, personal tragedy fed Toynbee's sense of cosmic despair. In February 1939 his mother died, and a month later his son Tony committed suicide. His wife's decision to leave him in 1942 completed the rout of disappointments both public and private. Depressed and self-absorbed, Toynbee barely noticed the coming of World War II.* He rediscovered the consolations of a faith in a transcendent God and briefly considered becoming a Roman Catholic. In 1940 he gave a public lecture at Oxford, later entitled "Christianity and Civilization," in which he unveiled his new conviction that it was religious rather than human progress that gave meaning to history. In it he employed a vivid and startling metaphor worthy of St. Augustine:

> If religion is a chariot, it looks as if the one which it mounts toward Heaven may be the periodic downfalls of civilizations on Earth. It looks as if the movement of civilizations may be cyclic and recurrent, while the movement of religion may be on a single continuous upward line.

---

* Still, he was careful to move to Oxford during the Blitz and avoid visits to London. His wife outright accused him of cowardice, a charge that, given his evasion of service in World War I, stung because it was probably true.

Indeed, Toynbee now concluded, "If our secular Western civilization perishes, Christianity may be expected not only to endure but to grow in wisdom and stature as the result of a fresh experience of secular catastrophe."[59]

These were strange words to utter in the midst of the Battle of Britain. In fact, Toynbee went so far as to suggest privately that surrender to Hitler might be preferable to more hatred and violence. "It would be possible to argue," he told friends, "that the world is in such desperate need of political unification . . . that it is worth paying the price of falling under the worst tyranny."[60] As events turned more favorable and Russia and America entered the war, Toynbee's sense of confidence in the future returned. However, his religious vision of the end of the West survived the war, coinciding with an explosion of his own personal celebrity after 1945.

Ironically, that popularity was based on a misunderstanding. By the war's end millions of readers had consumed the abridged version of his prewar *Study of History*, prepared by D.C. Somervell, with its focus on "challenge and response" and the inevitable rise of a secular universal state. Far from grasping Toynbee's pessimism regarding the West, many had concluded that he was prophesying a new, emerging universal civilization, with the United States at its head. This misinterpretation led to a lucrative lecture tour of the United States in 1948 and induced Henry B. Luce to put Toynbee's large, mournful face on the cover of *Time* magazine.

Toynbee was horrified. Like many European intellectuals, he was deeply ambivalent over the new role America would play in the postwar world. Figures on both the Right and Left had always seen the United States as the towering capitalist colossus, the ultimate end point of the modern West's powers of transformative materialism. They had recognized, too, that a kind of "translation of empire" from Europe to America had been under way since the nineteenth century, which two world wars had only confirmed.

Still, when after World War II the United States not only appeared as the dominant power in the world but seemed to dictate the balance of power in Europe itself, figures as diverse as Jean-Paul Sartre, Evelyn Waugh, Malcolm Muggeridge, and Arnold Toynbee were shocked and dismayed. They would see the Cold War not in terms of a struggle between Communism and freedom but as a geopolitical vise, squeezing Europe between two different kinds of tyranny. One was an expression of Asiatic barbarism and ruthless savagery, the other an expression of the modern West's own dark side: capitalism and philistinism.*[61] Toynbee always dismissed any notion that the Cold War constituted an ideological struggle. The differences between the Soviet Union and the United States were to his mind minimal. Indeed, Toynbee seems to have been the first postwar liberal thinker to characterize Communism as "a page torn out of the New Testament," a "Western heresy" that expressed most of the false thinking of the modern West, particularly its rejection of God. The Soviet Union's future seemed limited and insignificant to him, because it had irrevocably linked itself to material civilization's fate.

He saw the United States as the more serious threat to world peace. Toynbee's favorite term for Americans before the war had been "barbarians." In 1945 he had already predicted to his father-in-law Gilbert Murray that if a new war broke out, the Americans would be the aggressors.[62] Toynbee's books nowhere sold in greater quantities, nor were his lecture tours more successful, than in the United States. Yet America had come to represent everything Toynbee most despised about the modern West: its technological know-how, its bumptious self-confidence (this was the age of Eisenhower, Kennedy, and the New Frontier), and its capitalist base. He looked back wistfully to the time when America had been a debtor nation to Europe.[63] Now, in his view, America had become the world's arch-conservative power and the defender of a bankrupt Western cultural order.

America also represented another deadly tendency, that of acquisitive empire. Expanding on his neo-Augustinian vision, Toynbee cast the United States as the new Rome in an entirely negative sense. Just as imperial Rome "consistently supported the rich against the poor in all foreign communities that fell under her sway" and generated "inequality, injustice, and the least happiness of the greatest number," so was America set to do the same in the Cold War world. Indeed, by 1962 Toynbee

---

* On his first visit to the United States in the spring of 1946, Malcolm Muggeridge decided that "the whole show is a fraud" and that "the appalling melancholia induced by this country is due to the fact that the light of the spirit is quite out, making a kingdom of darkness, and my own spirit was correspondingly lightened."

was shrilly insisting that "America's decision to adopt Rome's role [was] deliberate" and would lead to the same fate.[64]

Toynbee counted the United States as one of two malign imperialist powers in the postwar world; the other was the state of Israel. "The United States and Israel," he wrote in 1969, "must be today the two most dangerous of the 125 sovereign states among which the land-surface of this planet is at present partitioned." In only twenty-four years of existence, Toynbee pointed out, Israel had already fought and won four wars against its neighbors. Military victory was always for Toynbee certain proof of moral deficiency: he suggested that, had America and Israel lost some wars rather than continually winning them, it might have been better for their souls. He suggested that Israel's occupation of Arab territory constituted as vicious and inhuman an act as Germany's occupation of Czechoslovakia and Poland. Indeed, Toynbee went even further; he suggested that modern Israelis were even worse than the Nazis because "the Jews knew, from personal experience, what they were doing" in persecuting the unfortunate Arabs, whereas the Germans presumably did not.[65]

In fact, Toynbee's attitude toward Jews and Judaism proved to be the most controversial of all his pronouncements on the fate and meaning of the modern West. He repeated Schopenhauer's charge of more than a century earlier that the worst features of Western civilization sprang from Judaic roots. Toynbee called Judaism the "fossil relic of a dead civilization" that had taken Christianity and the West on a disastrous wrong turn, inspiring the West's crass materialism and "consummate virtuosity in commerce and finance," and its insistence on a morality of law and stern taboos rather than the workings of the free spirit. Above all, the Jewish claim to being the chosen people had encouraged a Western attitude of arrogance toward other cultures, which Toynbee saw as the real origin of the Holocaust.* America, too, Toynbee argued, was tainted by the same vicious Judaic streak, as exemplified by its extermination of the Indians during its westward expansion and its record in the Vietnam War. Like another aging Bloomsbury member, Bertrand Russell, Toynbee was convinced that America's aims in Vietnam were

---

* In a 1948 essay, Toynbee blamed all the false and brutal political movements of the modern world on this baneful Jewish influence, including both Communism *and Nazism*.

basically colonialist and genocidal. "It is just conceivable," Toynbee wrote, "that by the time the present book appears [1969] the Vietnamese people will have been exterminated and Vietnam will have been made unhabitable."[66]

America and Israel were dangerous not just because they were violent, "militarist" powers. They also represented a dying, dissolving modern West. Their actions in Laos, Vietnam, and Palestine were not merely crimes, but "crimes that were also a moral anachronism." The contemporary world would have to be reorganized on an entirely new, non-Western basis if peace and harmony were to finally reign. "What shall we do to be saved?" Toynbee had asked in 1955. "In politics, establish a constitutional cooperative system of world government. In economics, find a working compromise . . . between free enterprise and socialism. In the life of the spirit, put the secular super-structure back on religious foundations."[67]

As volumes eight through eleven of *The Study of History* appeared between 1954 and 1958, Toynbee went on the offensive. He made himself the new prophet of the demise of Western civilization in its modern (especially American) mode and of a new spiritual stirring in the non-Western world that promised a future of universal peace and social justice. He went on endless lecture tours and authored such books as *The Challenge of Our Time*, *Mankind and Mother Earth*, *Man's Concern with Death*, and many others. The results were variable, if increasingly predictable—the output expressing what one not unsympathetic contemporary called his "knee-jerk liberal responses" to world events became so vast and repetititve that his publisher, Oxford University Press, had to ask him to stop writing so much because it was diluting overall sales.[68]

Toynbee proposed first of all staking the future of humanity on the United Nations, the successor to the League of Nations. If Toynbee the ancient historian saw America as the new Rome—brutal, ambitious, and expansive—then the United Nations was the modern equivalent of the confederations of Greek city-states banded together for mutual defense in the pre-Hellenistic world to promote universal peace while avoiding the hegemony of a single power. Of course, as Toynbee knew, these leagues had not been very successful. They had broken down in petty squabbles and remained vulnerable to marauding outside states

(like Macedonia and Rome herself). But Toynbee was willing to overlook these details, since the ultimate goal in the nuclear age had to be
reconciliation rather than confrontation: "Mankind must become one
family or destroy itself." Privately he added, "One has to admit history is
against us. . . . I can't think of a single case of the cooperative method
having done the trick." But in Toynbee's perspective, which was rooted
in Bloomsbury of the twenties, being good was more important than doing good. It was one's intentions, not the results, that ultimately
counted most. As the decline of the West accelerated, Toynbee asserted,
world government was "a foregone conclusion." The only alternative
was nuclear catastrophe: "Mankind has to choose between political unification and mass suicide."[69]

Meanwhile, Toynbee's prescribed path of spiritual progress was moving away from Western Christianity; all the "higher religions"—Hin-
duism, Buddhism, and Islam—were merely varying perspectives on a
unifying truth, that of the spiritual power of love. In a politically unified
world, these various faiths would inevitably merge into an ecumenical
religion of love, which would teach compassion and tolerance for diversity—the sort of agenda later adopted by liberal religious groups such as
the World Council of Churches.[70] But part of his outlook was the result
of his own burning sense of guilt. Western civilization was now, as he put
it, "on trial." In *The World and the West*, published in 1953 at the height
of the Korean War, Toynbee dwelt at length on the West's historic aggressiveness toward Asians, Africans, and other peoples. Adopting an
analogy that was fashionable at the time, Toynbee referred to the West
as a "radioactive" culture (recalling civilization's "radiation of destructive intensity" in *The Study of History*) whose contact with non-Western
societies through technology, religion, and politics "threatens to poison
the life of the society whose body social is being penetrated."[71]

The most virulent of these poisons, he believed, was nationalism. In
1921 Toynbee had gone to Crete for the League of Nations during the
Greek-Turkish war and had seen corpses and other effects of war firsthand. He convinced himself that the massacres sprang from modern
rather than ancient causes—namely, nationalist rivalry and hatred. The
blame for nationalist wars in the Third World, Toynbee decided, ultimately had to be laid at the West's door. The abolition of "parochial" nationalism and establishment of world government were, therefore, not

only the natural tendency of world history, but also the natural aspiration of all non-Western peoples. Since they vastly outnumbered Europeans and Americans, their ability to determine the shape of the world government seemed, like world government itself, a foregone conclusion. The West would now have to adjust at a practical level to its new, diminished role in the world.

Europe and America had to become in effect a creative minority, setting a good example for the rest of the world through their open-mindedness and tolerance so that a new spiritual age could dawn. Purposeful action and self-assertion, the forward-looking cycle of challenge and response, were now reserved for the peoples of the Third World. "Non-Western societies [have] in fact by now been successfully re-educated" in the realities of a global world, Toynbee concluded in 1948, drawing them "out of their ancestral shell" into a new future. Europeans and Americans, by contrast, "are the only people in the world whose outlook on history still remains pre-da Gama," that is, shaped by an orientation toward Europe and the "smug and slovenly illusion" of its dominance and importance. We must realize, he told his audience, that in the modern global setting "our own descendants" will cease to be Westerners in the traditional sense. The civilization Toynbee and his generation had known "will gradually be relegated to the modest place" history had originally assigned it.[72]


TOYNBEE'S LEGACY

At first glance, these remarks are striking and sobering, as Toynbee meant them to be. Toynbee died in 1975, having seen the process of decolonization and the end of the British Empire almost to their conclusion. In one of his last years he remarked to a journalist, "I would like to think I had done a useful job in persuading Western peoples to think of the world as a whole," by which he meant convincing them of their own relative insignificance.

Yet Toynbee's quietist perspective begged the crucial question: why had the arrogant, self-important, and ethnocentric West remained so powerful when past arrogant and ethnocentric civilizations, such as imperial China or Incan Peru, had collapsed in the face of outside competitors? One of Toynbee's self-confessed disciples, the American historian William L. McNeill, would supply the answer. As a graduate student McNeill had been so impressed with the majestic sweep and vision of *The Study of History* that after the war he went to Oxford to study at the feet of its author. In 1963 he produced an expanded and modified version of Toynbee's analysis of the modern world, *The Rise of the West*.

Like its intellectual predecessor, *The Rise of the West* was a best-seller; yet its spirit was very different. McNeill demonstrated that the West, far from being the arrogant and aloof civilization that Toynbee had portrayed, was distinguished among civilizations by its openness and receptivity to other cultures and peoples. This allowed it to borrow the tools it needed—religious institutions from the Middle East, Greek secular learning and science from the Arabs, technologies from the Chinese— and then successfully adapt them to its own purposes. In its own way, McNeill's *Rise of the West* returned comparative history to its origins in civil society theory. For McNeill as for his Enlightenment predecessors, the history of civilization is not about the growth or loss of cultural-spiritual vitality, but an ever increasing sociability and broadening of horizons: a continuous process of borrowing, invention, travel, and communication between disparate places and peoples. However, McNeill's thesis of adaptability also pointed to a different future for the West than Toynbee's. It suggested that the much vaunted collapse of the West from its own dead weight might not be imminent after all. Through its own flexibility and ability to react to changing conditions, the modern West would find a way to turn the rise of the Third World to its own advantage and so have a more decisive influence on the rest of the world than it had enjoyed at the height of the colonial era.

Toynbee himself was cold to this sort of conclusion.[73] He remained convinced that civilizations formed discrete entities with their own character and spirit, as well as their own trajectories and fates. This led him, like Du Bois and later multiculturalists, both to *underestimate* the degree to which people outside the West might actually want to live in accordance with "soulless Western materialism" and to *overestimate* the degree to which Westernization adhered to an imperialist model. For Toynbee, any compromise with the industrial West would mean an ignominious surrender of "true" cultural and spiritual values for those of Madison Avenue.

In the fifties and early sixties Toynbee's example inspired a whole se-

ries of works on the fate of civilization that centered on the West's di-
minishing role in the world. "If Western man wishes to survive," wrote
one such author, the economist James P. Warburg, "he will have to
learn—and learn very quickly—how to live in and with a world which
has forever escaped from his grasp." Warburg's *The West in Crisis* (1959),
J.G. de Beus's *The Future of the West* (1953), Ernest Hocking's *The Coming World Civilization* (1956), historian John Nef's *Looking for Civilization*
(1962), and Bertrand Russell's *Has Man a Future?* (1964) were all written to feed the market for the kind of speculative "the future as world
history" genre Toynbee had created. Their conclusions tended to center
on one principal theme: the need for a major shift in Western values in
order to deal with the new face of the world.

A representative example was Albert Schweitzer's *Philosophy of Civilization*, published hot on the heels of Toynbee's *Civilization on Trial* in
1950. The first sentence of the book contained more than an echo of
Toynbee: "We are living today under the sign of the collapse of civilization." The reason, Schweitzer claimed, was that since the nineteenth
century "the ethical ideas on which civilization was built have been
wandering about the world, poverty-stricken and helpless." The modern
West's economic and technological progress had taken away men's true
freedom, while the "spiritual life of the community" stood in serious
danger. "We have lost ourselves in outward progress," Schweitzer
lamented, meaning economic growth and affluence. We have allowed
"all advance in the moral life to come to a standstill."

Schweitzer's program for correction also closely resembled Toynbee's.
A new spiritual and ethical awakening was needed to counteract the
dangerous direction civilization had taken. This would involve a "passive self-perfecting effected by inward self-liberation (resignation)," to
counteract the West's emphasis on active self-perfection "between man
and man." For Schweitzer as for Toynbee, ethical progress becomes the
true basis of civilized life, "the development of man to a state of higher
organization and a higher moral standard." Spiritual progress means a
flowing of energy toward affirmation of the spiritual self (Toynbee's
etherealization of the self) and away from political or social institutions.
In fact, he argued, the two are pitted against one another. "Ethical
progress consists in making up our minds to think pessimistically of the
ethics in society," meaning specifically Western society.[74]

Resignation, "passive self-perfecting," and "etherealization": these were the components for the new Western self-image. At the same time that modern liberals embraced the goals and assumptions of welfare state New Liberalism, they gave up their self-confident, competitive edge. Toynbee's father-in-law, Gilbert Murray, coined a term for this: "failure of nerve."

> It is a rise of aeseticism, of mysticism, in a sense, of pessimism; [a] loss of self-confidence . . . and of faith in normal human effort: a despair of patient inquiry, a cry for infallible revelation. It is an atmosphere in which the aim of the good man is not so much to live justly, to help the society to which he belongs and enjoy the esteem of his fellow creatures, but rather . . . to be granted pardon for his unspeakable unworthiness, his immeasurable sins.[75]

Murray, the freethinking Oxford liberal, was speaking of the impact of Christianity on ancient Greek culture. But a failure of nerve applied even more aptly to his son-in-law—and to the wave of passivity and self-flagellation that was now overwhelming the twentieth-century liberal imagination.

Meanwhile, its opponent, cultural pessimism, was discovering a new boldness in the decades after World War II.

# PART THREE

# THE TRIUMPH OF
# CULTURAL PESSIMISM

◆

## CHAPTER 9

# THE CRITICAL PERSONALITY

## The Frankfurt School and Herbert Marcuse

Terror and civilization are inseparable.
—M. Horkheimer and T. Adorno, *The Dialectic of Enlightenment*, 1944

Karl Liebknecht and Rosa Luxemburg were fugitives on the run. On January 6, 1919, they had led bands of armed workers and Bolshevik activists calling themselves the Spartacist League* to seize control of the German government in Berlin. For nine days the Spartacist rebels had held the city at gunpoint, proclaiming their defiance of the Weimar Republic and its Social Democratic leadership. Then, soldiers and volunteer units—the *Freikorps*—moved in and began clearing the streets. By the fifteenth the last barricade had fallen and the leaders of Germany's failed Communist revolution had gone into hiding.

Ironically, Liebknecht and Luxemburg had opposed the uprising when it broke out, and only joined in so as not to be left behind in the tidal wave of revolt. Now they were hostages to its defeat. They managed to elude the army's elaborate manhunt until the night of the fifteenth, when a patrol from the Horse Guards Division found them in an apartment in the Wilmersdorf district. The soldiers brought them to the division's headquarters at the Eden Hotel for a brutal interrogation. Later, as they were being taken away, shaken and bruised, in the glare of a waiting car's headlights, a *Freikorps* veteran named Runge—the sort of

---

* Named after the leader of ancient Rome's most famous slave revolt in 71 B.C.

man admired and idealized by Spengler as a member of the new master race—lunged forward and struck Liebknecht with his rifle butt. As Liebknecht fell to the ground Runge also struck at Luxemburg, crushing her skull. In the pandemonium that followed, the two bodies were frantically dragged into the waiting cars, where they were shot and then dumped into the Landwehr Canal. Spartacist Week was over.[1]

The deaths of Liebknecht and Luxemburg and the failed workers' revolution set off a crisis in German Marxist thinking that later events would only make worse. Rosa Luxemburg had argued fervently that members of the German working class were natural revolutionaries and were only waiting for the right moment to overthrow their oppressors and gain their "day of salvation." Now leading Marxist theorists were not so sure. The old idea that socialism's victory over capitalism was a historical certainty, indeed part of history as progress, had been crushed under the jackboot heel of a more formidable adversary, the "revolution on the Right." Even the success of revolution in Russia in 1917 could not dispell these doubts, as German Communism retreated into an increasingly slavish obedience to Moscow and figures like Lenin (whom Luxemburg had deeply distrusted) and Stalin.

In the Weimar years, young left-wing intellectuals became skeptical of *all* institutions, including the Communist Party and the Social Democratic republic. Their tone was increasingly critical and bitter, reflected in the interwar writings of Kurt Tucholsky and Thomas Mann's brother, Heinrich.[2] Many (including Georg Grosz, Paul Klee, Walter Gropius, Kurt Weill, and Bertolt Brecht) turned from politics to the arts and academia. German universities, once a stronghold of old-fashioned conservatism, opened up under Weimar to a variety of influences, including Marxism. On "progressive" campuses like the University of Frankfurt, even avowed Communists were welcome. The founders of the so-called Frankfurt School, the Institute of Social Research, found there a haven from which they would launch a new Marxist form of cultural criticism that drew on old traditions but also included new and even more potent ideological weapons.

By 1920 the core assumptions of both historical and cultural pessimism—that mass democracy corrupts true political freedom; that technology and positivist science systematically degrade the human spirit; that industrial capitalism tears to tatters the social-cultural fabric of community (*Gemeinschaft*); and that all these trends bring an erosion of vitality and a decadence in arts and manners that spell the imminent end of the West—were now so engrained in discussions of modern culture and society that to deny them would have prompted doubt and suspicion. The Frankfurt School theorists had been born and raised on such pessimism. After the experience of the First World War and the publication of Spengler's best-selling *Decline of the West*, talking about the end of Western civilization had become as natural as breathing. The only subject left for debate was not whether the modern West was doomed but why.

The answer the Frankfurt School critics—Max Horkheimer, Theodor Adorno, Franz Neumann, Erich Fromm, and Herbert Marcuse—developed meant abandoning the old-fashioned Marxist faith in progress and scientific rationality for a far more despairing vision of the future. Marxism provided a concrete historical basis for a sweeping critique of bourgeois culture and "the technological rationality of modern civilization," and for explaining why even a Communist revolution would in the end fail to prevent the self-destruction of the West. Although Marx himself provided some ammunition for this new pessimistic "critical Marxism," especially in his unpublished early manuscripts that scholars had only recently rediscovered, the Frankfurt School actually turned to two non-Marxist thinkers for their most central and influential claims.

The first was Sigmund Freud, whose theories allowed the Frankfurt School to understand, as one member put it, "the mutilating effects by which humanity pays for its technocratic triumphs." The Franfurt critics concluded that Western capitalism systematically produced a neurotic and dysfunctional human type, who surfaced not just in liberal bourgeois society but among its right-wing fascist antagonists as well. Erich Fromm and Herbert Marcuse would later insist that any remaining hope for human freedom required overthrowing the bourgeois mechanisms of psychological *repression* as well as class *oppression*.

The other thinker was Nietzsche. Old-fashioned Marxists had once denounced the vitalist and elitist Nietzsche as the "philosopher of capitalism." However, in the late 1890s some young leftists joined the Nietzschean revival, announcing that the absolute freedom of the creative individual had to be part of a future egalitarian society. What drew the

Franfurt critics to Nietzsche, however, was not his message of vital and redemptive nihilism (which would inspire Nietzsche's twentieth-century French admirers) but his unflinching criticism of bourgeois values. Theodor Adorno called Nietzsche's works "a unique demonstration of the repressive character of Western culture" and said they "expressed the humane in a world in which humanity had become a sham." Nietzsche's attacks on Western logic and reason epitomized Adorno's own idea of "negative dialectics," and Adorno wrote many of his works in the short, sharp aphoristic style of *Human, All-Too-Human* and *Beyond Good and Evil*. Adorno and Horkheimer together turned Nietzsche into a central figure in the new Marxist pantheon, almost displacing Marx himself; in fact, at the end of his life Horkheimer admitted that Nietzsche was probably a greater thinker than Marx.[3]

However, by choosing Nietzsche and Freud as their models, the members of the Frankfurt School also unwittingly put the images and language of degeneration theory squarely in the middle of their critical Marxist program. All the ills of modern society that had been blamed on physiological degeneration—social decay, crime, insanity, suicide, neurosis, alcoholism, degradation of the arts, atavistic mass democratic politics, even anti-Semitism—were now the fault of capitalism and, by extension, the modern West.

The Frankfurt School proclaimed that Western civilization had been built around a deliberate degenerative strategy: that of crushing man's vital instincts through the rational control of nature, oneself, and others. The modern West's chief characteristic was its essential *lifelessness*. As Marcuse later put it, Nietzsche's "total affirmation of the life instinct" represented a "reality principle fundamentally antagonistic to that of Western civilization."[4] Liberation on the Frankfurt School's terms, therefore, meant giving up a view of life that stressed man's ability to use logic and reason to arrive at truth and his need to accommodate himself to a reasonable and natural social order in order to be happy and free.

Instead, human beings had to look to a deeper and more "negative" consciousness, in short, a Nietzschean consciousness. The Frankfurt School created a new cultural hero, the "critical" writer/teacher/intellectual. A direct descendant of the Romantic artist, he would use his typewriter or classroom to attack and expose the contradictions and evils of modern Western civilization. "Under the conditions of late capitalism," Horkheimer wrote in 1936, "truth has sought refuge among small groups of admirable men"—meaning himself and his friends. Later on, those same "admirable" critics would act as carriers of a new cultural pessimism, stemming this time from the political Left rather than the Right.

## CAPITALISM AND INTELLECTUALS: THE ORIGINS OF THE FRANKFURT SCHOOL

Ironically, the Institute of Social Research owed its very existence to capitalist wealth—considerable wealth, in fact, which sustained the activities of the Frankfurt School in four countries for nearly forty years.* The institute was the brainchild of Felix Weil, the son and heir of a German-Jewish millionaire and speculator. By his own description, Felix was a "salon Bolshevik" who decided in 1923 to use the fortune he had inherited to set up an institute at the University of Frankfurt as a forum for communicating Marxist dogma to the masses. That goal was reflected in its first director, Carl Grünberg, an old-school Marxist whose students were among the socialist founders of the Austrian republic in 1918.[5] However, Grünberg retired in 1929 and his successor, Max Horkheimer, was not part of the institute's original Communist contingent. Horkheimer's intellectual guides were more the leading modernist authors—Ibsen, Tolstoy, Zola—and philosophers—Edmund Husserl and Nietzsche—than they were Marx or Engels. The portrait that hung on Horkheimer's office wall when he was director was not of Karl Marx but of Arthur Schopenhauer.

Horkheimer and his allies in the institute, including Theodor Wiesengrund-Adorno, were also drawn to the Hungarian Marxist Georg Lukács, who had suggested that the eventual victory of the proletariat would resolve not only the contradictions of capitalism but modernity itself. They were particularly impressed by Lukács's revelation that bourgeois capitalism functioned as a totality, encompassing institutions, attitudes, and habits of mind as well as the means of

---

* Ironically, one of the first to point this out was Bertolt Brecht. Z. Tar, *The Frankfurt School*, p. 61, n. 1.

production—in fact, Lukács claimed, "the concept of totality, the all-pervasive supremacy of the whole over the parts" was the essence of Marxism as a social and historical theory. The Marxist theorist's job was to combat "the insidious effects of bourgeois ideology on the thought of the proletariat." By making workers aware of their present misery and their power to change it, by giving them a sense of their own "class consciousness," the intellectual provided an indispensable service to his working-class partners.[6]

Unlike Lukács, Horkheimer himself had no interest in promoting a revolution in the streets. Spartacist Week had proved the futility (and physical dangers) of that approach. For Horkheimer, the crucial figure in transforming the totality was no longer the worker but the intellectual; the socialist order "will be realized," he wrote in an early essay, "either by human beings trained in theory and determined to achieve better conditions, or not at all."[7] The belief in the primacy of "critical theory" for overthrowing the bourgeois concrete totality became the early unifying theme of Frankfurt School Marxism. Instead of stirring the masses to armed struggle, eagle-eyed intellectuals would devote themselves to exposing or "demystifying" the false relations of capitalist society, particularly its degradation of man's reason and spiritual wholeness.

The Frankfurt School version of "true" culture reflected more than a trace of traditional German academic snobbery, as well as Nietzsche's "republic of genius," where "one giant calls to another across the desert interval of time." Adorno in particular extolled the pursuit of original and innovative aesthetic forms, especially in avant-garde art and music.[8] But the Frankfurt critics also understood that conventional bourgeois culture was itself the product of a total historical process, capitalism's "alienation" of modern man as described in the newly discovered "Economic and Philosophical Manuscripts" of the young Karl Marx.

These had been written in 1844 when Marx was only twenty-five years old, but they remained unpublished until almost half a century after his death, in 1932. Their release to the public forced Marxists, including the members of the Frankfurt School (Herbert Marcuse was one of the first to work on them), to radically revise their thinking about the development of Marx's ideas. In 1844 Marx was still under Hegel's spell; in these early writings he suggested that the evils of capitalism were found not just in economic exploitation, with its low wages, destitution, and chronic unemployment. Capitalism's real dangers were spiritual, or as we would say today, psychological.

The division of labor in capitalist enterprise turned the product of the worker's labor into a lifeless commodity. What he makes is taken away and sold with no benefit to him (apart from his wages, which never reflect its full value). The bolts of cloth, iron pots, or brass pins he made no longer have any connection to him; he is "alienated" from his labor. The result, Marx claimed, is that "the worker feels himself only when he is not working; when he is working he does not feel himself."[9] The worker under capitalism surrenders his autonomy and humanity to the industrial process. Capitalism "reduces him to a machine," and eventually he is replaced by one. Marx concluded that the physical division of labor in capitalism results in the division of men's souls.

Consequently, the expansion of capitalist production can never benefit the worker; on the contrary, even as "the division of labor increases the productive power of labor and wealth and *refinement of society* [Marx's emphasis], it impoverishes the worker" both materially and spiritually, producing "idiocy and cretinism." The degenerative dynamics of capitalism could even be reduced to a simple and dogmatic formula. The more capitalism grows and expands, the more it must actually exploit and impoverish its workers, notwithstanding any material evidence to the contrary. In fact, capitalism's production of such "estranged men" does not stop with the working class, Marx argued. It necessarily includes the bourgeoisie, since no one is free from the transformation of things and men into commodities by the division of labor. "Each man is estranged from the others and . . . all are estranged from man's essence" under capitalism.[10]

The relation, if any, between the ideas of the young, Hegelianized Marx and the later, more materially minded Marx of *Das Kapital* became a matter of enormous and bitter debate to Marxists. However, the "Economic and Philosophical Manuscripts" succeeded in turning Karl Marx into a diagnostician of modern cultural decline. His concept of alienation seemed to anticipate the sociology of Durkheim, Weber, Sombart, and Simmel, not to mention degeneration theorists like Benedict Morel and Charles Féré. However, Marx also supplied a culprit to explain modern degeneracy: capitalism. The triumph of capitalism meant the degradation of the vital human spirit. The Frankfurt School quickly translated Marx's theory of alienation into the more familiar idioms of German cultural criticism and Nietzsche.

Theodor Adorno was impatient with traditional Marxism's neglect of cultural criticism: "There is," he wrote once, "more truth in Nietzsche's *Genealogy of Morals* than there is in Burkharin's ABC."[11] Capitalism had destroyed art by turning it into a commodity like soap and automobiles, he raged. The true spirit of creative art "cannot survive where it is fixed as a cultural commodity and doled out to satisfy consumer needs." Like Werner Sombart's technological culture, Adorno's capitalist "culture industry" mass-produces "candy-floss entertainment" that "stultifies mankind."[12] He developed an elaborate social theory of music to prove that jazz represented the victory of the mass-produced and mechanical over "genuine" artistic creativity (represented by the twelve-tone music of Schoenberg). Even whistling came under Adorno's scathing scrutiny: it represented the deformation of musical forms for popular consumption, and hence corrupted the aesthetic integrity of the musical composition.[13]

The Frankfurt Marxists in effect reversed Nordau's judgment of contemporary art. Truly "degenerate" art was not Arnold Schoenberg's atonal music or Picasso's cubist paintings but their "bourgeois" alternatives—John Philip Souza or jazz or Norman Rockwell or Mickey Mouse. As in Nietzsche's dismissal of Wagner, the fact that this kind of art appealed to a "stultified" mass public proved that it was corrupt and debased.*

When capitalism collapses, however, Horkheimer explained, "mankind will for the first time be a conscious subject and actively determine its own way of life." Culture, art, music, and literature will regain their genuine autonomy and life-enhancing powers. The problem in 1932 was that capitalism did not seem to be collapsing, at least not in any direction that would help to foster a new Marxist order. Instead, it was producing a revolution of a very different kind: that of the militarist, vitalist Right.

---

* Ultimately this argument becomes circular. Why are Norman Rockwell's paintings vulgar art? Because they appeal to a culturally debased public. What evidence is there that the public's taste is debased? Because it likes Norman Rockwell's vulgar paintings.

## CIVILIZATION AND THE NAZIS: THE DIALECTIC OF THE ENLIGHTENMENT

Hitler's rise to power caught nearly everyone on the Left by surprise. Communist Party doctrine in the interwar years taught that movements like Mussolini's Blackshirts and the Nazis represented the last stage of "late capitalism." Faced with economic ruin and the rise of the Soviet Union, it was asserted, the bourgeoisie were forced to turn to the brutality of fascism in order to hold on to power. The Frankfurt School's Franz Neumann stated that Nazism was "an affirmation of the living force of capitalist society."[14] However, everyone also assumed that fascism, too, would collapse and the working class would rally to the red banners of Communism. Instead the Nazis ascended triumphantly to power, with working-class and popular support. Their message of racial vitality and national rebirth had proved more successful than that of proletarian revolution and freedom.

To the crestfallen members of the Frankfurt School, National Socialism seemed the final victory of Nietzsche's debased last man. Adorno later described it as Germany's "leap into the abyss," just as Sigmund Freud saw it as the fulfillment of civilized man's death wish. "No one," Adorno wrote, "could fail to perceive the moment of mortal sadness, the half-knowing half-surrender to perdition [with] the torchlight processions and the beating drums."[15] Six weeks after Hitler was sworn in as chancellor, the Gestapo seized the library of the Institute of Social Research and closed its buildings. But Horkheimer and the others had already fled to Geneva, where they took refuge while waiting for visas to the United States. In the meantime they began to put forward a theory to explain why a supposedly civilized country like Germany had embraced an irrational, violent, and racist ideology with such devastating swiftness. In the end, they proclaimed that liberal capitalism "contained from *its very beginning* the tendency toward national socialism."[16]

Meanwhile Horkheimer and the institute took refuge in the United States. Only a year earlier, in 1935, its administrative director, Friedrich Pollock, had denounced New Deal America as a hotbed of fascism.[17] Now it became their place of refuge. Columbia University's president, Nicholas Butler, was a political conservative but also a strong believer in academic freedom and diversity (a point of view Herbert Marcuse would later attack as "repressive tolerance"). At the urging of his faculty, Butler gave the Marxist group a building on 117th Street, with offices for staff and visiting scholars. Horkheimer and Adorno were soon joined by two other institute members, Erich Fromm and Herbert Marcuse.

Ensconced in Morningside Heights amidst an unfamiliar sea of American affluence, Horkheimer's tiny coterie proceeded to shut their gates against the vibrant polyglot society that had taken them in. They became and remained an enclave of German exiles; now that they were out of reach of Hitler's goons, the institute's self-image took on heroic proportions. Horkheimer announced that the institute was now "the only group which can maintain the relatively advanced state of theory which has been achieved in Germany and advance it even further."[18] For the next fifteen years the institute at Columbia would become a conduit for German sociology and philosophy, as well as Marxist theory, into American intellectual life. Theory was paramount: Horkheimer always maintained a strong distaste for empirical research, stressing the virtues of "theoretical reason" over "mere facts," or what others might term empirical reality.*[19] Although as director Horkheimer made impressive claims about the institute's creating a new unity of the social sciences, in fact the only unity among the Frankfurt theorists was their desire to do away with bourgeois capitalism and its philistine values.

Horkheimer and Adorno convinced themselves that the nightmare they had escaped in Germany was not just an isolated case of mass hysteria. The Nazi episode represented something deeper and even more intractable: the final stage of Western civilization as a total process. All the modern West's characteristic forms of economic, social, political, and cultural life reflected the same goal: absolute control and domination. They referred to this controlling, expansive nature of Western civilization as the impulse toward "total integration." Spengler had called it the Faustian spirit of the West; in their 1944 book, *The Dialectic of Enlightenment*, Horkheimer and Adorno made it the driving force of progress.

"The fallen nature of modern man cannot be separated from social

---

* Those who disagreed on this point, such as Karl Wittfogel and Franz Neumann, were carefully kept at arm's length from the institute's policy-making decisions.

[and material] progress," they wrote. "On the one hand the growth of economic productivity furnishes the condition for a world of greater justice ... [on the other] the individual is wholly devalued in relation to the economic powers, which ... press the control of society to hitherto unsuspected heights."[20] The individual in Western culture becomes completely subordinate to the totalizing whole. He not only surrenders his political freedom to the state, he also loses all powers of independent action and thought. The "sickness" of Western culture "condemns the spirit to increasing darkness." Even the occasional dissident, even a Karl Marx, can no longer formulate his opposition except in the "impoverished and debased" formulae and categories of the exiting totality, which "strengthens the very power of the established order he is trying to break."[21]

This is why revolution always fails in the modern West, while fascism will always triumph. "Fascism is the truth of modern society," Horkheimer had proclaimed, "which theory realized from the beginning." The entire capitalist West stood on the same brink from which the Weimar Republic had fallen, helpless before the onslaught of the fascist military state and collectivized madness; "mankind, instead of entering into a truly human condition, is sinking into a new barbarism." Horkheimer and Adorno pointed beyond capitalism to its philosophical origins in the Western cult of rationality and reason. They asserted that "the present collapse of bourgeois civilization" was ultimately due to the Enlightenment. Contrary to its own self-image, the Age of Reason in the eighteenth century was not about reason at all, but rather about the pursuit of power over nature and human beings. "This very way of thinking ... contains the seed of the reversal universally apparent today." In other words, for Adorno and Horkheimer Nazism was the final product of the Enlightenment.[22]

This conclusion seems less startling when we realize that the Frankfurt School made a sharp distinction between a "good" and a "bad" Enlightenment. The first had produced the rational humanist philosophy of figures like Hume, Kant, and Hegel, as well as the critical skeptical spirit of Voltaire, which had been reborn with Nietzsche. This was the Age of Reason properly speaking, to which Adorno and Horkheimer saw themselves as the last true heirs. The second, however, had generated the modern obsession with science, technology, and number, which turns reason "into a thing, an instrument." This was the Enlightenment of Newton, Condorcet, Jeremy Bentham—and Adam Smith. Yet the two enlightenments are ultimately inseparable; their relationship is "dialectical." By trying to know the unknowable, "enlightenment tried to secure itself against the return of the mythic." The result was that the Western mind ended up alienating man from nature and himself.

Like Nietzsche, Horkheimer and Adorno begin the story of the decline of the West with the Greeks. Prerational myth and magic had preserved the unity of man and nature, which the Apollonian project of Greek philosophy destroyed.* Man's reason was set free, but he used that freedom to try to dominate everything that now seemed separate from himself and human reason, the so-called Other. Science, law, government, even language itself—all became instruments by which Western man reduced diversity to sameness, spontaneity to uniformity, and difference (defined as the Other) to multiform objects for control, like butterflies in a killing-jar.

The Enlightenment termed this totalizing process civilization or progress. The result, however, was not satisfaction but alienation. As Horkheimer and Adorno explain it, "men pay for the increase of their power with alienation, from that over which they exercise their power." This inspires them to seek even more power, with the same futile result; the upward ascent of progress is in reality an inward-turning *anakuklosis* of illusion and frustration. It becomes a trap that, like Max Weber's iron cage, man's own rational nature has built for him.[23] The Enlightenment brought this self-destructive Western culture of control up to its modern tempo. It gave the West's new dominant class, the bourgeoisie, a rationale or "myth" for the self-conscious pursuit of power, called the scientific method.[24] Everything is reduced to "equivalence," number, and system. It produces modern social science's emphasis on facts and empirical research, and liberal democracy's quantitative principle of one man–one vote. Underneath them all, however, is instrumental reason's dream of absolute power over the Other.

"A technological rationale is the rationale of domination itself,"

---

* Scientific man's mythological prototype, for Horkheimer and Adorno, is Odysseus, who overcame his supernatural enemies by means of his wits, generating the first form of "rational labor," i.e., the model for the scientist and entrepreneur.

which is why "the Enlightenment is totalitarian."[25] Reason finally reveals its true face on paper in the brutal sexual fantasies of the Marquis de Sade, Nietzsche's *fin de siècle* nihilism (Nietzsche serves as both hero and villain in Horkheimer and Adorno's account), the Gestapo interrogation cell, and Auschwitz's barbed wire and gas ovens. According to Horkheimer and Adorno, these are the logical outcome of the Europe that extolled science and progress. In Horkheimer and Adorno's memorable words, "terror and civilization are inseparable."[26]

Of course, one could object that the Enlightenment's supposed final product, Nazi Germany, was actually the self-declared enemy of Enlightenment liberalism and all its works, just as it championed *Kultur* over *Zivilisation*. However, Adorno and Horkheimer denied the significance of these claims. The crucial question in understanding the origins of the Nazi movement was not what Hitler and his associates claimed to be doing, but how they functioned as part of the total process. Having conquered and enslaved everything in sight, rationality in its late stages, Adorno and Horkheimer concluded, is forced to appeal to its opposite, violence and barbarism, in order to secure its final total victory. "In modern fascism, rationality has reached a point at which it is no longer satisfied with simply repressing nature; rationality now exploits nature by incorporating into its own system the rebellious potentialities of nature."[27] So even irrationality eventually becomes reason's dialectical instrument. This established a principle, and a useful rhetorical device, that became characteristic of other cultural pessimists besides the members of the Frankfurt School: the more things *seem* to be opposites (liberalism and fascism, affluence and poverty, free speech and censorship), the more they are actually the same.*

In any case, Adorno and Horkheimer had very little to say about the actual political origins of the fascist state. Instead, politics is only a function of what is really uppermost in their minds, the question of culture. They were convinced that modern technology was transforming art, music, and culture in industrial societies into a medium for "mass deception . . . neutralized and ready-made," according to a totalitarian po-

---

* This was a variation of what Hegel had called the "cunning of Reason," in which the World Spirit manages to advance historical progress even through its seeming opposite, for example, the liberty of the French Revolution through the military dictatorship of Napoleon.

litical program. To say that *The Dialectic of Enlightenment* took this degradation of culture by capitalism seriously would be a gross understatement:

> In the culture industry the individual is an illusion. . . . He is tolerated only so long as his complete identification with the generality is unquestioned.

> The blind and rapidly spreading repetition of words . . . links advertising and the totalitarian watch-word.

> The sound film, far surpassing the theater of illusion, leaves no room for imagination or reflection . . . forcing its victims to equate it directly with reality.

> Television aims at . . . derisively fulfilling the Wagnerian dream of the *Gesamtkunstwerk* . . . This process integrates all the elements of the production, from the novel (shaped with an eye to the film) to the last sound effect.

> Cartoons . . . confirm the victory of technological reason over truth. . . . Donald Duck in the cartoons and the unfortunate in real life get their thrashing so that the audience can learn to take their own punishment.

Their far-ranging cultural critique relied on the aesthetic theories of the maverick Walter Benjamin,* in many ways the most original of the Frankfurt group. Benjamin stressed the role of technology in transforming modern experience into "a never-ending series of shocks to the individual's consciousness." The typical modern man in Benjamin's view is like a character in a Franz Kafka novel: bewildered, lost, shell-shocked

---

* Born in 1892, Benjamin came to Marxism from the German Youth Movement, whose message of revolt against the bourgeoisie and of the need for a new community of spirit pushed many to fascism as well as to Communism. However, his allegiance to Marxism was only skin-deep. Benjamin's real hero was the French poet Charles Baudelaire; in fact, his theory of culture forms a bridge extending from the late Romantic rebellion of Baudelaire and the Decadents, to the similar impulses of German Expressionism and modernism, to "postmodern" critics such as Susan Sontag, Jean Baudrillard, and Gianni Vattimo. Julian Roberts, *Walter Benjamin* (London, 1982).

into passive conformity and emotional numbness—an abject picture of alienation.[28] Meanwhile, that same technology was transforming culture through mechanical reproduction, with photographs, films, records, and mass production of books. This trend again revealed modernity's "sense of the universal equality of things," since each copy of a photograph, a film, or a recording is exactly like the next.

The uniformity of mass reproduction destroyed forever what Benjamin called the "aura" of a work of art, the sense of reverence and awe before an object's uniqueness that made true artistic creativity possible.[29] In Benjamin's view, a photograph of the Venus de Milo made it impossible to look at the real Venus de Milo with any appreciation for its uniqueness, even as man's drastically foreshortened experience in modern society made him unable to create any genuine works of art on his own. Technology and capitalism spell the end of both art and the artist, he argued. The only way the creative individual can avoid becoming part of this system of aesthetic exploitation—a "whore" to its corrupting values—was paradoxically to abandon all claim to creativity or artistic independence, which only served to make him respectable in the eyes of the middle class. Instead, the artist must employ his talents and the new mass media to serve the proletariat in overthrowing the real cause of their mutual degradation—capitalism. This is a tall order, of course, and Benjamin kept the details vague; the possibility that in avoiding becoming a whore to bourgeois culture the artist might become a whore to Stalin's never seems to have occurred to him.[30]

Mention of Stalin raises the major problem the Frankfurt School never quite fully came to grips with. Marxism, which ought to have provided a way to escape from the rise of totalitarian society, had ended up producing its own form of totalitarianism in the Soviet Union. Adorno, Horkheimer, and their colleagues could never bring themselves to consider that brutal police states such as Hitler's Germany and Stalin's Russia may have had more in common with each other, and less in common with the Western capitalist values that were supposed to be the root of all evil, than critical theory made out. Instead, confronted by the undeniable truth of Stalinism, they allowed themselves to draw an even more pessimistic conclusion. *Every* society on the Western model, regardless of its actual ideology or the character of its rulers, advances inevitably to

the type of bleak totalitarianism made vivid in George Orwell's *1984*.*
Wherever soulless reason reigns, they asserted, tyranny inevitably takes
root.

This belief led them toward Toynbee's theory about superpower convergence. However, this convergence was not a hopeful or reassuring
trend. Instead, the United States and the Soviet Union were both examples of "advanced industrial societies," which were evolving into
twin rigid and interchangeable totalitarian states. Liberal democratic
principles and Marxist egalitarianism merely provided the window
dressing for the faceless bureaucratic elites that supervised both. The total police state was the natural consequence of Western-style economic
production; no advanced industrial society could maintain control
without a secret government apparatus and its attendant atrocities.[31]

Their pessimistic view of Cold War convergence dovetailed with the
views of another Marxist teaching at Columbia University, C. Wright
Mills. Together with Marcuse and Adorno, Mills would serve as one of
the intellectual mentors of the New Left. His works read like a compendium of the Frankfurt School and Brooks Adams. His most influential book, *The Power Elite* (1958), pointed to the same dangers of the
advanced industrial state but with a distinctively American paranoid
style (which would later be exploited by the film director Oliver Stone).
Mills presented America's Anglo-Saxon natural aristocracy as an entrenched, self-interested elite of old wealth, corporate businessmen,
technocrats, and Cold War admirals and generals. (Mills was writing
during Eisenhower's presidency.) Linked by wealth and old school ties
(Harvard, Yale, Groton, and West Point), they effected America's economic, political, and military decision-making through a single ruthless
"political directorate."[32] What Brooks Adams had only dreamed of,
"that one day we shall be reorganized by soldiers," Mills claimed had already come about.

This "military-industrial complex," however, was not distinctively
American. It reflected the modern nation's industrial and therefore foreign character. Like Stalin's Russia, the sins of Eisenhower's United

---

* Cf. Erich Fromm's disingenuous introduction to Orwell's novel in the New American Library edition (New York, 1949): "It would be most unfortunate if the reader smugly interpreted *1984* as another description of Stalinist barbarism, and if he did not see he means us, too."

States formed part of a larger historical totality. "There is," Mills wrote, "a fairly straight line running upward throughout the history of the West; that oppression and exploitation, violence and destruction, as well as the means of production, have been progressively enlarged and increasingly centralized." By means of a manipulative mass media, "the decline of politics as a genuine and public debate of alternative decisions," the loss of personal autonomy, and the commercialization of wishes and desires, the "power structure" had organized every aspect of American society to conceal its manipulative power. It made people think they made their own political decisions when in fact those decisions were made for them (what would later be termed "manufactured consent").[33] Crucial to this concealment, and hence to the functioning of the totality, was the role of ideology.

Mills, the Frankfurt School, and their heirs in the New Left used the term "ideology" to refer to the way in which people in advanced industrialized society imagine the world works, as opposed to the way it really works. The sociologist Karl Mannheim, who had taught at the University of Frankfurt in the twenties, explained that ideology in bourgeois society serves to disguise or "mystify" the real relations of economic production, class struggle, and political power. In the case of America, for example, it leads people to imagine that they are enjoying more control over their lives, with more affluence, more consumer choices, and more social and geographic mobility, when in fact they are being steadily enslaved to the demands of modern capitalism. In fact, the Frankfurt School saw ideology as the great supportive net that held mass industrial society together; without their ideological blinders, the masses would certainly rebel. "In certain situations," Karl Mannheim wrote, "the collective unconscious of certain groups obscures the real condition of society both to itself and others *and thereby stabilizes it* [emphasis added]."[34]

The term C. Wright Mills and later Marcuse used to describe this disguising, stabilizing ideology in America was "conservatism." American conservatism was above all a bourgeois ideology; in fact, being a conservative came to mean, in New Left terms, the same thing as being a liberal had meant to the Nietzscheans on the German Right. It implied a certain willful blankness regarding the emptiness of modern life, a blankness in the face of corruption and decline.[35] Communism under

Stalin had lost the capacity to unmask that false ideology. Instead it had generated its own false ideology, "authoritarian socialism," which it used to prop its own ramshackle, decaying industrial society.

The only alternative left to totalitarianism, then, was critical theory. To expect that the entire totalizing process of modern civilization would suddenly give way under critical theory's attacks would be naive and futile. In any case, according to the logic of *The Dialectic of Enlightenment*, the failure of Communism meant it was not possible to progress forward, since every extension of systematic rationality, even Marxism itself, only brings another form of the same rationalizing-totalizing deathtrap. The only escape is the individual Nietzschean act of criticism, what Horkheimer called "negative dialectics" and what Marcuse, borrowing a term from the French Surrealists, called "the Great Refusal." This was the intellectual's conscious decision not to subscribe to any of the values and conventions of bourgeois society, as a protest against its totalizing dream of power.

So even as late capitalism, in its prelude to dictatorship and fascism, herds the stupefied masses together into a mindless collectivity, critical thinking declares its independence. The intellectual positions himself to be neither "deep-rooted," that is, obedient like totalitarian and fascist ideologues to the political regime, nor "detached," that is, obedient like liberals to a dying cultural system. Instead, he is "negative," in the sense of assailing the status quo. But this is not a futile or merely symbolic gesture. The central tenet of the entire Frankfurt School, and of later figures like Marcuse and Jürgen Habermas, is that the radical critic's words are not idle chatter but a significant form of social action, because his protest against the totality preserves the possibility of an alternative in men's minds.[36]

One can see how this image of the heroic lone dissenter made sense in Nazi Germany, but it hardly applied to the realities of the United States in the forties and fifties, let alone to the "pre-fascist" Weimar Republic. In fact, one of Weimar's fundamental problems may have been an *overabundance* of critical words masquerading as "significant speech." However, to the Frankfurt School, words and deeds were on the same continuum. Indeed, verbal criticism of bourgeois society became a moral duty, even (or perhaps preferably) from the safety of the classroom or the pages of a scholarly journal. Since the negative critic, like

C. Wright Mills at Columbia or Herbert Marcuse at Brandeis University, had already declared his spiritual independence from a moribund social and cultural system, he was no longer part of it, even as it continued to pay his bills. In Frankfurt School terms, he no longer recognized its authority.

## AUTHORITARIAN CIVILIZATION: THE IMPACT OF FREUD

Is not the individual who functions normally, adequately, and healthily
as a citizen of a sick society—is not such a person sick?
    —Herbert Marcuse

In the end, the Frankfurt School's historical pessimism rested on a crude parallel between America and pre-Nazi Weimar: both were seen as life-less, mindless, late capitalist societies teetering on the brink of dictator-ship. Here Sigmund Freud proved as useful as Nietzsche. At first glance, Freud seems a surprising model for attacks on Western rationality and middle-class values. A liberal Jewish intellectual, Freud was a proud and unabashed member of the bourgeois medical profession. He considered his psychoanalytic theories to be part of the Western intellectual main-stream and a form of science. But to the Frankfurt School, Freud's works did not belong to science at all; they saw him as a fellow critic, one who celebrated the role of the unconscious and cast a dark light on human existence similar to that of novelists like Dostoyevsky and Franz Kafka. In this respect, the Frankfurt School pointed the way to Freud's future prominence in literary theory, as well as in psychology.[37]

Erich Fromm had been trained as a Freudian psychiatrist and in the late twenties became interested in merging Freudian theory with Marx-ism. He was not the first to do so: Freud's disciple Wilhelm Reich had made the same attempt, much to Freud's disgust and fury.[38] But whereas Reich limited himself to insisting that the end of capitalism would mean the end of neurosis, Fromm and his supporters at the Institute of Social Research gave the merger of Freud and Marx a more analytical thrust. They tried to describe the social psychology of late capitalism by reveal-ing its supposedly distorting effects on the individual and the family, particularly among workers.

"The more a society collapses economically, socially and psychologi-cally," Fromm wrote in 1937, "the greater are the differences in psychic structure in the various classes." The modern family, like late capitalism itself, was "in crisis," Fromm and Adorno concluded in their *Studies on Authority and the Family*. The effects were far-reaching and deadly, particularly on the individual. People emerged from the modern family as psychological cripples, particularly in their capacity to deal with authority and authority figures. An unthinking obedience to a variety of authority figures—among whom Adorno included "parents, older people, leaders, supernatural powers, and so forth"—emerges in late capitalist society, as people are conditioned to believe the lies used by the holders of power to disguise their manipulative exploitation.[39]

Thanks to the Frankfurt School, "authority" would become, like imperialism, a dirty word for Marxists and progressives (as in the bumper sticker that urges passers-by to "question authority"). However, the reason had less to do with politics than with psychoanalytic theory—one might even say degeneration theory. While the Enlightenment saw dependence on authority as the hallmark of primitive cultures, Fromm and Horkheimer argued, on the contrary, that the search for authority figures was the normal condition of human beings in the modern West. Sensing their own weakness and impotence under late capitalism, men instinctively turned to those who seemed to represent strength and power. "When the child," wrote Horkheimer, "respects in his father's strength a moral relationship and thus learns to love what his reason recognizes to be a fact, he is experiencing his first training for the bourgeois authority relationship."[40]

The typical modern family, then, involves "a sado-masochistic resolution of the Oedipus complex," producing a psychological cripple, the "authoritarian personality." The individual's hatred of the father is suspended and remains unresolved, becoming instead an attraction for strong authority figures whom he obeys unquestioningly. Like degeneracy, it is a form of atavism—Adorno later even used the term—that is most prominent in the lower classes.[41] Like Le Bon's man in the crowd, the authoritian personality looks to mass movements and charismatic leaders (such as Hitler or Mussolini) for a sense of direction and purpose. And as in Le Bon, this atavistic reversion is itself the product of progress, which is to say the socioeconomic forces of unchained democracy and modernity. Bourgeois society, which seems to extol individual autonomy, actually generates the opposite.

The masochistic bourgeoisie and their working-class clones passively yield to the demands of their sadistic political masters, just as they yield to the demands of capitalism's division of labor. "The human types that prevail today," Horkheimer intoned gloomily, "are not educated to get at the root of things . . . They are unable to think theoretically and to move beyond the simple registering of facts." Horkheimer's inevitable conclusion was that "the overwhelming majority of people" living in capitalist society "have no personality." So widespread, in fact, is this dynamic in modern society, Fromm added, that "the majority of people in our society" now consider "the bourgeois human being to be the 'normal' and natural one."[42]

Fromm carefully spelled out the political implications of this in *Escape From Freedom*, which was published in 1941, just before the United States entered World War II. "Freed from the bonds of pre-individualistic society"—or, we might say, from *Gemeinschaft*—the modern human being still "has not gained freedom in the positive sense of the realization of his individual self, that is, the expression of his intellectual, emotional, and sensuous potentialities." He is, in Marxist terms, alienated. That sense of alienation drove the German masses and citizens of other industrial societies to movements like National Socialism, instead of freeing themselves from the economic exploitation that was the real root of their misery. "In our own society," Fromm warned his fellow Americans, "we are faced with the same phenomenon that is fertile soil for the rise of Fascism everywhere: the insignificance and powerlessness of the individual." The modern American citizen is free to do only one of two things: he can "fall in step like a marching soldier or a worker on the endless belt. He can act; but the sense of independence, significance, has gone.*[43]

Fromm's theory of modern man's "fear of freedom" also laid the foundation for the institute's most ambitious undertaking, *The Authoritarian Personality*. Whereas Fromm's and Adorno's earlier conclusions about the psychology of late capitalism drew on German examples, *The Au-*

---

* Among other examples of the widespread "sense of fear and insignificance" in American society, Fromm pointed to the popularity of Mickey Mouse cartoons. The hero's ability to elude his stronger pursuer and exact revenge (here Fromm seems to have confused Mickey Mouse with Tom and Jerry) satisfied the spectator's deepest psychic needs: "That is how he feels and that is the situation with which he can identify himself."

*thoritarian Personality* was an American project. It first of all appealed to American ideals, suggesting that the authoritarian personality was the enemy of "democratic civilization." Published in 1948, it looked to the postwar American context: even though America had defeated fascism in World War II, the authors warned, the threat of its resurrection remained. This was because the personality disorders that had caused it had not disappeared—indeed, they were omnipresent. In this sense, their message was also implicitly anti-Cold War: fascism, rather than Communism, was the gravest threat to American traditional values in the postwar world.[44]

In an unusual departure, Adorno and his team also appealed to the American taste for quantitative methods in their study, presenting *The Authoritarian Personality* as a social scientific model with a high degree of predictability. But these objective, scientific trappings were in fact misleading. *The Authoritarian Personality* contained the harsh warning that fascism was finding a new home in America itself. This was hardly shocking news to the authors of *The Dialectic of Enlightenment*. Since America was the home of modernity's dominant values, of pragmatism and positivist science, it must also eventually become the epicenter of modern civilization's downward slide into fascism. However, this larger agenda was kept carefully hidden.

*The Authoritarian Personality* was conceived in 1939 as part of a larger joint project, with the Berkeley Public Opinion Study and the American Jewish Committee, dealing with anti-Semitism, the issue that the Frankfurt School rather belatedly realized was central to the entire Nazi episode in Germany.[45] The project was built around a series of questionnaires that tried to establish a psychological profile of the "potential fascist character" (amazingly, they had no interest in studying fascists themselves). The answers would supposedly reveal "trends which lay relatively deep within the personality," that is, beyond the reach of particular ideologies, particularly those that disposed their subjects to "express or be influenced by, fascist ideas."

The results seemed to warrant alarm. Anti-Semitism turned out to be only the visible edge of a dysfunctional personality revealed in the many "ethnocentric" and "conventional" attitudes of the general American population, as well as of a disquietingly submissive attitude toward authority of all kinds. "Despite our assumed enlightenment," Adorno explained in his introduction with an air of surprise, widespread racial and ethnic prejudices revealed the survival of "the incongruous atavism of ancient peoples" in modern society—although Adorno had just finished arguing in *The Dialectic of Enlightenment* that these prejudices were an essential part of modern society.

The essential traits of the potential fascist character were revealed to be a rigid commitment to dominant values (particularly regarding morality and religion), concern about being unobtrusive in behavior and appearance, a stress on efficiency, cleanliness, and success—in short, those of the stereotypical decent American citizen. These traits actually disguised "a pessimistic and contemptuous view of humanity" (exemplified by agreement with the statement, "Human nature being what it is, there will always be war and conflict"), "morbid fears of sexuality and spontaneous activity," a resistance toward out-groups and minorities, and a susceptibility to authority figures. Such an authoritarian personality, in the words of the most recent historian of the project, "identified himself with power, and appealed to democracy, morality, and rationality only in order to destroy them."[46]

Adorno and his researchers appealed to Freud for their diagnosis of this dysfunctional personality. Everything resulted from a weak ego and an externalized superego—which also happened to be the chief characteristics of man in mass industrial society. *The Authoritarian Personality* belonged to a cluster of postwar works—Jean-Paul Sartre's *Reflections on the Jewish Question*, David Reisman's *The Lonely Crowd*, and Alberto Moravia's novel *The Conformist*—which concluded that fascism and anti-Semitism appealed to deficient "other-directed" personalities, who were weak and devoid of inner integrity. However, Adorno and his colleagues were also reworking Lombrosian social science in a modern leftist context. "Abnormality" was defined by certain fixed and quantifiable traits measured on the so-called F-scale (F for fascism), which were then compared with a profile of the supposedly "normal" or healthy personality. But despite all the "scientific" and "clinical" measurements and charts in the manner of Lombroso and Galton, it soon became apparent to serious critics that the number of respondents (three thousand) and the selection of "key groups" had produced so unrepresentative a sample and such skewed data that the study was largely worthless.

For example, as in the smaller surveys of German workers in the thirties, that underpinned *Authority and the Family*, the questions were posed in such a way that any answer reflecting traditional values was interpreted as "authoritarian" (i.e., distorted) and hence potentially fascist.* On the other hand, the possibility that someone could be politically progressive and still susceptible to authority types was excluded. Indeed, persons inclined to leftist views were "proved" to be emotionally healthier and *happier* than their conservative counterparts in their personal as well as public lives. This was reflected in their openness, "capacity for love," sympathy for others, and understanding of reality. Those qualities made them supportive of progressive or socialist causes and impervious to authoritarian political movements. "If fear and destructiveness are the emotional sources of fascism," Adorno concluded, "*Eros* belongs to democracy," that is to say, to socialism.[47]

*The Authoritarian Personality* and its assumptions were all but demolished by other social scientists and critics.† But the term "authoritarian personality" caught on and proved useful for disarming critics of the Marxist Left. It allowed the Marxist to accuse his opponent, whether anti-Communist liberal or conservative, of being abnormal and actually an unconscious Nazi—just as Lombroso's criminal was really a degenerate, "a sick man." America, the totem of modern democratic culture, was actually "latently" fascist. The absence of a "genuine" fascist movement in America, like the absence of any "genuine" anti-Semitism, was in fact a sign of how far the corruption had spread. As Herbert Marcuse put it somewhat later, "The fact that we cannot point to an SS or SA here, simply means that they are not necessary in this country."[48]

In opposition to the conformist authoritarian personality stood the "openness" of the healthy personality, which Erich Fromm defined as the recognition that there are no higher values or authority than oneself. "Man is the center and purpose of his life." Fromm dismissed any notion that this self-anchored existence might lead to cultural anarchy or nihilism. Nihilism, Nietzsche had shown, was the result of the constraint of middle-class manners and mores on man's vitality, not the lack

---

* For example, a positive response to the statement, "Obedience and respect for authority are the most important virtues that children should learn" or "Young people sometimes get rebellious ideas, but as they grow older they ought to get over them and settle down."

† Especially Edward Shils, Herbert Hyman, and Paul Sheatsley. R. Christie and M. Jahora, *Studies in the Scope and Method of "The Authoritarian Personality"* (Glencoe, IL, 1954).

of them; once these were gone, untapped reservoirs of emotional strength and limitless self-creativity would be released. Yet if Fromm believed that Western man could still save himself and build a "sane society" (the title of his 1964 sequel to *Escape From Freedom*), Adorno had no such illusions. He had become obsessed with the dark heart of modern civilization, which he and Horkheimer had first revealed in *The Dialectic of Enlightenment*. The Second World War and the Holocaust led Adorno to conclude that genocide, like fascism, was a "deeply imprinted schema" within Western civilization's dream of reason and power.

Rationality's systematic organization of the Other leads inevitably to the extermination of the Other, in the form of Jews and other powerless, "marginal" groups. The pogrom was the ritual murder of civilization, Adorno grimly concluded. In the pogrom Western rationality turned back on itself, just as in the abuse of women. "The signs of powerlessness, sudden uncoordinated movements, animal fear, confusion, awaken the thirst for blood." The strong, "who must pay for their strength with an intense alienation from nature, and must always suppress their fear" into irrational rage, can only find release by preying on the weak, satisfying their blood lust "when they hear their victims utter over and over again the cry that they dare not themselves emit."[49]

The true root of this kind of overheated rhetoric lay not in Marxism but in the German Expressionist imagination.* Industrial civilization now loomed on the horizon like the jungle in Conrad's *Heart of Darkness*, an impenetrable shadowed maze of primitive terrors and monstrous images (like Baudelaire's gaslit Paris inhabited by skeletons and vampires, or Brecht's City of Mahagonny). Yet Adorno and Horkheimer's *fin de siècle* reading of anti-Semitism, far from underlining the horror of the Holocaust, actually drained it of specific meaning and context. Nazi anti-Semitism was not directed at Jews after all, they were saying, nor was it caused directly by anything in Nazi ideology or German society.

This view ignored the degree to which the Nazi program of genocide represented an extreme solution to what seemed an extreme crisis: the

---

* In fact, the section just quoted is reminiscent of a passage in José Ortega y Gasset's *Revolt of the Masses* (1930): "The mass acts on its own, it does so in one way, for it has no other: it lynches" (p. 116).

threat of Jewish pollution and racial catastrophe. The Holocaust was implicit in every theory of racial pessimism. Gobineau himself, in his *Essay on Inequality*, had described how the racial decline of Rome had been momentarily checked during the dictatorship of Sulla, when the vengeful tyrant ordered the massacre of his highborn opponents, thus coincidentally weeding out the weakest and most corrupt bloodlines of the Roman aristocracy. Gobineau had enjoyed the irony of the situation: a vicious man unwittingly saved his city by an ignorant act of cruelty. To Heinrich Himmler and his associates, there was no ignorance and no irony. In order to save the Aryan race from the destructive forces of *Zivilisation*, what choice did they have? The only thing required was to remain strong and "be hard," as Spengler might have said.

However, to the Frankfurt School the Holocaust was a function of a sterile industrial order and its typically atavistic human products, who directed their sadistic energies at anyone who was different or vulnerable. "The world of the concentration camps was not an exceptionally monstrous society," Herbert Marcuse would later write. "What we saw there was . . . the quintessence of the infernal society into which we are plunged every day."[50]

Adorno's most frequently quoted comment on the Holocaust was that there can be no poetry after Auschwitz. In fact, he had drawn that conclusion long before Auschwitz, as had his hero Nietzsche and even Brooks Adams, when he wrote that "no poetry can grow in the modern soil." In the end, the horrors of Auschwitz were not the result of the Nazis or anti-Semitism or even the authoritarian personality. At their epicenter lay a "sick" Western civilization, lashing out to corrupt or destroy everything in its lethal embrace.

## HERBERT MARCUSE: THE PROMISE OF UTOPIA

*The Dialectic of Enlightenment* appeared almost simultaneously with the D-day invasion, marking the beginning of the end for Hitler's empire. Within a year the capitalist powers of the West, led by the United States and Great Britain, had purged fascism from Western Europe, and the revolution on the Right retreated beyond the cultural horizon. In 1949 Horkheimer and Adorno left America to return to Germany. Despite their professed Marxism, they both decided against settling in Communist East Germany. Instead, they returned to the University of Frankfurt, where they reestablished the Institute of Social Research for the new postwar era.

Despite the end of the Nazi nightmare, Adorno's gloom about the future only deepened. In 1951 he published a series of Nietzsche-like reminiscences and aphorisms, significantly titled *Minima Moralia: Reflections From a Damaged Life*, which revealed the full depths of his bitterness and misanthropy. His despair went far beyond the memory of the Holocaust or the threat of nuclear catastrophe. Modern society, Adorno stated, had become totally devoid of meaning or worth. Every human emotion or quality was now debased by being part of the larger capitalist totality. Friendship, marriage, courtesy, a sense of privacy, and kindness were all extinct—"all the human worth of social mixing and participation merely masks a tacit acceptance of inhumanity."

Things were so bad Adorno almost became nostalgic about an earlier bourgeois era, before mass technology and television. "What was once good and decent in bourgeois values, independence, perseverance, forethought, circumspection, has been corrupted utterly." Even the classic liberal belief in private property was being destroyed, since the proliferation of goods in consumer society undermined a sense of pride in ownership. Instead, modern consumer goods, Adorno was convinced, all exhibit "the violent, hard-hitting, unresting jerkiness of Fascist maltreatment." Car doors and refrigerator doors have to be *slammed* to be closed, he pointed out, while sliding-glass windows have to be *shoved* open (unlike windows of the past, with their delicate, unassuming latches). All these modern technologies brutalized the human personality. "Which driver is not tempted," he exclaimed, "merely by the power of his engine, to wipe out the vermin of the street, pedestrians, children, and cyclists?"[51]

While Adorno fell into a despair as deep and unrelieved as Henry Adams's—the intellectual, he lamented, must live with "the shame of still having air to breathe, in hell"*—his younger colleague Herbert Marcuse assumed a different stance. Like Adorno and Horkheimer, Marcuse would stress the inevitable death of the West by its own hand,

---

* Of course, it must be pointed out that Adorno himself thrived in this hell, surrounded by respectful colleagues, accolades, and academic honors until his death in 1969.

not so much through totalitarianism (although that too was inevitable and important) as through the self-administered constipation of material affluence. But he would also prophesy what would come after: a new cultural order built on what the earlier Frankfurt School had called "the revolt of nature." That prophecy would make Marcuse one of the most influential gurus of the radical movement of the 1960s and the New Left and the Frankfurt School's first full-fledged cultural pessimist.

The revolt of nature was the social price civilization allegedly paid for its relentless repression of the life instinct. "The victory of civilization is too complete to be true," Horkheimer had proclaimed in *The Eclipse of Reason*. "Therefore adjustment in our times involves an element of resentment and repressed fury."[52] This results in sporadic outbursts of irrationalism in various forms, anti-Semitism being the core example, but also criminality and violence of all kinds. The revolt of nature became the hinge on which rationalizing civilization opens itself to its opposite—and hence briefly and inadvertently to its alternative. This was the possibility that Marcuse seized upon to build a new human future.

Marcuse's philosophy involved heady doses of various weighty German thinkers: Hegel and Martin Heidegger as well as Marx and Freud.[53] But in fact Marcuse's real instincts lay not in formal German philosophy but in the "insurrection of the sons against the fathers" of his generation of pre-1914 German youth. Marcuse wrote all his influential works in the years after World War II. However, they retained the reckless, iconoclastic outlook of the Expressionist rebellion of Hasenclever and Georg Heym, as well as Bertolt Brecht.

Marcuse's relationship to the Frankfurt School was in many ways similar to that of Marcus Garvey and W.E.B. Du Bois. It consisted of taking certain key doctrines and pushing them to their limits. The first was the disappearance of a revolutionary proletariat thanks to mindless bourgeois culture. Marcuse stridently expounded on this theme in his most widely read work, *One-Dimensional Man* (1964), which is largely an expansion of *The Dialectic of Enlightenment*'s grim picture of the nature of late capitalism, what others were now referring to as "the affluent society" and "postindustrial civilization." Soul-destroying *Zivilisation* had turned into the "consumer society," which disguises its true repressive nature behind a cornucopia of goods and services. As with Adorno and Horkheimer's totalizing late capitalism, what *seems* to be increasing personal freedom is actually the opposite; the middle class and workers often remain blissfully unaware of how unhappy they really are.* However, "the extension of exploitation to a larger part of the population, accompanied by a higher standard of living, is the reality behind the facade of the consumer society."[54]

"In the affluent society," Marcuse wrote, "capitalism has come into its own." Its degenerate victim is the faceless and affectless consumer, whom Fromm had twenty years earlier described as living "under the illusion that he knows what he wants, while he actually wants what he is *supposed* to want," and who squanders his leisure time buying products that "indoctrinate and manipulate." Consumerism, Marcuse wrote, "promotes a false consciousness which is immune against its falsehood," largely because it feels so good and anesthetizes its victim against deeper thought—like Horkheimer's bourgeoisie, the consumer is taught to recognize only superficial facts and appearances, not the social reality underneath.[55]

"Thus emerges a pattern of one-dimensional thought and behavior," Marcuse stated, which characterizes the modern West: "The people recognize themselves in their commodities: they find their soul in their automobiles, hi-fi set . . . The very mechanism which ties the individual to his society has changed, and social control is anchored in the new needs which it has produced."[56] This exploitative social control takes unexpected forms. One example is the welfare state, which keeps the poor well-fed when they should be hungry and in prerevolutionary tumult.[57] Another is a "repressive tolerance" toward dissident groups, by which liberal society extends civil liberties to critics in such a way that it neutralizes their negation. This allows liberal society, for example, to silence deadly enemies like Marcuse by openly publishing his works. This strategy renders his ideas ineffective (since his own words presumably make him appear strange and ridiculous), whereas censoring and arresting him would make him a martyr (Jean-Paul Sartre, with his free airtime on the state-controlled radio and television for denouncing the French government, faced much the same problem).

Tolerance of other points of view in the age of mass communication

---

* According to Hegel's notion of the "cunning of Reason," trends that seem to run counter to rational progress actually turn out to serve its ultimate purpose.

revealed the face of political tyranny in a new form, one "which may well be compatible with a 'pluralism' of parties, newspapers, 'countervailing powers,' &c." This is because this so-called liberal society is actually a new form of the totalitarian state. "For totalitarianism is not only a terroristic political coordination of society," Marcuse explained, "but also a non-terroristic economic technical coordination which operates through the manipulation of needs by vested interests." By these insidious devices, then, the consumer society manages to construct its own system of total control. The result is that "a comfortable, smooth, reasonable, democratic unfreedom prevails in advanced industrial civilization, a token of technological progress."[58] This was in fact the paradoxical nature of modern society that drove all the Frankfurt critics to distraction: it makes tyranny look and feel like freedom, and poverty like affluence. But it is totalitarian nonetheless, like its Stalinist Soviet counterpart.

If *One-Dimensional Man* expounded the pessimism of Adorno and Horkheimer, then *Eros and Civilization* (1955) recycled the Marxian Freud of Fromm and *The Authoritarian Personality*. Marcuse exploited the ambiguity of the term "repression," which can be used in a political sense but is also the term for the central psychological mechanism of Freud's theory of personality. Marcuse simply insisted that they are in fact one and the same thing.

Marcuse argued that civilization was indeed built on repression, as Freud had claimed in *Civilization and Its Discontents*. But Freud's mistake was to assume that the particular form Western civilization had taken, with its sublimation of the vital instincts through "slow and methodical work" and "unpleasurable postponement of gratification," was the only possible form of civilized life.[59] Freud failed to see that this repression was the characteristic product of a *capitalist* civilization. Buried in man's unconscious, Marcuse suggested, was a possible nonrepressive civilization in which the life instinct, Eros, would be unchained. Through the expansion of modern automation, for example, the machine permits "the painless gratification of needs" and makes possible "the reduction of the work day" to a minimum so as not to arrest human self-development. This "liberation of Eros could create new and durable work relations," Marcuse speculated, and exploitation would no longer be necessary.[60]

In short, technology might double back on its master and wipe out capitalism—a conclusion not so far removed from that of Marcuse's right-wing soulmate, Oswald Spengler. "The technological processes of mechanization and standardization might release individual energy into a yet uncharted realm of freedom beyond necessity." Human existence itself would be fundamentally altered; "the individual would be free to exert autonomy over a life that would be [entirely] his own."[61] Thanks to technology, Marx's alienated worker vanishes and a new man takes his place: a well-rounded individual who bears a startling resemblance to Friedrich Ratzel's nonspecialized German peasant and W.E.B. Du Bois's black folk.[62] However, "in order to become vehicles for freedom," Marcuse explained, "science and technology would have to change their present direction and goals." Instead of being deployed to make and do things, they would have to be used to enhance the "new sensibility—the demands of the life instincts." The new man steps into a nonrepressive civilization that produces nothing except an endless round of pleasurable self-satisfactions.

This may seem a rather farfetched utopia, a kind of socialist Nintendo arcade. But for Marcuse the term "utopia" was a positive one. A utopia was not a self-deluding fantasy but the critical mind's dismantling of a moribund social order on the basis of a deeper, rather than a mere empirical, truth.[63] Of course, achieving the "promise of utopia" would require a reduction in the standard of living, especially for the rich, but not enough to "militate against progress in freedom." But above all, it would require a total overthrow of the economic interests and the political institutions of advanced industrial society, as well as the ideology that sustained them.

Like the rest of the Frankfurt School, Marcuse saw no hope for revolution from the working class. Instead, he looked to the marginalized groups who are excluded from consumer society and hence immune to its blandishments, a "substratum of the outcasts and outsiders, the exploited and persecuted of other races and other colors, the unemployed and unemployable."[64] Marx himself had scornfully called this moblike group the *Lumpenproletariat*, a tool of demogogic reaction; now they became Marcuse's last hope. In his *Essay on Liberation* (1969), Marcuse summoned forth an alliance of "the young, the intelligentsia," blacks, welfare recipients, Third World revolutionaries, and New Left students, who would "break the historical continuum of injustice, cruelty, and silence." "The armed class struggle is waged outside" the mainstream of Western society, in the streets and ghettos, the rice paddies of Asia, and the mountains of Latin America.[65] "The Cuban revolution and the Viet Cong have demonstrated it can be done," Marcuse wrote in 1968. "There is a morality, a humanity, a will, and a faith which can resist and deter the gigantic technical and economic force of capitalist expansion" and what he called "the affluent monster."[66]

The sixties student revolt left the Institute of Social Research's old guard cold. When students in Frankfurt disrupted classes, Adorno did not hesitate to order them arrested; Horkheimer dismissed them as "left-wing fascists." But Marcuse's Nietzschean youth movement instincts led him to embrace the anti-Vietnam marchers and enlist them in his own cultural cause. He saw in them a new sensibility overthrowing the false promises of a sick consumer society. "A society is sick," he explained to an interviewer, "when its basic institutions and relations do not permit . . . the optimal development of individual needs,"[67] which meant capitalist America.

However, by 1970 Marcuse and his youthful revolutionary cadres learned that decadent and soulless capitalist America was not going to collapse at the first touch. They realized, as a biographer and admirer put it, that they were "facing a long and difficult struggle to transform the existing society." One difficulty was a certain lack of decorum on the part of his putative revolutionary allies. Once, when Marcuse was speaking at the Socialist Scholars Conference in New York on "Radicals and Hippies: Youth Responses to Industrial Society," Abbie Hoffman, dressed as a cowboy and sporting twin-cap pistols, burst in and marched up to the podium. Lighting up a joint, Hoffman challenged the guru of Eros to stop talking and start smoking.[68]

Another was Marcuse's own harsh, uncompromising views on politics—views that might even be termed authoritarian. Like Spengler, Marcuse had great contempt for the normal processes of democracy. His new utopia left no room for the endless haggling and give-and-take of debate. American society was so close to overt fascism, he wrote in 1968, and was in such a serious crisis, that total destruction seemed only a missile launch away. America and the West live in "an emergency situation" where the "extreme suspension of the right of free speech and free assembly is indeed justified." As he told a reporter for the BBC in

1968, the time had come for "the withdrawal of speech and assembly from groups and movements which promote aggressive policies, armament, chauvinism, discrimination on the grounds of race or religion, or which oppose the extension of public services, social security, health care, etc." In his *Critique of Pure Tolerance* he added that contrary to the "sacred liberalistic principle" of giving equal time to the other side in political debate, "there are issues in which there is 'no other side' . . . where 'the other side' is demonstrably 'regressive' and impedes possible improvement of the human condition."[69] Marcuse's appeal to an emergency situation bears an uncomfortable resemblance to the justifications for Hitler's emergency decrees in 1933. The resemblance is no coincidence. Like his cultural pessimist counterparts on the German revolution on the Right, Marcuse impatiently awaited the emergence of a new cultural order out of the rubble of the old liberal capitalist West.

Behind every prophet of decline lurks a vision of progress. This especially includes cultural pessimists. In the case of Marcuse and his ideological "counterculture" allies, progress meant a sweeping program of human self-actualization, reaching out beyond every boundary or taboo in typical or "normal" Western society (now defined as irremediably sick): gender, class, age, race, sexual preference. True human liberation would not only bring about the death of the consumer society and C. Wright Mills's power structure; it would also liquidate every false ideology, institution, and identity the modern West imposed on its hapless victims. "The established universe of discourse and behavior," as Marcuse had called it, required as much radical "negation" and revision as representative democracy and capitalism, since they too were parts of the same totality.

By Marcuse's death in 1975, American and Western society had not been transformed in the massive ways he and others on the New Left had hoped for. However, before he died Marcuse saw one more possibility of negation within the system. This was the university in affluent post-sixties America. Schools such as Berkeley, Brandeis, and Columbia had served as Marcuse's own base of operations, and he suspected that in the future they might serve as a safe haven for a countercultural Left during what the German radical Rudi Dutschke called "the Long March through the institutions."

At the end of his life Marcuse became deeply interested in feminism and supported the appointment of feminist theorists, as well as political radicals, to academic positions. When an interviewer asked him in 1974 if, in the aftermath of Watergate and the American withdrawal from Vietnam, the New Left was dead, he replied, "I don't think it's dead and it will resurrect"—in American universities.[70] This prediction, at least, turned out to be right.

## CHAPTER 10

# THE MODERN FRENCH PROPHETS

### Sartre, Foucault, Fanon

Men of the present day are born criminals.
—J.-P. Sartre

Marcuse and the Frankfurt School, with their hostile view of Western totalizing reason, helped to shape a new generation of cultural critics. However, the real home of the new cultural pessimism was
not Germany but France.

In 1900 a new professor of philosophy arrived at the Collège de
France in Paris, a young man of forty named Henri Bergson. Since the
beginning of the nineteenth century the university scene in Paris had
centered around the charismatic teacher, the intellectual guru. Bergson
was perfectly suited to the role. "His forehead enormous, his bright
eyes . . . like two lights under his thick eyebrows," an admirer gushed,
"his features [are] of a delicacy that emphasizes . . . the radiance of his
thought." His philosophical works were so evocatively written that he
would win the Nobel Prize for literature. His lectures at the Collège de
France, delivered without notes, drew crowds not only of students and
colleagues but of tourists, statesmen, and society hostesses as well. All
were aware they were witnessing a sea change in the direction of French
philosophy and intellectual life.[1]

The rebellious, romantic Paris of Gobineau and Gautier had given
ground, in the later nineteenth century, to the influence of thinkers and
writers like Comte, Durkheim, Pasteur, Hyppolite Taine, and Emile Zola

who extolled positivism and science. However, positivist France had also been haunted by the twin specters of degeneration, which troubled social scientists and members of the medical profession, and decadence, which had seduced the literary heirs of Baudelaire, among them the Symbolist poets and Paul Valéry. The French had coined the phrase *fin de siècle* to describe the atmosphere of the 1890s: "the impotent despair of a sick man" in the midst of affluence and plenty.

Bergson had decisively broken with the *fin de siècle* mood and the dominant orthodoxies of French philosophy and science. He had made himself the champion of a new, "higher" way of understanding the world around us based on intuition, spontaneity, and the animal instincts—which he termed the *élan vital*. Analytic reason was the instincts' servant not, as the scientist might imagine, its master. The solid but essentially lifeless realm of *mécanisme*, of nineteenth-century industrial society and science, required the motive force of nature's eternal *élan vital*.

Like a "rising wave," Bergson proclaimed, the *élan vital* swept through life and brought in its wake "potentialities without number . . . running through human generations, [and] subdividing itself into individuals."[2] Bergson's vitalism celebrated the individual's sharp and vivid experience of history as change, or "duration," the "continual progress of the past which gnaws into the future . . . [it] follows us at every instant; all that we have felt, thought and willed . . . pressing against the portals of consciousness." For Bergson, history has no objective meaning that waits to be grasped by reflective intelligence. Instead, the past has meaning only if it becomes part of our individual consciousness. That revelation is summed up in Jean-Paul Sartre's startled observation as he found himself caught up in the battle for France in July 1940: "History is all around me."

For those like Sartre who fell under Bergson's spell, past, present, and future reflect this vital force, which is aroused through experience—whether political, religious (religion was for Bergson the equivalent of Nietzsche's commitment to values), sexual, artistic, or martial—drawing to us all of humanity and nature. "I experience, therefore I am" might be the motto of the entire Bergsonian movement.

All the living hold together, and all yield to the same tremendous push . . . The whole of humanity, in space and in time, is one immense army galloping beside and before and behind each of us in an over-whelming charge able to beat down every resistance, and clear the most formidable obstacles, perhaps even death.[3]

On the eve of World War I, Bergson was the celebrated mentor of a generation of French students soon to be locked in combat with their German counterparts. Charles Péguy, Jacques Maritain, the novelist Alain-Fournier, the journalist Henri Massis, and many others found in Bergsonian vitalism a way to shake off not only bourgeois boredom but also pessimism about degeneration and cultural collapse. This "genera-tion of 1912," as Henri Massis called it, had "exiled self-doubt." Unlike their "decadent" elders, they were devoutly Catholic and intensely pa-triotic because they recognized the importance of faith, discipline, and commitment. Members of the generation of 1912 were above all men of action: "In all matters, it is his distinguishing characteristic to create or-der and harmony, just as his elders created disorder and ruins." Their hero Bergson publicly pronounced their appearance an evolutionary miracle, an unprecedented mutation in the human temperament. And like their hero, they breathed optimism, energy, and hope into every-thing they touched.

All these hopes were cruelly crushed within months of the outbreak of World War I. Many of Massis's models for this optimistic generation, like Charles Péguy, were killed in the first two months of fighting. Berg-son's image of an "overwhelming charge beating down every resistance" dissolved into futile massed infantry assaults under German machine guns, the agonies of Verdun, and finally, in 1917, mutiny. Ten percent of the adult male population of France died between 1914 and 1918. The survivors returned to a cultural atmosphere poisoned by failure and frus-tration and to a broken intellectual class that would escape into Dadaism, Surrealism (its guru André Breton was a war veteran), and embittered withdrawal. One of these embittered intellectuals, the twenty-five-year-old Pierre Drieu La Rochelle, said on his return from the front, "We haven't said our last word. More than one people will perish before we do."[4]

Sentiments like these opened the way for a French version of cultural pessimism. Intellectual life in Paris in the twenties and thirties exhibited the same disillusionment with the nineteenth century and progress that was eating away at the heart of Bloomsbury Britain and Weimar Germany. "We are Europe's defeatists," Louis Aragon announced proudly in 1925. "Western world, you are condemned to die." Although Bergson's own influence faded during this period, in a profound sense he set the stage for what followed. His exaltation of instinct over intelligence (Bergson's own terms) and vital experience over social conformism had become a common ground for French thinkers of both the Left and the Right. In the end, what united them all, from Sartre and Camus to Michel Foucault and Frantz Fanon, was Bergson's vitalist quest.

To intellectuals of the twenties and thirties, the old political choices no longer seemed to offer any solutions. Georges Bernanos, a survivor of the generation of 1912, wrote that "liberalism died at the first shot in the Great War."[5] On the French Right conservatives like Maurice Barrès and Charles Maurras were still fighting the battle of the Dreyfus Affair of a quarter-century earlier and railing against the "decadent" Third Republic. Younger conservatives like Pierre Drieu La Rochelle and the poet Robert Brasillach turned away from monarchism to embrace fascism. Fascism, they believed, would scour out the rot in modern France. "The only way to love France today," La Rochelle explained in the thirties, "is to hate it in its present form." Later he, Brasillach, and others would provide the intellectual cadre for the Vichy regime.[6]

The French Left, meanwhile, was enmeshed in the exhausting struggles between socialism and Communism. Communist intellectuals enjoyed virtually no influence in the two decades before World War II, while their socialist opponents turned meekly to pacifism and its illusory hopes. Only the direct threat of German fascism was able to draw the two camps together in the Popular Front of 1935 to '36, which briefly held power and then fell apart amid labor strikes and the Spanish Civil War, leaving both groups more embittered than before.

Left or Right, the politically committed reflected what one observer, Arthur Koestler, called "an enormous longing for a new human order." As in the rest of postliberal Europe, the lines between the French Left and Right became remarkably permeable, with figures flitting from one to the other with bewildering ease. The head of the Young Communists in the twenties, Jacques Doriot, left in 1934 to found the French Popular Party, which became the political vanguard of France's fascist movement. Marcel Déat quit the French Socialist Party in 1933 to create his own national socialist movement, which eventually also became a mainstay of Vichy's radical Right.[7] A later, notorious case was the young François Mitterrand, who associated himself with a fringe of Action Française and the French monarchists, eagerly serving under Vichy only to emerge as a socialist member of the Resistance in 1945.[8]

All these shifts were possible because, if French intellectuals were unclear about what they were *for*, they were very firm about what they were *against*. This was the "decadence of France," the title of a popular leftist diatribe published in 1931. "I am a fascist," Drieu La Rochelle explained in 1943, "because I have measured the progress of decadence in Europe." Decadence meant bourgeois capitalism, parliamentary democracy, and an American-style technological society.* As Denis de Rougemont (later to undergo his own political change of heart, moving from socialism to the political center) confided in his diary in 1936, the real enemy is not "the totalitarian peril" of Hitler and Bolshevism, but the "sort of thinking from which both Fascism and Stalinism necessarily grow. And that is liberal thought."[9]

In this sullen and uncertain atmosphere the new German philosophy exploded like shrapnel. First came Marxism in its "Western" form of the young Marx and George Lukács. Then, beginning in the early thirties, a Russian emigré named Alexandre Kojève ran a seminar at the Sorbonne that introduced Hegel to an entire generation of French intellectuals, including Raymond Aron, Maurice Merleau-Ponty, Georges Bataille, Jacques Lacan, and André Breton.† Kojève developed a sharply sardonic view of Hegel's universal history as progress, which perfectly suited the new post-Verdun disillusionment in France.[10] Western capitalism and democratic institutions had now triumphed over their alternatives, Kojève proclaimed with almost malicious glee. A Marxist revolution to achieve justice for the downtrodden was no longer possible (as German Marxism had learned in 1919) or even desirable. In-

---

* Bernanos described the dismal future of Western man this way in 1931: "Some little Yankee shoeshine boy, a kid with a rat's face, half Anglo-Saxon, half a Jew, with a trace of Negro ancestry in his maddened marrow . . . future master of a standardized planet."

† One of those who also signed up for Kojève's famous seminar in the thirties but did not attend was the young Leo Strauss.

stead, modern industrial society would propel people toward an ever increasing affluence and the free and equal status as individuals that they sought.

Everyone would eventually be bourgeoisified, Kojève explained; everyone would happily adjust to an increasingly homogeneous culture at the "end of history." But the human product of this final stage of civilization would be something much less than Hegel or any of his liberal and progressive heirs had imagined. Modern man was already, Kojève taught, Nietzsche's last man. He had become dull, bland, and lifeless. Hopelessly conformist, he had surrendered his own character and vitality to his social self, giving up his capacity to love and hate, to create and destroy. At the end of history, Kojève predicted, all the world will become America—a gloomy fate by any French measure.[11] Kojève's other master after Hegel, Friedrich Nietzsche, also had his French followers, as did two later innovative German thinkers, Edmund Husserl and Martin Heidegger. In the Paris of the twenties and thirties, insofar as thought was modern and avant-garde, it was German, not French.

Initially, the young Jean-Paul Sartre was far removed from these concerns. He was born in Poitiers in 1905 and grew up in comfortable and cultivated surroundings, with an adoring mother and a family with strong attachments to art, literature, and music (his grandfather was Albert Schweitzer's uncle). He was sent to Paris for the elite education reserved for the *haute bourgeoisie* of that era, attending the Lycée Henri IV and then, of course, the Sorbonne. His great desire was to become a poet in the style of the prewar French avant-garde of Baudelaire, the Symbolists, and Paul Valéry. Marcel Proust influenced his early outlook, as did Henri Bergson. "In Bergson," he wrote later, "I immediately found a description of my own psychic life." Like Arnold Toynbee, Sartre found in Bergson a justification for the inner life of art and spiritual enlightenment, shielded from the crass materialistic concerns of the outside world. The young Sartre's motto was the one that had dominated the French literary scene in Gobineau's era: *l'art pour l'art.*[12]

He was pulled out of this aesthete's hothouse by his former *lycée* classmate Raymond Aron. Aron had returned to Paris in 1931 after studying in Berlin with Edmund Husserl. As he explained to the astonished Sartre one day at an outdoor cafe, *this* glass, *this* table were now the subjects of philosophy. Husserl was telling his students to forget about the usual formal trappings of philosophical theory; instead, all true knowledge comes from our immediate intuition of things as they are. The outer limits of that intuition were put to the test by what Husserl called the "boundary situation"—that extreme and sudden moment when a pedestrian suddenly steps off the pavement in front of a car or when a grenade rolls into a soldier's foxhole. These moments of "unmediated Existence," Husserl had explained, strip away the superficial rationality with which we deal with the phenomena of ordinary life and force us to choose and act.

This stark "philosophy of Existence" was bound to appeal to a generation that had not been directly exposed to the horrors of World War I but still felt that same modernist urge for "absolute experience" and contact with reality—something they had been taught a restored bourgeois postwar world could no longer deliver. World War I had shattered the nerves of the older intellectual establishment. However, among the young avant-garde, the standard-bearers of modernism, the war only solidified their fascination with the irrational and violent as the vital opposites of civilized life. Nietzschean and non-Nietzschean alike praised man's propensity for killing and aggression as important parts of experience: "Cruelty," as Nietzsche had once explained, "permeates the entire history of higher culture."[13] In Britain authors like D.H. Lawrence and Wyndham Lewis became fascinated with aggressive violence, while in Germany intellectuals on both the Left (like Bertolt Brecht) and Right (like Oswald Spengler) explored its creative possibilities. Alexandre Kojève emphasized the necessity for bloodshed and revolt in the historical process, not as part of Darwin's struggle for survival but as part of man's underlying vital nature. History, Kojève proclaimed (not unlike Bergson), was a field of action not contemplation—another reason why the rise of an inert, complacent bourgeoisie marked the end of history.

Meanwhile, another influential Nietzschean, Martin Heidegger, completed this reorientation toward action and experience. Born in 1889, Heidegger had originally been trained as a theologian and philosopher but had rebelled against the dominant trends in German philosophy. Instead, he was profoundly influenced by Nietzsche's *Will to Power*, which he read on the eve of World War I. Heidegger's great achievement was to reconcile Nietzsche's nihilism and modernism's rejection of bourgeois taste (he was a great admirer of Van Gogh) with the mainstream German academic tradition. As one former student put it, in Heidegger "the chasm . . . between the academic and worldly forms of philosophy seemed to close up."[14]

His most influential book was *Being and Time*, published in 1927. Like his lectures at the University of Freiburg, it preached a doctrine of both escape and commitment—particularly escape from a Western modernity hopelessly mired in its own sterile rationality. The bourgeois West, Heidegger told his readers, had shut itself off from the rich "life world" initially opened up by Nietzsche's Dionysian Greeks.*[15] Heidegger rejected any mediation of reality or "Being" by normal institutions and analytic reason. Instead of analyzing the world, man had to throw himself into it. One of Heidegger's favorite terms was *Geworfenheit*, man's state of "being plunged" into the reality of his own time and place. In Heidegger's philosophy, "to be thrown into the stream of time is a fundamental and inalterable feature of our human situation."[16] Human history has no meaning in itself or any purpose that we can supply; like Heraclitus's (and Spengler's) endless flux, it is simply a river in which we either sink or swim.

Heidegger told his students that man's primary objective is not to try to understand and control events. Instead, man needs to recommit himself to values that allow him to act from within those events. By doing so, Heidegger taught, he can once again achieve "authenticity"—which he, like Kojève, suggested had virtually disappeared from the modern world. In France, Heidegger's words spread into an environment already prepared by Bergson's exaltation of *élan vital*, but with a crucial difference. Instead of the experience of the world around us serving as an affirmation of the self, as it did for Bergson, for Heidegger it becomes a source of negation and alienation because of the nature of the modern West.

Heidegger had read Spengler's *Decline of the West* with consuming interest when it appeared. Although he was critical of many of its assumptions, the book affected him profoundly and became, in effect, Heidegger's history of the West as well.[17] The disasters "of world history

---

* The similarity to *The Dialectic of Enlightenment* is striking and not coincidental—it reflects the hand of Nietzsche on both. Herbert Marcuse studied with Heidegger in the late twenties, while Adorno and Horkheimer both felt the power of Heidegger's ideas and targeted him as an important philosopher competitor.

in this century," Heidegger explained to his audiences, were the result of the Western "will to will." This is modern man's "unconditional objectification of everything present." Like his Frankfurt School contemporaries, he saw this relentless will to will symbolized by modern science. The consequences are horrifying: "the flight of the gods, the destruction of the earth, the standardization of man, the preeminence of the mediocre . . . the darkening of the world." He was forced to conclude: "The spiritual decline of the planet is so far advanced that the nations are in danger of losing the last bit of spiritual energy that makes it possible to see the decline . . . and appraise it as such."[18]

According to Heidegger, the Western rational animal had evolved into the mechanical laboring animal. Technology forces man and nature to work to the same rationalist timetable, the same "unreasonable demands" modern man makes of himself. The earth, once the sacred source of man's sense of being, was now treated as a commodity. Man extracted from the sacred earth iron and coal by the ton, while its forests were turned into lumber and pulp for reading matter for the mindless masses. The Rhine itself, that hallowed symbol of Germanic and Wagnerian myth, was diverted to create hydroelectric plants to power the capitalists' factories. Heidegger warned that rational civilization had shattered man's place in nature and sense of himself, leaving him "to the giddy whirl of his products so that he may tear himself to pieces and annihilate himself in empty nothingness."[19]

Heidegger's apocalyptic image of modernity as "a darkening of the world" and his attack on "metaphysical reason" as the enemy of Being shook Sartre to his core. Bergson's spiritualized *élan vital* must have seemed effete by comparison with this solid and elemental Being-there (*Dasein*) of man and raw nature, a celebration of Existence itself—the philosophy that Sartre would eventually call existentialism. In 1935, after returning to Paris from his own sojourn in German philosophy at the University of Berlin, he enthusiastically proclaimed that Husserl and Heidegger "have plunged man back into the world; they have given full measure to man's agonies and sufferings, and also to his rebellions." The most important lesson for Sartre was that the world is the place "whereby human reality discloses to itself what it is. Not a contemplation but a wisdom, a heroism." The new existentialist philosophy, Sartre believed, would produce "an ethics and a politics which are purely positive," in contrast to the "negative" bourgeois world represented by contemporary France.[20]

But this new positive politics, to Sartre's mind, had no connections to politics in the ordinary sense. During his stay in Berlin in 1933, he had remained oblivious to Hitler's and the Nazis' coming to power. Instead, existentialism was the affirmation of the ego as it is; in Heidegger's terms, the naked Being-in-Itself. Man is *in* the world, of course, and *of* the world, since there is no God or transcendent reality. But he is not *for* the world in any social or even moral sense. Man as a civilized being Sartre described as Being "for Others"; he allows the burdens of sociability and conventional institutions to define him instead of allowing himself full and free pursuit of his own values, or Being "for Itself." As Sartre put it, "Man encounters an obstacle only within the field of his freedom." The only constraints he meets are those he allows others to impose on him, which by their very nature deny his own existence and his true self.

Sartre's conception of freedom wiped away the last traces of the Enlightenment's belief in man as a naturally social being. It also fiercely negated the world as it is constituted by modernity. Life in that world is "absurd" (the term Sartre would make famous) because modern man has made it so. His reason has destroyed God and all intrinsic purpose just as Nietzsche, another of Sartre's heroes, had warned. Man's encounter with that empty absurdity produces a sense of "nausea," the title of Sartre's 1938 novel that laid the foundations for his later thinking.

Sartre's nausea is reminiscent of Heidegger's "giddy whirl" and, of course, Nietzsche's Zarathustra: "This nausea suffocates me. . . . We have tried to get away from the rabble . . . the shopkeeper's stench . . . Nausea! Nausea! Nausea!" However, it also contained an echo of Gautier and the French Romantics, with their fear of the *ennui* produced by modern life. The great sin of modern civilization is not that too much happens, as fretful historical pessimists like Jacob Burckhardt, Henry Adams, and Theodor Adorno complained, but too little. The main character in *Nausea* lives in a provincial bourgeois world, where life drags on with "a sort of sweetish sickness." It is a world of "upright citizens [with] your received ideas, your bank accounts and good manners . . . town counselors, doctors, economists."

Yet Sartre finds underneath this bland, empty facade an even more horrible truth. Despite the pretentions of religion, politics, and professional and family life, we are finally frighteningly alone in the world. Like the heroes in Sartre's novels, we have no resources other than ourselves. Man is, in another famous phrase, "*condemned* to be free" because he is also condemned to be alone. Here Sartre borrowed yet another term from Husserl and Heidegger, *Angst*, to describe the disturbing sense of anxiety that the solitude of total freedom produces in modern man, who is left feeling as if he carries the "weight of the world on his shoulders." To escape the agonies of *Angst* he tries, like Erich Fromm's mass man, to pretend he is not free. He constructs for himself the realm of "bad faith," where the negation of the Other, which is the foundation of freedom, turns inward against the self instead of outward at others. Bad faith is the constriction of man's vitality—like Freud's repression, it is also the basis of modern civilized life. But while Freud saw that constriction as necessary to contain man's own savage nature and self-debasement, for Sartre repression is all lies and hypocrisy, the victory of the bourgeois over the creative and authentic. Bad faith in Sartre's philosophy "arises most conspicuously in conjunction with bourgeois propriety and . . . the split between public feelings or actions and private ones."[21]

In the end, Sartre's existentialism uses Heidegger and Nietzsche to turn late Romantic contempt for the bourgeoisie into a life philosophy. For the free individual, life in modern society becomes a struggle against the bourgeois constraints of moral strictures and social roles.[22] Sartre's autobiography, *The Words*, recounts his own running battle against bourgeois hypocrisy and bad faith in his own family.* The model middle-class citizen is for Sartre a cheap con artist, always pretending to be someone he is not. He is, as Sartre puts it, "the person I *have to be* for the sake of others."

For example, we see our own dilemma in the surly waiter who dreams of being an actor and knows he is wasting his time—his resentment is *our* resentment at being straitjacketed in a world constructed on the false needs of others. Waiters were a favorite example for Sartre of the mechanisms of bad faith. The other was women, who appear in his

---

* In fact, as Sartre himself later admitted, his family had adored him and supported his every literary effort.

philosophical novels as harpies and sirens who tempt unwilling men to their doom in sterile relationships and marriage. Indeed, all the values of civilized life—sociability, complex social roles, politeness, even love—are for Sartre now merely traps (*L'Engrénage*, or "In the Mesh," was the title of one of his later screenplays) that destroy man's freedom.

Sartre's existentialism stated baldly that being with others in modern society—above all, submitting to their standards and beliefs—is a form of self-immolation. As a character remarks in his play *No Exit*, "Hell is other people." And what makes other people intolerable is precisely their own lack of authenticity and vitality, trapped as they are in a world of bad faith—"bogus on bogus," as another character suggests. So instead of struggling to survive in the world according to its own corrupt terms, freedom has to be found by breaking away from it. Albert Camus found a symbol for the meaninglessness of normal bourgeois routine in the myth of Sisyphus (the title of a 1955 essay), in which the hero struggles to push an enormous boulder to the top of a hill, only to have it roll back down so that he can push it up again—and again and again.

"Rising, streetcar, four hours of work," wrote Camus, "meal, sleep, and Monday Tuesday Wednesday Thursday Friday and Saturday according to the same rhythm." But then "one day the 'why' arises and everything begins in that weariness tinged with amazement. . . . It awakens consciousness and provokes what follows."[23] What follows is the act of existential rebellion, outlined in Camus's manifesto *L'homme Revolté*, or *The Rebel*. Man's awakened consciousness confronts the absurdity of modern bourgeois existence and he decides he can no longer have any dealings with it. By rejecting his situation he reignites his sense of himself as Being-for-Itself, which in turn reopens the possibility of injecting new meaning and purpose into his life. *L'homme revolté* becomes *l'homme engagé*, vitally reengaged in the world. However, finding that meaning requires a radical break, he must separate "the true from the false." No one changes the world, Camus and Sartre implied, by remaining on the streetcar and going on to a nine-to-five job.

But if we have already rejected all those values that connect us to others as false, where are these new meanings and purposes going to come from? This was the major weak point in the existentialist program, and Heidegger himself had revealed its dangers.

For Heidegger, authentic Being expressed itself on the political plane only as a "moment of vision," a breakthrough beyond modern man's self-limited fallen nature. Legitimacy, due process, constitutional forms, and other inauthentic constraints fall away, as man decides the moment has come to take action, regardless of consequences.[24] That moment, Heidegger decided, was 1932 and the man was Adolf Hitler. Heidegger believed that National Socialism would decisively overturn modernity's lack of depth and values and recapture "our historical-spiritual existence, in order to transform it into a new beginning." Nor was Heidegger bothered by the threat of Nazi violence and brutality: "The beginning must be begun again, more radically, with all the strangeness, darkness, insecurity that attend a new beginning"—even if that meant a return to barbarism.[25]

As rector of the University of Freiburg, Heidegger threw himself into the National Socialist revolution with enthusiasm. His activities on behalf of the Nazi regime that, even after 1945, he could not bring himself to repudiate are now well documented.[26] After the war they would cost him his rectorship and academic honors, as well as the friendship and respect of many colleagues and students (including Herbert Marcuse). Yet it says something about Sartre's own political naivete that he was oblivious to the lesson in this. He did not actually read Heidegger thoroughly until 1939, when the philosopher's name was already synonymous with the Nazi regime. Nonetheless, his immersion in Heidegger's thought was, in his own words, "providential." Sartre also confided in his diary that Heidegger's belief in politics as a personal commitment helped him "assume my destiny as a Frenchmen in the France of '40."[27]

## POSTWAR EXISTENTIALISM: SARTRE, MERLEAU-PONTY, AND COMMUNISM

All here is new, all must begin anew. And for me, too, a new life is beginning. A strange life . . .

   —Jean-Paul Sartre, *The Flies*

The collapse of France in twenty-two days in May and June 1940—its "strange defeat," in the words of one witness, the historian Marc Bloch—followed by the dreary years of German occupation and Resistance, and then by liberation and victory, restored to the nation's intellectual class some of the energies that World War I had taken away. But it was a bitter, desperate energy. Intellectual culture in France after 1945 was a culture under pressure. If the Frankfurt School took Weimar Germany to be the symbol of all that was wrong with Western civilization, then Sartre and his successors made Vichy their touchstone for criticism of the modern West. Modern society took shape as a hidden network of betrayers and collaborators, with bad faith lurking in every institution.

The war had permanently altered the political balance in French intellectual life, and with it the ideological grounding of antimodern thought. The Vichy intellectuals of the Right were discredited by their collaboration with the occupying Germans. Some, like Louis-Ferdinand Céline, fled abroad; others, like Charles Maurras and Robert Brasillach, were put on trial and convicted as traitors. Drieu La Rochelle committed suicide.[28] Writers and critics who wished to pursue their attacks on capitalism, industrial society, and democracy now lined up on the Left, as the French revolution on the Right lost all respectability.

The German invasion and occupation had also forced political choices among writers and scholars that they had hitherto avoided. Among them was Sartre. As he explained long afterwards, "The war really divided my life in two." Through his brief service in the army and internment in Germany, and then his work as a journalist for the Resistance movement, Sartre made contact with the world of practical action and purpose for the first time. His frigid and furious sense of isolation was at last dispelled. "I suddenly understood that I was a social being," Sartre wrote years later. "I became aware of the weight of the world and my ties with all the others and their ties with me."[29]

Although Sartre's own role in the French Resistance was never as risky or important as he later liked to pretend, it nonetheless forced a change in his philosophical outlook.[30] The experience taught Sartre how ordinary people can work together toward a common goal, and after the war he decided to come to grips with this discovery. Other people, he suddenly realized, were not hell but a form of salvation. He therefore proclaimed a new role for the writer and intellectual for the postwar period. The ideal of *l'art pour l'art* was a contradiction in terms: "Since the writer cannot escape his own time, we desire that he embrace it entirely . . . The writer is *situated* in his own epoch."[31] Sartre began groping for a definition of existential freedom that would allow him reintegration with the lives of other human beings so that, "by choosing myself, I choose Man."

In October 1945, buoyed by the defeat of fascism and his first trip to America, which temporarily exhilarated him with its energy and affluence, Sartre returned to a bleak grey Paris. He was scheduled to deliver a public lecture entitled "Existentialism Is a Humanism." When Sartre arrived at the lecture hall, the crowd was so large and desperate for a seat he could barely get inside and the lecture began an hour late. He spoke for two hours without notes and without stopping to the hushed throng, defending his earlier work and proclaiming that existentialism was not a doctrine of despair but "a doctrine based on optimism and action."

> Man begins by existing, finds himself, appears in the world, and then defines himself. If man, as the Existentialist conceives him, cannot be defined, this is because he is nothing to begin with. He will only *be* later, and he will be such as he has made himself.

Man could no longer be content with false ideals of God and human nature. Existentialism, Sartre said, would be the new creed for "the European of 1945," one that only taught him what he already knew, that he must "commit himself to his life . . . beyond which there is nothing."

The lecture made him instantly famous.[32] Its maxims—"Man is condemned to be free" and "We are alone without excuses"—became journalistic catchphrases almost overnight. Sartre moved into an intellectual eminence unequaled since Bergson. He became the guru for a generation uncertain about the direction of France and Europe after the Second World War and nervous about a future dominated by the Soviet Union and the United States. To his new admirers, Sartre's philosophy seemed to promise nothing less than a new liberal humanism purged of nineteenth-century hypocrisy and cant. With Simone de Beauvoir and Maurice Merleau-Ponty, Sartre founded a new political and literary journal called *Les Temps Modernes* ("Modern Times"), whose motto was "Man is total: totally committed and totally free." To defend this freedom against its enemies of every political persuasion was the writer's duty in the new postindustrial age.[33]

In his opening editorial, however, Sartre made it clear that his larger program remained the overthrow of the bourgeoisie. The key characteristic of modern civilization, Sartre explained, remained its false faith in the power of analytical reason. Since the Enlightenment and the nineteenth century, "the analytical turn of mind remains the official doctrine of bourgeois democracy." Like the Frankfurt School, Sartre saw this rationality as an irresistible instrument of destruction. Under reason's assault, organic and social "wholes vanish" and society is reduced "to the sum of the individuals who constitute it." Man's sense of solidarity disappears and he is left a solitary individual, "one pea in a can of peas," with a bundle of abstract rights and responsibilities.

This false individualism, like the entire notion of civil society, is built on the assumption that human nature has a universal character with definable universal qualities (a desire to better oneself, for example, or a natural inclination to act as a rational animal, to love one's family, and to abhor incest and murder). The liberal bourgeois notion of freedom "proclaims the identity of human nature through all varieties of situation," all of which appeals to "the analytical mind which conceives individuals outside their real conditions of existence. . . . and deceives itself about their solidarity." The problem with modern society, Sartre warned, was that it wants everyone to be the same, that is, to be bourgeois. "In fact," Sartre concluded, "one becomes bourgeois by choosing, once and for all, the analytical vision of the world, which tries to impose itself upon every man," capitalist or Communist, eastern or western, black or white.[34]

Instead, man in the postmodern age must look for a true individualism, the product of what Sartre calls his total situation. "Man," Sartre proclaimed in one of his most fateful pronouncements, "is only a situation," a summing up of his experiences, affections, and desires at any particular moment. "We are convinced that the analytical approach is dead," Sartre wrote, "and that its only role today is to trouble the revolutionary conscience and isolate men in favor of the privileged classes." Man "must free himself entirely, that is to say to become *other*, by working on his biological constitution as well as on his economic conditions, on his sexual complexes as well as his political reality."

Intellectuals have a key role to play in this reawakening of man's fullness of being "and the distant purpose we give ourselves," which is total liberation from bourgeois rationality. Like Marcuse, Sartre proposed a positive role for the modern critic as well as a negative one. "By taking sides" in the political conflicts of the day, Sartre declared, intellectuals and writers locate themselves in *their* own total situation. They turn contemplation into action and power. By making the people "aware of the eternal values implied in these social and political debates," they finally fulfill their purpose in the world. They "touch eternity."

For a brief moment Sartre had seemed about to embark into uncharted territory, toward a modernist version of humanism. But by 1950 his desire to avoid the embrace of the inauthentic bourgeois world drove him instead straight into the arms of the Communist Party. He and others later claimed that what prompted this *volte face* was the truth of Marxism itself. "It is not my fault if reality is Marxist," Sartre would say with a shrug.[35] Yet Sartre himself never actually read Marx very closely. His version of Communism had less to do with liberation through class struggle than with a personal heroic ideal. Although Sartre's famous lecture had prompted an angry reply from his former mentor Heidegger, who accused him of watering down "the philosophy of Existence" for the masses, in truth Heidegger's influence never left him. Instead, Sartre's young associate, Maurice Merleau-Ponty, showed him how a commitment to Communism could fulfill the conditions Heidegger had set for political commitment as a form of spiritual freedom.

Maurice Merleau-Ponty had traveled the typical intellectual terrain of the thirties, from Husserl and Nietzsche to Kojève and Heidegger, but without much result. Then during the war he met Sartre. The well-born Merleau-Ponty joined Sartre's bohemian Left Bank circle and became his intellectual right arm, serving as co-editor of *Modern Times*. His *Humanism and Terror* (1948) pointed the way to the unlikely merger of Stalinism and Sartre's existential humanism. Its basic point was deceptively simple. It is not possible to foresee the future, even with the help of Marxism, since the future is the instantaneous construction of individual decisions and actions. However, at certain times, when "the traditional ground of a nation or society crumbles, for better or worse, man must reconstruct human relations himself." He is forced to choose between two extremes. Merleau-Ponty suggested that Cold War politics had become a classic boundary situation, requiring "fundamental decisions from men where the risk is total."[36]

Either way, politics is a kind of gamble; if a policy or ideology fails, then its proponents are vilified. If it succeeds, then the cruelty and violence with which it was carried out are forgotten, as in France's celebration of Bastille Day as a national holiday. And since "violence is the common origin of all regimes" and "successful revolutions taken together have not spilled as much blood as empires . . . we should prefer revolutionary violence because it has a humanist future." The violence and terror of Stalinism were really only a more blatant and "honest" form of the violence and terror that underlay liberal capitalism. "The purity of [liberal] principles not only tolerates but even requires violence," Merleau-Ponty intoned. Hence, "a regime which acknowledges its violence *might* have in it more genuine humanity" than those of the bourgeois West, which try to disguise it by appeals to the rule of law.[37]

In praising Marxist "humanist" violence, Merleau-Ponty was saying something more than that the end justifies the means. He was setting the stage for the next development of French cultural pessimism, including Sartre's own. Institutions, individuals, and political regimes that ignore or violate civilized Western norms can *by that very act* claim moral superiority to their Western counterparts. The principle comes ultimately from Nietzsche's vitalist nihilism, in which the absence of moral scruples is a sign of spiritual health. It also reflects Heidegger's belief that it is the individual's act of choosing values that really matters, not what they are—or what their consequences may be for other human beings.

Sartre had emerged from the war firmly rejecting Communism, while Communist journalists in turn dismissed existentialism as a bourgeois ideology and devoted column space to vicious attacks on the *Modern Times* circle. In 1948 Sartre founded the Revolutionary Democratic Assembly (the RPR) to blaze a new trail for progressives and European intellectuals away from Cold War conflicts and toward "a new freedom reinforced by social justice." But then Sartre began moving toward an anti-anti-Communism, lashing out at the hypocrisy of modern capitalist institutions while avoiding any direct criticism of the Soviet Union. By 1949 he was refusing to appear at RPR meetings, which were attended by leading anti-Communists and even socialists such as Sidney Hook. The real threat to Europe, he had decided, was Americanization as the final stage of bourgeois Western values, not Soviet domination. Then in 1952 he published an essay entitled "Communism and Peace," in which he revealed that he embraced Merleau-Ponty's decision that moral authenticity demanded that "we must carry out the policy of the Communist Party."[38]

Beginning in 1952 *Modern Times* became virtually a party organ. Those who repeated reports about Soviet labor camps and atrocities, like Arthur Koestler, were all branded liars; when presented with incontrovertible evidence that the reports were true, both Sartre and Merleau-Ponty would argue that Soviet attempts to conceal their existence were proof that they at least were ashamed of having to resort to secret police and prisons, whereas these were an open and integral part of the West.* However, Sartre's espousal of Stalinism sprang less from admiration of the Soviet Union—although he gave plenty of evidence of that, declaring after a trip to Russia in 1954 that "there is total freedom of criticism in the USSR"—than dislike of its Western opponents, particularly the United States.

America now became the target of all the criticisms and excoriations intellectuals used to hurl at bourgeois European society. It epitomized what one of Sartre's circle, Henri Lefebvre, called "the bureaucratic society of controlled consumption." An editorial in the pro-Communist newspaper *Esprit* summed up not only Sartre's position but that of other French intellectuals: "What can one expect from a civilization that mocks and caricatures Western spiritual traditions and is propelling mankind into a horizontal existence, shorn of transcendence and depth?"[39] Even when Sartre publicly broke with Moscow four years later, he still insisted that the modern industrialized West had nothing to offer as a substitute. Looking back in 1975 he would remark, "I came to think that during the years of the cold war the Communists were right. The USSR—in spite of the mistakes we know it made—was not yet in a position to hold its own against America . . . That was why we could go along with what the Communists were saying, because on the whole, their objections to America were the same as ours."[40]

Since Soviet "mistakes" (including the murder of millions of its own citizens) had ruined its chances for providing a haven for existentialist politics, Sartre was forced to take on the American juggernaut alone.

---

* This would seem to contradict Merleau-Ponty's argument in *Humanism and Terror* about Marxist governments being more "honest" about their use of repressive violence. However, consistency on these points mattered less than an effective response to criticism of the Soviet Union.

America's global empire, he warned, was being assembled by means of its control over a global mass communications and technological network and the "world economic system." "This One World," as Sartre described it, was actually a nightmare of American cultural and political hegemony, enabling six percent of the earth's population to dominate the other ninety-four percent.[41] He began looking desperately for humanist alternatives. He turned to other Marxist countries, including Tito's Yugoslavia, Castro's Cuba, Ho Chi Minh's North Vietnam (declaring in 1967 that "the Vietnamese are fighting for all men, and the Americans against all men"), and still later Mao's China.[42] He also took up other anti-Western crusades. He led a host of leftist intellectuals in protests against France's war in Algeria in 1954 to '56 and embraced the cause of the Marxist FLN rebels—which led to his friendship with Frantz Fanon.*

Then, in May 1968, French university students in Paris and elsewhere started a massive strike and organized a series of demonstrations against the government. When French automobile workers joined them, the possibility that a general strike and revolution might sweep away the bourgeois establishment seemed genuine, at least to French intellectuals on the Left. Sartre was ecstatic; he went to talk to the striking students, who revered the sixty-year-old author of *No Exit, Being and Nothingness,* and *Critique of Dialectical Reason.* Even their slogans and posters seemed to echo his philosophy, including one that read: "We want nothing to do with a world where starvation can only be swapped for boredom."

When the demonstrations turned into riots, Sartre spoke on national radio in the students' defense. "The only anti-establishment force in our flabby Western countries is represented by the students. . . . These young people do not want to share . . . our cowardice, our weariness, our sluggishness and servility." The students "realized that the old bourgeois society was doomed," he wrote later, "and was only protecting itself from death with its policemen's clubs."[43]

But disappointingly, the crisis dissipated and the riots ended. The Re-

---

* By 1959 Sartre had also perfected the language of collective guilt in discussions of the West and the Third World: "The whole of French society is responsible for the Algerian War, and for the way it is being conducted (torture, internment camps, etc.)—the whole of society, including the men and women who have never stopped protesting against it."

nault workers called off their strike, the students returned to their classes, and the old "doomed" society again proved its resilience, carrying on as before. That resilience puzzled Sartre. "For two years after May 1968," he later explained, "I was still trying to understand what happened." In the end he decided that the revolution had not actually failed. What the French students had wanted was not power in the classic revolutionary sense of 1789 or 1917, but the abolition of power itself; in modern terms, this meant the end of all bourgeois constraints and social-economic relations. "For them, and for us today, it is the social structure itself which must be abolished, since it permits the exercise of power."

Therefore, as Sartre related in a self-interview in 1975, he refused to be pessimistic. He felt sure that a bigger revolution, in which "all powers have been done away with because each individual has full possession of himself," and a more profound new beginning than he or Heidegger or anyone else had anticipated was coming.[44]

## MICHEL FOUCAULT: REASON, POWER, AND THE END OF MAN

He was free which meant that he could look for no help either inside or
outside himself against his own freedom. He bent over the abyss and
became giddy at the sight . . .
    —J.-P. Sartre, *Baudelaire*

One of the French radical student groups that attracted Sartre's attention was the Proletarian Left, a self-proclaimed Maoist revolutionary cell. When the government tried to shut down their propaganda newspaper, *The Cause of the People* (which carried a large portrait of Mao on the masthead), Sartre eagerly lent his prestige to their cause. He became their honorary editor-in-chief and began passing out copies of *The Cause of the People* on Paris street corners while surrounded by television and camera crews. What appealed to Sartre was their revolutionary motto: "Violence, Spontaneity, and Morality"—the "moral society" being, to the French Maoists, one in which "man, no longer alienated, will be able to find himself in his real relationship with the group."[45]

The Maoists had also attracted the attention of another, younger radical intellectual, Michel Foucault. With his shaved head, rimless spectacles, leather jacket, and white turtleneck jerseys, Foucault struck a strange figure beside the long-haired Maoists and the dumpy, shabbily dressed Sartre. For Foucault, as for Sartre, 1968 had been a political awakening. However, his vision of a new beginning for modern man was, if anything, even more radical and Nietzschean.

Foucault proposed nothing less than a total overturning of the notions of reason and unreason, of truth and falsehood, and even of the human being as a spiritual and mental being. He believed that even Sartre's version of man as totally committed and totally free was, like the bourgeois notion of the individual, "an invention of recent date," and an illusion. The entire Western image of man, Foucault had written two years before the 1968 explosion, eventually "would be erased, like a face drawn in sand at the edge of the sea."[46]

In 1945, while Sartre was delivering his speech "Existentialism Is a Humanism," the nineteen-year-old Michel Foucault had arrived at the prestigious Lycée Henri IV in Paris in preparation for entering the university. His education there and at the university coincided with the height of Sartre's influence: his mentor, Jean Hyppolite, was a Sartre enthusiast, and his classmates Gilles Deleuze and Michel Tournier had both managed to get into Sartre's epoch-making lecture. But Foucault himself was drawn to the more stark and austere message of Sartre's German predecessors. In 1947 Martin Heidegger, now in disgrace, wrote a furious attack on Sartre's existential humanism, charging that it was inadequate for confronting the crisis of modern man in the grip of technology and mass culture. All forms of humanism, Heidegger proclaimed, lead inevitably to metaphysics, since they presuppose a human being with a fixed rational nature. Instead of freeing man, the humanist view actually reduces Being's infinite possibilities to the dim, stunted creature of the modern age.

For Foucault, that dim creature's true face seemed revealed in Samuel Beckett's celebrated play *Waiting for Godot*, which opened in Paris in 1953 and defined the new postwar theater. Beckett's characters were modernity's last man as described by both Nietzsche and Heidegger, awaiting that "metaphysics of presence," Godot (or God), who never arrives. Meanwhile they find themselves with nothing to do, nothing to say. They disguise their anxiety in a welter of self-important and meaningless chatter, all the while hoping that the mystery of life will be revealed to them—in vain.

Foucault later admitted that the play had been a revelation, leading him to break with a French intellectual scene that at the time seemed limited to "a horizon consisting of Marxism, existentialism, and [German] phenomenology."[47] It inspired him to move in a very different intellectual direction, rejecting Sartre not because he was pro-Stalinist or anti-Western but because his philosophy still contained the same bankrupt assumption about man as a self-regarding subject. The modern Western image of man, Foucault would assert, "is not a proposition to be defended but a product of social-historical processes," that is to say, of capitalist civilization.

Foucault's *The Order of Things* (1966) laid out his version of cultural pessimism in the form of an historical essay. Western man, with his self-regarding and innate moral nature, was the privileged creation of what Foucault called "the classical age": the secularized and secularizing seventeenth century and Enlightenment. As it was for the Frankfurt School (with which Foucault would later develop a mutual interest and rapprochement), Enlightenment reason becomes a merciless instrument of life-destroying dissection and analysis that ultimately turns on and demolishes what it creates. This includes its history of itself as a "history of man," in other words, the history of civil society.

The nineteenth-century fascination with history, personified in figures like Hegel, Ranke, and Burckhardt, revealed that all human activities—work, art, and politics, even thinking, speaking, and writing—are merely successive stages in an ongoing temporal process over which individuals have no control. The Western historical search for origins demonstrated the relativity of its own concepts and values: "None of the contents analyzed by [philosophy, sociology, psychology, and anthropology] can remain stable in itself or escape the movement of History," Foucault explained.[48]

"History constitutes, therefore," Foucault announced, "the chronological and geographic boundaries" for anthropology, sociology, and the other "sciences of man." But history also surrounds them "with a frontier which limits them and destroys, from the outset, their claim to validity within the element of universality." In other words, *all* history is Nietzschean history; the historicist impulse destroys any notion of Western man's privileged position by revealing the various points in time at which all his assumptions, beliefs, and values about himself began—and by implication, where they will end. Foucault concluded that "the human being no longer has any history; or rather, since he speaks, works, and lives, he finds himself interwoven in his own being with histories which are neither subordinate to him nor homogeneous with him." For Foucault, the individual finds himself subjected to a new form of alienation more profound than anything Marx or the Frankfurt School ever imagined. He is alienated from the very moment he enters into *any* relationship or institutional structure that can be analyzed or explained in historical terms, including his own knowledge of himself.

Being part of "history" for Foucault means being trapped within an artificial "finitude" (a point that both Plato and Saint Augustine would have appreciated). Since "all knowledge is rooted in a life, a society, and a language that has a history," everything we know or do is part of the same trap. Instead, Foucault decided, one had to look for freedom beyond the image of man as a rational being, since this had been "created" by the same totalizing structures from which one was supposed to escape. "Strangely enough," he wrote, "man . . . is probably no more than a rift in the order of things. . . . It is comforting, and a source of profound relief to think that man is only a recent invention, a figure not yet two centuries old, a new wrinkle . . . and that he will disappear again."[49] This conclusion provoked howls of outrage from the existentialist Left. However, Foucault simply carried the existentialists' assumptions to their logical conclusion: freedom from the bourgeois West must also require freedom from its most representative product, Western man himself. And like Sartre and the existentialists, Foucault believed that the free individual could still reemerge from the collapse of Western modernity—but shorn of his false humanity.

As an alternative, Foucault turned to two figures from the Surrealism of the twenties, George Bataille and Antonin Artaud. Bataille and Artaud united Nietzsche's iconoclastic nihilism with the images of death and violence contained in the poetry of Charles Baudelaire and that of his Decadent disciples. They argued for rejecting all forms of reason and morality as intolerable restrictions on the individual's creative freedom. Sadism, sex, violence, and even insanity have a fundamental value in themselves, Artaud and Bataille proclaimed, as raw expressions of man's vital instincts, which bourgeois society tries to contain and repress. Nietzsche's revaluation of all values became for them, and ultimately for

Foucault, an endless program of "transgression," a declaration of war against society through a celebration of crime and sexual deviance. The French Nietzschean man turns the world into what Artaud called "a theater of cruelty."

"It has been a long time," Artaud wrote in 1947, "since I had any control over my mind, and my subconscious rules me with impulses which come from the depths of my nervous rages and from the whirring of my blood." The subconscious mind retains our deepest vital energies, as Freud had recognized; however, for Artaud those instincts are in fact man's true, not merely his primitive or unformed, self. Lombroso's born criminal is in effect the human being at his fullest and most vital, whose energies release themselves "like stabs of a knife or flashes of lightning in a congested sky." Acts that civilization calls vicious and evil are in fact, Artaud declared in Nietzschean fashion, the highest forms of life: "Because life involves extension, thickness, heaviness, and matter, it involves, as a direct consequence, evil and all that is inherent in evil." The French Nietzscheans' hero (or rather antihero) was the Marquis de Sade; Sade's history of sexual atrocity and madness was celebrated as an epic example of man's struggle against the rationalizing and self-limiting forces of civilization.[50]

That insanity is a form of freedom became the basic assumption of Foucault's most widely read work, *Madness and Civilization* (1961). The dichotomy is significant; in the precapitalist West of the Middle Ages and Renaissance, Foucault claimed, insanity was understood to be part of the human condition, even an ironic comment on man's pretensions to autonomy and power. Then the classical age defined madness as the enemy of reason and hence the enemy of humanity, requiring rigid and brutal segregation of the insane and other "deviants" in asylums and hospitals. That process of "confinement," the categorizing, segregation, and exclusion of what seems foreign and hence threatening to the rationalizing self, defined for Foucault the Enlightenment mind and all of modern civilization. All of modern society is, for Foucault, a prison with modern man its inmate.

"The massive structures of bourgeois society and its values: Family-Child relations, centered on the theme of paternal authority; Transgression-Punishment relations, centered on the theme of immediate justice; Madness-Disorder relations, centered on the theme of social and moral order" are all creations of the unchained power of categorizing, discriminating, segregating reason of Western society.[51] Foucault reached the same conclusion about Western analytic reason as his predecessors. The spread of reason is a totalizing process; everything everywhere bears its unmistakable imprint. However, Foucault's critiques were presented not in dense philosophical treatises but in the guise of a series of Nietzschean histories or "genealogies," which revealed the historical origins of the "structured norms of existence" of modern life one by one.

Foucault's philosophical project was what Heidegger had termed an *Abbau*, a demolition or tearing down, a "deconstruction." Foucault's deconstruction spared no one, not even Marx, who turns out to be just another "fish in the water" of nineteenth-century bourgeois thought. History for Foucault reflexively reproduces Western reason's patterns of domination over and over again, as "the fundamental codes of a culture . . . governing its language, its schemas of perception, its exchanges, its techniques, its values, its hierarchy of practices." These cultural norms permit no exceptions and crush everything in their path—including ultimately their supposed beneficiary, the individual himself. In Western society, reason's disciplining power "now reaches the very grain of the individual, touches his body, intrudes into his gestures, his attitudes, his discourse."[52]

Yet at its deepest level, Foucault's history is also a vitalist history in the tradition of Nietzsche and Gobineau. The driving force behind this totalizing Western reason is will to power. Its social discipline, like its notions of knowledge, are only expressions of that will to power. "The relations of power that function in a society such as ours essentially rest upon a definite relation of forces that is established at a determinate, historically specifiable moment, in war and by war." Bourgeois society, like Gobineau's Aryan civilization, is arranged by the strong for the strong. However, "the strong" for Foucault are not a racial elite or human beings at all; they are the instinct for order and discipline itself, which is "reinscribed in social institutions, in economic inequalities, in language, in the bodies themselves of each and every one of us."[53]

Foucault attacked the conventional Western image of man precisely because he believed it subordinated our personal will to power to that of others. "Humanism is everything in Western civilization that restricts *the desire for power,*" which is to say our own will to power. A loping double movement—reason as will to power, transgression as the individual's vitalist challenge to that will to power—runs through all of Foucault's books. After *The Order of Things* his deconstructive enterprise rapidly expanded its scope, blasting loose the foundations of rational-scientific discourse in psychiatry, history, law and justice, and language itself. Every instance of Western man's search for knowledge turns out to be simply a construction of discourses of power, or "practices" of discipline and domination over unperceiving victims.[54]

Foucault's books impressed and overwhelmed his readers with their appearance of careful scholarship and research (although in fact that scholarship was faulty, even mendacious, at crucial points), creating a new and exhilarating genre for cultural pessimists everywhere.[55] "One must conduct an ascending analysis of power," Foucault later said, "starting, that is, from its infinitesimal mechanisms"—including seemingly innocuous ones such as the Western family, its furniture, its eating habits, even its notions of personal hygiene—"which each have their own history" and are "invested, colonized, utilized, involuted, transformed, displaced, extended by ever more general mechanisms and by forms of global domination."[56]

Even the notion of truth itself was a ruse of power. "We are subjected to the production of truth through power and we cannot exercise power except through the production of truth." Foucault added that "this is the case for every society," but in the modern West it takes particularly systematic and totalitarian forms. "Power never ceases its interrogation, its inquisition . . . In the last analysis, we must produce truth as we produce wealth." In any case, "power is everywhere, it is produced from one moment to the next, at every point, or rather in every relation of one point to another."[57]

Although Foucault shared an affinity with Adorno and Marcuse in his view of Western society and rationality as relentlessly totalitarian, he wandered further out into the Nietzschean wilderness. There is *no* escape, he concluded, from civilization's culture of surveillance and confinement. Like rats in a laboratory cage, we find ourselves the subjects of "supervision of the smallest fragment of life and the body . . . in the context of the school, the barracks, the hospital or the workshop."[58] Sartre's dream of freedom, Being-in-Itself, is for Foucault just another dead end;

his heroes who recognize their "total situation" are simply those rats that have been prodded into unthinking resentment and rage by the relentless pressures of that confinement and domination. Even in their rebellion they are still stuck in the cage, like everyone else.

Foucault's last project, *The History of Sexuality*, which he began in 1976, suggested that even our sexual desires are only the very deepest level of the tyranny that power as will to power imposes upon us through a rigid hierarchy of acceptable bodily pleasures. Foucault decided that the repressive bourgeois attitude toward sex could not be simply thrown off in a gesture of personal liberation, as Marcuse had fondly imagined. All forms of "normal" sexual desire, from married bliss to heterosexuality to masturbation and even Foucault's own homosexuality, were merely modes of complicity in our own confinement. Yet because sex does represent will to power at its final and deepest limit, like the underground sewers of a great and glittering metropolis, Foucault proposed that it provided an opportunity for escape. We could lift the manhole cover, as it were, and slip down into a new reality.

During his visits to the United States in the late seventies, Foucault became fascinated by San Francisco's gay scene with its bathhouses, leather bars, chains, whips, "glory holes," and sadomasochistic rituals. Sadomasochistic sex in particular represented what Foucault called a "limit-experience," an existentialist boundary situation in which the vitalist forces of the self could break from "falsification" of pleasure through genital-centered sex. Foucault had come to believe what Artaud had argued in the forties, that "the human body is an electric battery whose discharges have been castrated and repressed" by civilized taboos. That included the giving and taking of pain as a sexual ritual, in which, said another celebrant of the gay S/M scene, "the experience of extreme suffering points us to the frontiers of human behavior."*[59]

Under the whip or iron clamp the entire body becomes an energized playing field for a Nietzschean "game of truth." For Foucault, all relations, even with our own bodies, are part of that same struggle for power; there is no standpoint outside them and no valid moral constraints on the *libido dominandi* as it reaches out for power and "the end-

---

* Even erotic ritual castration can serve as transgression in this sense, a "de-centering of the subject" that frees the individual from conventional genital-centered views of sex.

lessly repeated nonexistence of gratification." When Foucault learned that he had contracted AIDS as the result of his pursuit of sexual transgression, that too became in his mind just another limit-experience: sex as a form of death, as well as the power to give death to others through sex. For at least two years after he contracted AIDS (from 1982 to 1984), Michel Foucault continued to visit his various gay orgy sites, knowingly passing the disease on to his anonymous partners. "We are inventing new pleasures beyond sex," Foucault told an interviewer—in this particular case, sex as murder.[60]

If Foucault's personal story seems chilling, it is only because he pursued his own philosophy to its logical extreme. As one biographer put it, "Foucault took Nietzsche's injunction, to become 'what one is,' very seriously," which is to say to become a being whose core is his own will to power.[61] In Foucault's nihilism every trace of ourselves that is shaped by others must be destroyed: our political, cultural, and sexual identities, our notions of right and wrong, sanity and madness, even what is true and false, all vanish. Ultimately even the person himself vanishes; only the restless and spasmodic will to power is left and—like Gobineau's Aryan warrior or Artaud's "evil" transgressor—its only justification is its own existence. "I am not of your world," Artaud wrote; "mine is the other side of everything that is, knows, and is aware of itself, desires, and makes itself."

## WHITE MASKS, BLACK VIOLENCE: FRANTZ FANON

History is the history of the working Slave.
    —Alexandre Kojève

A taste for violence and action as an antidote to cultural malaise became an integral part of French cultural pessimism. It decisively shaped its orientation toward politics, which in the postwar period meant the political Left. Sartre had turned against both the socialists and the French Communist Party because, he said, they no longer seemed interested in "the sound principle" of violent revolution. "In the Sixties," he complained, "no one talked about violence anymore," whereas Sartre talked about it endlessly. He preached to his students and radio and television audiences about "necessary violence," explaining that murders and crimes committed by oppressed peoples and individuals were not violence at all, but were justifiable responses to their total situation in bourgeois society.

Foucault, who had deplored the modern West as "war by other means," became attracted to the Maoists in the Proletarian Left precisely because they advocated terrorism as "people's justice." Foucault urged them to engage in random acts of violence against their bourgeois oppressors, whether guilty or innocent. Foucault grimly explained that the whole notion of innocence and guilt was part of the "incarceration" society of the bourgeois West. He often pointed to the French revolutionary September Massacre of 1792 and "the old Germanic custom" of sticking "the head of an enemy on a stake, for public viewing" as examples of this sort of people's justice.[62]

However, the figure most associated with the liberating power of violence was Frantz Fanon. A friend and admirer of Jean-Paul Sartre, Fanon very much subscribed to the postwar French assault on Western rationality. Fanon identified that corrupt Western totalizing process with colonialism and imperialism. His call for an onslaught of "holy violence" against European colonialism, led by a rootless and impoverished Third World lumpenproletariat of *fellahin*, gave Marcus Garvey's vision of an apocalyptic race war new, intellectually respectable force. The rituals of that holy violence—revolutions, assassinations, skyjackings, car bombings, and the burning of tire "necklaces"—were seen as acts of existential authenticity that would obliterate the West's empire of bad faith.

Born in 1925 in French Martinique, Frantz Fanon belonged to what Du Bois would have called the talented tenth of middle-class French-speaking black West Indians. He served with gallantry in the Free French forces in World War II, studied philosophy and psychology at the Sorbonne in Paris, and eventually become a doctor at a leading hospital in French Algeria. However, as in Du Bois's case, his race prevented full acceptance by the Europeans whom he admired. Fanon became deeply bitter over this fact; explaining his rejection turned into a consuming passion.[63] Race had become the determining issue in his life and the reason lay not with him, he decided, but the nature of Western culture.

His first book, *Black Faces, White Masks* (1954), asserted that Western civilization repressed not only its own passions, as Freud had said, but those of the peoples it colonized as well. White Europeans sensed the vitality and cultural health of the nonwhite races, particularly blacks like Fanon himself, and therefore placed them in a subordinate position. Whites then trained the nonwhite intellectual to think of his own culture as inferior and lacking in "civilized" values. By accepting this denigration of his own culture, the nonwhite intellectual in effect denied his own humanity. He became a neurotic, Fanon explained in clinical detail, and permitted the white man's unconscious fears of vitality to dictate his own life choices.

Fanon's high school French teacher, the poet Aimé Césaire, had already defined this issue in Sartre's existentialist terms. The nonwhite intellectual faced the same dilemma as Sartre's play-acting bourgeois, and must pretend to be someone he is not in order to evade the "absurdity" of white colonial domination. Instead, Césaire said, he needed to turn to his genuine, more authentic identity, what he and the Senegalese poet Louis Senghor called *négritude*, or "blackness."

The Negritude movement began among West African and Caribbean black intellectuals in Paris in the twenties, who sought to uncover a cultural identity in their shared Negro-African ancestry. They attempted to construct retrospectively a vitalist black *Kultur* to pit against an imperialist Western civilization. Louis Senghor, for example, spoke of the *forces vitales*—"this humming in our legs, this rising of the sap/which swells the buds in the youths' groins"—which lay at the basis of all precolonial African society. Césaire dismissed the West as "decadent and stricken" because of its class divisions and exploitative colonial empires: "A civilization which cheats on its principles is a moribund civilization." For Césaire and Senghor, Negritude exhibited the same unifying racial character as Aryan-Teutonic Germanism; like Du Bois's black soul, race was not biological but the sacred spiritual force that must eventually defeat its enemy, white *Zivilisation*.[64]

"I have found not only my situation, but *myself*," Fanon wrote in describing his discovery of Césaire's poetry. "I feel in myself a soul as large as the world, a soul as deep as the deepest rivers, my breast swells to infinity. And then," he added bitterly, "and then they [i.e., whites] recommend to me the modesty of a sick man."[65] Meanwhile, the process of decolonization was already under way. In May 1945 the Sétif massacre in French Algeria cost the lives of six thousand Muslims; in 1947 an uprising in Madagascar was put down with brutal severity, with nearly eighty thousand deaths. One year later war against French rule began in Indochina. For Césaire and the other Negritude artists, Sartre's existential rebel now became the anticolonial revolutionary.[66]

In 1948 Sartre published an anthology of poetry by Senghor, Césaire, and other Negritude writers entitled *Black Orpheus*. It bathed the anticolonial movement in publicity, not to mention glamor. Sartre revealed that Negritude was truly Heidegger's Being-in-Itself, brimming with creativity and authenticity.*[67] Predictably the black man (which meant the nonwhite man) possesses all the virtues that the narrow, constricted, industrial West has lost: oneness with nature, an intuitive sympathy for others as opposed to rational self-interest. But Sartre also brought before a wide audience for the first time a notion that would grow in influence. This was that imperialism was a system of not only economic and political but also cultural control over persons of color (Simone de Beauvoir would perform the same service for women in *The Second Sex* a year later). European culture laid a series of traps for unwary nonwhites—institutional, intellectual, and linguistic traps—that were all vehicles of white bad faith.[68]

Fanon became Sartre's admirer after reading the preface to *Black Orpheus*, although the two did not meet until 1961. By then Fanon was already sick with the illness that would eventually kill him. He had just finished what would be his final political testament, *The Wretched of the Earth*. He instructed his publisher: "Ask Sartre to write a preface. Tell him each time I sit down at my desk, I think of him [as someone] who writes such important things for our future but who as yet has found no readers"—or rather, no true readers besides Fanon himself.

In *The Wretched of the Earth* Fanon transformed Sartre's Being-for-Itself into the basis for a revolutionary apocalypse. The history of the West has reached the point of final dissolution. "Come, then, comrades, the European game has finally ended; we must find something differ-

---

* On encountering this black Africanism, Sartre adds, "one cannot help but think of the famous distinction which Bergson established between intelligence and intuition."

ent." Fanon rejected any notion of the new nations of Africa and Asia adopting the Western model of "modernization." "For centuries they have stifled almost the whole of humanity in the name of a so-called spiritual experience." Now Europe "is running headlong into the abyss; we would do well to avoid it with all possible speed."[69]

For Fanon, decolonization was the ultimate reality of history. The end of European empire was "the meeting of two forces, opposed to each other by their very nature," which will "change the order of the world." The central axis of this revolution, Fanon affirmed, was race not class. Whether bourgeois or worker, the white world is united in its exploitative oppression of nonwhites. On the other hand, the black world is not united but divided. There is a colonial black bourgeoisie, a parasitic class of lackeys who have linked themselves to the white culture and economy: Being-for-Others, in short. These are the advocates of nonviolence, peaceful compromise—and thus betrayal of true freedom.

Revolution's liberating force is found instead among the peasantry and dispossessed, the true wretched of the earth who are in effect for Fanon the *Volk*, an anchor for *Kultur* as well as revolution. An armed peasantry, rather than an industrial proletariat, will form the basis for a permanently politicized society precisely because they are the most distant and immune to the corrupting influence of Western institutions and ideas. This is the true vital face of the Third World. "Decolonization," he proclaimed, "is the veritable creation of new men. . . . the replacing of a certain 'species' of men by quite another." That is, the man created by the society—both colonial master and native—is replaced by the one created by liberation.[70]

Political and even economic freedom from the West can never be enough, Fanon asserted. True decolonization must be a complete destruction of the culture imposed by the former white rulers, including the goals of its politics and institutions: nationality, democracy, and the rule of law. Indeed, decolonization *requires* violence to break the totalizing spell. Freedom is "a murderous and decisive struggle" and "our historic mission is to sanction all revolts, all desperate actions, all those abortive attempts drowned in rivers of blood." This bloodshed is only just recompense for the violence of colonization: "To the saying, all natives are the same, the colonized reply, all settlers are the same." In the complicitous Western imperialist system, all are guilty and none are to be spared.

Fanon turned to Aimé Césaire for his model of the ritual purifying power of revolutionary violence:

> We were running like madmen, shots rang out . . . Blood and sweat cooled and refreshed us. . . . Then was the assault made on the master's house . . . We broke in the doors. . . . The master's room was brilliantly lighted, and the master was there, very calm . . . "It's you," he said very calm. It was I, even I, and I told him so, the good slave, the faithful slave, the slave of slaves, and suddenly his eyes were like two cockroaches, frightened in the rainy season. . . . I struck and the blood spurted; it was the only baptism I remember today.[71]

Sartre made his own direct contribution to this promise of vengeance in his preface, suggesting that the Third World political terrorist is actually "man recreating himself." Sartre tells his audience, "The rebel's weapon is proof of his humanity. To shoot down a European is to kill two birds with one stone, to destroy an oppressor and the man he oppresses at the same time . . . We were men at his expense, he makes himself man at ours: a different man; *of higher quality.*"[72]

Fanon's *Wretched of the Earth* provided intellectual cover for a generation of enthusiasts for Third World socialism—including Sartre himself. Revolutionary violence in far-off countries would serve as a source of both political liberation and cultural regeneration. Cuba, Vietnam, China (particularly during Mao's Cultural Revolution), and Khmer Rouge Cambodia promised to turn politics into the same cleansing, unifying force that National Socialism's revolution on the Right had promised: a spontaneous, vital, and invincible movement toward liberation from a dying West.

"We need only march, and charge," Fanon told an All-African Peoples Conference in 1958. Fanon even proposed organizing a Pan-African Legion, an army of black storm troopers who would sweep away European influence from one end of the continent to the other. "It is not even a question of strategy. . . . We have Africa with us. A continent is getting into motion while Europe is languorously asleep."[73] Of course, no such legion came into existence, and the struggle to expel the European presence from Africa would go on for another decade after Fanon's death in 1964. Independence itself would usher in an age not of liberation and triumph but of bloody civil wars, military coups, and squalid dictatorships. By 1975 more than half of all black African nations were under military rule.

Fanon's message, however, had less to do with African realities than with the cultural pessimism of Sartre. Submission to any Western values, no matter how much "false" personal freedom one gains, is a form of slavery and self-annihilation for whites as well as nonwhites. "Our precious sets of values begin to molt," Sartre exulted in the preface to *The Wretched of the Earth*, "on closer scrutiny you won't find one that isn't stained with blood. . . . the Parthenon, Chartres, the Rights of Man, the swastika. Now we know what these are worth."[74]

However, in their haste to abandon the West, Sartre and his disciples soon discovered that there was nowhere else to go. As the historian H. Stuart Hughes has explained, "If Frenchmen of the generation preceding Sartre's . . . had lived with too good a conscience to question their own values, in his case the process had been just the reverse; he had become so obsessed with the concept of bad faith, he had delivered himself over so totally to his conviction that he, like every other bourgeois intellectual, was ultimately at fault, that in the end he found no norm to live by."[75]

None, that is, except a naked vitalism, expressed through Foucault's nihilism or Fanon's revolutionary terror.

## CHAPTER 11

# THE MULTICULTURALIST IMPULSE

Hey, hey, ho, ho
Western culture's got to go.
—Jesse Jackson, 1987

A rnold Toynbee was probably the last historian with academic pretensions to take up the "decline of the West." By 1970 the issue itself no longer held the attention of intellectuals. But at the same time, the modern French cultural pessimists reveal how declinism moved from being an explicit issue, as it still was for Toynbee and Spengler, to an implicit one in modern critical thinking. Sartre, Foucault, Fanon, and their ideological offspring, such as Gilles De Leuze, Jacques Derrida, and Félix Lyotard, were teaching that Western institutions, Western-style rationality, language, and "discourse," and even the Western image of man himself were all a cultural dead end. All genuine freedom came from denying or transgressing against those Western boundaries, they proclaimed. Humanity had to look beyond the limits modern European civilization set on the authentic self.

Those criticisms, as well as those of Marcuse and the Frankfurt School, served as a springboard for a new wave of anti-Western, anti-European ideologies. One of these became multiculturalism. Multiculturalism has looked to a wide gallery of cultural pessimists for its inspiration: W.E.B. Du Bois, Marcus Garvey, Adorno, Marcuse, and the Frankfurt School, as well as Sartre, Foucault, and Frantz Fanon. In multiculturalism, the classic *symptoms* of Western decline—its rationality that tramples out vitality, its totalizing political institutions, capitalist economy, and degenerate mass culture—as well as earlier *antidotes* to decline—racism, imperialism, Darwinian nationalism, fascism—are lumped together to epitomize the West as a uniquely malign force in history. For the multiculturalist, Western civilization is entirely *Zivilisation*; there is no *Kultur* at its heart.

The origins of the terms of these old debates, and their limitations, are forgotten. However, the perennial hope of progress still guides the multiculturalist critic when he looks to the future. He and other cultural pessimists still tend to uphold the idea of political liberty as a measure of personal liberation, usually in the form of demands for "genuine" democratic institutions. Hegel's vision of freedom as the fully self-contained individual, with a "consciousness of his own being," continues to direct efforts to end modern alienation and achieve full "self-realization" for men, women, blacks, homosexuals, and other groups.

The Enlightenment emphasis on "politeness" also takes on a new relevance, in terms of the hope for tolerance of "diversity" and for a new brotherhood of humankind. Condorcet's and Herder's vision of a future universal civilization survives in the ideal of "one world"—although stripped of its primary Western attributes, of course—and an end to divisive nationalisms.[1] Similarly, the hopes of earlier critiques of progress also survive in multicultural forms. Rousseau's vision of primitive collective virtue is transformed into a vision of a socialistic community with guaranteed equality for all members, regardless of race, color, or gender. Romantic vitalism and Nietzsche's Overman reemerge as the energy and vitality that a "whole" and healthy racial identity provides for the individual. Indeed, one of the key issues in multiculturalism's critique of the modern West, that of identity, is part of that Romantic vitalist legacy.

However, all of these "progressive" goals now require the unraveling of Western hegemony. Western civilization, once the driving force of human progress, is now treated as its greatest obstacle. Under the circumstances, it hardly seems extreme to assert, as Susan Sontag did in 1967, that "the truth is that Mozart, Pascal, Shakespeare, parliamentary government, the emancipation of women . . . don't redeem what this particular civilization has wrought on the world. The white race is the cancer of human history."

By the seventies, European cultural pessimism reached an important fermentation stage. Despite the deaths of its leading figures—Kojève in 1968, Adorno in 1969, Horkheimer in 1973, Marcuse in 1975, Heidegger in 1976, and Sartre in 1980 (C. Wright Mills and Fanon had passed on a decade earlier)—their ideas became institutionalized on college campuses in America and at universities in Europe. The historian John Patrick Diggins has suggested separating the New Left of the sixties from the rise of what he calls the Academic Left, which formulated its radicalism in the classroom rather than in the streets.[2] However, the distinction is misleading. Each flowed effortlessly into the other, particularly given their angle of attack on mainstream liberal institutions. The Frankfurt School's critical theory shaped much of the outlook of the New Left, while heroes of the New Left such as C. Wright Mills, Noam Chomsky, and Sartre provided additional fuel for condemning the West as totalizing and totalitarian. As a result, American radicals found themselves looking at the affluent society around them with skepticism—and fear. Worrying about mindless consumerism and mass culture, capitalism's destruction of tradition and value, dehumanizing government and technology, and the rising specter of a technocratic police state now became the ideological duty of the Left, not the Right.[3]

Noam Chomsky's radicalism stems ultimately from C. Wright Mills, with a bracing admixture of other thinkers. According to Chomsky, America is run by the malign conspiratorial forces of big capitalism, government, and the Pentagon "power elite." To keep its position, the power elite is forced "to deprive democratic political structures of substantive content" in order to "deflect any political challenge to established privilege and authority. The general public must be reduced to its traditional apathy and obedience" through a degraded mass culture, manipulative political elections (or "manufactured consent"), and a mind-numbing, conformist system of thought control via the mass media.[4]

Abroad, America in the twentieth century (like Spengler's British Empire) had erected an expansive empire in alliance with international capitalist interests, through "terror states" in Latin America, genocidal violence in Asia, and its equally violent surrogate in the Middle East, Israel.[5] Like Marcuse, Mills had regularly compared the United States with the Soviet Union, claiming that they were virtually indistinguishable from each other as advanced industrial societies. For Chomsky, the closest historical parallel to America is Nazi Germany. Its military-based state capitalism is determined to "deter democracy" at home and abroad and maintain an international network of brutal terror and force. Even the school system serves as a training ground for "troops that will enforce the muted, unending terms of the status quo in the coming years of a projected American century."[6] However, this American empire is in fact a doomed enterprise, Chomsky warns. As Chomsky told an interviewer in 1987: "Some societies are so organized that they lead themselves to a quite predictable destruction . . . The U.S. is such an example of 'inevitable, global' suicide."[7]

Another radical critic, Jonathan Kozol, fashioned a dismal picture of modern America from many of the same elements. In 1975 Kozol concluded that America was "a rich, benevolent, sophisticated, murderous, well-mannered and exquisite social order." From childhood Americans are trained to be "morally impotent." Kozol explained, "Lifelong technological insulation [has] numbed our power to fathom and capability to feel." In short, American life is what Nietzsche would call decadent; it is one in which "life no longer lives in the whole." America's long-standing faith in progress serves as a particularly deadening influence, Kozol charged. It disguises the individual's powerlessness and the vast social and economic inequities in American life. Quoting Albert Camus, that "progress, paradoxically, can be used to justify conservatism," Kozol insisted that American history gives an optimistic rather than a realistic view of industrial society: "Auschwitz, Selma, My Lai, Kent State are ignored or treated as historical aberrations" rather than as normal and inevitable occurrences in modern life. "Atrocities, real and repeated, proliferate in this social order."[8]

Like Chomsky, Mills, and Marcuse, Kozol observed a power elite building an authoritarian regime without need for direct coercion or repression. "Physical threat and massive presence of police," he states, "are used here only as a last resort," except in the inner city and against blacks. For Kozol, the most evident proof of America's moral corruption is its treatment of American Negroes. Enslavement, racial brutality, discrimination, and exploitation are revealed as the true face of American society, just as Du Bois had once called World War I the true face of the West. "All white people, I think, are implicated in these things so long as we participate in American life in a normal way and attempt to go on leading normal lives."[9]

Another radical critic, Christopher Lasch, consciously reframed old *Kulturkritik* themes in the psychoanalytic language of the Frankfurt School. He began his 1979 book, *The Culture of Narcissism*, with a now familiar description of how "a crisis of confidence" had seized America and other capitalist countries, producing "a mood of pessimism," while "the political crisis of capitalism reflects a general crisis of western culture.* Liberalism, Lasch declared, is "politically and intellectually bankrupt"; in its place, postindustrial America has created a postmodern "culture of narcissism, . . . which in its decadence has carried the logic of individualism to the extreme." Like Freud's narcissist neurotic, the modern American lives in a self-enclosed world that lacks cultural depth. Lasch summed up this degenerate type in a passage that recalls Werner Sombart's attacks on German liberalism or Spengler's deprecations of *Zivilisation*:

> The new narcissist is haunted not by guilt but by anxiety. . . . Liberated from the superstitions of the past, he doubts even the reality of his own existence. Superficially relaxed and tolerant . . . [but] fiercely competitive in his demand for appropriation and acclaim . . . he demands immediate gratification and lives in a state of restless, perpetually unsatisfied desire.

Quoting Adorno and Erich Fromm, Lasch also ripped into American popular culture and the mass media, which helped to inspire this culture of emptiness and unsatisfied desire. "According to Erich Fromm, Americans had lost the capacity for spontaneous feeling, even for anger."[10] For Lasch, the solution lies not in socialism but in a return to instinct in a Nietzschean sense. Local communities and neighborhoods will become expressions of *Gemeinschaft*, battling science, technology, and the "corporate state." This cultural rejuvenation might fracture into separate racial communities, Lasch admitted; however, "the advantages of community cohesion" outweigh "the dangers of racial separatism."[11] At the same time, Lasch doubted whether this "dying culture" could in fact be saved. "Modern capitalism," he declared, "not only elevates narcissists

---

*For the complete quotation, see the Introduction.

to prominence" in politics and cultural life, but "elicits and reinforces narcissistic traits in everyone." It forms, in other words, a totality (in the Frankfurt School sense) from which there is no escape, while "the custodians of culture hope, at bottom, merely to survive its collapse."[12]

Even as radicals were busy condemning America and the West in the vocabulary of cultural pessimism, liberals themselves moved toward a resigned historical pessimism. The so-called North–South debate of the seventies assumed many of Arnold Toynbee's concerns about the future of a Western-dominated globe, as well as his postliberal guilt. European and American economists such as René Dumont, Barbara Ward, Robert Heilbroner, and Lester Thurow urged their countries to submit to a major restructuring of the planet's economic resources. The North (meaning America, Western Europe, and Japan) was consuming too many resources, they warned, while the Third World was left with too few. Every drop of oil or loaf of bread consumed by a Westerner represented food taken from the mouths of starving Africans or Asians, a view summed up in René Dumont and Bernard Rozier's *The Hungry Future* (1969): "The children of backward countries . . . never attain their full promise, or . . . have died of kwashiorkor, because the fish meal that may have saved them has fed the chickens gorged by the rich."

Robert Heilbroner's *An Inquiry into the Human Prospect* (1974) explained that the role of a liberal intelligentsia in the modern world was "to prepare the West" for a future redefinition of "the legitimate boundaries of power and permissible sanctuaries of freedom" in a world of shrinking resources.[13] The belief that the global future requires a diminished Western role is still an article of faith among enlightened liberals. Twenty years later, Paul Kennedy quoted a Singapore diplomat on "the arithmetic of Western folly":

> The West has 800 million people; the rest make up almost 4.7 billion . . . no Western society would accept a situation where 15 percent of its population legislated for the remaining 85 percent.

Paul Kennedy urged Western countries to strike a new North–South deal before they are finally overwhelmed by Fanon's wretched of the earth.[14]

Other critics, like Jean-Paul Sartre, forthrightly embraced those wretched of the earth as the new humanity of the future. Orientalism's noble savage reemerged as the Third World peasant or ghetto dweller: impulsively compassionate, stronger in body, mind, and spirit, and with more energy and integrity than his degenerate Western counterparts. The seventies saw the birth of "radical chic," as "political pilgrims" traveled from Europe and America to Cuba, Nicaragua, China, and Angola to discover the same regenerative virtues Du Bois had professed to see in Kwame Nkrumah's Ghana. Sartre found Cuba's leaders Fidel Castro and Che Guevara to be the fulfillment of his authentic man, unifying thought and action, art and politics. Castro's revolution had, Sartre announced, "rolled back the limits of the possible." As another visitor remarked, "You come away with your faith in the human race restored."[15]

The Third World personality, "the person of color," turned out to have the vitality needed to bring renewal not only to his own, postcolonial culture but to that of exhausted whites as well. Norman Mailer said after his Cuban visit in 1963, "We were a league of silent defeated men. You [Castro] were aiding us, giving us psychic ammunition . . . in that desperate silent struggle . . . against the cold insidious cancer of the power that governs us."[16] Still later, Hollywood films such as *Dances With Wolves* and *The Old Gringo* would extend that same redemptive theme, with whites immersing themselves in the primitive virtues of a Native American or Latino Arcadia and finding spiritual enlightenment and release.

Like the exotic Orient of the early nineteenth century, the Third World, especially in its organized, "socialist" forms, presented a sharp contrast with the world of the West. On a trip to Hanoi in 1970 Susan Sontag praised her "charming and dignified" Vietnamese hosts, whose "grace, variety, and established identity" contrasted sharply with the "dehumanized individuals" and "living dead" produced by "inorganic, dead, coercive, authoritarian" American culture. "A small nation of handsome people . . . is being brutally and self-righteously slaughtered . . . by the richest and most grotesquely overarmed, most powerful country in the world." She was forced to conclude that "America has become a criminal, sinister country."[17]

This Third World exoticism also took explicitly declinist forms. A work such as *The Promise of the Coming Dark Age* (1976) by historian L.S. Stavrianos managed to bridge the gap between the exoticists' yearning for cultural renewal and the liberal defeatism of Toynbee. As in the Christian Dark Ages following imperial Rome's collapse, Stavrianos argued, the coming collapse of Western hegemony will release nonwhite peoples from cultural and economic bondage and launch a new era of peace and prosperity. This non-Western prosperity would be achieved not through capitalism (Japan is not mentioned anywhere in Stavrianos's book) but through collectivist societies on a "southern" Third World model. Stavrianos extolled the virtues of Tanzania under Julius Nyrere (just as Tanzania's agricultural output was falling by one-third), Communist China during the Cultural Revolution and under the Gang of Four, and Cambodia under Pol Pot. These new "democratic societies" generated, Stavrianos concluded, a "true liberation of spirit and energy" that would touch the other peoples of the earth.[18]

Revelations about the Cambodian "killing fields" and the death toll from the Cultural Revolution later dampened some of the ardor for Third World Communism. But anti-Western cultural pessimism and its polemical tools remained sharp as ever. These would be perfected in the American context in the guise of "promoting diversity."

## MULTICULTURALISM IN AMERICA: IDENTITY AND CIVILIZATION

Power without some sense of oneself is to me another kind of instability, and black people would then become exactly what white people have become.
—Nikki Giovanni, 1973

Proponents of multiculturalism usually inveigh against the traditional image of America as a melting pot. They suggest instead the metaphor of a patchwork quilt, in which individual ethnic elements blend together but retain their distinct character.[19] Yet that same ambiguous (and confusing) melting pot image had been created in reaction against an earlier declinist trend, the nativist fear of "race suicide" aroused by waves of immigration. The melting pot image suggested that these immigrants from southern and eastern Europe, including Jews, could all become Americans as healthy and normal as any Anglo-Saxon or Nordic physical type. Being an American was a question of social and cultural integration, not racial integrity.[20]

The melting pot owed its success to the waning of Anglo-Saxonism. By 1930 race theories were falling into discredit and disfavor, first among intellectuals and then among political elites. Outside of the South, the Ku Klux Klan steadily lost support and members. Even within the South, official resistance to integration began to appeal not to racial arguments but to "local tradition" and states' rights. Fears of race mixing as a threat to "Anglo-Saxon democracy" were now banished to the hinterland and the margins of American society.[21] But at the same time that racial theories lost their power to explain "the American character," a new social psychological one appeared that would prove crucial to multiculturalism: identity theory.

The modern notion of identity takes its force from the same Romantic rejection of material progress that spawned a belief in the vital power of *Kultur*. The notion that individual identity is rooted in some unique personal self had no place in the early Enlightenment. For Voltaire, David Hume, and Adam Smith, personality develops from the interactions between social life and our innate rational faculties and moral sentiments. Civil society theory held that the human being is who he is because he is both a rational and a social animal. Hume compared the mind to a theater in which multiple characters move back and forth; diversity was something experienced on the inside rather than on the outside. "Identity" simply referred to the individual's realization that, regardless of these inner changes, he is the same person throughout.[22]

To the German and English Romantics, this cut-and-dried picture sacrificed man's organic and vital connections with nature and his own physical being. As a result, the poet Wordsworth and others warned, the human being becomes an emotionless, affectless machine (not unlike Marx's alienated worker), his life entirely determined by the circumstances around him. He becomes superficial, empty, and weak, easily led by the wishes and desires of others—what the Enlightenment had called "manners." German critics like Paul de Lagarde said that the individual produced entirely by society's manners lacked depth; Nietzsche called him an emotional cripple. Sociologists like David Riesman would later describe him as the "other-directed personality." Instead, man must be reunited with his true identity, an inner self or ego in which, as Freud argued, the vital springs of Eros resist all social formation.[23]

In the forties Freud's disciple Erik Erikson popularized the term "identity formation" to describe the interaction between this irreducible, directing/choosing ego and the demands placed on the personality by society and others. The healthy personality, that is, the well-formed identity, is built on a balance between the two. "Identity is responsible for the individual's maintaining an inner solidarity with the ideals and aspirations of social groups," Erikson stated, while at the same time preserving his sense of uniqueness.[24] But at crucial historical junctures, Erikson warned, the needs of the self and those of society will stand in opposition. The result is an "identity crisis." Erikson predicted that these identity crises will be particularly acute in modern society, because rapid economic and social changes, which vastly expand the range of new opportunities for individuals, also demand "self-made identities ready to grasp many choices" or social roles.

A series of American sociologists* took up the theme of identity and self-image in their writings in the fifties, while others looked for other models to explain how modern society affects the individual's sense of identity. Inevitably the discussion forced scholars to take a new look at the challenges that old and new immigrant groups had faced in adapting to an alien American environment and modern social and economic realities. Will Herberg's *Protestant Catholic Jew* moved the issue of identity and "ethnicity," as this pre-Americanized identity was now being called, to front and center. However much he may be pushed into the maelstrom of modern American society, Herberg argued, the immigrant will—indeed must—retain some form of "social identification" with his original ethnic group as a matter of self-preservation. The melting pot had become a "triple melting pot." "To be a Protestant, a Catholic, or a Jew," Herberg said, "are today the alternative ways of being an American."[25]

Erik Erikson himself (who was a refugee from Nazi Germany) stressed that American society could liberate the outsider from prior "tribal" and national identifications. At the same time it could also push certain groups beyond their ability to cope and adapt; the examples he turned to were Sioux Indians and American blacks. In fact, the distance from

---

*Including David Riesman's *The Lonely Crowd*, Irving Goffman's *Presentation of Self in Everyday Life*, Colin Wilson's *The Outsider*, Anselm Strauss's *Mirrors and Masks: The Search for Identity*, and Will Herberg's *Protestant Catholic Jew*.

Erik Erikson and modern man's identity crisis to Erich Fromm and capitalism's systematic creation of dysfunctional selves or "identities" was small.

By the sixties the American melting pot seemed more and more the enemy of identity: modern American society's most celebrated characteristics—its promise of personal material success, its mobility, its unparalleled opportunities for personal freedom—undermined the stability of self. Identity, as one sociology textbook of the time explained, was "all the things a person may legitimately and reliably say about himself—his status, his name, his personality, his past life." But that identity cannot survive a rapidly changing social context—modernity's swirl of alienation, frustration, and depersonalization. "If the social context is unreliable, it follows that he cannot say anything legitimately and reliably about himself." He will be forced to rely on the evaluations of others, which are just as unreliable and, most importantly, reflect the needs of others rather of the person himself.[26]

Particularly if he is black. Liberal sociologists, beginning with Erikson himself, all agreed that the central problem for American Negroes was possessing "self-esteem" in a society that treated him as inferior and dealt a mortal blow to his identity formation even in the best of circumstances. Thomas Pettigrew's 1964 *Profile of the American Negro* focused almost entirely on the issue of social psychology. For the Negro, life in America is a "rude jolt" and a series of "identity-shocks" in which he feels himself to be thoroughly American in thought and manner but is constantly devalued in the eyes of others. Although he believes in equality of opportunity and the American Dream as much as anyone else, Pettigrew pointed out, in the media and everyday life he sees only whites enjoying success and status and his fellow blacks reduced to shining shoes and holding the towel in men's rooms. Given the evident contradictions in his own life and the lack of "positive role models" (as they would later be called), he is forced to believe himself to be inferior, regardless of the success of integration. Jonathan Kozol even argued that mainstream American education represented "a sentence of death" for Negroes because of its implicitly racist bias and disregard for their sense of identity and group consciousness.[27]

A host of black writers joined the chorus. Ralph Ellison, Richard

Wright, and James Baldwin had been exposed to Frantz Fanon and to Sartre's notions of authenticity and Being-for-Itself versus Being-for-Others. They now insisted that the black man in America, like Frantz Fanon's black in French colonial Africa, is forced to wear a mask, an identity that is not his own but is assigned by whites.* The Negro's authentic sense of self has been taken away, Wright and others argued, by the need of white racism to keep him in a subordinate position. James Baldwin even argued that whites would never be able to admit blacks to true equality because that would destroy *their* identity, constructed on the myth of racial superiority.[28]

Although Pettigrew, James Baldwin, and others stressed the unique experience of American Negroes, their claims about loss of identity served as the basic paradigm for all the discussions of identity and multiculturalism that were to come. By definition the social forces distorting the identity of Negroes were not limited to blacks, any more than Marx's theory of alienation was limited to workers. According to Baldwin, blacks fully recognize what white Americans only dimly perceive, that the American Dream is actually a nightmare of alienation, violence, and a struggle for superiority in which "identity is almost impossible to achieve and people are perpetually attempting to find their feet on the shifting sands of status."

Baldwin argued that the American Negro and his rebellion against meaninglessness through drugs, crime, and (by 1965) riots makes him "the key figure in his country" because he reveals a fundamental human truth: "This depthless alienation from oneself and one's people, is, in sum, the American experience."[29] Radical theorist and educator Edgar Z. Friedenberg even turned this fear of alienation into an argument for integration. Assimilating its blacks, he charged, gave American society its last chance "to transfuse into itself a stream of people whose moral vision has been . . . preserved and sharpened by exclusion from [the] opportunities for self-betrayal and self-advancement" that capitalism had forced upon everyone else.[30] To racial pessimists at the turn of the century, the presence of the Negro had threatened national degeneration

---

*The influence of this view can be assessed in the use of the terms "mask" and "identity" in Shelby Steele's *Content of Our Character* (1990).

through race suicide. To cultural pessimists in the sixties and seventies, his presence seemed the last hope for *preventing* national degeneration through capitalist civilization.

In 1959, Norman Mailer penned a prophetic essay for *Esquire* magazine entitled "The White Negro." It was a paean of praise to the Beat Generation and Greenwich Village hipsters, the precursors of what would later be termed, "the counterculture." Mailer pronounced them rebels against civilization's "Faustian urge to dominate nature." They rebelled, he said, through the orgiastic release of their own vital natures by means of jazz, sex, drugs, and crime. Their model was the Negro, who survived in oppressive white society by "following the needs of his body" and living "for his Saturday night kicks." The American Negro "kept for his survival the art of the primitive," which could serve as a model of survival for whites as well. "In this wedding of the white and the black," Mailer said, "it was the Negro who provided the cultural dowry." By living for the moment, through their "burning consciousness of the present" as opposed to a tradition-bound past or a progress-ordered future, the Negro and the hipster shared the same vitalist will to power as "the existentialist, the psychopath, the saint, the bullfighter, and the lover."[31]

Mailer's Negro lived in a realm of Nietzschean nihilism, of Being-for-Itself. Other commentators, however, saw the Negro's future in more volkish terms. Escape from a corrupting mainstream American culture meant doing what Herberg and others seemed to be saying ethnic groups like Jews and Italians were doing: turning to a prior identity in order to discover one's "roots." Writers like Ralph Ellison and sociologists like Joyce Ladner had extolled a rich and vibrant black cultural identity at the same time that they argued for integration and assimilation with white Americans. However, the most important formative element of this black identity was essentially negative: a long, wretched history of chattel slavery, racist violence, and W.E.B. Du Bois's longing for a lost community in Africa. The American black identity was an identity forged in fire and blood—not unlike the Romantic German nationalism Du Bois had encountered in the 1890s.

Du Bois himself became a fashionable figure among young black intellectuals. The murder of Martin Luther King, Jr., in 1968 and frustration with the lack of progress in integration led a new generation of black leaders to look for alternatives. Black radicals turned to both Du

Bois and Marcus Garvey, who had argued that American blacks could never be fully equal to whites until they had built their own separate black community. Malcolm X pointed the way toward this resegregation of American society, and his murder in 1967 made him a martyr for the new black separatist radicals. Roy Innis, like Garvey a black West Indian, pushed the Committee on Racial Equality (CORE) toward a program of black separatism over the protests of its original president, James Farmer. Another West Indian, Stokely Carmichael, did the same with the Student Nonviolent Coordinating Committee, or SNCC. Carmichael emulated the Black Muslims (who were already heavily imbued with Garveyite ideas) and borrowed their slogan "Black is beautiful" and their phrase "soul brother" as part of a new political agenda, Black Power.

As a result the question of black identity moved in a direction neither Erikson nor Herberg could have predicted—nor, given Erikson's own experience in fascist Germany, was it one they would have approved. Stokely Carmichael defined Black Power as "a call for black people in this country to unite, to recognize their heritage, and to build a sense of community." In order to become an effective political force in the United States, he contended, blacks must achieve "self-identity" and "self-determination" as a group, not as individuals. The result would be a rising black consciousness, "an attitude of brotherly, communal responsibility among all black people for one another."[32]

But Black Power also meant "that black people see themselves as part of a new force, sometimes called 'the Third World,' that we see our struggle as closely related to liberation struggles around the world." Carmichael quoted Fanon's pronouncement that "the United States of America has become a monster, in which the taints, the sickness, and the inhumanity of Europe have grown to appalling dimensions."[33] Black America must realize, Carmichael wrote, that it is in effect a colony of white America. The urban ghetto exists because it offers "opportunities for profit" for parasitic white businessmen, sociologist Kenneth B. Clark had argued in *The Dark Ghetto*, reinforcing Carmichael's colonialist model.* In the face of black resistance, "whites tend to view their inter-

---

*The similarities to Hobson's parasitic empire are striking. Later, those parasites on the black ghetto would turn out to be the Jews and, still later, the Koreans.

ests in a particularly united, solidified way," forming what Carmichael (echoing C. Wright Mills) called "the white power structure." Blacks must now form the same unified political movement, he insisted.

Its character would be familiar to any reader of Werner Sombart or Arthur Moeller van den Bruck. True black *Kultur* rejects all white bourgeois standards, since "the values of that class are in themselves antihumanist" and racist; in fact, any black person who adopts "American middle class standards and values" ceases to be black.[34] It rejects liberalism with its mealymouthed belief in compromise and interracial unity, and it rejects capitalism, looking instead to build a community based "on free people, not free enterprise." Black Power also reflected the Garveyite perspective that blackness could be a vehicle for mass mobilization and the destruction of a decadent white civilization. Carmichael urged blacks to "create new values" in Heidegger's sense. Like his counterparts in the German revolution on the Right, Carmichael saw his own era as "a time of dynamism" in which new forms of authority and power must be substituted for old. The rise of the Black Power movement would sweep away the "outmoded structures and institutions" of the past, Carmichael predicted, including racism. Its motto would be "Modernization, not moderation."[35]

Carmichael's volkish black nationalism and creation of new values required, as the Black Muslims insisted, shedding a false enslaving identity for a true (i.e., authentic) one rooted in black Africa. This included shedding that most obvious sign of identity, one's name. So just as Malcolm Little dropped his "slave name" for a simple X, representing his lack of identity in a white racist society, the boxer Cassius Clay reemerged as Muhammad Ali, the basketball star Lew Alcindor as Kareem Abdul Jabbar, and the beat poet LeRoi Jones as Imamu Amiri Baraka (ignoring for the moment that Islamic names reflected an identity imposed by an earlier slave-owning elite, the Arabs). Carmichael himself became Kwame Touré, after two African dictators of the sixties, Sekou Touré of Guinea and Du Bois's failed Pan-African savior, Kwame Nkrumah.

Despite hopes for a revolutionary mass movement, Black Power remained as much a matter of personal cultural identity as political power. It provided the individual with the same message as its German volkish or French Negritude counterparts: any assimilation into mainstream civilization threatens one's vital and organic group identity. The aim of white society, Negritude author Alioune Diop reminded readers, was "to make the individual . . . torn from the background natural to him and which brought out his own personality, agree to replace his habits of thinking, feeling, and acting by others," the false values of an alien white community.[36] In opposition to this cultural usurpation, Black Power adopted as its slogan Du Bois's term "soul," without reflecting much on its affinity with German racial ideologies and Nazi *Kultur*.

Instead, the new black identity was presented in the familiar form of American evangelical Christianity. In 1970 the black psychologist William Cross, in an often-quoted paper, described the individual's transition from Negro to black identity in quasi-religious terms, as a conversion. However, its specific elements were all taken directly from the German tradition of cultural pessimism. Cross stated that the Negro who identifies with mainstream American values is politically naive, a believer in the Protestant work ethic, dependent on white authority figures or role models, and conformist in his social and religious habits. In short, he is Adorno's authoritarian personality in black skin, the Uncle Tom stereotype that applied to Martin Luther King, Jr., (whom black radicals, we must remember, despised with a passion) as well as to Clarence Thomas. This deracinated Negro prefers to be called an American citizen or a "civilized" human being, rather than what he is, a black person.

However, as the truth of his situation is explained to him by his black peers, he undergoes the crucial change. "His heart pounding, hands sweating, and eyes filled with tears, the person speaks for the first time the magic words: 'Black is beautiful.' " He realizes he has been brainwashed by his true enemy, the white man. "Black rage" is the result, inspiring an obsessive search for his true or authentic identity, which has been buried by his white enemies. A "Negro is dying," Cross exclaimed, "and a Black American is being resurrected."[37]

The result is a startling transformation. He enjoys a rebirth of vitality that reads like a combination of Ernst Haeckel and Erich Fromm. He is now creative ("professional artists speak of a profound and fundamental change in the quality of their work"), imaginative, and politically active. "The person shifts from a preference for individualism to mutualism or collectivism. A constant theme of selflessness, dedication, and commitment is evident." He is overwhelmed with feelings of self-love and self-esteem, as well as love for others, since his old Western identity "suppressed affective outputs." His sense of community with other blacks is affirmed as he addresses them as "brothers" and "sisters," a community built not on rational self-interest (as in the American political community) but on affective bonds. His new heroes are Malcolm X, W.E.B. Du Bois, Marcus Garvey, Angela Davis—and Frantz Fanon.

He also prepares for political mobilization in accordance with his new self-image. Although he recognizes that violent revolution on the total scale preached by Fanon is not feasible in America, he will forthrightly adopt a rhetoric that involves "confrontation, bluntness, and directness" in dealing with his former white oppressors and asserting his new and vital self-image. Verbal violence as a form of cultural vitality overlaps with physical violence as part of the same black anti-Western *Kultur*. Turning the pages of Eldrige Cleaver's *Soul on Ice*, George Jackson's *Soledad Brother*, or the poetry of LeRoi Jones, one meets with a delight in violence both as a cleansing, purifying process (as in Frantz Fanon's "holy violence") *and* as an affirmation of vital cultural identity. The black inner-city criminal thug took on the glamorous image of Frantz Fanon's *fellah* or revolutionary guerrilla cadre, as urban street gangs reorganized themselves as the Black Panthers. In a notorious passage, Norman Mailer had even praised the vitalism and "courage" of these hoodlums when they murder neighborhood store owners. "For one murders not only a weak fifty-year-old man," he wrote, "but an institution as well," namely, private property. Mailer concluded that "the hoodlum is therefore daring the unknown, and no matter how brutal the act, it is not altogether cowardly."[38]

The formerly degenerate urban criminal had now been turned into the vital urban guerrilla. The convicted California murderer George Jackson saw Fanon's invocations of violence as perfectly appropriate for combating racism in the United States, which he, like other radicals, now dubbed "Amerika" to underline American society's alleged affinities with Nazi Germany. "Violence is not supposed to work in Amerika," Jackson said. "Why not? A bullet fired from an assault rifle in the hands of a Vietnamese liberation fighter will kill a pig in Vietnam. Why won't it kill a pig in the place where pigs are made?" Nor did Jackson neglect the declinist dimension:

Western civilization is dying because it's tied to an economic system that was decadent a hundred years ago. . . . Its seemingly remarkable ability to return from crisis is not proof of natural durability. Rather it is proof of a destructive will to power at any cost.[39]

For Jackson, Cleaver, and other Black Power extremists, black violence reflected a vitalism that was also, as it was for Nietzsche and the German Expressionists, a breakthrough to reality. "The magic dance in the street," according to LeRoi Jones. "Run up and down Broad Street niggers take the shit you want. All the stores will open if you will say the magic words. The magic words are: Up against the wall mother fucker this is a stick up! . . . Our brothers are moving all over, smashing at jellywhite faces. We must make our own World, man, our real world, and we can not do this unless the white man is dead."[40]

In the last analysis, this stereotyped image of American culture as "sick" owed its existence to critics from the New Left.* America now displayed all the characteristics of a decadent modernity, or *Zivilisation*, as well as a decaying Faustian empire. Noam Chomsky, Michael Parenti, Richard Barnet, and Richard Slotkin all explained that American culture glorified violence, imperialism, and genocide. It practiced a vicious form of capitalism and technological repression (described by Leo Marx in *The Machine in the Garden*), a bankrupt liberalism (scathingly criticized by Roberto Unger), a manipulative consumerism (laid bare by Christopher Lasch and William Leach), as well as racism and a hatred of *all* minorities and subordinate groups. Not only blacks but American Indians, Jews, Chinese, Japanese, Mexicans, Hispanics, and women suffered unendurable humiliations at the hands of mainstream American society.[41]

In this sense it was a typical Western society. In 1979 critic Edward Said explained that all of Western culture was a culture of imperialism. A disciple of Foucault, Chomsky, and the Frankfurt School—he quotes Adorno as well as Fanon in his later works—Said proposed that the entire West since the Enlightenment formed a vast totalizing "discourse on the Other," which is to say on nonwhite peoples. The American and European imperialist adventures of the nineteenth century were prepared

---

*Cf. George Jackson's angry Marcuse-like outburst: "What can we do with a people who have gone through the authoritarian process and come out sick to the core?!!"

well ahead of time, both in an institutional and a moral sense. "Race theory, ideas about primitive origins and primitive classifications, modern decadence, the progress of civilization, the destiny of the white (or Aryan) races, the need for colonial territories—all these were elements" in Said's view of "an imposing edifice of learning and culture" created in order to "raise Europe or a European race to dominion over non-European portions of mankind"—as well as over women, the poor, the insane, and the delinquent *inside* Europe.

The West sees the world exclusively in terms of "a rigidly binomial opposition of 'ours and theirs,' " or the Self against the Other. In modern times, Said charged, "this opposition was reinforced not only by anthropology, linguistics, and history, but . . . by the rhetoric of high cultural humanism." The negativizing, totalizing "Western gaze . . . shuts out even as it includes, compresses, and consolidates." In the end, *no* Western discourse about blacks, Arabs, Vietnamese, or American Indians is possible without inevitably invoking this European impulse to subordinate, control, and slaughter. Even reading about the Bedouins or Africans in a standard anthropological text or history book, Said implies, moves us one step closer to wanting to kill them.[42]

Said's views proved immensely influential, implying, among other things, that all histories written by Westerners shared a single negativizing perspective. From Gibbon to Toynbee, the entire enterprise had been only an imperialist sham. Nonwhites now required a new kind of universal history that would enable them to escape Western "structures of violence and violation" but would also rescript the history of the West in accordance with the canons of cultural pessimism.

## MULTICULTURAL HISTORIES: FROM MIRRORS TO APOCALYPSE

Americanization on the old melting pot model, for example, now looked like a deliberate process of cultural genocide—"genocide" because it destroyed group identities and hence the soul.[43] By the mid-eighties the first multiculturalist historians were writing racialized accounts of American civilization that turned Madison Grant inside out. The United States was indeed the original foundation of a white Aryan Anglo-Saxon cultural hegemony—along with its attendant racist myths. Everyone who was not a White Protestant male had been systematically denied any identity in American society, since (and Gobineau and Nietzsche would have agreed) all ruling classes construct their civilization according to their own self-image. The views of a Henry Adams regarding Jews, of a Lothrop Stoddard regarding Italians and eastern European immigrants, or of an Ernest Siever Cox regarding blacks turned out to be not dissident visions of American civilization (as their holders thought them to be), but typical and representative.

Historian Gary B. Nash described the arrival of European colonists in North America as a stark clash of cultural identities. Indian tribes like the Iroquois lived a cultural ideal very different from (and, Nash implies, far superior to) that of the white interlopers. "The European idea of male dominance and female subordination in all things was conspicuously absent in Iroquois society." Men and women functioned as comparative equals, Nash asserted.*[44] The Native American was an "autonomous individual" who was "loyal to the group but independent and aloof." Nash quoted an early-nineteenth-century Quaker's claim that among the Iroquois, "liberty in its fullest extent becomes their ruling passion." The Iroquois warrior turns out to be Houston Stewart Chamberlain's Teuton, with an instinct for loyalty combined with a love of freedom.[45] If the Iroquois practiced an early form of egalitarian socialism, white Europeans, by contrast, were acquisitive, competitive, and obsessed with their own self-interest and personal ambition. Native American culture emphasized "the band, lineage, and community," and the autonomy of the individual was balanced by a sense of "social responsibility." In European culture selfish, possessive individualism reigns supreme.

Nash's frontier, like Turner's, served to unleash American vitality, with disastrous results. The scramble for land in the rapidly expanding American empire broke the last remaining European constraints on acquisitive culture, such as Puritanism. "Having gained something [by settling in North America]," Nash writes, "the typical colonist wanted more." However, this desire for more was not unique to America, Nash concedes, but formed part of the entire modern Western outlook. Similar developments streamed out of Enlightenment Europe, with its "new

---

*Nash claims, for example, that women played "an important part" in war-making, citing as proof that women made the moccasins and foodstuffs for warring expeditions.

model of economic and social life" based on "the notion that the market mentality was preferable to the older corporate society of persons finely attuned to the public good." In other words, *Gemeinschaft* had yielded to capitalist *Gesellschaft*, corrupting the American spirit from the start.[46]

"A competitive, entrepreneurial spirit began to take hold" in America, bringing "a material success that contained within it the seeds of social strain," with inequalities of wealth among whites as well as between whites and nonwhites, particularly black slaves. However, where these other groups lagged in material success they triumphed in cultural vitality, infusing American culture with their racial seed and values (Negro music and dialect, Native American material culture) and making it distinct from its European counterpart.

The dean of American multicultural historians, Ronald Takaki, presents a grand synthesis of these cultural pessimist themes. The progress of American history is the construction of a routinizing, totalizing, racist capitalist hegemony, which Takaki sees (borrowing from Max Weber) as a series of cultural iron cages. "As white men in power separated themselves from the king in the War of Independence," he states, they constructed a new political identity, becoming repressed, affectless "republican machines" who proceeded to wreak havoc on themselves as well as others.

All of Takaki's representative American figures—Thomas Jefferson, Benjamin Rush, Andrew Jackson, and George Custer—appear as classic degenerates, sexually twisted and driven by dark obsessions and profound psychological weaknesses. The American founders were sick in mind and body, Takaki implies, while their "external aggressiveness signified inner torment." By stealing Indian and Mexican lands and exploiting black and Asian labor, white Anglo-Saxons created a monstrous industrial and imperialist order. Brooks Adams's quasi-fascist "new empire" turns out to be not a reactionary crank's last fantasy but the ironclad heart of American civilization. "Demonic in force and nature," Takaki concludes, "it took them into an irrational quest for power and destruction."[47]

All the while non-Wasps, "the vast surging, hopeful army of workers—men and women of all races and ethnicities—were denied the class consciousness, the feeling of community, and the power of collective action"—in short, denied a sense of identity—by the insidious lie that American civilization rested on individual equality of opportunity rather than group solidarity. Like Du Bois, Takaki sees racism and capitalism as historical allies, not antagonists, and unlike Herberg, Nathan Glazer, and earlier students of ethnicity, he no longer distinguishes the self shaped by American society from the prior self rooted in ethnicity. Both are, in Foucault's terms, "historicized," that is, they are the predetermined products of a particular time and place—the experience of oppression and exclusion.

Exclusion is a key concept for multiculturalist history. The exclusion of nonwhites and nonmales in American and Western society made them *invisible*; the task of traditional American history, Takai assures us, was to keep them invisible. It did this by focusing on institutions, such as politics and economics, that were dominated by white males—thus confirming their own identity at the expense of others. The multicultural scholar must now render those excluded groups visible and restore their lost identities. Ronald Takaki remarks, "What Gloria Steinem termed the 'revolution from within' must ultimately be grounded in unlearning much of what we have been told about America's past and substituting a more *inclusive* and accurate history of all the peoples of America." Inclusion in turn requires holding up a "different mirror of history" to nonwhites, one that reflects their collective experience of oppression and exclusion.[48]

To the trained multiculturalist, Western strategies of exclusion enjoy a subtlety and complexity that seem to defy credulity. The West's racism and "construction of race" turn out to be its most crucial characteristics, even if race is not being explicitly discussed. Paul Gilroy, for example, argues that the entire history of modern Britain is an elaborate attempt on the part of whites to *avoid* discussing the multitudes of nonwhite Asians and Africans who inhabited their empire. The black American novelist Toni Morrison can assert that "in virtually all of this nation's great debates, nonwhites and women figure powerfully, although their presence may be disguised, denied, or obliterated."[49] The very fact that nonwhites and nonheterosexual males are not mentioned in traditional histories or textbooks becomes proof of how important they actually were. As Edward Said explained, and as Du Bois had hinted decades before, modern Western culture is really about imperialism and exclusion, even when it is not.

An inclusive history of America brings forward virtually every separate ethnic identity to be found in American society. (Takaki even solemnly notes the Iroquois League's declaration of war against Germany, Italy, and Japan during World War II as proof of their autonomous opposition to fascism.[50]) Every identity, that is, except Anglo-Saxon whites. Maya Angelou's 1992 Inauguration Day poem, "On the Pulse of Morning," mentions the Irish, Scandinavians, blacks, women, Hispanics, Native Americans, West Indians—everyone except the ethnic group that originally created the American republic. History as diversity, then, comes to mean a "reverse exclusion": pushing Anglo-Saxon white males and their institutions out of memory, or at least showing them to be dependent on those groups that have been subordinated to their cultural and political control.[51]

The ongoing task of inclusion involves a radical shift, not just in a political sense but in the view of America as a social-cultural enterprise. Takaki's multiculturalist history, for example, is not about different ethnic groups succeeding in reaching the American Dream but about their failure to do so—and it embraces that failure, which protects the individual against absorption into the demonic iron cages that form American civilization.*[52] To serious advocates like Stanley Aronowitz, the multiculturalist revolution includes abandoning all notions of American citizenship or of equating "the United States with what freedom and democracy really signify."

Instead, persons must learn to opt for "cultural citizenship," in which a subgroup identity (black, woman, Latino) serves as an escape from narrow and oppressive American cultural structures. This in turn frees the individual to identify with subgroups in other countries (such as Africa or Mexico) or to partake of "international women's solidarity." "In short," Aronowitz asserts, "cultural citizenship signifies a community of the oppressed and a statement that the nation-state [such as the United States of America] is symbolic of the oppressor."[53] Similarly, Toni Morrison expresses perplexity that "Jews in this country, by and large,

---

*This is one reason why Takaki furiously denies any evidence that Asian Americans have managed to succeed in American life: their success would not only undermine his claim that the United States is an irremediably racist society, but would also destroy their Korean, Chinese, and Japanese identities by making them Americans—once again, a collective act of cultural genocide.

have become white. They behave like white people rather than Jewish people."[54]

The whole point of studying multicultural American history for ethnic groups and subgroups is to learn about their identity, not as rational creatures faced by contingency ("I can be anyone I want to be") but as part of communities shaped by historical necessity ("I am who I always had to be"). The individual exchanges a conformist-style American individualism for an individualism built on a "counterhegemonic" identity. He no longer has to believe in an organic "essentialism" undergirding that identity; it is enough merely to be recognizable as one of the oppressed in order to generate an anti-Western self. For the original subcultural group in racist America, blacks, this means the emergence of a vital black culture that takes its cue from opposition to the desiccated white one. To sociologist Thomas Kochman, American blacks turn out to be more ostentatious, physical, spontaneous, spiritual, and emotionally committed than their white counterparts. In Nietzschean terms, ironically, it is the ex-masters who exhibit a lifeless slave morality and the ex-slave who exemplifies Nietzsche's master morality.*[55]

Black Studies guru Houston Baker has defended rap music in the same terms. "Rap is like a rich stock garnered from the sudden simmering of titanic B-boy/B-girl energies. Such energies were diffused over black cityscapes." Baker also describes the same energy in "wilding," and in the murderous mass rape of a white female jogger in Central Park in 1987, as the vital overthrow of the white man's attempt to tame nature by constructing a park in the first place. Just as in *The Genealogy of Morals* Nietzsche's blond beast emerges "from a disgusting procession of murder, arson, rape, and torture, exhilarated and undisturbed of soul, as if it were no more than a student's prank," so do young blacks joyfully bring the reality of terror to the white power structure (as Nietzsche wrote, "That lambs dislike great birds of prey does not seem strange").[56]

This vital black identity, however, now intersects with the identities of other oppressed, exploited, and dominated groups. Joyce Ladner ar-

---

*Although Kochman presents Nietzsche's "exalted, proud states of the soul" in dry sociological language: "The hand-to-hand exchange that blacks call 'giving skin' is invigorated by its connection to inner impulses and feelings and one's spiritual connection with others in the group."

gued in the sixties that preserving black identity would be most crucial for black women, since they had suffered most from exploitation and slavery. Hence, writers Toni Morrison, Rita Dove, and Maya Angelou present themselves not only as black writers, but as black women writers; Nikki Giovanni is not only a black woman writer, but a black lesbian writer; while Audre Lord is not only a black woman and a black lesbian writer, but a black lesbian writer of West Indian descent: a total of four historicized "subaltern" identities (five if one includes poet/intellectual).[57]

With the proliferation of intersecting counterhegemonic identities also comes the possibility of conflict with other recognized elements of the oppressed that reflect one or another element of white "patriarchalist" *Zivilisation*. Bell Hooks, for example, defines for herself a black feminism separate from white feminism. Since the majority of college-educated liberal feminists are also participants in the white capitalist order, she observes, it is not surprising that "much feminist literature . . . is both racist and sexist in its content" and fails to recognize the special victimized position of black women since slavery. The same applies to black males. "Men of *all* races in America bond on the basis of their common belief that a patriarchal social order is the only viable foundation of society." But now, Hooks happily proclaims, that order is in a state of "slow ideological and material collapse." About to vanish, she predicts, are "the White supremacist patriarchal family structure as we have historically known it" and the structures of domination it generated.[58]

So while the multicultural revolution in America is unmistakably a revolution on the Left, its dominant images of change still come from the earlier revolution on the Right. Vital *Kultur* will reemerge from the ruins of *Zivilisation* as new multicultural identities replace the old. Of course, a new type of political and legal system must replace the old one, but this too involves more than just the transition from capitalism to socialism. According to Du Bois biographer Manning Marable, "multicultural democracy demands new types of power-sharing." Majority rule must be abandoned, since historically it was merely a ploy for maintaining traditional white hegemony (as in Lani Guinier's *Tyranny of the Majority*). Multicultural democracy also involves "the re-allocation of resources necessary to create economic and social development for those who have been systematically excluded and denied"—which means the redistributive welfare state.[59]

At the same time, the relation between the old and new orders remains a matter of cultural shift, not violent overthrow—in this sense, Sartre would recognize multiculturalism as part of the "long movement in which power is dismantled." Edward Said has suggested that simply by recognizing "the complete centrality of the West . . . how totalizing is its form, how all-enveloping its attitudes and gestures, how it shuts out even as it includes, compresses, and consolidates," it becomes possible to undermine its ideological foundations. This also requires a Toynbee-like recognition on the part of whites that their day—and their culture—is done. "Some day soon, surely much sooner than most people realize, white Americans will become a minority group," author Ellis Cose claims. This must force a healthy Nietzschean-style revaluation of all values, he insists, including the traditional view of America as a melting pot. If America's most pressing problem to E.A. Ross was race suicide, to Cose it is "race sickness"— meaning the insistence on a uniform American cultural identity.[60]

For commentators like Ellis Cose and Andrew Hacker, the alternative is catastrophe. Since Du Bois, critics of American race relations have always conjured up the image of an apocalyptic racial war plunging the nation into the abyss—Garvey, Ernest Siever Cox, Elijah Mohammed have all played with the same language of a racial Armageddon. Cornel West pays a deeper and more self-conscious tribute to this apocalyptic heritage in *Race Matters*. He assures us that we are indeed "passing through a time as horrifying as any experienced in this country. We live in a time of cultural disarray and social decay, an age filled with ruins and fragments." He takes a grim pleasure in describing how white *Zivilisation*, that is, American capitalist society, is swiftly unraveling, its arrogance humbled and the forces of reaction (Reagan, Bush, William Bennett) doomed to destruction. But from those "ruins and fragments," Cornel West concludes, must and will arise a new recognition of the need for racial equity and social justice. The result will be a new "politics of conversion," in which whites and nonwhites will draw together in "dramatic narratives of reconciliation." West denies that his hopes are naive or utopian; however, he does move the future of multicultural America from a vitalist transvaluation of values to the rule of the saints from the Book of Revelation.

This is not surprising, given his own fascination with the black American religious tradition. West describes himself as a "prophetic Christian freedom fighter," even though Christian religious traditions themselves "are, for the most part, reactionary or repressive, and repulsive." Instead, what attracts him to Christianity is precisely its apocalyptic force, which defines history from the perspective of the excluded victim. "The culture of the wretched of the earth," West says, "is religious," that is to say apocalyptic, revealing to believers why and how the oppressed will overcome their oppressors and obliterate their secular power.

The prophetic-apocalyptic view of history also undercuts any notion that material progress points the way to social progress; or that economic freedom might be a prerequisite for other types of freedom; or that genuine human progress involves men and women assuming some responsibility for their own fate. As a self-professed Marxist and a multiculturalist prophet, West prefers a future in which a multiracial and socialist Zion replaces the bankrupt Babylon of materialist and capitalist America, like Saint Augustine's eternal city of God replacing a vanquished Rome:

> That most glorious society and celestial city of God's faithful, which is partly seated in the course of these declining times ... is a pilgrim amongst the wicked ... until 'righteousness be turned into judgment' [and] by that obtains the last victory, and is crowned in the perfection of peace.[61]


## REVERSING THE POLES: AFROCENTRISM

At this point we leave Africa, not to mention it again. For it is no historical part of the world, it has no movement or development to exhibit.
    —G.F. Hegel, 1830

Every race has its soul and every soul its race.
    —Alfred Rosenberg, 1930

In the case of Cornel West, the multiculturalist revolt reveals something unexpected. In trying to escape the murderous grip of Western civilization and its false promises of progress, one turns to other, earlier (if unavoidably Western) views of history—particularly those that see man not as freed by history as a secular process but trapped by it. All the West is corruption because all history is ultimately corruption. *Homo ethnicus* is, like Saint Augustine's Christian and Cornel West's black American, "a pilgrim amongst the wicked." He finds himself wandering past institutions, "ruins and fragments," with which he has no meaningful connection. Like medieval or ancient man, he is profoundly timebound. While waiting for some great millennial breakthrough, he must struggle against blind Fate, of which the modern West turns out to be only one aspect. The best example of this sense of being adrift, or bound to Fortune's wheel, is the contemporary Afrocentrist movement.

The origins of Afrocentrism lie deep in Romantic primitivism: its acknowledged godfather is, surprisingly, not some strident black nationalist or African scholar in exile but Napoleon's aristocratic companion on his expedition to Egypt, Constantine de Volney. In his *Ruins* Volney speculated that the original home of monotheism, Thebes, was not originally part of Egypt but of the ancient kingdom of Ethiopia. "There a people, now forgotten, discovered, while others were yet barbarians, the elements of the arts and sciences; a race of men now rejected from society for their *sable skin and frizzled hair*, founded those civil and religious systems which still govern the universe."[62]

Volney's vision of an ancient community of black men guarding a superior esoteric knowledge strongly resounded in nineteenth-century black nationalism. It inspired James Pennington and Hosea Easton to envision a mighty black Ethiopian civilization predating the emergence of Europe from barbarism. In 1848 black nationalist Henry H. Garnet announced that "when these representatives of our race were filling the world with amazement, the ancestors of the now proud and boasting Anglo-Saxons . . . abode in caves underground, either naked or covered with the skins of wild animals."[63]

At the same time, the impenetrability of the African continent had prevented Europeans from discovering the treasures and ruins of ancient Africa until late in the century; for this reason, Africa had played almost no part in the Orientalist imagination.[64] Then, in 1851, Heinrich Barth became the first Western traveler to visit Timbuktu, and the translation of African Arabic texts began. Largely ignored by European scholars, these discoveries encouraged black scholars such as Pennington and Easton, who could now refute the claims of "race scientists" like

Josiah Nott that Negroes were incapable of civilization because they had never produced one.

The claim that Ethiopia and Egypt were both black civilizations had been circulating for nearly sixty years when W.E.B. Du Bois wrote his Pan-Africanist tract, *The Negro*. In 1939 Du Bois reissued *The Negro* under the title of *Black Folk Then and Now* and included a lengthy section on the black origins of Egyptian civilization. Du Bois was now convinced that Egypt served as the crucial starting point or "cradle" not only of Western civilization but of black history as well. These speculations reached Paris in the twenties via the Harlem Renaissance, as American expatriates Alain Locke and Claude McKay spread the idea of "the New Negro," as well as other aspects of Du Bois's work, to the French-speaking black poets and writers who would later form the Negritude movement.[65]

Then, in 1948, came the appearance of *Black Orpheus*, in which Sartre created the image of a resurgent black African civilization throwing off its white oppressors and their technological capitalist culture. However, *Black Orpheus* prompted a split within the Negritude movement itself. One faction, including Aimé Césaire and Frantz Fanon, followed Sartre's revolutionary Marxism. The other rejected the clamor for a Marxist revolution to begin in the colonies as just another form of cultural subordination. Its spokesman, the Senegalese student Cheikh Anta Diop, turned instead to a radical Pan-Africanism with deep vitalist roots.

The most essential requirement of a Pan-Africanist history, like an Aryanist or Pan-Germanic history, is a moment of pure origin from which all subsequent developments derive their character, whether as triumph or decline. Diop turned Negritude and older Pan-Africanist elements into a complete theory of civilization, with the diffusion of a vital and superior black culture to the rest of the world. Diop divided humanity into two types: southerners (Negro-Africans) and "Aryans," which included Semitic peoples, Mongoloids, and American Indians. Aryans formed patriarchal societies, characterized by the political suppression of women and a lust for warfare. They celebrated materialism, individualism, and pessimism. Southerners, by contrast, were matriarchal, creating a unified community of free and equal people who were creative and idealistic and who lived by the rules of social collectivism instead of competitive capitalism. In every aspect of their lives, Negro-Africans radiated vitality and optimism.

Diop claimed that archeological evidence overwhelmingly supported the thesis that Egyptians were racial southerners or Negroes; hence, the very first civilization in history was not only African in origin but deeply conscious of its own racial powers. "On numerous bas-reliefs," Diop wrote, "we see that, under the Eighteenth Dynasty, all the specimens of the White Race were placed behind the Blacks; in particular, the 'blond beast' of Gobineau and the Nazis, a tattooed savage, dressed in animal skins . . . occupied the last rung of humanity."[66] However, the truth of the black race creating civilization was carefully hidden or suppressed by European scholars such as Hegel, Gobineau, Carus, and Klemm in order to maintain the fiction of white supremacy.[67]

Diop's Afrocentrist history was at bottom a strong visceral reaction against a long tradition of European racism and condescension toward black Africa. However, it presented African civilization in the same Romantic historicist terms. Diop, like Gobineau and his predecessors, made race a vehicle of cultural vitality, generating civilizing structures in political, social, and economic institutions.[68] Diop's race history soon attracted the interest of the Black Power movement and the new Black Studies programs on college campuses. Joyce Ladner had already announced the "death of white sociology" as a means of understanding the American black experience and identity; a black replacement needed new affirmative principles. As Maulana Karenga put it in Introduction to Black Studies, "Multiculturalism is a critical thought and practice which cannot and should not be left to established order theorists." Now Diop provided an instant universal history to act as a new framework. Nor did he neglect the crucial issue of identity: the Afrocentric theory of civilization would empower the black with a sense of ethnic pride and power, just as (presumably) earlier theories of civilization had empowered whites.

The basic premise of all Afrocentric theories is that Egyptian civilization, in Diop's words, "descended from Nubia and the heart of Africa." Afrocentrists do not, as it is sometimes charged, suggest that all human history begins with Egypt; instead, history begins with a black African Kultur, while civilization represents the diffusion of a single Gobineau-style cultural template, which is black African and sub-Saharan. Its elements only became visible to the non-African world through the ancient kingdom of Egypt (or Kemet, the preferred term among younger Afrocentrists). Old Dynastic Egypt is this sub-Saharan culture's *Zivilisation* in the Spenglerian sense, the rich fruit of black African vitality. It represents, as Spengler would have said, "rigidity following expansion, . . . petrifying world-city following mother-earth," and as such already contains the seeds of its own doom.

Afrocentrists, like their Pan-Africanist predecessors, argue that race welds African history into a cultural whole, uniting Egyptians, Ethiopians, and sub-Saharan peoples into a single continuous *Volk*. "Because of this essential identity of genius, culture, and race," Diop announced, "today all Negroes can legitimately trace their culture to ancient Egypt and build a modern culture on that foundation."[69] That culture is intellectually richer, more vital, and more profound than either its Western or Asian competitors. According to Yosef ben-Jochannan, the black Egyptians created the first systems of writing, mathematics, medicine (including the original Hippocratic oath), politics, monumental architecture, and religion, as well as all the philosophic concepts whites later falsely attributed to the Greeks—including the idea of the atom. "This is the legacy of the African continent to the nations of the world," George James says in *Stolen Legacy*, which "laid the foundations of modern progress."

Later, the Greeks and other whites managed to steal all these civilized skills from the African man, leaving him in darkness. When he heard this, the liberal historian Arthur Schlesinger asked skeptically, "How does one lose knowledge by sharing it?" The answer is simple: because culture in the Afrocentric version is not based on knowledge but on racial vitality. As in Gobineau, the only way a lower race can acquire it is surreptitiously, whether by racial mixing or theft and pillage.[70]

Egypt had served as Africa's portal to the barbarian world beyond—and the portal through which those barbarians would take their revenge on their black-skinned superiors. To an Afrocentrist such as Chancellor Williams or John Henrik Clarke, history is as much about conquest, empire, and the struggle between stronger and weaker races as it was to Madison Grant or Gobineau, or even Carus and Klemm. If history's underlying continuity is that of a black African culture, its discontinuities are the periodic interruption of that vital flow by nomadic non-African peoples, first Semites and Arabs, then European whites.

Chancellor Williams sees the course of Egyptian history as a struggle for racial purity by a black "master race," as he calls it, against its Semitic neighbors, a struggle that, in Gobinian fashion, it inevitably loses. The last Egyptians were, he concluded, virtually reduced to a mulatto race. Egypt of the later dynasties became a true *Völkerchaos* melting pot, "as the Blacks were pushed to the bottom of the social, economic, and political ladder wherever and whenever the Asians and their mulatto offsprings gain control."[71] It was from this decadent, mongrelized Egypt (half Semitic, half Negroid) that, according to ben-Jochannan, "the European—presently called 'Caucasian'—got his first peep into what is today called Western civilization."[72]

The former black master race became the despised prey of its inferiors, and the history of the master race now split in two. One half became part of a great "black diaspora" to America, Europe, and Asia as slaves, while "those in Africa had, during the half-night of the centuries, declined from what in some cases had been great civilizations of their own, reverting deeper and deeper into primitive life, barbarism, and, in many cases, extreme savagery." Chancellor Williams explains that the result was that they "became easy objects of conquest and domination" by Western men. As their civilizations and traditions collapsed, black people "lost all memory of their illustrious history." They "were encouraged to believe . . . that they never had a past worth remembering; else where was its written record?" Once again, written evidence represents a lie; the only true evidence is found in the soul.[73]

Meanwhile, the whites who snatched up the remnants of Egyptian civilization now created their own degenerate copy. The great intellectual achievements and wisdom now lost their vitality; in European hands they turned dry and lifeless. Europeans were unable to grasp the higher spiritual truth of black culture, and so "truth itself [became] material." The universe was viewed only in mechanical, not vital terms, Chancellor Williams explained:

So it came about that the very science upon which the Enlightenment had so much relied to spearhead total progress, went forward with the development of *only one part of man*, leading to chance the cultivation . . . of those finer, humanizing qualities which truly distinguish man from beast.

The result, Williams concluded (turning to Erich Fromm for support), is that "modern, Western man, is morally and spiritually bankrupt, and therefore unfitted to lead the 20th century world toward a better day."*[74]

Modern history in Afrocentric terms becomes Houston Stewart Chamberlain's struggle between a resurgent black racial vitality and its spiritually bankrupt white antagonists. Wherever we see vitality and human progress, there we find the black race or at least one of its cultural survivals—including ancient China, in an interesting parallel to Gobineau's claims of an omnipresent Aryan civilizing race.[75] Wherever we find degeneracy, violence, cruelty, and chaos there we find the white man, who spends his time covering up any evidence of his parasitic dependence on African civilization. Racist scholars insist that Egyptian mummies are not Negroids, for example, while others claim that white men were the first to discover the New World. In fact, as Ivan van Sertima contended in *They Came Before Columbus* in 1976, black Africans reached its shores as early as A.D. 800 and—in a spectacular display of transcontinental cultural vitality—created the Olmec civilization.[76]

As Marcus Garvey had argued forty years earlier, white history is by its very nature antiblack, like imperialism itself. Standard history, according to Molefi Asante, is "killing our children by killing their minds."[77] As such, it forms part of the next step in the white genocidal conspiracy: the myth of integration, which whites believe, according to Chancellor Williams, "will effectively check the alarming development of pride in race, a sense of cultural identity with one's blood line." When that fails, whites are forced to fall back on a final line of defense. This is "the Plan," the mass genocidal extermination of blacks through drugs, ghettoization, violent crime, and AIDS. Since all these social problems take a disproportionate toll on blacks, as Leonard Jeffries points out, they "certainly have to be looked at as part of a larger conspiratorial

---

*Instead, Williams concluded, the future lies with the nation of Ghana, which through "providential favor" has the mission of "reversing the destructive trend of present-day civilization." Williams wrote *The Rebirth of African Civilization* in 1961 and dedicated it, ironically enough, to Kwame Nkrumah.

process." The Plan provides one more example of the white attempt to prevent the forward march of black vitality through history by using "black lives and psyches as the seemingly endless fodder in a system set up by white males for the benefit of white males."[78]

"At the heart of history," Molfani Karenga writes, "is the struggle against others who threaten human life, freedom, and development," which means capitalism, racism, fascism, apartheid, and colonialism.[79] The black man's struggle is not a Marxist or Darwinian struggle but a vitalist one. Afrocentrism returns us to the age of Romantic racism. In its choice of opponents—Hegel, Cuvier, Gobineau, Champollion, Lothrop Stoddard, Charles Darwin—and supporters—Volney, the French Egyptologist Gaston Maspero, the German anthropologist Leo Frobenius, and Nietzsche's colleague at the University of Basel and a leading proponent of the matriarchal theory of civilization, Johann Bachofen—it reflects a former era of thinking about race, civilization, and history.*

Like their Aryanist counterparts, Afrocentrists believe that cultural vitality must flow from a single original source, which is also the source of spiritual health. "Blackness is more than a biological fact," writes Molefi Asante. "It functions as a commitment to a historical project that places the African person back on center and, as such, it becomes an escape to sanity." Alfred Rosenberg put it this way in 1930: "The race-bound *Volksseele* is the measure of all our thought, longing of will and activities; it is the last measure of our value." This vital flow produces a unified Afrocentric view of the universe, not unlike the one extolled by Chamberlain, Rosenberg, and the Ariosophists.[80] As in Ratzel and Du Bois, Africanness produces a well-rounded individual, a healthy and "wholistic" personality. Unlike whites, the Afrocentric "person does not look for external powers; those powers inhere in him as an extension of the future of those who had gone before."[81] He embodies that other key principle, soul. "Soul is the vitality the researcher brings to the Afrocentric method," allowing him to grasp a higher truth than his white counterparts, with their obsession with evidentiary proof—proof, for example, that Negroes voyaged to America. Vitality alone is enough to

---

*As a result, Leonard Jeffries's racial theory of civilization becomes a parody not only of Diop but of Gustav Carus. Blacks, not whites, become the original "sun people," radiating spiritual warmth and creativity, while Caucasians are the "ice people," emotionally frigid, materialistic, and aggressive, who bring the three D's, "domination, destruction, and death."

explain it; as Karenga says, "If Europeans could reach America by accident, why couldn't Africans reach it by design and skill?"

In short, the very strangeness of the theory to the corrupt Western mind is a function of its ultimate truth. This assumption reaches its height in the work of Frances Cress Welsing. Her writings are an eclectic mix, with Afrocentric history, Jean-Paul Sartre, Freud, Max Weber, the Frankfurt School, and degenerationist theory all making brief appearances before melding into the whirl of her vitalist race theory, "the key to the colors." For Welsing, all white people are depigmented albinos. Since they lack the necessary melanin for color skin they also, by definition, lack cultural vitality. Western civilization, then, is the collective product of a race of degenerates whose genetic defects are played out in the psychological dysfunctions of modern society—its narcissism, it alienation, its *Angst*—and other diseased cultural forms.*[82]

Like her Ariosophist predecessors, Welsing pauses to dwell on the significance of the biblical parable of Adam and Eve's expulsion from the Garden. This moment, the beginning of secular history, allegorizes the white man's shame of living in a world "where the human norm is to have hue." Jesus himself was a black hero whose sexual potency is symbolized by the cross, a schematic representation (according to Welsing) of an erect penis and testicles. However, Jesus was lynched so that the genetically inferior whites could be saved by devouring his blood and flesh, and thus his potency.[83] His totemic sacrifice is, in effect, the Freudian founding moment of Western culture; and its civilization, like its religion, is a vast conspiracy of racial degenerates to cannibalize black genetic vitality. White envy of the black penis appears in various symbolic forms: the penchant for gun ownership, nuclear missiles, cigarettes (especially among white women feminists who smoke as a sign of liberation), and the Washington Monument. Even the chessboard becomes a symbolic racial battleground, with the black player allowed to move first on alternating black and white squares but the white player, naturally, always guaranteed to win.[84]

Race history, such as Francis Parker Yockey's *Imperium* or Alfred

---

*Among these are a fetishlike cult of dog ownership and Christianity. These "cults" are treated as forms of irrational fetishism—and the fact that God is actually "dog" spelled backwards does not pass unnoticed.

Rosenberg's *Myth of the Twentieth Century*, has always rejected empirical research in exchange for a mythic vision. The world of verifiable facts becomes unimportant because a deeper vital truth lies underneath. As a form of universal history, Afrocentrism follows the same prophetic pattern. As one of its practitioners states, Afrocentrism "takes whatever data are available and squeezes enough truth from them as circumstances will allow" in order to bolster racial identity and self-esteem.[85] In doing so, however, it has merely created an inverted image of Western racial pessimism, just as the multiculturalist mirrors the nihilistic precepts of Western cultural pessimism.

## CHAPTER 12

# ECO-PESSIMISM

## *The Final Curtain*

Men come and go, cities rise and fall, whole civilizations appear
and disappear—the earth remains, slightly modified. . . . Man is
a dream, thought an illusion, and only rock is real. Rock and
sun.

—Edward Abbey, *Desert Solitaire*, 1988

The idea of decline makes its latest appearance as modern environmentalism. As an ideology, environmentalism springs from complex origins and comes in historical-pessimist and cultural-pessimist
forms. On one side, it sustains nineteenth-century fears of technology
and degeneracy as well as liberal self-doubt. On the other, it rests on the
assumption that pollution, exploitation of resources, and environmental
damage are specifically Western problems and mark the modern West's
terminal stage. "Industrial society finally, mercifully chokes on its own
dung pile," as one activist put it, and "civilization [passes] into history."[1]

In the seventies, environmentalism acquired a powerful dose of cultural pessimism derived from by-now-familiar sources: Herbert Marcuse, Martin Heidegger, and Michel Foucault. Like their predecessors in
the twenties and thirties, environmental pessimists were prepared to
turn from analysis to action. When Michel Foucault predicted that the
Western image of man "would be erased, like a face drawn in sand at the
edge of the sea," he may not have realized that certain radical environmentalists were prepared to take him literally.

## TECHNOPOLIS IN DECLINE: THE WESTERN
## OVERTHROW OF NATURE

Remember that I am thy creature: I ought to be thy Adam; but I am
rather the fallen angel, whom thou drivest from joy for no misdeed.

—Mary Shelley, *Frankenstein*, 1818

Enlightenment man had equipped himself with science and the mechanical arts as an expression of his basic harmony with nature, understood as natural law. Diderot's *Encyclopedia*, the bible of the French
Enlightenment, was filled with plates illustrating technology and industrial processes, which were understood to be reasonable expressions of
civil society's progress.[2] All that changed with the Romantics' rejection
of nature as a lawful or rational order. Mary Shelley's *Frankenstein*
(1818) is the precursor of both the science fiction and the horror novel.
It moves us to the frontier of Romanticism's new view of man as part of
an irrational nature and presents the first elements of what would eventually become the environmentalist vitalist formula.

*Frankenstein* is drenched in the vitalism and *Lebensphilosophie* of the
German Romantics. As Baron Frankenstein admits, "The world was to
me a secret which I desired to divine." Understanding nature's life
forces becomes an obsession; the search for the "secrets of heaven and
earth" leads Frankenstein to reject positive science and turn to medieval alchemy and magic—the ancient occult origin of vitalism.
Frankenstein envisions himself a Prometheus who has learned to manipulate the "life principle" in order to create life. However, he finds he
has become a Pandora instead. Far from harmonizing himself with the
life forces of nature, Frankenstein summons them forth only to have
them turn against him. Like the dinosaurs in the film *Jurassic Park*, the
products of modern science disastrously exceed its expectations.
Frankenstein's creation, like man himself, is in his creator's image. But
that image turns out to be monstrous and fulfills its own destiny by destroying them both.

The most lasting image of this negative Romantic view of science, of
rational man versus vital nature, was the machine. From Francis Bacon
to Saint-Simon, technology had been seen as an essential aspect of
progress precisely because it seemed to express the opposite of man's de-

structive tendencies. Machines enabled human beings to create infinite wealth without the need for conquest or exploitation. Romantic vitalism spoiled this perspective forever. Technology was now an entirely mechanical process, devoid of any human value or spiritual uplift. Indeed, "technics" (as Spengler called it) formed the crucial link between science and capitalism's dehumanizing division of labor and specialization: for Spengler, Sombart, and the German antitechnic cultural critics, the machine stood with capitalism and *Zivilisation* as the enemies of organic *Kultur*.

By the second half of the nineteenth century Western man's technological advance was beginning to look like a preordained, impersonal, almost oppressive order, even to some of its admirers. Its devices seemed to take on a life of their own, like Frankenstein's monster. The image of science and technology as the "sorcerer's apprentice" of progress sprang up at exactly the same time and place as the first stirrings of Western declinism: in the Paris of the 1840s and '50s, in the science fiction novels of Jules Verne.

Jules Verne was originally a writer of historical romances in the style of Sir Walter Scott and Alexandre Dumas. However, Verne then turned his expansive imagination loose on nineteenth-century technology. His most famous character, Captain Nemo, first appeared in 1868 in *Twenty Thousand Leagues Under the Sea*. Nemo shows how the disillusioned Romantic artist becomes the modern mad scientist. Nemo has severed all ties with humanity and civilization, he tells his visitors. "I am not what you would call a civilized man! I've broken with all of society for reasons which I alone can appreciate. I therefore don't obey its rules, and I advise you never to refer to them again in front of me!"

Living beneath the sea in his submarine *Nautilus*, Nemo maintains a library filled with scientific works but, like Doctor Frankenstein's, with "no politics or economy." Nemo's consuming obsession is for the ocean as a living being:

The sea is everything. It covers seven-tenths of the globe. Its breath is pure and healthy. It is an immense desert where man is never alone, for he can feel life quivering all about him. The sea is . . . movement and love; it is the living infinite, as one of your poets has said. . . . Only there can one be independent! Only there do I have no master! There I can be free!

On a submarine voyage around the globe, Verne's narrator feels the underwater world's vital power. It teems with exotic flora and fauna, vast forests, and breathtaking mountainscapes of coral and carpets of algae and mollusks. In the end, the ocean beckons as a more potent life world than the one above. When Nemo and his guests find the ruins of the lost continent of Atlantis, it reminds the narrator of the puny stature of mankind in comparison with the powers of a violent, ever-changing nature. However, Nemo himself is convinced that the growth of man's power has gone too far. By 1875, in *Mysterious Island*, Nemo has turned into nature's avenging angel. He cruises the world's oceans, sinking the warships of leading European powers in an eternal vendetta against modern man's pride and hubris. The underlying danger is not science itself but those who use it; as Nemo tells the narrator in *Twenty Thousand Leagues*, "What the world needs is not new continents, but new men!"

Verne's Nemo suggested that the progressive man of science also had his ruthless streak, bordering on misanthropic violence. In one of Verne's last novels, *Robur the Conqueror* (1881), the scientist becomes a Caesarian builder of empire who ruthlessly uses his mechanical invention, a heavier-than-air airship, to destroy his less "advanced," "nonscientific" rivals, European balloonists. Robur himself—with his stark spheroid head, thick black hair like steel wool, triangular-shaped torso, and "bellows-like" lungs, carries the stigmata of his links to the mechanical, rather than the natural, world. Scientific genius (which Cesare Lombroso compared to madness and degeneracy in its "abnormality") pushes man beyond his own civilized restraints and limits. The scientist as law maker has become the law breaker.[3]

Verne never loses sight of the inevitability of progress. As a character in *Mysterious Island* warns Nemo, "Civilization never recedes, the law of necessity ever forces it onward." But it does not have to be a very pleasant prospect. That same ambivalence appears in the works of that other pioneer of the science fiction genre, H.G. Wells. His contemporary opponents, including Arnold Toynbee, used to dismiss him as a fatuous optimist on the future of progress and science. But his novels belie that reputation. In *The War of the Worlds* (1898), human technological hubris proves a puny opponent to a superior race of conquerors from Mars; in *The Food of the Gods* (1904), a scientific experiment to create a super-growth hormone produces catastrophic results. However, in *The Time Machine* (1895) and *The Island of Doctor Moreau* (1896) Wells combined his ambivalence about scientific progress with another familiar theme, that of degeneration.

The inventor of the time machine and narrator of the story finds himself transported to the remote future (A.D. 802,801, to be exact), to a society that is a degenerationist parable of hypercivilization. The effete ruling class, the Eloi, live in terror of their atavistic subordinates, the Morlocks, with their "pale, chinless faces, and great, lidless, pinkish-grey eyes," which they need to see in the deep subterranean caverns where they live and work. The Morlocks are hapless slaves of the Eloi, producing everything their masters need to live in comfort. Although the narrator feels sympathy for their plight (Wells was, after all, a socialist), he also notices "something inhuman and malign" about the Morlocks. "Instinctively I loathed them," he confesses. The Morlocks are not a race of slaves waiting to lose their chains. They are a race of permanent degenerates for whom freedom no longer has any meaning.

The narrator soon realizes that the social division of industrial civilization into capital and labor has been perpetuated over thousands of years, creating two different races of beings. "Above the ground you have the Haves, pursuing pleasure and comfort and beauty, and below ground the Have-nots." His own faith in progress is shaken. "The great triumph of Humanity I had dreamed of took a different shape in my mind. . . . Instead, I saw a real aristocracy, armed with a perfected science and working to a logical conclusion the industrial system of today. Its triumph had not been simply a triumph over nature, but a triumph over nature and the fellow-man." Like Charles Murray in *The Bell Curve*, Wells foresees a future divided between a permanent underclass and a "cognitive elite." But in Wells's version, technology and evolution have produced a double degenerative process. While the Morlocks are trapped forever in drudgery and ignorance, the Eloi elite have lost all self-motivation and creativity as a result of their reliance on technology, as well as experiencing a "general dwindling in size, strength, and intelligence."*

*The Island of Doctor Moreau* drives home the same point. Doctor Moreau's godlike experiments in surgically changing animals into men (atavism in reverse) go horribly wrong, producing instead a series of agonized, resentful monstrosities, the Beast-People. "The study of Nature," the narrator concludes gloomily in a Verne-like passage, "makes men at last remorseless as Nature"; more importantly, when he manages to escape back to industrial London and meets "the blank expressionless faces of people on trains and omnibuses," he finds he cannot distinguish these "animals half-wrought into the outward image of human souls" from the monstrous menagerie of the evil Doctor Moreau. "I go in fear," he tells the reader. "I feel as though the animal was surging up through them; that presently the degradation of the Islanders will be played over and over again on a larger scale."

Wells saw in science and technology a new kind of revolt against nature. This was not Verne's romantic conquest but an assault directed against the biological imperative of evolution itself, and one that must eventually exact its revenge. As with so many of his generation, Wells feared that evolution and progress were moving in opposite, not parallel directions. Modern man's increasingly artificial environment would eventually leave him defenseless against "the unknown implacable," nature's own latent destructive powers, which are revealed in all their hideous force in *The War of the Worlds*.

After two world wars Wells's pessimism grew into the apocalyptic gloom of his last important work, *The Mind at the End of Its Tether*. It was written in the same year as *Dialectic of the Enlightenment* and Heidegger's *Question Concerning Technology*. In all three books, the victory over fascism seems not the end of a long nightmare but the beginning of a new one. "This world is at the end of the tether," Wells told his readers, "the end of everything we call life is close at hand and cannot be evaded." Perhaps after the death of man, Wells speculates, some new species better adapted to nature's plan will arise. But for *Homo sapiens* there is only an inevitable extinction: "There is no way out or

---

*The same hypercivilized species reappears in Aldous Huxley's *Brave New World*, with its Alphas and Betas ruling over the proletarian Gammas, Deltas, and Epsilons.

round or through. . . . Our universe is not merely bankrupt; there remains no dividend at all; it has not simply been liquidated; it is going clean out of existence. . . ." The explosion of the atomic bomb at Hiroshima only seemed to confirm his pessimism, as it did for many others of his generation.*

For other critics, technology itself became the ultimate form of barbarism. When Henry Adams stood before the giant dynamo at the 1900 Chicago Exposition—"revolving at vertiginous speed, and barely murmuring"—he saw not just a machine but an "occult mechanism." It seemed to trigger the human being's primordial instinct to bow before "silent and infinite force," as the medieval peasant bowed before statues of the Virgin or the primitive savage before his totem. H.G. Wells himself published a short story, "The Lords of the Dynamos," in which a colored native from the tropics actually does believe the great humming generator to be a deity. When the machine inadvertently kills his white master, he decides that this is a ritual of human sacrifice. ("Never had Azuma-zi seen a man killed so swiftly and pitilessly. The big humming machine had slain its victim without wavering for a second from its steady beating. It was indeed a mighty god.")[4]

In the modernist version of technological pessimism, the machine destroys man's humanity by casting him into an artificial, fluorescent-lit cultural darkness. This barbaric reversion underlies the antitechnic vision of the modern West we find in critics such as Walter Benjamin, Lewis Mumford, and Jacques Ellul in *The Technological Society*:

> Men now live in conditions that are less than human. Consider the concentration of our great cities, the slums, the lack of space, air, of time, the gloomy streets and sallow lights that confuse night and day. Think of our dehumanized factories, our unsatisfied senses, our working women, our estrangement from nature. Life in such an environment has no meaning. . . . Yet we call this progress.[5]

In Roberto Vacca's phrase, the modern West forms a new, technological "dark ages," which traps humanity in ignorance and impotence.[6]

---

*This scenario, too, would become a favorite motif for science fiction writers: the atomic weapon as modern man's "sorcerer's apprentice," returning him to a savage, primordial state, both as wielder of that power in films such as *Dr. Strangelove* and as its victim, as in *The Planet of the Apes*, *A Canticle for Liebowitz*, *A Clockwork Orange*, and many others.

However, Jacques Ellul also distinguished between the machine, which is culturally neutral, and technology, which integrates the machine into the social order. Technology and its fate are inseparable from the fate of this society that develops and uses it, which is to say the industrial West. To critics in the fifties and sixties, the value of technology, computers, and mass communications was inseparable from capitalism and its mechanisms of exploitation, as well as the material destructive power of its arsenals of nuclear missiles. In short, technology becomes the modern West: the same ugly characteristics, the same malign power—and the same vulnerability to decline. Adorno wrote, "Spengler saw in the downfall of the West the promise of a golden age of engineers. The prospect coming into view, however, is the downfall of technology itself." To quote one of the directors of Worldwatch: "It is only a question [of] which will collapse first, the global economy or its ecological support system."[7]

Just as Western capitalism, technology, and self-interested liberalism has posed a challenge to vital *Kultur*, these same elements now pose an analogous threat to vital nature. Two large ideological camps appeared, each of which employed these old sets of oppositions in new ways. The first pitted progress and science *against* technology, that is, against "normal" Western capitalist values, which must either come to an end or be integrated into a new, higher vision for humanity. Like other late liberals, these environmentalists turned for salvation to a postcapitalist global order, in which acquisitive and destructive Western values lose out to more humane ones.

The second camp formed environmentalism's own version of cultural pessimism. To these heirs of Nietzsche, Heidegger, and the Frankfurt School, normative Western science, even Western man himself, turns out to be the root of the problem rather than the solution.

## APOCALYPSE AND THE NEW GREEN ORDER

Earth is threatened by destruction on a world-wide scale, and only if we all work together can we defeat the forces of evil: drought and flooding, ultraviolet radiation and smog, cancer and famine, all brought on by the three horsemen of the apocalypse—the greenhouse effect, ozone depletion, and nuclear winter.

—David Fisher, *Fire and Ice*, 1990

The notion of civilization rests on a firm rejection of the apocalyptic view of history. Enlightenment thinkers believed that the apocalyptic prophet, like the religious fanatic, was the enemy of humane civilized values; both were willing to wreck ordinary working institutions for the sake of a personal, and therefore unverifiable, vision of God's purposes. The eighteenth century emphasized the importance of reason in human affairs, because without a firm rational grounding for our beliefs we tend to become the victims of our fears and anxieties. As David Hume explained, "The mind of man is subject to certain unaccountable terrors and apprehensions, proceeding from the unhappy situation of private or public affairs, from ill health, from a gloomy and melancholy disposition. In such a state of mind, where real objects of terror are wanting, the soul . . . finds imaginary ones, to whose power and malevolence it sets no limits."[8]

In 1968 Paul Ehrlich published *The Population Bomb*. Although other books, such as Rachel Carson's *Silent Spring* (1963) and Ehrlich's own *Science and Survival*, had argued that modern technological "progress" was now endangering lives rather than saving them, no one had presented the future in such sweeping, all-encompassing, dire terms—even apocalyptic terms. *The Population Bomb* predicted "certain" world mass starvation by 1975 unless the world's population growth was halted. "The battle to feed all of humanity is over," Ehrlich's first sentence read. "In the 1970's the world will undergo famines—hundreds of millions of people will starve to death in spite of any crash programs." At best, he predicted, America and Europe would have to undergo "mild" food rationing within the decade, even as starvation and riots swept across Asia, Latin America, Africa, and the Arab countries. At worst, the turmoil in a foodless Third World could set off a series of international crises, leading to thermonuclear war.

This world crisis was about to be unleashed because of overpopulation, Ehrlich warned. Progress in medicine and health care, a Green Revolution in agriculture, and global mobility in transportation and communication had allowed population growth to place an intolerable strain on the earth's resources, not just in terms of food and pollution but in the demand for more technology to improve standards of living, which in turn increases population. Ehrlich turned the technological future into a classic *anakuklosis*—in Barry Commoner's words, the "closing circle." Ehrlich also predicted that overpopulation would bring intolerable pressure to bear on the new nations of the postcolonial world. "The chances of war increase with each addition to the population," Ehrlich suggested, "increasing competition for dwindling resources and food."[9] While this competition posed the most danger for the Third World, Ehrlich argued paradoxically that efforts at population control had to begin in the United States, where it was not a serious problem. The reason was that America had to serve as a model of civilizational restraint and "selflessness" for developing countries to emulate in population control. "The 'selfless' actions necessary to aid the rest of the world and stabilize the population are our only hope for survival," he explained.

Echoing Arnold Toynbee, Ehrlich argued: "We are the most influential superpower; we are the richest nation in the world. At the same time we are also just one country on an ever-shrinking planet. . . . Ways must be found to bring home to all the American people the reality of the threat to their way of life—indeed to their very lives." Ehrlich rejected the idea of introducing sterilants or antireproductive hormones into the national water supply, since these would prompt a widespread outcry. Instead, he proposed specific incentives such as imposing a luxury tax on baby cribs, diapers, and toys to penalize Americans who selfishly insisted on having more babies. A federal Bureau of Population and Environment would have to be established, while national laws requiring sex education in schools and guaranteeing abortion on demand would be important steps in the same direction.[10]

Ehrlich recognized that no existing political system could carry out so ambitious a reversal of standard Eurocentric priorities. The future of humanity required a radical shift from "a growth-oriented and exploitative system to one focussed on stability and conservation," as well as the overturning of institutions that perpetuated the old self-destructive system—the Catholic Church, the Judeo-Christian ethic, and multinational corporations. Ehrlich envisaged a future "planetary regime," with the United Nations transformed into a vast international agency for population and environmental resources, which would institute mass forced sterilization programs and, if need be, break up Third World countries into more environmentally sustainable units.[11]

If Ehrlich's plans seemed ambitious ("Coercion?" he wrote. "Perhaps, but coercion in a good cause.") Barry Commoner's *The Closing Circle*

(1971) was even more far-reaching. Commoner predicted that the earth's mineral and fossil fuel resources would be exhausted by the end of the century because the West was using them up too quickly. To Commoner, "plundering the planet" had become the imperative of Western civilization; its dynamic of economic growth and progress would inevitably bring catastrophic pollution and depletion of resources. Just as capitalism was for Marxists a system of appropriation from workers, so was it now a system of appropriation from the planet itself.

"The earth is polluted neither because man is some kind of especially dirty animal nor because there are too many of us. The fault lies with human society—with the ways in which society has elected to win, distribute, and use the wealth that has been extracted by human labor. . . ." For "society" we are to read "Western society." For Commoner, even more than for Ehrlich, the redistribution of resources in a new one-world order was as much a moral as a practical necessity. The economic burden of such a new order would fall most heavily on postindustrial technological societies such as the United States. But this is also "a kind of justice," he concluded, because it was precisely those societies whose economic advance had come at the expense of others.[12]

Commoner's and Ehrlich's conclusions were of a piece with the 1972 Club of Rome report, *The Limits to Growth*, which foresaw an end to economic growth everywhere by the twenty-first century. The *raison d'être* of modern Western-style countries (such as Japan) would soon disappear, the authors warned, with unpredictable results. That same year two leading voices in the North–South debate, René Dubos and Barbara Ward, weighed in with a book entitled *Only One Earth*, the implication being that Western industrial countries acted as if there were more than one. Dubos and Ward warned that "our sudden, vast accelerations—in numbers, in the use of energy and new materials, in urbanization, in consumptive ideals, in consequent pollution—have set technological man on a course" that put the survival of the planet at risk.[13]

Ehrlich, Dubos, Ward, and the Club of Rome were pushing for more than just environmental protection or restraints on Western influence over the Third World. They wanted a "political world order that is morally and socially responsible"—meaning the end of economic and technological change according to the normal Western model. They called for new international bodies to impose a rational order on the unpredictable postmodern technocapitalist *anakuklosis*, which, like fortune's wheel, eluded human control. According to a report published in 1980, economic development "involves a profound transformation of the entire economic and social structure" of a society, usually for the worse. Development was dislocating and disruptive, shattering "cultural identities" and leaving a trail of human wreckage behind it. One author, Alvin Toffler, coined a new phrase for its traumatic effects: "future shock."*[14]

A new model of development was therefore needed, one that would lead not to "chaos" (meaning economic activity running beyond the control of government planners) but to stability as conceived by the late-liberal mind. In 1980, World Bank president Robert McNamara and former German Chancellor Willi Brandt assembled an Independent Commission on International Development Issues for UN Secretary Kurt Waldheim.† Although Paul Ehrlich's dire predictions of twelve years earlier had failed to materialize, the commission's mood had not improved:

> At the beginning of the 1980's the world community faces much greater dangers than at any time since the Second World War. It is clear the world economy is now functioning so badly that it damages both the immediate and the longer-run interests of all nations. The problems of poverty and hunger are becoming more serious; there are already 800 million absolute poor and their numbers are rising; shortages of grain and other foods are increasing the prospect of hunger and starvation; fast-growing population . . . will cause much greater strains on the world's food and resources.

There is a real danger, the commission warned, that by the year 2000 starvation, overpopulation, and overurbanization will be widespread, "if

---

*Toffler's phrase not only reminds us of Walter Benjamin's view of technological society. It is also reminiscent of the discussion of "shell shock" during the First World War as a form of degenerative disease.

†The panel members included former Treasury Secretary Peter Peterson, publisher Katherine Graham of the *Washington Post*, former prime ministers Olaf Palme of Sweden and Edward Heath of Great Britain, as well as leading economists and Third World politicians.

a new major war has not already shaken the foundations of what we call world civilization."[15]

Part of the solution was for newly emerging nations to give up trying to be like their rich Western counterparts. "One must avoid the persistent confusion of growth with development," the Brandt Commission urged. Instead, "we strongly emphasize that the prime objective of development is to lead to self-fulfillment and creative partnership in the use of a nation's productive forces and its full human potential." The other part was a worldwide "emergency program" for the eighties, involving a global food program, an international energy program, and "effective national laws and international codes of conduct" requiring a "sharing of technology" among rich and poor nations, as well as restrictions on the activities of transnational corporations.[16]

Like their postliberal counterparts at the end of the nineteenth century, the modern liberal concern was not that unfettered capitalism failed to produce wealth; the problem was that it produced too much and placed it in the wrong hands (in this case, the populations of the rich industrialized North). The Western nations' basic outlook was overly "materialist and based on a belief in the automatic growth of the gross national product and of what they regard as living standards." The Western nations needed to recognize that "the world is a system" on the classic organicist model, with "many different components interacting with one another." The Brandt Commission and others proposed a "new international order" that, with its regulatory agencies and multilateral bodies, "can be seen as a constantly changing process in which forethought and negotiation operate constantly to establish an overall balance between all its elements, whether individual or collective."[17]

Just as historical pessimists like Burckhardt and Henry Adams had believed that capitalism would dry up the sources of human creativity and thought, so were advocates of sustainable development convinced that normal capitalism would dry up the sources of raw materials. These worries gave birth to the notion of sustainable economic development. A sustainable economy, according to a Worldwatch Institute report in 1991, was one that did not stretch beyond available resources: "Such an economy has a population that is stable . . . an energy system [that does not produce] greenhouse gases . . . and a level of material demand that neither exceeds the sustainable yield of forests, grasslands, or fisheries nor systematically destroys the other species with which we share the planet."[18]

A sustainable economy looked beyond "the narrow economic view of the world" of businessmen and economists, who analyze the world in abstract terms—"savings, investment, and growth." Ecologists, by contrast, "study the complex and ever-changing relationships of living things with their environment." Ecologists understand the notion of "natural limits to growth." Worldwatch admitted that "building an environmentally sustainable economy could revolutionize nearly every facet of human existence." Of course, "the transition to an ecologically secure world" would require mobilizing the full powers of the state, as well as international agencies such as the United Nations. However, "at issue is whether we are collectively ready to undertake the struggle that is needed to bring a new world into being" and save the planet.[19]

In the meantime, the range of malign effects of Western *Zivilisation* on the earth grew like toxic mushrooms. The threat of carcinogens produced by industry (although they represented only eight percent of all cancer deaths) and of nuclear and toxic waste, acid rain, ozone depletion, and finally the greenhouse effect—all were not just tangible dangers to health and safety, but the results of older cultural patterns and assumptions that had to be rethought or abandoned—particularly in the West.

Jonathan Schell brought the same perspective to bear on nuclear weapons in *The Fate of the Earth*. He was not only interested in nuclear disarmament as a political or diplomatic issue; his concern was with the health of a civilization that had produced them in the first place: "A society that systematically fails to take any steps to save itself cannot be called psychologically well." Schell claimed that the presence of nuclear weapons "makes us sick" in both a literal and a Nietzschean sense, since it exposes a cultural decadence that sets us on the brink of self-annihilation.[20]

In nuclear power Western science confronts the limits of its own progress. "Scientists, as they erect the steadily growing structure of scientific knowledge . . . feel no 'sorrow' or 'moral embitterment' or any 'taint of corruption' that supposedly undoes all human achievements." Instead, technological progress represents an "invulnerable, inhuman order obtruding into our changeable and perishable human realm." Like

Gobineau's Incas or the inhabitants of Volney's Nineveh or Saint Augustine's Rome, we had come to believe in our own immortality—until the advent of nuclear weapons. "Seen as a planetary event," Schell wrote, "the rising tide of human mastery over nature has brought about a categorical increase in the power of death on earth . . . [man's] power to encroach on life . . . came to threaten the balance of the entire planetary system of life."[21]

But instead of confronting this danger, Schell lamented, normal political institutions have ignored it: "The upholders of the status quo defend the anachronistic structure of their thinking, and seek to block the revolution in thought and action which is necessary if mankind is to go on living."[22] Schell argued that the end to the threat of nuclear holocaust requires the end of nationalism—"we must lay down our arms, relinquish sovereignty, and found a political system for the peaceful settlement of international disputes." Survival also requires full acceptance of the "ecological principle," the realization of "the oneness of the earth as a system of support for life."* "Our modest role," he concluded, "is not to create ourselves but only to preserve ourselves." He warned balefully:

> The alternative is to surrender ourselves to absolute and eternal darkness; a darkness in which no nation, no society, no ideology, no civilization will remain; in which never will a child be born; in which never again will human beings appear on the earth, and there will be no one to remember that they ever did.[23]

The popularity of this new apocalypticism became so widespread that even Senator George Mitchell of Maine published an environmental tract entitled *The World on Fire*, in which he discussed the "four horsemen" of environmental disaster that threatened the planet (adding one more horseman to David Fisher's unholy trio) and argued for a massive governmental effort to restructure the American economy on a sustainable basis. The United States, he concluded, like other industrial nations, now had to fit itself within an ecologically safe model of "global development." Jonathan Schell agreed: "There was a time when the no-

---

*"An organism's ability to renew itself during its lifetime depends upon . . . a balanced, self-reproducing, slowly changing whole. The ecosphere of the earth . . . is the largest of the living configurations . . . and [a] balanced, self-perpetuating system in its own right. . . ."

tion of a world order was thought to be a utopian vision. We can see now that, in many respects, it is a hellish necessity."[24]

Little wonder that by 1991 Worldwatch Institute's writers compared the planet to the sinking *Titanic* and Americans to its complacent passengers in their "inability to comprehend the scale of the ongoing degradation of the planet and how it will affect [their] future." By then, the notion that the Western model of economic development and national self-determination posed a dire threat to the survival of the planet had virtually become conventional wisdom in liberal circles. But this only made earlier pessimists like Paul Ehrlich even gloomier. "Growth of the physical economies in rich nations," he wrote in 1991, "must now be recognized as the disease, not the cure." Ehrlich added that this "growth will soon come to a halt in the developed world" because international markets can no longer support the production of more goods.

Development, even in its modest sustainable form, had become a Western curse on the rest of the world. An environmentally sound society in Ehrlich's terms meant explicitly rejecting what he saw as all the key values of Western society: growth, affluence, and private enterprise, along with "racism, sexism, religious prejudice, and xenophobia." "Unless these divisive traits can be managed," Ehrlich warned, "they could cripple attempts to develop the global cooperation needed to create a new civilization."[25] "A new civilization": Ehrlich's vision of the future now reflected modern ecology's call for a new cultural order to replace its old, moribund predecessor. The passing of the West, ecology's more radical proponents in the seventies and eighties announced, would open the doors to a vital, holistic human community rooted in a "new" organic vision of nature. That radical revision culminated in the influential Deep Ecology movement, which described itself as "going beyond the so-called factual scientific level to the level of Self and Earth wisdom."[26]

Of course, this was not a new order at all. Modern ecology's hopes of creating a new self to replace the old Western one, the artificial creation of *Zivilisation*, replayed the same enthusiasms that had animated every modern cultural regeneration movement since the German Romantics. In fact, vitalist life philosophy, which had underpinned both Gobineau's racial Aryan and Nietzsche's Overman, has more than a casual link to the contemporary ecology movement. Ecologists managed to rehearse the same arguments that divided Nietzscheans and other cultural pessimists in Germany between the wars and that centered around the motto, "Back to the soil."

## DECIVILIZING MAN: GERMAN CULTURAL PESSIMISM AND THE ECOLOGY MOVEMENT

Back to the Pleistocene!
> —Earth First! slogan

Ernst Haeckel invented the term "ecology" in 1866 as part of his vitalist biological monism. Ecology described the "science of relations between organisms and their environment," which Haeckel believed formed the basic network of life. In Haeckel's evolutionary holism, nature in all its variety and diversity formed a single totality, an infinite substance with no beginning or end—only the same evolutionary life force appearing everywhere and in everything, including man. In his own mind, Haeckel had finished off any notion that nature or man possessed some higher divine essence. Instead, everything in the cosmos formed an ever-evolving process, without purpose or design, "Our monistic view," he wrote, "not only involves, on its positive side, the essential unity of the cosmos and the causal connection of all phenomena . . . but it also, in a negative way, marks the highest intellectual progress, in that it definitely rules out the three central dogmas of metaphysics— God, freedom [of will], and immortality."[27]

In fact, Haeckel hoped his monistic philosophy would replace Christianity's God worship with the worship of nature, just as it would replace selfish individualism with a new ethical monism, in which all would recognize that their interests and the interests of the community were one and the same. Christianity, Haeckel believed, "has contributed not only to an extremely injurious isolation from our glorious mother nature, but also to a regrettable contempt of all other organisms." Haeckel even argued that in the monistic view, animals should enjoy equal status to men as fellow sentient, social, and even (in the case of the higher vertebrates) rational creatures. Haeckel's early version of "animal rights" formed part of his campaign against the anthropocentric view of nature, that "boundless presumption of conceited man" that "has misled him into making himself 'the image of God.' "[28]

Haeckel's monism proved popular and influential. His views on the ecological approach to nature, as well as on eugenics, spread through prewar Germany and beyond. He directly inspired a number of scientists and thinkers to take up his vitalist calling. They included the Nobel Prize chemist Wilhelm Ostwald, who became president of the Monist League; Hans Driesch, professor of philosophy at Heidelberg; and the zoologist Konrad Lorenz, whose studies of animal behavior (the best known is *On Aggression*) stressed Haeckel's notion that animal and habitat—including man and *his* environment—form a single unit.* Haeckel's vitalism had also helped to inspire Oswald Spengler's notion of the life force in world cultures, while in England it heavily influenced another figure on the radical Right, the novelist D.H. Lawrence.

At the same time, the German Youth Movement found a similar route back to nature in German Romanticism's strong antitechnic strain. Although Haeckel himself had fused together mechanical and organic nature as aspects of the same evolutionary life force (which lovers of military technology like Ernst Jünger came to appreciate), others took vitalist ecology in a very different direction. After the 1913 youth rally in the Meissner Mountains, one of its spokesmen, the young Nietzschean Ludwig Klages, wrote an influential essay entitled "Man and Life." Klages proclaimed that progress as a rational enterprise was at an end. "What is generally seen as the advance of history, or as progress, is in fact the gradual domination of the spirit over life, which must end with the annihiliation of the latter."[29]

By "spirit" Klages meant the will to power. Unlike his master Nietzsche but anticipating Foucault, Klages believed the will to power and Western rationality to be aspects of the same malign force. Will to power was not the product of man's organic vitality but of mind and the desire to kill life. "Man, as bearer of the spirit, has torn himself apart along with the planet which gave him birth." For Klages, rational man stood at the opposite pole from natural man; one pointed toward what Klages called "the rape of nature" and spiritual death, symbolized by the Jews. The other pointed toward "Dionysiac intoxication" and life.[30]

After World War I, all these elements fostered a series of back-to-

---

*Driesch's own disciples included two figures on the Nietzschean Right, Ernst Jünger and José Ortega y Gasset, author of *The Revolt of the Masses*.

nature movements in Germany that inevitably pressed their way into political movements—including Hitler's National Socialist Party. One of these was "organic" farming, which rejected chemical fertilizers as part of lifeless technological society. In the twenties the biologist Rudolf Steiner launched a program of "biodynamic agriculture," which viewed agriculture in Haeckel-like terms as a holistic enterprise between man, plant, and soil. As Alfred Rosenberg and the Nazi Nordicists attacked the "false spirituality" of Christianity and appealed to a return to the Aryan's original reverence for nature, back-to-nature types suddenly saw the National Socialists' Aryan man as heralding the new organic man, bonded to his race, his soil, and his environment. Eugen Diedrichs, one of the organizers of the 1913 Youth Movement celebration, became an early Nazi. Ludwig Klages tried to join as well (he was thrown out because he was, like Ernst Haeckel, a pacifist). One radical group, the *Artamanen*, or "guardians of the soil," even carried banners with pictures of Gandhi and Tolstoy (in their role as spokesmen for peasants) on one side and swastikas on the other.[31]

The interplay among these various antitechnic groups tended to be complicated and often obscure, just as in the ecology movement today. Houston Chamberlain and other volkish thinkers had disliked Haeckel for his evolutionary view of nature. So did Hitler himself. However, Hitler's minister of agriculture, Walter Darré, took up the cause of organic farming as part of "blood and soil" Aryanism. "The peasant," Oswald Spengler had written in *The Decline of the West*, "is the eternal man." Just as the virtuous German peasant farmer formed the model for the new Reich, Darré believed, so should German agriculture reflect the same organic bonds. His chief ally in Hitler's inner circle was Rudolf Hess, a vegetarian, a practitioner of homeopathic medicine, and a passionate convert to the cause of biodynamic farming.[32]

Many other Nazi enthusiasms would reappear in the seventies and eighties. Heinrich Himmler (who had been a chicken farmer before becoming head of Hitler's SS bodyguard) experimented with organic farming and sponsored organic herbal gardens for his SS. New recruits in the SS were taught "a reverence for animal life" that, one modern historian has suggested, reached "near Buddhist proportions."[33] Himmler also saw to it that antivivisection regulations became law under the Third Reich (even as euthanasia became compulsory for "useless mouths" among humans), while the official symbol of the SS became the oak leaf, representing the regenerative powers of nature.

The various strands of German environmentalism between the wars may have differed in how nature was understood—whether in terms of monistic materialism, Dionysian eros, or biodynamic vitalism—but they all agreed on their principal enemy: the modern technological capitalist West. Everyone, regardless of political stripe, would have concurred with National Bolshevik Ernst Niekisch's pronouncement in 1931:

> Technology is the rape of nature. It brushes nature aside. It cunningly tricks nature out of one piece of land after another. When technology triumphs, nature is violated and desolated. Technology murders life and strikes down, step by step, the limits established by nature.[34]

Even those who later celebrated technology's place in the new German cultural order, like Spengler and Ernst Jünger, insisted that it had to be reintegrated in a new, vitalist form. Others, like Martin Heidegger, turned the "back to the soil" antitechnic critique into a key component of antimodern thought.

Heidegger had been profoundly influenced by Klages's Nietzschean attack on technological capitalism.* Heidegger would spend days and weeks climbing in the mountains, and often appeared in class and at Nazi Party rallies dressed in alpine garb and open shirt. He viewed modernity's loss of touch with nature as part of modern man's loss of Being, which technology epitomized: "The object-character of technological domination spreads itself ever more quickly, ruthlessly, and completely." Heidegger complained that not only does Western technology "establish all things as producible in the process of production," it also "delivers the products of production by means of the market." Hence, through technological capitalism "the humanness of man and the thingness of things dissolve into the calculated market value of a market which spans the whole earth."

Heidegger insisted that man had to become the steward, not the master, of nature. Through poetry and art modern man could restore his sense of "the simple onefold of earth and sky, divinity and mortals." The

---

*That influence came via the philosopher Max Scheler, who was a follower of Klages and the author of *Man's Place in the Cosmos*, published in 1928.

new man would learn to abandon technology and consumerism and accept his humble place in the unity of nature. "Self-assertive man," he wrote in 1926, "whether or not he knows and wills it as an individual, is the functionary of technology."[35]

Heidegger's student Herbert Marcuse brought these assumptions to his own view of "post-scarcity society" in One-Dimensional Man. Its bold images of a technological capitalism poised to subjugate the vital energies of man as well as nature infused German cultural pessimism into the New Left. Marcuse galvanized American conservationist sentiments on the Left, which derived from the writings of figures like Henry David Thoreau and John Muir. The New Left's attacks on American capitalism included its systematic "degradation" of the natural, whether in sexual terms (a favorite topic of Haeckel's, who strongly advocated free love) or in terms of the environment. In 1969 radical students at Berkeley created the so-called Peoples' Park, organizing a "conspiracy of the soil" to reclaim the land from capitalist property relations. One radical even claimed that trees were like other exploited minorities in America, such as blacks, Vietnamese, and hippies.[36]

Marcuse's ideas decisively influenced the most blatant example of volkish environmentalism of the sixties, Charles Reich's The Greening of America. Industrial capitalist America was now facing its own self-destruction, the Yale professor announced in 1970. Disorder, corruption, "absence of community," a meaningless culture, and "uncontrolled technology and the destruction of the environment" had left most Americans with a sense of powerlessness. American blacks "long ago felt their deprivation of identity and potential for life." Now the white middle class felt the same. "Stand in a commuter train," Reich wrote, choosing a favorite image of cultural pessimists, "and see the blank, hollow faces. We do not look at faces very often in America, even less than we look at ruined rivers and devastated hills."

However, Reich assured his readers, "there is a revolution coming" that will "bring a renewed relationship of man to himself, to other men, to society, to nature, and the land." In true Nietzschean fashion, this revolution will be spearheaded by the young. Acting as the carriers of unblemished vitality, American youth will shatter the artificial bonds of technological society with their rock music, clothing and hairstyles, and sexual freedom as well as their instinct for nature. Much like German youth or Martin Heidegger, "members of the new generation seek out the beach, the woods, and the mountains." Echoing an ancient Aryanist theme, Reich added that "the forest is where they come from, it is the place where they feel closest to themselves, it is renewal. Nature is not some foreign element. Nature is them."[37]

However, the thinker who ultimately separated ecological pessimism from its blood-and-soil associations and turned it into a pillar of the New Left was Murray Bookchin. An admirer of the nineteenth-century anarchist tradition and a close student of earlier antitechnic critics such as Lewis Mumford and Paul Goodman, Bookchin embraced Marcuse's idea that postscarcity society represented a profoundly new and dangerous development for civilization. In 1966 Bookchin published *Crisis of the Cities*, in which he predicted that America's industrial cities were spreading "like a rampant cancer" into the hinterland, destroying wilderness, agricultural land, and waterways. Technological civilization, he claimed, was placing "an intolerable burden" on the environment, or what Lewis Mumford had called the "biosphere."

Like Marcuse, however, Bookchin also thought that new technologies such as wind power could bring "land and city into a rational and ecological synthesis." For Bookchin and later environmental radicals, technology has two edges. One, the hard edge, had ruined the environment and provided the driving engine of industrial capitalism—automobiles, chemicals, fossil fuels, and nuclear power. The soft edge, by contrast, not only preserves natural resources but also undercuts the forces of concentrated, large-scale capital. It includes preindustrial technologies of all kinds, solar power, wind power, and for some very recent converts, personal computers.*

Of all the offshoots of the New Left, environmentalism proved to be the most broadly successful. On April 22, 1970, its popularity took official shape with the celebration of Earth Day. In scenes reminiscent of the 1913 German Youth Movement meeting in the Meissner Mountains, thousands of students, hippies, and teenagers gathered in teach-ins and rallies. The wave of popular enthusiasm attracted mainstream

---

*Soft technology's great spokesman, Fritz Schumacher, was an anti-Nazi German refugee who nonetheless held many of the same back-to-the-soil views of his rightist counterparts. His most famous book, *Small Is Beautiful* (1973), is a compendium of Weimar-style environmentalist views.

conservation groups and thrust figures from the antipollution movement, such as Barry Commoner, Paul Ehrlich, and René Dubos, permanently into the limelight. It drew support from the American political establishment, including President Richard Nixon. Its original organizer, Senator Gaylord Nelson of Wisconsin, explained that "Earth Day may be a turning point in American history. It may be the birth of a new American ethic that rejects the frontier philosophy that the continent was put here for our plunder."[38]

Beginning in 1970, Congress enacted a series of far-reaching environmental regulations and laws, beginning with the Clean Air Act. Only seven months after Earth Day, President Nixon set up the Environmental Protection Agency, which was charged with treating "air pollution, water pollution, and solid wastes as part of a single problem." At the same time, the environmental movement received a heady transfer of energy from the New Left. Groups such as the Natural Resources Defense Council (founded in 1970) and the Environmental Defense Fund led the way by aggressively lobbying in the style of civil rights lawyers' groups in the sixties. Old-fashioned conservation organizations like the Sierra Club, Audubon Society, and Wilderness Society took on new radicalized members, who would dictate the environmental agenda over the next two decades.

Still other groups, such as Greenpeace (founded in 1971), allied themselves more openly with militant leftist politics by taking direct action against "enemies of the environment" such as seal hunters and nuclear engineers. Like its interwar German counterparts, Greenpeace rejected both capitalist society and mainstream political categories. However, it proved most successful with European leftist youth (as did the German environmentalist Green Party, which ran its first slate of candidates in 1977). Others hearkened back to Bookchin's anarchist roots. Antitechnic demands for a return to the soil spawned various experimental communes—at least two thousand in thirty-four states by 1970. Some of these hippie communes would later take their rejection of modern society's conventions to unexpected extremes, such as Charles Manson's murderous "family" in California and Jim Jones's Jonestown in Guyana.* However, at the time they seemed to support

---

*Or in a more recent offshoot, David Koresh's Branch Davidians.

the conclusion of Charles Reich that youth was about to voluntarily re-nounce alienating Western capitalism and technological society for a more natural, and purer, existence.[39]

By the second large Earth Day celebration, in 1990, cultural pes-simism's critique of technological capitalism was becoming largely ac-cepted in mainstream American society. Yet many environmental groups were still unhappy with the lack of more radical change. Dennis Hayes, the original organizer of the 1970 events, lamented: "How could we have fought so hard, and won so many battles, only to find ourselves now on the verge of losing the war?"[40] Others suggested that the entire premise of mainstream environmentalism—in Worldwatch's Lester Brown's words, "making industrialist society safe for human life"—was not part of the solution but part of the problem.

For years figures like Bookchin and the Norwegian philosopher Arne Naess had been calling for a totally different direction for environmen-talism. "There are political potentials in this movement," Naess wrote in 1973, "which should not be overlooked and which have little to do with pollution and resource depletion." Naess lamented that main-stream environmentalism "does not ask what kind of society would be the best for maintaining a particular eco-system." Instead, he called for a new direction, which he termed "deep ecology," that would correct the cultural assumptions that had produced pollution in the first place. Like Haeckel's monism, Naess's deep ecology meant abandoning an anthro-pocentric view of the environment for a "biocentric" view. Like Heideg-ger's philosophy of existence, it involved a transformation not only of society but of man himself. "The modern Western self," Naess ex-plained, "is defined as an isolated ego striving narrowly for hedonistic gratification or . . . individual salvation in this life or the next." This false self-image "robs us of the beginning of our search for our unique spiritual/biological personhood" through oneness with nature.[41]

Murray Bookchin's *The Modern Crisis* pointed to the challenge of bringing to heel modern man's "market society and the vicious mental-ity it breeds." Pollution, industrial degradation of the environment, acid rain, global warming, and nuclear militarism on a massive scale were all the egregious products of Western capitalism. "Capitalism, I would ar-gue, is the cancer of society."[42] Echoing Heidegger, Bookchin asserted that it reduces all relations between human beings, and between human beings and the earth, to commodities. Capitalism "parasitizes and threatens to annihilate every social domain that harbored ties of mutuality and collective concern."

As a consequence, it leaves a trail of environmental and cultural destruction in its wake. The United States, he observed, is "the most illiterate, uninformed society in the developed world." Unconsciously recalling Gobineau's description of France in the 1850s, Bookchin stated: "Every day life has steadily acquired almost bovine characteristics. Society is little more than a pasture and people a herd grazing on a diet of trivialities and petty pursuits."[43] Meanwhile, "so-called socialist societies like the Soviet Union and China" have ended up in the same predicament because of their acceptance of the image of man as an economic being. Instead, human survival requires a new "ethical stance," which he called "social ecology." This was a philosophy of "participation" in which "animals and plants foster each other's survival, fecundity, and well-being" in a noncompetitive way. It celebrates "differentiation" of species and natural variety "without structuring differences into a hierarchical order."[44]

Bookchin's social ecology displays almost all the characteristics of Haeckel's monistic evolution. It views "life as active, interactive, procreative, relational, and contextual." It sees change as an organic process, not a mechanical or linear one, so that "each form emerges out of its predecessor—the later and more complex generally incorporating the earlier and simpler ones, whether internally"—as with embryonic development, a favorite example of Haeckel's—"or as part of a community." Out of this social ecology arises an egalitarian communitarian ideal in which all members, men and women, well-fed and poor, white and nonwhite, share the same communal spirit. This harmonious biocommunity stands in sharp contrast to the dynamics of civil society, which is profoundly antinatural, according to Bookchin (despite its Enlightenment-derived claims to be following nature's laws). Instead, primitive and precapitalist societies stand as the new model for the future.

For Bookchin, primitive man and nature formed a rich matrix of "fecundity and well-being." Men and women shared as equals (like Gary Nash's Iroquois), enjoying a truly participatory role in decision-making. They understood the dangers of competitive individualism, shunning trade and pronouncing profit-making a sin.[45] In one sense, Bookchin admires the Enlightenment for the same reason Haeckel did, because "it brought the human mind down from heaven to earth, from the realm of the supernatural to the natural." It "fostered a clear-eyed secular view toward the dark mythic world that festered in feudalism, religion, and royal despotism." However, "capitalism warped those goals."[46] It turned "reason into a harsh industrial rationalism focused on efficiency rather than a high-minded intellectuality . . . it used science to quantify the world and dualize thought and being . . . it used technology to exploit nature, including human nature." As Adorno had written in *Negative Dialectics*, "No universal history leads from savagery to humanitarianism, but there is one leading from the slingshot to the megaton bomb."

However, the most immediate danger Bookchin saw in 1987 was that economic and technological change might improve people's lives without forcing any fundamental cultural revision. Bookchin argued that a genuine revolution in attitudes and values was needed that would "alter every thread of the social fabric, including the way we experience reality." Bookchin looked forward to a future "ecological society, structured around a confederal Commune of communes, each of which is shaped to conform with the ecosystem and bioregion in which it is located." Everyone will engage in organic farming and use solar and wind power. New technologies will be employed in "an artistic way," freeing up time for other activities: "gardening, the crafting of objects, reading, recitations," and experimental mixed farming for biological diversity. The notion of ownership, even collective ownership, will disappear, replaced by "a holistic approach to an ecologically oriented economy." Instead, "everyone would function as a citizen, not as a self-interested ego," committing himself to a sense of oneness with the community—and with nature.[47]

Bookchin's ideas owed a great deal to the tradition of utopian socialism; however, Friedrich Ratzel's well-rounded peasant, as well as the ecstatic aspirations of the German Youth Movement, also make a shadowy appearance in his bioregional communism. And now there was a living link to man's organic roots: existing primitive societies around the world. For environmentalist writer Edward Abbey, "a superior race" is the human community that "has done the least harm to the earth, to other forms of life, to humans, to each other." By that standard, Abbey concluded, "the only superior races would be the Aborigines of Australia, the Bushmen of Africa, maybe the Hopis of Arizona."[48]

The ecology movement's technological pessimism inverted the relationship between society and the environment defined by Toynbee, and going back at least to Thomas Buckle and Hegel. They had held that the struggle to dominate and control nature predominates in the early stages of civilization; later on, more, if not most, of man's efforts are directed at perfecting his own powers. Now Bookchin and others were asserting that Western history "has not been a unilinear advance from one stage to another . . . in an untroubled ascent to ever-greater control over" nature. On the contrary, he charges, "prehistory may have allowed for alternatives before the emergence of patricentric warrior societies . . . that might have seen a more benign social development than the one that formed our own history."[49]

The ecologist sees civilization as a deliberate rather than a necessary struggle against nature. Another Haeckel disciple, Oswald Spengler, had written that civilization is "death following life . . . petrifying world-city following mother earth." This, too, becomes the ecologist's history. Western man's remote forebears expressed "an organic relationship with nature" that modern civilization has erased. Modern man is a *latecomer* whose civilized efflorescence denies vitality. Just as Columbus's discovery of the New World symbolized for Spengler the birth of the Faustian will for expansion and space, so did his intrusive arrival among the peoples inhabiting North America seem to the new ecologists the starting point for the West's history of plundering the planet. The white man is the latecoming gate-crasher—and the gates he crashes are the gates of paradise.

This debt to Spengler and cultural pessimism goes unacknowledged in Kirkpatrick Sale's *1492: Conquest of a Continent* (1990). But Sale does insert Columbus explicitly as Faustian man, quoting Christopher Marlowe's *Doctor Faustus*:

> O what a world of profit and delight,
> Of power, of honor, of omnipotence . . .
> All things that move between the quiet poles
> Shall be at my command.

Columbus, Sale concludes, "is the figure who more than any other, provided the legacy by which European civilization came to dominate the American world for five centuries with consequences, we now realize, involving nothing less than issues of life and death."[50] For Sale, 1492 was the beginning of the Europeans' victory over nature through degradation and exploitation. "This was the sort of victory upon which the premise of America was based," he argues.

Post-Columbian America became a "battlefield," not so much between Europeans and Indians as between Western man and the environment. Europeans turned the earth's products into commodities—gold, silver, sugar, lumber, tobacco, cotton. The opening of the West became one long environmental catastrophe. "Its opulent beneficiary" was European civilization; its overseas empires enabled European man "to multiply, thrive, and dominate the earth as no single species ever has."[51] For Sale, Europeans are nature-haters; they are cut off from life. The peoples they conquered, on the other hand, the Native Americans, reflected a superior cultural vitalism—not only in their artistic attributes but also in their social and moral institutions. This is a startling new direction for cultural pessimism, but one typical of the radical environmentalists: primitive man's chief advantage is not that he is crude and vital but that he is sophisticated and advanced, at least in his dealings with Mother Earth.

Sale's Indians fit this new stereotype. They are well-nourished, enjoy gender equality, are equipped with systems of agriculture, medicine, and even technologies superior to those of Europeans.* Whatever wars they had were invariably mild and short. Sale's Native Americans are truly noble savages: they even have the foresight to be energy efficient. Above all, their lives are governed by a religion that dictates a balance with nature and the biosphere and has no destructive notion of human progress, or even improvement. This stands in foresquare opposition to the white barbarian newcomer, who is dirty and smelly, violent and hypocritical, born of "a culture that did not know the earth is alive and all beavers brothers."[52]

---

*The bow and arrow being superior to the musket in that it is safer for its user—the OSHA test, as it were, of technological progress.

Kirkpatrick Sale, like Bookchin, rejects the notion that civilization is in some sense an outgrowth or inevitable transformation of an earlier stage of primitive culture. Primitive society enjoys a *Kultur* that has no conceptual link to *Zivilisation* and therefore remains uncontaminated by its superficial values. Indeed, any instinct that might produce such a destructive impulse is warded off by a spirituality that is, again, not anthropocentric but biocentric, that is, it views man as the insignificant creature he actually is. Radical environmentalism does not merely repudiate the idea of human improvement and of man as a social being (that is, a being with certain individual needs—physical, moral, cultural—that must be satisfied in cooperation with others in order for him to be happy.) Cultural pessimism had already completed that task—a quick glance at Nietzsche or Sartre or even Rousseau makes that clear.

The radical ecologist goes further by saying that even if human beings have these needs *they do not matter.* Deep Ecology claims that "man's vital material needs" are actually much smaller than "technocratic-industrial society" leads us to believe. We could all easily eat less, drink less, do less—and presumably think and desire less. Bookchin specifically invokes the image of the beehive as the ideal community, in which the individual is entirely lost within the functioning of the organic whole. Instead, what matters is man's relationship to a nonhuman nature. And since the attributes that make for civilized life—a sense of private possessions, a rational self-interest expressed in commercial exchange, a desire for cultural activities as outlets for our passions—put us on the bottom step of Commoner's closing circle, they have to be suppressed, as they are (or at least seem to be) in the "organic societies" of primitive peoples, where trade is a sin and self-assertion an evil.[53]

If ecologists tend to be more interested in the Hopi Indians or the Penan hunter-gatherers of Borneo or the !Kung San bushmen than in the great non-Western civilizations of the Afrocentrist or Orientalist, it is because these survivals from the Stone Age "stand as an alternative to the civilization complex." Peoples such as the Chinese and Zulus, the Aztecs and Mayas, all took the fateful step toward civilization's cycle of self-destruction. In a profound sense, they invited the degradation they suffered at the hands of the white man. Indigenous peoples of the rain forest and savannah plains, by contrast, retain their primeval innocence. As such, they serve an important political purpose, as models for the antitechnic, no-growth society of the future. "The path to environmental modesty is not utopian," says radical activist Chris Manes, "it is being lived this minute by millions of tribal peoples around the world."[54]

To Stanley Diamond in The Search for Primitive, "the longing for a primitive mode of existence" is not limited to ecologists or romantic ecotourists but is "consonant with fundamental human needs." It is civilization, he states, that is out of sync:

> Civilization may be regarded as a system in internal disequilibrium; technology or ideology or social organization are always out of joint with each other—that is what propels the system along a given track. Our sense of movement, of incompleteness, contributes to the idea of progress.

Hence, he triumphantly concludes, "the idea of progress is generic to civilization."[55]

These notions prompt Jerry Mander to claim in In the Absence of the Sacred (1991) that the tribal way of life is not the result of ignorance but of a deliberate rejection of technology, science, and its cultural assumptions (productivity, the work ethic, the subduing of nature). In other words, it is not that the Iroquois or Uruburu cannot build airports or nuclear reactors but that, at a deep level, they have chosen not to do so. Mander's contented and unassuming Native American peoples, "living lightly on the planet" and sharing the bounty of nature based on "an older, alternative, nature-based philosophy," point the way to man's future: "It is the native societies, not our own, that hold the key to survival."[56]

Even for Rousseau, primitive harmony with nature had only been a dream, an ideal at best. But ecological cultural pessimists assert that the processes of civil society themselves will bring it about, thanks to technology's self-destruction and the inevitable reversion to primitive conditions. In Good News (1980) the wilderness writer Edward Abbey predicted that "the military-industrial state will disappear from the surface of the Earth within fifty years," followed by "the triumph of love, life and rebellion." Abbey helped to inspire the Earth First! movement with his 1975 novel The Monkey Wrench Gang, in which a group of renegade environmentalists stall construction of a highway through the wilderness by sabotaging trucks, earth movers, and other equipment. The monkeywrenchers consciously imitate Viet Cong guerrillas, even to the point of resorting to gunplay in order to elude capture. Edward Abbey made no apologies when Earth First! turned his message into direct action; he even composed their official ecotage manual, *Eco-Defense.* In a profound sense, he is the intellectual twin of the Unabomber. The fantasies Abbey spun in his writings the Unabomber translated into deeds.

Abbey advocated a radical and total rejection of what he called "syphilization." His dominant images of modern society are of lifelessness and death. A visit to lower Manhattan in 1956 presented Abbey with the spectacle of "cold frozen tomblike grandeur: a fearsome and inhuman spectacle, more like Death Valley and Skull Canyon than human habitation." He wrote afterwards, "our civilization has obviously entered its Tiberian phase—the barbarian mass in the East [i.e., the Soviet Union and China] merely waiting."[57]

Like Captain Nemo, Abbey felt the vital power of organic nature, which man's presence jarred and disturbed.* Abbey was well aware of his own links to the tradition of cultural pessimism: "Heidegger in his alpine cabin. Zarathustra in his cave. Jesus in the wilderness. Nietzsche alone in his madness."[58] He rejected the sentimental humanitarian appeals of other ecologists ("you can *not* change human nature without mutilating human beings") and attacked the American welfare state as passionately as he did the "warfare state." He also fantasized about striking back. Traveling in 1959 down Glen Canyon, which was soon to be dammed into a lake, Abbey mused:

How much dynamite, we wondered aloud to each other, would be needed to destroy the dam? How delightful and just, we imagined, to have our dynamite so integrated into the dam's wiring system, that when the president or the secretary of the interior and the governor, together

---

*"Looking out on this panorama of light, space, rock, and silence," Abbey wrote, visiting a spot along the Colorado River where a suicidal man had tried to jump to his death, "I am inclined to congratulate the dead man on his choice of jumping-off place; he had good taste. He had good luck—I envy him his manner of going; to die alone, on a rock under sun at the brink of the unknown, like a wolf, like a great bird, seems to me very good luck indeed." Quoted in Rik Scarce, *Ecowarriors* (Chicago, 1990), p. 243.

with their swarms of underlings, the press and hordes of tourists [gathered], it would be the white pudgy finger of the biggest bigshot, pressing the little black button . . . that would blow to smithereens the official himself, his guests, the tourists, the bridge, and Glen Canyon Dam.[59]

Shortly before his death, Abbey had a Volney-like vision of a new postmodern civilization emerging from the rubble of the old, consisting of "scattered human populations modest in number that live by fishing, hunting, food-gathering, small-scale farming and ranching" who will "assemble yearly in the ruins of the great cities for annual festivals of moral, spiritual, artistic, and intellectual renewal. . . ."[60] Of course, some unnamed catastrophe has by then presumably thinned out an overpopulated planet to enable Abbey's arcadian paradise to come into existence. But, again, catastrophic destruction, especially if self-induced, is never bad news for the cultural pessimist. It represents opportunity—as part of pessimism's apocalyptic inheritance.

## GREEN UNIVERSAL HISTORIES: JEREMY RIFKIN AND ALBERT GORE

Ecological pessimism presents us with an anticivilized "universal history." Jeremy Rifkin's *Beyond Beef* (1992) does the same thing but in reverse. Instead of man's agrarian communities supplanting his older nomadic ones, thus sealing the doom of the planet by his appetite for arable acres, it is the agricultural community that lives lightly on the land. Agrarian man forms a peaceful, vegetarian society worshiping life, not taking it. The intruder into this Garden of Eden, Rifkin theorizes, is the nomadic herdsman with his wandering flocks and technology of the horse. He plunders his neighbors in his greed for cattle; the earth is for him his free range—his "empire of liberty," as it were. "Much of Western history," Rifkin writes, "is an account of the on-going struggle between two groupings, one herdsman, the other agriculturalist, the first depending on grass, the other on grain," to the advantage of the former.[61]

When Kurgan horsemen descended into the Fertile Crescent from the central Asian steppes in 4000 B.C., Rifkin claims, they imposed their character on the lands they conquered. "Fiercely independent, militaristic, detached from the land, acquisitive, and utilitarian . . . they were the great invaders, the feared horsemen of the north." They were also prototypical capitalists, ruthlessly desiring to "capture, possess, and exploit" the land.[62] And who were these wanderers? The Indo-Europeans: Germans, Romans, Greeks, Hindu Brahmins, and Persians—Gobineau's Aryans, in fact. So the Aryan warrior makes yet another appearance, this time in the unfamiliar guise of an agent of *Zivilisation*, not *Kultur*.

These cattle-herding Aryan conquerors (Rifkin enjoys pointing out that the Sanskrit word for battle means "desire for cattle") prepared "the ground for modern capitalism and the colonial era in world history." Rifkin argues that "a radical new form of economics was being readied for the world stage, one based on ruthless acquisition and later justified by naked self-interest." From Attila the Hun to the mounted Spanish conquistadores to the beef-eating culture of eighteenth-century commercial Britain (where "the taste for fat was synonymous with the taste for opulence, for power and privilege"), a cultural inheritance of herding and military prowess pointed the way to Western domination of the globe.

Like a carnivorous plague, it spread its herds of flatulent, methane-gas-producing cattle across the Eurasian landmass and the Americas. Even the nineteenth-century meat-packing plant has its place in world history, as the ancestor of the modern industrial process: it was a "disassembly line" functioning within "a profit-driven, utilitarian framework."[63] Today, Rifkin concludes, "they line up at McDonald's in cities around the world, the utilitarian spirit of the age drowning out any reservations they might entertain about the Faustian bargain they are entering into." Rifkin even quotes a Japanese executive who said, "If we eat hamburgers for a thousand years, we will become blond. And when we become blond we will conquer the world."[64]

Meanwhile, man and earth pay the price—through deforestation, global warming, high cholesterol combined with mass starvation, not to mention the glorification of the violence of the cattleman—as Rifkin's cattle empire turns into Gary Nash's and Richard Slotkin's frontier of violence. In short, Western man's technological prowess proves to be a function of his corrupt culture, rather than (as older cultural pessimists like Nietzsche and Marcuse had argued) vice versa. This makes it possible for the eco-pessimist to invalidate the cultural efforts not only of Western man but of the rest of the species as well. This is precisely what Albert Gore will do in *Earth in the Balance.*

Gore's contribution, like Senator George Mitchell's earlier *World on Fire,* demonstrates how widespread the assumptions of environmental pessimism, in both their late-liberal and more radical forms, have become. *Earth in the Balance* is also self-consciously, even earnestly, philosophical; it claims to be as much about the nature and origin of Western culture as about the environment. The names Nietzsche, Heidegger, Fromm, Adorno, and Sartre do not grace its pages but their presence is palpable.* Their pessimistic view of Western culture prompts a further judgment on Gore's part. It is not just Western man but human beings as rational beings who are ultimately at fault: their impulses as social creatures and culture-bearers *at every level* guarantee their self-destruction. By this long-winding retreat, the fear of the decline of the West leads inevitably to a rejection of the very process that the notion of civilization had once stood for.

The term "civilization" appears constantly in *Earth in the Balance.* For Gore, civilization equals technology; they are essentially one and the same. The civilizing process involves the progressive alienation of human beings from their natural environment, until we finally reach today's desperate plight. "Modern industrial civilization, as presently organized, is colliding violently with our planet's ecological system." Its "vast technological power" has constituted a "ferocious" and deliberate assault on the planet and its resources. Now the old assumptions on which modern civilization's rise was built have proved hollow; the destruction of all living things can only be averted by a shift in the values of civilization itself.[65]

So far, so familiar. But Gore's modern civilization is also Nietzsche's civilization, distorting and destroying human spiritual power and the sense of the sanctity of the world around us. It is shallow; "the pursuit of happiness and comfort" are its paramount values, along with "the consumption of an endless stream of shiny new products." This leads us to

---

*However, the names of Walter Benjamin and Merleau-Ponty do. *Earth in the Balance*, pp. 203, 384.

"forget what we really feel and abandon the search for authentic purpose and meaning in our lives." Civilization is also inauthentic in a Sartre-Heidegger sense, trapped in "the frenzied destruction of the natural world" and the "obsession with inauthentic substitutes for direct experience with real life."

As in Bookchin, modern gender roles, with the "dominance" of male over female, are the egregious product of this separation of Western man from nature. Gore even compares the modern West to a dysfunctional family, whose warped children—ourselves—cannot separate themselves from the false gratifications it offers: "The food on the supermarket shelves, the water in the faucets in our homes, the shelter and sustenance, the clothing and purposeful work, our entertainment, even our identity—all these our civilization provides, and we dare not even think about separating ourselves from such beneficence."[66] Dysfunctional or sick—the Nietzschean element is obvious. The morality (in Nietzsche's sense) of this dysfunctional family, "the unwritten rules that govern our relationship to the environment," has been inherited and "passed down from one generation to the next" since Descartes and the Scientific Revolution. But the true origins, Gore reveals to us, go back even further, to Plato and the Greeks and the fateful rational heritage that has shaped Western metaphysics and science.

Inspired by Plato's example, "the new modern person pointed decisively upward," Gore explains, "away from nature, away from earth." This forgetfulness of Being, as Heidegger would put it, marks the most important "fundamental shift in Western thinking—which in a very real sense marks the beginning of modern history." By giving human beings increasing dominance over nature and matter, this spiritually dead *Zivilisation* impairs "the ability to feel our connections to the natural world." Separating mind from body, and the Other from the self, Western man became what Descartes said he was: a ghost in the machine. At times Gore can even sound like Bergson, bemoaning the loss of "a direct connection to the vividness, vibrancy, and aliveness of the rest of the natural world."[67] To compensate for his spiritual emptiness, man begins a frenzied assault on the earth itself; this is reminiscent of Adorno's description of anti-Semitism in *The Dialectic of Enlightenment*, in which those "who must pay for their strength with an intense alienation from nature" can find relief only "by preying on the weak"—in this case nature itself. Pollution, global warming, ozone depletion are the egregious results.

Old-fashioned Romantic vitalism also surfaces in Gore's book, in a specifically ecological guise: the so-called Gaia thesis, which has clearly had a profound impact on his thinking. This is the theory of James Lovelock and others that the planet Earth is literally alive, the biosphere forming a single organism with a life principle and self-regulating mechanisms making up its ecology. This unified and unifying life force, of course, existed three and a half billion years before the appearance of man as a species. Given humanity's egregious record since in "fouling the nest and posing a threat to the total life of the planet," the Gaia theorist is prompted to seriously pose the question, "Does man have a place on the planet?" After due reflection, Lovelock is forced to conclude that yes, he does. But the human being is an afterthought, an intrusive latecomer (not unlike Kirkpatrick Sale's Columbus) with an uncertain purpose within Gaia's living whole, which moves and grows without paying him much notice: "Any species that adversely affects the environment is doomed, but life goes on."[68]

For Gore this vision of a vitalist Gaia invokes a "spiritual response" as he reflects on the "deeper meaning" of the environmental crusade. It leads him to a kind of Haeckel-like pantheism, in which, "by experiencing nature in its fullest—our own and that of all creation—we can glimpse an infinite image of God." This vitalist truth, he notes, has been reflected in all the world's religions (except, perhaps, Western Christianity).* Indeed, throughout *Earth in the Balance* Gore points to religion rather than science as the source of true insight into nature's vital order. Even that old citadel of vitalism, *Kultur*, fails in this regard; indeed, it soon becomes apparent that man-made culture is nature's first and foremost enemy.

Gore's vitalism is, like Haeckel's, entirely biological. *All* culture, not only Western civilization but even that of Rousseau's noble savage, stands more or less pitted against the natural order. In Gore's ecological anthropology, human beings' cultural ascent begins with the production

---

*Gore hedges on this last point. Compare *Earth in the Balance*, p. 265 with pp. 260–61.

of symbolic representations of the world in myth, cave paintings, and stone tools, by which "we learn to manipulate the world itself." Culture is power over nature, whether we are making an arrowhead or a moon shot. "Whenever *any* technology is used to mediate our experience of the world, we gain power but we also lose something in the process," namely the immediacy of being.[69]

Technology in its modern form is merely an extreme extension of the tendency in all human culture, even the most primitive, to gain power over the environment. In this Gore agrees with the Oxford zoologist Jonathan Kingdon's radical vision in *Self-Made Man* (1993), in which the entire biological evolution of man is driven by his "lust for new tools" and technology. Since his emergence from the other primates, Kingdon sadly concludes, *Homo sapiens* has been Faustian man; whether Stone Age bushman, aborginal basket weaver, or Eskimo seal hunter, he is a born trasher of his environment whose insatiable appetite to change and transform nature brings him in the postmodern age to the point of imminent extinction.[70]

Gore is similarly forced to conclude that the threat to the planet is not just Western civilization but human civilization itself.[71] Gore pushes cultural pessimism to a new extreme, concluding that the human community was doomed from the very start. Gore's world history is the struggle between man and nature, but now it is nature that sets the pace rather than man. Nature, rather than any virtue or vice in man, becomes the driving force behind the collapse of civilizations past and present.

Other historians of climate and human geography have recently made the same claim. Ecobiologist David Attenborough has speculated that the real cause of Rome's collapse was not moral or economic or political collapse but deforestation.[72] Gore himself relies on the example of the Mayas as a parable for modern times: a sophisticated and urbanized culture, equipped with mathematics and astronomy, whose agricultural revolution was ruthlessly swept away by an eleventh-century global warming that brought climatic changes and soil erosion. That same climatic shift, Gore speculates, also melted the ice floes blocking the Scandinavian fjords and allowed the Vikings to reach Iceland and North America. The Vikings, the Germanic invasions, the rise of Egypt, and the fall of Mycenae and Rome—the great world-historical shifts of Romantic historiography all turn out to have been impossible without the permission of Gaia, as it were, and favorable weather. In this green universal history, we also get our final glimpse of the Indo-European peoples: setting off on their great trek not because of any inner vitality or racial restlessness, but in order to escape drought in the Central Asian steppes.[73]

## EPILOGUE: THE END OF MAN

In Toynbee's terms, the process of challenge and response has been turned inside out. Whether one looks to Rome's heedless deforestation, ancient China's abuse of its river systems, or the contemporary clearing of the rain forests, it is the human community that poses the challenge to nature, and it is nature's *élan vital* that provides the response. Floods, typhoons, global warming—Gaia strikes back. Foucault's image of the end of man, "a face drawn in sand at the edge of the sea," suddenly looms as a literal possibility.

The Deep Ecology movement has forthrightly rejected any notion that human beings have rights superior to those of any other species on the planet. Since human civilization has assumed the opposite, it constitutes an ongoing crime against the rights of the earth. "For thousands of years, Western culture has become increasingly obsessed with the idea of *dominance*," write authors William Devall and George Sessions: dominance of rich over poor, men over women, the West over non-Western cultures, and humans over nature. Deep Ecology seeks to dispel those illusions of dominance; instead there must be an "awakening of wholes greater than the sum of their parts," including the whole of the earth. Quoting Henry David Thoreau (and unconsciously echoing Michel Foucault), they assert that the world "is no place for man-worship."[74]

Deep Ecology's principles return us again to Haeckel's monism. There is no essential difference between the human and nonhuman halves of life. Biocentric equality assumes "all organisms and entities in the eco-sphere, as parts of the interrelated whole, are equal in intrinsic worth." Human beings, monkeys, whales, turtles, bees, and insects form a single ecocommunity. "The balance [between human and nonhuman habitats] has long been tipped in favor of humans," Arne Naess suggests. "Now we must shift the balance back to protect the habitat of other species."

Deep Ecology's radical renunciation of human claims to the planet galvanized the Earth First! founders. "It's not enough to save the remaining 10% of wilderness that remains," Dave Foreman, editor of *Earth First! Newsletter*, told a conference of ecologists. "It's time to restore it, to take it back." He even summoned up a kind of neo-Gobinian elite, "a warrior society to rise up out of the Earth and throw itself in front of the juggernaut of destruction, to be antibodies against the human pox" that has dominated the planet since man's first appearance. Like their counterparts in the radical animal rights movement, Earth Firsters see the issue of driving human beings out of wilderness areas as fundamentally a moral one. Radical ecologist Bill Devall has even compared cutting down trees to sending Jews to Auschwitz. Traditional environmental groups are "complicit" in these criminal practices, it is claimed, since they represent an "environmental humanism" that is one of "the last sputtering candles of the Enlightenment."[75]

Acts of civil disobedience—ecotage such as tree-spiking in the forests of the Pacific Northwest and kidnapping and releasing animals from laboratories—all become "points of resistance" that will provide "the springboard to deconstructing the values, like progress, to which civilization grants privilege." Earth First! radicals like Christopher Manes explicitly compare their program to Foucault's de-centering of Western humanism. They are also well aware of their long-term impact. As Dave Foreman puts it, "I think that the role of an avant garde group is to throw out ideas that are objected to as absurd or ridiculous at first, but end up trickling into the mainstream and becoming more accepted over time." This had been the case with the Gaia thesis, which radicals now frown on as being *too* human-friendly.[76]

This extremism has raised the ire of more pacific figures like Murray Bookchin, who has accused Earth First! of indulging in "eco-fascism."[77] On the other hand, the German Greens have condoned violence "against objects"—such as animal rights groups throwing paint on fur coats—as part of civil disobedience. In 1990 Earth First! activists tore down electricity towers in central California as part of their "monkey-wrenching" protest against Earth Day (the symbol of environmental humanism). Power went out for a hundred and forty thousand customers; other activists have hinted at a guerrilla war against loggers in the Northwest. Praise of violence is not unknown to political movements springing out of cultural pessimism: witness the German Nietzscheans and Frantz Fanon. However, Earth First!'s ecological pessimism has drifted very far from the familiar landmarks of *Kultur* and race, even in their contemporary multiculturalist forms. Man, it turns out, is the only creature who is *not* rooted on the planet. In the end he "lives lightly on the land" (in Jerry Mander's phrase) because as a biological species he is the unwanted latecomer. His anomalous presence, some theorize, may even have brought normal biological evolution of species to a stop.[78]

Man, then, is the ultimate stranger, "traditionless, utterly matter-of-fact, religionless, clever, unfruitful"—this is Spengler describing the degenerate world-city man in *The Decline of the West*. Deep ecology's *Homo sapiens* corresponds to Werner Sombart's trader or J.A. Hobson's capitalist Jew: a parasite, "a locust-like blight on the planet," according to deep ecologist Gary Snyder, to whom human history is one of "ravaging this precious, beautiful planet." And Gaia's final solution to this threat? "Nature will be able to reconstitute itself once the top of the food chain is lopped off—meaning us."[79] Activist Judi Bari has concluded, "I believe the Earth is going to rise up and throw us off . . . The Earth's failure to be able to sustain this kind of life will cause it to collapse. I'm sure life will survive that," she adds, "but I don't know that humans will. I don't know if we deserve to."[80]

Some radicals have even seriously hypothesized that humanity is a virus in the biosphere that requires a countervirus. This is AIDS; Christopher Manes in 1987 called HIV "the necessary solution" to human destruction of the planet. "To paraphrase Voltaire," he said, "if the AIDS epidemic didn't exist, radical environmentalists would have to invent one."[81] One recent best-selling book, by no means a piece of extremist propaganda, has suggested that super deadly viruses such as Ebola and Marburg are also part of the biosphere's reaction against "the human parasite" and the "cancerous rot-outs" of advanced industrial societies, which will incessantly spread their infectious poisons across the planet unless they are stopped.[82] In this ultimate declinist vision, not only modern society but man himself will soon be finally, mercifully extinct. His frenzied destruction of his environment, his plundering of the planet, all come to an end; the meaningless chatter of *Zivilisation* ceases.

The last word belongs to Haeckel's English disciple, D.H. Lawrence:

Birkin looked at the land, at the evening, and was thinking: "Well, if mankind is destroyed, if our race is destroyed like Sodom, and there is this beautiful evening with the luminous land and trees, I am satisfied. . . . Let mankind pass away—time it did. . . . Humanity doesn't embody the utterance of the incomprehensible any more. Humanity is a dead letter. . . . Let humanity disappear as quick as possible."[83]

# AFTERWORD

In his book *The Good Society and Its Discontents*, Robert Samuelson points out that modern Americans live a strange paradox. On the one hand, their material life has improved dramatically in the four decades since the end of World War II. Average life expectancy in 1930 was 58 years for men, 61 years for women. In 1990 it was 71 years for men, 79 years for women. Median family income in 1940 was $18,000 measured in 1993 dollars; in 1990 it was more than $39,000. Today the United States and other industrial economies grow on average at twice or three times the rate that they did in the nineteenth century. Taken in conjunction with its twin victories over fascism in World War II and communism in the Cold War, democratic capitalism represents an extraordinarily successful chapter in the history of human civilization.

Our public mood, on the other hand, clashes sharply with this underlying reality. It is no longer possible to attribute what Samuelson calls Americans' "unwarranted pessimism" to traumatic events like Vietnam, Watergate, or the assassination of John F. Kennedy. People remain disillusioned and fearful of the future long after these events have passed into history and even as the Cold War specter of imminent nuclear annihilation has faded. When he asked himself why, Samuelson blamed the failure of our modern "entitlement society" to meet its own utopian expectations. "Our overall sense of letdown," he concludes, "stems from the gap between our idealized society and the one we actually experience." He even draws a comparison to the Gilded Age, when American optimism and faith in progress seemed similarly crushed by the forces of industrial change.[1]

Samuelson may be right when he says that a sense of "failure and disappointment are preordained," but it is not as a result of disappointed expectations. The reasons lie deeper. The truth is that since the 1970s Americans have been living in a culture steeped in self-doubt and the anti-Western assumptions of cultural pessimism. The radical environmentalism that produced the Unabomber is only the most glaring example. Similar beliefs underlie our current attitudes toward corporate capitalism, with its vision of the tobacco lobby, nuclear power lobby, and arms lobby all supposedly poised to exploit, cheat, and poison the general public (those same assumptions drove the debate over NAFTA as well). Radical multiculturalism implies that American society systematically produces race hatreds and social inequities, while cultural pessimism's various other offshoots and branches insist that our society is irremediably racist, sexist, imperialist, homophobic, phallocentric, greedy, and proto-totalitarian; or alternatively (for those on the political Right), corrupt, decadent, mindless, hedonistic, apathetic, morally bankrupt, as well as proto-totalitarian.

In effect, the very things modern society does best—providing increasing economic affluence, equality of opportunity, and social and geographic mobility—are systematically deprecated and vilified by its direct beneficiaries. None of this is new or even remarkable. Contemporary headlines proclaiming that the computer revolution will produce "two nations" of rich and poor reproduce a debate over industrial society that reaches back to the 1840s. The current furor over immigration both in America and in Europe merely revisits the pessimistic fears of *fin de siècle* degenerationists such as Gustav Le Bon and E.A. Ross. America's perceived failures are in fact the failures that nineteenth-century intellectuals attributed to their own industrial civilization. The crucial difference is that these criticisms are now embedded in the fabric of mass culture. We live in an era of pop pessimism, with all the problems and limitations that cultural perspective tends to create.

Contemporary pessimism does not surface just in gloomy tracts like Allan Bloom's *The Closing of the American Mind* or Robert Bork's *Slouching Toward Gommorah*. We see it popularized in futuristic films like *The*

*Road Warrior, Total Recall, Waterworld,* and *Escape from New York,* whose implicit messages are all derived from cultural pessimist models. They present a future in which traditional standards of barbarism and civilization are deliberately inverted. "Normal" civil society has become repressive, decadent, devoid of creativity, and profoundly antinatural: its technologies have led it to the brink of destruction, if (as in *The Terminator* and *The Road Warrior*) they have not already destroyed it. Those individuals vital and strong enough to struggle against society's self-destructive tide are portrayed as living on its margins: as petty criminals, rogue cops, and social vagrants, the cultural underclass whom Nietzsche termed "the immoralists."

The modern action hero is (in a favorite Weimar phrase) "a wanderer between two worlds," that of modern decadence and the higher reality that lies beyond it. He tends to be rude, crude, and inarticulate, as proof of his uncontaminated vitality, while villains invariably speak with sophisticated, civilized accents. In fact, today's action heroes are all cardboard cutouts from the pages of Nietzsche. Their dynamic will to power dwarfs their corrupted civilized environment and ultimately destroys it. Their creators supply them with ample sex, violence, and obscene language as signs of their underlying vitality, while normal society shatters into chaotic fragments of broken glass, exploding cars and airliners, and demolished buildings.

The same pessimistic themes persist in rock music and on MTV. Camille Paglia has pointed out the close similarities between the aristocratic dandy of 1830s Paris—the world of Gobineau and Gautier—and the modern rock star. The truth is that our modern bad boy rock star is the direct descendant of the cultural rebel of Baudelaire, who establishes his own vitality by a defiant display of decadence. *Fin de siècle* aesthetes, like the modern rocker, viewed their own society as hopelessly decadent and unworthy of their respect, but the material trappings of that decadence then served as a springboard for artistic creativity. In a similar fashion, musicians such as Madonna use decadent images of sexuality and sado-masochism in order to generate an antibourgeois, vital self, while performers such as Howard Stern accomplish the same thing by exploiting images of the grotesque and perverse. In the case of "gansta rap," we even cross the line into the Nietzschean wilderness of nihilistic violence and a vitality "beyond good and evil," and neo-Nazi heavy metal bands remind us of the original affinity between Nietzsche and Gobineau, between cultural pessimism and racial pessimism.

In the action movie *Broken Arrow*, a character says, "You're out of your mind." The other replies: "Yeah, ain't it cool?" This is the contemporary Nietzschean spirit. Yet today we have the sense that it has also outworn its welcome. Complaints about our degraded and degrading "mass culture" multiply, even as almost against their will our educational institutions and entertainment and news media find themselves returning repeatedly to those same themes. These include not just violence and sex as expressions of vitality, but all the assumptions of historical pessimism that underpin cultural pessimism: the "failure" of modern democracy, the loss of identity in mass society, the threat of corporate capitalism and the computerized police state, the life-threatening dangers of too much technology and science (in industry and the economy) or too little (in medicine and health), and a constantly "vanishing" middle class. From universities and public policy institutes to daytime talk shows, we are the heirs to the modern idea of decline in its strange twin form.

Cultural pessimism is the reverse image of historical pessimism, just as the idea of decline is the reverse image of the idea of progress. The historical pessimist sees civilization's virtues under attack from malign and destructive forces that it cannot overcome; cultural pessimism claims that those forces form the civilizing process from the start. The historical pessimist worries that his own society is about to destroy itself, the cultural pessimist concludes that it deserves to be destroyed. The historical pessimist sees "disaster in the pole star," as Henry Adams put it: the cultural pessimist looks forward to disaster, since he believes something better will rise from its ashes.

Perhaps the most salient feature of the twentieth century has been the tremendous upsurge of this cultural pessimism, not just in the realm of ideas, but directly into the arena of politics and culture. Before the Second World War its political character was that of the extreme Right. It took hold of figures like Georges Sorel, who helped to inspire the Italian fascist movement, and Marcus Garvey, who imitated it. In France it animated a series of fascist writers and intellectuals who had the opportunity to put their ideas into practice during the Vichy regime. In Germany, of course, it inspired "the revolution on the Right" and the rise of National Socialism. Writers like Wyndham Lewis and Ezra Pound, and political figures like Oswald Mosley and Gerald L.K. Smith, even emerged in the two centers of civilized liberal values, England and the United States. When combined with the bloody imperatives of racial pessimism, cultural pessimism helped to produce the totalitarian nightmare of Nazi Germany.

World War II and the Holocaust should have spelled the defeat of cultural pessimism, and for a brief spell it seemed they had. There was a revival of interest in Western history and its humanist heritage. Popular works like Will and Ariel Durant's *The Story of Civilization* and Herbert J. Muller's *The Idea of Freedom* and *The Uses of the Past* gave readers a strongly positive view of Western man's artistic and intellectual heritage, while William O'Neill's *The Rise of the West* rewrote Toynbee's world history in a new, more optimistic key. Ernst Cassirer's *The Myth of the State*, Karl Popper's *The Open Society and Its Enemies*, and Frederich von Hayek's *Road to Serfdom* all tried to show how modern Europeans had veered away from their nineteenth-century liberal roots and toward political tyranny. In *The Vital Center*, Arthur Schlesinger, Jr., pointed out the virtues of a liberal Western society and culture that was now under assault from another form of totalitarianism, Soviet Communism, while Lionel Trilling's *The Liberal Imagination* revealed how much "the open society" depends on a delicate balance between conventional moral certainties and creative doubt.

Yet the roots of cultural pessimism remained. Existentialism, modernism, critical Marxism, and various other avant-garde movements kept its basic assumptions safe from critical scrutiny. Then the Vietnam War in the sixties and economic malaise in the seventies played much the same role that World War I and the Great Depression had played four decades earlier in weakening public confidence in modern Western society and its values. The way was open for a new wave of cultural criticism, emanating this time from the far left. Like its predecessor, the cultural pessimism of the Left argued that the modern West was in crisis and about to destroy itself, raising the possibility of something new to take its place. As Martin Heidegger had announced in his rectoral address in 1933 celebrating the advent of Hitler, "The beginning still *is*. It does not lie behind us, as something that was long ago, but stands before us."

Despite their political differences, the two movements are more alike that different. Critical Marxism, multiculturalism, postmodernism, and radical environmentalism not only share many of the same heroes as the earlier "revolution on the Right"—Friedrich Nietzsche, Georges Sorel, Martin Heidegger, Arthur Schopenhauer—but also share the same contempt for the liberal, rational traditions of post-Enlightenment Europe. They spurn any notion of "normal" social progress according to a Western model. Like their rightist predecessors, they see belief in the autonomy of the individual; in the possession of private property as a fundamental natural right; in science and technology as conducive to human happiness rather than otherwise; and in the pursuit of happiness as an essentially *rational* activity—as a source of corruption, exploitation, and death. If Herbert Marcuse, Toni Morrison, Ronald Takaki, Michel Foucault, Noam Chomsky, Edward Said, and Murray Bookchin seem startlingly new and radical to their admirers, their words seem all too familiar to others.

But the cultural pessimism of the Left also brought, as we have seen, a startling reversal of analytic poles. Instead of imperialism and militarism serving as antidotes to debilitating liberal civilization, they are, as suggested by W.E.B. Du Bois, presented as normal expressions of it. Instead of white Nordic man serving as the bearer of cultural and racial vitality, it is Third World nonwhites who now perform that role. Instead of seeing modern technology as the antithesis of the Aryan cultural tradition, authors like Jeremy Rifkin argue that it has been its most characteristic product and ally. While cultural pessimism of the Right castigated the physical degenerate and sexual deviant as typical products of a "decadent" West, cultural pessimism on the Left celebrates and extols them.

This is the face of cultural pessimism today. Its primary base is, notoriously, among intellectuals and what is sometimes called the "new class": teachers, students, artists, writers, and members of the media. It is by no means a mass political movement. Of course, neither was right-wing cultural pessimism in its initial stages, when it caught the imagination of intellectuals, artists, and university professors and students in

European universities on the eve of World War I. Then the war weakened the self-confidence of their opponents and gave the Right the opportunity to mold politics in their own radical image, through the Brownshirts, Blackshirts, and other fascist political organizations. We can already see something of the ugly side of today's cultural pessimism as a mass movement in Afrocentrism—which has prompted an angry backlash from old-line liberals like Arthur Schlesinger, Jr., in *The Disuniting of America*. We see it in the activities of radical environmentalism, such as the Unabomber and Earth First! eco-warriors whom more "moderate" environmentalists like Murray Bookchin characterize as "eco-fascists."

This is not to say that these movements pose the same danger that fascism or Nazism did. Making *that* sort of prediction would, of course, involve falling into the same trap that declinists and other alarmists invariably end up in. But it should remind us of a salient point: that the cultural pessimist uses the historical pessimist in order to gain a secure foothold in popular culture. Without Jacob Burckhardt's gloomy vision of the European future, Nietzsche's nihilist vitalism would have seemed ludicrous. Without an Oswald Spengler pronouncing the bourgeois West extinct, the German revolution of the Right would have lacked its sense of historical inevitability. When an Arnold Toynbee or Paul Kennedy or Kevin Phillips or Robert Bork solemnly writes our civilization's epitaph, the cultural pessimists gather to celebrate at the wake.

Do we conclude, then, that anyone with misgivings about the direction of modern society should keep silent, or that such misgivings are fanciful or the result of self-delusion? Certainly not. The effects of rapid industrialization in the nineteenth century were in fact deeply disruptive and inflicted pain on large numbers of people. Certainly the survivors of World War I were entitled to feel shaken by their experience in the trenches and to ask whether the society that had sent them there deserved their loyalty. The Holocaust and the large numbers of people, great and small, implicated in committing it, or at least allowing it to happen, can make the phrase "European civilization" die on our lips.

It is legitimate to deplore certain trends and developments in any society as malign or destructive. However, it is quite another thing to draw, or allow to be drawn, a picture that suggests that these problems have such deeply rooted causes that they are unsolvable, or have such far-reaching implications that only a drastic overhaul of the society or culture *as a whole* can fix them. Yet this was precisely what large numbers of Western intellectuals did at the end of the nineteenth century and again in the century that followed. It is this assumption—that modern Western civilization functions as a whole, and that its problems require holistic, not piecemeal, solutions—which lies at the heart of both the pessimistic persuasion and its optimistic counterpart, the blind faith in Progress.

The nineteenth century became addicted to the notion that societies form systematic wholes, in which every part performs some useful function or operation. Philosophers, sociologists, and historians treated societies in mechanical or organic terms: they functioned either like a machine or a living organism or (as in the case of Herbert Spencer) both. The social group was more than just an aggregate of individuals; the social group or nation or civilization had an existence of its own, with its own life-cycle, and was governed by its own laws. The laws of social development and change were analogous to physical laws governing material bodies, making it possible to speak of the "social sciences," or *sciences humaines*.

These deterministic assumptions encouraged a host of grand schemes for understanding history, of which Marxism is only the most notorious example. Every event, past, present, and future, had to play a defining part within a larger whole that developed according to its own rules, apart from the wishes and inclinations of individuals.[2] Hence, World War I and the Great Depression did not exist in isolation or have discreet causes: they arose from the balance of relationships within the systematic whole, such as "the crisis of late capitalism" or "the death throes of European imperialism." Similarly, aspects of social life such as popular culture, intellectual and artistic activities, and moral attitudes were assumed to reflect the larger health of the totality. Terms like "health," "growth," and "sickness" as applied to a society and civilization—even the notion of "crisis" or the breaking point of a body's fever—reflect this same organicist bias.

It was this holistic view of society that the declinist tradition inherited and exploited. It encouraged the use of such metaphors as "parasite," "disease," and "cancer" for describing undesirable changes in the social fabric. They underpin every notion of Romantic vitalism and racial pessimism, from the ideas of Gobineau and Nietzsche to those of the Afrocentrists, as well as contemporary cultural pessimism. Sartre's existentialism, Heidegger's Philosophy of Being, Foucault's analysis of will to power, and Edward Said's totalizing Western gaze all start with the assumption that modern Western society forms an interconnected whole or total process, which cannot be understood or attacked in a piecemeal fashion but only through a radical "break."

The eco-pessimist makes the same assumption with regard to the biosphere: the organic-holistic approach is the key to the radical ecologist's view of man and nature. In the same vein, multiculturalism has become a haven for every sort of nineteenth-century historical determinism. The notion that social groups are never merely aggregates of their members, and that "we must study the history of the [social] group, its traditions and institutions, if we are to understand and explain it as it is now," once propped up Romantic nationalist history and universal histories of civilization from Hegel to Toynbee.[3] Now it has become dogma among feminists, proponents of African-American studies, and other minority group-identities. Without it, in fact, much of the multiculturalist program would collapse under its own weight.

So our contemporary radicals and so-called progressives turn out not to be so progressive after all. The Unabombers, Albert Gores, Cornel Wests, Noam Chomskys, Toni Morrisons, and Edward Saids are actually throwbacks to a nineteenth-century view of society in which the modern West is a predetermined whole created by the impersonal forces of race, class, gender, and nation. An alternative view of society and social action, one that stems from the Enlightenment and an earlier humanist tradition, is not much in evidence these days.

This book has been primarily about the idea of civilizational decline and the rise of cultural pessimism. But in some ways, ironically, it has also turned out to be a history of another kind of decline—the decline of the liberal humanist image of man and society, of its morals and values, in the face of its various opponents. Decline might not be the best term. A better metaphor might be that of a grand recessional, as the luminous exponents of the liberal Western tradition one by one abandoned the stage, and eugenicists, racists and racial pessimists, fascists, modernists, and multiculturalists took over.

That older tradition involves much more than just a blind confidence in progress and in the superiority of Western civilization over any alternative. The liberal humanist recognizes that civil society, like all human institutions, has been deliberately constructed to fulfill various purposes, purposes necessarily supplied by individuals acting in concert. Race, class, and gender do not in fact determine the direction of society and history: they operate on the surface of things. The real forces for change lie in the choices we make as individuals, the actions they set in motion, and their consequences for others. The most characteristic product of the Western humanist tradition is the free and autonomous individual—who is also the cultural pessimist's worst enemy.

The cultural pessimist always confronts the durability of "atomizing" Western institutions—capitalism, technology, democratic politics, the basic rules of law and morality—with a sense of frustration. How can an oppressive, artificial, fraudulent monolith so obviously doomed to failure continue to prosper and even expand its influence? Yet that durability, and its continuing appeal, is closely related to its individualistic bias operating as a source of *strength* rather than weakness. Humanism assumes that since people generate conflicts and problems in society, they can also resolve them, and it concentrates on supplying people with the material, moral, and cultural tools to do so.

As Tocqueville remarked to Gobineau after reading his *Essay on Inequality,*

> Yes, I sometimes despair of mankind. Who doesn't. . . . I have always said that it is more difficult to stabilize and maintain liberty in our new democratic societies than in certain aristocratic societies in the past. But I shall never dare to think it impossible. And I pray to God lest He inspire me with the idea that one might as well give up trying.[4]

Tocqueville's nineteenth-century liberalism was in a sense the culmination of that humanist tradition. Undeniably, it generated its own forms of orthodoxy and complacency, which prompted a backlash. What Tocqueville in 1853 already sensed in Gobineau's ideas has now largely come to pass. Modern pessimism has done more than just counterbalance excessive optimism regarding the future; it has managed to wreck our faith in the idea of civilization itself. Our real problem is not that our popular culture is filled with obscenities or trivialities, but that no one seems able to present the necessary intellectual grounds for an alternative.

In the end, the whole debate over "the decline of the West" presents us with a false set of choices. The alternative to historical pessimism about the future of modern society is *not* optimistic complacency: they are opposite sides of the same holistic view. The alternative to cultural pessimism is not some sort of megatrend "third wave" or other futurological adventure of authors like Warren Wagar and Alvin Toffler. The classical liberal view originally sprang up precisely because its adherents recognized the dangers of insisting that individuals have significance only if they are part of a larger whole. In earlier times, that holistic-organic model had been "the great chain of being," in which a person's status was assigned by God and nature and enforced by political authority. Enlightenment thinkers rebelled against this sort of social determinism; John Locke defined this position of "being under the determination of some other than himself" without that individual's consent as a form of tyranny. One of the great blessings of the civilizing process, the Enlightenment concluded, is that it raises humans above that servile status by making them aware of their individual rights, interests, and powers as well as free from irrational passions and fears.[5]

The Middle Ages had given that awesome power of directing the fate of the individual to God and His representatives on earth—popes and kings; the nineteenth century gave it instead to history, first as progress, then as decline. However, the Enlightenment had posed the really revolutionary question: What if society is not an organism with a predetermined course and lifespan, but is made up of individual organisms, each with the power to more or less shape his own destiny? Then society's future is not the product of some inevitable law of Progress, or Decrepitude; it is what the society's members decide to make of it. At one stroke, the *anakuklosis* is broken and the cycle of disillusion and despair dispelled—not out in the world, but where it actually exists, in the minds of men and women.

# NOTES

## Introduction

1. Lasch, *Culture of Narcissism*, p. xiv.
2. Kennedy, *Rise and Fall of the Great Powers*, pp. xvi, xviii, xxiii.
3. K. Phillips, *Arrogant Capital*, pp. xii–xiii.
4. West, *Race Matters*, pp. 18; 6.
5. Kennon, *Twilight of Democracy*; Graham Fuller, *The Democracy Trap* (New York, 1991); Jean B. Elshtain, *Democracy on Trial* (New York, 1995); Victor Kamber, *Giving Up on Democracy* (Washington, DC, 1995); Daniel Lazare, *The Frozen Republic* (New York, 1996); Rose L. Martin, *The Selling of America* (Santa Monica, CA, 1973); David Calleo, *The Bankrupting of America* (New York, 1992); Edward Luttwak, *The Endangered American Dream* (New York, 1993); and William Grieder, *Who Will Tell the People?* (New York, 1989).
6. Murray and Herrnstein, *Bell Curve*, pp. 510, 526; 509.
7. Gore, *Earth in the Balance*, pp. xii, 295.
8. *Ibid.*, pp. 12, 183.
9. *Ibid.*, pp. 1, 367.
10. *Washington Post*, September 19, 1995, special section entitled "The Unabomber: Industrial Society and Its Future," pp. 1–5.
11. Spengler, *Decline of the West*, Vol. 1, p. 40.
12. Historian Ernest Tuveson has even argued that the modern idea of progress actually spring from Christian doctrines of the millenium and the return of Christ's kingdom: that progress, even in its Marxist version, is a secularized version of the Apocalypse. See *Millenium and Utopia: A Study in the Background of the Idea of Progress*.

## Chapter 1

1. Bury, *Idea of Progress*; Teggart, *Theory and Processes of History*; Van Doren, *Idea of Progress*; Nisbet, *History of the Idea of Progress*. See also A. J. Todd, *Theories of Social Progress* (New York, 1918).
2. *Iliad*, trans. E.V. Rieu (Harmondsworth, 1950), p. 231.

3. Zimmer, *Philosophies of India*, p. 106; Levin, *Myth of the Golden Age in the Renaissance*, pp. 9–10.
4. Quoted in H. Frankfurt, *Ancient Egyptian Religion* (Chicago, 1948), p. 143.
5. Sophocles, *Oedipus at Colonus*, 608–15 (the translation in mine).
6. Horace, *Odes*, Bk. I, XXIX, pp. 41–48 (the translation is by John Dryden).
7. Polybius, *The Rise of the Roman Empire* (Harmondsworth, 1979), pp. 309–10.
8. Ezell, *Fortune's Merry Wheel*; Patch, *Goddess Fortune in Medieval Literature*.
9. G. Karl Galinsky, *The Heracles Theme: Adaptations of the Hero in the Literature from Homer to the Twentieth Century* (Totowa, NJ, 1972); Patch, *Goddess Fortune in Medieval Literature*; Pocock, *Machiavellian Moment*.
10. Cf. *Peloponnesian War*, B. One, Ch. 1, and Edelstein, *Idea of Progress in Classical Antiquity*, pp. 30–31.
11. A.C. Prudentius (b. 384 A.D.), quoted in Dawson, *Making of Europe*, p. 40.
12. Yates, *Astraea*; Burke, *Images of the Sun King*.
13. Tuveson, *Millennium and Utopia*.
14. "To the Christian Nobility of the German Nation," in *Three Treatises by Martin Luther*, pp. 35, 86.
15. E.g., Tully, *A Discourse Concerning Property*.
16. Vico, *New Science of History*.
17. Davie, *Philosophers of the Scottish Enlightenment*; Hont and Ignatieff, eds. *Wealth and Virtue*.
18. Quoted in Pocock, *Virtue, Commerce, and Liberty*, p. 49.
19. Cf. Burke's remarks on women and the development of chivalry in *Reflections on the Revolution in France*, and Muller, *Adam Smith in His Time and Ours*, pp. 126–30.
20. "Sensus communis," in *Characteristics* (1711; New York, 1967), p. 46.
21. Robertson, *The Progress of Society in Europe*, p. 67.
22. Burrow, Collini, and Winch, *That Noble Science of Politics*, pp. 54–55.
23. Smith, *Wealth of Nations* (Harmondsworth, 1970), B. III, p. 508.
24. Guizot, *The History of Civilization in Europe*, p. 11.
25. Quoted in Laffey, *Civilization and Its Discontented*, p. 22.
26. Quoted in Bury, *Idea of Progress*, p. 167.
27. On Fichte, see Nisbet, *History of the Idea of Progress*, pp. 274–75; the quotation from Dugald Stewart is in *That Noble Science of Politics*, p. 35.
28. Meek, ed., *Turgot on Progress, Sociology and Economics*, pp. 55–59.
29. See Becker, *Heavenly City of the Eighteenth-Century Philosophers*.
30. Gibbon, *Decline and Fall*, Vol. 2, pp. 267; 442–43.
31. See Pocock, "David Hume and the American Revolution: Thoughts of a Dying North Briton," in *Virtue, Commerce, and Liberty*, pp. 125–41.
32. The so-called Gothic revival in architecture and art was part of the same melancholy obsession. Rosenblum, *Transformations in Late-Eighteenth-Century Art*, pp. 112–20.
33. Volney, *Ruins* (1787; English translation, 1802), Vol. 1, pp. 6–8.
34. Schneps, *Vorläufer Spenglers*.
35. Quoted in Schwartz, *Century's End*, p. 149.
36. Rousseau, *Discourse on Inequality*, pp. 115, 122.
37. Hegel, *Philosophy of History*, p. 17.
38. *Ibid.*, pp. 105–06; 18.
39. *Ibid.*, p. 456.
40. Popper, *Open Society and Its Enemies*, Vol. 2, p. 58.
41. Quoted in Nisbet, *History of the Idea of Progress*, p. 281.

42. Hegel, *Philosophy of Right*, Section 155.
43. "Socialism: Utopian and Scientific," in Feuer, ed., *Marx and Engels: Basic Writings on Politics and Philosophy*, p. 111.
44. Quoted in J.E. Sullivan, *Prophets of the West: An Introduction to the Philosophy of History* (New York, 1970), pp. 64–65.
45. Quoted in Nisbet, *History of the Idea of Progress*, p. 255.
46. Bury, *Idea of Progress*, p. 310.
47. Newman, *The Idea of a University*, p. 189.
48. E.g., Lévy-Bruhl, *Primitive Mentality* (Boston, 1922).
49. Quoted in Pick, *Faces of Degeneration*, p. 178, n. 5.
50. Fleming, *John William Draper and the Religion of Science*.
51. Wordsworth's lines are from *The Preludes*, begun in 1799 and finished in 1805. Blake's and Turner's views are described in K. Clark, *Civilisation*, pp. 308–09.
52. Schenk, *Mind of the European Romantics*, p. 32.
53. Kenneth Clark, *The Gothic Revival* (London, 1932).
54. Jennings, *Pandemonium*.
55. Mendilow, *Romantic Tradition in British Political Thought*, pp. 61, 69.
56. R. Gilman, *Decadence*.
57. Quoted in Buckley, *Triumph of Time*, p. 71.
58. Quoted in Swart, *Sense of Decadence*, p. 48.
59. Juvenal, *Satire VI*, 292–93 (the translation is mine).
60. Rousseau, *Discourse on the Arts and Sciences*, pp. 18–19.
61. Nietzsche, *Case of Wagner*, p. 170.
62. Quoted in Beckson, ed., *Aesthetes and Decadents*, p. xxx; Hansen, *Disaffections and Decadence*, pp. 4–5.
63. *Intimate Journals*, p. 56.

## Chapter 2

1. "Memoires de Louis de Gobineau," quoted in Biddiss, pp. 11–12.
2. Boissel, *Comte de Gobineau*, p. 54.
3. Poggioli, *Theory of the Avant Garde*.
4. Schamber, *Artist as Politician*, p. 135.
5. Quoted in Del Caro, *Nietzsche Contra Nietzsche*, p. 41. On antibourgeois themes, see C. Graña, *Modernity and Its Discontents*.
6. Quoted in Swart, *Sense of Decadence*, p. 75.
7. Graña, *Modernity and Its Discontents*, pp. 92–93.
8. Gautier, "Preface to *Mademoiselle de Maupin*," in E. Weber, ed., *Movements, Currents, Trends*, pp. 76–103. See also Siegel, *Bohemian Paris*.
9. Schwab, *Oriental Renaissance*, p. 430.
10. *Intimate Journals*, p. 75.
11. *Ibid.*, p. 91.
12. Biddiss, p. 17.
13. Tocqueville, *European Revolution*, p. 193.
14. *Ibid.*, pp. 202, 203; Gobineau, *Essay on the Inequality of the Human Races*, p. 62.
15. Price, *French Second Republic*.
16. Gregor-Dellin, *Wagner*.
17. Quoted in Buenzod, *La Formation*, p. 270.
18. Biddiss, p. 100.

19. Harris, *Rise of Anthropological Theory*.
20. Mosse, *Toward the Final Solution*, pp. 28–29; Voegelin, *Die Rassenidee in der Geiste-geschichte von Ray bis Carus*.
21. Bainton, *Racial Theories*, pp. 19–22.
22. E.g., Curtin, *Image of Africa*; Bainton, *Idea of Race and Race Theory*.
23. Buenzod, *La Formation*, p. 234.
24. Gobineau, *Inequality of Human Races*, p. 206; Spring, *Vitalism of Count de Gobineau*.
25. Schwab, *Oriental Renaissance*, pp. 35–36.
26. Levitine, *Dawn of Bohemianism*.
27. Quoted in Poliakov, *Aryan Myth*, p. 197.
28. Quoted in Biddiss, p. 117.
29. Gobineau, *Essai*, pp. 171–72; 170.
30. *Ibid.*, Cf. Nietzsche, *Genealogy of Morals*, First Essay, Sections 2–11, esp. pp. 29–33.
31. Gobineau, *Essai*, p. 174.
32. *Ibid.*, Vol. 2, pp. 860–61.
33. *Ibid.*, p. 683.
34. Quoted in Biddiss, p. 127.
35. Gobineau, *Golden Flower*, p. 19. *The Golden Flower* is a compilation of the prefaces to each section of *The Renaissance*, published separately by Ludwig Schemann in 1912.
36. Some scholars have seen Gobineau's reading of Thierry as the beginning of his interest in race; Buenzod, *La Formation*, pp. 286–92.
37. Gobineau, *Essai*, p. 167.
38. *Essai*, Vol. 2, p. 870.
39. Quoted in Mosse, *Toward the Final Solution*, p. 54.
40. Cf. Pott, *Die Ungleichheit menschlicher von Grafen*.
41. M. Lémonon, "La diffusion en Allemagne des idées de Gobineau sur les races," in Crouzet, ed., *Arthur de Gobineau, Cents Ans Après*, p. 12; Boisseu, *Comte de Gobineau*, p. 126.
42. "Conclusion générale," in Gobineau, *Essai*, Vol. 2, p. 862.
43. Palmer, *The Two Tocquevilles*.
44. Tocqueville, *European Revolution*, pp. 309–10.
45. Letter of 7 November 1853 in Tocqueville, *European Revolution*, p. 228.
46. Letter of 30 July 1856 in *Ibid.*, pp. 291–92.
47. *Essay*, Vol. 2, p. 680.
48. Letter of 20 March 1856 in Tocqueville, *European Revolution*, p. 285.
49. Boissel, *Comte de Gobineau*, p. 321.
50. *Ibid.*, p. 320.
51. Stern, *Politics of Cultural Despair*, pp. 56–57.
52. Chickering, *We Men Who Feel Most German*, pp. 239–41.
53. Quoted in Mosse, *Toward the Final Solution*, p. 105.
54. E.g., Tocqueville, *European Revolution*, p. 186.
55. Field, *Evangelist of Race*, p. 210; R. Hankins, *Racial Basis of Civilization*, pp. 55–57.
56. H.S. Chamberlain, *The Foundations of the Nineteenth Century* (1899), Vol. I, pp. 388, 574–75.
57. See Gay, *Freud, Jews and other Germans*.
58. Quoted in Poliakov, *Aryan Myth*, p. 317.
59. Quoted in Field, *Evangelist of Race*, pp. 217–18, 222.

60. Although we do not know whether Hitler actually received a copy or not. Mosse, *Toward the Final Solution*, p. 56.
61. Hitler, *Mein Kampf*, pp. 289–90.
62. Field, *Evangelist of Race*, p. 445.


*Chapter 3*

1. Gossman, *Orpheus Philologus*, pp. 8–9.
2. Quoted in Gooch, *History and Historians in the Nineteenth Century*, p. 126; Burckhardt, *Force and Freedom*, p. 73.
3. Leonard Krieger, *Ranke The Meaning of History* (Chicago, 1977); T. von Laue, *Leopold Ranke: The Formative Years* (Princeton, 1950).
4. Ranke, "The Great Powers," reprinted in von Laue, *Leopold Ranke*, p. 217.
5. Burckhardt, *Force and Freedom*, p. 49.
6. Ranke, "A Dialogue on Politics," reprinted in von Laue, *Leopold Ranke*, p. 180.
7. *Ibid.*, pp. 162–63.
8. H. White, *Metahistory*, pp. 170–71.
9. Craig, *Triumph of Liberalism*, pp. 248–49.
10. Burckhardt, *Force and Freedom*, pp. 36–37.
11. *Ibid.*, p. 19.
12. *Ibid.*, pp. 229–31; 124; 92, 96, 238.
13. Burckhardt, *On History and Historians*, p. 220; *Force and Freedom*, p. 263.
14. Quoted in Trevor-Roper, Introduction, Burckhardt, *On History and Historians*, p. xvi.
15. Burckhardt, *Force and Freedom*, pp. 263, 265.
16. Burckhardt, *Civilization of the Renaissance in Italy*, pp. 441; 22.
17. Gobineau, *The Renaissance*, p. 67.
18. Cf. Burckhardt, *Force and Freedom*, p. 132.
19. Pletsch, *Young Nietzsche*.
20. *Ibid.*, pp. 104–05.
21. Nietzsche, *Ecce Homo*, p. 286.
22. Burckhardt, *On History and Historians*, p. 218.
23. *Ibid.*, p. 32; *Force and Freedom*, p. 132.
24. Burckhardt, *Letters*, p. 23.
25. Burckhardt, *On History and Historians*, pp. 235–56.
26. Quoted in Tracy Strong, "Nietzsche and Politics," in R. Solomon, ed., *Nietzsche: A Collection of Critical Essays* (Garden City, NY, 1973), p. 282. See also T. Strong, *Nietzsche and the Politics of Transfiguration*.
27. Nietzsche, *Thus Spake Zarathustra*, p. 97. Cf. Kaufmann, *Nietzsche: Philosopher, Psychologist, Antichrist*.
28. Pletsch, *Young Nietzsche*, p. 97.
29. Gregor-Dellin, *Wagner*, pp. 385–87.
30. Nietzsche, *Ecce Homo*, pp. 243, 247.
31. Schwab, *Oriental Renaissance*, p. 430.
32. Letter to H. von Preen, 27 September 1870, in Burckhardt, *Letters*, p. 144.
33. Hollinrake, *Nietzsche, Wagner, and the Philosophy of Pessimism*, p. 59.
34. Nietzsche, "Schopenhauer as Educator," in *Untimely Meditations*, p. 148.
35. Nietzsche, "On the Uses and Disadvantages of History for Life" and "Schopenhauer as Educator," in *Untimely Meditations*, pp. 65, 148, 149.
36. Nietzsche, "Schopenhauer as Educator," in *Untimely Meditations*, p. 158.

37. Peter Heller, *Studies on Nietzsche* (Bonn, 1980), p. 172.

38. Nietzsche, "On the Uses and Disadvantages of History for Life," in *Untimely Meditations*, p. 76.

39. Nietzsche, "Schopenhauer as Educator," in *Untimely Meditations*, p. 111.

40. Nietzsche's revisionist view of the Greeks was heavily influenced by Burckhardt's lectures on Greek culture that began in May 1872. K. Schlechta, "The German 'Classicist' Goethe as Reflected in Nietzsche's Works," in O'Flaherty, Sellner, and Helm, eds., *Studies in Nietzsche and the Classical Tradition*, p. 151.

41. Nietzsche, *Birth of Tragedy*, p. 110.

42. Quoted in Manthey-Zorn, *Dionysus: The Tragedy of Nietzsche*, p. 29. For the Romantic origins of Nietzsche's treatment of cultural and aesthetic issues in *The Birth of Tragedy*, see Del Caro, *Nietzsche Contra Nietzsche*, esp. pp. 47–49 and 131–32.

43. Nietzsche, "On the Uses and Disadvantages of History for Life," in *Untimely Meditations*, p. 95.

44. Gregor-Dellin, *Wagner*, p. 410.

45. Quoted in the Introduction to Nietzsche, *Untimely Mediations*, pp. xxvi–xxvii.

46. Burckhardt, *Letters*, pp. 187; 186. How much of Nietzsche's collapsing health was due to physiological causes, including syphilis, as some historians have claimed, and how much to psychological ones, such as the loss of faith in his hero, Richard Wagner? The evidence for this theory is presented in Gregor-Dellin, *Wagner*, pp. 451–55.

47. Nietzsche, "On the Uses and Disadvantages of History for Life," in *Untimely Meditations*, p. 84; Nietzsche, *Case of Wagner*, pp. 170, 179.

48. Letter of 13 September 1883 in Burckhardt, *Letters*, p. 209.

49. Nietzsche, *Ecce Homo*, p. 290.

50. Schacht, *Nietzsche*, p. 220.

51. Nietzsche, *Will to Power*, p. 450.

52. Nietzsche, *The Anti-Christ*, p. 127.

53. Nietzsche, *Will to Power*, p. 30.

54. Nietzsche, *Beyond Good and Evil*, pp. 201–02.

55. Cf. Boisseul, *Comte de Gobineau*, p. 259: W. D. Williams, in *Nietzsche and the French* (Oxford, 1952), p. 140, stresses the influence of *The Renaissance*. Nietzsche's sister, Elisabeth Förster-Nietzsche, also mentions her brother's interest in Gobineau in her *Life of Nietzsche*, Vol. 2, pp. 382–83. Of course, Elisabeth's testimony regarding her brother's intellectual preferences are not always to be taken at face value, and the fact that Nietzsche does not mention Gobineau in any of his published works has led others to doubt Gobineau's role in Nietzsche's thinking (e.g., Kaufmann, *Nietzsche*, p. 296, n. 97). Nonetheless, it is interesting that while Nietzsche accepted the Aryan Indo-European theory of civilization, he deliberately distanced himself from any notion of Aryan-Teuton equivalence—which suggests his source was Gobineau himself, rather than his German nationalist followers.

56. Nietzsche, *Beyond Good and Evil*, pp. 41, 203.

57. Ibid., pp. 204, 205.

58. Nietzsche, *Genealogy of Morals*, p. 33.

59. Cf. Nietzsche, *Genealogy of Morals*, pp. 30–31; *Beyond Good and Evil*, p. 209.

60. Nietzsche, *Twilight of the Idols*, trans. R. Hollingdale, p. 58; *Gay Science*, Aphorism 130 (on Nietzsche's hatred of racial anti-Semitism, see Kaufmann, *Nietzsche*, pp. 42–46; *Will to Power*, pp. 22–23).

61. Nietzsche, *Genealogy of Morals*, pp. 44; 36. The reference to Chinese is again significant, since it closely follows Gobineau's observation in *The Inequality of Human Races* that the Chinese constitute the perfect middle class.
62. Nietzsche, *Will to Power*, pp. 14–15.
63. Nietzsche, *Thus Spake Zarathustra*, p. 18.
64. Ibid., p. 255.
65. Ibid., p. 286.
66. Nietzsche, *Twilight of the Idols*, quoted in Kaufmann, *Nietzsche*, p. 316.
67. Danto, "Eternal Recurrence," in Solomon, ed., *Nietzsche*, pp. 316–21; Kaufmann, *Nietzsche*, p. 327; *Gay Science*, Aphorism 341.
68. Cf. Förster-Nietzsche, *Life of Nietzsche*, Vol. 2, pp. 382–83; Verrecchia, *La Catastrofe di Nietzsche a Torino*, pp. 60–61.
69. Nietzsche, *The Anti-Christ*, trans. R. Hollingdale, pp. 186–87; *Ecce Homo*, p. 344.
70. Hayman, *Nietzsche: A Life*, pp. 302–04.
71. Ibid., p. 326; *Selected Letters of Friedrich Nietzsche*, ed., C. Middleton (Chicago, 1969), pp. 345–47.
72. Nietzsche, *Will to Power*, pp. 3, 71; 14–15.
73. Burckhardt, *Letters*, p. 209.
74. Quoted in Trevor-Roper, Introduction, *On History and Historians*, p. xx.

## Chapter 4

1. Lombroso-Ferrera, *Criminal Man*, pp. xiv–xv.
2. Nordau, *Degeneration*, p. 16.
3. As, for example, S. Gilman, *Difference and Pathology*, and Showalter, *Sexual Anarchy*.
4. Pick, *Faces of Degeneration*, p. 121.
5. S. G. Gilman, "Political Theory and Degeneration: From Left to Right, From Up to Down," in Gilman and Chamberlain, eds., *Degeneration*, esp. pp. 174–79.
6. On Darwin and theories of progress, see Mandelbaum, *History, Man, and Reason*, pp. 77–92; G. Jones, *Social Darwinism*; and Himmelfarb, *Darwin and the Darwinian Revolution*, pp. 413–26.
7. Quoted in Pick, *Faces of Degeneration*, p. 178.
8. Darwin, *Origin of Species*, quoted in Mandelbaum, *History, Man, and Reason*, p. 82.
9. Cf. Pick, *Faces of Degeneration*, p. 198, n. 49, and G. Jones, *Social Darwinism*, p. 7.
10. Maudsley, *Body and Mind*, p. 52.
11. Villa, *Il Deviante et I suòi segni*, pp. 144–45.
12. These are described in Lombroso-Ferrera, *Criminal Man*, pp. 222–25, 231–49.
13. Quoted in Pick, *Faces of Degeneration*, p. 126.
14. Quoted in Gould, *Mismeasure of Man*, p. 125.
15. Lombroso-Ferrera, *Criminal Man*, p. 245.
16. Nye, *Crime, Madness, and Politics in Modern France*, pp. 100–21.
17. Pick, *Faces of Degeneration*, p. 114–15.
18. See Lombroso-Ferrera, *Criminal Man*, pp. 142, 150.
19. Lombroso, *Crime*, p. 427.
20. For example, Parmelee, *Criminology*.
21. Pick, *Faces of Degeneration*, pp. 146–47.
22. Quoted in Nye, *Crime, Madness, and Politics in Modern France*, p. 105.
23. Chevalier, *Laboring Classes and Dangerous Classes*.
24. Swart, *Sense of Decadence*, p. 124.
25. Pick, *Faces of Degeneration*, pp. 71–72.

26. Féré, *Dégénéresçence et Criminalié*, pp. 70, 94–96.
27. *The Debacle*, pp. 176–77.
28. Stoker, *Dracula*, p. 27; Kline, *Dracula and the Degeneration of Women*; and Pick, *Faces of Degeneration*, pp. 167–74.
29. Stoker, *Dracula*, p. 346.
30. Ibid., pp. 326; 220.
31. G.S. Jones, *Outcast London*, and Walkowitz, *City of Dreadful Delights*.
32. Quoted in Pick, *Faces of Degeneration*, p. 223.
33. Ibid., p. 20.
34. Nordau, *Three Conventional Lies of Civilization*, p. 6.
35. Pick, *Faces of Degeneration*, p. 27, and Peter Bade, "Art and Degeneration: Visual Icons of Corruption," in Gilman and Chamberlain, eds., *Degeneration*, pp. 220–40.
36. Nordau, *Three Conventional Lies*, p. 283.
37. Ibid., p. 364.
38. E. Weber, *France Fin de Siècle*, pp. 213–33.
39. Mosse, *Confronting the Nation*, p. 165.
40. Le Bon's *L'homme et les sociétés* (1881), quoted in Durkheim, *Division of Labor*, p. 60.
41. LeBon, *The Crowd*, p. 36.
42. Quoted in Shearer West, *Fin de Siècle* (Woodstock, N.Y., 1994), p. 35.
43. M. Weber, *Protestantism and the Spirit of Capitalism*, pp. 181–82; Horowitz and Maely, eds., *Barbarism of Reason*.
44. "Suicide and Birthrates" (1887), quoted in Nye, *Crime, Politics, and Madness in Modern France*, p. 147.
45. Durkheim, *Suicide*, pp. 367; 323. See also R. Nye, "Sociology and Degeneration: The Irony of Progress," in Chamberlain and Gilman, eds., *Degeneration*, pp. 60–63.
46. Durkheim, *Division of Labor*, pp. 53, 242; 337; 51.
47. Nordau, *Three Conventional Lies*, p. 360.
48. From *Cours de Philosophie Positive* (1830), quoted in Durkheim, *Division of Labor*, pp. 358–59.
49. Freeden, *New Liberalism*.
50. Quoted in Pick, *Faces of Degeneration*, p. 223.
51. G. Jones, *Social Darwinism*, p. 99; Kelly, *Descent of Darwin*; and Pickens, *Eugenics and the Progressives*.
52. Galton, *Hereditary Genius*.
53. Quoted in Forrest, *Francis Galton*, p. 235.
54. See G. Jones, *Social Darwinism*, pp. 6–9, 102–03.
55. Lankester, *Degeneration*, quoted in Pick, *Faces of Degeneration*, p. 218.
56. Quoted in Pickens, *Eugenics and the Progressives*, p. 27, and Solway, *Demography and Degeneration*, p. 21.
57. G. Jones, *Social Darwinism*, p. 106; Gould, *Mismeasure of Man*, pp. 75–76; Pick, *Faces of Degeneration*, p. 165.
58. Cf. Kevles, *In the Name of Eugenics*.
59. W.R. Greg, "On the Failure of Natural Selection in Man," *Fraser's Magazine* (1868), quoted in G. Jones, *Social Darwinism*, p. 102.
60. L.P. Curtis, *Apes and Angels*.
61. Barkan, *Retreat of Scientific Racism*.
62. L. Clark, *Social Darwinism in France*, pp. 154–58.
63. Mosse, *Toward the Final Solution*, pp. 58–61.
64. S. Gilman, *Freud, Race, and Gender*, pp. 20, 101.
65. Lombroso, *Antisemitism and the Jews* (1893), discussed in S. Gilman, *ibid*, p. 101.

66. Haeckel, *Riddle of the Universe*, pp. 1–2, 8.
67. Darwin, *Evolution of Man* (New York, 1896).
68. Haeckel, *Riddle of the Universe*, pp. 350–52.
69. Gasman, *Scientific Origins of National Socialism*. For a modified view of Haeckel's connections to neo-Gobinian ideas, see Kelly, *Descent of Darwin*. Haeckel's eugenics became enormously influential, even reaching as far as China. See Dikötter, *Discourse of Race in Modern China*, pp. 138–40.
70. Proctor, *Racial Hygiene*, pp. 14–15; Mosse, *Toward the Final Solution*, pp. 80–81.
71. A Ploetz, *Social Anthropology* (1913), quoted in Field, *Evangelist of Race*, p. 213.
72. Goodrick-Clarke, *Occult Roots of Nazism*, pp. 51, 90–96; Hillel and Henry, *Of Pure Blood*.
73. Proctor, *Racial Hygiene*, pp. 41–42; Weindling, *Health, Race and German Politics*, p. 503.
74. Quoted in Pick, *Faces of Degeneration*, p. 91 (my emphasis).
75. S. Gilman, "Sexology, Psychoanalysis, and Degeneration," in Gilman and Chamberlain, eds., *Degeneration*, pp. 80–83; Gay, *Freud: A Life for Our Time*, pp. 48–49.
76. Quoted in Gay, *Freud: A Life for Our Time*, p. 412.
77. Gould, *Ontogeny and Phylogeny*.
78. Rieff, *Freud*, p. 219.
79. Derek Freeman, *Margaret Mead and Samoa: Making and Unmaking of an Anthropological Myth* (Cambridge, MA, 1983).
80. Freud, *Civilization and Its Discontents*, pp. 16–17.
81. *Ibid.*, p. 19.
82. *Ibid.*, p. 42.

Chapter 5

1. Tuveson, *Redeemer Nation*; Bloch, *Visionary Republic*.
2. George Berkeley, "Verses on the Prospect of Planting Arts and Learning in America," quoted in Tuveson, *Redeemer Nation*, p. 94.
3. Hendrickson and Tucker, *Empire of Liberty*.
4. "Fourth of July address, 1821," in Lefeber, ed., *John Quincy Adams*, pp. 42–44.
5. E.g., *Federalist Papers*, p. 144. Timothy Dwight, "The Conquest of Canaan," quoted in Tuveson, *Redeemer Nation*, p. 107.
6. Quoted in Mathiopoulos, *History and Progress*, p. 128.
7. Marcell, *Progress and Pragmatism*, p. 18.
8. Hostadter, *Social Darwinism in American Thought*, and Bannister, *Social Darwinism: Science and Myth*.
9. Lombroso-Ferrera, *Criminal Man*, p. 183; Barkan, *Retreat of Scientific Racism*, pp. 105–06; Boller, *American Thought in Transition*; Mathiopoulos, *History and Progress*, p. 117.
10. Wood, *Creation of the American Republic*, p. 35.
11. *Ibid.*, p. 571.
12. J. Adams, "Defense of the American Constitutions," in *Political Writings*, pp. 160–63; Wood, *Creation of the American Republic*, pp. 571–74; J. Adams, "Dissertation," in *Political Writings*, p. 6.
13. Hostadter, *Paranoid Style*, p. 29.
14. "Letter to John Taylor of Caroline," in J. Adams, *Works*, Vol. VI, p. 480.
15. H. Adams, *Education*, p. 13.
16. Letter of February 17, 1909, in H. Adams, *Selected Letters*, p. 509.

17. Ibid., pp. 33–34. For a sympathetic view of the development of gentility and American political culture, see Bushman, *Refinement of America*.
18. H. Adams, *Degradation of the Democratic Dogma*, p. 10.
19. H. Adams, *Education*, p. 192.
20. H. Adams, *Degradation of the Democratic Dogma*, pp. 129, 283.
21. Quoted in Cater, ed., *Henry Adams and His Friends*, p. 134.
22. Quoted in Himmelfarb, *Idea of Poverty*, p. 199.
23. Beringause, *Brooks Adams*, p. 97.
24. H. Adams, *Education*, p. 60.
25. E. Digby Baltzell, *The Protestant Establishment* (New York, 1964).
26. Quoted in Mathiopoulos, *History and Progress*, p. 115.
27. George, *Progress and Poverty*, pp. 533–34.
28. Rothman, *Politics and Power*, Ch. 8.
29. A. Hoogenboom, "Spoilsmen and Reformers: Civil Service Reform and Public Morality," in Morgan, ed., *Gilded Age: A Reinterpretation*, p. 73.
30. Letter to Taylor, in H. Adams, *Selected Letters*, p. 205; Wood, *Creation of the American Republic*, p. 578.
31. See Chapter 53 in James Bryce's *American Commonwealth* entitled, "Why the Best Men Do Not Go into Politics," Vol. 2, pp. 65–71.
32. Eliot, *Five American Contributions*, pp. 92–93, 138.
33. Letter to John Bright, May 1869, in H. Adams, *Selected Letters*, p. 107.
34. H. Adams, *Education*, p. 266; *Selected Letters*, p. 103.
35. Samuels, *Young Henry Adams*, p. 180; H. Adams, *Education*, p. 294.
36. Quoted in H.A. McDougall, *Racial Myth in English History: Trojans, Teutons and Anglo-Saxons* (Hanover, NH, 1982), p. 121.
37. Burrow, Collini, and Winch, *That Noble Science*, p. 158–60; Samuels, *Young Henry Adams*, pp. 257–58.
38. Quoted in Samuels, *Young Henry Adams*, pp. 353, 385.
39. Quoted in Pocock, *Machiavellian Moment*, p. 536.
40. John Kasson, *Civilizing the Machine: Technology and Republican Values in America, 1776–1900* (New York, 1976).
41. Nock, *Memoirs of a Superfluous Man*, p. 112.
42. Quoted in Lynn, *Visions of America*, p. 67.
43. George, *Progress and Poverty*, p. 10.
44. Beringause, *Brooks Adams*, p. 55.
45. Keller, *Affairs of State*, pp. 350, 365.
46. Anderson, *Brooks Adams: Constructive Conservative*.
47. Samuels, *Henry Adams*, p. 339.
48. Beringause, *Brooks Adams*, p. 72.
49. Ibid., pp. 98–99.
50. Cf. Chamberlain, *Farewell to Reform*.
51. H. Adams, *Degradation of the American Dogma*, p. 91.
52. Quoted in Samuels, *Henry Adams: The Major Phase*, p. 112.
53. Quoted in Wood, *Creation of the American Republic*, p. 571.
54. Letter of May 14, 1895, quoted in Beringause, *Brooks Adams*, p. 115.
55. B. Adams, *Law of Civilization and Decay*, pp. 58–59.
56. Ibid., p. 60.
57. The phrase "untrammeled capitalism" is from Charles Beard's Introduction to *The Law of Civilization and Decay*, p. 40.
58. B. Adams, *Law of Civilization and Decay*, pp. 60–61, 324.

59. *Ibid.*, p. 61.
60. May 7, 1898, in Ford, *Letters of Henry Adams*, Vol. II, p. 177–78.
61. *Ibid.*, p. 72.
62. Quoted in Cater, ed., *Henry Adams and His Friends*, p. 184.
63. H. Adams, *Selected Letters*, p. 305.
64. Quoted in Beringause, *Brooks Adams*, p. 155.
65. *Ibid.*, p. 160.
66. H. Adams, *Education*, pp. 300–01.
67. H. Adams, "The Tendency of History," in *Degradation of the Democratic Dogma*, p. 133; Leers, *No Place of Grace*, p. 296.
68. F. J. Turner, "Significance of the Frontier," in *Frontier and Section*, p. 62.
69. B. Adams, *America's Economic Supremacy*, p. 82.
70. Pocock, *Machiavellian Moment*, p. 542; Healy, *U.S. Expansionism*, pp. 131, 200.
71. Beard, Introduction to B. Adams, *Law of Civilization and Decay*, p. 45.
72. *Theodore Roosevelt and the Idea of Race.*
73. Quoted in Beringause, *Brooks Adams*, p. 274.
74. B. Adams, *America's Economic Supremacy*, p. 134.
75. *Ibid.*, p. 135.
76. H. Adams, *Selected Letters*, pp. 331–32; 384–85; 397–98.
77. B. Adams, *America's Economic Supremacy*, p. 80.
78. Cf. Croly, *Promises of American Life.*
79. Anderson, *Brooks Adams: Constructive Conservative*, p. 97.
80. Croly, *Promise of American Life*, pp. 274–75; Noble, *Paradox of the Progressive Mind*, pp. 60–61.
81. Contrary to the claims of Horsman, *Race and Manifest Destiny.*
82. *Letters*, Vol. II, p. 46. Pearson's influence on Brooks Adams was profound. See Beringause, *Brooks Adams*, pp. 166–67.
83. B. Adams, *Law of Civilization and Decline*, p. 325.
84. Higham, *Send These to Me*, p. 5.
85. Higham, *Strangers in the Land.*
86. Quoted in Tomisch, *A Genteel Endeavor*, p. 83.
87. Kraut, *Silent Travelers.*
88. *Passing of the Great Race*, Introduction, p. xxxiii.
89. Stoddard, *Racial Realities in Europe*, pp. 19–21.
90. Tucker, *Dragon and the Cross*, p. 6.
91. Wade, *Fiery Cross*, p. 165.
92. Higham, *Send These to Me*, pp. 56–58.
93. On Yockey's extraordinary life see George and Wilcox, *Nazis, Communists, Klansmen*, pp. 252–53. *Imperium* was originally published under the pseudonym Ulich Varange, obviously to evoke images of Aryan-Teutonic vitality.
94. Mintz, *Liberty Lobby*, pp. 36–38.

## Chapter 6

1. Du Bois, "Dusk of Dawn," in *Writings*, p. 582.
2. Lewis, *W.E.B. Du Bois*, p. 18.
3. Gatewood, *Aristocrats of Color.*
4. Williamson, *New People.*
5. Bainton, *Idea of Race*, pp. 47–59.
6. E.g., Horsman, *Race and Manifest Destiny*, passim.

7. As in Robert Shufeldt's 1907 book, *The Negro: A Menace to American Civilization*.
8. Lewis, *W.E.B. Du Bois*, pp. 56–63; W.E.B. Du Bois, "Dusk of Dawn," in *Writings*, p. 577.
9. McPherson, *Abolitionist Legacy*, pp. 308–09.
10. E.g., De Marco, *Social Thought of W.E.B. Du Bois*, and D. D. Bruce, "W.E.B. Du Bois and the Idea of Double Consciousness."
11. Quoted in Lewis, *W.E.B. Du Bois*, p. 134.
12. Ringer, *Decline of the German Mandarins*, pp. 146–48.
13. Schmoller, *Mercantile System*, pp. 2–3; Ringer, *Decline of the German Mandarins*, p. 147.
14. Smith, *Politics and the Sciences of Culture in Germany*, p. 182.
15. Simmel, *Conflict in Modern Culture*, p. 11.
16. Cf. Berlin, *Vico and Herder*.
17. Quoted in Ringer, *Decline of the German Mandarins*, p. 100; Muller, *Other God That Failed*, p. 62.
18. Tönnies, *Community and Society*.
19. Smith, *Politics and the Sciences of Culture in Germany*, p. 138.
20. Quoted in Appiah, "Uncompleted Argument: Du Bois and the Illusion of Race," in Gates, ed., *"Race," Writing, and Difference*, pp. 23–24.
21. Du Bois, "Souls of Black Folk," in *Writings*, p. 512.
22. Moses, *Alexander Crummell*, pp. 294–96.
23. H. M. Turner, *Respect Black*, pp. 74–75.
24. Moses, *Alexander Crummell*, p. 263.
25. Quoted in Lewis, *W.E.B. Du Bois*, p. 170.
26. Du Bois, *Du Bois Speaks*, p. 49.
27. Du Bois, "Conservation of Races," in *W.E.B. Du Bois: A Reader*, pp. 825; 817, 821.
28. Quoted in Lewis, *W.E.B. Du Bois*, p. 263.
29. Du Bois "Conservatism of the Races," in *W.E.B. Du Bois: A Reader*, p. 24.
30. Smith, *Politics and the Sciences of Culture of Germany*, pp. 126–28, 189.
31. Williamson, *Crucible of Race*, p. 411; Du Bois, "Dusk of Dawn," in *Writings*, p. 662.
32. Du Bois, *The Negro*, p. 9.
33. *Ibid.*, pp. 14, 24.
34. *Ibid.*, p. 18.
35. *Ibid.*, pp. 21–24.
36. *Ibid.*, p. 137. Also pp. 132, 133; 124, 138.
37. *Ibid.*, p. 29.
38. *Ibid.*, p. 242.
39. *Darkwater*, pp. 49–50; Lewis, *W.E.B. Du Bois*, p. 565.
40. Du Bois, "The Negro's Fatherland," in *W.E.B. Du Bois: A Reader*, p. 652.
41. Du Bois, *Black Reconstruction*, p. 5.
42. *Darkwater*, p. 49; Foner, p. 51; Du Bois, "Dusk of Dawn," in *Writings*, pp. 659; 658.
43. *Darkwater*, p. 41.
44. Appiah, "Uncompleted Argument: Du Bois and the Illusion of Race," in Gates, ed., *"Race," Writing, and Difference*, pp. 21–37.
45. E.g., "Jefferson Davis as a Representative of Civilization," p. 811.
46. Du Bois, *Black Reconstruction*, pp. 15–16.
47. *Darkwater*, p. 39.
48. *Ibid.*, p. 49.
49. Du Bois, "Dusk of Dawn," in *Writings*, pp. 646–47, 648; 639.

50. Rampersad, *Art and Imagination of W.E.B. Du Bois*, p. 203.
51. Quoted in Ibid., p. 213.
52. Quoted in Bainton, *Idea of Race*, p. 155.
53. Du Bois, "Dusk of Dawn," in *Writings*, pp. 648, 662.
54. Quoted in J. White, *Black Leadership*, p. 93.
55. Garvey, *Life and Lessons*, p. 268.
56. Garvey, *Philosophy and Opinions*, Vol. II, p. 68.
57. Ibid., p. 14.
58. Ibid., p. 90; *Life and Lessons*, p. 147.
59. Cf. Speech of September 26, 1920, in *Marcus Garvey and UNIA Papers*, Vol. III, pp. 22–28
60. Garvey, *Philosophy and Opinions*, Vol. I, p. 37.
61. Garvey, *Marcus Garvey and UNIA Papers*, Vol. II, p. 128.
62. Ibid., pp. 13, 129, Garvey, *Life and Lessons*, p. 5.
63. J. White, *Black Leadership*, p. 90.
64. Garvey, *Life and Lessons*, pp. lviii–lix.
65. Garvey, *Philosophy and Opinions*, lxxiv–lxxvii; Stein, *World of Marcus Garvey*, p. 225.
66. Garvey, *Philosophy and Opinions*, p. lxxv.
67. Garvey, *Life and Lessons*, passim.
68. Quoted in Lincoln, *Black Muslims in America*, p. 62.
69. Malcolm X, *Autobiography*, pp. 269–70.
70. Sewell, *Garvey's Children*, pp. 61–62.
71. Quoted in Lewis, *W.E.B. Du Bois*, p. 316.
72. Du Bois, *Color and Democracy*.
73. Du Bois, *The World and Africa*, p. 1.
74. G. Horne, *Black and Red* (New York, 1983), p. 317.
75. Du Bois, *Speeches and Addresses*, p. 181.
76. Ibid., pp. 236–37.
77. Nkrumah, *Africa Must Unite*, p. xvi.
78. Record, *Race and Radicalism*.
79. Rampersad, *Art and Imagination of W.E.B. Du Bois*, p. 256.
80. Hollander, *Political Pilgrims*, pp. 126, 166.

## Chapter 7

1. Nietzsche, *Thus Spake Zarathustra*, p. 75; Hayman, *Nietzsche: A Life*, pp. 334–37.
2. Macintire, *Forgotten Fatherland*.
3. Peters, *Zarathustra's Sister*.
4. Aschheim, *The Nietzsche Legacy*, p. 23.
5. Quoted in *ibid.*
6. Spengler, *Selected Letters*, p. 50.
7. Wohl, *Generation of 1914*, pp. 126–29.
8. Rudolf Pannwitz, quoted in Aschheim, *Nietzsche Legacy*, p. 76.
9. Spengler, *Selected Letters*, p. 70.
10. Koktanek, *Oswald Spengler in Seiner Zeit*, p. 63.
11. See Kaufmann, Introduction to Nietzsche, *Will to Power*, pp. xiii–xviii. Ibid., p. 544.
12. Simmel, *Conflict in Modern Culture*, p. 18.
13. Stern, *Politics of Cultural Despair*, p. 234.

14. Ringer, *Decline of the German Mandarins*; Jarausch, *Students, Society, and Politics in Imperial Germany*.

15. Cf. Ringer, *Decline of the German Mandarins*, pp. 48–50. See also Barnouw, *Weimar Intellectuals and the Threat of Modernity*.

16. The issue is also summarized in Elias, *History of Manners*, Vol. 1 of *The Civilizing Process*, pp. 8–10.

17. Nietzsche, *Will to Power*, p. 75.

18. Herf, *Reactionary Modernism*, pp. 133–151.

19. Eksteins, *Rites of Spring*, p. 117.

20. Simmel, *Conflict in Modern Culture*, p. 281.

21. *Third Reich* (1923; English trans. 1934; New York, 1971), pp. 87, 90.

22. Mann, *Reflections of a Non-Political Man*, p. 46.

23. Quoted in Ringer, *Decline of the German Mandarins*, pp. 183–84.

24. Simmel, "Sociological Significance of the Stranger," in K. Wolff, *Sociology of Georg Simmel* (New York, 1950), pp. 322–27.

25. Spengler, *Decline of the West*, p. 379.

26. Sombart, *Towards a New Social Philosophy*, p. 32.

27. Mann, *Reflections of a Non-Political Man*, p. 36.

28. Fennelly, *Twilight of the Evening Lands*, p. 13.

29. Cecil, *Myth of the Master Race*, pp. 23–25.

30. Cf. Chickering, *We Men Who Feel Most German*, pp. 95–97.

31. Mann, *Reflections of a Non-Political Man*, p. 34.

32. E.g. Nietzsche, *Gay Science*, pp. 57–58; *Will to Power*, p. 78.

33. Chickering, *We Men Who Feel Most German*, pp. 285–88.

34. Spengler, Preface to *Decline of the West*, Vol. I, p. xv.

35. Bridgwater, *Poet of Expressionist Berlin*, pp. 116, 130; Stern, *Politics of Cultural Despair*, p. 237.

36. Quoted in R. Wohl, *Generation of 1914*, p. 42.

37. Quoted in Johnson, *Modern Times*, p. 12.

38. Quoted in Muller, *Other God That Failed*, p. 61.

39. Simmel, *Conflict in Modern Culture*, p. 281.

40. Spengler, *Decline of the West*, p. xiv.

41. Spengler, *Decline of the West*, Vol. I, pp. 21; 3.

42. Ibid., pp. 18, 24.

43. Ibid., pp. 22, 106–07.

44. Spengler, *Decline of the West*, Vol. II, pp. 90, 165.

45. Ibid., pp. 100; 95.

46. Spengler, *Decline of the West*, Vol. I, pp. 28, 106–7.

47. Ibid., p. 31.

48. Ibid., p. 360.

49. Ibid., p. 40.

50. Ibid., pp. 20–21.

51. Spengler, *Decline of the West*, Vol. II, pp. 46; 44.

52. Mann, *Reflections of a Non-Political Man*, p. 33.

53. Spengler, *Decline of the West*, p. 37.

54. Spengler, *Selected Letters*, p. 31; Spengler, *Decline of the West*, Vol. II, p. 49.

55. Hitler, *Mein Kampf*, p. 163.

56. Spengler, *Selected Letters*, p. 28.

57. Ibid., p. 80.

58. *Ibid.*, p. 69.
59. Quoted in Wohl, *Generation of 1914*, p. 53.
60. Quoted in Holmes, *Anatomy of Anti-Liberalism*, p. 37.
61. Mann, *Diaries 1918–1939*, pp. 61–64; Mann, *Letters*, p. 90.
62. Monk, *Ludwig Wittgenstein*, pp. 315–17.
63. Described in Hughes's Introduction to the abridged edition of Spengler, *Decline of the West*, p. xvi.
64. Spengler, *Selected Letters*, p. 94.
65. Contrary to Struve, *Elites Against Democracy*.
66. Spengler, "Prussianism and Socialism," in D.O. White, ed., *Oswald Spengler, Selected Essays* (Chicago, 1967), pp. 17–18; Spengler, *Selected Letters*, p. 69.
67. "Prussianism and Socialism," p. 3.
68. Spengler, *Selected Letters*, p. 94.
69. Spengler, *Decline of the West*, Vol. II, p. 464.
70. *Ibid.*, pp. 441–42, 506.
71. Quoted in Ringer, *Decline of the German Mandarins*, p. 223.
72. "Prussianism and Socialism," p. 11; Herf, *Reactionary Modernism*, pp. 65–67.
73. "Prussianism and Socialism," p. 130.
74. Spengler, *Selected Letters*, pp. 818; 184.
75. Struve, *Elites Against Democracy*, p. 273.
76. Quoted in *ibid.*, p. 258.
77. Hitler's remarks to Walter Rauschning quoted in Toland, *Life of Adolf Hitler*, Vol. I, p. 331.
78. Koktanek, *Oswald Spengler in Seiner Zeit*, pp. 304–05.
79. Sombart, *Towards a New Social Philosophy*, p. 5.
80. Hitler, *Mein Kampf*, p. 255.
81. Giles, *Students and National Socialism in Germany*.
82. Quoted in Ringer, *Decline of the Mandarins*, p. 439.
83. Ott, *Martin Heidegger: A Political Life*; Holmes, *Anatomy of Antiliberalism*, pp. 37–39; Muller, *Other God That Failed*, pp. 261–62.
84. Spengler, *Hour of Decision*, pp. xiii–xv.
85. H. Schaeder to A. Alpers, Spengler, *Selected Letters*, p. 295.
86. Mann, *Diaries: 1918–1939*, p. 261.

## Chapter 8

1. Toynbee, *Civilization on Trial*, pp. 8–9.
2. Arnold, *Selected Prose*, p. 211.
3. Arnold, "Popular Education of France" (1861), in *Selected Prose*, p. 121.
4. Cf. Himmelfarb, *Idea of Poverty*, Ch. XX, and G.M. Young, *Portrait of an Age: Victorian England*.
5. Von Arx, *Progress and Pessimism*.
6. See Himmelfarb, *Idea of Poverty*, passim.
7. Marcus, *Engels, Manchester, and the Working Class*.
8. Quoted in Himmelfarb, *Poverty and Compassion*, p. 276.
9. Quoted in Buckley, *Triumph of Time*, p. 72.
10. Plant and Vincent, *Philosophy, Politics, and Citizenship*, p. 35.
11. E.g., Barker, *Traditions of Civility*.
12. T. H. Green, *Lectures*, pp. 194–212; 200.

13. Quoted in Himmelfarb, *Poverty and Compassion*, pp. 250–51; Henry Jones, quoted in Vincent and Plant, p. 26.

14. Henry Jones, *The Working Faith of a Social Reformer* (London, 1910), p. 114.

15. Quoted in Plant and Vincent, *Philosophy, Politics, and Citizenship*, p. 119.

16. Burrow, Collini, and Winch, *That Noble Science of Politics*, pp. 257–59; Kadish, *Apostle Arnold*, pp. 39–45.

17. Toynbee, Sr., *Progress and Poverty, A Criticism of Mr. Henry George*, p. 53. The emphasis on "sinned" is mine.

18. Quoted in Collini, *Liberalism and Socialism*, p. 55; Webb quoted in Himmelfarb, *Poverty and Compassion*, p. 362; Tawney, *Acquisitive Society*, passim, esp. pp. 30–1.

19. Compare Harold Laski's *Law and Justice in Soviet Russia* (London, 1935) with Muggeridge's description of the *Manchester Guardian's* benign attitude toward the "Soviet experiment" in *Chronicles of Wasted Time: The Green Stick*, pp. 172-74

20. Semmel, *Imperialism and Social Reform*.

21. Paul Rich, *Race and Empire in British Politics*, 2nd ed. (Cambridge, 1990), p. 21.

22. J. Townsend, *J. A. Hobson*, p. 144.

23. Feuer, *Imperialism and the Anti-Imperialist Mind*, pp. 10, 74–75.

24. Buchan, *Pilgrim's Way*, pp. 120–21.

25. Toynbee, *Experiences*, pp. 199; 193.

26. Wohl, *Generation of 1914*, pp. 111–13.

27. Quoted in Parry, *Arnold Toynbee and the Crisis of the West*, p. 95.

28. McNeil, *Arnold Toynbee*, pp. 65–66, 67–68, 73–75.

29. *Diary of Virginia Woolf: Volume One 1915–1919* (New York, 1977), p. 108.

30. Toynbee, *Acquaintances*, p. 114.

31. Cf. Nicholson, *Peace-Making 1919*; on the origins of the League of Nations see Johnson, *Modern Times*, pp. 30–31.

32. J. Kendle, *Round-Table Movement*, p. 18; Lionel Curtis, *Commonwealth of Nations*, Part One.

33. Rich, *Race and Empire in British Politics*, p. 61.

34. Toynbee, *Experiences*, p. 220–21.

35. Kidd, *Principles of Western Civilization*, p. 161.

36. Toynbee, *Experiences*, pp. 267–70.

37. Toynbee, "The Dwarfing of Europe," in *Civilization on Trial*, pp. 98–99.

38. McNeil, *Arnold Toynbee*, p. 41.

39. Toynbee, *Reconsideration*, Vol. XII of *Study of History*.

40. Toynbee, "The Study of History: What I Am Trying to Do," in Ashley-Montagu, ed., *Toynbee and History*, p. 5.

41. Toynbee, *Study of History*, pp. 15, 52.

42. Cf. Popper, *Open Society and Its Enemies*, Vol. I, p. 232 (n. 45).

43. Toynbee, *Study of History*, p. 190.

44. *Ibid.*, pp. 65–66, 87.

45. *Ibid.*, pp. 99, 201.

46. *Ibid.*, p. 198.

47. *Ibid.*, pp. 276, 277.

48. *Ibid.*, pp. 286, 288.

49. *Ibid.*, p. 304.

50. *Ibid.*, p. 190.

51. *Ibid.*, p. 142.

52. *Ibid.*, pp. 553–54.

53. *Ibid.*, pp. 206–07.
54. E.g., review in *Times Literary Supplement* discussed in McNeil, *Arnold Toynbee*, p. 177.
55. Toynbee, *Study of History*, p. 554.
56. Kedourie, *Chatham House Version*, and Rowse, *All Souls and Appeasement*.
57. Rowse, *All Souls and Appeasement*, p. 38; McNeil, *Arnold Toynbee*, pp. 173–74.
58. Quoted in McNeil, *Arnold Toynbee*, p. 185.
59. Toynbee, *Civilization on Trial*, pp. 235–36.
60. Quoted in McNeil, *Arnold Toynbee*, p. 174.
61. Muggeridge, *Like It Was*, p. 222.
62. McNeil, *Arnold Toynbee*, p. 199.
63. Toynbee, *Experiences*, p. 258.
64. Toynbee, *America and the World Revolution*, pp. 92–93.
65. Toynbee, *Experiences*, pp. 234–35; F. Schweitzer, "Toynbee and Jewish History," in MacIntire and Perry, *Toynbee: Reappraisals*, pp. 208–09.
66. Toynbee, *Experiences*, p. 264.
67. *Ibid.*, p. 267; Toynbee, "Does History Repeat Itself?", in *Civilization on Trial*, p. 39.
68. McNeil, *Arnold Toynbee*, p. 256; the "knee jerk" remark is attributed to W.L. White in *Toynbee: Reappraisals*, p. 138, n. 5.
69. Ashley-Montagu, ed., *Toynbee and History*, p. 11; McNeil, *Arnold Toynbee*, p. 199; Toynbee, *Change and Habit*, p. 138.
70. *Toynbee: Reappraisals*, p. 135.
71. Toynbee, *World and the West*, pp. 68–69.
72. Toynbee, *Civilization on Trial*, pp. 158; 63; 79.
73. McNeil, *Mythohistory*, pp. 194–95.
74. A. Schweitzer, *Philosophy of Civilization*, pp. 292–94, 328.
75. G. Murray, *Five Stages of Greek Religion* (1925; New York, 1955), p. 119.

## Chapter 9

1. Watts, *The Kings Depart*, pp. 271–72.
2. Istvan Deak, *Weimar's Left-Wing Intellectuals* (Berkeley, 1968).
3. Quoted in Aschheim, *Nietzsche Legacy*, p. 185.
4. *Ibid.*, p. 186.
5. Wiggershaus, *Frankfurt School*, p. 22.
6. Lukács, *History and Class Consciousness*, pp. 27; 10–12; Lichtheim, *Georg Lukács*.
7. Quoted in Wiggershaus, *Frankfurt School*, p. 49.
8. Adorno, *Introduction to the Sociology of Music*.
9. Karl Marx, "Economic and Philosophic Manuscripts," in *Early Writings*, pp. 326, 327; 286–87.
10. *Ibid.*, pp. 332; 330.
11. Quoted in Tar, *Frankfurt School*, p. 207, n. 4. Bukharin's work was a standard catechism of Bolshevik Marxist ideas published in the twenties.
12. Adorno and Horkheimer, *Dialectic of Enlightenment*, p. xv.
13. Wiggershaus, *Frankfurt School*, pp. 297; 245.
14. Adorno, *Minima Moralia*, p. 104.
15. Quoted in Hughes, *Sea Change*, p. 106.
16. "The Jew in Europe," quoted in Tar, *Frankfurt School*, pp. 76–79; Wiggershaus, *Frankfurt School*, p. 162.

17. Wolin, *Terms of Cultural Criticism*, p. 47; Wiggershaus, *Frankfurt School*, p. 149.
18. *Ibid.*, p. 158.
19. *Ibid.*, pp. 117–18; 383.
20. Adorno and Horkheimer, *Dialectic of Enlightenment*, Introduction, p. xiv.
21. *Ibid.*, pp. xiv–xv.
22. *Ibid.*, pp. 7–10.
23. *Ibid.*, pp. 43–44.
24. *Ibid.*, p. xix.
25. Adorno and Horkheimer, *Dialectic of Enlightenment*, pp. 6–7.
26. *Ibid.*, 121.
27. Quoted in Tar, *Frankfurt School*, p. 87.
28. Cf. Benjamin's essay "Franz Kafka," in *Illuminations*, pp. 111–40.
29. Benjamin, "The Work of Art in the Age of Mechanical Reproduction," in *Illuminations*, p. 223–24.
30. Cf. Barnouw, *Weimar Intellectuals and the Threat of Modernity*, pp. 172–93.
31. Cf. Marcuse, *Soviet Marxism: A Critical Analysis*.
32. Mills, *Power Elite*, p. 296.
33. *Ibid.*, pp. 23, 274, 317.
34. *Ideology and Utopia*, p. 40.
35. Mills, *Power Elite*, p. 360.
36. E.g., Habermas, *Theory of Communicative Action*.
37. Hoffman, *Freudianism and the Literary Mind*; Moller, *Freudian Reading*.
38. On Reich, see Rieff, *Triumph of the Therapeutic*, Ch. 6.
39. Adorno, et al., *Authoritarian Personality*, p. 231.
40. Horkheimer, "Authority and the Family," in *Critical Theory*, p. 109.
41. Adorno, et al., *Authoritarian Personality*, pp. 664–65.
42. Horkheimer, *Critical Theory*, p. 109; Wiggershaus, *Frankfurt School*, p. 153; Horkheimer, *Eclipse of Reason*, p. 119.
43. Fromm, *Escape From Freedom*, p. 153.
44. Adorno, et al., *Authoritarian Personality*, pp. 1–2.
45. Cf. Tar, *Frankfurt School*, pp. 181–89.
46. Wiggershaus, *Frankfurt School*, p. 414; Adorno, et al., *Authoritarian Personality*, p. 249.
47. Adorno, et al., *Authoritarian Personality*, p. 976.
48. Quoted in Kellner, *Herbert Marcuse*, p. 296.
49. Quoted in Wiggershaus, *Frankfurt School*, p. 339.
50. Quoted in Cranston, ed., *Prophetic Politics*, p. 88.
51. Adorno, *Minima Moralia*, pp. 34, 39, 40.
52. Horkheimer, *Eclipse of Reason*, p. 94.
53. As outlined in A. MacIntyre, *Marcuse* (New York, 1970).
54. Marcuse, *One-Dimensional Man*, p. 7; quoted in Kellner, *Herbert Marcuse*, p. 293.
55. Marcuse, *Essay on Liberation*, p. 7; Fromm, *Escape From Freedom*, p. 278; Kellner, *Herbert Marcuse*, p. 293.
56. Marcuse, *One-Dimensional Man*, p. 9.
57. A point developed in Frances Fox Piven and Richard Cloward, *Regulating the Poor* (New York, 1971).
58. Marcuse, *One-Dimensional Man*, pp. 3; 1.
59. Marcuse, *Eros and Civilization*, pp. 110, 140.
60. *Ibid.*, pp. 138–39, 140.

61. Marcuse, *One-Dimensional Man*, p. 2.
62. Marcuse, *Essay on Liberation*, p. 20.
63. Cf. Kolakowski, *Varieties of Marxism*, Vol. 3, p. 399.
64. Marcuse, *One-Dimensional Man*, pp. 256–57.
65. Marcuse, *Essay on Liberation*, p. 7.
66. Marcuse, et al., *Critique of Pure Tolerance*, pp. 107–09; Kellner, *Herbert Marcuse*, p. 289.
67. Marcuse, *Negations*, p. 251.
68. Kellner, *Herbert Marcuse*, p. 299; R. Radosh, "On Hanging Up the Old Red Flag," in J. Bunzel, ed., *Political Passages*, p. 224.
69. Marcuse, et al., *Critique of Pure Tolerance*, Postscript, p. 120.
70. Quoted in Kellner, *Herbert Marcuse*, pp. 292, 300–01.

## Chapter 10

1. Quoted in Hughes, *Consciousness and Society*, pp. 114–15.
2. Bergson, *Creative Evolution*, p. 294.
3. *Ibid.*, pp. 7, 293–94, 295.
4. Wohl, *Generation of 1914*, pp. 8–9, 27.
5. *Diary of My Times*, p. 65.
6. Quoted in Paxton, *Vichy France*, p. 146.
7. *Ibid.*, pp. 253–56.
8. Péan, *Une Jeunesse Francaise*.
9. Paxton, *Vichy France*, p. 146; Judt, *Past Imperfect*, pp. 20; 16.
10. Roth, *Knowing and History*.
11. Drury, *Alexandre Kojève*, pp. 43–44.
12. Cohen-Solal, *Sartre*, p. 57. See also Pilkington, *Bergson and His Influence*.
13. Nietzsche, *Genealogy of Morals*, p. 66.
14. Gadamer, *Philosophical Hermeneutics*, pp. 136–37.
15. Wiggershaus, *Frankfurt School*, pp. 101–04, 593–96.
16. Quoted in Cassirer, *Myth of the State*, p. 293.
17. Barash, *Martin Heidegger and the Problem of Historical Meaning*, esp. pp. 146–60.
18. Heidegger, *Introduction to Metaphysics*, pp. 37; 31.
19. Richard Wolin, *The Politics of Being* (New York, 1990), p. 139; for the remarks on the Rhine river, see Holmes, *Anatomy of Anti-Liberalism*, p. 124.
20. Cohen-Solal, *Sartre*, pp. 92, 93; Sartre, *War Diaries*, pp. 49, 185.
21. Quoted in Charmé, *Vulgarity and Authenticity*, p. 54.
22. See Johnson, *Intellectuals*, pp. 225–27.
23. Jean-Paul Sartre, *Myth of Sisyphus and Other Essays* (New York, 1969), pp. 12–13.
24. On Heidegger's decisionism, see Wolin, *The Politics of Being*, esp. pp. 28–40.
25. Heidegger, *Introduction to Metaphysics*, p. 32.
26. Farias, *Heidegger and Nazism*; Ott, *Martin Heidegger: A Political Life*.
27. Sartre, *War Diaries*, pp. 182, 186–87.
28. Lottman, *The Purge*.
29. Sartre, "Self-Portrait at Seventy," in *Life/Situations*, pp. 47–48.
30. Johnson, *Intellectuals*, pp. 230–31.
31. Sartre, *Situations*, Vol. 2, p. 12.
32. Cohen-Salal, *Sartre*, pp. 251–52.

33. Sartre, *Situations*, Vol. 1, pp. 26–28.
34. All quotations come from the English translation in E. Weber, *Movements, Currents, Trends*, pp. 465–76.
35. Quoted in Wolin, *The Terms of Cultural Criticism*, p. 132.
36. *Humanism and Terror*, pp. xvi–xvii.
37. *Ibid.*, p. xv.
38. Quoted in Hayman, *Writing Against: A Biography of Sartre*, p. 229.
39. Quoted in Judt, *Past Imperfect*, p. 196.
40. Sartre, *Life/Situations*, p. 50.
41. Sartre, *Between Marxism and Existentialism*, pp. 82–83.
42. *Ibid.*, pp. 75, 83.
43. Cohn-Solal, *Sartre*, pp. 459–60; Sartre, *Life/Situations*, p. 163.
44. Sartre, "Self-Portrait at Seventy," in *Life/Situations*, p. 84.
45. *Life/Situations*, pp. 170–71.
46. Foucault, *Order of Things*, p. 387.
47. Quoted in Eribon, *Foucault*, pp. 20–21.
48. Foucault, *Order of Things*, p. 370.
49. *Ibid.*, p. xxiii.
50. E.g., Bataille, *Literature and Evil*, pp. 105–25.
51. Foucault, *Madness and Civilization*, p. 274.
52. Quoted in Miller, *Passion of Michel Foucault*, p. 301.
53. Foucault, *Power/Knowledge*, p. 90.
54. Foucault, *The Birth of the Clinic*, trans. Alan Sheridan (London, 1973); *Discipline and Punish: Birth of the Prison* (London, 1977); *The Archeology of Knowledge* and *Order of Discourse* (London, 1972).
55. Detailed in J. G. Merquior, *Foucault* (London, 1985), pp. 56–75.
56. Foucault, *Power/Knowledge*, p. 99.
57. *Ibid.*, pp. 93–94; Foucault, *History of Sexuality* (New York, 1978), p. 93.
58. Quoted in J. G. Merquior, *Foucault* (London, 1985), p. 90.
59. Geoff Mains, *Urban Aboriginals*, quoted in Miller, *Passion of Michel Foucault*, p. 268.
60. Miller, *Passion of Michel Foucault*, pp. 293, 375–81.
61. *Ibid.*, p. 384.
62. *Ibid.*, p. 205.
63. Perinbaum, *Holy Violence*; Gendzier, *Frantz Fanon: A Critical Study*; Caute, *Frantz Fanon*.
64. "Discourse on Colonialism" (1950), quoted in von Grunebaum, *French African Literature*, p. 13; Ba, *The Concept of Negritude in the Poetry of Leopold Sedar Senghor*, pp. 45–48.
65. Quoted in Moikobu, *Blood and Flesh*, p. 82.
66. E.g., Césaire, *Les Armes Miraculeuses* (The Miraculous Guns).
67. Sartre, *Black Orpheus*, p. 44.
68. *Ibid.*, p. 25.
69. Fanon, *Wretched of the Earth*, pp. 311–12.
70. *Ibid.*, p. 35.
71. *Ibid.*, p. 207; Césaire, *Les Armes Miraculeuses*, quoted in *ibid.*, p. 88.
72. *Ibid.*, pp. 22, 24.
73. Fanon, *Toward the African Revolution*, p. 18.
74. *Ibid.*, p. 27.
75. Hughes, *Obstructed Path*, p. 221.

Chapter 11

1. Cf. Said, *Culture and Imperialism*, p. 18.
2. Diggins, *Rise and Fall of the American Left*, pp. 290–95.
3. Cf. Wolin, *The Terms of Cultural Criticism*, and Lasch, *True and Only Heaven*.
4. Chomsky, *Necessary Illusions*.
5. For example, Klare, *War Without End*, p. 13.
6. Chomsky, *American Power and the New Mandarins*, p. 310.
7. Quoted in Hollander, *Anti-Americanism*, p. 69.
8. *Ibid.*, pp. 69; 33.
9. Kozol, *Death at an Early Age*, p. 12.
10. Lasch, *Culture of Narcissism*, pp. xvi, 64.
11. Lasch, *True and Only Heaven*, p. 403.
12. Lasch, *Culture of Narcissism*, p. 235.
13. Richard Heilbroner, *An Inquiry into the Human Prospect* (New York, 1974), pp. 137–38.
14. In *Atlantic Monthly*, December 1994.
15. Quoted in Hollander, *Political Pilgrims*, p. 246.
16. *Ibid.*, p. 210.
17. Quoted in Hollander, *Anti-Americanism*, p. 67.
18. Stavrianos, *Promise of the Coming Dark Age*.
19. E.g., Katz and Taylor, eds. *Eliminating Racism*, passim.
20. Gleason, *Speaking of Diversity*; Sollors, *Beyond Ethnicity*.
21. Cf. Dees, *Hate on Trial*.
22. E.g., Locke, *Essay Concerning Human Understanding*, Vol. 1, pp. 456–63; Hume, *A Treatise of Human Nature*, Book I, Section 6.
23. Langbaum, *Mysteries of Identity*.
24. Erikson, *Childhood and Society*; Paul Roazen, *Erik Erikson: The Power and Limits of a Vision* (New York, 1976), p. 24.
25. Herberg, *Protestant-Catholic-Jew*, p. 258.
26. Klapp, *Collective Search for Identity*, p. 5.
27. Pettigrew, *Profile of the American Negro*, pp. 6, 8, 9–11, Kozol, *Death at an Early Age*, p. 11.
28. Baldwin, *Fire Next Time*, pp. 9–10.
29. Quoted in Moikubu, *Blood and Flesh*, p. 85.
30. Quoted in Kozol, *Death at an Early Age*, p. 181.
31. Mailer, *Advertisements for Myself*, pp. 303–08.
32. Carmichael, *Black Power*, pp. 44, 46; viii.
33. Fanon, *Wretched of the Earth*, p. 313.
34. Carmichael, *Black Power*, pp. 40–41; 30.
35. *Ibid.*, pp. 181; 164–65.
36. Quoted in Moikubu, *Blood and Flesh*, p. 79.
37. The following comes from Cross, "The Negro-to-Black Conversion Experience," in Ladner, *Death of White Sociology*, pp. 267–86.
38. Mailer, *Advertisements for Myself*, p. 504.
39. *Blood in My Eye*, pp. 34, 92.
40. Jones/Baraka, *LeRoi Jones/Amiri Baraka Reader*, p. 224.
41. Slotkin, *Regeneration Through Violence* and *Gunfighter Nation*; Chomsky, *Deterring Democracy*; Leo Marx, *Machine in the Garden*; Leach, *Land of Desire*; Finn, *Politics of History*; Nash, *Race and Revolution*; and Brownmiller, *Against Our Will*.

42. Said, *Orientalism*, p. 227.
43. Carlson, *The Americanization Syndrome*, pp. 10–12.
44. Nash, *Red, White, and Black*, pp. 21–22.
45. Compare Nash, *ibid.*, and H. S. Chamberlain, *Foundations*, Vol. 1, pp. 574–77.
46. Nash, *Red, White, and Black*, p. 215.
47. Takaki, *Iron Cages*, pp. 20–21, 40–42, 269, 304; ix–x.
48. *Ibid.*, pp. 179, 269; Takaki, *A Different Mirror*, p. 426.
49. Morrison, *Race-ing Justice, En-gendering Justice*, p. xix.
50. *Ibid.*, p. 388.
51. Angelou, *On the Pulse of the Morning*.
52. Cf. Takaki, *Iron Cages*, pp. 292–99.
53. Aronowitz and Giroux, *Education Still Under Siege*, p. 171.
54. Morrison, *Conversations*, p. 256.
55. Kochman, *Black and White Styles in Conflict*, p. 110.
56. Baker, Jr., *Black Studies, Rap, and the Academy*, pp. 87; 46.
57. Lord, *Zami: A New Spelling of My Name*.
58. Hooks, *Ain't I a Woman*, pp. 191; 99; *Breaking Bread* (with Cornel West), p. 103.
59. Marable, *Black America*, p. 13.
60. Cose, *Nation of Strangers*, p. 218.
61. Saint Augustine, *City of God*, Vol. 1, Bk. 1, Ch. 1.
62. Volney, *Ruins*, I, pp. 32–34.
63. Quoted in Moses, *Roots of Black Nationalism*, p. 64.
64. Cf. Davidson, *Search for Africa*.
65. Vaillant, *Black, French, and African*, pp. 93–100.
66. Diop, *African Origin of Civilization*, p. 49.
67. On this, see Bernal, *Black Athena*, Vol. 1.
68. Diop, *Civilization or Barbarism? An Authentic Anthropology*.
69. Diop, *African Origin of Civilization*, p. 140.
70. Schlesinger, *Disuniting of America*, p. 79.
71. Williams, *Destruction of Black Civilization*, pp. 73, 74; 54.
72. Ben-Jochannan, *Africa: Mother of Western Civilization*, p. 345.
73. Williams, *Rebirth of African Civilization*, p. 69.
74. *Ibid.*, p. 71.
75. Khamit-Kush, *What They Never Told You in History Class*, p. 204.
76. Van Sertima's claims are summarized in Karenga, *Introduction to Black Studies*, pp. 110–14.
77. Quoted in Schlesinger, *Disuniting of America*, p. 62.
78. *Amsterdam News*, quoted in Taylor, *Paved with Good Intentions*, p. 101.
79. Karenga, *Introduction to Black Studies*, pp. 70, 73.
80. Asante, *Afrocentric Idea*, p. 125; *Kemet, Afrocentricity, and Knowledge*, pp. 90; 89.
81. Asante, *Afrocentric Idea*, p. 185.
82. Welsing, *Isis Papers*, p. 23.
83. *Ibid.*, p. 69.
84. *Ibid.*, p. x.
85. Wilson Carruthers, quoted in Bernal, *Black Athena*, Vol. 1, p. 436.

*Chapter 12*

1. Quoted in Manes, *Green Rage*, p. 42.
2. Hankins, *Science and the Enlightenment*.

3. Martin, *Mask of the Prophet*, p. 170.
4. Wells, *The Door in the Wall and Other Stories*, p. 119.
5. Ellul, *Technological Society*, pp. 4–5.
6. Vacca, *The Coming Dark Ages*.
7. Quoted in Fisher, *Fire and Ice*, p. 152.
8. Hume, *On the Standard of Taste and Other Essays*, p. 146.
9. Ehrlich, *Population Bomb*, p. 48.
10. *Ibid.*, pp. 130, 132.
11. *Ibid.*, p. 151.
12. Commoner, *The Closing Circle*, pp. 283–84.
13. Dubos and Ward, *Only One Earth*.
14. Toffler, *Future Shock*; Kuklick, *Savage Within*, pp. 165–74.
15. Brandt, et al. *North-South: A Program for Survival* (Cambridge, MA, 1980), pp. 267; 11.
16. *Ibid.*, pp. 23, 288.
17. *Ibid.*, p. 268.
18. Brown, et al., *Saving the Planet*, p. 11.
19. *Ibid.*, p. 181.
20. Schell, *Fate of the Earth*, p. 8.
21. *Ibid.*, pp. 23, 103, 111.
22. *Ibid.*, pp. 161–62.
23. *Ibid.*, pp. 226; 178.
24. Quoted in Schwartz, *Century's End*, p. 287.
25. Ehrlich, *Healing the Planet*, pp. 12, 243; 242.
26. Devall and Sessions, *Deep Ecology*, p. 65.
27. Quoted in DeGrood, *Haeckel's Theory of the Unity of Nature*, p. 47.
28. Haeckel, *Riddle of the Universe*, p. 363.
29. Bramwell, *Ecology in the 20th Century*, p. 180.
30. On Klages, see Aschheim, *Nietzsche Legacy*, pp. 79–81.
31. Bramwell, *Ecology in the 20th Century*, pp. 177–80; on the Artamanen and Himmler's SS, see Mosse, *Crisis of German Ideology*, pp. 116–20.
32. Bramwell, *Blood and Soil*.
33. Bramwell, *Ecology in the 20th Century*, p. 204.
34. Quoted in *ibid.*, p. 184.
35. Heidegger, *Poetry, Language, Thought*, pp. 114–15, 116.
36. Gottlieb, *Forcing the Spring*, p. 102.
37. Reich, *Greening of America*, pp. 2–8, 165, 284.
38. Quoted in Manes, *Green Rage*, pp. 46–47.
39. Reich, *Greening of America*, pp. 3–4, 165, 284.
40. Quoted in Brown, et al., *Saving the Planet*, p. 21.
41. Quoted in Devall and Sessions, *Deep Ecology*, p. 66.
42. Bookchin, *The Modern Crisis*, p. 30.
43. *Ibid.*, p. 6.
44. *Ibid.*, p. 25.
45. *Ibid.*, p. 29.
46. Bookchin, *Remaking Society*, p. 166.
47. *Modern Crisis*, pp. 22–23; *Remaking Society*, pp. 194–95.
48. Abbey, *Confessions of a Barbarian*, p. 337.
49. *Remaking Society*, p. 22.
50. Sale, *1492: The Conquest of Paradise*, quoting Marlowe's *Doctor Faustus*, pp. 264; 5.

51. *Ibid.*, pp. 289; 4.
52. *Ibid.*, pp. 301, 320.
53. Devall and Sessions, *Deep Ecology*, p. 6; Bookchin, *Ecology of Freedom*, pp. 46–48.
54. Manes, *Green Rage*, pp. 238; 123.
55. *Ibid.*, pp. 238–39.
56. Mander, *In the Absence of the Sacred*, p. 387.
57. Abbey, *Confessions of a Barbarian*, p. 138.
58. *Ibid.*, p. 307.
59. *Ibid.*, p. 152.
60. "Response to Schmookler on Anarchy," quoted in Manes, *Green Rage*, p. 241.
61. Rifkin, *Beyond Beef*, p. 25.
62. *Ibid.*, pp. 28, 32.
63. *Ibid.*, pp. 62–63.
64. *Ibid.*, p. 271. The quotation comes from Boas and Chain, *Big Mac: The Unauthorized Story of McDonald's* (New York, 1976), p. 177.
65. Gore, *Earth in the Balance*, p. 269.
66. *Ibid.*, pp. 222, 232; 231.
67. *Ibid.*, pp. 252, 220–21; 220.
68. Allaby, *Guide to Gaia*; quoted in Dobson, *Green Political Thought*, p. 43.
69. Gore, *Earth in the Balance*, pp. 197–99, 203 (my emphasis).
70. Kingdon, *Self-Made Man*, esp. conclusion.
71. Gore, *Earth in the Balance*, p. 35.
72. Fagan, *Journey From Eden*; Ponting, *A Green History of the World*; Attenborough, *First Eden*.
73. Gore, *Earth in the Balance*, pp. 64–65.
74. Devall and Sessions, *Deep Ecology*, p. 66.
75. Manes, *Green Rage*, pp. 75, 84, 176; 162.
76. For examples, see Devall and Sessions, *Deep Ecology*, p. 6, and Dobson, *Green Political Thought*, pp. 45–47.
77. Bookchin and Foreman, *Defending the Earth*, p. 39.
78. Soule, *Conservation Biology*.
79. Quoted in Gore, *Earth in the Balance*, p. 217.
80. Quoted in *Ecowarriors*, p. 266.
81. Bookchin and Foreman, *Defending the Earth*, p. 80.
82. Preston, *Hot Zone*, p. 287.
83. Lawrence, *Women in Love*, p. 52.

### Afterword

1. Samuelson, *The Good Society and Its Discontents* (New York, 1995), p. 49.
2. Popper, *Poverty of Historicism*, pp. 17, 22.
3. *Ibid.*, p. 18.
4. Tocqueville, *European Revolution*, pp. 309–10.
5. A.J. Lovejoy, *The Great Chain of Being* (New York, 1964); Locke, *Essay Concerning Human Understanding*, Book II, p. 392.

# BIBLIOGRAPHY

Abbey, Edward. *Confessions of a Barbarian: Selections from the Journals of Edward Abbey.* South End Press, Boston, 1994.
———. *The Monkey Wrench Gang.* Lippincott, Philadelphia, 1975.
Adams, Brooks. *America's Economic Supremacy.* Harper and Brothers, New York, 1947.
———. *The Law of Civilization and Decay.* Introduction by Charles Beard. Vintage Books, New York, 1955.
Adams, Henry. *The Degradation of the Democratic Dogma.* Edited by Brooks Adams. Macmillan, New York, 1949.
———. *The Education of Henry Adams.* Modern Library, New York, 1931.
———. *Letters 1892–1918.* Houghton Mifflin, Boston, 1938.
———. *Selected Letters.* Edited by Ernest Samuels. Harvard University Press, Cambridge, MA, 1992.
Adams, John. *Political Writings.* Edited by George Peck. Macmillan, New York, 1985.
———. *Works.* Volume VI. Little, Brown, Boston, 1856.
Adorno, Theodor. *Introduction to the Sociology of Music.* Seabury Press, New York, 1976.
———. *Minima Moralia. Reflections From a Damaged Life.* Trans. E.F.N. Jephcott. NLB, London, 1974.
———. *Negative Dialectics.* Trans. E.B. Ashton. Seabury Press, New York, 1973.
———; Frenkel-Brunswick, E.; Levinson, D.; and Sanford, R.N. *The Authoritarian Personality.* W.W. Norton, New York, 1949.
———, and Horkheimer, Max. *The Dialectic of Enlightenment.* Trans. J. Cumming. Herder and Herder, New York, 1944.
Allaby, Michael. *Guide to Gaia.* E.P. Dutton, New York, 1991.
Almond, G.; Chodorow, M.; and Pearce, R.H., eds. *Progress and Its Discontents.* University of California Press, Los Angeles, 1982.
Anderson, Thornton. *Brooks Adams: Constructive Conservative.* Cornell University Press, Ithaca, NY, 1954.
Angelou, Maya. *On the Pulse of the Morning.* Random House, New York, 1993.
Appiah, A. "The Uncompleted Argument: Du Bois and the Illusion of Race." In H.L. Gates, ed. *"Race," Writing, and Difference.* University of Chicago Press, Chicago, 1986.

Arnold, Matthew. *Selected Prose*. Penguin Books, Harmondsworth, 1980.

Aron, Raymond. *Introduction to the Philosophy of History*. Trans. G.J. Irwin. Beacon Press, Boston, 1962.

———. *Marxism and the Existentialists*. Simon and Schuster, New York, 1970.

Aronowitz, Stanley, and Giroux, Henry. *Education Still Under Siege*. Bergen and Garvey, Westport CT, 1993.

Asante, Molefi. *The Afrocentric Idea*. Temple University Press, Philadelphia, 1987.

———. *Kemet, Afrocentricity, and Knowledge*. Africa World Press, Trenton NJ, 1990.

Aschheim, Steven. *The Nietzsche Legacy in Germany 1890–1990*. University of California Press, Berkeley, 1992.

Ashley-Montagu, M., ed. *Toynbee and History*. Porter Sargent, Boston, 1956.

Attenborough, David. *The First Eden: The Mediterranean World and Man*. Little, Brown, Boston, 1987.

Ba, S.W. *The Concept of Negritude in the Poetry of Leopold Sedar Senghor*. Princeton University Press, Princeton, NJ, 1973.

Bainton, Michael. *The Idea of Race and Race Theory*. Cambridge University Press, Cambridge, 1985.

———. *Racial Theories*. Cambridge University Press, Cambridge, 1987.

Baker, Houston, Jr. *Black Studies, Rap, and the Academy*. University of Chicago Press, Chicago, 1993.

Baldwin, James. *The Fire Next Time*. Dell, New York, 1962.

Bannister, Robert. *Social Darwinism: Science and Myth in Anglo-American Social Thought*. Temple University Press, Philadelphia, 1979.

Barash, Jeffrey A. *Martin Heidegger and the Problem of Historical Meaning*. M. Nijhoff, Dordrecht, 1988.

Barkan, Elazar. *The Retreat of Scientific Racism*. Cambridge University Press, Cambridge, 1992.

Barker, Ernest. *Traditions of Civility*. Cambridge University Press, Cambridge, 1922.

Barnouw, Dagmar. *Weimar Intellectuals and the Threat of Modernity*. University of Indiana Press, Bloomington, 1988.

Barzun, Jacques. *The Culture We Deserve*. Wesleyan University Press, Middletown, CT, 1989.

Bataille, Georges. *Literature and Evil*. Trans. A. Hamilton. M. Boyars, London and New York, 1985.

Baudelaire, Charles. *Intimate Journals*. Trans. Christopher Isherwood.

———. *Selected Writings on Art and Literature*. Trans. P. Charvet. Penguin Books, Harmondsworth, 1992.

Becker, Carl. *The Heavenly City of the Eighteenth-Century Philosophers*. Yale University Press, New Haven, CT, 1957.

Beckson, Karl, ed. *Aesthetes and Decadents of the 1890's*. Academy Publishers, Chicago, 1981.

Belford, Barbara. *Bram Stoker: A Biography of the Author of 'Dracula'*. Knopf, New York, 1996.

Benda, Julien. *The Treason of the Intellectuals*. Trans. R. Aldington. W. W. Norton, New York, 1969.

Bendix, R. *Max Weber: An Intimate Portrait*. University of California Press, Berkeley, 1977.

Ben-Jochannan, Y.A.A. *Africa: Mother of Western Civilization*. Black Classics Press, Baltimore, 1988.

Benjamin, Walter. *Illuminations*. Trans. H. Zohn. Edited by Hannah Arendt. Schocken Books, New York, 1978.

Bercovitch, Sacvan. *The American Jeremiad.* University of Wisconsin Press, Madison, 1978.

Bergson, Henri. *Creative Evolution.* Trans. A. Mitchell. Henry Holt, New York, 1911.

Beringause, Arthur. *Brooks Adams: A Biography.* Knopf, New York, 1955.

Berlin, Isaiah. *Against the Current: Essays in the History of Ideas.* Viking Press, New York, 1980.

———. *Vico and Herder.* Viking Press, New York, 1976.

Bernal, Martin. *Black Athena: The Afroasiatic Roots of Classical Civilization.* Volume 1. Rutgers University Press, New Brunswick, NJ, 1987.

Bernanos, Georges. *Diary of My Times.* Macmillan, New York, 1938.

Beziau, R., ed. *Arthur de Gobineau: Etudes Critiques 1842–1847.* Klincksieck, Paris, 1984.

Biddiss, Michael. *Father of Racist Ideology: The Social and Political Thought of Count Gobineau.* Weybright and Talley, New York, 1970.

———, ed. *Gobineau: Selected Political Writings.* Harper and Row, New York and London, 1970.

Bloch, Ruth. *Visionary Republic: Millennial Themes in American Thought 1756–1800.* Cambridge University Press, Cambridge, 1985.

Bloom, Allan, *The Closing of the American Mind.* Simon and Schuster, New York, 1987.

Boissel, J. *Gobineau (1816–1882).* Gallimard, Paris, 1982.

Boller, P.R. *American Thought in Transition: The Impact of Evolutionary Naturalism 1865–1900.* University of Chicago Press, Chicago, 1969.

Bookchin, Murray. *The Ecology of Freedom.* Cheshire Books, Palo Alto, CA, 1982.

———. *The Modern Crisis.* Black Rose Books, Montreal, 1987.

———. *Remaking Society.* Black Rose Books, Montreal, 1989.

———, and Foreman, David. *Defending the Earth: A Dialogue.* South End Press, Boston, 1991.

Borden, C., and Jackman, J.C., eds. *The Muses Flee Hitler: Cultural Transfer and Adaptation.* Smithsonian Press, Washington, DC, 1983.

Bowler, Peter. *Evolution: The History of an Idea.* University of California Press, Berkeley, 1989.

———. *The Invention of Progress: The Victorians and the Past.* Basil Blackwell, Oxford, 1989.

———. *The Non-Darwinian Revolution: Reinterpreting a Historical Myth.* Johns Hopkins University Press, Baltimore, 1988.

Bradley, F.H. *Ethical Studies.* Bobbs-Merrill, Indianapolis and New York, 1951.

Bramwell, Anna. *Blood and Soil: Walter Darré and Hitler's Green Party.* Kensal, Bourne End, 1985.

———. *Ecology in the 20th Century: A History.* Yale University Press, New Haven, CT, 1989.

Brandt, Willy, et al. *North-South: A Program for Survival.* MIT Press, Cambridge, MA, 1980.

Brantlinger, Patrick. *Bread and Circuses: Theories of Mass Culture as Social Decay.* Cornell University Press, Ithaca, NY, 1983.

Bridgewater, Patrick. *Poet of Expressionist Berlin: The Life and Work of Georg Heym.* Libris, London, 1991.

Broderick, Francis. "German Influence on the Scholarship of W.E.B. Du Bois." *Phylon* 19 (1958), 367–71.

Bromwich, David. *A Choice of Inheritance: Self and Community from Edmund Burke to Robert Frost.* Harvard University Press, Cambridge, MA, 1989.

Brown, Lester; Flavin, C.; and Postel, S. *Saving the Planet.* W. W. Norton, New York, 1991.

Brownmiller, Susan. *Against Our Will: Men, Women, and Rape.* Simon and Schuster, New York, 1975.

Bruce, D.D. "W.E.B. Du Bois and the Idea of Double Consciousness." *American Literature* 64 (1992), 299–309.

Bryce, James. *The American Commonwealth.* 2 vols. MacMillan, London, 1891.

Buchan, John. *Pilgrim's Way: An Essay in Recollection.* Houghton Mifflin, Boston, 1940.

Buck-Morss, Susan. *The Origins of Negative Dialectics.* Free Press, New York, 1977.

Buckley, J.H. *The Triumph of Time.* Harvard University Press, Cambridge, MA, 1967.

Buenzod, Janine. *La Formation de la Pensée de Gobineau et L'Essai sur l'inégalité des races humaines.* A.-G. Nizet, Paris, 1967.

Burckhardt, Jacob. *The Civilization of the Renaissance in Italy.* Trans. S. Middlemore. Harper and Row, New York, 1958.

———. *Force and Freedom.* Edited by J.H. Nicolls. Meridian Books, New York, 1955.

———. *Letters of Jacob Burckhardt.* Edited by A. Dru. Pantheon Books, New York, 1955.

———. *On History and Historians.* Trans. H. Zohn. Introduction by H.R. Trevor-Roper. Harper and Row, New York, 1965.

Burke, Peter. *Images of the Sun King.* Yale University Press, New Haven, CT, 1990.

Burrow, John; Collini, Stefan; and Winch, Donald. *That Noble Science of Politics: A Study in Nineteenth-Century Intellectual History.* Cambridge University Press, Cambridge, 1983.

Bury, J.B. *The Idea of Progress: An Inquiry into Its Origins and Growth.* Dover Publications, New York, 1955.

Bushman, Richard. *The Refinement of America.* Knopf, New York, 1992.

Camus, Albert. *The Myth of Sisyphus and Other Essays.* Trans. J. O'Brien. Knopf, New York, 1969.

Carlisle, Rodney. *The Roots of Black Nationalism.* Kennikat Press, Port Washington, NY, 1975.

Carlson, Robert. *The Americanization Syndrome: A Quest for Conformity.* St. Martin's Press, New York, 1987.

Carmichael, Stokely. *Black Power.* Random House, New York, 1967.

Carter, A.E. *The Idea of Decadence in French Literature 1830–1900.* University of Toronto Press, Toronto, 1958.

Cassirer, Ernst. *The Myth of the State.* Yale University Press, New Haven, CT, 1979.

Cater, Harold, ed. *Henry Adams and His Friends.* Houghton Mifflin, Boston, 1947.

Caute, David. *Frantz Fanon.* Viking Press, New York, 1970.

Cecil, Robert. *The Myth of the Master Race: Alfred Rosenberg and Nazi Ideology.* Dodd Mead, New York, 1972.

Césaire, Aimé. *Les Armes Miraculeuses.* Gallimard, Paris, 1949.

Chamberlain, John. *Farewell to Reform: The Rise, Life, and Decay of the Progressive Mind in America.* John Day, New York, 1933.

Charmé, Stuart. *Vulgarity and Authenticity: Dimensions of Otherness in the World of Jean-Paul Sartre.* University of Massachusetts Press, Amherst, 1991.

Chevalier, Louis. *Laboring Classes and Dangerous Classes in Paris During the First Half of the Nineteenth Century.* Trans. F. Jellinek. Howard Fertig, New York, 1973.

Chickering, Roger. *We Men Who Feel Most German: The Pan-German League 1891–1902.* Princeton University Press, Princeton, NJ, 1980.

Chomsky, Noam. *American Power and the New Mandarins.* Pantheon Books, New York, 1967.

———. *Deterring Democracy.* Verso, New York and London, 1991.

———. *Necessary Illusions: Thought Control in Democratic Societies.* South End Press, Boston, 1989.

Christie, R., and Jahora, M. *Studies in the Scope and Method of 'The Authoritarian Personality.'* Free Press, Glencoe, IL, 1954.

Clark, Kenneth. *Civilisation.* Harper and Row, New York, 1970.

Clark, Linda. *Social Darwinism in France.* University of Alabama Press, Montgomery, 1984.

Cleaver, Eldridge. *Soul on Ice.* McGraw-Hill, New York, 1968.

Cohen-Solal, Annie. *Sartre: A Life.* Knopf, New York, 1987.

Collier, Peter, and Timms, Edward, eds. *Visions and Blueprints: Avant Garde Culture and Radical Politics in Early-Twentieth-Century Europe.* Manchester University Press, Manchester, 1988.

Collingwood, R.G. *The Idea of History.* Oxford University Press, Oxford, 1957.

Collini, Stefan. *Liberalism and Socialism: L.T. Hobhouse and Political Argument in England 1880–1915.* Harvard University Press, Cambridge, MA, 1979.

Commoner, Barry. *The Closing Circle.* Knopf, New York, 1971.

Conan Doyle, Arthur. *The Annotated Sherlock Holmes.* Edited by W. Baring-Gould. C.N. Potter, New York, 1967.

Cose, Ellis. *A Nation of Strangers.* William Morrow, New York, 1992.

Craig, Gordon. *The Triumph of Liberalism: Zurich in the Golden Age 1830–1860.* Scribner, New York, 1988.

Cranston, Maurice, ed. *Prophetic Politics.* Simon and Schuster, New York, 1970.

Croly, Herbert. *The Promise of American Life.* Belknap Press, Cambridge, MA, 1965.

Crook, D.P. *Benjamin Kidd: Portrait of a Social Darwinist.* Cambridge University Press, Cambridge, 1984.

Cross, William. "The Negro-to-Black Conversion Experience." In J. Ladner, ed., *The Death of White Sociology,* 267–86. Vintage Books, New York, 1973.

Crouzet, M., ed. *Arthur de Gobineau, Cents Ans Après: Colloque du Centenaire.* L. Minard, Paris, 1990.

Curtin, Philip. *The Image of Africa: British Ideas and Action 1780–1850.* University of Wisconsin Press, Madison, 1964.

Curtis, L.P. *Apes and Angels: The Irish in Victorian Caricature.* Newton, Abbot, David and Charles, Washington, DC, 1971.

Curtis, Lionel. *The Commonwealth of Nations.* Part One. MacMillan, London, 1916.

Danto, Arthur. "The Eternal Recurrence." In Robert Solomon, ed., *Nietzsche. A Collection of Critical Essays,* 316–21. Anchor Press, Garden City, NY, 1973.

Davidson, Basil. *The Search for Africa. History, Culture, and Politics.* Times Books, New York, 1994.

Davie, G. E., ed. *Philosophers of the Scottish Enlightenment.* Edinburgh University Press, Edinburgh, 1981.

Dawson, Christopher. *The Making of Europe.* World Publishing Company, Cleveland and New York, 1956.

Dees, Morris. *Hate on Trial.* Villard Books, New York, 1993.

Degler, Carl. *In Search of Human Nature: The Decline and Revival of Darwinism in American Social Thought.* Oxford University Press, Oxford, 1991.

————. *Neither Black Nor White: Slavery and Race Relations in Brazil and the United States*. Macmillan, New York, 1971.

DeGrood, D.H. *Haeckel's Theory of the Unity of Nature*. B.R. Gruner, Amsterdam, 1982.

Del Caro, Adrian, *Nietzsche Contra Nietzsche*. Louisiana State University Press, Baton Rouge, 1989.

De Marco, Joseph B. *The Social Thought of W.E.B. Du Bois*. University Press of America, Lanham, MD, 1983.

Devall, Bill, and Sessions, George. *Deep Ecology*. G. M. Smith, Salt Lake City, UT, 1985.

Diggins, John P. *The Rise and Fall of the American Left*. W. W. Norton, New York, 1992.

Dijkstra, Bram. *Idols of Perversity*. Oxford University Press, Oxford and London, 1986.

Dikötter, Frank. *The Discourse of Race in Modern China*. Stanford University Press, Stanford, CA, 1992.

Diop, Cheikh Anta. *The African Origin of Civilization*. Trans. Mercer Cook. Lawrence Hill, Chicago, 1974.

————. *Civilization or Barbarism? An Authentic Anthropology*. Lawrence Hill, Chicago, 1991.

Dobson, Andrew. *Green Political Thought: An Introduction*. Unwim Hyman, London, 1990.

Dowling, Linda. *Language and Decadence in the Victorian Fin de Siècle*. Princeton University Press, Princeton, NJ, 1986.

Drury, Shadia B. *Alexandre Kojève: The Roots of Postmodern Politics*. St. Martin's Press, New York, 1994.

Du Bois, W.E.B. *Against Racism. Unpublished essays, papers, addresses, 1887–1961*. Ed. H. Aptheker. University of Massachusetts Press, Amherst, 1985.

————. *Black Reconstruction in America*. Russell and Russell, New York, 1966.

————. *Color and Democracy*. Kraus-Robinson Organization, Millwood, NY, 1983.

————. *Du Bois Speaks*. Edited by P. Foner. Pathfinder Press, New York, 1970.

————. *Dark Princess*. Kraus-Robinson Organization, Millwood, NY, 1974.

————. *Darkwater*. AMS Press, New York, 1969.

————. *Dusk of Dawn*. Kraus-Robinson Organization, Millwood, NY, 1975.

————. *The Negro*. Kraus-Robinson Organization, Millwood, NY, 1975.

————. *W.E.B. Du Bois: A Reader*. Edited by D.L. Lewis, Henry Holt, New York, 1995.

————. *Writings*: Literary Classics (Viking Press), New York, 1986.

————. *The World and Africa*. International Publishers, New York, 1965.

Dubos, René, and Ward, Barbara. *Only One Earth*. W. W. Norton, New York, 1972.

Durkheim, Emile. *The Division of Labor in Society*. Trans. G. Simpson. Free Press, New York, 1964.

————. *Suicide: A Study in Sociology*. Trans. G. Simpson. Free Press, New York, 1966.

Dyer, Thomas. *Theodore Roosevelt and the Idea of Race*. Louisiana State University Press, Baton Route, 1980.

Edelstein, Ludwig. *The Idea of Progress in Classical Antiquity*. Johns Hopkins University Press, Baltimore, 1967.

Ehrlich, Paul. *The Population Bomb*. Ballantine Books, New York, 1971.

———— and Barbara. *Healing the Planet*. Addison-Wesley, Reading, MA, 1991.

Eksteins, Modris. *Rites of Spring: The Great War and the Birth of the Modern Age*. Black Swan Press, London, 1990.

Elias, Norbert. *The History of Manners*. Volume 1 of *The Civilizing Process*. Trans. E. Jephcott. Pantheon Books, New York, 1978.

Eliot, Charles W. *Five American Contributions to Civilization*. New York, 1897.

Ellul, Jacques. *The Technological Society*. Vintage Books, New York, 1964.

Eribon, Didier. *Foucault.* Trans. R. Wing. Harvard University Press, Cambridge, MA, 1991.

Erikson, Erik. *Childhood and Society.* W. W. Norton, New York, 1963.

Ezell, J. *Fortune's Merry Wheel: The Lottery in America.* Harvard University Press, Cambridge, MA, 1960.

Fagan, Brian. *The Journey from Eden: The Peopling of Our World.* Thames and Hudson, New York, 1990.

Fanon, Frantz. *Toward the African Revolution: Political Essays.* Grove Press, New York, 1967.

———. *The Wretched of the Earth.* Trans. C. Farrington. Grove Press, New York, 1968.

Farías, Victor. *Heidegger and Nazism.* Temple University Press, Philadelphia, 1989.

Fennelly, J.F. *Twilight of the Evening Lands: Oswald Spengler a Half-Century Later.* Brookdale Press, New York, 1972.

Féré, Charles. *Dégénérescence et Criminalité.* Paris, 1880.

Feuer, Lewis. *Imperialism and the Anti-Imperialist Mind.* Transaction Publishers, New Brunswick, NJ, 1989.

———, ed. *Marx and Engels: Basic Writings on Politics and Philosophy.* Doubleday, New York, 1959.

Field, G. *Evangelist of Race: The Germanic Vision of Houston Stewart Chamberlain.* Columbia University Press, New York, 1981.

Fischer, Kurt. *History and Prophecy: Oswald Spengler and the Decline of the West.* Peter Lang, Frankfurt and New York, 1989.

Fisher, David. *Fire and Ice.* Harper and Row, New York, 1990.

Fiske, John. *A Century of Science and Other Essays.* Houghton Mifflin, Boston, 1900.

Fleming, Donald. *John William Draper and the Religion of Science.* University of Pennsylvania Press, Philadelphia, 1972.

Forrest, D.W. *Francis Galton: The Life and Work of a Victorian Genius.* Taplinger Publishers, New York, 1974.

Förster-Nietzsche, Elisabeth. *Life of Nietzsche.* 2 vols. Trans. P. Cohn. Sturgis and Walton, New York, 1915.

———; Jessen, P.; and Rath, P. *Bücher und Wege von Büchern: Friedrich Nietzsches Bibliotek.* W. Spemann, Berlin and Stuttgart, 1900.

Foucault, Michel. *Madness and Civilization.* Trans. R. Howard. Vintage Books, New York, 1973.

———. *The Order of Things. An Archeology of the Human Sciences.* Vintage Books, New York, 1973.

———. *Power/Knowledge: Selected Interviews and Other Writings 1972–1977.* Edited by Colin Gordon. Pantheon Books, New York, 1980.

Freeden, Michael. *The New Liberalism: The Ideology of Social Reform.* Oxford University Press, Oxford, 1978.

Freud, Sigmund. *Beyond the Pleasure Principle.* Trans. J. Strachey. W. W. Norton, New York, 1975.

———. *Civilization and Its Discontents.* Trans. J. Strachey. W. W. Norton, New York, 1961.

———. *Moses and Monotheism.* Trans. K. Jones. Vintage Books, New York, 1967.

Fromm, Erich. *Escape From Freedom.* Avon Books, New York, 1965.

Gadamer, Hans Georg. *Philosophical Hermeneutics.* Trans. D. Linge. University of California Press, Berkeley, 1977.

Gale, Richard M., ed. *The Philosophy of Time.* Doubleday, New York, 1967.

Galton, Francis. *Hereditary Genius*. London, 1866.

Garofalo, Raphaele. *Criminology*. Little, Brown, Boston, 1914.

Garvey, Marcus. *Marcus Garvey and UNIA Papers*. University of California Press, Berkeley, 1983.

————. *Life and Lessons of Marcus Garvey*. 7 vols. Edited by R.A. Hill and B. Blair. University of California Press, Berkeley, 1987.

————. *Philosophy and Opinions of Marcus Garvey*. Atheneum Press, New York, 1992.

Gasman, Daniel. *The Scientific Origins of National Socialism*. MacDonald, London, 1971.

Gatewood, Willard. *Aristocrats of Color: The Black Elite 1880–1920*. University of Indiana Press, Bloomington, 1990.

Gay, Peter. *Freud: A Life for Our Time*. W. W. Norton, New York, 1988.

————. *Freud, Jews, and Other Germans: Masters and Victims in Modernist Culture*. New York, 1978.

Gendzier, I. *Frantz Fanon: A Critical Study*. Pantheon Books, New York, 1973.

George, Henry. *Progress and Poverty*. Modern Library, New York, 1964.

George, J., and Wilcox, L. *Nazis, Communists, Klansmen, and Others on the Fringe*. Prometheus Books, Buffalo, NY, 1992.

Gibbon, Edward. *Decline and Fall of the Roman Empire*. 3 vols. Modern Library, New York, 1932.

Giles, G.J. *Students and National Socialism in Germany*. Princeton University Press, Princeton, NJ, 1985.

Gilman, Richard. *Decadence: The Strange Life of an Epithet*. Farrar, Straus and Giroux, New York, 1979.

Gilman, Sander. *Difference and Pathology: Stereotypes of Sexuality, Race, and Madness*. Cornell University Press, Ithaca, NY, 1985.

————. *Freud, Race, and Gender*. Princeton University Press, Princeton, NJ, 1993.

————, and Chamberlain, J.E., eds. *Degeneration: The Dark Side of Progress*. Columbia University Press, New York, 1985.

Gilroy, Paul. *The Black Atlantic: Modernity and Double Consciousness*. Harvard University Press, Cambridge, MA, 1993.

Gleason, Philip. *Speaking of Diversity: Language and Ethnicity in Twentieth-Century America*. Johns Hopkins University Press, Baltimore, 1992.

Gobineau, Joseph Arthur, comte de. *Essai sur L'Inégalité des Races Humaines*. 2 vols. H. Juin. Belfond, Paris, 1967.

————. *The Golden Flower*. Trans. B.K. Rodman. Books for Libraries, Freeport, NY, 1924.

————. *The Inequality of Human Races*. Trans. A. Collins. Putnam, New York, 1915.

Gooch, G.P. *History and Historians in the Nineteenth Century*. Beacon Press, Boston, 1959.

Goodrick-Clarke, Nicolas. *The Occult Roots of Nazism*. Cambridge University Press, Cambridge, 1992.

Gore, Albert. *Earth in the Balance*. Houghton Mifflin, Boston, 1992.

Gossman, Lionel. *Orpheus Philologus: Bachofen versus Mommsen on the Study of Antiquity*. Proceedings of the American Philosophical Society, Philadelphia, 1983.

Gottlieb, Robert. *Forcing the Spring*. Island Press, Washington, DC, 1993.

Gould, Stephen Jay. *The Mismeasure of Man*. W. W. Norton, New York, 1981.

————. *Ontogeny and Phylogeny*. Harvard University Press, Cambridge, MA, 1977.

Graña, Cesare. *Modernity and Its Discontents*. Harper and Row, New York, 1964.

Grant, Madison. *Conquest of a Continent*. Scribner, London and New York, 1933.

————. *Passing of the Great Race*. Scribner, New York, 1921.

Green, Martin. *Mountain of Truth: The Counterculture Begins. Ascona 1900–1920*. University of New England Press, Hanover, PA, 1986.

Green, Thomas Hill. *Lectures on the Principles of Political Obligation*. Edited by P. Harris and J. Morrow. Cambridge University Press, Cambridge, 1986.

———. *Prolegomena to Ethics*. Edited by A.C. Bradley. Thomas Crowell, New York, 1969.

Gregor-Dellin, Martin. *Wagner: His Life, His Work, His Century*. Harcourt Brace Jovanovich, New York, 1983.

Griffiths, Richard. *The Reactionary Revolution: The Catholic Revival in French Literature, 1870–1914*. F. Unger Publishers, New York, 1965.

Guizot, François. *Historical Essays and Lectures*. Edited by Stanley Mellon. University of Chicago Press, Chicago, 1972.

———. *History of Civilization in Europe*. New York, 1855.

Guterman, N., and Lowenthal, L. *Prophets of Deceit*. Pacific Books, Palo Alto, CA, 1970.

Gutman, Robert. *Richard Wagner: The Man, His Mind, and His Music*. Harcourt, Brace, and World, New York, 1968.

Habermas, Jürgen. *Knowledge and Human Interests*. Trans. J. Shapiro. Beacon Press, Boston, 1971.

———. *The Theory of Communicative Action*. Trans. T. McCarthy. Beacon Press, Boston, 1981.

Haeckel, Ernst. *The Riddle of the Universe*. Harper and Bros., New York and London, 1900.

Hamilton, Alexander; Jay, John; and Madison, James. *The Federalist Papers*. Edited by Isaac Kramnick. Penguin Books, Harmondsworth, 1988.

Hankins, R. *The Racial Basis of Civilization. A Critique of the Nordic Doctrine*. Knopf, New York, 1926.

Hankins, Thomas. *Science and the Enlightenment*. Cambridge University Press, Cambridge, 1987.

Hansen, Eric. *Disaffections and Decadence: A Crisis in French Intellectual Thought 1848–1898*. University Press of America, Washington, DC, 1979.

Harris, Marvin. *The Rise of Anthropological Theory: A History of Theories of Culture*. Crowell, New York, 1968.

Harris, Ruth. *Murder and Madness: Medicine, Law, and Society in the Fin de Siècle*. Oxford University Press, Oxford, 1989.

Hayman, Ronald. *Nietzsche: A Critical Life*. Oxford University Press, New York, 1980.

———. *Writing Against: A Biography of Sartre*. Weidenfeld and Nicholson, London, 1986.

Healy, David. *U.S. Expansionism: The Imperialist Urge in the 1890's*. University of Wisconsin Press, Madison, 1970.

Hegel, G. F. *The Philosophy of History*. Trans. J. Sebree. Dover Publications, New York, 1956.

———. *The Philosophy of Right*. Trans. H. Nisbet. Cambridge University Press, Cambridge, 1991.

Heidegger, Martin. *An Introduction to Metaphysics*. Trans. Ralph Manheim. Doubleday, New York, 1961.

———. *Poetry, Language, Thought*. Trans. A. Hofstadter. Harper and Row, New York, 1975.

Heilke, T. *Voegelin on the Idea of Race*. Louisiana University Press, Baton Rouge, 1990.

Hendrickson, D.C., and Tucker, R.W. *Empire of Liberty: The Statecraft of Thomas Jefferson*. Oxford University Press, Oxford, 1990.

Herberg, Will. *Protestant-Catholic-Jew.* University of Chicago Press, Chicago, 1983.

Herf, Jeffrey. *Reactionary Modernism: Technology, Culture, and Politics.* Cambridge University Press, Cambridge, 1984.

Higham, John. *Send These to Me: Immigrants in Urban America.* Johns Hopkins University Press, Baltimore, 1984.

———. *Strangers in the Land: Patterns of American Nativism 1860–1925.* Atheneum Press, New York, 1974.

Hillel, M., and Henry, C. *Of Pure Blood.* Trans. E. Mossbacher. McGraw-Hill, New York, 1976.

Himmelfarb, Gertrude. *Darwin and the Darwinian Revolution.* Doubleday, Garden City, NY, 1959.

———. *The Idea of Poverty: England in the Early Industrial Age.* Vintage Books, New York, 1983.

———. *Poverty and Compassion: The Moral Imagination of the Late Victorians.* Vintage Books, New York, 1991.

Hitler, Adolf. *Mein Kampf.* Trans. R. Manheim. Houghton Mifflin, New York, 1962.

Hocking, William E. *The Coming World Civilization.* Harper, New York, 1956.

Hoffman, Frederick. *Freudianism and the Literary Mind.* Louisiana State University Press, Baton Rouge, 1959.

Hofstadter, Richard. *The Paranoid Style in American Politics and Other Essays.* Knopf, New York, 1965.

———. *Social Darwinism in American Thought.* Beacon Press, Boston, 1955.

Hollander, Paul. *Anti-Americanism: Critiques at Home and Abroad, 1965–1990.* Oxford University Press, Oxford and New York, 1992.

———. *Political Pilgrims.* University Press of America, Lanham, MD, 1990.

Hollingdale. R.J. *Nietzsche: The Man and His Philosophy.* Louisiana State University Press, Baton Rouge, 1965.

Hollinrake, Roger. *Nietzsche, Wagner, and the Philosophy of Pessimism.* Allen and Unwin, Boston and London, 1982.

Holmes, Stephen. *Anatomy of Anti-Liberalism.* Harvard University Press, Cambridge, MA, 1993.

Hont, I., and Ignatieff, N., eds. *Wealth and Virtue.* Cambridge University Press, Cambridge, 1983.

Hooks, Bell. *Ain't I a Woman: Black Women and Feminism.* South End Press, Boston, 1981.

———, and West, Cornel. *Breaking Bread: Insurgent Black Intellectual Life.* South End Press, Boston, 1991.

Hooton, Earnest. *The American Criminal: An Anthropological Study.* Harvard University Press, Cambridge, MA, 1939.

Horkheimer, Max. *Critical Theory: Selected Essays.* Trans. M. J. O'Connell. Seabury Press, New York, 1972.

———. *The Eclipse of Reason.* Oxford University Press, Oxford and London, 1947.

———. *Gesammelte Schriften. Band 3: 1931–1936; Band 4: 1936–1941.* S. Fischer Verlag, Frankfurt am Main, 1988.

Horowitz, A., and Maely, T. eds. *The Barbarism of Reason: Max Weber and the Twilight of Enlightenment.* University of Toronto Press, Toronto, 1994.

Horsman, Reginald. *Race and Manifest Destiny.* Harvard University Press, Cambridge, MA, 1978.

Hughes, H. Stuart. *Consciousness and Society. The Reorientation of European Social Thought 1890–1930.* Vintage Books, New York, 1977.

———. *The Obstructed Path: French Social Thought in the Years of Desperation 1930–1960*. Harper & Row, New York, 1968.

———. *Oswald Spengler*. Transaction Publishers, New Brunswick, NJ, 1992.

———. *The Sea Change: The Migration of Social Thought 1930–1965*. Harper and Row, New York, 1975.

Hume, David. *On the Standard of Taste and Other Essays*. Edited by J. Lenz. Bobbs-Merrill, Indianapolis and New York, 1965.

———. *A Treatise of Human Nature*. Edited by L. A. Selby-Bigge. Clarendon Press, Oxford, 1978.

Huntington, Samuel. "Clash of Civilizations?" *Foreign Affairs* (Summer 1993).

Jackson, George. *Blood in My Eye*. Random House, New York, 1972.

———. *Soledad Brother: Prison Letters of George Jackson*. Coward-McCann, New York, 1970.

Jarausch, Karl. *Students, Society, and Politics in Imperial Germany*. Princeton University Press, Princeton, NJ, 1982.

Jay, Martin. *The Dialectical Imagination*. Little, Brown, Boston, 1973.

Jennings, Hugh. *Pandaemonium: The Coming of the Machine as Seen by Contemporary Observers 1660–1886*. Free Press, New York, 1985.

Johnson, Paul. *Intellectuals*. Harper and Row, New York, 1988.

———. *Modern Times*. Harper and Row, New York, 1983.

Jones, David A. *The History of Criminology: A Philosophical Perspective*. Greenwood Press, Westport, CT, 1986.

Jones, Gareth Stedman. *Outcast London*. Oxford University Press, Oxford, 1971.

Jones, Greta. *Social Darwinism and English Thought*. Harvester Press, Brighton, 1980.

Jones, Leroi/Amiri Baraka. *The LeRoi Jones/Amiri Baraka Reader*. Thunder's Mouth Press, New York, 1991.

Jordan, Thomas. *The Degeneracy Crisis and Victorian Youth*. State University of New York Press, Albany, NY, 1993.

Judt, Tony. *Past Imperfect: French Intellectuals 1944–1956*. University of California Press, Berkeley, 1992.

Kadish, Alon. *Apostle Arnold: The Life and Death of Arnold Toynbee 1852–1883*. Duke University Press, Durham, NC, 1986.

Kahan, Alan. *Aristocratic Liberalism: The Social and Political Thought of Jacob Burckhardt, John Stuart Mill, and Alexis de Tocqueville*. Oxford University Press, Oxford, 1992.

Kalikoff, Beth. *Murder and Moral Decay in Victorian Popular Literature*. UMI Research Press, Anne Arbor, MI, 1986.

Karenga, Maulana. *Introduction to Black Studies*. University of Sankore Press, Los Angeles, 1993.

Kasson, John. *Civilizing the Machine: Technology and Republican Values in America 1776–1900*. Grossman Publishers, New York, 1976.

Katz, P., and Taylor, D., eds. *Eliminating Racism: Profiles in Controversy*. Plenum Press, New York, 1988.

Kaufmann, Walter. *Nietzsche: Philosopher, Psychologist, Antichrist*. Princeton University Press, Princeton, NJ, 1968.

Kedourie, Elie. *The Chatham House Version and Other Middle Eastern Studies*. Weidenfield and Nicholson, London, 1970.

Keller, M. *Affairs of State: Public Life in Late-Nineteenth-Century America*. Harvard University Press, Cambridge, MA, 1977.

Kellner, Douglas. *Herbert Marcuse and the Crisis of Marxism*. University of California Press, Berkeley, 1984.

Kelly, Alfred. *The Descent of Darwin: The Popularization of Darwin in Germany 1860–1914.* University of North Carolina Press, Chapel Hill, 1981.

Kendle, J. *The Round-Table Movement and Imperial Union.* University of Toronto Press, Toronto, 1975.

Kennedy, Paul. *The Rise and Fall of the Great Powers.* Random House, New York, 1987.

———, and Connelly, Patrick. "Must It Be the West Against the Rest?" *Atlantic Monthly* (December 1994), 61–84.

Kennon, Patrick. *The Twilight of Democracy.* Doubleday, New York, 1995.

Kevles, Daniel. *In the Name of Eugenics: Genetics and the Uses of Human Heredity.* Knopf, New York, 1985.

Khamit-Kush, I. *What They Never Told You in History Class.* N.p., 1983.

Kidd, Benjamin. *Principles of Western Civilization.* MacMillan, London, 1902.

Kingdon, Jonathan. *Self-Made Man: Human Evolution from Eden to Extinction?* Wiley, New York, 1993.

Klapp, Orrin. *The Collective Search for Identity.* Holt, Rinehart and Winston, New York, 1969.

Klare, Michael. *War Without End: American Planning for the Next Vietnams.* Vintage Books, 1972.

Klein, Lawrence. "The Third Earl of Shaftesbury and the Progress of Politeness." *Eighteenth Century Studies* 18:2 (1984), 186–214.

———. "Liberty, Manners and Politeness in Early 18th Century England." *Historical Journal* 32:3 (1989), 583–605.

Kline, Salli. *Dracula and the Degeneration of Women.* CMZ-Verlag, Pheinbach-Merzbach, 1992.

Kochman, Thomas. *Black and White Styles in Conflict.* University of Chicago Press, Chicago, 1981.

Koktanek, Anton. *Oswald Spengler in Seiner Zeit.* Beck, Munich, 1968.

Kolakowski, Lezek. *Varieties of Marxism.* 4 vols. Oxford University Press, Oxford, 1964.

Kozol, Jonathan. *Death at an Early Age: The Destruction of the Hearts and Minds of Negro Children in Boston Public Schools.* Houghton Mifflin, Boston, 1967.

———. *The Night Is Dark and I Am Far From Home.* Houghton Mifflin, Boston, 1975.

Kraut, Alan. *Silent Travelers: Germs, Genes, and the "Immigrant Menace."* Basic Books, New York, 1994.

Kroeber, A.L. *A Roster of Civilizations and Cultures.* Aldine Press, Chicago, 1962.

Kuhl, Stefan. *The Nazi Connection.* Oxford University Press, Oxford, 1994.

Kuklick, Henrika. *The Savage Within: The Social History of British Anthropology 1885–1945.* Cambridge University Press, Cambridge, 1991.

Laffey, John. *Civilization and Its Discontented.* Black Rose Books, Montreal, 1993.

Langbaum, R. *The Mysteries of Identity: A Theme in Modern Literature.* Oxford University Press, New York and Oxford, 1977.

Lasch, Christopher. *The Culture of Narcissism.* W. W. Norton, New York, 1978.

———. *The True and Only Heaven: Progress and Its Critics.* W. W. Norton, New York, 1994.

Laski, Harold. *Faith, Reason, and Civilization.* Viking Press, New York, 1944.

———. *Reflections on the Revolution of Our Time.* Viking Press, New York, 1943.

Lawrence, D.H. *Women in Love.* Penguin Books, Harmondsworth, 1979.

Leach, William. *Land of Desire: Merchants, Power, and the Rise of a New American Culture.* Pantheon Books, New York, 1993.

Le Bon, Gustav. *The Crowd.* Fisher and Unwin, London, 1910.

Leers, Jackson. *Fables of Abundance: A Cultural History of Advertising in America*. Basic Books, New York, 1994.

———. *No Place of Grace: Antimodernism and the Transformation of American Culture, 1880–1920*. Harvard University Press, Cambridge, MA, 1981.

Lefeber, Walter, ed. *John Quincy Adams and American Continental Empire*. Quandral Books, Chicago, 1965.

Lehman, David. *Signs of the Times: Deconstruction and the Fall of Paul de Man*. Simon and Schuster, New York, 1991.

Lester, J.A. *Journey Through Despair 1880–1914: Transformations in British Literary Culture*. Princeton University Press, Princeton, NJ, 1968.

Levin, Henry. *The Myth of the Golden Age in the Renaissance*. University of Indiana Press, Bloomington, 1969.

Levitine, George. *The Dawn of Bohemianism: The Barbu Rebellion and Primitivism in Neoclassical France*. Pennsylvania State University Press, University Park and London, 1978.

Lévy-Bruhl, Lucien. *Primitive Mentality*. Beacon Press, Boston, 1922.

Lewis, Daniel L. *W.E.B. Du Bois: Biography of a Race 1868–1919*. Henry Holt, New York, 1993.

Lichtheim, George. *Georg Lukács*. Viking Press, New York, 1970.

Lifton, Robert Jay. *The Nazi Doctors*. Basic Books, New York, 1986.

Lincoln, C. Eric. *Black Muslims in America*. 3rd ed. Africa World Press, Trenton, NJ, 1994.

Locke, John. *Essay Concerning Human Understanding*. Volume 1. Edited by J. A. St. John. London, 1902.

Lombroso, Cesare. *Crime: Its Causes and Remedies*. Little, Brown, Boston, 1918.

———. *The Female Offender*. New York, 1895.

———. *The Man of Genius*. New York, 1891.

Lombroso-Ferrera, Gina. *The Criminal Man, According to the Classification of Cesare Lombroso*. Patterson Smith, Monclair, NJ, 1972.

Lord, Audre. *Zami: A New Spelling of My Name*. Crossing Press, Trumansburg, NY, 1982.

Lottman, Herbert. *The Purge*. William Morrow, New York, 1986.

Lukács, Georg. *History and Class Consciousness*. Trans. R. Livingstone. MIT Press, Cambridge, MA, 1971.

Luther, Martin. *Three Treatises*. Fortress Press, Philadelphia, 1966.

Lynch, Hollis. *Edward Wilmot Blyden: Pan-Negro Patriot*. Oxford University Press, London, 1967.

Lynn, Kenneth S. *Visions of America*. Greenwood Press, Westport, CT, 1973.

McIntire, C.T., and Perry, Marvin. *Toynbee: Reappraisals*. University of Toronto Press, Toronto, 1989.

McNeil, William. *Arnold Toynbee: A Life*. Oxford University Press, New York, 1989.

———. *Mythohistory and Other Essays*. University of Chicago Press, Chicago, 1986.

———. *The Rise of the West*. University of Chicago Press, Chicago, 1963.

McPherson, James. *The Abolitionist Legacy*. Princeton University Press, Princeton, NJ, 1975.

MacIntire, Ben. *Forgotten Fatherland: The Search for Elisabeth Nietzsche*. Farrar, Straus and Giroux, New York, 1992.

Mahon, Michael. *Foucault's Nietzschean Genealogy: Truth, Power, and the Subject*. State University of New York Press, Albany, NY, 1992.

Mailer, Norman. *Advertisements for Myself*. New American Library, New York, 1960.

Mandelbaum, Maurice. *History, Man and Reason: A Study in Nineteenth-Century Thought*. Johns Hopkins University Press, Baltimore, 1971.

Mander, Jerry. *In the Absence of the Sacred.* Sierra Club Books, San Francisco, 1991.

Manes, Christopher. *Green Rage. Radical Environmentalism and the Unmaking of Civilization.* Little, Brown, Boston, 1990.

Mann, Thomas. *Diaries 1918–1939.* Trans. Richard and Clara Winston. Knopf, New York, 1982.

———. *Letters of Thomas Mann.* Edited and translated by Richard and Clara Winston. Knopf, New York, 1975.

———. *Reflections of a Non-Political Man.* Trans. W. Morris. F. Ungar, New York, 1983.

Mannheim, Karl. *Ideology and Utopia.* Trans. L. Wirth and E. Shils. Harcourt Brace, New York, 1936.

Manthey-Zorn, B. *Dionysius: The Tragedy of Nietzsche.* Greenwood Press, Westport, CT, 1975.

Marable, Manning. *Black America: Multicultural Discourse in the Age of Clarence Thomas and David Duke.* Open Media Press, Westfield, NJ, 1992.

Marcell, D. W. *Progress and Pragmatism: James, Dewey, Beard, and the American Idea of Progress.* Greenwood Press, Westport, CT, 1974.

Marcus, Steven. *Engels, Manchester, and the Working Class.* Vintage Press, New York, 1974.

Marcuse, Herbert. *Eros and Civilization.* Beacon Press, Boston, 1955.

———. *Essay on Liberation.* Beacon Press, Boston, 1969.

———. *Negations: Essays in Critical Theory.* Free Association, London, 1988.

———. *One-Dimensional Man.* Beacon Press, Boston, 1991.

———. *Soviet Marxism: A Critical Analysis.* Columbia University Press, New York, 1958.

———; Moore, Barrington; and Wolff, R.P. *A Critique of Pure Tolerance.* Beacon Press, Boston, 1969.

Martin, Andrew. *The Mask of the Prophet: The Extraordinary Fictions of Jules Verne.* Oxford University Press, Oxford and New York, 1990.

Martin, Rose. *The Selling of America.* Fidelis Publishers, Santa Monica, CA, 1973.

Marx, Karl. *Early Writings.* Edited by Quinton Hoare. Vintage Press, New York, 1975.

Marx, Leo. *The Machine in the Garden: Technology and the Pastoral Ideal in America.* Oxford University Press, New York, 1974.

Mason, Jim. *An Unnatural Order.* Simon and Schuster, New York, 1993.

Mathiopolous, Margarita. *History and Progress: In Search of the American and European Mind.* Praeger, New York, 1989.

Matthew, H.C.G. *The Liberal Imperialists.* Oxford University Press, London, 1973.

Maudsley, Henry. *Body and Mind: An Inquiry into their Connection and Mutual Influence.* New York, 1886.

Meek, Ronald, ed. *Turgot on Progress, Sociology and Economics.* Cambridge University Press, Cambridge, 1973.

Mendilow, J. *The Romantic Tradition in British Political Thought.* Barnes and Noble, New York, 1986.

Merleau-Ponty, Maurice. *Humanism and Terror.* Trans. J. O'Neill. Beacon Press, Boston, 1969.

Midgley, Mary. *Beast and Man: The Roots of Human Nature.* Cornell University Press, Ithaca, NY, 1978.

Miller, James. *The Passion of Michel Foucault.* Simon and Schuster, New York, 1993.

Mills, C. Wright. *The Power Elite.* Oxford University Press, London and New York, 1956.

Mintz, H. *The Liberty Lobby and the American Right.* Greenwood Press, Westport, CT, 1985.

Moikobu, J.M. *Blood and Flesh: Black Americans and African Identification*. Greenwood Press, Westport, CT, 1981.

Moller, Lis. *The Freudian Reading*. University of Pennsylvania Press, Philadelphia, 1991.

Mommsen, Wolfgang. *Max Weber and German Politics 1890–1920*. University of Chicago Press, Chicago, 1984.

Monk, Raymond. *Ludwig Wittgenstein: The Duty of Genius*. Free Press, New York, 1990.

Morgan, H., ed. *The Gilded Age: A Reappraisal*. Syracuse University Press, Syracuse, NY, 1963.

Morris, Charles. *The Aryan Race: Its Origin and Its Achievements*. Chicago, 1892.

Morrison, Toni. *Conversations with Toni Morrison*. Edited by Danille Taylor-Guthrie. University Press of Mississippi, Jackson, 1994.

———. *Race-ing Justice, En-gendering Justice*. Pantheon Books, New York, 1992.

Moses, Wilson. *Alexander Crummell*. Oxford University Press, New York and Oxford, 1989.

———. *Classical Black Nationalism*. New York University Press, New York, 1986.

Mosse, George. *Confronting the Nation: Jewish and Western Nationalism*. Brandeis University Press, Hanover and London, 1993.

———. *Crisis of German Ideology*. Grosset and Dunlap, New York, 1964.

———. *Toward the Final Solution: A History of European Racism*. H. Fertig, New York, 1978.

Muggeridge, Malcolm. *Chronicles of Wasted Time: The Green Stick*. William Morrow, New York, 1973.

———. *Like It Was: The Diaries of Malcolm Muggeridge*. Edited by J. Bright-Holmes. William Morrow, New York, 1981.

Muller, Jerry Z. *Adam Smith in His Time and Ours*. Basic Books, New York, 1992.

———. *The Other God That Failed*. Princeton University Press, Princeton, NJ, 1987.

Murray, Charles, and Herrnstein, Richard. *The Bell Curve*. Free Press, New York, 1994.

Nash, Gary. *Race and Revolution*. University of Wisconsin Press, Madison, 1990.

———. *Red, White, and Black: The Peoples of Early North America*. Prentice Hall, Englewoods Cliffs, NJ, 1992.

Negri, Antimo. *Nietzsche storia e cultura*. Armando Armando, Rome, 1977.

Nettleship, Richard L. *Lectures on the Republic of Plato*. Macmillan, London, 1967.

Newman, John Henry. *The Idea of a University*. Reinhardt, New York and Toronto, 1960.

Nicholson, Harold. *Peacemaking 1919*. Grosset and Dunlap, New York, 1965.

Nietzsche, Friedrich. *The Anti-Christ*. Trans. R. J. Hollingdale. Penguin Books, Harmondsworth, 1968.

———. *Beyond Good and Evil*. Trans. Walter Kaufmann. Random House, New York, 1966.

———. *The Birth of Tragedy* and *The Case of Wagner*. Trans. Walter Kaufmann. Random House, New York, 1967.

———. *Ecce Homo* and *The Genealogy of Morals*. Trans. Walter Kaufmann. Random House, New York, 1969.

———. *The Gay Science*. Trans. Walter Kaufmann. Random House, New York, 1974.

———. *Selected Letters of Friedrich Nietzsche*. Trans. and ed. C. Middleton. Chicago, 1969.

———. *Thus Spake Zarathustra*. Trans. Walter Kaufmann. Viking Penguin, New York, 1978.

———. *Untimely Meditations*. Trans. R.J. Hollingdale. Cambridge University Press, Cambridge, 1983.

————. *The Will to Power*. Trans. Walter Kaufmann. Random House, New York, 1968.

Nisbet, Robert. *The History of the Idea of Progress*. Basic Books, New York, 1980.

Nkrumah, Kwame. *Africa Must Unite*. Praeger, New York, 1963.

Noble, David W. *The Paradox of the Progressive Mind*. University of Minnesota Press, Minneapolis, 1958.

Nock, Arthur J. *Memoirs of a Superfluous Man*. Harper and Brothers, New York, 1943.

Nordau, Max. *Degeneration*. Introduction by G.L. Mosse. University of Nebraska Press, Lincoln, 1993.

————. *Three Conventional Lies of Civilization*. London, 1884.

Nye, Robert S. *Crime, Madness, and Politics in Modern France: The Medical Concept of National Decline*. Princeton University Press, Princeton, NJ, 1984.

O'Flaherty, J.; Sellner, T.; and Helm, E., eds. *Studies in Nietzsche and the Classical Tradition*. University of North Carolina Press, Chapel Hill, 1976.

Ortega y Gasset, José. *The Revolt of the Masses*. W. W. Norton, 1960.

Ott, Hugo. *Martin Heidegger: A Political Life*. Trans. A. Blunden. Basic Books, New York, 1993.

Palmer, Robert R. *The Two Tocquevilles: Father and Son*. Princeton University Press, Princeton, NJ, 1987.

Parmelee, Maurice. *Criminology*. Macmillan, New York, 1926.

Parry, Marvin. *Arnold Toynbee and the Crisis of the West*. University Press of America, Washington, DC, 1982.

Patch, Howard. *The Goddess Fortune in Medieval Literature*. Octagon Books, New York, 1967.

Paxton, Robert. *Vichy France: Old Guard and New Order*. Columbia University Press, New York, 1972.

Payne, Robert. *The Life and Death of Adolf Hitler*. Praeger, New York, 1973.

Péan, Pierre. *Une Jeunesse Francaise: Francois Mitterrand 1934–1947*. Fayard, Paris, 1994.

Perinbaum, B. Marie. *Holy Violence: The Revolutionary Thought of Frantz Fanon*. Three Continents Press, Washington, DC, 1982.

Peters, H.F. *Zarathustra's Sister*. Crown Books, New York, 1974.

Pettigrew, Thomas. *A Profile of the Negro American*. Van Nostrand, Princeton University Press, Princeton, NJ, 1964.

Phillips, D.C. *Holistic Thought in Social Science*. Stanford University Press, Stanford, CA, 1976.

Phillips, Kevin. *Arrogant Capital*. Little, Brown, Boston, 1994.

Pichois, Claude. *Baudelaire*. Trans. Graham Robb. Hamish Hamilton, London, 1989.

Pick, Daniel. *Faces of Degeneration: A European Disorder c.1848–c.1918*. Cambridge University Press, Cambridge, 1989.

Pickens, Donald. *Eugenics and the Progressives*. Vanderbilt University Press, Nashville, TN, 1968.

Pierrot, Jean. *The Decadent Imagination 1880–1900*. University of Chicago Press, Chicago, 1981.

Pilkington, A.E. *Bergson and His Influence: A Reassessment*. Cambridge University Press, Cambridge, 1976.

Pittock, Murray. *Spectrum of Decadence: Literature of the 1890's*. Routledge, London, 1993.

Plant, Raymond, and Vincent, Andrew. *Philosophy, Politics, and Citizenship: The Life and Thought of the British Idealists*. Basil Blackwell, Oxford, 1984.

Pletsch, Carl. *Young Nietzsche: Becoming a Genius.* Free Press, New York, 1992.

Pocock, J.G.A. *The Machiavellian Moment: Florentine Political Thought and the Atlantic Republican Tradition.* Princeton University Press, Princeton, NJ, 1975.

———. *Virtue, Commerce, and Liberty.* Cambridge University Press, Cambridge, 1985.

Poggioli, Renato. *The Theory of the Avant Garde.* Harvard University Press, Cambridge, MA, 1968.

Poliakov, Leon. *The Aryan Myth.* Trans. E. Howard. Basic Books, New York, 1974.

Ponting, Clive. *A Green History of the World: The Environment and the Collapse of Great Civilizations.* Penguin Books, New York, 1992.

Popper, Karl. *The Open Society and Its Enemies.* 2 vols. Princeton University Press, Princeton, NJ, 1971.

———. *The Poverty of Historicism.* Harper and Row, New York, 1964.

Pott, A.N. *Die Ungleichheit menschlicher Rassen hauptsächlich vom Sprachwissenschäftlichen Standpunkte . . . von des Grafen von Gobineau gleichnämigen Werke.* Berlin, 1856.

Praz, Mario. *The Romantic Agony.* Oxford University Press, London, 1933.

Preston, Richard. *The Hot Zone.* Random House, New York, 1994.

Price, Roger. *The French Second Republic: A Social History.* Cornell University Press, New York, 1983.

Proctor, Richard. *Racial Hygiene: Medicine under the Nazis.* Harvard University Press, Cambridge, MA, 1988.

Quigley, Carroll. *The Evolution of Civilizations: An Introduction to Historical Analysis.* Liberty Press, Indianapolis, IN, 1979.

Radosh, Ronald. "On Hanging Up the Old Red Flag." In J. Bunzel, ed., *Political Passages*, 213–38. Free Press, New York, 1988.

Rampersad, A. *The Art and Imagination of W.E.B. Du Bois.* Harvard University Press, Cambridge, MA, 1976.

Ranke, Leopold von. "The Great Powers" and "Dialogue on Politics." In Theodore von Laue, ed., *Leopold Ranke: The Formative Years*, 152–80, 181–218. Princeton University Press, Princeton, NJ, 1950.

Record, W. *Race and Radicalism: The NAACP and the Communist Party in Conflict.* Cornell University Press, Ithaca, NY, 1964.

Reich, Charles, *The Greening of America.* Bantam Books, New York, 1971.

Rich, Paul. *Race and Empire in British Politics,* 2nd ed. Cambridge University Press, Cambridge, 1990.

Rieff, Philip. *Freud: The Mind of the Moralist.* Doubleday, New York, 1961.

———. *The Triumph of the Therapeutic.* Harper and Row, New York, 1968.

Rifkin, Jeremy. *Beyond Beef: The Rise and Fall of the Cattle Culture.* E.P. Dutton, New York, 1992.

Ringer, Fritz. *Decline of the German Mandarins.* Harvard University Press, Cambridge, MA, 1968.

Robertson, William. *The Progress of Society in Europe.* University of Chicago Press, Chicago, 1972.

Rosenblum, Robert. *Transformations in Late-Eighteenth-Century Art.* Princeton University Press, Princeton, NJ, 1967.

Roth, Michael. *Knowing and History. Appropriations of Hegel in Twentieth-Century France.* Cornell University Press, Ithaca, NY, 1988.

Rothman, D.J. *Politics and Power: The United States Senate 1869–1901.* Harvard University Press, Cambridge, MA, 1966.

Rousseau, Jean Jacques. *Discourse on the Arts and Sciences.* Trans. V. Gourevitch. Harper and Row, New York, 1990.

————. *Discourse on Inequality.* Trans. Maurice Cranston. Penguin Books, Harmondsworth, 1984.

Rowse, A. L. *All Souls and Appeasement.* Alfred Leslie, London, 1961.

Said, Edward. *Culture and Imperialism.* Knopf, New York, 1993.

————. *Orientalism.* Vintage Press, New York, 1979.

Sale, Kirkpatrick. *1492: The Conquest of Paradise.* W. W. Norton, New York, 1992.

Samules, Ernest. *Henry Adams.* Harvard University Press, Cambridge, MA, 1989.

————. *Henry Adams: The Major Phase.* Harvard University Press, Cambridge, MA, 1964.

————. *Henry Adams: The Middle Years.* Harvard University Press, Cambridge, MA, 1958.

————. *Young Henry Adams.* Harvard University Press, Cambridge, MA, 1948.

Sanders. Ronald. *Lost Tribes and Promised Lands: The Origins of American Racism.* Little, Brown, Boston, 1978.

Sartre, Jean Paul. *Anti-Semite and Jew.* Trans. G. Becker. Schocken Books, New York, 1976.

————. *Being and Nothingness.* Trans. H. Barnes. Routledge, London, 1989.

————. *Between Marxism and Existentialism.* Trans. G. Becker, NLB, London, 1974.

————. *Black Orpheus.* Trans. S.W. Allen. Présence Africaine, Paris, 1963.

————. *The Communists and Peace. With a Reply to Claude Lefort.* Braziller, New York, 1968.

————. *Existentialism.* Trans. B. Frechtman. Philosophical Library, New York, 1947.

————. *Life/Situations: Essays Written and Spoken.* Trans. P. Auster and L. Davis. Pantheon Books, New York, 1977.

————. *Nausea.* Trans. L. Alexander. R. Bentley Press, Cambridge, MA, 1979.

————. *No Exit and Three Other Plays.* Vintage Books, New York, 1955.

————. *Situations.* Volumes 1 and 2. Gallimard, Paris, 1948.

————. *The War Diaries: November 1939–March 1940.* Trans. Q. Hoare. Pantheon Books, New York, 1984.

Schacht, Richard. *Nietzsche.* Routledge and Kegan Paul, London, 1983.

Schamber, E.N. *The Artist as Politician: The Relationship Between the Art and the Politics of the French Romantics.* University Press of America, Lanham, MD, 1984.

Schell, Jonathan. *The Fate of the Earth.* Avon Books, New York, 1982.

Schenk, H.G. *The Mind of the European Romantics.* Constable, London, 1966.

Schlesinger, Arthur. *The Disuniting of America: Reflections on a Multicultural Society.* W. W. Norton, New York, 1993.

Schmoller, Gustav von. *The Mercantile System and Its Historical Signficance.* P. Smith, New York, 1931.

Schneps, Hans. *Vorläufer Spenglers. Studien zum Geschichtspessimismusim 19. Jahrhundert.* E.J. Brill. Leiden, 1953.

Schopenhauer, Arthur. *Essays and Aphorisms.* Trans. R.J. Hollingdale, Penguin Books, Harmondsworth, 1976.

Shufeldt, Robert. *The Negro: A Menace to American Civilization.* Library Resources, Chicago, 1970.

Schwab, Raymond. *The Oriental Renaissance: Europe's Rediscovery of India and the East, 1680–1880.* Columbia University Press, New York, 1984.

Schwartz, Hillel. *Century's End: A Cultural History of the Fin de Siècle from the 990's to the 1990's.* Doubleday, New York, 1990.

Schweitzer, Albert. *The Philosophy of Civilization.* Macmillan, New York, 1950.

Semmel, Bernard. *Imperialism and Social Reform: English Social-Imperial Thought 1895–1914.* Harvard University Press, Cambridge, MA, 1960.

Sewell, Tony. *Garvey's Children.* Africa World Press, Trenton, NJ, 1990.

Shaftesbury, Anthony Ashley Cooper, Third Earl of. *Characteristics.* Bobbs-Merrill, Indianapolis, IN, 1967.

Sheridan, Alan. *Michel Foucault: The Will to Truth.* Tavistock Publications, London and New York, 1980.

Showalter, Elaine. *Sexual Anarchy: Gender and Culture at the Fin de Siècle.* Viking Press, New York, 1993.

Siegel, Jerrold. *Bohemian Paris.* Princeton University Press, Princeton, NJ, 1982.

Simmel, Georg. *The Conflict in Modern Culture and Other Essays.* Trans. Peter Etzkorn. Teachers College Press, New York, 1968.

———. *The Sociology of Georg Simmel.* Trans. and edited by Kurt H. Wolff. Free Press of Glencoe, London, 1950.

Slotkin, Richard. *Gunfighter Nation: The Myth of the Frontier in Twentieth-Century America.* Atheneum, New York, 1992.

———. *Regeneration Through Violence.* Wesleyan University Press, Middletown, CT, 1973.

Smith, Woodruff H. *Politics and the Sciences of Culture in Germany.* Oxford University Press, Oxford, 1991.

Sollors, Werner. *Beyond Ethnicity: Consent and Descent in American Culture.* Oxford University Press, Oxford, 1986.

Solway, R.A. *Demography and Degeneration.* University of North Carolina Press, Chapel Hill, 1990.

Sombart, Werner. *Towards a New Social Philosophy.* Princeton University Press, Princeton, NJ, 1937.

Soule, Michael. *Conservation Biology. The Science of Science and Diversity.* Sinauer Associates, Sunderland, MA, 1980.

Spackman, Barbara. *Decadent Genealogies: The Rhetoric of Sickness from Baudelaire to D'Annunzio.* Cornell University Press, Ithaca, NY, 1989.

Spengler, Oswald. *Briefe 1913–1936.* Edited by A. Koktanek. Beck, Munich, 1963.

———. *The Decline of the West.* Trans. C.F. Atkinson. Knopf, New York, 1959.

———. *The Hour of Decision.* Trans. C.F Atkinson, Knopf, New York, 1934.

———. *Man and Technics.* Trans. C.F. Atkinson. Knopf, New York, 1932.

———. *Selected Essays.* Trans. Donald White. H. Regnery, Chicago, 1967.

———. *Selected Letters of Oswald Spengler 1913–1936.* Trans. Arthur Helps. Knopf, New York, 1966.

Spring, Gerald. *The Vitalism of Count de Gobineau.* Institute of French Studies Press, New York, 1932.

Stavrianos, L. S. *The Promise of the Coming Dark Age.* W. H. Freeman, San Francisco, 1976.

Stein, Judith. *The World of Marcus Garvey.* Louisiana State University Press, Baton Rouge, 1986.

Stepan, Nancy. *The Idea of Race in Science: Great Britain 1800–1960.* Archon Books, Hamden, CT, 1982.

Stern, Fritz. *The Politics of Cultural Despair.* Doubleday, New York, 1964.

Sternhell, Zev. *Neither Right Nor Left: Fascist Ideology in France.* Trans. David Maisel. University of California Press, Berkeley and Los Angeles, 1986.

Stoddard, Lothrop. *Clashing Tides of Colour.* Scribner, London, 1935.

———. *Racial Realities in Europe.* Scibner, London, 1924.

Stoker, Bram. *Dracula.* Signet Books, New York, 1992.

Strong, Tracy. *Nietzsche and the Politics of Transfiguration.* University of California Press, Berkeley, 1975.

Struve, Walter. *Elites Against Democracy: Leadership Ideals in Bourgeois Political Thought in Germany 1890–1933*. Princeton University Press, Princeton, NJ, 1973.

Swart, K.W. *The Sense of Decadence in Nineteenth-Century France*. M. Nijhoff, The Hague, 1964.

Takaki, Ronald. *A Different Mirror: A History of Multicultural America*. Little, Brown, Boston, 1993.

———. *Iron Cages: Race and Culture in Nineteenth-Century America*. Knopf, New York, 1993.

Tar, Zoltan. *The Frankfurt School*. Basil Wiley, New York, 1977.

Tawney, R.H. *The Acquisitive Society*. Harcourt Brace, New York, 1920.

Taylor, Jared. *Paved with Good Intentions: The Failure of Race Relations in Contemporary America*. Carroll and Graff, New York, 1992.

Teggart, F. J. *Theory and Processes of History*. University of California Press, Berkeley and Los Angeles, 1941.

Tilly, James. *A Discourse Concerning Property: John Locke and His Adversaries*. Cambridge University Press, Cambridge, 1980.

Tocqueville, Alexis de. *The European Revolution* and *Correspondence with Gobineau*. Trans. J. Lukács. Greenwood Press, Westport, CT, 1974.

Toffler, Alvin. *Future Shock*. Random House, New York, 1970.

Toland, John. *Adolf Hitler*. Volume 1. Doubleday, New York, 1976.

Tomisch, J. *A Genteel Endeavor: American Culture and Politics in the Gilded Age*. Stanford University Press, Stanford, CA, 1971.

Tönnies, Ferdinand. *Community and Society*. Trans. Charles Loomis. Michigan State University Press, East Lansing, 1957.

Townsend, Jules. *J.A. Hobson*. Manchester University Press, London and Manchester, 1990.

Toynbee, Arnold, Sr. *Progress and Poverty. A Criticism of Mr. Henry George . . . by the late Arnold Toynbee, M.A.* London, 1883.

Toynbee, Arnold. *Acquaintances*. Oxford University Press, London, 1967.

———. *America and the World Revolution*. Oxford University Press, Oxford and London, 1962.

———. *Change and Habit: The Challenge of Our Time*. Oxford University Press, New York, 1969.

———. *Civilization on Trial*. Oxford University Press, Oxford and London, 1948.

———. *Experiences*. Oxford University Press, London, 1967.

———. *Reconsiderations*. Vol. 12 of *A Study of History*, Oxford University Press, London, 1961.

———. *A Study of History*. 12 vol. Oxford University Press, London, 1934–61.

———. *A Study of History*. Abridgement of Vols. 1–6. Edited by D. C. Somervell. Oxford University Press, New York and London, 1947.

———. *A Study of History*. Abridgement of Vols. 7–10. Edited by D. C. Somervell. Oxford University Press, New York and London, 1957.

———. *The World and the West*. Oxford University Press, New York and London, 1953.

Trevor-Roper, Hugh. "Arnold Toynbee's Millennium." In *Men and Events*, 299–324. Harper and Brothers, New York, 1957.

Trilling, Lionel. *The Liberal Imagination*. Viking Press, New York, 1950.

———. *Matthew Arnold*. Meridian Books, Cleveland and New York, 1965.

Tucker, R.K. *The Dragon and the Cross: The Rise and Fall of the Ku Klux Klan in Middle America*. Archon Books, Hamden, CT, 1991.

Turner, Frederick J. *Frontier and Section: Selected Essays of Frederick Jackson Turner.* Prentice-Hall, Englewood Cliffs, NJ, 1961.

Turner, Henry M. *Respect Black: Writings and Speeches of Henry McNeal Turner.* Edited by E.S. Redkey. Arno Press, New York, 1971.

Tuveson, Ernest. *Millennium and Utopia: A Study in the Background of the Idea of Progress.* University of California Press, Berkeley, 1949.

———. *Redeemer Nation: The Idea of America's Millennial Role.* University of Chicago Press, Chicago, 1968.

Vacca, Roberto. *The Coming Dark Age.* Doubleday, Garden City, NY, 1971.

Vaillant, J.G. *Black, French, and African: A Life of Leopold Sedar Senghor.* Harvard University Press, Cambridge, MA, 1990.

Vajk, J. Peter. *Doomsday Has Been Cancelled.* Peace Press, Culver City, CA, 1978.

Van Doren, Charles. *The Idea of Progress.* Praeger, New York, 1967.

Vattimo, Gianni. *The End of Modernity.* Johns Hopkins University Press, Baltimore, 1988.

Verrechia, A. *La Catastrofe di Nietzsche a Torino.* G. Einaudi, Turin, 1978.

Vico, Giambattista. *The New Science of History.* Cornell University Press, Ithaca, NY, 1959.

Villa, R. *Il Deviante e I suòi segni. Lombroso e la nàscita dell'antropologia criminale.* F. Angeli, Milan, 1985.

Vincent, Theodore. *Black Power and the Garvey Movement.* Ramparts Press, Berkeley, CA, 1971.

Voegelin, Eric. *Die Rassenidee in der Geistesgeschichte von Ray bis Carus.* Junkers und Dunnhaupt, Berlin, 1933.

Volney, Constantine François de. *A New Translation of Volney's 'Ruins.'* Garland Publishing, New York, 1979.

Von Arx, Jeffrey. *Progress and Pessimism: Religion, Politics, and History in Late-Nineteenth-Century Britain.* Harvard University Press, Cambridge, MA, 1985.

Von Grunebaum, G.E. *French African Literature: Some Cultural Implications.* Mouton, The Hague, 1964.

Wade, W.C. *The Fiery Cross.* Simon and Schuster, New York, 1987.

Wagar, W. Warren. *Building the City of Man: Outlines of a World Civilization.* W.H. Freeman, San Francisco, 1971.

Walkowitz, Judith. *City of Dreadful Delights.* Cambridge University Press, Cambridge, 1991.

Wanklyn, H.G. *Friedrich Ratzel.* Cambridge University Press, Cambridge, 1961.

Warbug, James P. *The West in Crisis.* Doubleday, Garden City, NY, 1959.

Watts, Richard. *The Kings Depart.* Simon and Schuster, New York, 1968.

Weber, Eugen, ed. *France: Fin de Siècle.* Harvard University Press, Cambridge, MA, 1986.

———. *Movements, Currents, Trends: Aspects of European Thought in the Nineteenth and Twentieth Centuries.* D. C. Heath, Lexington, MA, 1992.

Weber, Max. *On Charisma and Institution Building. Selected Essays.* Edited by S. N. Eisenstadt. University of Chicago Press, Chicago, 1968.

———. *Protestantism and the Spirit of Capitalism.* Trans. T. Parsons. Scribner's Sons, New York, 1958.

Weindling, Paul. *Health, Race, and German Politics.* Cambridge University Press, Cambridge, 1989.

Wells, H. G. *The Door in the Wall and Other Stories.* David Godine, Boston, 1980.

Welsing, Frances C. *The Isis Papers: The Keys to the Colors.* Third World Press, Chicago, 1991.

West, Cornel. *Race Matters.* Beacon Press, Boston, 1993.

White, Hayden. *Metahistory: The Historical Imagination in Nineteenth-Century Europe.* Johns Hopkins University Press, Baltimore. 1973.

White, John. *Black Leadership in America 1895–1968.* Longmans, London, 1985.

Whitney, Lois. *Primitivism and the Idea of Progress.* Octagon Books, New York, 1965.

Wieseltier, Leon. "Against Identity." *The New Republic* 211:22 (November 28, 1994), 24–32.

Wiggershaus, Rolf. *The Frankfurt School.* Trans. M. Robertson. MIT Press, Cambridge, MA, 1994.

Williams, Chancellor. *The Destruction of Black Civilization.* Third World Press, Chicago, 1987.

———. *The Rebirth of African Civilization.* Third World Press, Chicago, 1993.

Williamson, Joel. *The Crucible of Race.* Oxford University Press, Oxford, 1964.

———. *New People: Miscegenation and Mulattos in the United States.* Free Press, New York, 1980.

Winch, Donald. *Adam Smith's Politics.* Cambridge University Press, Cambridge, 1978.

Wohl, Robert. *The Generation of 1914.* Harvard University Press, Cambridge, MA, 1979.

Wolf, Leonard, ed. *The Essential Dracula.* Plume Books, New York, 1993.

Wolin, Richard. *Labyrinths: Explorations in the Critical History of Ideas.* University of Massachusetts Press, Amherst, 1995.

———. *The Politics of Being.* Columbia University Press, New York, 1990.

———. *The Terms of Cultural Criticism.* Columbia University Press, New York, 1992.

Wood, Gordon. *Creation of the American Republic 1776–1787.* W. W. Norton, New York, 1972.

X, Malcolm. *Autobiography of Malcolm X.* Edited by Alex Haley. Ballantine Books, New York, 1964.

Yates, Francis. *Astraea: The Imperial Theme in the Sixteenth Century.* Routledge and Kegan Paul, London, 1974.

Yockey, Francis Parker. *Imperium.* Noontide Press, Sausalito, CA, 1969.

Young, G.M. *Portrait of an Age: Victorian England.* Oxford University Press, London and New York, 1977.

Zimmer, Henry. *Philosophies of India.* Edited by Joseph Campbell. Princeton University Press, Princeton, NJ, 1951.

Zinn, Howard. *The Politics of History.* Little, Brown, Boston, 1970.

Zola, Emile. *The Debacle.* Trans. L. Tancock. Penguin Books, Harmondsworth. 1970.

# ACKNOWLEDGMENTS

More people participated in making and shaping this book than I can possibly remember to thank. But I'm going to try.

First and foremost, I must thank the History Department at George Mason University for freeing me from my teaching responsibilities so that I could embark on the book in the first place. For the past three years colleagues and students there have been helpful and solicitous, and they always seemed to understand when my writing demanded time that rightfully belonged to them.

Thanks are also due to the graduate students who attended my George Mason seminar in the autumn of 1995, and to my students at the Smithsonian and Johns Hopkins University, whose suggestions and comments contributed more to the book than they might think.

Lionel Gossman, Carl Pletsch, and Michael Scammell took time to answer inquiries in the early stages of my research. For their helpful advice, I say thank you.

The following people read and commented on various chapters or sections of the book: Steven Beller, Jack Censer, Jane Censer, Marion Deshmukh, Jeffrey Herf, Barbara Herman, Lanny Knight, Michael O'Malley, and John Orrens. Jerry Z. Muller not only read key chapters, but provided a sympathetic sounding board during the whole project, and encouraged me to go on where others would have feared to tread. He and everyone else helped to give the book whatever virtues it has. It would have been even better if I had used more of their ideas and criticims. As it is, the flaws that remain are my responsiblity, not theirs.

Joyce Hackett read an early version of the manuscript. I profited immeasurably from her comments and criticism. Conversations with Robert Artigiani, Richard Breitman, Alan Kraut, Orest Ranum, and many others also helped to shape the direction of my work.

My father, Arthur Herman, Sr., not only read chapters and gave expert advice on philosophical matters about which I knew nothing, but seemed to relish the project as much as I did. Carol and Fred Warshofsky gave me invaluable guidance and inspiration from the beginning. Fred served as my mentor throughout the project, and taught me the difference between writing a book and being a writer.

Adam Bellow, my editor at The Free Press, turned out to be everything an editor should be. He has been patient and quietly confident, when others (including myself) were not. Someone once said the best thing an editor can do is to make his author believe that he, and no one else, can write the book he's writing. In all our conversations, Adam did that above everything else, and I will be always be grateful for it.

My other debt is to Glen Hartley and Lynn Chu. It was Glen Hartley who originally suggested to me a book on the decline of the West, although the project has gone off in directions I'm sure he never imagined. He and Lynn have been among my biggest supporters from start to finish. Without them, there literally would not be a book.

Finally, there is my wife, Beth. She suffered and endured all the ups and downs that go with a book of this sort, and when my own strength ran out, she always found some of her own to give me.

# INDEX

501